Fodor's Arizona

"When it comes to information on regional history, what to see and do, and shopping, these guides are exhaustive."

—*USAir Magazine*

"Usable, sophisticated restaurant coverage, with an emphasis on good value."

—Andy Birsh, *Gourmet Magazine* columnist

"Valuable because of their comprehensiveness."

—*Minneapolis Star-Tribune*

"Fodor's always delivers high quality...thoughtfully presented...thorough."

—*Houston Post*

"An excellent choice for those who want everything under one cover."

—*Washington Post*

Fodor's Travel Publications, Inc.
New York • Toronto • London • Sydney • Auckland
http://www.fodors.com/

Fodor's Arizona

Editors: Chelsea S. Mauldin and Kristen D. Perrault

Editorial Contributors: Robert Andrews, Jenner Bishop, Robert Blake, Judy Blumenberg, David Brown, Suzanne Carmichael, Audra Epstein, Edie Jarolim, Mark Hein, Gregory McNamee, Heidi Sarna, Helayne Schiff, Mary Ellen Schultz, M. T. Schwartzman (Gold Guide editor), Susana C. Sedgwick, Dinah Spritzer, and Stephen Wolf

Creative Director: Fabrizio LaRocca

Associate Art Director: Guido Caroti

Photo Researcher: Jolie Novak

Cartographers: David Lindroth, Mapping Specialists

Cover Photograph: Rob Boudreau/TSW

Text Design: Between the Covers

Copyright

ISBN 0-679-03171-5

Special Sales

Fodor's Travel Publications are available at special discounts for bulk purchases for sales promotions or premiums. Special editions, including personalized covers, excerpts of existing guides, and corporate imprints, can be created in large quantities for special needs. For more information, contact your local bookseller or write to Special Markets, Fodor's Travel Publications, 201 E. 50th Street, New York, NY 10022. Inquiries from Canada should be directed to your local Canadian bookseller or sent to Random House of Canada, Ltd., Marketing Dept., 1265 Aerowood Drive, Mississauga, Ontario L4W 1B9. Inquiries from the United Kingdom should be sent to Fodor's Travel Publications, 20 Vauxhall Bridge Road, London, England SW1V 2SA.

PRINTED IN THE UNITED STATES OF AMERICA

10 9 8 7 6 5 4 3 2 1

CONTENTS

Maps

ON THE ROAD WITH FODOR'S

WE'RE ALWAYS THRILLED to get letters from readers, especially when they sound like this:

It took us an hour to decide what book to buy and we now know we picked the best one. Your book was wonderful, easy to follow, very accurate, and good on pointing out eating places, informal as well as formal. When we saw other people using your book, we would look at each other and smile.

Our editors and writers are deeply committed to making every Fodor's guide "the best one"—not only accurate but always charming, brimming with sound recommendations and solid ideas, right on the mark in describing restaurants and hotels, and full of fascinating facts that make you view what you've traveled to see in a rich new light.

About Our Writers

Our success in achieving our goals—and in helping to make your trip the best of all possible vacations—is a credit to the hard work of our extraordinary writers.

Jenner Bishop is a L.A.–based freelance writer whose months in Phoenix have convinced her that Arizona may be her spiritual home. When not evaluating the quality of hotel-bathroom amenities, searching for the elusive javelina, or checking out the clientele at the Valley's finest drag bars, she tours with her funk band, Fistfulls of Aspirin.

Edie Jarolim, who wrote the "North-Central Arizona" and "Tucson and Southern Arizona" chapters, abandoned her senior editor's desk at Fodor's in 1992 to settle among the saguaros in Tucson. Her articles about Arizona have appeared in *Arizona Highways, Bride's* magazine, and *The Wall Street Journal,* among other publications.

Susana C. Sedgwick is a writer and explorer. She has traveled all over the world, particularly in South America, where among other adventures she paddled 2,000 miles down the Amazon River in a dugout canoe. She is a member of the Explorer's Club in New York and a Fellow of the Royal Geographical Society in London, England. When she is not traveling, Susana splits her time between New York and Arizona.

We'd also like to thank the people who have assisted in preparing this guide: Marjorie Magnusson of the Arizona Office of Tourism, whose helpfulness is matched only by her cheerfulness, Jean E. McKnight of the Tucson Convention and Visitors Bureau, Frank Miller of the Sedona Chamber of Commerce, L. Greer Price, Information Specialist at Grand Canyon National Park, and City of Phoenix Park Ranger Dave Stamper for his expertise on rattlesnakes, Gila monsters, and scorpions. In Phoenix, thanks to Kim Chmel of KC Marketing Communications, Casey Fabig for sharing his encyclopedic knowledge of Phoenix bike trails, Paul Potts for all his nightlife tips and expertise, Georgiana Marie for her warm hospitality, and most of all to Terri Sinclair, without whom updating the chapter would not have been possible.

New This Year

This year we've reformatted our guides to make them easier to use. Each chapter of *Arizona '97* begins with brand-new recommended itineraries to help you decide what to see in the time you have; a section called When to Tour points out the optimal time of day, day of the week, and season for your journey. You may also notice our fresh graphics, new in 1996. More readable and more helpful than ever? We think so—and we hope you do, too.

Also new this year are maps of Sedona and Prescott, as well as revised Tucson maps, to correspond with our expanded coverage of these areas, and Phoenix writer Jenner Bishop's brand-new section on Tempe, a bustling college town with great shopping, lively cafés, and interesting architecture on the ASU campus. Gregory McNamee—a specialist on the Arizona outdoors who has written books and articles for *Arizona Highways, Outside,* and Sierra Club Books, among others—has reviewed each chapter with an expert local eye and added information on recreation, ecology, and geology.

Also check out Fodor's Web site (http://www.fodors.com/), where you'll find travel information on major destinations around the world and an ever-changing array of travel-savvy interactive features.

How to Use This Book

Organization

Up front is the **Gold Guide.** Its first section, **Important Contacts A to Z,** gives addresses and telephone numbers of organizations and companies that offer destination-related services and detailed information and publications. **Smart Travel Tips A to Z,** the Gold Guide's second section, gives specific information on how to accomplish what you need to in Arizona as well as tips on savvy traveling. Both sections are in alphabetical order by topic.

Chapters in *Arizona '97* are arranged from the top of the state down, starting with the Grand Canyon, moving to the Navajo and Hopi reservations in the northeast, then looking at the center of the state before moving to Phoenix, Tucson, and the south. Each city chapter begins with an Exploring section, which is subdivided by neighborhood; sights are listed in alphabetical order. Each regional chapter is divided by geographical area; within each area, towns are covered in logical geographical order, and attractive stretches of road and minor points of interest between them are indicated by the designation *En Route.* Throughout, Off the Beaten Path sights appear after the places from which they are most easily accessible. And within town sections, all restaurants and lodgings are grouped together.

To help you decide what to visit in the time you have, all chapters begin with recommended itineraries; you can mix and match those from several chapters to create a complete vacation. The A to Z section that ends all chapters covers getting there, getting around, and helpful contacts and resources.

At the end of the book you'll find Portraits, wonderful essays about Native American history, desert life, and shopping in Arizona, followed by suggestions for pretrip reading, both fiction and nonfiction, and movies on tape with Arizona as a backdrop.

Icons and Symbols

★ Our special recommendations
✕ Restaurant
🏨 Lodging establishment
✕🏨 Lodging establishment whose restaurant warrants a detour
⛺ Campground
🦆 Rubber duckie (good for kids)
☞ Sends you to another section of the guide for more info
✉ Address
☎ Telephone number
FAX Fax number
⏲ Opening and closing times
🎟 Admission prices (those we give apply only to adults; substantially reduced fees are almost always available for children, students, and senior citizens)

Numbers in white and black circles—② and ❷, for example—that appear on the maps, in the margins, and within the tours correspond to one another.

Dining and Lodging

The restaurants and lodgings we list are the cream of the crop in each price range. Price charts appear in the Pleasures and Pastimes section that follows each chapter introduction.

Hotel Facilities

We always list the facilities that are available—but we don't specify whether they cost extra: When pricing accommodations, always ask what's included. Unless otherwise noted, all rooms have a private bath.

Restaurant Reservations and Dress Codes

Reservations are always a good idea; we note only when they're essential or when they are not accepted. Book as far ahead as you can, and reconfirm when you get to town. Unless otherwise noted, the restaurants listed are open daily for lunch and dinner. We mention dress only when men are required to wear a jacket or a jacket and tie. Look for an overview of local habits under Dining in Smart Travel Tips A to Z and in the Pleasures and Pastimes section that follows each chapter introduction.

Credit Cards

The following abbreviations are used: **AE,** American Express; **D,** Discover; **DC,** Diners Club; **MC,** MasterCard; and **V,** Visa.

Don't Forget to Write

You can use this book in the confidence that all prices and opening times are based on information supplied to us at press time; Fodor's cannot accept responsibility for any errors. Time inevitably brings changes, so always confirm information when it matters—especially if you're making a detour to visit a specific place. In addition, when making reservations be sure to mention if you have a disability or are traveling with children, if you prefer a private bath or a certain type of bed, or if you have specific dietary needs or any other concerns.

Were the restaurants we recommended as described? Did our hotel picks exceed your expectations? Did you find a museum we recommended a waste of time? If you have complaints, we'll look into them and revise our entries when the facts warrant it. If you've discovered a special place that we haven't included, we'll pass the information along to our correspondents and have them check it out. So send your feedback, positive *and* negative, to the Arizona Editor at 201 East 50th Street, New York, New York 10022—and have a wonderful trip!

Karen Cure
Editorial Director

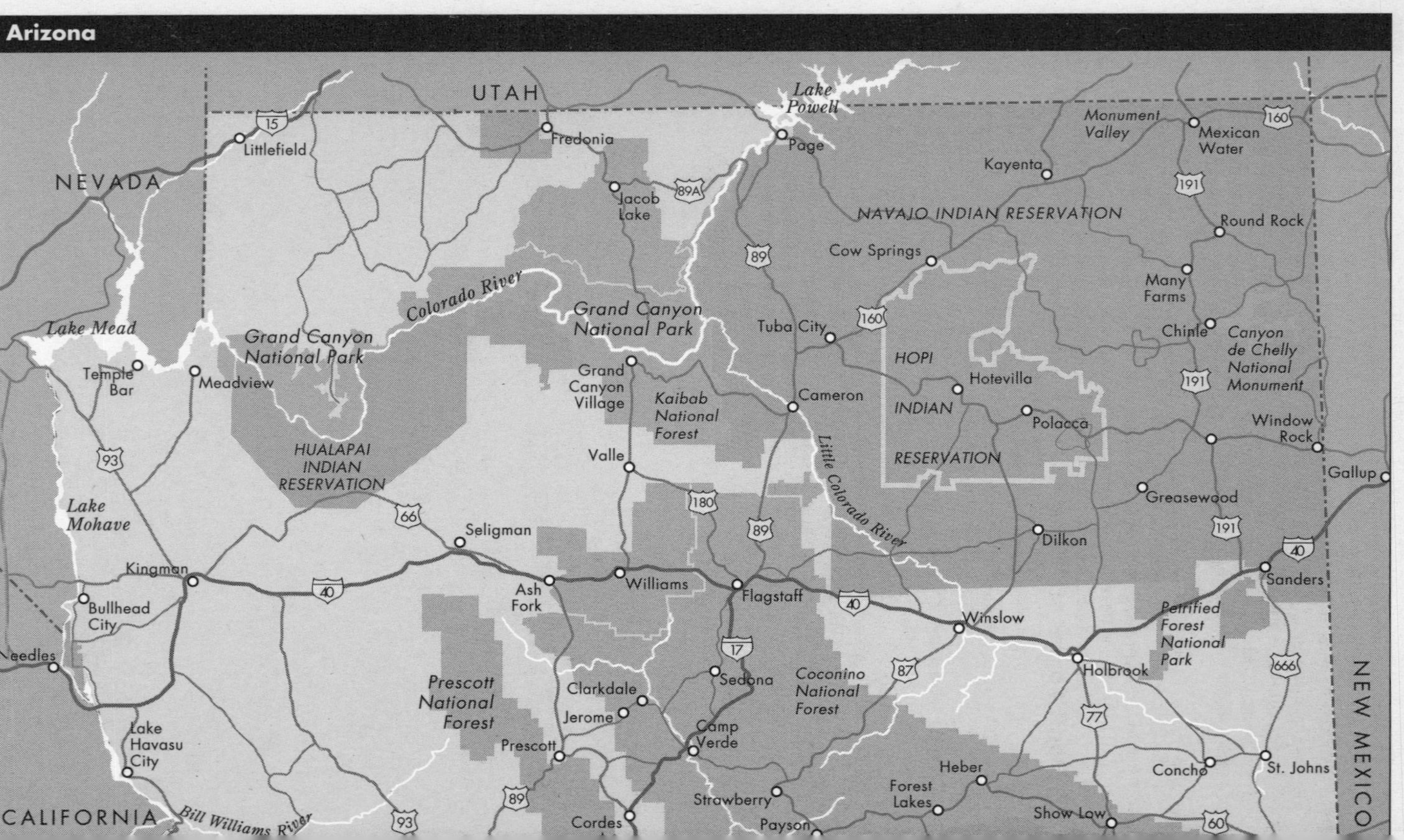
Arizona
UTAH
NEVADA
NEW MEXICO
CALIFORNIA
Littlefield
Fredonia
Jacob Lake
Lake Powell
Page
Monument Valley
Mexican Water
Kayenta
NAVAJO INDIAN RESERVATION
Round Rock
Cow Springs
Many Farms
Chinle
Canyon de Chelly National Monument
Lake Mead
Colorado River
Grand Canyon National Park
Temple Bar
Meadview
Grand Canyon Village
Kaibab National Forest
Tuba City
Cameron
HOPI INDIAN RESERVATION
Hotevilla
Polacca
Window Rock
Gallup
HUALAPAI INDIAN RESERVATION
Valle
Little Colorado River
Greasewood
Dilkon
Sanders
Lake Mohave
Seligman
Kingman
Ash Fork
Williams
Flagstaff
Winslow
Holbrook
Petrified Forest National Park
Bullhead City
Needles
Prescott National Forest
Clarkdale
Jerome
Sedona
Coconino National Forest
Camp Verde
Prescott
Lake Havasu City
Bill Williams River
Cordes
Strawberry
Payson
Heber
Forest Lakes
Show Low
Concho
St. Johns
15
89A
89
160
191
93
66
180
40
17
87
77
666
60

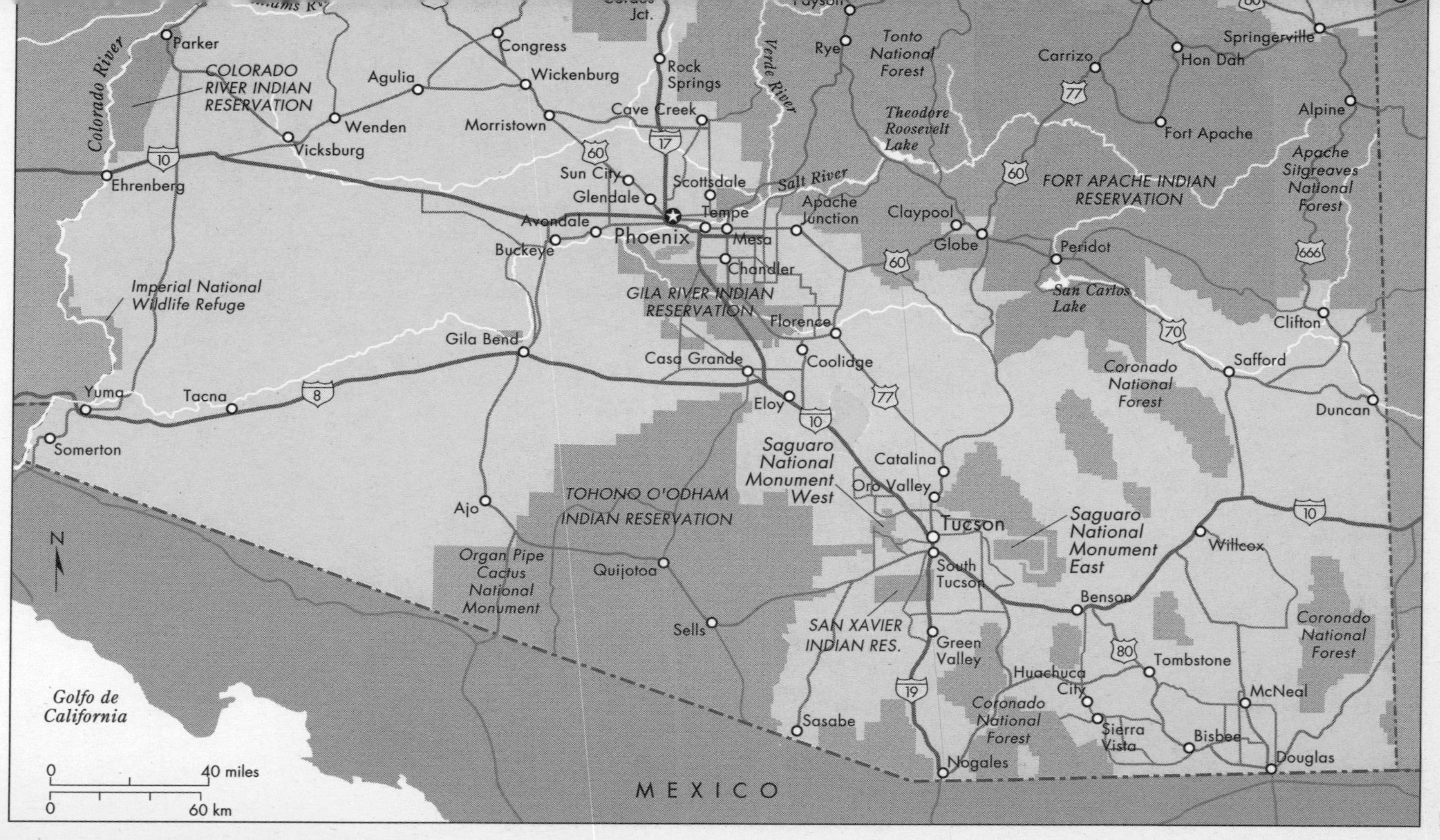
Parker
COLORADO RIVER INDIAN RESERVATION
Colorado River
Congress
Wickenburg
Agulia
Wenden
Vicksburg
Morristown
Ehrenberg
Rock Springs
Cave Creek
Verde River
Rye
Tonto National Forest
Theodore Roosevelt Lake
Carrizo
Hon Dah
Springerville
Alpine
Fort Apache
Apache Sitgreaves National Forest
FORT APACHE INDIAN RESERVATION
Sun City
Glendale
Scottsdale
Salt River
Tempe
Apache Junction
Claypool
Globe
Peridot
Avondale
Phoenix
Mesa
Buckeye
Chandler
San Carlos Lake
Clifton
Imperial National Wildlife Refuge
GILA RIVER INDIAN RESERVATION
Florence
Gila Bend
Casa Grande
Coolidge
Coronado National Forest
Safford
Duncan
Yuma
Tacna
Eloy
Somerton
Saguaro National Monument West
Catalina
Oro Valley
TOHONO O'ODHAM INDIAN RESERVATION
Ajo
Tucson
Saguaro National Monument East
Willcox
South Tucson
Organ Pipe Cactus National Monument
Quijotoa
Benson
Sells
SAN XAVIER INDIAN RES.
Green Valley
Tombstone
Coronado National Forest
Huachuca City
McNeal
Coronado National Forest
Golfo de California
Sasabe
Sierra Vista
Bisbee
Douglas
Nogales
0
40 miles
0
60 km
MEXICO
N

The United States

ONTARIO
CANADA
QUÉBEC
NEW BRUNSWICK
Fredericton
Québec
MAINE
Augusta
Montréal
Ottawa
Montpelier
VT.
Concord
N.H.
Boston
MASS.
R.I.
Providence
Lake Superior
MINNESOTA
Duluth
WISCONSIN
MICHIGAN
Lake Huron
Lake Michigan
St. Paul
Minneapolis
Green Bay
Toronto
Lake Ontario
Albany
Hartford
Hudson R.
Buffalo
NEW YORK
Lake Erie
CONN.
New York
Milwaukee
Lansing
Madison
Detroit
Cleveland
PENNSYLVANIA
N.J.
Trenton
IOWA
Chicago
Pittsburgh
Harrisburg
Philadelphia
Des Moines
Omaha
OHIO
INDIANA
ILLINOIS
MD
Dover
Baltimore
DEL.
Annapolis
Columbus
Indianapolis
Springfield
WEST VIRGINIA
Washington, D.C.
Charleston
Cincinnati
Richmond
Topeka
Kansas City
Jefferson City
St. Louis
Louisville
Frankfort
Norfolk
VIRGINIA
Mississippi R.
Ohio R.
MISSOURI
KENTUCKY
Raleigh
Nashville
NORTH CAROLINA
TENNESSEE
Tulsa
ARKANSAS
Memphis
Columbia
SOUTH CAROLINA
Little Rock
Tennessee R.
Atlanta
Savannah R.
Birmingham
GEORGIA
ATLANTIC OCEAN
MISSISSIPPI
Savannah
Montgomery
Jackson
ALABAMA
Jacksonville
Baton Rouge
Mobile
Tallahassee
FLORIDA
New Orleans
Orlando
Houston
LOUISIANA
Bahama Islands
Miami
Nassau
Gulf of Mexico
N
0
500 miles
0
800 km

IMPORTANT CONTACTS A TO Z

An Alphabetical Listing of Publications, Organizations, and Companies That Will Help You Before, During, and After Your Trip

A

AIR TRAVEL

The major gateways to Arizona include Phoenix Sky Harbor International (☎ 602/273–3300), about 3 mi east of Phoenix city center, and Tucson International Air Terminal (☎ 520/573–8000), about 8½ mi south of the central business area. Flying time is 5½ hours from New York, 3½ hours from Chicago, and 1¼ hours from Los Angeles.

CARRIERS

TO PHOENIX➤ Contact **Alaska Airlines** (☎ 800/426–0333), **American** (☎ 800/433–7300), **America Trans Air** (☎ 800/225–2995), **America West** (☎ 800/235–9292), **Arizona Airways** (☎ 800/274–0662), **Continental** (☎ 800/525–0280), **Delta** (☎ 800/221–1212), **Frontier Air** (☎ 800/432–1359), **Northwest** (☎ 800/225–2525), **Reno Air** (☎ 800/736–6247), **Southwest** (☎ 800/435–9792), **TWA** (☎ 800/221–2000), **United** (☎ 800/241–6522), **USAir** (☎ 800/428–4322), and **Western Pacific** (☎ 800/930–3030).

TO TUCSON➤ Contact **Air California** (☎ 800/237–6225), **American** (☎ 800/433–7300), **America West** (☎ 800/235–9292), **Continental** (☎ 800/525–0280), **Delta** (☎ 800/221–1212), **Northwest** (☎ 800/225–2525), **Reno Air** (☎ 800/736–6247), and **United** (☎ 800/241–6522).

FROM THE U.K.➤ **Delta** (☎ 0800/414–767) flies from London's Gatwick Airport via Atlanta, **Continental Airlines** (☎ 0800/776–464 or 01293/776–464) from Gatwick via Houston and from Manchester via Newark, and **American Airlines** (☎ 0345/789–789) from Heathrow via Chicago.

COMPLAINTS

To register complaints about charter and scheduled airlines, contact the U.S. Department of Transportation's **Aviation Consumer Protection Division** (✉ C-75, Washington, DC 20590, ☎ 202/366–2220). Complaints about lost baggage or ticketing problems and safety concerns may also be logged with the **Federal Aviation Administration (FAA) Consumer Hotline** (☎ 800/322–7873).

LOW-COST CARRIERS

For inexpensive, no-frills flights, contact **Midwest Express** (☎ 800/452–2022), **Reno Air** (☎ 800/736–6247), and **Southwest Airlines** (☎ 800/435–9792).

PUBLICATIONS

For general information about charter carriers, ask for the Department of Transportation's free brochure **"Plane Talk: Public Charter Flights"** (✉ Aviation Consumer Protection Division, C-75, Washington, DC 20590, ☎ 202/366–2220). The Department of Transportation also publishes a 58-page booklet, **"Fly Rights,"** available from the Consumer Information Center (✉ Supt. of Documents, Dept. 136C, Pueblo, CO 81009; $1.75).

For other tips and hints, consult the Consumers Union's monthly **"Consumer Reports Travel Letter"** (✉ Box 53629, Boulder, CO 80322, ☎ 800/234–1970; $39 1st year).

WITHIN ARIZONA

Within the state, **America West Express/Mesa** (☎ 800/235–9292) operates regularly scheduled flights from Phoenix to Flagstaff, Prescott, Lake Havasu, Laughlin, Kingman, Sierra Vista, and Yuma; **Skywest** (☎ 800/453–9417) flies from Phoenix to Page/Lake Powell and Yuma.

B

BETTER BUSINESS BUREAU

Contact the **Better Business Bureau** in Phoenix (✉ 4428 N.

12th St., Phoenix, AZ 99503, ☎ 602/264–1721) and Tucson (✉ 3620 N. 1st Ave., Suite 136, Tucson, AZ 85719, ☎ 602/888–5353). For other local contacts, consult the **Council of Better Business Bureaus** (✉ 4200 Wilson Blvd., Suite 800, Arlington, VA 22203, ☎ 703/276–0100, FAX 703/525–8277).

BUS TRAVEL

Greyhound (☎ 800/231–2222) provides service to many Arizona destinations from most parts of the United States.

C

CAR RENTAL

The major car-rental companies represented in Arizona are **Alamo** (☎ 800/327–9633; in the U.K., 0800/272–2000), **Avis** (☎ 800/331–1212; in Canada, 800/879–2847), **Budget** (☎ 800/527–0700; in the U.K., 0800/181181), **Dollar** (☎ 800/800–4000; in the U.K., where it is known as Eurodollar, 0990/565656), **Hertz** (☎ 800/654–3131; in Canada, 800/263–0600; in the U.K., 0345/555888), and **National InterRent** (☎ 800/227–7368; in the U.K., where National is known as Europcar InterRent, 01345/222525). Rates in Arizona begin at $35 a day and $129 a week for an economy car with unlimited mileage. This does not include tax on car rentals, which is 14.05%.

RENTAL WHOLESALERS

Contact **Auto Europe** (☎ 207/828–2525 or 800/223–5555).

CHILDREN & TRAVEL

FLYING

Look into **"Flying with Baby"** (✉ Third Street Press, Box 261250, Littleton, CO 80163, ☎ 303/595–5959; $4.95 includes shipping), cowritten by a flight attendant. **"Kids and Teens in Flight,"** free from the U.S. Department of Transportation's Aviation Consumer Protection Division (✉ C-75, Washington, DC 20590, ☎ 202/366–2220), offers tips on children flying alone. Every two years the February issue of ***Family Travel Times*** (☞ Know-How, *below*) details children's services on three dozen airlines. **"Flying Alone, Handy Advice for Kids Traveling Solo"** is available free from the American Automobile Association (AAA) (✉ send SASE legal-size: Flying Alone, Mail Stop 800, 1000 AAA Dr., Heathrow, FL 32746).

KNOW-HOW

Family Travel Times, published quarterly by Travel with Your Children (✉ TWYCH, 40 5th Ave., New York, NY 10011, ☎ 212/477–5524; $40 per year), covers destinations, types of vacations, and modes of travel.

LOCAL INFORMATION

A Family Guide to Arizona, by Catherine Dunes (✉ Kids Touring Arizona, 4201 W. Villa Maria Dr., Glendale, AZ 85308, ☎ 602/439–2324; $6.95), contains Arizona-related fun facts, games, puzzles, and palatable educational information.

LODGING

All **Holiday Inns** (☎ 800/465–4329) allow children under age 19 to stay free when sharing a room with an adult, and some offer family plans, whereby children under 12 can eat free from special children's menus. **Westin La Paloma Hotel** in Tucson (☎ 800/228–3000) has supervised activities year round for children ages 6 months–12 years, as well as junior tennis camps for kids 5–14 years old in summer. From Thanksgiving through April, the **Tanque Verde Guest Ranch** (☎ 800/234–3833), also in Tucson, offers activities for children 4–11, including horseback-riding lessons, tennis, and nature walks in the daytime and arts and crafts and games in the evening. In the Phoenix area, the **Pointe Hilton Resort at Squaw Peak** (☎ 800/934–1000) runs its Coyote Camp for children ages 4–12 year-round, including such activities as arts and crafts, hiking, swimming, and cooking. The **Phoenician Resort** (☎ 800/888–8234) in Scottsdale has supervised indoor and outdoor activities for children 5–12 as well as junior golf and tennis clinics for kids 5–14 throughout the year; Scottsdale's **Hyatt Regency** (☎ 800/233–1234) also offers a full range of supervised daytime activities, geared for kids 3–12; in addition, there are evening sessions each Friday and Saturday. All of the above resorts also have baby-sitting services.

TOUR OPERATORS

Contact **Grandtravel** (✉ 6900 Wisconsin Ave., Suite 706, Chevy Chase, MD 20815, ☎ 301/986–0790 or 800/247–7651), which has tours for people traveling with grandchildren ages 7–17; or **Rascals in Paradise** (✉ 650 5th St., Suite 505, San Francisco, CA 94107, ☎ 415/978–9800 or 800/872–7225).

CUSTOMS

CANADIANS

Contact **Revenue Canada** (✉ 2265 St. Laurent Blvd. S, Ottawa, Ontario K1G 4K3, ☎ 613/993–0534) for a copy of the free brochure **"I Declare/Je Déclare"** and for details on duty-free limits. For recorded information (within Canada only), call ☎ 800/461–9999.

U.K. CITIZENS

HM Customs and Excise (✉ Dorset House, Stamford St., London SE1 9NG, ☎ 0171/202–4227) can answer questions about U.K. customs regulations and publishes a free pamphlet, **"A Guide for Travellers,"** detailing standard procedures and import rules.

D

DISABILITIES & ACCESSIBILITY

COMPLAINTS

To register complaints under the provisions of the Americans with Disabilities Act, contact the U.S. Department of Justice's **Disability Rights Section** (✉ Box 66738, Washington, DC 20035, ☎ 202/514–0301 or 800/514–0301, FAX 202/307–1198, TTY 202/514–0383 or 800/514–0383). For airline-related problems, contact the U.S. Department of Transportation's **Aviation Consumer Protection Division** (☞ Air Travel, *above*). For complaints about surface transportation, contact the Department of Transportation's **Civil Rights Office** (✉ 400 7th St. SW, Room 10215, Washington DC, 20590 ☎ 202/366–4648).

GETTING AROUND

BY BUS➢ **Greyhound** (☎ 800/752–4841, TTY 800/345–3109), which provides service to many destinations in Arizona, will carry a person with disabilities and a companion for the price of a single fare.

BY TRAIN➢ **Amtrak** (✉ National Railroad Passenger Corp., 60 Massachusetts Ave. NE, Washington, DC 20002, ☎ 800/872–7245) advises that you request redcap service, special seats, or wheelchair assistance when you make reservations. Also note that not all stations are equipped to provide these services. All passengers with disabilities are entitled to a 15% discount on the lowest fare, and there are special fares for children with disabilities as well. Contact Amtrak for a free brochure that outlines services for older travelers and people with disabilities.

BY CAR➢ **Avis** (☎ 800/331–1212), **Hertz** (☎ 800/654–3131), and **National** (☎ 800/328–4567) can provide hand controls on some rental cars with advance notice.

LOCAL INFO

For information on accessible facilities at specific parks and sites in Arizona, contact the **Southern Arizona Group Office** (☎ 602/640–5250).

ORGANIZATIONS

TRAVELERS WITH HEARING IMPAIRMENTS➢ The **American Academy of Otolaryngology** (✉ 1 Prince St., Alexandria, VA 22314, ☎ 703/836–4444, FAX 703/683–5100, TTY 703/519–1585) publishes a brochure, "Travel Tips for Hearing Impaired People."

TRAVELERS WITH MOBILITY PROBLEMS➢ Contact the **Information Center for Individuals with Disabilities** (✉ Box 256, Boston, MA 02117, ☎ 617/450–9888; in MA, 800/462–5015; TTY 617/424–6855); **Mobility International USA** (✉ Box 10767, Eugene, OR 97440, ☎ and TTY 541/343–1284, FAX 541/343–6812), the U.S. branch of a Belgium-based organization (☞ *below*) with affiliates in 30 countries; **MossRehab Hospital Travel Information Service** (☎ 215/456–9600, TTY 215/456–9602), a telephone information resource for travelers with physical disabilities; the **Society for the Advancement of Travel for the Handicapped** (✉ 347 5th Ave., Suite 610, New York, NY 10016,

☎ 212/447–7284, FAX 212/725–8253; membership $45); and **Travelin' Talk** (✉ Box 3534, Clarksville, TN 37043, ☎ 615/552–6670, FAX 615/552–1182), which provides local contacts worldwide for travelers with disabilities.

TRAVELERS WITH VISION IMPAIRMENTS➤ Contact the **American Council of the Blind** (✉ 1155 15th St. NW, Suite 720, Washington, DC 20005, ☎ 202/467–5081, FAX 202/467–5085) for a list of travelers' resources or the **American Foundation for the Blind** (✉ 11 Penn Plaza, Suite 300, New York, NY 10001, ☎ 212/502–7600 or 800/232–5463, TTY 212/502–7662), which provides general advice and publishes **"Access to Art"** ($19.95), a directory of museums that accommodate travelers with vision impairments.

IN THE U.K.

Contact the **Royal Association for Disability and Rehabilitation** (✉ RADAR, 12 City Forum, 250 City Rd., London EC1V 8AF, ☎ 0171/250–3222) or **Mobility International** (✉ rue de Manchester 25, B-1080 Brussels, Belgium, ☎ 00–322–410–6297, FAX 00–322–410–6874), an international travel-information clearing-house for people with disabilities.

PUBLICATIONS

Several publications for travelers with disabilities are available from the **Consumer Information Center** (✉ Box 100, Pueblo, CO 81009, ☎ 719/948–3334). Call or write for its free catalog of current titles. The Society for the Advancement of Travel for the Handicapped (☞ Organizations, *above*) publishes the quarterly magazine **"Access to Travel"** ($13 for 1-year subscription).

Fodor's ***Great American Vacations for Travelers with Disabilities*** (available in bookstores, or ☎ 800/533–6478; $18 plus $4 shipping) details accessible attractions, restaurants, and hotels in U.S. destinations. The 500-page ***Travelin' Talk Directory*** (✉ Box 3534, Clarksville, TN 37043, ☎ 615/552–6670, FAX 615/552–1182; $35) lists people and organizations who help travelers with disabilities. For travel agents worldwide, consult the ***Directory of Travel Agencies for the Disabled*** (✉ Twin Peaks Press, Box 129, Vancouver, WA 98666, ☎ 360/694–2462 or 800/637–2256, FAX 360/696–3210; $19.95 plus $3 shipping). The Sierra Club publishes ***Easy Access to National Parks*** (✉ Sierra Club Store, 85 Second St., San Francisco, CA 94105, ☎ 415/977–5630 or 800/935–1056, FAX 415/977–5795; $16 plus $4 shipping).

TRAVEL AGENCIES & TOUR OPERATORS

The Americans with Disabilities Act requires that all travel firms serve the needs of all travelers. That said, you should note that some agencies and operators specialize in making travel arrangements for individuals and groups with disabilities, among them **Access Adventures** (✉ 206 Chestnut Ridge Rd., Rochester, NY 14624, ☎ 716/889–9096), run by a former physical-rehab counselor.

TRAVELERS WITH MOBILITY PROBLEMS➤ Contact **Hinsdale Travel Service** (✉ 201 E. Ogden Ave., Suite 100, Hinsdale, IL 60521, ☎ 708/325–1335), a travel agency that benefits from the advice of wheelchair traveler Janice Perkins; and **Wheelchair Journeys** (✉ 16979 Redmond Way, Redmond, WA 98052, ☎ 206/885–2210 or 800/313–4751), which can handle arrangements worldwide.

TRAVELERS WITH DEVELOPMENTAL DISABILITIES➤ Contact the nonprofit **New Directions** (✉ 5276 Hollister Ave., Suite 207, Santa Barbara, CA 93111, ☎ 805/967–2841) and **Sprout** (✉ 893 Amsterdam Ave., New York, NY 10025, ☎ 212/222–9575), which specializes in custom-designed itineraries for groups but also books vacations for individual travelers with developmental disabilities.

TRAVEL GEAR

The **Magellan's** catalog (☎ 800/962–4943, FAX 805/568–5406) includes a section devoted to products designed for travelers with disabilities.

DISCOUNTS & DEALS

AIRFARES

For the lowest airfares to Arizona, call ☎ 800/FLY–4–LESS. Also try ☎ 800/FLY–ASAP.

CLUBS

Contact **Entertainment Travel Editions** (✉ Box 1068, Trumbull, CT 06611, ☎ 800/445–4137; $28–$53, depending on destination), **Great American Traveler** (✉ Box 27965, Salt Lake City, UT 84127, ☎ 800/548–2812; $49.95 per year), **Moment's Notice Discount Travel Club** (✉ 7301 New Utrecht Ave., Brooklyn, NY 11204, ☎ 718/234–6295; $25 per year, single or family), **Privilege Card** (✉ 3391 Peachtree Rd. NE, Suite 110, Atlanta, GA 30326, ☎ 404/262–0222 or 800/236–9732; $74.95 per year), **Travelers Advantage** (✉ CUC Travel Service, 49 Music Square W, Nashville, TN 37203, ☎ 800/548–1116 or 800/648–4037; $49 per year, single or family), or **Worldwide Discount Travel Club** (✉ 1674 Meridian Ave., Miami Beach, FL 33139, ☎ 305/534–2082; $50 per year for family, $40 single).

STUDENTS

Members of Hostelling International–American Youth Hostels (☞ Students, *below*) are eligible for discounts on car rentals, admissions to attractions, and other selected travel expenses.

PUBLICATIONS

Consult ***The Frugal Globetrotter,*** by Bruce Northam (✉ Fulcrum Publishing, 350 Indiana St., Suite 350, Golden, CO 80401, ☎ 800/992–2908; $16.95 plus $4 shipping). For publications that tell how to find the lowest prices on plane tickets, *see* Air Travel, *above*.

DRIVING

For up-to-date information on highway conditions and road closings throughout the state, call ☎ 520/573–7623.

G

GAY & LESBIAN TRAVEL

ORGANIZATIONS

The **International Gay Travel Association** (✉ Box 4974, Key West, FL 33041, ☎ 800/448–8550, FAX 305/296–6633), a consortium of more than 1,000 travel companies, can supply names of gay-friendly travel agents, tour operators, and accommodations.

PUBLICATIONS

The 16-page monthly **"Out & About"** (☎ 212/645–6922 or 800/929–2268, FAX 800/929–2215; $49 for 10 issues and quarterly calendar) covers gay-friendly resorts, hotels, cruise lines, and airlines. Also consult Fodor's **Gay Guide to the USA** by Andrew Collins (available in bookstores, or by ☎ 800/533–6478; $19.50 plus $4 shipping).

TOUR OPERATORS

Toto Tours (✉ 1326 W. Albion Ave., Suite 3W, Chicago, IL 60626, ☎ 312/274–8686 or 800/565–1241, FAX 312/274–8695) offers group tours to worldwide destinations.

TRAVEL AGENCIES

The largest agencies serving gay travelers are **Advance Travel** (✉ 10700 Northwest Fwy., Suite 160, Houston, TX 77092, ☎ 713/682–2002 or 800/292–0500), **Islanders/Kennedy Travel** (✉ 183 W. 10th St., New York, NY 10014, ☎ 212/242–3222 or 800/988–1181), **Now Voyager** (✉ 4406 18th St., San Francisco, CA 94114, ☎ 415/626–1169 or 800/255–6951), and **Yellowbrick Road** (✉ 1500 W. Balmoral Ave., Chicago, IL 60640, ☎ 312/561–1800 or 800/642–2488). **Skylink Women's Travel** (✉ 2460 W. 3rd St., Suite 215, Santa Rosa, CA 95401, ☎ 707/570–0105 or 800/225–5759) serves lesbian travelers.

I

INSURANCE

IN CANADA

Contact **Mutual of Omaha** (✉ Travel Division, 500 University Ave., Toronto, Ontario M5G 1V8, ☎ 416/598–4083 or 800/465–0267).

IN THE U.S.

Travel insurance covering baggage, health, and trip cancellation or interruptions is available from **Access America** (✉ 6600 W. Broad St., Richmond, VA 23230, ☎ 804/285–3300 or 800/334–7525), **Carefree Travel Insurance** (✉ Box 9366, 100 Garden City Plaza, Garden City, NY 11530, ☎ 516/294–0220 or 800/323–3149), **Near Travel Services** (✉ Box 1339, Calumet City, IL

60409, ☎ 708/868-6700 or 800/654-6700), **Tele-Trip** (✉ Mutual of Omaha Plaza, Box 31716, Omaha, NE 68131, ☎ 800/228-9792), **Travel Guard International** (✉ 1145 Clark St., Stevens Point, WI 54481, ☎ 715/345-0505 or 800/826-1300), **Travel Insured International** (✉ Box 280568, East Hartford, CT 06128, ☎ 203/528-7663 or 800/243-3174), and **Wallach & Company** (✉ 107 W. Federal St., Box 480, Middleburg, VA 22117, ☎ 540/687-3166 or 800/237-6615).

IN THE U.K.

The **Association of British Insurers** (✉ 51 Gresham St., London EC2V 7HQ, ☎ 0171/600-3333) gives advice by phone and publishes the free pamphlet **"Holiday Insurance and Motoring Abroad,"** which sets out typical policy provisions and costs.

L

LODGING

APARTMENT & VILLA RENTAL

Among the companies to contact are **Property Rentals International** (✉ 1008 Mansfield Crossing Rd., Richmond, VA 23236, ☎ 804/378-6054 or 800/220-3332, FAX 804/379-2073) and **Rent-a-Home International** (✉ 7200 34th Ave. NW, Seattle, WA 98117, ☎ 206/789-9377 or 800/488-7368, FAX 206/789-9379, rentahomeinternational£msn.com). Members of the travel club **Hideaways International** (✉ 767 Islington St., Portsmouth, NH 03801, ☎ 603/430-4433 or 800/843-4433, FAX 603/430-4444, info@hideaways.com; $99 per year) receive two annual guides plus quarterly newsletters and arrange rentals among themselves.

B&BS

Arizona B&B organizations include **Mi Casa Su Casa** (✉ Box 950, Tempe 85280, ☎ 602/990-0682 or 800/456-0682, FAX 602/990-3390), **Bed & Breakfast Inn Arizona** (✉ 8900 E. Via Linda, Suite 101, Scottsdale 85258, ☎ FAX 602/860-9338, reservations only 800/266-7829), and the **Arizona Association of Bed and Breakfast Inns** (✉ Box 7186, Phoenix 85012, ☎ 602/277-0775). The Arizona Office of Tourism (☞ Visitor Information, *below*) has a statewide list of bed-and-breakfasts.

CAMPING

Individual campgrounds should be contacted before travel for suggestions as to specific equipment to bring, as well as necessary reservations, advance deposits, and permits. Most state parks have a 15-day maximum-stay limit. For further details, contact the **National Park Service** (✉ 202 E. Earll Dr., Suite 115, Phoenix 85012, ☎ 602/640-5250), **Bureau of Land Management** (✉ Box 16563, Phoenix 85011, ☎ 602/650-0528), **Arizona State Parks Department** (☞ National and State Parks, *below*), **Apache Sitgreaves National Forest** (✉ 309 S. Mountain Ave., Springerville 85938, ☎ 520/333-4301), **Coconino National Forest** (✉ 2323 E. Greenlaw La., Flagstaff 86004, ☎ 520/527-3600), **Coronado National Forest** (✉ Federal Bldg., 300 W. Congress St., Tucson 85701, ☎ 520/670-4552), **Williams-Forest Service Visitor Center** (✉ 200 W. Railroad Ave., Williams 86046, ☎ 520/635-4061), **Prescott National Forest** (✉ 344 S. Cortez St., Prescott 86303, ☎ 520/771-4700, TTY 520/771-4792), or **Tonto National Forest** (✉ 2324 E. McDowell Rd., Phoenix 85006, ☎ 602/225-5200). The **National Forest Service hot line** (☎ 602/225-5296) gives recorded information on road conditions.

DUDE RANCHES

Contact the Arizona Office of Tourism (☞ Visitor Information, *below*) for the names and addresses of dude ranches throughout the state.

HOME EXCHANGE

Some of the principal clearinghouses are **HomeLink International/Vacation Exchange Club** (✉ Box 650, Key West, FL 33041, ☎ 305/294-1448 or 800/638-3841, FAX 305/294-1148; $78 per year), which sends members five annual directories, with a listing in one, plus updates; **Intervac International** (✉ Box 590504, San Francisco, CA 94159, ☎ 415/435-3497, FAX 415/435-7440; $65 per year), which publishes four annual directories.

M

MONEY

ATMS

For specific **Cirrus** locations in the United States and Canada, call ☎ 800/424–7787. For U.S. **Plus** locations, call ☎ 800/843–7587 and enter the area code and first three digits of the number from which you're calling (or of the calling area in which you want to locate an ATM).

N

NATIONAL AND STATE PARKS

A variety of passes are available for senior citizens, travelers with disabilities, and frequent visitors. The passes can be purchased at any park that charges admission or obtained by mail from the **National Park Service** (✉ Dept. of the Interior, Washington, DC 20240).

For a complete listing of all state parks and their facilities, contact the **Arizona State Parks Department** (✉ 1300 W. Washington St., Phoenix 85007, ☎ 602/542–4174).

P

PACKING

For strategies on packing light, get a copy of ***The Packing Book,*** by Judith Gilford (✉ Ten Speed Press, Box 7123, Berkeley, CA 94707, ☎ 510/559–1600 or 800/841–2665, FAX 510/524–4588; $7.95 plus $3.50 shipping).

PASSPORTS & VISAS

U.K. CITIZENS

For fees, documentation requirements, and emergency passports, call the **London Passport Office** (☎ 0990/210410). For U.S. visa information, call the **U.S. Embassy Visa Information Line** (☎ 01891/200–290; calls cost 49p per minute or 39p per minute cheap rate) or send a self-addressed, stamped envelope to the **U.S. Embassy Visa Branch** (✉ 5 Upper Grosvenor St., London W1A 2JB). If you live in Northern Ireland, write to the **U.S. Consulate General** (✉ Queen's House, Queen St., Belfast BTI 6EO).

PHOTO HELP

The **Kodak Information Center** (☎ 800/242–2424) answers consumer questions about film and photography. The ***Kodak Guide to Shooting Great Travel Pictures*** (available in bookstores; or contact Fodor's Travel Publications, ☎ 800/533–6478; $16.50 plus $4 shipping) explains how to take expert travel photographs.

R

ROCKHOUNDING

The **Department of Mines and Mineral Resources** (✉ 1502 W. Washington St., Phoenix 85007, ☎ 602/255–3795) is an excellent source of information about specimens that can be found in each part of the state.

S

SAFETY

"Trouble-Free Travel," from the AAA, is a booklet of tips for protecting yourself and your belongings when away from home. Send a stamped, self-addressed, legal-size envelope to Trouble-Free Travel (✉ Mail Stop 75, 1000 AAA Dr., Heathrow, FL 32746).

SENIOR CITIZENS

EDUCATIONAL TRAVEL

The nonprofit **Elderhostel** (✉ 75 Federal St., 3rd Floor, Boston, MA 02110, ☎ 617/426–7788), for people 55 and older, has offered inexpensive study programs since 1975. Courses cover everything from marine science to Greek mythology and cowboy poetry. Fees for programs in the United States and Canada, which usually last one week, run about $300, not including transportation.

ORGANIZATIONS

Contact the **American Association of Retired Persons** (✉ AARP, 601 E St. NW, Washington, DC 20049, ☎ 202/434–2277; annual dues $8 per person or couple). Its Purchase Privilege Program secures discounts for members on lodging, car rentals, and sightseeing, and the AARP Motoring Plan (☎ 800/334–3300) furnishes domestic trip-routing information and emergency road-service aid for an annual fee of $39.95 ($59.95 for a premium version). Senior-citizen travelers can also join the AAA for emergency road service and other travel benefits (☞ Driving, *above, and* Discounts & Deals *in* Smart Travel Tips A to Z).

Additional sources for discounts on lodgings, car rentals, and other travel expenses, as well as helpful magazines and newsletters, are the **National Council of Senior Citizens** (✉ 1331 F St. NW, Washington, DC 20004, ☎ 202/347–8800; annual membership $12) and Sears's **Mature Outlook** (✉ Box 10448, Des Moines, IA 50306, ☎ 800/336–6330; annual membership $14.95).

SPORTS

BASEBALL

During spring training, the **Chicago Cubs** play at Hohokam Park in Mesa (☎ 602/964–4467), the **Oakland Athletics** at Phoenix Municipal Stadium (☎ 602/392–0074), the **San Francisco Giants** at Scottsdale Stadium (☎ 602/990–7972), the **California Angels** at Diablo Stadium in Tempe (☎ 602/438–9300), and the **Milwaukee Brewers** at the Compadre Stadium in Chandler (☎ 602/895–1200). Both the **San Diego Padres and the Seattle Mariners** train at Peoria Stadium (☎ 602/878–4337) in another Phoenix suburb. The **Colorado Rockies** play at Tucson's Hi-Corbett Field (☎ 520/327–9467). For current information on all aspects of Cactus League baseball, contact the **Mesa Convention and Visitor's Bureau** (✉ 120 North Center St., Mesa 85201, ☎ 602/827–4700 or 800/283–6372).

BICYCLING

Call the county **Parks and Recreation Department** in the area you're visiting for information on nearby bike paths. **The Arizona Bicycle Club, Inc.** (✉ Box 7191, Phoenix, AZ 85011, ☎ 602/264–5478 or 602/279–6674) publishes a schedule of the many bicycle races that take place throughout the state.

FISHING

Fishing licenses are required and can be obtained from the **Arizona Game and Fish Department** (✉ 2221 W. Greenway Rd., Phoenix 85023, ☎ 602/942–3000). For permission to fish San Carlos Lake on the San Carlos Indian reservation call ☎ 520/475–2343.

GOLF

For a list of Arizona's golfing facilities, contact the **Arizona Golf Association** (✉ 7226 N. 16th St., Suite 200, Phoenix 85020, ☎ 602/944–3035 or 800/458–8484).

HIKING

The **Backcountry Office** (☎ 520/638–7888) provides hikers with trail details, weather conditions, and packing suggestions for the Grand Canyon. For hikers who prefer to travel with a group, the **Sierra Club** (☎ 602/253–8633) leads a variety of wilderness treks. Contact the local chapters in Phoenix, Tucson, Kingman, Prescott, Sedona, Flagstaff, and Yuma for information on guided hikes in these area.

RIVER RAFTING

Contact the **Arizona Office of Tourism** (☞ Visitor Information, *below*) for an extensive list of rafting outfits, or *see* Tour Operators, *below.*

SKIING

For cross-country skiing, **Arizona Snowbowl & Flagstaff Nordic Center** (☎ 520/779–1951), **North Rim Nordic Center** (☎ 520/526–0924 or 800/525–0924 outside AZ), **Williams Ski Area** (☎ 520/635–9330), and miles of crisscrossing trails around **Alpine** (✉ Alpine Ranger District, ☎ 520/339–4384) are recommended. Equipment and instruction are readily available. We advise making reservations in the busy season.

For downhill skiing, **Sunrise Park Resort** in McNary (☎ 800/554–6835), owned and operated by the White Mountain Apache Indians, encompasses three mountain peaks and is the state's largest ski area. **Arizona Snowbowl** (☞ *above*), and **Mt. Lemmon Ski Valley** (☎ 520/576–1321), near Tucson, are also popular. Though they aren't as impressive as those in the Rockies, ski resorts cater to all levels and provide instruction and equipment rental.

TENNIS

Arizona offers a multitude of tennis opportunities, from hard courts at city parks and university campuses to full-scale programs at ultraposh tennis-oriented resorts, such as **John Gardiner's Tennis Ranch** (✉ 5700

E. McDonald Dr., Scottsdale 85253, ☎ 602/948–2100 or 800/245–2051), one of the country's best. Most hotels either have their own courts or are affiliated with a private or municipal facility.

STUDENTS

GROUPS

A major tour operator specializing in student travel is **Contiki Holidays** (✉ 300 Plaza Alicante, Suite 900, Garden Grove, CA 92640, ☎ 714/740–0808 or 800/266–8454).

HOSTELING

In the United States, contact **Hostelling International–American Youth Hostels** (✉ 733 15th St. NW, Suite 840, Washington, DC 20005, ☎ 202/783–6161 for reservations worldwide or 800/444–6111 for reservations at U.S. hostels using a credit card, FAX 202/783–6171); in Canada, **Hostelling International–Canada** (✉ 205 Catherine St., Suite 400, Ottawa, Ontario K2P 1C3, ☎ 613/237–7884); and in the United Kingdom, the **Youth Hostel Association of England and Wales** (✉ Trevelyan House, 8 St. Stephen's Hill, St. Albans, Hertfordshire AL1 2DY, ☎ 01727/855215 or 01727/845047). Membership (in the U.S., $25; in Canada, C$26.75; in the U.K., £9.30) gives you access to 5,000 hostels in 77 countries that charge $5–$40 per person per night.

ORGANIZATIONS

A major contact is the **Council on International Educational Exchange** (✉ mail orders only: CIEE, 205 E. 42nd St., 16th Floor, New York, NY 10017, ☎ 212/661–1450, info@ciee.org). The **Educational Travel Centre** (✉ 438 N. Frances St., Madison, WI 53703, ☎ 608/256–5551 or 800/747–5551, FAX 608/256–2042) offers rail passes and low-cost airline tickets, mostly for flights that depart from Chicago.

In Canada, also contact **Travel Cuts** (✉ 187 College St., Toronto, Ontario M5T 1P7, ☎ 416/979–2406 or 800/667–2887).

T

TOUR OPERATORS

Among the companies that sell tours and packages to Arizona, the following are nationally known, have a proven reputation, and offer plenty of options.

GROUP TOURS

DELUXE➢ **Globus** (✉ 5301 S. Federal Circle, Littleton, CO 80123-2980, ☎ 303/797–2800 or 800/221–0090, FAX 303/795–0962), **Maupintour** (✉ Box 807, Lawrence, KS 66047, ☎ 913/843–1211 or 800/255–4266, FAX 913/843–8351), and **Tauck Tours** (✉ Box 5027, 276 Post Rd. W, Westport, CT 06881, ☎ 203/226–6911 or 800/468–2825, FAX 203/221–6828).

FIRST-CLASS➢ **Brendan Tours** (✉ 15137 Califa St., Van Nuys, CA 91411, ☎ 818/785–9696 or 800/421–8446, FAX 818/902–9876), **Caravan Tours** (✉ 401 N. Michigan Ave., Chicago, IL 60611, ☎ 312/321–9800 or 800/227–2826), **Collette Tours** (✉ 162 Middle St., Pawtucket, RI 02860, ☎ 401/728–3805 or 800/832–4656, FAX 401/728–1380), **Gadabout Tours** (✉ 700 E. Tahquitz Canyon Way, Palm Springs, CA 92262, ☎ 619/325–5556 or 800/952–5068), and **Mayflower Tours** (✉ Box 490, 1225 Warren Ave., Downers Grove, IL 60515, ☎ 708/960–3793 or 800/323–7604, FAX 708/960–3575).

BUDGET➢ **Cosmos** (☞ Globus, *above*).

PACKAGES

Independent vacation packages are available from major tour operators and airlines. Contact **Adventure Vacations** (✉ 10612 Beaver Dam Rd., Hunt Valley, MD 21030-2205, ☎ 410/785–3500 or 800/638–9040, FAX 410/584–2771), **Certified Vacations** (✉ Box 1525, Fort Lauderdale, FL 33302, ☎ 305/522–1414 or 800/233–7260), **Continental Vacations** (☎ 800/634–5555), **Delta Dream Vacations** (☎ 800/872–7786), **SuperCities** (✉ 139 Main St., Cambridge, MA 02142, ☎ 617/621–0099 or 800/333–1234), **TWA Getaway Vacations** (☎ 800/438–2929), **United Vacations** (☎ 800/328–6877), and **USAir Vacations** (☎ 800/455–0123). **Gogo Tours,** in Ramsey, New Jersey, and **Kingdom Tours,** based in Plains, Pennsylvania, sell packages to Arizona only through travel agents.

Also contact **Amtrak**'s Great American Vacations (☎ 800/321–8684).

FROM THE U.K.

Companies offering packages to Arizona include **British Airways Holidays** (✉ Astral Towers, Betts Way, London Rd., Crawley, West Sussex RH10 2XA, ☎ 01293/723–121), **Jetsave Travel Ltd.** (✉ Sussex House, London Rd., East Grinstead, West Sussex RH19 1LD, ☎ 01342/312–033), **Key to America** (✉ 1–3 Station Rd., Ashford, Middlesex TW15 2UW, ☎ 01784/248–777), **Kuoni Travel** (✉ Kuoni House, Dorking, Surrey RH5 4AZ, ☎ 01306/742–222), and **Premier Holidays** (✉ Premier Travel Centre, Westbrook, Milton Rd., Cambridge CB4 1YG, ☎ 01223/516–688).

Travel agencies that offer cheap fares to Arizona are **Trailfinders** (✉ 42–50 Earl's Court Rd., London W8 6FT, ☎ 0171/937–5400), **Travel Cuts** (✉ 295a Regent St., London W1R 7YA, ☎ 0171/637–3161; ☞ Students, *above*), and **Flightfile** (✉ 49 Tottenham Court Rd., London W1P 9RE, ☎ 0171/700–2722).

THEME TRIPS

ADVENTURE➤ Packages from **American Southwest Tours** (✉ Box 4300, Durango, CO 81302, ☎ 970/247–2955 or 800/644–5755) combine rafting, mountain biking, and hiking. **American Wilderness Experience** (✉ Box 1486, Boulder, CO 80306, ☎ 303/444–2622 or 800/444–3833, FAX 303/444–3999) offers rafting, cattle driving, hiking, camping, and other adventures. **Smithsonian Study Tours and Seminars** (✉ 1100 Jefferson Dr. SW, Room 3045, MRC 702, Washington, DC 20560, ☎ 202/357–4700, FAX 202/633–9250) conducts hiking, rafting, and camping trips. **Trek America** (✉ Box 189, Rockaway, NJ 07866, ☎ 201/983–1144 or 800/221–0596, FAX 201/983–8551) includes biking, hiking, camping, and other adventures in its western programs, which are geared to ages 18–38. **World Wide River Expeditions** (✉ 153 E. 7200 S, Midvale, Utah 84047, ☎ 801/566–2662 or 800/231–2769, FAX 801/566–2722) offers rafting trips.

ARCHAEOLOGY➤ **American Southwest Tours** (☞ *above*) will arrange for you to join a professional dig. A nonprofit educational organization, the **Archaeological Conservancy** (✉ 5301 Central Ave. NE, No. 1218, Albuquerque, NM 87108-1517, ☎ 505/266–1540), conducts tours of southwestern ruins with an emphasis on Native American culture. **Crow Canyon Archaeological Center** (✉ 23390 Country Rd. K, Cortez, CO 81321, ☎ 970/565–8975 or 800/422–8975, FAX 970/565–4859) explores Native American culture and ruins. **Earthwatch** (✉ Box 403, 680 Mount Auburn St., Watertown, MA 02272, ☎ 617/926–8200 or 800/776–0188, FAX 617/926–8532, info@earthwatch.org, http://www.earthwatch.org) recruits volunteers to serve in its EarthCorps as short-term assistants to scientists on research expeditions. **Nature Expeditions International** (✉ Box 11496, Eugene, OR 97440, ☎ 503/484–6529 or 800/869–0639, FAX 503/484–6531, NaturExp@aol.com) explores Native American culture. **Southwest Ed-Ventures** (✉ Four Corners School of Outdoor Education, Box 1029, Monticello, UT 84535, ☎ 800/525–4456 or 801/587–2156, FAX 801/587–2193) visits rarely viewed native ruins and rock art in the Southwest.

BICYCLING➤ Road and mountain biking tours of Arizona are available from **Backroads** (✉ 1516 5th St., Berkeley, CA 94710-1740, ☎ 510/527–1555 or 800/462–2848, FAX 510/527–1444, goactive@Backroads.com) and **Timberline** (✉ 7975 E. Harvard, No. J, Denver, CO 80231, ☎ 303/759–3804 or 800/417–2453, FAX 303/368–1651). **Cycle America** (✉ Box 485, Cannon Falls, MN 55009, ☎ 507/263–2665 or 800/245–3263, http://www.cycleamerica.com) operates tours of Arizona and coast-to-coast rides.

CULTURAL➤ **Southwest Ed-Ventures** (☞ Archaeology, *above*) employs local artists and authors as tour guides. Art and culture are the focus of several itineraries planned by **American Southwest Tours** (☞ Adventure, *above*).

DRIVING➤ Custom-tailored itineraries for independent travelers can be arranged by **Off the Beaten Path** (✉ 109 E. Main St., Bozeman, MT 59715, ☎ 406/586–1311 or 800/445–2995, FAX 406/587–4147). Itineraries include stays at distinctive inns and ranches, visits to unique cultural attractions such as ruins and historical sites, and meals in the region's best restaurants.

DUDE RANCHES➤ **American Wilderness Experience** (☞ Adventure, *above*) books ranches from luxurious to rustic. Also contact **Off the Beaten Path** (☞ Driving, *above*).

GOLF➤ Packages including accommodations, confirmed tee times, and golfing fees are sold by **Golfpac** (✉ Box 162366, Altamonte Springs, FL 32716-2366, ☎ 407/260–2288 or 800/327–0878, FAX 407/260–8989) and **Stine's Golftrips** (✉ Box 2314, Winter Haven, FL 33883-2314, ☎ 941/324–1300 or 800/428–1940, FAX 941/325–0384, golftrip@cris.com).

HEALTH➤ **Spa-Finders** (✉ 91 5th Ave., No. 301, New York, NY 10003-3039, ☎ 212/924–6800 or 800/255–7727) represents several spas in Arizona.

HIKING➤ **Backroads** (☞ Bicycling, *above*) guides hikers through the Sonoran Desert and Chiricahua Mountains. Also try **Timberline** (☞ Bicycling, *above*).

HORSEBACK RIDING➤ Trips with overnight stays in rustic inns and lodges are operated by **FITS Equestrian** (✉ 685 Lateen Rd., Solvang, CA 93463, ☎ 805/688–9494 or 800/666–3487, FAX 805/688–2943). Riding trips including deluxe camping or lodge accommodations are offered by **American Wilderness Experience** (☞ Adventure, *above*).

KAYAKING➤ Kayaking trips in the Grand Canyon are sold by **Orange Torpedo Trips** (✉ Box 1111, Grants Pass, OR 97526-0294, ☎ 541/479–5061 or 800/635–2925, FAX 541/471–0995).

MOTORCYCLING➤ **Western States Motorcycle Tours** (✉ 1823 W. Seldon La., Phoenix, AZ 85021, ☎ FAX 602/943–9030) leads rides through the Southwest, including the Grand Canyon.

MUSIC➤ **Dailey-Thorp Travel** (✉ 330 W. 58th St., No. 610, New York, NY 10019-1817, ☎ 212/307–1555 or 800/998–4677, FAX 212/974–1420) has opera packages that include lodging, dining at fine restaurants, and sightseeing.

NATIVE AMERICAN HISTORY➤ **American Southwest Tours** (☞ Adventure, *above*) emphasizes Native American history in its various itineraries. **Crow Canyon Archaeological Center** (☞ Archaeology, *above*) visits the homes and studios of Native American jewelers, potters, weavers, sand painters, and kachina carvers. **Southwest Ed-Ventures** (☞ Archaeology, *above*) explores Navajo and Ute culture.

RIVER RAFTING➤ For trips on the Colorado River, try **Action Whitewater Adventures** (✉ Box 1634, Provo, UT 84603, ☎ 800/453–1482, FAX 801/375–4175, rafting@xmission.com), **Canyoneers** (✉ Box 2997, Flagstaff, AZ 86003, ☎ 602/526–0924 or 800/525–0924), **Grand Canyon Dories** (✉ Box 67, Angels Camp, CA 95222, ☎ 209/736–0811 or 800/877–3679, FAX 209/736–2902), and **OARS** (✉ Box 67, Angels Camp, CA 95222, ☎ 209/736–4677 or 800/346–6277, FAX 209/736–2902; reservations@oars.com, http:/www.oars.com). Rafting on the Salt River Canyons is the specialty of **Far Flung Adventures** (✉ Box 377, Terlingua, TX 79852, ☎ 915/371–2489 or 800/359–4138, FAX 915/371–2325).

WALKING➤ **Country Walkers** (✉ Box 180, Waterbury, VT 05676-0180, ☎ 802/244–1387 or 800/464–9255, FAX 802/244–5661) takes a leisurely look at the Sonoran Desert.

ORGANIZATIONS

The **National Tour Association** (✉ NTA, 546 E. Main St., Lexington, KY 40508, ☎ 606/226–4444 or 800/755–8687) and the **United States Tour Operators Association** (✉ USTOA, 211 E. 51st St., Suite 12B, New

York, NY 10022, ☎ 212/750–7371) can provide lists of members and information on booking tours.

PUBLICATIONS

Contact the USTOA (☞ Organizations, *above*) for its **"Smart Traveler's Planning Kit."** Pamphlets in the kit include the "Worldwide Tour and Vacation Package Finder," "How to Select a Tour or Vacation Package," and information on the organization's consumer protection plan. Also get a copy of the Better Business Bureau's **"Tips on Travel Packages"** (✉ Publication 24-195, 4200 Wilson Blvd., Arlington, VA 22203; $2). The National Tour Association will send you **"On Tour,"** a listing of its member operators, and a personalized package of information on group travel in North America.

TRAIN TRAVEL

The *Southwest Chief* operates daily between Los Angeles and Chicago, stopping in Kingman, Flagstaff, and Winslow. The *Sunset Limited* travels three times each week between Los Angeles and Miami, with stops at Yuma, Phoenix, Tempe, Coolidge, Tucson, and Benson. For details, contact **Amtrak** (☎ 800/872–7245).

TRAVEL GEAR

For travel apparel, appliances, personal-care items, and other travel necessities, get a free catalog from **Magellan's** (☎ 800/962–4943, FAX 805/568–5406), **Orvis Travel** (☎ 800/541–3541, FAX 703/343–7053), or **TravelSmith** (☎ 800/950–1600, FAX 415/455–0554).

TRAVEL AGENCIES

For names of reputable agencies in your area, contact the **American Society of Travel Agents** (✉ ASTA, 1101 King St., Suite 200, Alexandria, VA 22314, ☎ 703/739–2782), the **Association of Canadian Travel Agents** (✉ Suite 201, 1729 Bank St., Ottawa, Ontario K1V 7Z5, ☎ 613/521–0474, FAX 613/521–0805) or the **Association of British Travel Agents** (✉ 55-57 Newman St., London W1P 4AH, ☎ 0171/637–2444, FAX 0171/637–0713).

V

VISITOR INFORMATION

The **Arizona Office of Tourism** (✉ 1100 W. Washington St., Phoenix 85007, ☎ 602/542–8687 or 800/842–8257, FAX 602/542–4068, http://www.arizonaguide.com) can send a comprehensive tourist kit as well as information on the 14 tribal councils, a map of reservations, and a list of addresses and phone numbers. The **Hopi Tribe Office of the Chairman** (✉ Box 123, Kykotsmovi 86039, ☎ 520/734–2441, FAX 520/734–2435) and the **Navajoland Tourism Department** (✉ Box 663, Window Rock 86515, ☎ 520/871–6659 or 520/871–7371, FAX 520/871–7381) can inform you of upcoming tribal activities.

W

WEATHER

For current conditions and forecasts, plus the local time and helpful travel tips, call the **Weather Channel Connection** (☎ 900/932–8437; 95¢ per minute) from a touch-tone phone.

The ***International Traveler's Weather Guide*** (✉ Weather Press, Box 660606, Sacramento, CA 95866, ☎ 916/974–0201 or 800/972–0201; $10.95 includes shipping), written by two meteorologists, provides month-by-month information on temperature, humidity, and precipitation in more than 175 cities worldwide.

SMART TRAVEL TIPS A TO Z

Basic Information on Traveling in Arizona & Savvy Tips to Make Your Trip a Breeze

A

AIR TRAVEL

If time is an issue, **always look for nonstop flights,** which require no change of plane. If possible, **avoid connecting flights,** which stop at least once and can involve a change of plane, even though the flight number remains the same; if the first leg is late, the second waits.

For better service, **fly smaller or regional carriers,** which often have higher passenger satisfaction ratings. Sometimes they have such in-flight amenities as leather seats or greater legroom, and they often have better food.

CUTTING COSTS

The Sunday travel section of most newspapers is a good place to look for deals.

MAJOR AIRLINES➢ The least-expensive airfares from the major airlines are priced for round-trip travel and are subject to restrictions. Usually, you must **book in advance and buy the ticket within 24 hours** to get cheaper fares, and you may have to **stay over a Saturday night.** The lowest fare is subject to availability, and only a small percentage of the plane's total seats are sold at that price. It's smart to **call a number of airlines, and when you are quoted a good price, book it on the spot**—the same fare may not be available on the same flight the next day. Airlines generally allow you to change your return date for a $25 to $50 fee. If you don't use your ticket, you can apply the cost toward the purchase of a new ticket, again for a small charge. However, most low-fare tickets are nonrefundable. To get the lowest airfare, **check different routings.** If your destination has more than one gateway, **compare prices to different airports.**

FROM THE U.K.➢ To save money on flights, **look into an APEX or Super-PEX ticket.** APEX tickets must be booked in advance and have certain restrictions. Super-PEX tickets can be purchased right at the airport.

ALOFT

AIRLINE FOOD➢ If you hate airline food, **ask for special meals when booking.** These can be vegetarian, low-cholesterol, or kosher, for example; commonly prepared to order in smaller quantities than standard fare, they can be tastier.

SMOKING➢ Smoking is not allowed on flights of six hours or less within the continental United States. Smoking is also prohibited on flights within Canada. For U.S. flights longer than six hours or international flights, **contact your carrier regarding its smoking policy.** Some carriers have prohibited smoking throughout their system; others allow smoking only on certain routes or even certain departures of that route.

C

CAMERAS, CAMCORDERS, & COMPUTERS

IN TRANSIT

Always keep your film, tape, or disks out of the sun; never put these on the dashboard of a car. Carry an extra supply of batteries, and **be prepared to turn on your camera, camcorder, or laptop computer for security personnel** to prove that it's real.

X-RAYS

Always **ask for hand inspection at security.** Such requests are virtually always honored at U.S. airports. Photographic film becomes clouded after successive exposure to airport x-ray machines. Videotape and computer disks are not by X-rays, but **keep your tapes and disks away from metal detectors.**

CAR RENTAL

CUTTING COSTS

To get the best deal, **book through a travel agent who is willing to shop around.** When pricing cars, **ask where the rental lot is located.** Some off-airport locations offer lower rates—even though their lots are only minutes away from the terminal via complimentary shuttle. You also may want to **price local car-rental companies,** whose rates may be lower still, although service and maintenance standards may not be as high as those of a national firm. Ask your agent to **look for fly-drive packages,** which also save you money, and **ask if local taxes are included** in the rental or fly-drive price. These can be as high as 20% in some destinations. Don't forget to find out about required deposits, cancellation penalties, drop-off charges, and the cost of any required insurance coverage.

Also **ask your travel agent about a company's customer-service record.** How has it responded to late plane arrivals and vehicle mishaps? Are there often lines at the rental counter, and—if you're traveling during a holiday period—does a confirmed reservation guarantee you a car?

INSURANCE

When driving a rented car, you are generally responsible for any damage to or loss of the rental vehicle, as well as any property damage or personal injury that you cause. Before you rent, **see what coverage you already have** under the terms of your personal auto insurance policy and credit cards.

For about $14 a day, rental companies sell protection, known as a collision- or loss- damage waiver (CDW or LDW), that eliminates your liability for damage to the car; it's always optional and should never be automatically added to your bill.

Companies renting cars in Arizona have the initial responsibility for damage caused to third parties, after which the renter's personal auto or other liability insurance covers the loss. This may seem like unlimited protection for the renter, but state law caps the amount that the car-rental company must pay. If you do not have auto insurance or an umbrella insurance policy that covers damage to third parties, purchasing CDW or LDW is highly recommended.

U.K. CITIZENS

In the United States you must be 21 to rent a car; rates may be higher if you're under 25. You'll pay extra for child seats (about $3 per day), compulsory for children under five, and for additional drivers (about $2 per day). To pick up your reserved car you will need the reservation voucher, a passport, a U.K. driver's license, and a travel policy that covers each driver.

SURCHARGES

Before you pick up a car in one city and leave it in another, **ask about drop-off charges or one-way service fees,** which can be substantial. Note, too, that some rental agencies charge extra if you return the car before the time specified on your contract. To avoid a hefty refueling fee, **fill the tank just before you turn in the car**—but be aware that gas stations near the rental outlet may overcharge.

CHILDREN & TRAVEL

Many large resorts and dude ranches offer special activities for children, and many offer baby-sitting services. Children of all ages are enthralled by the Wild West flavor around Tucson and the southeastern part of the state, with Tombstone ranking as a particular favorite. If you're driving on long desert stretches, take along plenty of games and snacks.

When traveling with children, **plan ahead** and **involve your youngsters** as you outline your trip. When packing, **include a supply of things to keep them busy** en route (☞ Children & Travel *in* Important Contacts A to Z). On sightseeing days, try to **schedule activities of special interest to your children,** like a trip to a zoo or a playground. If you **plan your itinerary around seasonal festivals,** you'll never lack for things to do. In addition, **check local newspapers for special events** mounted by public libraries, museums, and parks.

BABY-SITTING

For recommended local sitters, **check with your hotel desk.**

DRIVING

If you are renting a car, don't forget to **arrange for a car seat when you reserve.** Sometimes they're free.

FLYING

As a general rule, infants under two not occupying a seat fly for free. If your children are two or older **ask about special children's fares.** Age limits for these fares vary among carriers. Rules also vary regarding unaccompanied minors, so again, check with your airline.

BAGGAGE➤ In general, the adult baggage allowance applies to children paying half or more of the adult fare.

SAFETY SEATS➤ According to the FAA, it's a good idea to **use safety seats aloft** for children weighing less than 40 pounds. Airline policies vary. U.S. carriers allow FAA-approved models but usually require that you buy a ticket, even if your child would otherwise ride free, since the seats must be strapped into regular seats. However, some airlines may require you to hold your baby during takeoff and landing—defeating the seat's purpose.

FACILITIES➤ When making your reservation, **request for children's meals or freestanding bassinets** if you need them; the latter are available only to those seated at the bulkhead, where there's enough legroom. If you don't need a bassinet, **think twice before requesting bulkhead seats**—the only storage space for in-flight necessities is in inconveniently distant overhead bins.

GAMES

Milton Bradley and Parker Brothers have travel versions of some of their most popular games, including Yahtzee, Trouble, Sorry, and Monopoly. Prices run $5 to $8. Look for them in the travel section of your local toy store.

LODGING

Most hotels allow children under a certain age to stay in their parents' room at no extra charge; others charge them as extra adults. Be sure to **ask about the cutoff age.**

CUSTOMS & DUTIES

To speed your clearance through customs, **keep receipts for all your purchases abroad** and **be ready to show the inspector what you've bought.** If you feel that you've been incorrectly or unfairly charged a duty, you can **appeal assessments in dispute.** First ask to see a supervisor. If you are still unsatisfied, **write to the port director** of your point of entry, sending your customs receipt and any other appropriate documentation. The address will be listed on your receipt. If you still don't get satisfaction, you can take your case to customs headquarters in Washington.

IN CANADA

If you've been out of Canada for at least seven days, you may bring in C$500 worth of goods duty-free. If you've been away for fewer than seven days but for more than 48 hours, the duty-free allowance drops to C$200; if your trip lasts between 24 and 48 hours, the allowance is C$50. You cannot pool allowances with family members. Goods claimed under the C$500 exemption may follow you by mail; those claimed under the lesser exemptions must accompany you.

Alcohol and tobacco products may be included in the seven-day and 48-hour exemptions but not in the 24-hour exemption. If you meet the age requirements of the province or territory through which you reenter Canada, you may bring in, duty-free, 1.14 liters (40 imperial ounces) of wine or liquor *or* 24 12-ounce cans or bottles of beer or ale. If you are 16 or older, you may bring in, duty-free, 200 cigarettes, 50 cigars or cigarillos, and 400 tobacco sticks or 400 grams of manufactured tobacco. Alcohol and tobacco must accompany you on your return.

An unlimited number of gifts with a value of up to C$60 each may be mailed to Canada duty-free. These do not affect your duty-free allowance on your return. Label the package "Unsolicited Gift—Value Under $60." Alcohol and tobacco are excluded.

IN THE U.K.

From countries outside the EU, including the United States, you may import, duty-free, 200 cigarettes, 100 cigarillos, 50 cigars, or 250 grams of tobacco; 1 liter of spirits or 2 liters of fortified or sparkling wine or liqueurs; 2 liters of still table wine; 60 milliliters of perfume; 250 milliliters of toilet water; plus £136 worth of other goods, including gifts and souvenirs.

IN THE U.S.

Visitors age 21 or over may import the following into the United States: 200 cigarettes or 50 cigars or 2 kilograms of tobacco; 1 U.S. liter of alcohol; gifts to the value of $100. Restricted items include meat products, seeds, plants, and fruits. Never carry illegal drugs.

D

DINING

Make advance reservations at better restaurants, and don't be misled by the casual lifestyle—**ask about dress codes** first to avoid being turned away at the door. A few establishments, including some at more elegant resorts, require men to wear a jacket and tie.

DISABILITIES & ACCESSIBILITY

Most of the region's national parks and recreation areas have wheelchair-accessible visitor centers, rest rooms, campsites, and trails, and more are being added every year. Even so, when discussing accessibility with an operator or reservationist, **ask hard questions.** Are there any stairs, inside *or* out? Are there grab bars next to the toilet *and* in the shower/tub? How wide is the doorway to the room? To the bathroom? For the most extensive facilities, meeting the latest legal specifications, **opt for newer accommodations,** which more often have been designed with access in mind. Older properties or ships must usually be retrofitted and may offer more limited facilities as a result. Be sure to **discuss your needs before booking.**

DISCOUNTS & DEALS

You shouldn't have to pay for a discount. In fact, you may already be eligible for all kinds of savings. Here are some time-honored strategies for getting the best deal.

LOOK IN YOUR WALLET

When you **use your credit card to make travel purchases,** you may get free travel-accident insurance, collision damage insurance, medical or legal assistance, depending on the card and bank that issued it. Visa and MasterCard provide one or more of these services, so **get a copy of your card's travel benefits.** If you are a member of the AAA or an oil-company-sponsored road-assistance plan, always **ask hotel or car-rental reservationists for auto-club discounts.** Some clubs offer additional discounts on tours, cruises, or admission to attractions. And don't forget that auto-club membership entitles you to free maps and trip-planning services.

SENIORS CITIZENS & STUDENTS

As a senior-citizen traveler, you may be eligible for special rates, but you should mention your senior-citizen status up front. If you're a student or under 26 can also get discounts, especially if you have an official ID card (☞ Senior-Citizen Discounts *and* Students on the Road, *below*).

DIAL FOR DOLLARS

To save money, **look into "1-800" discount reservations services,** which often have lower rates. These services use their buying power to get a better price on hotels, airline tickets, and sometimes even car rentals. When booking a room, always **call the hotel's local toll-free number** (if one is available) rather than the central reservations number—you'll often get a better price. Ask the reservationist about special packages or corporate rates, which are usually available even if you're not traveling on business.

JOIN A CLUB?

Discount clubs can be a legitimate source of savings, but you must use the participating hotels and visit the participating attractions in order to realize any benefits. Remember, too, that you have to pay a fee to join, so **determine if you'll save enough to warrant your membership fee.** Before booking with a club, **make sure the hotel or other supplier isn't offering a better deal.**

DRIVING

Major approaches from the east and west are I–40, I–10, I–8, and U.S. 60. Main north–south routes are I–17, I–10 (from

Phoenix to Tucson), and U.S. 89. Other artery roads are U.S. 70 and U.S. 64 (U.S. 160 in Arizona) from the east.

Most highways into the state are good to excellent, with easy access, roadside facilities, rest stops, and scenic views. The speed limit on the freeways is now 75 mph, but **don't drive much faster than the limit**—police use sophisticated detection systems to catch violators.

At some point you will probably pass through one or more of the state's 23 Indian reservations. Roads and other areas within reservation boundaries are under the jurisdiction of reservation police and governed by separate rules and regulations. **Observe all signs and respect Indians' privacy.** Be careful not to hit any animals, which often wander onto the roads; the penalties can be very high.

PRECAUTIONS

DUST STORMS➢ These usually occur mid-July to mid-September (the monsoon months), just before thunderstorms hit, causing extremely low visibility. If you're on the highway, **pull as far off the road as possible, turn off your headlights, and wait for the storm to subside.**

FLASH FLOODS➢ They may sound apocalyptic or overly cautious, but warnings about flash floods should not be taken lightly. Sudden downpours send torrents of water racing into low-lying areas so dry that they are unable to absorb such a huge quantity of water so quickly. The result is powerful walls of water suddenly descending upon these low-lying areas, devastating anything in their paths. If you see rain clouds or thunderstorms in the area, stay away from dry riverbeds (also called arroyos or washes). If you find yourself in one, get out quickly. If you're with a car in a long gulley, leave your car and climb out of the gulley. You simply won't be able to outdrive a speeding wave. The idea is to **get to higher ground immediately when it rains.** Major highways are mostly floodproof, but some smaller roads dip through washes. If showers are nearby, look before you cross. Washes filled with water should not be crossed until you can see the bottom. By all means, don't camp in these areas at any time, interesting as they may seem.

DESERT HEAT➢ Vehicles and passengers should be well equipped for searing summer heat in the low desert. If you're planning to drive through the desert, **carry plenty of water, a good spare tire, a jack, and emergency supplies.** If you get stranded, stay with your vehicle and wait for help to arrive.

FRAGILE DESERT LIFE➢ The dry and easily desecrated desert floor takes centuries to overcome human damage. Consequently, it is illegal for four-wheel-drive and all-terrain vehicles and motorcycles to travel off established roadways.

H

HIKING

Be sure to take the following precautions when you go for a hike of any length.

SUN PROTECTION

Wear a hat and sunglasses and put on sun block to protect against the burning Arizona sun. And **watch out for heatstroke.** Symptoms include headache, dizziness, and fatigue, which can turn into convulsions and unconsciousness and can lead to death. If someone in your party develops any of these conditions, have one person seek emergency help while others move the victim into the shade, wrap him or her in wet clothing (is a stream nearby?) to cool him or her down.

DEHYDRATION

This underestimated danger can be very serious, especially considering that one of the first major symptoms is the inability to swallow. It may be the easiest hazard to avoid, however; simply **drink every 10–15 minutes,** up to a gallon of water per day in summer.

ANIMAL BITES

Wherever you're hiking, particularly between April and October, **keep a lookout for rattlesnakes.** You're likely not to have any problems if you maintain distance from snakes that you see—they can strike only half of their length, so a 6-

foot clearance should allow you to stay unharmed, especially if you **don't provoke them.** If you are bitten by a rattler, don't panic. Just get to a hospital within 2–3 hours of the bite. Keep in mind that 30%–40% of bites are dry bites, where the snake uses no venom (still, get thee to a hospital). **Avoid night hikes without rangers,** when snakes are on the prowl and less visible. You may want to pick up a kit called the Extractor for use if bitten.

Scorpions and Gila monsters are really less of a concern, since they strike only when provoked. To avoid scorpion encounters, **don't put your hands where you can't see with your eyes:** under rocks and in holes. Likewise, if you move a rock to sit down, make sure that scorpions haven't been exposed. Campers should shake out shoes in the morning, since scorpions like warm, moist places. If you are bitten, see a ranger about symptoms that may develop. Chances are good that you won't need to go to a hospital. Children are a different case, however: Scorpion stings can be fatal for them. Always try to keep an eye on what they may be getting their hands into to avoid the scorpion's sting. Gila monsters are relatively rare, but they are most active between April and June, when they do most of their hunting.

HYPOTHERMIA

Temperatures in Arizona can vary widely from day to night—as much as 40°F. Be sure to **bring enough warm clothing for hiking and camping, along with wet weather gear.** Exposure to the degree that body temperature dips below 95°F produces the following symptoms: chills, tiredness, then uncontrollable shivering and irrational behavior, with the victim not always recognizing that he or she is cold. If someone in your party is suffering from any of this, wrap him or her in blankets and/or a warm sleeping bag immediately and try to keep him or her awake. The fastest way to raise body temperature is through skin-to-skin contact in a sleeping bag. Drinking warm liquids also helps.

POTABLE WATER

Never drink from any stream, no matter how clear it may be. Giardia organisms can turn your stomach inside out. The easiest way to purify water is to **dissolve a water purification tablet** in it. Camping-equipment stores also carry purification pumps. **Boil water for 15 minutes,** a reliable method, if time- and fuel-consuming.

I INSURANCE

Travel insurance can protect your monetary investment, replace your luggage and its contents, or provide for medical coverage should you fall ill during your trip. Most tour operators, travel agents, and insurance agents sell specialized health-and-accident, flight, trip-cancellation, and luggage insurance as well as comprehensive policies with some or all of these coverages. Comprehensive policies may also reimburse you for delays due to weather—an important consideration if you're traveling during the winter months. Some health-insurance policies do not cover preexisting conditions, but waivers may be available in specific cases. Coverage is sold by the companies listed in Important Contacts A to Z; these companies act as the policy's administrators. The actual insurance is usually underwritten by a well-known name, such as the Travelers or Continental Insurance.

Before you make any purchase, **review your existing health and homeowner's policies** to find out whether they cover expenses incurred while traveling.

BAGGAGE

Airline liability for baggage is limited to $1,250 per person on domestic flights. On international flights, it amounts to $9.07 per pound or $20 per kilogram for checked baggage (roughly $640 per 70-pound bag) and $400 per passenger for unchecked baggage. Insurance for losses exceeding the terms of your airline ticket can be bought directly from the airline at check-in for about $10 per $1,000 of coverage; note that it excludes a rather extensive list of items, shown on your airline ticket.

COMPREHENSIVE

Comprehensive insurance policies include all the coverages described above plus some that may not be available in more specific policies. If you have purchased an expensive vacation, especially one that involves travel abroad, comprehensive insurance is a must; **look for policies that include trip delay insurance,** which will protect you in the event that weather problems cause you to miss your flight, tour, or cruise. A few insurers will also sell you a waiver for preexisting medical conditions. Some of the companies that offer both these features are Access America, Carefree Travel, Travel Insured International, and TravelGuard (☞ Insurance *in* Important Contacts A to Z).

FLIGHT

You should **think twice before buying flight insurance.** Often purchased as a last-minute impulse at the airport, it pays a lump sum when a plane crashes, either to a beneficiary if the insured dies or sometimes to a surviving passenger who loses his or her eyesight or a limb. Supplementing the airlines' coverage described in the limits-of-liability paragraphs on your ticket, it's expensive and basically unnecessary. Charging an airline ticket to a major credit card often automatically provides you with coverage that may also extend to travel by bus, train, and ship.

U.K. TRAVELERS

According to the Association of British Insurers, a trade association representing 450 insurance companies, it's wise to **buy extra medical coverage when you visit the United States.** You can buy an annual travel insurance policy valid for most vacations during the year in which it's purchased. If you are pregnant or have a preexisting medical condition, make sure you're covered before buying such a policy.

TRIP

Without insurance, you will lose all or most of your money if you cancel your trip, regardless of the reason. Especially if your airline ticket, cruise, or package tour is nonrefundable and cannot be changed, it's essential that you **buy trip-cancellation-and-interruption insurance.** When considering how much coverage you need, look for a policy that will cover the cost of your trip plus the nondiscounted price of a one-way airline ticket should you need to return home early. Read the fine print carefully, especially sections that define "family member" and "preexisting medical conditions." Also **consider default or bankruptcy insurance,** which protects you against a supplier's failure to deliver. Be aware, however, that if you buy such a policy from a travel agency, tour operator, airline, or cruise line, it may not cover default by the firm in question.

L

LODGING

Arizona's hotels and motels run the gamut—from world-class resorts to budget chains, and from historic inns, bed-and-breakfasts, and mountain lodges to dude ranches, campgrounds, and RV parks. And there is plenty of camping. Most nationwide and international companies are represented within the state. Large resorts offer extensive recreational and dining facilities, while modest motels may provide nothing more than a small swimming pool and complimentary coffee. **Make reservations well in advance for the high season**—winter in the desert south and summer in the high country. Tremendous bargains can be found off-season, when even the most exclusive establishments cut their rates by half.

APARTMENT & VILLA RENTAL

If you want a home base that's roomy enough for a family and comes with cooking facilities, **consider taking a furnished rental.** This can also save you money, but not always—some rentals are luxury properties (economical only when your party is large). Home-exchange directories list rentals—often second homes owned by prospective house swappers—and some services search for a house or apartment for you (even a castle if that's your fancy) and handle the paperwork. Some send an illustrated catalog; others send photographs only of specific properties, sometimes at a charge; up-front registration fees may apply.

CAMPING

You can choose from a feast of federal, state, Native American, and private campgrounds in virtually all parts of the state. Facilities range from deluxe parks with swimming pools and recreation rooms to primitive backcountry wilderness sites. Most campgrounds provide toilets, drinking water, showers, and hookups. Camping is also permitted in Arizona's seven national forests, but be forewarned that they have no facilities whatsoever.

GEAR➢ **Pack according to season, region, and length of trip.** Basics include a sleeping bag, a tent (optional, and forbidden in some RV parks), a camp stove, cooking utensils, food and water supplies, a first-aid kit, insect repellent, sunscreen, a lantern, trash bags, a rope, and a tarp. In case you forget something, almost every camping item is available for sale or rent at one of Arizona's many sporting-goods shops.

PRECAUTIONS➢ Don't forget to **shake out your shoes** in the morning after climbing out of your sleeping bag, since scorpions like warm, moist places. Also, keep in mind that flash floods after sudden rain showers are extremely dangerous, sending water hurtling through low-lying areas. For your safety, **avoid camping in or next to dry riverbeds, washes, arroyos, etc.**

DUDE RANCHES

Down-home western lifestyle, cooking, and activities are the focus of guest ranches, situated primarily in Tucson and Wickenburg. Some are resortlike properties where guests are pampered, whereas smaller family-run ranches expect *everyone* to join in the chores. Horseback riding and other outdoor recreational activities are emphasized. Most dude ranches are closed in summer.

HOME EXCHANGE

If you would like to find a house, an apartment, or some other type of vacation property to exchange for your own while on holiday, **become a member of a home-exchange organization,** which will send you its updated listings of available exchanges for a year and will include your own listing in at least one of them. Arrangements for the actual exchange are made by the two parties involved, not by the organization.

M

MONEY

ATMS

CASH ADVANCES➢ Before leaving home, **make sure that your credit cards have been programmed for ATM use.**

N

NATIONAL PARKS

If you are a frequent visitor, senior citizen, or traveler with a disability, you can **save money on park entrance fees** by getting a discount pass. The Golden Eagle Pass can be a good deal if you plan to visit several parks during your travels. Priced at $25, it entitles you and your companions to free admission to *all* parks for a year. It does not cover additional park fees such as those for camping or parking. Both the Golden Age Passport, for U.S. citizens or permanent residents 62 or older, and the Golden Access Passport, for travelers with disabilities, entitle holders to free entry to all national parks plus 50% off fees for the use of all park facilities and services except those run by private concessionaires. Both passports are free; you must show proof of age and U.S. citizenship or permanent residency (such as a U.S. passport, driver's license, or birth certificate) or proof of disability. All three passes are available at all national park entrances.

P

PACKING FOR ARIZONA

Wear casual clothing and resort wear in Arizona. When in more elegant restaurants in larger cities, as well as in dining rooms of some resorts, most men wear jackets and appropriate pants (few places require ties). Dressy casual wear is appropriate for women even in the nicest places—take along a silky blouse and chunky silver jewelry and you'll fit in almost anywhere.

Stay cool in cotton fabrics and light colors. T-shirts, polo shirts, sundresses, and lightweight shorts, trousers, skirts, and blouses are right for summer. **Bring sun hats, swimsuits, sandals, and sunscreen**—mandatory warm-weather items. **Bring a sweater and a warm jacket in winter,** particularly for high-country travel—anywhere around Flagstaff and north of it. And **don't forget jeans and sneakers or sturdy walking shoes**; they're important year-round.

Take along appropriate sports gear, although tennis, golf, ski, and horseback-riding equipment is readily available for rental.

Bring an extra pair of eyeglasses or contact lenses in your carry-on luggage, and if you have a health problem, **pack enough medication** to last the trip. It's important that you **don't put prescription drugs or valuables in luggage to be checked,** for it could go astray.

LUGGAGE

Airline baggage allowances depend on the airline, the route, and the class of your ticket; ask in advance. In general, on domestic flights you are entitled to check two bags. A third piece may be brought on board, but it must fit easily under the seat in front of you or in the overhead compartment. In the United States, the FAA gives airlines broad latitude regarding carry-on allowances, and they tend to tailor them to different aircraft and operational conditions. Charges for excess, oversize, or overweight pieces vary.

SAFEGUARDING YOUR LUGGAGE➢ Before leaving home, **itemize your bags' contents** and their worth, and label them with your name, address, and phone number. (If you use your home address, cover it so that potential thieves can't see it readily.) Inside each bag, **pack a copy of your itinerary.** At check-in, **make sure that each bag is correctly tagged** with the destination airport's three-letter code. If your bags arrive damaged—or fail to arrive at all—file a written report with the airline before leaving the airport.

PASSPORTS & VISAS

CANADIAN CITIZENS

No passport is necessary to enter the United States.

U.K. CITIZENS

British citizens need a valid passport to enter the United States. If you are staying for fewer than 90 days and traveling on a vacation, with a return or onward ticket, you probably will not need a visa. However, you will need to fill out the Visa Waiver Form, 1-94W, supplied by the airline.

It is advisable that you **leave one photocopy of your passport's data page** with someone at home and keep another with you, separated from your passport, while traveling. If you lose your passport, promptly call the nearest embassy or consulate and the local police; having the data-page information can speed replacement.

S

SENIOR-CITIZEN DISCOUNTS

To qualify for age-related discounts, **mention your senior-citizen status up front** when booking hotel reservations, not when checking out, and before you're seated in restaurants, not when paying the bill. Note that discounts may be limited to certain menus, days, or hours. When renting a car, **ask about promotional car-rental discounts**—they can net even lower costs than your senior-citizen discount.

For $10, U.S. residents age 62 or older can pick up a Golden Age Passport. In addition to lifetime free admission to national parks, the pass allows a 50% discount on park facilities and services (excluding those run by private concessionaires).

SHOPPING

Keep in mind that the high quality of Native American arts and crafts is reflected in the prices they fetch. Bargaining is the exception, not the rule. In general, the best buys are to be had in the fall, after most of the tourists have gone home. Many uniquely southwestern products—chili pepper strings or locally produced salsas—make inexpensive souvenirs.

STUDENTS ON THE ROAD

To save money, **look into deals available through student-oriented travel agencies.** To qualify, you'll need to have a bona fide student ID card. Members of international student groups are also eligible (☞ Students *in* Important Contacts A to Z).

T

TELEPHONES

LONG-DISTANCE

The long-distance services of AT&T, MCI, and Sprint make calling home relatively convenient and let you avoid hotel surcharges; typically, you dial an 800 number in the United States.

TIME

Arizona sets its clocks to mountain standard time—two hours earlier than eastern standard, one hour later than Pacific standard. However, from April to October, when other states switch to daylight saving time, Arizona does *not* change its clocks; during this portion of the year, the mountain standard hour in Arizona is the same as the Pacific daylight hour in California. To complicate matters, the vast Navajo reservation in the northeastern section of the state *does* observe daylight saving time, so that from April to October it's an hour later on the reservation than it is in the rest of the state. Finally, the Hopi reservation, whose borders fall within those of the Navajo reservation, stays on the same non-Navajo, non–daylight saving clock as the remainder of the state.

TOUR OPERATORS

A package or tour to Arizona can make your vacation less expensive and more hassle-free. Firms that sell tours and packages reserve airline seats, hotel rooms, and rental cars in bulk and pass some of the savings on to you. In addition, the best operators have local representatives available to help you at your destination.

A GOOD DEAL?

The more your package or tour includes, the better you can predict the ultimate cost of your vacation. Make sure you know exactly what is covered, and **beware of hidden costs.** Are taxes, tips, and service charges included? Transfers and baggage handling? Entertainment and excursions? These can add up.

Most packages and tours are rated deluxe, first-class superior, first class, tourist, or budget. The key difference is usually accommodations. If the package or tour you are considering is priced lower than in your wildest dreams, **be skeptical.** Also, **make sure your travel agent knows the accommodations** and other services. Ask about the hotel's location, room size, beds, and whether it has a pool, room service, or programs for children, if you care about these. Has your agent been there in person or sent others you can contact?

BUYER BEWARE

Each year a number of consumers are stranded or lose their money when operators—even very large ones with excellent reputations—go out of business. To avoid becoming one of them, take the time to **check out the operator**—find out how long the company has been in business and ask several agents about its reputation. Next, **don't book unless the firm has a consumer-protection program.** Members of the USTOA and the NTA are required to set aside funds for the sole purpose of covering your payments and travel arrangements in case of default. Nonmember operators may instead carry insurance; look for the details in the operator's brochure—and for the name of an underwriter with a solid reputation. Note: When it comes to tour operators, **don't trust escrow accounts.** Although there are laws governing those of charter-flight operators, no governmental body prevents tour operators from raiding the till.

Next, **contact your local Better Business Bureau and the attorney general's offices** in both your own state and the operator's; have any complaints been filed? Finally, **pay with a major credit card.** Then you can cancel payment, provided that you can document your complaint. Always **consider trip-cancellation insurance** (☞ Insurance, *above*).

BIG VS. SMALL➢ Operators that handle several

hundred thousand travelers per year can use their purchasing power to give you a good price. Their high volume may also indicate financial stability. But some small companies provide more personalized service; because they tend to specialize, they may also be more knowledgeable about a given area.

USING AN AGENT

Travel agents are excellent resources. In fact, large operators accept bookings made only through travel agents. But it's good to **collect brochures from several agencies** because some agents' suggestions may be skewed by promotional relationships with tour and package firms that reward them for volume sales. If you have a special interest, **find an agent with expertise in that area**; ASTA can provide leads in the United States. (Don't rely solely on your agent, though; agents may be unaware of small-niche operators, and some special-interest travel companies only sell direct.)

SINGLE TRAVELERS

Prices are usually quoted per person, based on two sharing a room. If traveling solo, you may be required to pay the full double-occupancy rate. Some operators eliminate this surcharge if you agree to be matched up with a roommate of the same sex, even if one is not found by departure time.

TRAVEL GEAR

Travel catalogs specialize in useful items that can **save space when packing** and make life on the road more convenient. Compact alarm clocks, travel irons, travel wallets, and personal-care kits are among the most common items you'll find.

U

U.S. GOVERNMENT

The U.S. government can be an excellent source of travel information. Some of this is free, and some is available for a nominal charge. When planning your trip, **find out what government materials are available.** For just a couple of dollars, you can get a variety of publications from the Consumer Information Center in Pueblo, Colorado. Free consumer information also is available from individual government agencies, such as the Department of Transportation and the U.S. Customs Service. For specific titles, *see* the appropriate publications entry in Important Contacts A to Z, *above.*

W

WHEN TO GO

When you travel to Arizona depends on whether you prefer scorching desert or snowy slopes, elbow-to-elbow resorts or wide-open territory. Our advice: **visit during spring and autumn,** when the temperatures are milder and the crowds have thinned out.

Winter is prime time in the central and southern parts of the state. The weather is sunny and mild, and the cities bustle with travelers escaping the cold. Conversely, northern Arizona—including the Grand Canyon—can be wintry, with snow, freezing rain, and subzero temperatures; the road to the Grand Canyon's North Rim is closed during this time.

Arizona's desert regions sizzle in summer, and travelers and their vehicles should be adequately prepared. Practically every restaurant and accommodation is air-conditioned, though, and you can get great deals on tony southern Arizona resorts you might not be able to afford in high season. Summer is also a delightful time to visit northern Arizona's high country, when temperatures are 18°F–20°F lower than they are down south.

CLIMATE

Phoenix averages 300 sunny days and 7 inches of precipitation annually. Tucson gets all of 11 inches of rain each year, and the high mountains see about 25 inches. The Grand Canyon is usually cool on the rim and about 20°F warmer on the floor. During winter months, approximately 6–12 inches of snow falls on the North Rim; the South Rim receives half that amount.

The following average daily maximum and minimum temperatures for two major cities in Arizona offer a representative range of temperatures in the state.

Climate in Arizona

TUCSON

Jan.	64F	18C	May	89F	32C	Sept.	96F	36C
	37	3		57	14		68	20
Feb.	68F	20C	June	98F	37C	Oct.	84F	29C
	39	4		66	19		57	14
Mar.	73F	23C	July	101F	38C	Nov.	73F	23C
	44	7		73	23		44	7
Apr.	82F	28C	Aug.	96F	36C	Dec.	66F	19C
	51	11		71	22		39	4

FLAGSTAFF

Jan.	41F	5C	May	66F	19C	Sept.	71F	22C
	14	–10		33	1		41	5
Feb.	44F	7C	June	77F	25C	Oct.	62F	17C
	17	– 8		41	5		30	– 1
Mar.	48F	9C	July	80F	27C	Nov.	51F	11C
	23	– 5		50	10		21	– 6
Apr.	57F	14C	Aug.	78F	26C	Dec.	42F	6C
	28	– 2		48	9		15	– 9

1 Destination: Arizona

THE GRAND CANYON STATE

ARIZONA IS an ancient land, visibly etched by the passage of the earth and the human race through time. Aeons of our planet's story are written in the deep, multicolored walls of the Grand Canyon and the cathedral-like stone spires of Monument Valley. Ages of human history echo in the hidden grandeur of Canyon de Chelly, the "sky villages" perched atop Hopi reservation mesas, and the prehistoric ruins of Montezuma Castle and Casa Grande.

At the same time, Arizona is a lively hub of modern life, a quickening center in the emerging web of communications and trade, travel, and recreation that links western North America with the Pacific Rim. Phoenix, the state capital and the metropolitan center of the Southwest, is America's ninth-largest and fastest-growing city.

Visitors usually wonder about the desert: How hot is it? What should we wear? Is it safe? These are intelligent questions about a place where summer daytime temperatures often exceed 100°F (38°C), major rivers run underground, and the native flora are spiny cactus and thorny scrub.

What few people realize is that Arizona has two deserts. The low desert (roughly the southwestern third of the state) is indeed arid and dotted with tall saguaro cacti, but the high desert—the northeastern tier, with the Grand Canyon and Navajo and Hopi lands—is a savanna-like plain, thousands of feet above sea level and mantled in snow all winter. The middle third of Arizona is not desert at all but rather mountainous terrain, with alpine lakes and the world's largest ponderosa pine forest.

Even with—and partly because of—its low-desert climate, Arizona has an irresistible draw. Long one of the nation's prime tourist destinations, visited annually by millions from around the world, in the past two decades Arizona has been one of America's fastest-growing states, with tens of thousands of immigrants arriving each year.

That growth transformed Phoenix from a farming town of 60,000 in 1940 to an urban center of 1 million by 1990. It also doubled and redoubled the population of Tucson, the "Old Pueblo" in the southern part of the state. Yet Arizona remains a place of boundless vistas, with more than 80% of its land in U.S. and state parks and preserves or Native American reservations. Whether they are in the deserts or the mountains, Arizona's small towns still have vast spaces between them.

The state has also retained much of its rich Native American and Spanish colonial heritage. More Native Americans live here than in any other state, and the Hopi village of Oraibi is the oldest continuously inhabited community in North America. Mexican and Central American families continue to immigrate, many following routes opened by Spanish explorers a century before the Pilgrims landed. Numerous Tucson families trace their lineage to Mexican pioneers who arrived in the days of the American Revolution.

Visitors can readily see some of the gifts modern Arizona has received from these ancient cultures: the Native American and Spanish names of most of its mountains and rivers, plants, and animals, even its streets and the pervasive influence of Hopi and Mexican architecture in homes and public buildings. Other aspects of this heritage appear only after some study: in the canals that carry Arizona's mountain streams into the low desert and the legal system that gives husband and wife equal shares in their "community property."

One part of Arizona's cultural heritage that almost everyone gets to share is the relaxed pace and style of living: In almost everything, from clothing to art, from home decor to meals, the desert dwellers of each era have learned to prize the unhurried and the informal, to accept the calming lessons of the heat and the majestic landscape. Leave your tie and tails at home and, even if you're on business, plan to take time out: Lean back for a leisurely late lunch during the hottest part of the day; stretch out under a patio awning beside a pool or fountain during the long, cool evenings.

And wherever you take your siesta, cast your eye toward the horizon: You'll see deep skies and luminous, gold-edged sunsets; the towering silhouettes of buttes and mountain ranges, their rugged surfaces subtly alive with shifting shadows and pastel colors; a forest of widely spaced saguaro cacti, standing firm like many-armed sentinels amid sketchy creosote and ocotillo bushes while birds and lizards dart from one spiny haven to the next; or the long, green bowl of a mountain meadow, dusted with poppy clusters and blue lupine beds, edged with shimmering aspens. Arizonans and visitors alike never tire of watching the play of sun and shadows on some corner of this magnificent land.

Mark Hein

Mark Hein is an editor and a writer in the features department of the *Arizona Republic.*

WHAT'S WHERE

The Grand Canyon and Northwest Arizona

In the face of this vast marvel, words can be hard to come by—except on the subject of recommendations: Go to the North Rim. It may take longer to get there, and it is closed in winter to all but cross-country skiers, but you will be rewarded by having a Wonder of the World more to yourself. In and around the state's northwest corner, Lake Mead, the Hoover Dam, and the gambling halls of Laughlin, Nevada, have their appeals, too.

The Northeast

This sprawling corner of the state is the home of the Navajo Nation and Hopi Reservation. Native American crafts draw some visitors, as does interest in gaining an understanding of the lives, past and present, of some of our land's true founding mothers and fathers. Along with the living Navajo and Hopi reservations, ancient Pueblo ruins at Betatakin, Keet Seel, and Canyon de Chelly are haunting, unforgettable sights. (☞"The Native Southwest" *in* Chapter 7 for cultural background to ancestral and contemporary inhabitants.) And don't forget about Monument Valley, the bizarre and fascinating Petrified Forest National Park and Painted Desert, and activities at another man-made lake, Lake Powell, when planning your trip.

North-Central Arizona

Jerome and Prescott are two of the state's most popular towns for their Wild West history, some of it bawdy and outrageous, all of it interesting, and for their place in yet another wondrous, beautiful locale. Sedona's red rocks, recognizable for the roles that they played in numerous Hollywood westerns, are as captivating as they are easy to hike. Flagstaff has become more of a destination in its own right, with historic buildings, an increasing number of good restaurants, and nightlife. Outside of the city, ancient Native American dwellings at Wupatki and Walnut Canyon national monuments and Sunset Crater are windows onto the world of a thousand years past.

Phoenix and Central Arizona

The ever-widening Phoenix metropolitan area provides a tremendous variety of activities for almost all interests. Hike in the Valley of the Sun's superb desert parks, golf on championship courses, dine at the restaurants where Southwestern cuisine was born, or experience the last word in pampering at world-class spas and resorts. The White Mountains are a nearby escape, with Old West towns, the stunning Salt River Canyon, and more great hiking.

Tucson and Southern Arizona

Tucson may have buried most of its Spanish roots, but some remnants of the adobe days in its El Presidio neighborhood provide a pleasant architectural diversion. And there is great Mexican food. Outside of town, the Mission San Xavier del Bac, an architectural and art-historical masterpiece, is set in the midst of the Tohonó O'odham Reservation, where Native American crafts are also available. Farther from the city, visit the legendary Tombstone and other mining towns, and pop over the border to Agua Prieta, Mexico. For nature and bird lovers, Ramsey Canyon, Organ Pipe National Monument, and Chiracahua National Monument have fascinating flora and fauna and great hiking. Chiracahua is a particularly unique zone where species from the Southwest, the Chiracahua Mountains, and Mexico all live amid forests and volcanic rock formations.

PLEASURES AND PASTIMES

Ballooning

If you're so inclined, floating in a balloon can be a delight. In both Phoenix and Tucson pilots will take you up over metropolitan areas as well as the Sonoran Desert. Some go up year-round, though most fly only in cooler months. Tours last about an hour and are customarily followed by a champagne celebration.

Baseball

Baseball fans visiting Arizona in March have a chance to watch major-league teams during spring training. Exhibition games begin in early March, but the eight Cactus League teams start practice at training camps as much as three weeks earlier. Their free drills—held in the morning before an exhibition game—are fun to watch, and there's a good chance you might be able to chat with the players before or after these sessions. In some cases, reserved seats sell out the fall before an upcoming season, but you can almost always get general admission seats on the day of the games.

Bicycling

Desert trails, the open road, and mountain passes provide a tremendous variety of great cycling. We recommend riding in cooler months, of course—a desert road in summer is like a frying pan.

Boating and Lake Activities

You may be surprised to find so many lakes in what most consider a desert state. In fact, Arizonans own more boats per capita than residents of any other state. The two national recreational areas, Glen Canyon (Lake Powell) in north-central Arizona and Lake Mead (including Lake Mohave) in the northwest, have marinas, launching ramps, and boat and ski rentals. At both lakes you can take a paddle-wheeler tour or take the wheel yourself in a fully equipped houseboat. Lake Havasu, fed by the Colorado River in the western part of the state, is another favored site for boating, waterskiing, windsurfing, and jetskiing. London Bridge, which was moved block by block from England and reassembled here, is a surreal vision at this lakeside resort. Be sure to call ahead on the availability of rental equipment.

Saguaro and Canyon lakes, just east of Scottsdale, offer good boating and waterskiing for those based in the Phoenix area who are looking for a convenient day trip.

Canoeing. Swift currents without rapids make the daylong Topock Gorge trip on the Colorado River a favorite outing. Beginning at Topock, canoeists travel through a wildlife refuge to Castle Rock at the top end of Lake Havasu. Another route, made dramatic by the Black Canyon cliffs, is along the Colorado River below Hoover Dam to Willow Beach.

River Rafting. Rafting and kayaking trips down the Colorado River and through the Grand Canyon keep some visitors returning year after year. Trips run from one day to two weeks and operate during the summer season. Other rafting expeditions run on the Salt and Verde rivers, through the Sonoran Desert, near Scottsdale.

Other Water Sports. Swimmers can plunge into a cool mountain lake or splash in the acres and acres of water at one of the recreational megaresorts. Virtually every hotel and motel has a swimming pool of some size, and nearly all Arizona cities have at least one public pool. Or, cavort in man-made waves at a number of water parks around Phoenix, including Water World and Golfland/Sunsplash (in Mesa), and even surf the 3- to 5-foot-high waves at Big Surf in Tempe. Tubing is popular along the Salt River, east of Mesa.

Dining

Outside of major cities, Arizona cuisine leans mainly toward western-style steaks, barbecued ribs and beans, biscuits with gravy, and chuck-wagon–type fare. The Navajo taco (beans, tomatoes, lettuce, and cheese on Indian fry bread) and a few Hopi recipes served on the reservation combine Native American and Mexican food traditions. Mexican food is plentiful everywhere in the state. Phoenix and Tucson offer Continental dining, an eclectic mix of ethnic eateries, and, most important, the acclaimed Southwestern cuisine, using local ingredients with a style at once classic and innovative.

Fishing

Fish virtually jump out of Arizona's cool mountain streams, major rivers, and manmade lakes and are especially plentiful at Colorado River resorts. Rainbow, brown, brook, and cutthroat trout, as well as catfish, crappie, bass, pike, and bluegill, are the primary game. San Carlos Lake is tops for bass, and trout are plentiful at Lees Ferry. Fishing licenses *are* required.

Golf

Your clubs certainly won't gather dust in Arizona. Aside from the big-draw Phoenix and Tucson opens (☞ Festivals and Seasonal Events, *below*), golfers flock to this state to tee off at the myriad top-ranked private and municipal courses. Year-round desert courses offer cheaper greens fees during the summer, and those in the northern part of the state usually shut down for winter. Just about every resort has its own course or is affiliated with a private club.

Hiking

Throughout the state, hikers can choose from trails that wind through the desert, climb mountains, meander past supernal rock formations, delve deep into forests, or circumnavigate cities. Whatever your choice of direction, you'll find thousands of miles of marked paths through unforgettable landscapes, many of which you'll find in parks and around national monuments.

Be prepared when you do hike—*see* Smart Travel Tips A to Z for important precautions to take before setting out.

Horseback Riding

Traveling by horseback through the somewhat wild West or the scenic high country is perhaps the most appropriate way to explore Arizona. Stables offer a selection of mountain or desert trail rides lasting a half day, two days, or as long as two weeks. In northern regions the season is from May through October. If riding is the focus of your Arizona holiday, you might consider staying at a dude ranch, where you can saddle up every day.

National and State Parks and Monuments

National Parks. Arizona's three national parks are the granddaddy Grand Canyon National Park (1,218,375 acres), Petrified Forest National Park (93,533 acres), and the U.S.'s newest, Saguaro National Park (91,327 acres). The Grand Canyon, northwest of Flagstaff, is one of the Seven Natural Wonders of the World. Travelers come from all parts of the globe to hike, camp, raft, helicopter, or simply ooh and aah at the spectacular views and ever-changing colors, shadows, and light. Petrified Forest National Park, east of Flagstaff, features rainbow-color petrified logs, tree fragments, and chunks of rock—preserved-in-stone remnants of a forest dating from the dinosaur age. Saguaro National Park, which flanks Tucson's east and west sides, supports the most specimens in the United States of the towering saguaro (suh-*wah*-ro) cactus, which can live more than 200 years.

National Monuments. Southwest of Tucson on the Mexican border, Organ Pipe National Monument abounds in examples of the saguaro's many-armed cactus cousin. For Native American ruins in scenic settings, visit Canyon de Chelly near the New Mexico border, Walnut Canyon National Monument and Wupatki National Monument in the Flagstaff area, Tuzigoot National Monument south of Sedona, and Navajo National Monument's Keet Seel and Betatakin (beh-*tah*-tah-kin) near Monument Valley. Little-visited spots of unusual beauty include Sunset Crater Volcano National Monument, west of Flagstaff, its black lava flows contrasted against a lush green forest, and Chiricahua National Monument in the southeast, where odd rock formations preside over woods that simultaneously celebrate spring and autumn.

State Parks. Arizona's state parks range from relatively small Slide Rock (54 acres), near Sedona, to 13,000-acre Lake Havasu; both feature water-based activities. Boating and water-sports enthusiasts also like to congregate at Alamo Lake State Park, north of Wenden; Roper Lake State Park, at the foot of Mt. Graham in the southeast; and Lyman Lake State Park, in the White Mountains area. Catalina and Picacho Peak state parks, near Tucson, and Lost Dutchman State Park, east of Phoenix, are the best bets for desert activities. Painted Rocks State Park, west of Gila Bend, is distinctive for its Native American rock carvings. Those interested in the lively frontier history of this state should enjoy Riordon Historical State Park in Flagstaff, Jerome State Historic Park and Fort Verde State Historic Park in north-central Arizona, and Tombstone Courthouse State Historic Park and Yuma Territorial Prison State Historic Park, both in the south.

Fragile Life. Don't be tempted to pull any of Arizona's century-old saguaro cacti out by the roots. The state flower is protected by law, as are most slow-growing desert plants and flowers. Theft or vandalism carries stiff penalties. Similarly, the dry and easily desecrated desert floor takes centuries to overcome human damage. Consequently, it is illegal for four-wheel-drive and all-terrain vehicles and motorcycles to travel off established roadways.

Native American Culture

Watching Native American festivals and exploring the remains of earlier settlements can be a rewarding part of a trip to Arizona—we recommend any effort to enhance your understanding of aspects of Native American culture on your trip. (For more information on Native Americans past and present, *see* "The Native Southwest" *in* Chapter 7.)

Rockhounding

Arizona is rock-hound heaven, its deserts and mountains laden with a dazzling variety of rocks and minerals: agate, jasper, tourmaline, petrified wood, quartz, turquoise, amethyst, precious opal, fire agate, and more. The Department of Mines and Mineral Resources has a fine Mining and Mineral Museum as well as a rockhounding reference library. Remember, however, to inquire about restrictions before you fill your pockets. Taking rocks is illegal on the Navajo and Hopi reservations, for example.

You can purchase rocks and minerals at specialty shops or at one of the state's year-round rock and gem shows. The largest shows are held in Quartzsite, about 19 mi from the California border, and in Tucson, generally from late January to mid-February.

Shopping

Many tourists come to Arizona for no other reason than to purchase fine Native American jewelry and crafts. Collectibles include Navajo rugs and sand paintings, Hopi kachina dolls (intricately carved and colorful representations of Hopi spiritual beings) and pottery, Tohonó O'odham (Papago) basketry, and Apache beadwork, as well as the highly prized silver and turquoise jewelry produced by several different tribes. Many of these items are sold in big-city shops and malls, but going directly to the reservation often gives shoppers additional rewards.

Museums and trading posts on the Navajo and Hopi reservations in the state's northeastern region offer introductions to crafts and their history and have gift shops where you can make purchases; especially worth visiting are the Hubbell and Cameron trading posts, the Navajo Arts and Crafts Enterprises, and the Hopi Cultural Center. Demonstrations of silversmithing, rug-weaving, and pottery-making techniques are often held on the premises. Roadside stands also offer wares for sale.

You can find exquisite baskets and other crafts of the Tohonó O'odham at the plaza outside the San Xavier Mission on the outskirts of Tucson, as well as at shops in Sells, the tribe's headquarters, about 60 mi southwest of Tucson. Apache beadwork, baskets, wood carvings, and jewelry are sold at reservation trading posts in the eastern part of the state.

Skiing

Cross-country and downhill skiing are both worthy winter pastimes in Arizona, even if they don't quite match the scale of the Rockies. Flagstaff Nordic Center, Mormon Lake Ski Touring Center southeast of Flagstaff, the North Rim Nordic Center, and miles of crisscrossing trails around Alpine are good places for cross-country skiing. The three peaks of Sunrise Park Resort in McNary are owned and operated by the White Mountain Apache Indians and constitute the state's largest ski area. Other popular areas are Arizona Snowbowl near Flagstaff and Mt. Lemmon Ski Valley near Tucson.

Tennis

Tennis lovers abound in Arizona, and you can find numerous opportunities to play the game. The dryness of the air makes for some of the best climate for tennis anywhere.

What's New in Arizona

The new $47 million **Arizona Science Center** opened in Phoenix in 1996. The 40,000-square-foot indoor/outdoor exhibit space is a delight for kids of all ages—blow 4-foot-wide bubbles, see the stars at the planetarium, take in a flick on the 50-foot-high Iwerks movie screen, and learn about our miracle planet through a variety of other interactive displays.

The **Phoenix Museum of History** moved into ultramodern, glass-and-steel quarters at Heritage and Science Park in 1996. Get a healthy dose of regional history, tour interactive exhibits, or play Sniff That Barrel (to guess its contents) at a replica of a 1860's general store.

FODOR'S CHOICE

Activities and Wonders

★ **Grand Canyon, North Rim.** The only way to get to know the canyon, to feel the force of it open you right up, is to hike or ride a mule down through all of those geological years to the bottom of the great chasm.

★ **Canyon de Chelly National Monument, Navajo Nation, the Northeast.** The silence and harmony with which these ancient cliff dwellings exist in their surroundings are truly profound—as they must have been for the canyon's inhabitants 700 and more years past.

★ **Sedona's red rocks.** Picnic or hike among Sedona's natural monuments and just feel the wonder of the place—it's the real reason to visit here.

★ **Desert Botanical Gardens, Phoenix.** An early morning walk through the desert gives perhaps the best, and most pleasant, view of the lives of its flora and fauna.

★ **Signal Hill, Saguaro National Park, Tucson.** The fascinating petroglyphs (rock art) made by the Hohokam people are among the state's numerous living testaments of the mythological figures and symbols of the first Americans.

Scenic Drives

★ **Point Sublime, North Rim, Grand Canyon.** The dirt road out to the point provides one of the most awe-inspiring panoramic views you'll have from a car, anywhere.

★ **U.S. 163 from Kayenta, Arizona, to the Goosenecks of the San Juan River in southern Utah.** This drive through the archetypal Wild West landscape of Monument Valley ends in a winding, water-carved canyon of the San Juan River, a unique counterpart to the Grand Canyon.

★ **Flagstaff to Sedona via Oak Creek Canyon, North-Central Arizona.** Another stunning canyon, this one quiet and tree-lined on its low end, towering and majestic as it looks toward Sedona, marks the transition from northern Arizona's Colorado Plateau to the southern desert landscape.

★ **Jerome to Prescott, North-Central Arizona.** The winding road through Prescott National Forest is one of Arizona's most breathtaking mountain drives—precipitous at times, but beautiful.

★ **Texas Canyon, Southern Arizona.** Does one ever tire of canyons? We don't think so, especially when they are hung with giant boulders apparently defying their great mass in astonishing formations, as in this one, east of Tucson.

★ **Tucson to Kitt Peak, Tucson and Southern Arizona.** About 20 mi southwest of Tucson, upon entering the Tohonó O'odham reservation, you enter the heart of the desert. In the distance looms the sacred Baboquivari Peak, a symbol of the deep-feeling Native American worldview that remains in sight as you climb the sides of Kitt Mountain.

Shopping

★ **Cameron Trading Post, Grand Canyon.** One of the state's historic trading posts, this one has a wide variety of Hopi, Navajo, and Pueblo jewelry, rugs, baskets, and pottery, along with Navajo tacos at its restaurant next door.

★ **Hubbell Trading Post, Ganado, the Northeast.** Established in 1878 by a big-hearted New Mexican, this National Historic Site specializes in Navajo rugs, existing, as it does, on the Navajo Reservation.

★**Tlaquepaque Mall, Sedona, North-Central Arizona.** Worth a visit as much for its architecture and Mexican village design as for its shopping, Tlaquepaque houses Sedona's most exclusive boutiques and their variety of splendid wares.

★**Main Street, Scottsdale.** From the touristy to the genuine, including Mexican imports and Thursday evening Art Walks (October–May), this is Scottsdale's own western version of one of America's favorite pastimes.

★**Tubac, Southern Arizona.** Arizona's first Euramerican town, Tubac is a great spot, with an artists' community, lots of history, numerous shops, and good values.

Restaurants

★**Chistopher's, Phoenix.** Christopher Gross offers the Valley's finest French cuisine. His flawlessly prepared and sauced creations are worthy of the Champs-Elysées. *$$$–$$$$*

★**Heartline Café, Sedona, North-Central Arizona.** What some might call hippie haute cuisine—because they love it, of course—includes tasty grilled food, inventive pizza, and southwestern dishes in a pleasant, friendly atmosphere. *$$–$$$*

★**Such Is Life, Phoenix.** Come to Moises Treves's corner of Phoenix to taste cactus, chicken Maya, garlic shrimp—yes, delicious regional Mexican food. *$$*

★**Café Poca Cosa, Tucson.** Ooh, those tropical colors, and ooh, what fantastic Sonoran Mexican cooking—especially if you like chicken mole. You won't find any excesses of cheese here. *$–$$*

★**Los Dos Molinos, Phoenix.** Pure, hot New Mexico–style cooking graces colorful tile tables in this bustling, white-adobe cantina. Be careful: the fresh, homemade green- and red-chile salsas can rip your lips off. *$*

★**Prescott Brewing Company, Prescott, North-Central Arizona.** The name doesn't lie: Four draughts are brewed on the premises and are served up along with a menu of good pub fare—even vegetarians will be pleasantly surprised. *$*

Hotels and B&Bs

★**The Phoenician, Phoenix.** French-provincial decor, fine European paintings, gleaming marble, and spacious rooms make this the swankest joint in town. A two-acre desert garden shelters hundreds of cacti and succulents, and Windows on the Green offers some of the best Southwest cuisine in the city. *$$$$*

★**Arizona Inn, Tucson.** With almost all that you would want from a landmark inn—period furnishings, fireplaces, quiet and friendly service, even a downtown location on property of its own—you won't be disappointed with a stay here. *$$$–$$$$*

★**Briar Patch Inn, Sedona, North-Central Arizona.** It may not be in the heart of Sedona's red rocks, but its lovely Oak Creek Canyon location alongside the laughing water, and so many touches, sets the Briar Patch apart. *$$$–$$$$*

★**Wahweap Lodge at Lake Powell, the Northeast.** A central and well-equipped location for Lake Powell recreation, Wahweap has cruises; river excursions; boat, ski, and tackle rentals; and a restaurant that make for a nearly all-in-one resort. *$$$*

★**Grand Canyon Lodge, North Rim, Grand Canyon.** We've said it once, and we'll say it again—come to the North Rim to avoid the crowds and *enjoy* the mighty abyss. While you're here, why not stay in the historic, rustic Grand Canyon Lodge, with spectacular views of you-know-what. *$–$$$*

★**Casa Tierra Bed & Breakfast, Tucson.** In an adobe brick building, this friendly bed-and-breakfast outside of town is a great desert getaway, highly recommended. *$$*

★**Cameron Trading Post at Cameron, Grand Canyon.** This may well be the best base, or even jumping-off point, for both the Grand Canyon, North and South rims, and Navajo-Hopi country, all with its own trading-post–style charm. *$–$$*

FESTIVALS AND SEASONAL EVENTS

WINTER

JAN. 1➢ Tempe's nationally televised **Fiesta Bowl Footbowl Classic** kicks off the year with a match between the nation's top two college teams.

JAN.➢ At the **Phoenix Open Golf Tournament** in Scottsdale, top players compete at the Tournament Players Club. The **Tucson Open,** the other top PGA event, is cohosted by Tucson National Golf & Conference Resort and Starr Pass Golf Club.

JAN.➢ The **Dixieland Jazz Festival** at Lake Havasu City uses London Bridge as the backdrop to traditional Dixieland sounds and more, including a parade, dancing on a riverboat, and Sunday-morning gospel.

JAN.–FEB.➢ **Parada del Sol Rodeo and Parade,** a popular state attraction on Scottsdale Road, features lots of dressed-up cowboys and cowgirls, plus horses and floats.

EARLY FEB.➢ The **Quartzsite Pow Wow Gem and Mineral Show** is a gigantic flea market, held the first Wednesday through Sunday of the month in Quartzsite, about 19 mi from the California border (take I–10 west of Phoenix and then turn north on AZ 95). It attracts more than 100,000 buyers and sellers of rocks, minerals, gems, and related crafts and supplies.

FEB.➢ At **O'odham Tash** in Casa Grande, Native American tribes from around the country host parades, native dances, a rodeo, costume displays, and food stands.

FEB.➢ History comes to life during **Wickenburg Gold Rush Days,** when the Old West town puts on a rodeo, dances, gold-panning demonstrations, a mineral show, and other activities.

FEB.➢ **La Fiesta de los Vaqueros** features the world's longest "non-mechanized" parade—horses pull floats and carry dignitaries—launching a four-day rodeo at the Tucson Rodeo Grounds.

FEB.➢ The huge **Tucson Gem and Mineral Show** attracts rock hounds—amateur and professional—from all over the world who come to buy, sell, and display their geological treasures and to attend lectures and competitive exhibits.

SPRING

MAR.➢ The highlight of the **Ostrich Festival** in Chandler is a race of the big birds; it also features a parade, crafts and food booths, and a petting zoo.

MAR.➢ For the **Lost Dutchman Gold Mine Superstition Mountain Trek** in Apache Junction, the Dons of Arizona search for the legendary lost mine, pan for gold, and eat lots of barbecue to keep up their strength. There are crafts demonstrations and fireworks, too.

MAR.➢ In Phoenix, the **Heard Museum Guild Indian Fair and Market** is a prestigious juried show of Native American arts and crafts that brings together participants from all over the Southwest. Visitors can also enjoy Native American foods, music, and dance.

APR.➢ Tucson hosts the **International Mariachi Conference,** four days of mariachi music, along with cultural and educational exhibits.

APR.➢ During the **Route 66 Fun Run Weekend,** in Seligman/Topock, the historic road between Chicago and Los Angeles is feted with classic car rallies, hot-rod and antique-car shows, and various other events—including a 1950s hop.

APR.➢ **Yaqui Easter** is celebrated in old Pasqua Village (Tucson) on the Saturday nights preceding Palm Sunday and Easter Sunday. Visitors are welcome to watch traditional Yaqui dances and ceremonies.

APR.➢ Bisbee's **La Vuelta de Bisbee** is Arizona's largest bicycle race and attracts top racers from around the country to the hills of the historic mining town. The 1995 race was used to select riders for the 1996 U.S. Olympic cycling team.

MAY➢ On **Rendezvous Days,** the townspeople of Williams reenact the annual trek to town by 1800s mountain traders. Events include a steak fry and a Buckskinners black powder shoot.

MAY➢ A two-day tournament, the **Lake Havasu Western Outdoor News Striper Derby** is the largest in Arizona, drawing fishing teams from as far away as Michigan and Idaho.

MAY–JUNE➢ At Flagstaff's **Trappings of the American West Festival,** the featured attraction is cowboy art—everything from painting and sculpture to cowboy poetry readings.

SUMMER

JUNE➢ Festivities of **Old West Day/Bucket of Blood Races,** in Holbrook, include arts and crafts, western dress, and Native American song and dance, in addition to the 10-kilometer fun run and 20-mile bike ride from Petrified Forest National Park to Holbrook.

LATE JUNE OR EARLY JULY➢ The **All Indian Powwow** and **Native American Arts Fair** are held in Flagstaff the weekend before July 4. Tribes from around the world present dance performances and competitions, and an international array of crafts is displayed and sold.

JULY➢ **Prescott Frontier Days and Rodeo,** billed as the world's oldest rodeo, finds big crowds and an equally big party on downtown Whiskey Row.

JULY➢ At the **Loggers/Sawdust Festival** in Payson, loggers from the United States and Canada test their skills and strength. Family fun includes a greased pole climb and a fire-extinguisher water fight.

JULY➢ The **Native American Arts & Crafts Festival,** in Pinetop/Lakeside brings storytellers, dancers, musicians, and artists together for two days in a beautiful mountain setting.

AUG.➢ The **Payson Rodeo** draws top cowboys from around the country to compete for top prizes in calf- and steer-roping contests at what they call the world's oldest continuous rodeo.

AUG.➢ Flagstaff's **Festival in the Pines** is a gathering of painters, potters, musicians, and other artists from around the United States. They vie with carnival rides and food vendors for the crowd's attention.

AUTUMN

SEPT.➢ At the **Jazz on the Rocks Festival** in Sedona, six or seven ensembles perform in a spectacular red-rock setting.

SEPT.➢ The **Navajo Nation Annual Tribal Fair** is the world's largest Native American fair. Held in Window Rock, it includes a rodeo, traditional Navajo music and dances, food booths, and an intertribal powwow.

OCT.➢ Phoenix's massive **Arizona State Fair** features games, rides, exhibits, livestock, art shows, and other entertainment.

OCT.➢ Spicy food lovers revel at **La Fiesta de Los Chiles,** Tucson's two-day salute to the chile, which is cooked, hung, made into art, and otherwise celebrated.

OCT.➢ At **Tombstone's Helldorado Days,** the town relives the spirited Wyatt Earp era and the shoot-out at the OK Corral.

OCT.➢ A weeklong event, **London Bridge Days** includes a triathlon, a parade, and a variety of contests in Lake Havasu City.

NOV.➢ Exhibits at the **Heard Museum Native American Art Show** in Phoenix feature fine tribal arts and crafts from across the state.

NOV.➢ In Lake Havasu City's **Havasu Classic Outboard World Championships,** various classes of racing boats tear up the water competing for prize money and trophies.

NOV.➢ During the **Thunderbird Balloon Classic & Air Show,** one hundred or more balloons participate in Glendale's colorful race.

DEC.➢ The **Arizona Temple Christmas Lighting** in Mesa finds more than 300,000 lights illuminating the walkways, reflection pool, trees, and plants at the Arizona Temple Gardens and Visitors Center.

DEC.➢ The waters of Lake Powell alight with the **Festival of Lights Boat Parade** as dozens of illuminated boats glide from Wahweap Lodge to Glen Canyon Dam and back.

DEC.➢ For the three days of **Old Town Tempe Fall Festival of the Arts,** the downtown area closes to traffic for art exhibits, food booths, music, and other entertainment.

2 The Grand Canyon and Northwest Arizona

To appreciate the Grand Canyon, you must see it. Not even the finest photographs pack a fraction of the impact of a personal glimpse of this vast, beautiful scar on the surface of our planet—277 miles long, 18 miles across at its widest spot, and more than a mile below the rim at its deepest point. The Grand Canyon is the quintessence of the high drama of the American western landscape. In and around the state's northwest corner, Lake Mead, the Hoover Dam, and the gambling halls of Laughlin, Nevada, have their appeals, too.

By William E. Hafford and Edie Jarolim

Updated by Susana Sedgwick

ALTHOUGH MILLIONS of words have been devoted to describing the Grand Canyon, writers have generally conceded that the earth's greatest gorge is beyond the scope of language. Southwestern author Frank Waters has come closer than most to capturing its power. "It is the sum total," he writes, "of all the aspects of nature combined in one integrated whole. It is at once the smile and frown upon the face of nature. In its heart is the savage, uncontrollable fury of all the inanimate Universe, and at the same time the immeasurable serenity that succeeds it. It is Creation."

More than 65 million years ago, a great wrenching of the earth pushed the land in the region of the canyon up into a domed tableland, today called the Colorado Plateau. Then the Colorado River, racing south through present-day Utah, began chewing at the uplifted region. The river is responsible for much of the erosion, but many side gullies and canyons were formed by melting snow and fierce rainstorms that sent water rushing into the gorge through smaller tributaries. Softer rock formations were washed away by the Colorado and carried to the distant sea; the harder formations remained as great cliffs and buttes. Above the twisting line of river are otherworldly stone monuments with colors that range from muted pastels to deep purples, vibrant yellows, fiery reds, and soft blues. This palette shifts with the hours: What you see at mid-morning is repainted by the setting sun.

This is also a land of ancient peoples. In some of the deepest, most inaccessible reaches of the Grand Canyon, evidence of early human habitation exists. Stone ruins high in the cliffs reveal the archaeological secrets of cultures some 8,000 to 10,000 years old. In higher country above both North and South rims are the remains of prehistoric Pueblo settlements active until about AD 1300. It is believed that a period of harsh and sustained drought, coupled with the effects of climatic change, soil erosion, and heavy use of local resources, caused the people to seek more favorable lands. Today's Hopi Indians, who live on mesas about 150 mi east of the canyon, along with New Mexican Pueblo people, view themselves as descendants of the earlier inhabitants. The former dwellings are, as a result, sacred homes of ancestral spirits.

In the year 1540, a band of Spanish soldiers under the command of Captain García López de Cárdenas became the first white men to look into the canyon. The members of the expedition, dispatched by Francisco Coronado to find the fabled golden cities of Cibola, found the Grand Canyon instead. Spanish Franciscan missionary and explorer Francisco Tomás Garcés visited a Havasupai Indian village in the canyon in 1776, and Lieutenant Joseph Ives went on an official mission for the U.S. government to explore the area in 1857. But no one thought it worth much attention until 1869, when John Wesley Powell, a one-armed adventurer and scholar, put rough-hewn boats into the Colorado and let the swirling white water of the mighty river take him along its length.

During the last years of the 19th century, almost all development at or near the canyon was related to mining. In fact, the earliest trails down into the canyon were built by miners searching for precious minerals. Shortly after the beginning of the 20th century, the Santa Fe Railroad completed a line to the South Rim of the canyon, ushering in the era of tourism. In 1903 Theodore Roosevelt visited and drew public interest to the site. It was declared a national park in 1919. Today close to 5 million visitors come each year from around the world to peer into this gorge in amazement.

Your first view of the Grand Canyon will last a lifetime. After a half dozen lookouts, however, your sense of wonder will begin to diminish—it's difficult to establish a personal relationship with so much grandeur. Traveling along the rim, you will soon tire of putting your nose up against all of this beauty, safely, almost antiseptically, peering in. By all means stop along the rim, but we can't encourage you strongly enough to take a walk, however brief, into the canyon itself. A 20-minute descent into the maw of this abyss will open up a totally new perspective and permit you to get close to the canyon in a way that is impossible at the rim.

Pleasures and Pastimes

Cross-Country Skiing

The North Rim Nordic Center (☞ Outdoor Activities and Sports *in* The North Rim, *below*) boasts the largest groomed-trail wilderness skiing system in the United States: 50 mi of regularly groomed trails and 21.7 mi of marked backcountry trails within the 1.6-million-acre Kaibab National Forest. The center's trails offer plenty of challenges, including the 8.7-mile Tater Ridge Trail and the appropriately named Adrenaline Alley, a mile-long screamer that gauges one's talent for dodging tree trunks. The Point Imperial guided tour, offered every Sunday, leads skiers across unmarked open country and over steep hills to the very edge of the Grand Canyon. Several ski packages are offered, including one that involves an overnight at a remote yurt (a heated dome-shape cabin). The instruction here is superb and lures cross-country skiers from all over the world who want to brush up on their techniques—and see the canyon.

Dining

Throughout Grand Canyon country and the vast areas of northwestern Arizona, restaurants cater to tourists who generally move from one place to another at a good clip. Most establishments offer standard American fare, prepared quickly and offered at reasonable prices. An exception to this general rule is the world-class restaurant and service at El Tovar, the oldest hotel in the canyon. In contrast to the civilized elegance of El Tovar, but equally appealing in its own way, is the family-style restaurant at Phantom Ranch, set at the bottom of the canyon; the menu may be limited, but the food tastes like ambrosia after a rugged hike down to the Inner Gorge.

Restaurants are open daily unless otherwise noted, and dress throughout this recreational area is casual (though you may want to don your hole-free jeans for the tony El Tovar dining room).

CATEGORY	COST*
$$$$	over $25
$$$	$17–$25
$$	$10–$17
$	under $10

**per person, excluding drinks, service, and 5% sales tax*

Hiking

Hiking trails are numerous, and scenery is always spectacular around the Grand Canyon. Opportunities range from leisurely walks on well-defined paths through level or easy-rolling country to arduous, multi-day treks to the bottom of the canyon—and across to the other rim if you'd like. At the very least, a short hike down any of the trails will give you an incredible spatial feeling of the canyon. In addition to some of the most popular trails outlined in the chapter, national park rangers or visitor-center personnel will gladly provide you with hiking information and local maps of trails of varying difficulty.

Lodging

The Fred Harvey Company opened the world-famous El Tovar Hotel on the rim of the canyon in 1905, heralding the beginning of Grand Canyon Village. Now there are more than 900 motel and hotel rooms in the Village, but the ever-increasing visitor population makes even that number of accommodations insufficient in summer. The North Rim is less crowded but has limited lodging facilities. You would be well advised to make reservations as soon as your itinerary has been decided, even as early as six months in advance. The South Rim's National Park Service Visitor Center, just outside Grand Canyon Village, posts the availability of hotel rooms inside the park and in the nearby town of Tusayan. (Note: The former tend to be high on rustic atmosphere but low on amenities; if you're looking for modern conveniences, you're better off in Tusayan.) If you can't find accommodations in the immediate area of the South Rim, you'll probably find something in the nearby communities of Williams or Flagstaff (☞ Flagstaff and Environs *in* Chapter 4). For those going to the North Rim, we list lodgings in the sparsely populated Arizona Strip country on the approach to the North Rim on U.S. 89A. Prices at many of the hotels and motels in Grand Canyon country are lower in spring, fall, and winter.

CATEGORY	COST*
$$$$	over $110
$$$	$85–$110
$$	$60–$85
$	under $60

**All prices are for a standard double room, excluding 5.5%–6.7% tax.*

Mountain Biking

Mountain-bike enthusiasts revel in the network of park-service dirt access roads that lace the North Rim, among them a 17-mile muscle tester that leads to Point Sublime, overlooking the inner canyon's Granite Gorge and its fierce rapids. A network of Jeep trails fans out north of Point Sublime, leading to other vistas to the west; mountain bikers who follow those trails are likely to have the place to themselves during most of the year.

Rafting

Many people who have made the white-water trip down the Colorado River through the Grand Canyon say it is the adventure of a lifetime. White-water trips embark from Lees Ferry, below Glen Canyon Dam near Page, Arizona. Trips that run the length of the canyon (a distance of more than 200 mi) can last from three days to three weeks. Shorter trips, also starting at Lees Ferry, let passengers off at Phantom Ranch at the bottom of the Grand Canyon (about 100 mi). These pass through a great amount of white water, including Lava Falls rapids (on longer trips), considered the wildest navigable rapids in North America. For those who would like a more tranquil turn on the Colorado, there are also one-day, quiet-water raft trips debarking from just below Glen Canyon Dam near Page.

Exploring the Grand Canyon and Northwest Arizona

The Grand Canyon stretches across northwest Arizona. Its popular South Rim includes the Village Rim, East Rim Drive, and West Rim Drive. The drive to the less-visited North Rim, in the Arizona Strip (a 12,000-square-mile tract of land isolated from the rest of the state by the Colorado River), takes in views of the Painted Desert to the east. Havasu

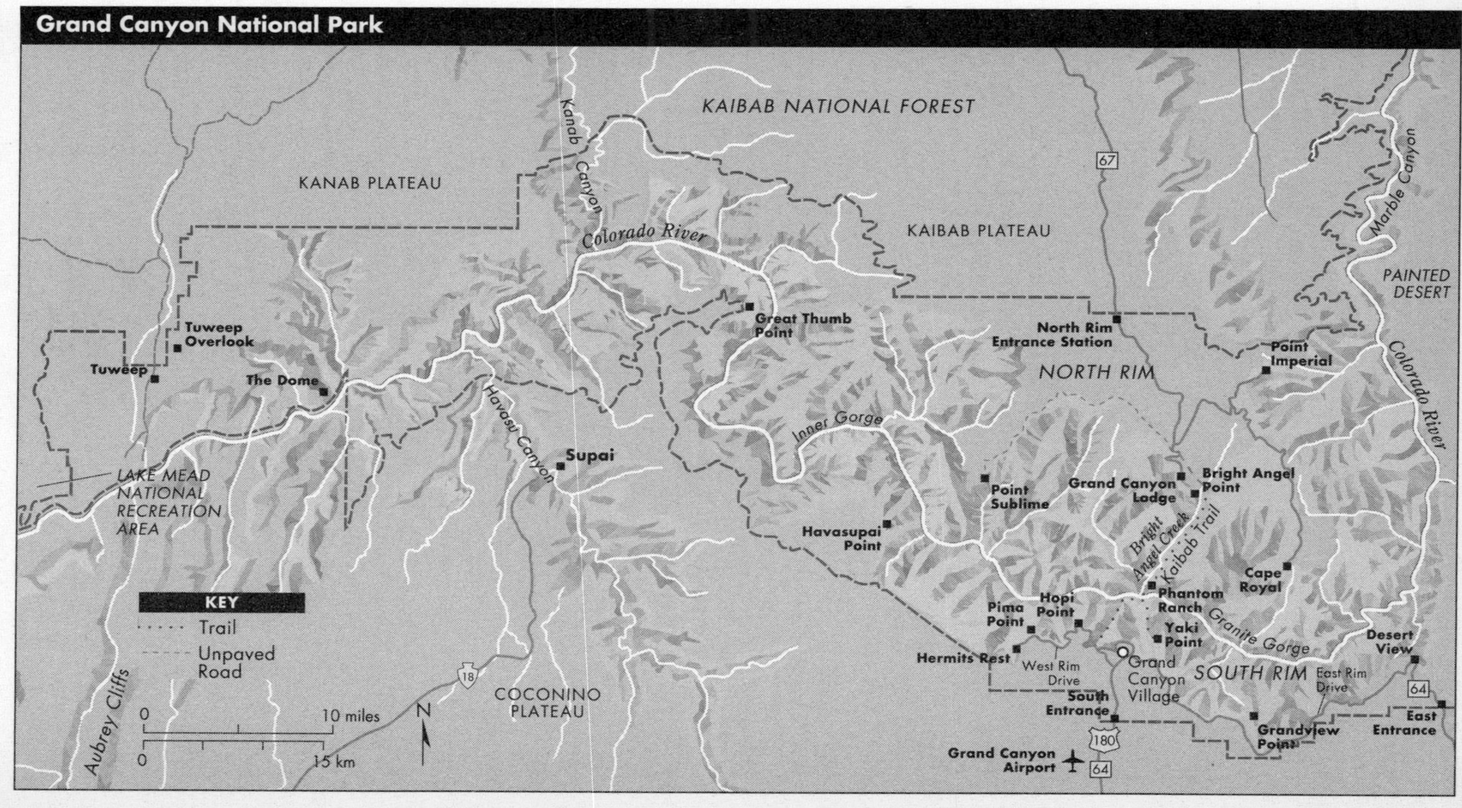
Grand Canyon National Park
KAIBAB NATIONAL FOREST
KANAB PLATEAU
KAIBAB PLATEAU
Kanab Canyon
Colorado River
Marble Canyon
PAINTED DESERT
67
Great Thumb Point
North Rim Entrance Station
Point Imperial
NORTH RIM
Tuweep Overlook
Tuweep
The Dome
Inner Gorge
Havasu Canyon
Supai
LAKE MEAD NATIONAL RECREATION AREA
Point Sublime
Grand Canyon Lodge
Bright Angel Point
Bright Angel Creek
Kaibab Trail
Havasupai Point
Cape Royal
Phantom Ranch
Pima Point
Hopi Point
Yaki Point
Granite Gorge
Desert View
Hermits Rest
West Rim Drive
Grand Canyon Village
SOUTH RIM
East Rim Drive
South Entrance
64
East Entrance
Grandview Point
180
Grand Canyon Airport
KEY
Trail
Unpaved Road
18
COCONINO PLATEAU
Aubrey Cliffs
0
10 miles
0
15 km
N

Canyon, south of the middle part of the national park, provides another respite from the crowds. To the northwest is Lake Mead, the largest man-made body of water in the United States, formed by the construction of giant Hoover Dam.

Great Itineraries

A visit of three days will make hurried travelers feel they have "done" the Grand Canyon; a lengthier stay of 10 days or so is enough to make most visitors feel like old hands—particularly if they've been able to experience some white-water rafting on the Colorado River. Budgeting a few extra days will allow for a trip to the Lake Mead area.

Numbers in the text below correspond to points of interest on the Grand Canyon National Park, The South Rim and West Rim Drive, The North Rim, and Northwest Arizona and Lake Mead maps.

IF YOU HAVE 2 OR 3 DAYS

Spend the first night in Williams ⑮. The next morning, board the historic Grand Canyon Railway, which takes you to the South Rim of the canyon. Spend the afternoon visiting Grand Canyon Village and then perhaps take in the informative IMAX film in nearby Tusayan (taxis or a shuttle bus will take you there). Spend the night at Grand Canyon Village and the next morning take a tour of the Village Rim ⑨–⑭ or build up an appetite with a short hike before lunch, then take the 3:15 train back to Williams.

If you don't want to be at the Grand Canyon itself, try hiking in the less-frequented Havasu Canyon. Hike 8 mi down into the canyon to the small village of Supai and the Havasupai Lodge. You'll want to spend at least two days in this hiker's heaven. On the morning of the third day, give yourself plenty of time and water to climb back out of the canyon, or consider riding up by mule.

IF YOU HAVE 4 OR 5 DAYS

You will have time to ponder the marvels of the Grand Canyon, both from above as well as from below. After a night at the Grand Canyon Village, take the mule-pack expedition down the Bright Angel Trail ⑬, stopping along the way for a picnic lunch on a plateau with breathtaking views. Arrive at Phantom Ranch for dinner and a night's sleep, then return by mule pack to the South Rim and another night or two in the Grand Canyon area.

IF YOU HAVE 7 TO 10 DAYS

You will have time for a memorable expedition of hiking the canyon as well as experiencing the thrill of white-water rafting along the Colorado River. If time allows, drive through the Arizona Strip to the North Rim. Alternatively, head to the to the northwest to visit Lake Mead ㊷ and view Hoover Dam ㊵.

When to Tour the Grand Canyon and Northwest Arizona

If you can arrange it, try to visit the Grand Canyon in the fall or spring. You might encounter cold weather during those periods, but chances are good that most of the days will be clear and will range from pleasantly cool to warm. In autumn and spring, when the crowds have thinned, reservations are much easier to arrange, and in some cases, prices drop. Or consider a winter visit. Snow on the ground only enhances the site's sublime beauty. Note: A drive to the North Rim is not possible during the winter, when heavy snows close the area's highways and facilities.

THE SOUTH RIM AND ENVIRONS

Both the South Rim and the North Rim areas of the Grand Canyon were established as recreational and sightseeing enclaves under the direction of the National Park Service. Unfortunately, most of Grand Canyon Village at the South Rim was laid out before the park service existed, so the area is not well equipped to accommodate the large crowds that converge on the area every summer (and increasingly throughout the spring and fall).

In truth, the South Rim is a bit of a circus in summer. It's hard to commune with one of nature's great spectacles when you've just spent two hours looking for a parking spot (there are only 1,400 spaces for the approximately 6,000 cars that enter each day) and are now being asked to step out of the range of someone's video camera. Not even a descent into the canyon itself guarantees a getaway at this time of year. For your sake as well as that of the canyon, it's best to avoid the South Rim in its busiest season.

Approaching the South Rim

Numbers in the margin correspond to points of interest on the South Rim and East Rim Drive map.

Because the approach to the South Rim of the Grand Canyon is across the relatively level surface of the 7,000-foot Coconino Plateau, you won't
❶ see the great gorge until you're practically at its edge. **Mather Point,** approximately 4 mi from the south entrance, gives you the first glimpse of the canyon from one of the most impressive and accessible vista points on the rim. This overlook, named for the National Park Service's first director, Stephen Mather, affords an extraordinary view of the Inner Gorge and of numerous buttes that rise out of the eroded chasm: Wotan's Throne, Brahma Temple, Zoroaster Temple, and many others. The Grand Canyon Lodge, on the North Rim, is almost directly north from Mather Point and only 10 mi away—yet you have to drive nearly 210 mi to get from one spot to the other.

★ ❷ The **National Park Service's Visitor Center,** in Grand Canyon Village, has something for even the most independent traveler. The center orients you to many facets of the site, and it's an excellent place for gathering information, whether you're interested in escapist treks or group tours. Park rangers are on hand to answer questions and aid in planning Grand Canyon excursions; short movies and slide shows on the canyon are presented regularly; and a bookstore carries a wide variety of printed matter and videotapes. A daily schedule for ranger-led hikes and evening lectures is also posted here.

A separate exhibit area offers an intriguing profile of the area's natural and human history. The first inhabitants were probably nomadic Paleo-Indians, arriving more than 10,000 years ago. Artifacts that were found in caves deep in the canyon were left by a later Archaic culture. They are perfectly preserved figurines of animals, made from willow twigs more than 4,000 years ago—thus predating Homeric Greece by 1,000 years. About 2,200 years ago, ancestral Pueblo culture began to develop around the canyon. The museum also traces the arrival of early Spanish explorers, including Captain García López de Cárdenas, leader in 1540 of the first expedition of white men to see the Grand Canyon, and of John Wesley Powell, the first person to travel through the canyon by boat. Various crafts that have navigated the white-water rapids of the Colorado River are on display. ✉ *East side of Grand Canyon Village, about 1 mi east*

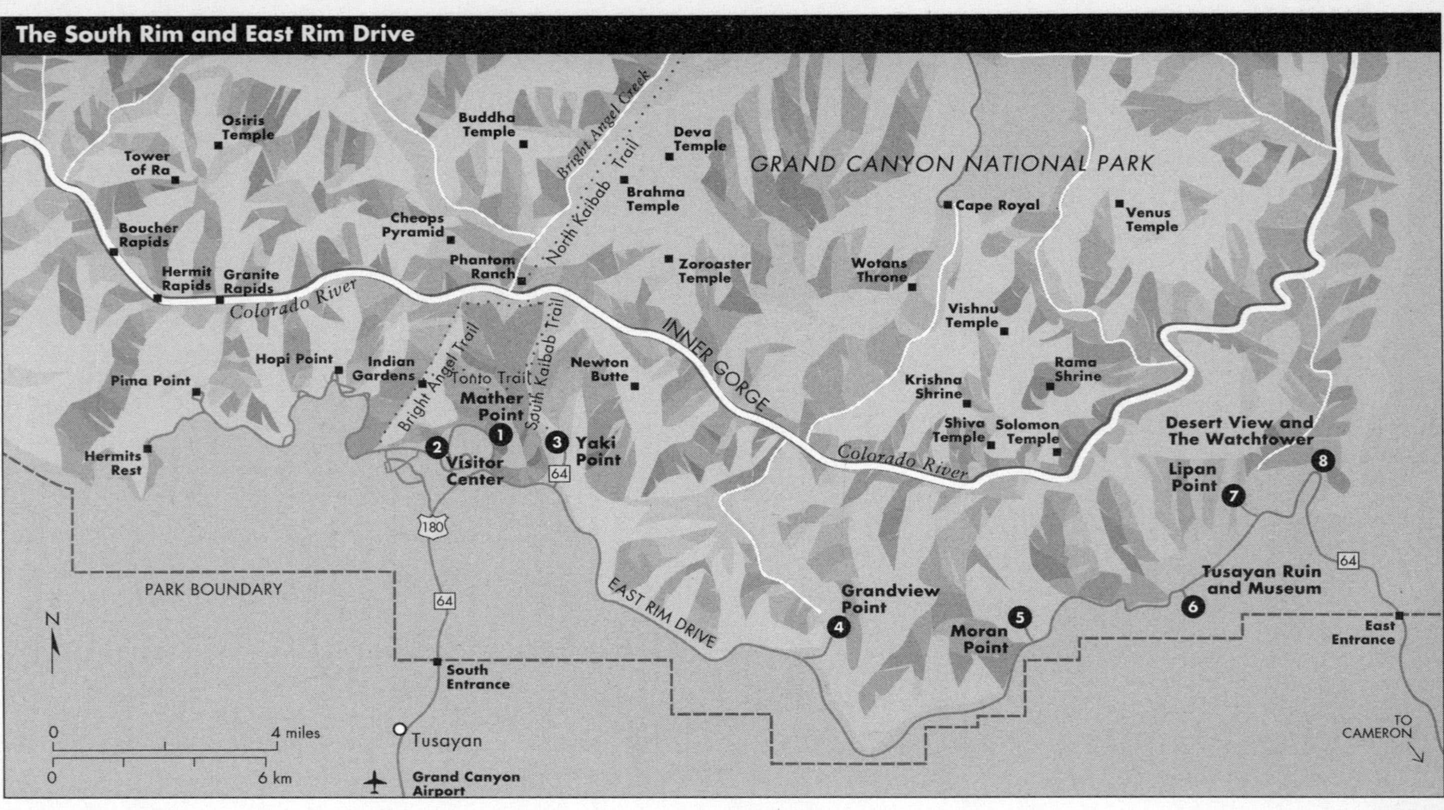
The South Rim and East Rim Drive
GRAND CANYON NATIONAL PARK
Osiris Temple
Tower of Ra
Buddha Temple
Deva Temple
Brahma Temple
Bright Angel Creek
North Kaibab Trail
Cape Royal
Venus Temple
Boucher Rapids
Cheops Pyramid
Phantom Ranch
Zoroaster Temple
Wotans Throne
Hermit Rapids
Granite Rapids
Colorado River
Vishnu Temple
Bright Angel Trail
South Kaibab Trail
Tonto Trail
Hopi Point
Indian Gardens
Newton Butte
INNER GORGE
Rama Shrine
Krishna Shrine
Pima Point
Mather Point
Shiva Temple
Solomon Temple
Desert View and The Watchtower
Hermits Rest
Visitor Center
Yaki Point
Lipan Point
64
180
PARK BOUNDARY
EAST RIM DRIVE
Grandview Point
Moran Point
Tusayan Ruin and Museum
East Entrance
South Entrance
Tusayan
Grand Canyon Airport
TO CAMERON
N
0
4 miles
6 km

of El Tovar Hotel, ☎ *520/638–7888.* 🎟 *Free.* ⏲ *Memorial Day–Labor Day, daily 8–6; rest of yr, daily 8–5.*

Outdoor Activities and Sports

HIKING

If you'd like a little exercise and great overlooks of the canyon, it's an easy hike from the back of the visitor center to the El Tovar Hotel (☞ The Village Rim, *below*). Walk through a pretty wooded area for about a half mile, and then the path will parallel to the rim for another half mile or so. The wide dirt trail is more or less level all the way, though at this altitude, even slight inclines require more effort.

Lodging

CAMPING

⛺ **Flintstone Bedrock City.** Thirty miles south of the Grand Canyon National Park, Flintstone Bedrock City offers 28 tent sites and 32 partial RV hookups in a cartoon-kitsch setting off a major thoroughfare. Basic rates are $12 per site for two people; add $2 for electricity hookup, $2 for water hookup, and $1.50 for each additional person. Facilities include a gift shop full of Flintstone-obilia and a diner, as well as pay showers. ✉ *Grand Canyon Hwy., HC 34, Box A, Williams 86046,* ☎ *520/635–2600.* ⏲ *Apr.–Oct. (may open earlier or close later, depending on weather).*

⛺ **Ten X Campground.** Run by the Forest Service, Ten X is about 9 mi south of the Grand Canyon National Park. It offers 70 family sites plus a group site (available for groups of up to 100 people), water, and pit toilets for $10 per day but no hookups or showers. No reservations are accepted (except for the group site). ✉ *Kaibab National Forest, Tusayan Ranger District, Box 3088, Grand Canyon 86023,* ☎ *520/638–2443.* ⏲ *May 1–Sept. 30.*

East Rim Drive

The breathtaking East Rim Drive proceeds east for about 25 mi along the South Rim from Grand Canyon Village to Desert View. Before beginning the drive, consider stopping to see the exhibits and attend the free mini lectures offered by park naturalists at Yavapai Observation Station, ¾ mi east of the visitor center. There are four posted picnic areas along the route and rest rooms at Tusayan Museum and Desert View.

3 **Yaki Point,** east of Grand Canyon Village on AZ 64, provides an exceptional view of Wotan's Throne, a majestic flat-top butte named by François Matthes, a U.S. Geological Survey scientist who developed the first topographical map of the Grand Canyon. Due north is Buddha Temple, capped by limestone; Newton Butte, with its flat top of red sandstone, lies to the east. At Yaki Point the popular **Kaibab Trail** starts the canyon descent to the Inner Gorge, crosses the Colorado over a steel suspension bridge, and wends its way to rustic Phantom Ranch (☞ Dining and Lodging, *below*), the only lodging facility at the bottom of the Grand Canyon. You might take this opportunity to hike a short distance down the Kaibab Trail, just to get a feel for a descent into the canyon. If you plan to go more than a mile, carry water with you (☞ Hiking *in* Outdoor Activities and Sports, *below*). If you encounter a mule train, be aware that the animals have the right-of-way. Move to the inside of the trail and wait as they pass.

4 About 7 mi east of Yaki Point, **Grandview Point,** at an altitude of 7,496 feet, supports large stands of ponderosa pine, piñon pine, oak, and juniper. The view from here is one of the finest in the canyon. To the northeast is a group of dominant buttes, including Krishna Shrine, Vishnu Temple, Rama Shrine, and Shiva Temple. A short stretch of the Col-

orado River is also visible. Directly below the point and accessed by the Grandview Trail is Horseshoe Mesa, where you can see ruins of the Last Chance Copper Mine. Grandview Point was also the site of the Grandview Hotel, constructed in the 1890s but closed in 1908; logs salvaged from the hotel were used for the Kiva Room of the Desert View Watchtower (☞ *below*).

5 **Moran Point,** about 5 mi east of Grandview Point, was named for American landscape artist Thomas Moran, who painted Grand Canyon scenes from many points on the rim but was especially fond of the play of light and shadows from this location. He first visited the canyon with John Wesley Powell in 1873, and his vivid canvases helped persuade Congress to create a national park at the Grand Canyon. Moran Point is a favorite spot for photographers.

Three miles east of Moran Point, on the south side of the highway, is
6 the entrance to **Tusayan Ruin and Museum,** which offers evidence of early habitation in the Grand Canyon and information about the lifestyles of ancestral Pueblo people. The partially intact rock dwellings here were occupied for roughly 20 years by a group of about 30 Indian hunters, farmers, and gatherers. They moved elsewhere, like so many others, pressured by drought and depletion of natural resources to find better settlements. A museum and a bookstore display artifacts, models of the dwellings, and exhibits on modern tribes of the region. Free 30-minute guided tours—as many as five during the summer, fewer in winter—are given daily. ✉ *East Rim Dr., 3 mi east of Moran Point,* ☎ *520/638–2305.* 🎫 *Free.* ⏲ *Daily 9–5.*

7 **Lipan Point,** 1 mi northeast of Tusayan Ruin, is the canyon's widest point. From here you can get an astonishing visual profile of the gorge's geologic history, with a view of every eroded layer of the canyon.

★ 8 At 7,500 feet, the highest point on East Rim Drive, **Desert View** and **The Watchtower** offer a climactic final stop. From the top of the 70-foot stone-and-mortar watchtower, built in 1932 by the Fred Harvey Company and the Santa Fe Railroad in the style of Native American structures, even the muted pastel hues of the distant Painted Desert to the east and the 3,000-foot-high Vermilion Cliffs rising from a high plateau near the Utah border are visible. In the chasm below, angling away to the north toward Marble Canyon, a powerful stretch of the Colorado River reveals itself. The Watchtower houses a glass-enclosed observatory with powerful telescopes, as well as galleries decorated with reproductions of ancient Indian pictographs, and a curio shop where paintings, jewelry, and other handicrafts by contemporary Native American artists are sold. ✉ *The Watchtower,* ☎ *520/638–2736; trading post,* ☎ *520/638–2360.* 🎫 *Free; 25¢ to climb Watchtower.* ⏲ *Daily 8–7 or 8–8 in summer, daily 9–6 in winter.*

Dining and Lodging

$$ ✕ **The Steak House.** This is a typical southwestern steak house—right down to the cowhide–pattern tablecloths, massive brick fireplace, displays of Native American and western art, and John Wayne bar lined with memorabilia of the actor. The food is western, too, with lots of mesquite-grilled steaks, ribs, and barbecued chicken entrées; the more adventurous might try the rattlesnake appetizer. Portions are large. ✉ *Tusayan, 2 mi south of Grand Canyon entrance, across from IMAX Theater,* ☎ *520/638–2780. No credit cards. Sometimes closed in Jan. No lunch.*

$ ✕🏨 **Phantom Ranch.** Built on the site of an earlier hunting camp in 1932, this group of wood-and-stone buildings is set among a grove of cottonwood trees at the bottom of the canyon. For hikers (who need a backcountry permit to come down here), dormitory accommodations—20 beds for men and 20 for women—are available, as are two cabins (one sleeps 4 people, the other 10). There are also seven cabins reserved exclusively for mule riders; lodging, meals, and mule rides are offered as a package (☞ Guided Tours *in* the Grand Canyon and Northwest Arizona A to Z, *below*). The restaurant at Phantom Ranch, probably the most remote eating establishment in the United States, has a limited menu. All meals are served family style, with breakfast, dinner (including a selection for vegetarians), and box lunches available. Arrangements—and payment—for both food and lodging should be made 9 to 11 months in advance. ✉ *Box 699, Grand Canyon 86023,* ☎ *520/638–2401 (reservations) or 520/638–2631 (switchboard). 4 dormitories with shared bath and two cabins for hikers, 7 cabins with shower outside for mule riders. Dining room. AE, D, DC, MC, V.*

$$$$ **Best Western Grand Canyon Squire Inn.** In Tusayan, about 2 mi south of the national park entrance, this motel lacks some of the historic charm of the older lodges at the canyon rim, but it offers a much longer list of amenities—including a bowling alley, a small cowboy museum in the stylish lobby, and an upscale gift shop. The spacious, cheerful rooms are nicely appointed with southwestern-style furnishings. Ask for one with a view of the woods; others face the highway. ✉ *Box 130, Grand Canyon 86023,* ☎ *520/638–2681 or 800/622–6966,* FAX *520/638–2782. 250 rooms, 4 rooms accessible to people with disabilities. Coffee shop, dining room, lounge, pool, beauty salon, sauna, 2 tennis courts, bowling, exercise room, billiards, video games, travel services. AE, D, DC, MC, V.*

$$$ **Quality Inn.** The design of this facility in Tusayan is unexpected for a chain motel: First-floor rooms can be entered either from a standard drive-up door or from an attractive atrium featuring a spa and lounge. Accommodations, done in soothing shades of light blue, peach, or tan, are also well designed, offering small seating areas, coffeemakers, two sinks, and (unusual for this area) minibars. An all-you-can eat buffet breakfast at the full-service restaurant is a good way to fortify yourself for a day at the canyon. ✉ *Box 520, AZ 64 and U.S. 180, Grand Canyon 86023,* ☎ *520/638–2673 or 800/221–2222,* FAX *520/638–9537. 176 rooms. Restaurant, lounge, pool. AE, D, DC, MC, V.*

CAMPING

Bright Angel. This free campground is en route to Phantom ranch, close to the bottom of the canyon. There are toilet facilities and running water but no showers. A backcountry permit is required to stay here and also serves as your reservation. ✉ *Contact the Backcountry Office, Box 129, Grand Canyon 86023,* ☎ *520/638–7888.*

Desert View Campground. Twenty-three miles east of Grand Canyon Village off AZ 64, Desert View offers RV and tent sites, flush toilets, and water but no hookups. The cost is $10 per site, with no reservations. It's open from May through October. ✉ *Box 129, Grand Canyon 86023,* ☎ *520/638–7888.*

Grand Canyon Camper Village. In Tusayan, this campground has 250 RV hookups, some partial, some full ($23 for two people, plus $2 for each additional person over the age of 12) and 100 tent sites ($15 for two people). ✉ *Box 490, Grand Canyon 86023,* ☎ *520/638–2887.*

Indian Garden. About halfway down the canyon is this free campground, located en route to Phantom Ranch. Running water and toilet facilities are available, but there are no showers. A backcountry permit, which serves as a reservation, is required. ✉ *Contact the Backcountry Office, Box 129, Grand Canyon 86023,* ☎ *520/638–7888.*

Outdoor Activities and Sports

HIKING

South Kaibab Trail, starting near Yaki Point on East Rim Drive near Grand Canyon Village, connects at the bottom of the canyon (after the Kaibab Bridge across the Colorado) with the North Kaibab Trail. Plan on two to three days if you want to hike the gorge from rim to rim (if you do this, we recommend that you descend from the North Rim, as it is more than 1,000 feet higher than the South Rim). South Kaibab Trail is steep, descending 4,800 feet in just 7 mi, with no water or campgrounds (there are portable toilets at Cedar Ridge, 2.2 mi from the trailhead) and very little shade. The trail corkscrews down through some spectacular geology, closely following the 300-million-year-old Supai and Redwall formations; look for (but don't remove) fossils in the limestone when you take your frequent water breaks. If you're going back up to the South Rim, ascend Bright Angel Trail. Accommodations for hikers along the way include the campgrounds at Indian Garden and Bright Angel, or Phantom Ranch (☞ Dining and Lodging, *above*).

HORSEBACK RIDING

You can rent extremely gentle horses at the **Apache Stables** at Moqui Lodge (☎ 520/638–2891 or 520/638–2424) in the village of Tusayan. The cost is $22 an hour, $36 for two hours. A four-hour East Rim ride goes for $57.50, a campfire horse and haywagon ride for $27 ($7.50 if you ride in the wagon rather than on your own horse). Children 6 and up are permitted on the hour-long ride, 10 and up on the two-hour ride, 14 and up on the half-day trip. The stables are open in March, and rides are offered, weather permitting, through the end of November. Moqui Lodge is open from mid-February through the end of November.

Shopping

Desert View Trading Post (✉ East Rim Dr., near the Watchtower at Desert View, ☎ 520/638–2360) sells a mix of traditional southwestern souvenirs and authentic Native American pottery.

The Village Rim

Numbers in the margin correspond to points of interest on the South Rim and West Rim Drive map.

The Village Rim can be explored on foot (about 1 mi round-trip); a paved pathway over level ground runs along the rim. Cars can be left at the nearby El Tovar parking lot.

9 **Hopi House,** a multistoried structure of rock and mortar, was modeled after buildings found in the Hopi village of Oraibi, Arizona, the oldest continuously inhabited community in the United States (☞ The Hopi Mesas *in* Chapter 3). Part of an attempt by the Fred Harvey Company to encourage Southwest Indian crafts at the turn of the century, Hopi House was established as one of the first curio stores in the Grand Canyon. It has the air of a museum, with some artifacts too priceless to sell today, but it remains one of the best-stocked gift shops in the vicinity.

A few yards to the west of Hopi House is the most renowned hotel in
★ 10 the nation's national-park system, the historic **El Tovar Hotel.** Built in 1905 to resemble the great hunting lodges of Europe, this massive log structure underwent a major renovation in 1991, and it retains the ambience of its early days. If the weather is cool, stop in front of the massive stone fireplace to warm your hands. The rustic lobby, with its numerous stuffed and mounted animal heads, is a great place for people-watching, and the back porch affords a front-row seat for the spectacle of the canyon.

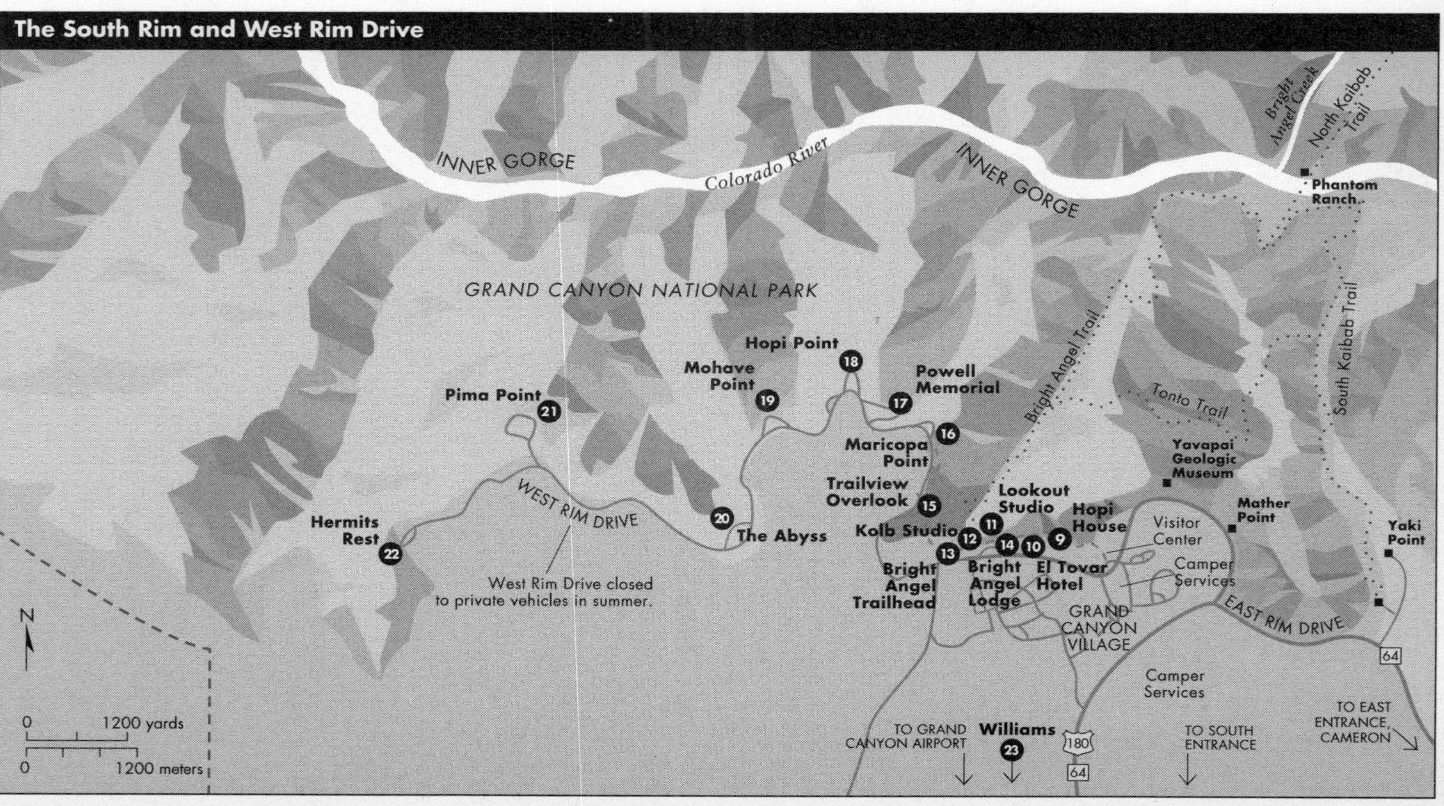
The South Rim and West Rim Drive
INNER GORGE
Colorado River
INNER GORGE
Bright Angel Creek
North Kaibab Trail
Phantom Ranch
GRAND CANYON NATIONAL PARK
Bright Angel Trail
Tonto Trail
South Kaibab Trail
Hopi Point
18
Mohave Point
19
Powell Memorial
17
Pima Point
21
16
Maricopa Point
Trailview Overlook
15
Yavapai Geologic Museum
Lookout Studio
11
Hopi House
9
Mather Point
Visitor Center
Kolb Studio
12
14
10
13
Camper Services
Yaki Point
Hermits Rest
22
WEST RIM DRIVE
20
The Abyss
Bright Angel Trailhead
Bright Angel Lodge
El Tovar Hotel
GRAND CANYON VILLAGE
EAST RIM DRIVE
West Rim Drive closed to private vehicles in summer.
N
64
Camper Services
0 1200 yards
0 1200 meters
TO GRAND CANYON AIRPORT
Williams
23
180
64
TO SOUTH ENTRANCE
TO EAST ENTRANCE, CAMERON

★ 11 A trail at the rim leads west toward **Lookout Studio.** Built in 1914 to compete with the Kolbs' photographic studio (☞ *below*), the building was designed by architect Mary Jane Colter to resemble a Hopi pueblo. Today it's a combination lookout point, museum, and gift shop, and it has an extensive collection of geologic samples from around the world as well as many fossil specimens. An upstairs loft provides another excellent overlook into the mighty gorge below.

12 A half dozen yards west of Lookout Studio are a few steps that descend to the **Kolb Studio,** built in 1904 by the Kolb brothers as a photographic workshop; it's now a bookstore and art gallery. If you look out the window, you can see Indian Gardens, where, in the days before a pipeline was installed, Emery Kolb descended some 3,300 feet each day to get the water he needed to develop his prints. Perhaps the exercise was beneficial: He operated the studio until he died in 1976 at age 95.

★ 13 **Bright Angel Trailhead,** a few feet from Kolb Studio, is the starting point for perhaps the best-known of all the trails that descend to the bottom of the canyon. It was originally a bighorn sheep path and was later used by the Havasupai Indians; in 1890–91 it was widened for prospectors trying to reach mining claims in the canyon. Today Bright Angel Trail is a well-maintained avenue for mule and foot traffic. If you intend to go very far—the trail descends 5,510 feet to the Colorado River—you should be prepared with proper shoes, clothing, equipment, and water (☞ Hiking *in* Sports and the Outdoors, *below*); discuss your intentions with the park-service representatives at the visitor center before you go.

14 Directly east of Bright Angel Trailhead are railroad tracks over which the Santa Fe trains once passed. Here you'll see the barn that houses some of the tour mules; it's worth a brief stop, especially if children are along. Farther east is **Bright Angel Lodge,** which was built in 1935 of Oregon pine logs and native stone; there are rustic cabins set off from the main building. It's a good place to people-watch, especially in the area of the "geologic" fireplace, made of regional rocks arranged in the order in which they are layered in the Grand Canyon. A history room displays memorabilia from early years at the South Rim.

NEED A BREAK? For light snacks—cold sandwiches, sweets, and soft drinks—try the **Soda Fountain** (☎ 520/638-2631) in the Bright Angel Lodge. It has the distinction of selling the most Breyer's ice cream in the United States.

Dining and Lodging

$$$$ ★ ✕🏨 **El Tovar Hotel.** Built in 1905 of native stone and heavy pine logs, El Tovar is reminiscent of a grand European hunting lodge. As when it first opened, the hotel is operated by the Fred Harvey Company. It still maintains its excellent reputation for service, though at a time when indoor plumbing is no longer a luxury, rooms don't seem as posh as they might have in the past. Some are rather small, but all are nicely appointed, and a number offer canyon views. For decades the hotel's world-class restaurant has enjoyed a reputation for fine food served in a classic 19th-century room of hand-hewn logs and beamed ceilings. The Southwest-inspired menu changes seasonally but includes a daily vegetarian special along with innovatively prepared fish, poultry, and meat dishes: Free-range chicken breast with smoked tomato pine-nut sauce or grilled salmon with tomatillo salsa might be among your dinner options. ✉ *Box 699, Grand Canyon 86023,* ☎ *520/638–2401 (reservations) or 520/638–2631 (switchboard),* FAX *520/638–9247. 70 rooms, 10 suites. Bar, dining room, room service. AE, D, DC, MC, V.*

$-$$$$ ★ ✕ **Bright Angel Lodge.** Designed by Mary Jane Colter for the Fred Harvey Company in 1935, this log-and-native-stone structure sits within a few yards of the canyon rim and offers rooms in the main lodge (most with shared baths) or in the quaint cabins (some with fireplaces and/or canyon views) that are scattered among the pines. Don't come for luxury but for a historic structure that blends superbly with the spectacular natural environment, and for bargain prices. The Bright Angel coffee shop is open for breakfast, lunch, and dinner; the more upscale but still casual—especially compared to the El Tovar dining room—Arizona Steak House serves dinner only. ✉ *Box 699, Grand Canyon 86023,* ☎ *520/638–2401 (reservations) or 520/638–2631 (switchboard),* FAX *520/638–9247. 11 rooms with bath, 13 rooms with ½ bath, 6 rooms with shared bath, 42 cabins with bath. Restaurant, bar, coffee shop, beauty salon. AE, D, DC, MC, V.*

$$–$$$ **Grand Canyon National Park Lodges.** The Fred Harvey Company has seven lodges on the South Rim. Of them, El Tovar and Bright Angel (☞ *above*) are outstanding, but Maswik Lodge, Yavapai Lodge, Moqui Lodge, Kachina Lodge, and Thunderbird Lodge are all comfortable, if not luxurious. The setting, rather than the amenities, is the draw here. (Note: It's a good idea to bring a flashlight; the dimly lit, wooded grounds can be rather difficult to negotiate in the evening.) In addition to lodge rooms, Maswik offers rustic cabins ($). Moqui, which is only open from March through November, is on U.S. 180, just outside the national park; the others are in Grand Canyon Village. ✉ *Box 699, Grand Canyon 86023,* ☎ *520/638–2401 (reservations) or 520/638–2631 (switchboard),* FAX *520/638–9247. 855 rooms with bath. Restaurant, 2 cafeterias (at Yavapai Lodge and Maswik Lodge). AE, D, DC, MC, V.*

CAMPING

Mather Campground. In Grand Canyon Village, Mather Campground has 97 RV and 190 tent sites (no hookups), flush toilets, water, showers, and a laundromat; the cost is $10 per site. It's open year-round; no reservations are accepted from December to March. ✉ *Reservations through Mistix, Box 85705, San Diego, CA 92138,* ☎ *800/365–2267 or 619/452–0150 outside the U.S.*

Trailer Village. This campground is open year-round and is located in Grand Canyon Village. It has 78 RV sites with full hookups for $17 per site. ✉ *Box 699, Grand Canyon 86023,* ☎ *520/638–2401 (reservations) or 520/638–2631 (switchboard),* FAX *520/638–9247.*

Outdoor Activities and Sports

HIKING

One of the most popular and scenic hiking paths from the South Rim to the bottom of the canyon (9 mi), the well-maintained Bright Angel Trail was used in the late 1800s as a route to mining claims. There are rest houses—which are equipped with water in the summer—for hikers at the 1½- and 3-mile points and at Indian Gardens. Water is also available at Bright Angel Campground, 6.7 mi below the trailhead. Plateau Point, about 175 feet below Indian Gardens, is a good turnaround point for a day hike. Bright Angel Trail is the easiest of all footpaths into the canyon, but because the climb out from the bottom is an ascent of 5,510 feet, the trip should be attempted only by those in good physical condition and should be avoided in summer due to extreme temperatures. The top of the trail can be icy in winter. Note that you will be sharing the trail with mule trains, which have the right-of-way.

Nightlife and the Arts

Unless you head for nearby Williams or Flagstaff after dark, nightlife in this part of the Southwest consists of watching a full moon above the soaring buttes of the Grand Canyon, roasting marshmallows over a crackling fire, crawling into your bedroll beside some lonely canyon trail, or attending a free evening program on the history of the Grand Canyon. Dinner at **El Tovar Restaurant** (there is an excellent wine list) would be a memorable evening. In addition, the following Grand Canyon properties have cocktail lounges: **El Tovar Hotel** (piano bar), **Bright Angel Lodge** (live entertainment), **Maswik Lodge** (sports bar), and **Moqui Lodge** (live entertainment). Call ☎ 520/638–2401 for reservations and further information (☞ Dining and Lodging, *above*).

Similarly, there's little in the way of cultural events in the area, but every September the **Grand Canyon Chamber Music Festival** (✉ Box 1332, Grand Canyon 86023, ☎ 520/638–9215) is held in the Shrine of the Ages auditorium at the South Rim visitor center. Call or write for schedule information and advance tickets. A **lecture series** on scientific topics, cosponsored by the National Park Service and the Grand Canyon Association, is scheduled to coincide with the chamber music festival; ask for details at any of the area lodges or at the visitor center. It's also worth checking out the **art gallery** at the Kolb Studio, just west of Bright Angel Lodge; a variety of painting, photograph, and craft exhibits are featured here from around April 15 through November 30.

Shopping

At the South Rim, nearly every lodging facility and retail store offers Native American artifacts and Grand Canyon souvenirs. In truth, you'll find that after visiting a few of the curio and jewelry shops, all the merchandise begins to look alike. However, the items at most of the lodges and at major gift shops are authentic. The **El Tovar Hotel Gift Shop** (✉ near the rim in Grand Canyon Village, ☎ 520/638–2631) carries Native American jewelry, rather expensive casual wear, and souvenir gifts. **Hopi House** (✉ east of El Tovar Hotel, ☎ 520/638–2631), which opened in 1905, still offers one of the widest selections of Native American artifacts—some of museum quality and not for sale—in the vicinity of the Grand Canyon. **Verkamp's** (✉ across from El Tovar Hotel, ☎ 520/638–2242) is in a historic (1906) building where a huge buffalo head surveys those browsing the fine artwork and crafts.

West Rim Drive

Originally called Hermit Rim Road, West Rim Drive was constructed by the Santa Fe Company in 1912 as a scenic tour route. Cars were banned on the road because they frightened horses pulling the open-top touring stages. Ten scenic overlooks spread out over an 8-mile leg. Since you have to return on the same road, consider stopping at half of the overlooks on the way out and the others on the way back; access to the lookout points is easy from both sides of the road.

In the summer months West Rim Drive is closed to auto traffic because of congestion. From Memorial Day weekend to October 1, a free shuttle bus makes most of the stops described below (☞ Getting Around *in* The Grand Canyon and Northwest Arizona A to Z, *below*).

15 **Trailview Overlook** affords a dramatic view of the Bright Angel and Plateau Point trails as they zigzag down the canyon. In the deep gorge to the north flows Bright Angel Creek, one of the few permanent tributary streams of the Colorado River in the region. If you turn and look away from the canyon toward the south, you'll have a wonderful, unobstructed view of the distant San Francisco Peaks, Arizona's highest mountains (the tallest is 12,633 feet), as well as of Bill Williams Mountain (on the horizon) and Red Butte (about 15 mi south of the canyon rim).

16 Less than a mile from Trailview Overlook, **Maricopa Point** merits a stop not only for the arresting scenery, which features a clear view of the Colorado River below, but also for its towering headframe of an early Grand Canyon mining operation. On the rim to your left, as you face the canyon, are the Orphan Mine and, in the canyon below, a mine shaft and cable lines leading up to the rim. The copper ore in the mine, which started operations in 1893, was of excellent quality, but the cost of removing it from the canyon finally brought the venture to a halt.

★ 17 About a half mile beyond Maricopa Point, the large granite **Powell Memorial** stands as a tribute to the first man to ride the wild rapids of the Colorado River through the canyon in 1869. John Wesley Powell, a one-armed Civil War hero and explorer, measured, charted, and named many of the canyons and creeks of the river. It was here that the dedication ceremony for Grand Canyon National Park took place on April 3, 1920.

18 From **Hopi Point** (elevation 7,071 feet) you can see a large section of the Colorado River; although it appears as a thin line from here, the river is nearly 350 feet wide below this overlook. Across the canyon to the north is Shiva Temple, which, until 1937, remained an isolated section of the Kaibab Plateau. In that year, Harold Anthony of the American Museum of Natural History led an expedition to the rock formation in the belief that it supported life that had been cut off from the rest of the canyon. Imagine the expedition members' surprise when they found an empty Kodak film box on top of the temple.

19 Four-fifths of a mile to the west of Hopi Point, **Mohave Point** also affords spectacular views of the Colorado River. In addition, Granite and Salt Creek rapids can be seen from this spot.

20 **The Abyss** is one of the most awesome stops on West Rim Drive, revealing a sheer canyon drop of 3,000 feet to the Tonto Platform in the gorge below. From here, you'll also see several impressive isolated sandstone columns, the largest of which is called the Monument.

21 **Pima Point** provides a bird's-eye view of the Tonto Platform and the Tonto Trail, which wends its way through the canyon for more than 70 mi. If you look down on the plateau toward the west, you may be able to see the foundations of an old tourist camp built in the first decade of the century and used until 1930. Also to the west, two dark, cone-shape mountains—Mt. Trumbull and Mt. Logan—are visible on clear days. They rise in stark contrast to the surrounding flat-top mesas and buttes.

★ 22 **Hermits Rest,** the westernmost viewpoint, and the Hermit Trail that descends from it (☞ *below*) were named for the "hermit" Louis Boucher, a 19th-century prospector who had a number of mining claims and a roughly built home down in the canyon. Canyon views from here include Hermit Rapids and the towering cliffs of the Supai and Redwall formations. The stone building at Hermits Rest sells curios and refreshments and provides the only rest rooms on West Rim Drive.

Outdoor Activities and Sports

HIKING

The 9-mile Hermit Trail beginning at Hermits Rest (8 mi west of Grand Canyon Village) is steep, unmaintained, and suitable only for experienced long-distance hikers. The trail is in generally good condition, but there is a tricky spot—a short section damaged by rock slides in 1993. No water is available along the way. The route leads 8½ mi down to the Colorado River and has inspiring views of Hermit Gorge and the Redwall and Supai formations. Six miles from the trailhead you'll come across the now abandoned Hermit Camp, which the Santa Fe Railroad ran as a tourist camp from 1913 until 1934.

Williams

23 *55 mi south of Grand Canyon Village, 30 mi west of Flagstaff. On I–40 and AZ 64. Use I–40 exits 161, 163, or 165.*

Often considered just a jumping-off point for the Grand Canyon (it's only an hour away from the South Rim by car and a little over two hours by train), Williams retains its own funky frontier charm, despite a proliferation of motels and fast-food restaurants on its main street (named, like the town itself, after mountain man Bill Williams). Due to its elevation of 6,700 feet, the area is wooded and pleasantly temperate in summer, and in winter a small ski area operates (☞ Outdoor Activities and Sports, *below*). Many of the neon signs on Bill Williams Avenue hark back to the days when it was better known as Route 66. Indeed, Williams was not bypassed by I–40 until 1984, making it the last town in America to be served by the legendary "Mother Road." Reasonably priced antiques shops and retailers selling Native American crafts and jewelry line this main drag, where a number of historic buildings have been restored and period lampposts installed.

The **Williams Visitor Center,** which also houses the Chamber of Commerce and Forest Service office, is a good resource for information about the area and is an interesting structure in its own right. Built in 1901, it was the original passenger-train depot, and its brick walls still show graffiti scrawled by early railroad workers and hoboes. ✉ *200 W. Railroad Ave. at Grand Canyon Blvd., Williams 86046,* ☎ *520/635–1418 or 520/635–4061,* FAX *520/635–1417.* ⏲ *Daily 8–5.*

Once a tough, turn-of-the-century town of saloons, bordellos, and opium dens, Williams gained some respectability with the construction of one of the first Harvey Houses, the original Fray Marcos, completed in 1908. It is said to be the first poured-concrete building in Arizona. The bordello is now a bed-and-breakfast, the saloon and opium den are a Mexican restaurant, and the Fray Marcos is an 89-room luxury hotel. Visitors to Williams can travel a nostalgic steam train back through time, with only the drama of local actors to remind them of rowdy times past.

The **Grand Canyon Railway,** originally owned by the Santa Fe Railroad line, sent its first passenger train from Williams to the Grand Canyon in 1901. Eighty-eight years and many incarnations later, the iron horse ran again and, since then, has continued to chug across the 65-mile stretch of tracks through lovely prairie, ranch, and national park land to the South Rim of the Grand Canyon. The vintage train departs daily from the Williams Depot and arrives at the Grand Canyon Railway Depot, the last functioning log-cabin railroad depot in the U.S. (☞ Guided Tours *in* The Grand Canyon and Northwest Arizona A to Z, *below*).

Even if you don't take the train, it's worth visiting the **Williams Depot,** built in 1908 to replace the terminal where the visitor center now resides. Attractions here include a passenger car and the locomotive of a turn-of-the-century steam train, a gift shop where you can find kitsch souvenirs like a tie that plays "I've Been Working on the Railroad," a café (open for breakfast only), and the small Railroad Museum, which is next to the depot in the original dining room of the old Harvey House. The museum hosts an interesting collection of old railroad and Harvey girl photographs and is a good place to learn a little about the history of the Grand Canyon Railway, which once carried American presidents, Franklin D. Roosevelt among them, on their whistle-stop campaigns through the West.

Small children should enjoy the **Grand Canyon Deer Farm,** 8 mi east of Williams on I-40, at Exit 171. Visitors can pet and feed the deer, including the tiny fawns born every June and July. There are also pygmy goats, llamas, and other animals to pet. ✉ *100 Deer Farm Rd., Williams 86046,* ☎ *520/635–4073.* *$5.* *Mar.–May, daily 9–dusk; June–Aug., daily 8–dusk; Sept.–Oct., daily 9–dusk; Nov.–Feb., daily 10–5 in good weather.*

Dining and Lodging

$–$$ ✕ **Pancho McGillicuddy's.** Originally the Cabinet Saloon, this restaurant is on the National Register of Historic Places. Gone are the spitoons and pipes—the smoke-free dining area now has Mexican decor, which sets the scene for such specialties as armadillo eggs, the local name for deep-fried jalapeños stuffed with cheese. ✉ *141 Railroad Ave., Williams 86046,* ☎ *520/635–4150. MC, V.*

$–$$ ✕ **Rod's Steak House.** You can't miss this steak house with the plastic Angus cow out front, set along old Route 66. Obviously the emphasis here is on meat—sizzling mesquite-broiled steaks are the specialty of the house. A children's menu is available. ✉ *301 E. Bill Williams Ave.,* ☎ *520/635–2671 or 800/562–5545. D, MC, V.*

$ ✕ **Tiffany's Restaurant and Lube Lounge.** This old gas station turned restaurant is full of Route 66 icons: 1950s gas pumps, hub caps, neon signs, and black-and-white photos of "the way it used to be." This lively, fun spot draws all ages, who come for the Italian specials, including pizza. The bar-lounge is open until 1 AM. ✉ *233 W. Bill Williams Ave., Williams 86046,* ☎ *520/635–2445. AE, DC, MC, V.*

$$$$ **The Fray Marcos Hotel.** Across from the train station, this new hotel has been designed to resemble the depot's original Fray Marcos lodge. Neoclassical Greek columns flank the grand entrance, which leads into a spacious lobby with a 35-foot-high ceiling, maple wood balustrades, an enormous flagstone fireplace, and gigantic oil paintings of the Grand Canyon, beautifully rendered by local artist Kenneth McKenna. Bronzes by Frederick Remington, from the private collection of hotel owners Max and Thelma Biegert, also adorn the lobby. Rooms are tastefully decorated in southwestern style and have large bathrooms. Adjacent to the lobby is Spenser's, a pub that features an ornate bar, hand-carved in England; light meals are served here after 4 PM. ✉ *235 N. Grand Canyon Blvd., Williams 86046,* ☎ *520/635–4010 or 800/843–8724. 89 rooms. Pub. AE, DC, MC, V.*

$$$ **The Ramada Inn, "Canyon Gateway."** At the east entrance to town, this member of the Ramada chain has comfortable rooms, a good restaurant, and live country-and-western bands in summer. ✉ *642 E. Bill Williams Ave., Williams 86046,* ☎ *520/635–4431 or 800/462–9381. 96 rooms. Restaurant, pool, hot tub, live entertainment weekends. AE, D, DC, MC, V.*

$$ **The Red Garter.** This small bed-and-breakfast is in a tastefully restored bordello dating to 1897. It has four quaint bedrooms; ask for one of the "Best Girl" rooms, which have their own sitting rooms overlooking the train tracks. Included in the room rate is a Continental breakfast at the bakery on the premises. Even if you don't stay here, the bakery's fresh goodies make it worth a stop. ✉ *137 W. Railroad Ave., Williams 86046,* ☎ *520/635–1484 or 800/328–1484. 4 rooms with private bath. AE, D, MC, V.*

Outdoor Activities and Sports

FISHING

Fishing for trout, crappie, catfish, and small-mouth bass is popular at a number of lakes surrounding Williams. For information on obtaining a fishing license, contact the **Arizona Game and Fish Department**

(☞ Fishing *in* The Grand Canyon and Northwest Arizona A to Z, *below*).

SKIING

Unrepentant downhillers can hit the slopes at the **Williams Ski Area** (✉ Box 953, Williams 86046, ☏ 520/635–9330), open when there's snow in the region (usually mid-December through March); take South 4th Street for 2 mi, and then turn right at the sign and go another 1½ mi. There are four groomed runs (including one for beginners) and other downhill trails as well as areas suitable for cross-country enthusiasts.

Havasu Canyon

For those who want to get away from the crowds, Havasu Canyon, south of the middle part of the national park, possesses a Shangri-la–like beauty. It is the home of some 500 Havasupai, a tribe that has populated this beautiful, isolated country for centuries. Spectacular waterfalls as high as 200 feet cascade over red cliffs, spilling blue-green water into immense travertine pools surrounded by thick foliage and sheltering trees. Eight-mile-long **Hualapai Trail** twists into the canyon along the edges of sheer rock walls. To reach Havasu Canyon, take I–40 west of Williams 44 mi to Seligman. From there, go 34 mi west on AZ 66 until you come to Indian Route 18. This junction will be the last chance to fill up with gas on the final 63 mi north to the head of the Hualapai Trail. Be sure to call ahead if you plan to hike the 8-mile-trail into the canyon—or ride a horse or mule down for about $70. You'll definitely want to spend the night if you're hiking or riding (☞ Dining and Lodging, *below*). The hurried can take a helicopter: **Papillon Helicopters** (☏ 800/528–2418) offers a one-way flight (leaving from Tusayan) for $150 or a round-trip package for $385 per person, which includes the ground and landing fee, as well as the horseback and guide fee. From November 1 through May 1 there is a winter rate of $285 per person, either for a day excursion or stay overnight. All visitors are charged a $12 fee to enter the Havasupai tribal lands. ✉ *Contact Havasupai Tourist Enterprise, Supai 86435,* ☏ *520/448–2141 for general information or* ☏ *520/448–2111 for lodging reservations.*

Dining and Lodging

$$$ ✕🏨 **Havasupai Lodge.** The lodge and restaurant at the bottom of Havasu Canyon, operated by the Havasupai tribe, offers clean, comfortable rooms at about $80 for a double (this rate is in addition to the $12 per person fee to enter the Havasupai tribal lands). The restaurant serves three meals a day, generally sandwiches and fast-food-type fare, and a special daily meal; dinner prices are about $8–$10. ✉ *Supai 86435,* ☏ *520/448–2111 (lodge), or 520/448–2981 (restaurant). 24 rooms. No credit cards; call for payment guidelines and/or restrictions.*

CAMPING

For information about camping in Havasu Canyon, call the **Havasupai Tourist Enterprise** (☏ 520/448–2121).

THE NORTH RIM AND ENVIRONS

The North Rim, in the isolated Arizona Strip, draws only about 10% of the Grand Canyon's visitors but is every bit as gorgeous as the South Rim. From southern Arizona, there's only one highway into this area, 210 mi of lonely road to the north and west of Flagstaff. Set in deep forest near the 9,000-foot crest of the Kaibab Plateau, the North Rim is, for many visitors, worth the extra miles. But truth to tell, there's virtually no place along either rim or in the depths of the Grand Canyon that will fail to startle and impress you.

The Drive to the North Rim

Numbers in the margin correspond to points of interest on the North Rim map.

This trip is not an option during the winter, when heavy snows block highway access to the North Rim and facilities are closed.

This long drive—about 210 mi, whether you start out from Grand Canyon Village on the South Rim of the canyon or from Flagstaff—is the best way to get to the North Rim and offers plenty to see along
24 the way. It begins at the **Cameron Trading Post,** on U.S. 89, 1 mi north of the junction with AZ 64 (which you will be on if you're coming from Grand Canyon Village) and 53 mi north of Flagstaff. Founded in 1916, this historic trading post, one of the few remaining in the Southwest, has an extensive stock of Native American jewelry, rugs, baskets, and pottery. Most of the items sold here are made by nearby Navajo and Hopi artisans, but some are created by New Mexico's Zuni and Pueblo Indians. In addition to the main building, which sells wares in all price categories, there's also a separate gallery that offers more expensive, museum-quality goods.

NEED A BREAK? The **Cameron Trading Post** restaurant (☎ 520/679–2231) serves American food that ranges from light snacks to complete dinners; don't miss the huge Navajo tacos on fry bread, heaped with cheese, chopped meat, guacamole, and salad. The high-ceiling room, decorated with Native American art and furniture, is an appealing setting, but service can be a bit slow; if you're in a rush, try the newer cafeteria next door (open high-season only), where you can get hot and cold sandwiches and other buffet-style fare.

The route north on U.S. 89 affords a wide and unobstructed view of
25 the **Painted Desert** off to the right. The desert, which covers thousands of square miles and extends far to the south and east, is a vision of harsh beauty, with windswept plains and mesas, isolated buttes, and barren valleys in delicate patterns of soft pastels. In the few places in which there is vegetation, it is mostly desert scrub, which provides sustenance for only the hardiest wildlife. Most of the undulating hills belong to the Chinle formation, deposited more than 200 million years ago and containing countless fossil records of ancient plants and animals.

About 30 mi north of the Cameron Trading Post, the Painted Desert country gives way to soaring sandstone cliffs that run for many miles off to the right. Brilliantly hued, and ranging in color from light pink
26 to deep orange, the **Echo Cliffs** rise to well over 1,000 feet in many places. They are also essentially devoid of vegetation, but in a few isolated places high up, you'll spot thick patches of tall cottonwood and poplar trees, nurtured by springs and water seepage from the rock escarpments.

At Bitter Springs, 60 mi north of Cameron, U.S. 89A branches off from U.S. 89, running north and providing views of **Marble Canyon,** actually the beginning of the Grand Canyon. Like the rest of the Grand Canyon, Marble Canyon has been carved by the force of the Colorado
27 River. Traversing a gorge nearly 500 feet deep is **Navajo Bridge,** a narrow steel span built in 1929; until the bridge at Glen Canyon Dam was constructed in 1959, this was the only bridge crossing the Colorado for the 600 mi from Moab, Utah, to the Hoover Dam. Formerly used for car traffic, it now functions only as a pedestrian overpass; a newer, wider bridge, built 120 feet downriver, was dedicated in the summer of 1995. An interpretive area and rest rooms are being designed for a

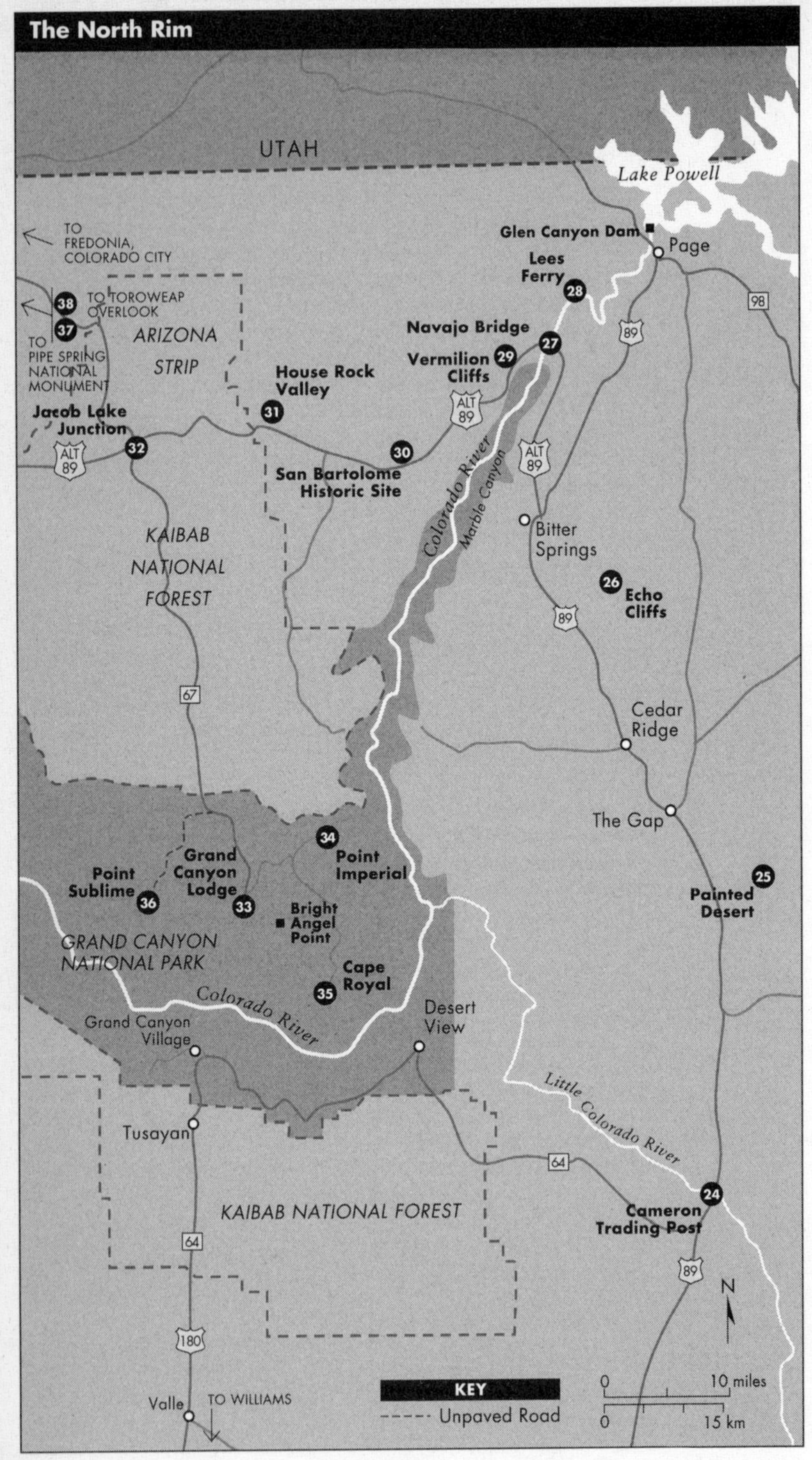
The North Rim
UTAH
Lake Powell
Glen Canyon Dam
Page
Lees Ferry
28
TO FREDONIA, COLORADO CITY
38
37
TO TOROWEAP OVERLOOK
TO PIPE SPRING NATIONAL MONUMENT
ARIZONA STRIP
Navajo Bridge
27
Vermilion Cliffs
29
House Rock Valley
31
Jacob Lake Junction
32
30
San Bartolome Historic Site
Colorado River
Marble Canyon
Bitter Springs
26
Echo Cliffs
KAIBAB NATIONAL FOREST
Cedar Ridge
The Gap
34
Point Imperial
Grand Canyon Lodge
33
Point Sublime
36
Bright Angel Point
25
Painted Desert
GRAND CANYON NATIONAL PARK
Cape Royal
35
Colorado River
Grand Canyon Village
Desert View
Little Colorado River
Tusayan
24
Cameron Trading Post
KAIBAB NATIONAL FOREST
Valle
TO WILLIAMS
KEY
Unpaved Road
0
10 miles
0
15 km
N

former parking lot near the old bridge, which is listed on the National Register of Historic Places.

At Marble Canyon Lodge, about a mile past Navajo Bridge, is a turnoff
★ 28 for historic **Lees Ferry,** 3 mi away. Situated on a sharp bend in the Colorado River at a break in the surrounding Echo Cliffs, Lees Ferry is considered mile zero of the river, the point from which all distances on the river system are measured. It's also at the eastern edge of Arizona Strip country (☞ Arizona Strip, *below*), and it was one of the last areas in the mainland United States to be completely charted. This spot was first visited by non–Native Americans in 1776, when Spanish priests Fray Francisco Atanasio Domínguez and Fray Silvestre Velez de Escalante tried but failed to cross the Colorado. Explorer John Wesley Powell also visited in 1870 on an expedition with Mormon leaders. After the ferry was established, it became part of the Honeymoon Trail, a gateway to Utah for young couples who wanted their civil marriages in Arizona sanctified at the Latter-Day Saints temple in St. George. It also became a crossing and a supply point for miners and other pioneers who shaped much of the American West.

Lees Ferry retains a number of vestiges of the mining era, but it's now primarily known as the spot where most of the Grand Canyon river rafts put into the water. In addition, huge trout lurk in the river near here, so there are several places to pick up angling gear and/or a guide. If you go out on your own, be sure you have an Arizona fishing license before casting a line (☞ Fishing *in* Outdoor Activities and Sports, *below*).

Heading west from Navajo Bridge, you'll be treated to views of some of the world's most spectacular geologic formations. Rising to the
★ 29 right of the highway are the sheer **Vermilion Cliffs,** in many places more than 3,000 feet high.

As you continue the journey to the North Rim, the immense blue-green bulk of the Kaibab Plateau stretches out before you. About 18 mi past
30 Navajo Bridge, a sign directs you to the **San Bartolome Historic Site,** an overlook with a series of plaques that tell the story of the Domínguez-Escalante expedition of 1776.

31 At **House Rock Valley,** a large road sign announces the House Rock Buffalo Ranch, operated by the Arizona Division of Wildlife. A 23-mile dirt road leads to the home of one of the largest herds of American bison in the Southwest. You may drive out to the ranch, but be aware that you may not see any buffalo—the expanse of their range is so great that they frequently cannot be spotted from a car.

About 25 mi west of Marble Canyon, U.S. 89A starts climbing to the top of the Kaibab Plateau, heavily forested, rife with animals and birds, and more than 9,000 feet at its highest point. The rapid change from barren desert to lush forest is dramatic. At an elevation of 7,900 feet,
32 the **Jacob Lake junction** is a good place to stop for groceries and gas. The forest service's **Kaibab Plateau Visitor's Center** (☎ 520/643–7298) is open at Jacob Lake from May 1 through mid-October. AZ 67 runs south from the junction to the North Rim, a distance of 44 mi; the route passes through one of the thickest stands of ponderosa pine in the United States. Visitors frequently see mule deer and, once in a while, catch a glimpse of rare Kaibab squirrels; you can recognize them by their all-white tails and by the long tufts of white hair on their ears.

Dining and Lodging

$$ ✕▣ **Cliff Dwellers Lodge.** Originated in 1949 in the Marble Canyon area of the Arizona Strip, this dining and lodging complex sits right at the foot of the Vermilion Cliffs. Rooms in the modern motel building

are attractive and clean. ✉ *AZ 89A, 9 mi west of Navajo Bridge, HC 67–30, Marble Canyon 86036,* ☎ *520/355–2228 or 800/433–2543,* FAX *520/355–2229. 21 rooms. Restaurant, bar, grocery. D, MC, V.*

$$ ✕🏨 **Jacob Lake Inn.** This modest but clean complex, on 5 acres in Kaibab National Forest (at the junction of U.S. 89A and AZ 67, 45 mi north of the North Rim), is a good option for lodging in the area. Both basic cabins and standard drive-up units are available. All rooms have modern, motel-style appointments, with some rustic touches; most overlook the highways. The bustling lodge center, a popular stop for those heading to the North Rim, has a grocery, a coffee shop, a restaurant, and a large gift shop. ✉ *Jacob Lake 86022,* ☎ *520/643–7232. 11 motel units, 3 family units, 22 cabins. Restaurant, café, grocery. AE, D, DC, MC, V.*

$–$$ ★ ✕🏨 **Cameron Trading Post.** In 1993 the 1930s-era inn abutting the historic trading post was razed and replaced by a two-building motel complex. Rooms still have southwestern-style decor, attractive hand-carved oak furniture, tile baths, and balconies overlooking the Colorado but now have such contemporary amenities as remote-control TVs. The original native-stone landscaping—including fossilized dinosaur tracks—was retained, as was the small, well-kept garden with lilacs, roses, and crab apple trees. A recently built cafeteria designed to serve the tour-bus trade is unusually well fitted, with an antique back bar and light fixtures; the older dining room, with its original tinwork ceilings, kiva fireplace, and beautiful oak sideboards, offers hearty meals at good prices. The trading post is on the Navajo reservation, so no alcohol is served here. ✉ *Box 339, Cameron 86020,* ☎ *520/679–2231 or 800/338–7385, ext. 414;* FAX *520/679–2350. 66 rooms, 4 suites. Restaurant, cafeteria, grocery. AE, DC, MC, V.*

$–$$ ★ ✕🏨 **Marble Canyon Lodge.** This Arizona Strip lodge opened in 1929, on the same day the Navajo Bridge was dedicated. It is currently owned by Jane Foster, who first came here in 1950 with her father. Three types of accommodations are available: rooms with lace curtains, brass beds, and hardwood floors in the original building; standard motel rooms in the newer building across the street; and apartments (which can sleep up to eight) in a 1991 complex. Guests can sit on the porch swing of the native-rock lodge building and look out on the Vermilion Cliffs and the desert, or they can play the piano that was brought over on Lees Ferry in the 1920s. Zane Grey and Gary Cooper are among the well-known guests who have stayed here. ✉ *½ mi west of Navajo Bridge on AZ 89A, Marble Canyon 86036,* ☎ *520/355–2225 or 800/726–1789,* FAX *520/355–2227. 63 units. Restaurant, coin laundry, private airstrip. D, MC, V.*

$ ✕🏨 **Lees Ferry Lodge.** Geared toward the Lees Ferry trout-fishing trade, this lodge will outfit you, guide you, and freeze your catch (if it's legal size). At the end of the day you can sit out on one of the garden patios of this rustic building, constructed of native stone and rough-hewn beams in 1929. Rooms are charming, if a bit quirky in their plumbing. The hotel's Vermilion Cliffs Bar and Grill is a popular gathering spot for the men and women who pilot and guide the river rafts through the Grand Canyon, and it serves good American fare—especially the steaks and seafood—in an authentic western setting. ✉ *4 mi west of Navajo Bridge on AZ 89A, HC 67, Box 1, Marble Canyon 86036,* ☎ *520/355–2231. 8 rooms with shower, 5-person trailer with bath. Restaurant. MC, V.*

CAMPING

⛺ **Cameron RV Park.** This park, open year-round, is adjacent to the Cameron Trading Post, with its restaurant, grocery store, even a butcher shop and post office. The fee with hookup is $14 per day. ✉

On U.S. 89, 26 mi southwest of Tuba City, ☎ *520/679–2231 or 800/338–7385.*

⛺ **Demotte Campground.** This forest service campground is outside the park, 16 mi north of the rim. It has 22 single-unit RV and tent sites, but no hookups, for $10 per day. There are interpretive campfire programs in summer. No reservations are accepted. It opens between mid-May and early June and closes in October. ✉ *Southwest Natural and Cultural Heritage Association, Box 620, Fredonia 86022,* ☎ *520/643–7395 (off-season), 520/643–7633 (in season).*

⛺ **Jacob Lake Campground.** At the junction of U.S. 89A and AZ 67, 45 mi north of the North Rim, this campground has family and group RV and tent sites (no hookups) for $10 per vehicle per day. In summer, rangers present interpretive programs in the evening. No reservations are accepted (except for groups of 10 or more). It's open year-round, but there are no facilities or running water in winter; fees are only charged from mid-April through October. ✉ *Southwest Natural and Cultural Heritage Association, Box 620, Fredonia 86022,* ☎ *520/643–7395 (off-season), 520/643–7633 (in season).*

⛺ **Kaibab Lodge Camper Village.** On AZ 67, ¼ mile south of Jacob Lake junction, this campground has 50 tent sites ($10 for two people) and 80 RV and trailer sites ($20 for a pull-through with full hookups, $10 without hookups). Firepits and more than 70 picnic tables are available in this wooded spot, located near a gas station, store, and restaurant. Reservations are accepted. It's open mid-May to November, weather permitting. ✉ *Box 3331, Flagstaff 86003,* ☎ *520/643–7804 in season, 520/526–0924 or 800/525–0924 (outside AZ) in winter,* FAX *520/527–9398.*

Outdoor Activities and Sports

FISHING

In the vicinity of Lees Ferry, just across Marble Canyon Bridge on U.S. 89 (the route to the North Rim), the Colorado River is known for huge, German brown and rainbow trout. Marble Canyon Lodge (☞ Dining and Lodging, *above*), near Lees Ferry, carries Arizona fishing licenses. If you'd like to apply for a license in advance, contact the **Arizona Game and Fish Department** (☞ Fishing *in* The Grand Canyon and Northwest Arizona A to Z, *below*). For details on fishing regulations, check with the **Backcountry Office** (☞ Hiking *in* The Grand Canyon and Northwest Arizona A to Z, *below*). **Lees Ferry Anglers** (✉ HC 67, Box 2, Marble Canyon, AZ 86036, ☎ 520/355–2261 or 800/962–9755 outside AZ) offers guided fishing trips, including lunch, starting from $225 per day; it is the only guide service in the area that practices year-round catch and release.

Shopping

The huge **Cameron Trading Post** (✉ U.S. 89, 1 mi north of junction with AZ 64, ☎ 520/679–2231 or 800/338–7385) stocks crafts of the Navajo, Hopi, Zuni, and New Mexico Pueblo peoples. The vast array of goods and prices will satisfy everyone's taste and purse, but it helps to come armed with knowledge of Native American artisanship if you're looking at high-ticket items. An outlet of the **Navajo Arts and Crafts Enterprises** (✉ U.S. 89 at the junction with AZ 64, ☎ 520/679–2244) stocks fine authentic Navajo products.

The North Rim

★ 33 The historic **Grand Canyon Lodge** is, literally, at the end of the road (AZ 67). A massive stone structure built in 1928 by the Union Pacific Railroad, the lodge is listed on the National Register of Historic Places. Inside, the huge lounge area with hardwood floors and high, beamed ceilings affords a marvelous view of the canyon through massive plate-glass windows. On warm days visitors sit in the sun and drink in the surrounding beauty at an equally spacious outdoor viewing deck.

★ The trail to **Bright Angel Point,** one of the most awe-inspiring overlooks on either rim, starts on the grounds of the Grand Canyon Lodge and proceeds along the crest of a point of rocks that juts into the canyon for several hundred yards. The walk is only 1 mi round-trip, but it's an exciting trek because there are sheer drops just a few feet away on each side of the trail. In a few spots, where the route is extremely narrow, metal railings along the path ensure visitors' safety. The trail is quite safe, but visitors have been known to clamber out to precarious perches to have their pictures taken. Be very careful: There have been tragic falls at the Grand Canyon.

The **Transept Trail** begins near the corner of the lodge's east patio. This 3-mile (round-trip) trail stays near the rim for part of the distance; then it plunges into the forest, ending at the North Rim Campground and General Store, 1½ mi from the lodge.

NEED A BREAK? Lunch, dinner, or a snack in the huge, high-ceiling, rock-and-log dining room of the **Grand Canyon Lodge** (☎ 520/638–2611) is an integral part of the North Rim experience; the food is good and reasonably priced. Or, if you don't want to go in for a meal, just buy a drink at the lodge's Pizza Place, sit out on the viewing deck, and watch the sun set over the canyon.

Eleven miles northeast of Grand Canyon Lodge is one of the North
34 Rim's most popular lookouts, **Point Imperial,** the highest vista point (elevation 8,803 feet) at either rim, offering magnificent views of both the canyon and the distant country for many miles around: the Vermilion Cliffs to the north, the 10,000-foot Navajo Mountain to the northeast in Utah, the Painted Desert to the east, and the Little Colorado River canyon to the southeast.

★ 35 **Cape Royal,** another popular lookout, is about 23 mi southeast of Grand Canyon Lodge. From the parking lot at the road's end it's a short, scenic walk on a paved road to this southernmost viewpoint on the North Rim. In addition to a large slice of the Grand Canyon, Angel's Window, a giant, erosion-formed hole, can be seen through the projecting ridge of Cape Royal. At Angel's Window Overlook, ⅓ mile north of here, **Cliff Springs Trail** starts its 1-mile route (round-trip) through a forested ravine. The trail, narrow and precarious in spots, passes ancient dwellings, winds beneath a limestone overhang, and terminates at Cliff Springs, where the forest opens on another impressive view of the canyon walls.

An excellent option for those who want to get off the beaten path, the
36 trip to **Point Sublime** is intended only for visitors driving vehicles with high-road clearance (pickups and four-wheel-drive vehicles). It is also necessary to be properly equipped for wilderness road travel: Check with a park ranger or at the information desk at Grand Canyon Lodge before taking this journey. The road winds for 17 mi through gorgeous high country to Point Sublime, an overlook that lives up to its name. You may camp here, but only after obtaining a permit from the Backcountry Office at the park ranger station (☞ Hiking *in* The Grand Canyon and Northwest Arizona A to Z, *below*).

Dining and Lodging

$–$$$ ★ ✕🏨 **Grand Canyon Lodge.** This historic property offers a range of accommodations in a setting of extraordinary beauty; constructed mainly in the 1920s and '30s, it's the premier lodging facility in the remote, sparsely populated North Rim area. The main building has massive limestone walls and timbered ceilings. Additional lodging options include small, very rustic cabins; larger cabins (some with a canyon view and some with two bedrooms); and traditional motel rooms in newer units. The hotel's huge, high-ceiling dining room offers spectacular views and the kitchen prepares very good food; you might find marinated pork kebabs, grilled swordfish, or linguine with cilantro on the surprisingly sophisticated dinner menu. ✉ *TW Recreational Services, Box 400, Cedar City, UT 84721,* ☎ *801/586–7686 (reservations) or 520/638–2611 (switchboard),* FAX *801/586–3157. 40 rooms, 54 western cabins (for up to 5 people), 82 frontier cabins (up to 3 people), 21 pioneer cabins (4 or 5 people), 4 cabins accessible to travelers with disabilities, all with bath. Bar, dining room, cafeteria. AE, D, MC, V.*

$$ **Kaibab Lodge.** In a lovely wooded setting just 5 mi from the entrance to Grand Canyon National Park's North Rim, this 1920s property offers rustic cabins with plain, motel-style furnishings. When they're not out looking into the abyss, guests can sit around the lodge's huge stone fireplace (it can be chilly up here in spring and early fall). In winter, when the canyon is closed, many folks come up for Nordic skiing (☞ Outdoor Activities and Sports, *below*). The lodge is open mid-May to early November for the summer season and early December to early April for the skiing season. ✉ *AZ 67, HC 64, Box 30, Fredonia 86022,* ☎ *520/638–2389 or 800/525–0924 (for reservations in winter). 24 cabins with shower. Restaurant. D, MC, V.*

CAMPING

North Rim Campground. This is the only designated campground inside Grand Canyon National Park on the North Rim. Located 3 mi north of the rim, it has 83 RV and tent sites (no hookups) for $10 per day. It's open mid-May to the end of October. ✉ *Reservations through Mistix, Box 85705, San Diego, CA 92138,* ☎ *800/365–2267 or 619/452–0150 outside the U.S.*

Outdoor Activities and Sports

CROSS-COUNTRY SKIING

In season, when the road to the national park is closed, the **North Rim Nordic Center** (✉ c/o Canyoneers, Inc., Box 2997, Flagstaff 86003, ☎ 520/526–0924 or 800/525–0924 outside AZ) transports visitors via a SnoVan—a contraption made up of the battered shell of a van perched atop an ungainly half-track fitted with skis where the front tires would be—from Jacob Lake to the Kaibab Lodge, a 20-mile trip (it takes 1½ hours). Call or write for information on packages.

HIKING

The North Kaibab Trail (☞ Outdoor Activities and Sports *in* East Rim Drive, *above*) is the only maintained trail into the canyon on the North Rim.

MULE RIDES

Canyon Trail Rides (☎ 801/679–8665 preseason, ☎ 520/638–2292 after May 15 at Grand Canyon Lodge) operates short mule rides suitable for children on the easier trails along the North Rim. A one-hour ride, available to those 6 and older, runs about $12. Half-day trips on the rim or into the canyon (minimum age 8) cost $35; full-day trips (minimum age 12), which include lunch, go for $85. These excursions are very popular, so try to make reservations in advance. Rides are available daily from May 15 to October 15.

Shopping

The North Rim, far less commercial than the South Rim, has only one gift shop, at the Grand Canyon Lodge (☞ Dining and Lodging, *above*), where you'll find some better-quality items mixed in with a largely schlocky selection of souvenirs.

Arizona Strip

The Arizona Strip is the 12,000-square-mile northwestern portion of the state, cut off from the rest of Arizona by the giant scar created by the Colorado River as it comes out of Utah and winds its way through the Grand Canyon to the western border of the state. Sometimes called the American Tibet because it's so isolated, the area boasts only two small towns: the farming and lumbering community of Fredonia and, near the Utah border, the polygamous Mormon town of Colorado City. Their combined population is less than 7,000, and fewer than 700 permanent residents—including 150 members of the Kaibab-Paiute tribe—live in the rest of the strip.

37 One of the main destinations in the area is **Pipe Spring National Monument,** 90 mi from the North Rim. Pipe Spring, 14 mi beyond Fredonia, is one of the few reliable sources of water in the Arizona Strip. The park features a restored rock fort and ranch, with exhibits of southwestern frontier life; in summer there are living-history demonstrations that focus on such things as ranching operations or weaving. The fort was completed in 1871 to fend off Indian attacks (which never came because a peace treaty was signed before it was finished), and it was originally built as a ranch for the managers sent to oversee the Mormon church's tithed herds. It ended up functioning mainly as headquarters for a dairy operation and in 1871 became the first telegraph station in the Arizona territory. Also on-site is a well-stocked bookstore and gift shop, a coffee shop, and a visitor center with exhibits. About a half mile north of the monument is a campground, picnic area, and—opened in 1994—a casino run by the Kaibab-Paiute tribe. The slots draw busloads of people to this remote spot. ✉ *HC 65, Box 5, Fredonia 86022,* ☎ *520/643–7105.* 🎟 *$2.* ⏲ *Historic structures daily 8–4:30; visitor center/museum daily 8–5.*

Six miles back toward Fredonia from Pipe Spring on AZ 389, a dirt road
38 leads some 50 mi south to **Toroweap Overlook.** You'll be riding through starkly beautiful, uninhabited country. Toroweap, a lonely and awesome overlook, is one of the narrowest stretches of the canyon (less than 1 mi across) and also the point with the deepest sheer cliff (more than 3,000 feet straight down). From this vantage point, you can see upstream to sedimentary ledges, cliffs, and talus slopes. Looking downstream, you can see miles of the lava flow that forms steep deltas, some of which look like black waterfalls frozen on the cliff. Be sure you have plenty of gas, drinking water, good tires, and a reliable car; a high-clearance vehicle (one that sits high up off the ground, like a pickup truck) is best for this trip. Don't try to go in wet weather, when the dirt road is likely to be washed out. There's a ranger station near the rim as well as a primitive campground. If you plan to return the same day, you should make motel reservations in advance at one of the Arizona Strip motels (☞ Dining and Lodging *in* The Drive to the North Rim, *above*).

NORTHWEST ARIZONA, LAKE MEAD, AND LAUGHLIN

If the Grand Canyon is the most dramatic natural attraction in northwest Arizona, it is by no means all there is to see. Towns like Kingman hark back to the glory days of old Route 66, while the ghost towns of Chloride and Oatman bear testament to the mining madness that once reigned in the region. Water-sports fans, or those who just want to laze on a houseboat, will enjoy Lake Mead, just across the Nevada border, or Lake Havasu, over which London Bridge surrealistically presides. Another bridge across the Colorado leads to Nevada and the casinos of Laughlin, more low-key and casual than those of Las Vegas. And if you need an antidote to the Grand Canyon, visit Hoover Dam, the towering monument to that age-old human endeavor: the control of nature.

Numbers in the margin correspond to points of interest on the Northwest Arizona and Lake Mead map.

Kingman

39 *112 mi west of Williams.*

Kingman is surrounded by mountains on three sides and host to the longest remaining stretch of Route 66. In this town the neon-lined roadway is named for native son Andy Devine, the gravelly-voiced actor who played sidekick in innumerable westerns. Because I–40, U.S. 93, AZ 68, and Route 66 all converge in Kingman, which is also served by Amtrak, Greyhound, and America West airlines (offering three flights a day from Phoenix), it is a hub for local attractions like Hoover Dam, Laughlin, and Lake Havasu.

The **Kingman Area Chamber of Commerce** (✉ 333 W. Andy Devine Ave., Box 1150, Kingman 86402, ☎ 520/753–6106) carries T-shirts, postcards, and the usual brochures to acquaint you with local attractions. The **Mohave Museum of History and Arts** (✉ 400 W. Beale St., ☎ 520/753–3195) includes an Andy Devine Room; an exhibit of carved Kingman turquoise; and a diorama depicting the expedition of Lt. Edward Beale, who led his ill-fated camel-cavalry unit to the area in search of a wagon road along the 35th parallel. The **Bonelli House** (✉ 430 E. Spring St.; call the Mohave Museum, *above,* for information), an excellent example of the Anglo-Territorial architecture popular in 1915, is one of 62 buildings in the business district listed on the National Register of Historic Places. A 15-mile drive from town up Hualapai Mountain Road will take you to **Hualapai Mountain Park,** where more than 2,200 wooded acres at elevations ranging from 6,000 to 8,400 feet host 6 mi of hiking trails as well as picnic areas, rustic cabins, and RV and tenting areas; contact the Mohave County Parks Department (☎ 520/753–0739) for details.

OFF THE BEATEN PATH

OATMAN – A worthwhile detour from Kingman, the ghost town of Oatman is reached via old Route 66 (now 68). It's a straight shot across the Mohave Desert valley for a while, but then the road narrows and winds precipitously for about 15 mi through the Black Mountains. The main street of this former gold-mining town is right out of the Old West; in fact, a number of films, including *How the West Was Won,* were shot here. You can wander into one of the three saloons or visit the Oatman Hotel, where Clark Gable and Carole Lombard honeymooned in 1939 after they were secretly married in Kingman, but the burros that often come in from nearby hills and meander down the street are the town's real draw; a couple of stores sell hay to visitors who want to feed these "wild" beasts.

Lodging

There are some 35 motels in Kingman (pop. about 13,000), most of them along Andy Devine Avenue.

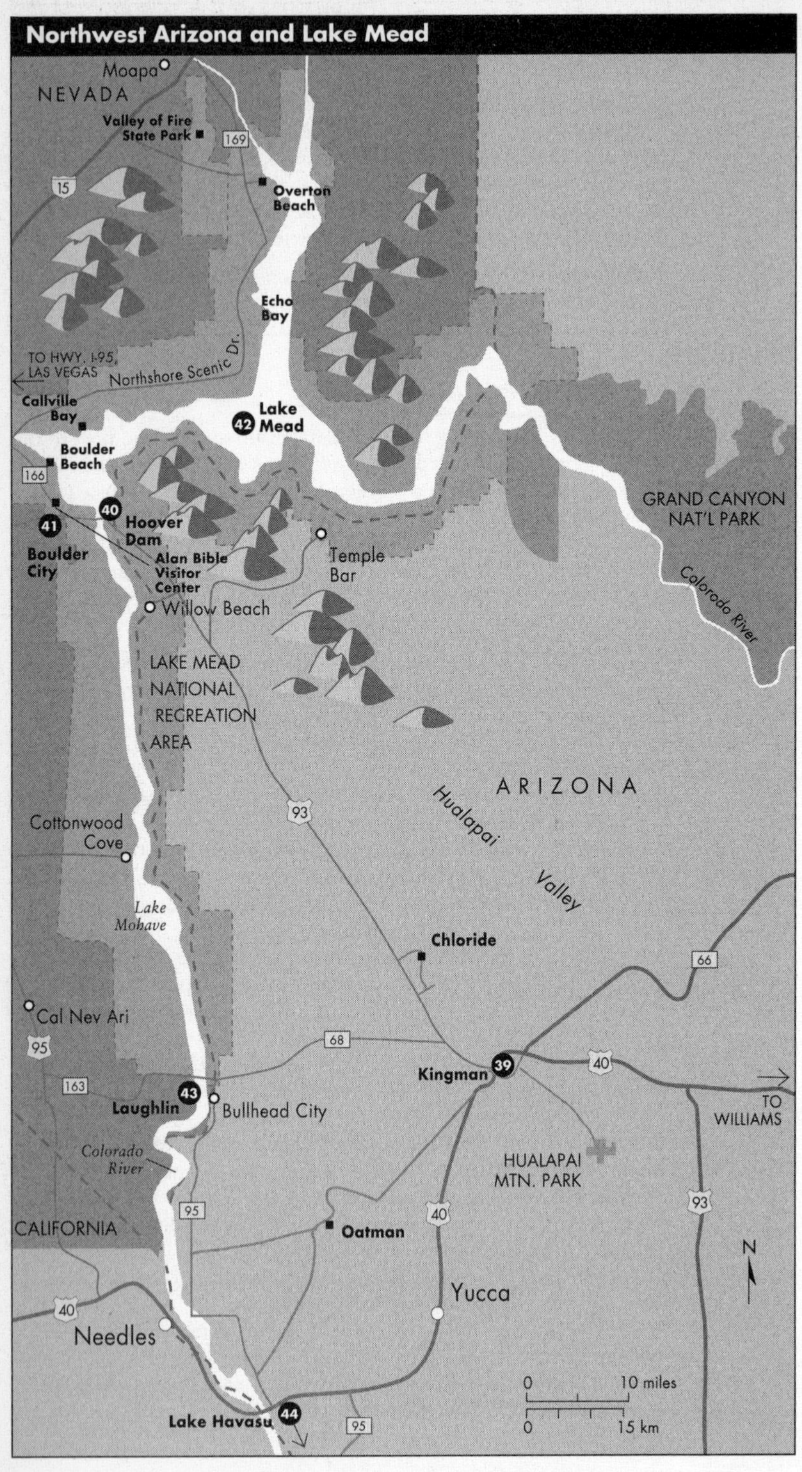
Northwest Arizona and Lake Mead
Moapa
NEVADA
Valley of Fire State Park
169
15
Overton Beach
Echo Bay
TO HWY. I-95, LAS VEGAS
Northshore Scenic Dr.
Callville Bay
Lake Mead
42
Boulder Beach
166
40
Hoover Dam
41
Boulder City
Alan Bible Visitor Center
Temple Bar
GRAND CANYON NAT'L PARK
Colorado River
Willow Beach
LAKE MEAD NATIONAL RECREATION AREA
ARIZONA
Hualapai Valley
93
Cottonwood Cove
Lake Mohave
Chloride
66
Cal Nev Ari
95
68
39
Kingman
40
163
43
Laughlin
Bullhead City
TO WILLIAMS
Colorado River
HUALAPAI MTN. PARK
95
40
93
CALIFORNIA
Oatman
N
Yucca
40
Needles
0
10 miles
0
15 km
44
Lake Havasu
95

Quality Inn. This chain member has comfortable rooms and a spiffy coffee shop stocked with Route 66 memorabilia. ✉ *1400 E. Andy Devine Ave., Kingman 86401,* ☎ *520/753–4747 or 800/221–2222. 98 rooms. Coffee shop. AE, D, DC, MC, V.*

En Route If you're heading on to Hoover Dam and Lake Mead, take U.S. 93 north; you'll come to a marked turnoff for the ghost town of **Chloride,** which takes its name from a type of silver ore mined in the area. Many buildings were lost to fires that ravaged the town in its heyday, but some historic treasures still stand, including the old bank vault, now a museum; the 1890 Jim Fritz house; and the Tennessee Saloon, now a general store and dance hall. Don't miss the huge murals painted on the rocks at the outskirts of town by western artist Roy Purcell, who worked the mines here in his youth.

Lake Mead and Hoover Dam

67 mi northwest of Kingman.

40 The visual impact of **Hoover Dam**'s incredible mass and height often compels visitors to make this the first stop on a visit to the Lake Mead area. Created to control floods and to generate electricity, the dam is 727 feet high (the equivalent of a 70-story building) and 660 feet thick (more than the length of two football fields). Its construction required 4.4 million cubic yards of concrete, enough to build a two-lane highway from San Francisco to New York. Every year more than 700,000 people take the Bureau of Reclamation's guided tour, which takes visitors deep inside the structure for a look at its inner workings; tours leave every few minutes from the exhibit building at the top of the dam. A huge new visitor center, which opened on the Nevada side in June, 1995, contains a theater with three revolving sections, an exhibition gallery, an observation tower, and a much-needed five-story parking garage. ✉ *Lake Mead,* ☎ *702/294–8367. Free. Entrance fee and guided tour $6. Memorial Day–Labor Day, daily 8–7:30 (last tour at 6:15); rest of yr, daily 9–5 (last tour at 4:15). Hrs may change; call ahead.*

41 About 8 mi west of Hoover Dam on U.S. 93, **Boulder City,** Nevada, is a small, pleasant town with a movie theater, numerous gift shops and eateries, and a small hotel. Developed in the early 1930s to house the 4,000 Hoover Dam workers and to deter them from spending their hard-earned dollars on wine, women, and Las Vegas, Boulder City is the only community in Nevada where gambling is illegal. When the dam was completed, the city served as a center for the management and maintenance of the site. The **Boulder City Chamber of Commerce** (✉ 1497 Nevada Hwy., Boulder City, NV 89005, ☎ 702/293–2034) has information about the town and nearby attractions.

Just northeast of Boulder City, at the intersection of U.S. 93 (also called Nevada Highway here) and Lakeshore Scenic Drive (NV 166), is the **Alan Bible Visitor Center** (✉ 601 Nevada Hwy., Boulder City, NV 89005, ☎ 702/293–8906), the best place to become acquainted with the Lake Mead area.

Lakeshore Scenic Drive (NV 166) wends its way along the shore of
42 **Lake Mead,** the largest man-made body of water in the United States, with a surface covering 229 square mi and an irregular shoreline extending for 550 mi. It was formed when Hoover Dam was built in 1935 to hold back the Colorado River. Recreation areas with marinas include Boulder Beach, Callville Bay, Echo Bay, and Overton Beach.

Outdoor Activities and Sports

BOATING

If you didn't bring your own boat, your rental options include houseboats, patio boats, fishing boats, and ski boats—pick up a list of marinas at the Alan Bible Visitor Center (☞ *above*). Houseboat rentals are available at **Callville Bay Resort and Marina** (☎ 800–255–5561) or at **Echo Bay Resort** (☎ 702/394–4000 or 800/752–9669). Smaller boats are available at these locations and at **Lake Mead Resort** (✉ Boulder Beach, ☎ 702/293–3484), in addition to other marinas.

CRUISES

For those who want to leave the navigating to someone else, a 1½-hour cruise of the Hoover Dam area on a 250-passenger stern-wheeler is available through **Lake Mead Cruises** (✉ Lake Mead Marina, near Boulder Beach, ☎ 702/293–6180). A 15-mile motorized raft trip on the Colorado from the base of Hoover Dam down Black Canyon to Willow Beach is offered by **Gray Line Tours** (☎ 702/384–1234 or 800/634–6579).

Laughlin

43 *32 mi west of Kingman.*

Don Laughlin opened the first casino here in 1966, but the town didn't really take off until the early 1980s. Though often considered just a smaller version of Las Vegas, Laughlin has a character of its own. It generally attracts older, retired travelers who spend at least part of the winter in Arizona and other folks who prefer the low-pressure, low-minimum tables, the cheap food, the low-cost rooms, and the slots galore. The dealers are generally friendlier, the bettors more relaxed, and, especially compared to the shuttered rooms in Las Vegas, Laughlin casinos have a bright, airy, open feeling, lent by large picture windows that overlook the Colorado.

When you've finished at the tables, Laughlin's outdoor activities include water sports, golf, tennis, and strolls along the tree-lined River Walk. The **Laughlin Chamber of Commerce** (✉ 1725 Casino Dr., Box 77777, Laughlin, NV 89028, ☎ 702/298–2214 or 800/227–5245) can provide further information on the area, which is currently served by America West, Arizona Airways, Reno Air, and United Express airlines.

Gambling

The gambling halls lining Casino Drive include **Riverside Resort** (✉ 1650 S. Casino Dr., ☎ 702/298–2535 or 800/227–3849), **Flamingo Hilton** (✉ 1900 S. Casino Dr., ☎ 702/298–5111 or 800/352–6464), **Regency Casino** (✉ 1950 S. Casino Dr., ☎ 702/298–2439), **Edgewater** (✉ 2020 S. Casino Dr., ☎ 702/298–2453 or 800/677–4837), **Colorado Belle** (✉ 2100 S. Casino Dr., ☎ 702/298–4000 or 800/458–9500), **Pioneer Hotel** (✉ 2200 S. Casino Dr., ☎ 702/298–2442 or 800/634–3469), **Ramada Express** (✉ 2121 S. Casino Dr., ☎ 702/298–4200 or 800/272–6232), **Golden Nugget** (✉ 2300 S. Casino Dr., ☎ 702/298–7111 or 800/237–1739), **Gold River** (✉ 2700 S. Casino Dr., ☎ 702/298–2242 or 800/835–7903), and **Harrah's** (✉ 2900 S. Casino Dr., ☎ 702/298–4600 or 800/447–8700).

Lake Havasu

44 *19 mi south of Laughlin.*

Lake Havasu is renowned for hosting London Bridge. A brilliant stroke of entrepreneurship turned what might have been just another desert town on the Colorado into a crowd-drawing curiosity: When the City of London put the sinking bridge up for sale in 1967, developer Robert

McCulloch decided it would make the perfect centerpiece for the community he had planned on the shores of the lake. He bought the historic bridge for nearly $2.5 million, had it dismantled stone by stone, shipped, and precisely reassembled (all 10,000 tons of it) to span a narrow arm of Lake Havasu.

An Olde English theme is played to the hilt here: A Tudor-style village replete with pub, red London telephone booths, and other Britobilia abuts the base of the bridge. But Havasu City is on a lake, and in Arizona after all, so the sunshine, water sports, and fishing can amuse visitors after they've seen the surprising span. The weather is wonderful in spring, fall, and winter, but summers often see temperatures that exceed 100°F. Among the recreational opportunities on and around 45-mile-long Lake Havasu are houseboat, ski-boat, Jet Ski, and sailboat rentals; marinas, RV parks, and campgrounds; and golf, tennis, and guided fishing expeditions. Those who are interested in exploring the desert—including old mines and a wildlife refuge—might consider booking a four-wheel-drive tour (☞ Outdoor Activities and Sports, below).

Dining and Lodging

The area has more than 20 lodging establishments—from inexpensive roadside motels to posh resorts—and more than 40 restaurants, from fast-food emporiums to fine dining establishments. For more information on Lake Havasu City, contact the **Lake Havasu Visitor and Convention Bureau** (✉ 1930 Mesquite Ave., Suite 3, Lake Havasu City 86403, ☎ 520/453–3444 or 800/242–8278).

Outdoor Activities and Sports

Outback Off-Road Adventures (✉ 1350 McCulloch Blvd., ☎ 520/680–6151) offers four-wheel-drive desert tours.

THE GRAND CANYON AND NORTHWEST ARIZONA A TO Z

Arriving and Departing

By Bus

Greyhound Lines (☎ 800/231–2222) provides bus service from all points in the United States to Flagstaff or Williams, both considered gateway communities to the Grand Canyon.

From either Flagstaff or Williams, bus service to the South Rim of the Grand Canyon is offered by **Nava-Hopi Tours** (☎ 520/774–5003 or 800/892–8687).

By Car

If you are driving to Arizona from the east, or coming up from the southern part of the state, the best access to the Grand Canyon is from Flagstaff. You can take U.S. 180 northwest (81 mi) to Grand Canyon Village on the South Rim. Or, for a scenic route with stopping points along the canyon rim, drive north on U.S. 89 from Flagstaff, and then turn left at the junction of AZ 64 (52 mi north of Flagstaff) and proceed west for an additional 57 mi.

To visit the North Rim of the canyon, proceed north from Flagstaff on U.S. 89 to Bitter Springs; then take U.S. 89A to the junction of AZ 67, which leads to the North Rim, a distance of approximately 210 mi from Flagstaff.

If you are crossing Arizona on I–40 from the west, your most direct route to the South Rim is on AZ 64 (U.S. 180), which runs north from Williams for 58 mi to Grand Canyon Village.

By Plane

AIRLINES

The many carriers that fly to the Grand Canyon from Las Vegas include **Air Nevada** (☎ 800/634–6377), **Air Vegas** (☎ 800/255–7474), **Las Vegas Airlines** (☎ 800/634–6851), and **Scenic Airlines** (☎ 800/634–6801 or 800/535–4448).

From Phoenix, **Scenic Airlines** (☞ *above*) offers two daily flights to Grand Canyon Airport. Phoenix Sky Harbor Airport is served by virtually all the major U.S. commercial airlines (☞ Phoenix A to Z *in* Chapter 5).

TWA Express (☎ 800/221–2000) has daily service from Los Angeles's LAX to Grand Canyon Village.

AIRPORTS

McCarran International Airport (☎ 702/261–5743) in Las Vegas is the primary air hub for flights to **Grand Canyon National Park Airport** (☎ 520/638–2446). You can also make connections into the Grand Canyon from **Sky Harbor International Airport** (☎ 520/273–3300) in Phoenix.

FROM THE AIRPORT

The **Tusayan/Canyon Airport Shuttle** (☎ 520/638–0821) operates between Grand Canyon Airport and the nearby towns of Tusayan and Grand Canyon Village; it makes hourly runs daily between 8:15 AM and 5:15 PM, with additional trips in the summer months.

Fred Harvey Transportation Company (☎ 520/638–2822 or 520/638–2631) offers 24-hour taxi service at Grand Canyon Airport, Grand Canyon Village, and the nearby village of Tusayan; taxis also make trips to other destinations in and around Grand Canyon National Park.

By Train

Amtrak (☎ 800/872–7245) provides daily service to Arizona from both the east and west, with its most convenient stop (for Grand Canyon access) at Flagstaff. From Flagstaff, bus connections can be made for the final leg of the trip to the South Rim through **Nava-Hopi Tours** (☞ By Bus, *above*).

You can also finish your journey on a scenic rail trip. Travel from Flagstaff to Williams by bus—the cost is included in the price of the Amtrak ticket—and then continue to the Grand Canyon on a beautifully restored steam train of the Grand Canyon Railway (☞ Guided Tours, *below*).

Getting Around

By Car

Most of Arizona's scenic highlights are many miles apart, and an automobile is the most practical mode of transportation for touring the state. However, you won't really need a car if you're planning to visit only the Grand Canyon's most popular area, the South Rim. Many people choose to fly to the Grand Canyon and then hike, catch a shuttle or taxi, or sign on for bus tours or mule rides in Grand Canyon Village.

Keep in mind that summer car traffic leading to the South Rim is heavy—badly congested in the vicinity of Grand Canyon Village and the various parking areas along the rim. If you visit from October through April, you should experience only light to moderate traffic in the vicinity of the canyon. The more remote North Rim has no services available from late October through mid-May. Reaching elevations of more than 8,000 feet, the road is open for day use only until the first heavy snowfall of the year (generally in November or December), at which point roads close until spring. The South Rim stays open to auto traffic all year, though access to the West Rim is restricted in summer because of overcrowded roads.

CAUTION – When driving off major highways in low-lying areas, watch for rain clouds. Flash floods from sudden summer rains can be deadly (☞ Driving Precautions *in* Smart Travel Tips A to Z *for more information*).

By Shuttle Bus

In summer, free shuttle service on the South Rim is offered by the **National Park Service** (☎ 520/638–7888). Generally this service runs shuttles around Grand Canyon Village and the West Rim approximately every 15 minutes from 6:30 AM to 6:45 PM, late May through September. In addition, during these months free shuttles go to Yaki Point on a more limited basis. **Mayflower,** under the aegis of the National Park Service, runs a year-round shuttle taking hikers from the Backcountry Office (across from the visitor center), Maswik Lodge, and Bright Angel Lodge to South Kaibab Trailhead at Yaki Point; there are two departures every morning. Check for times upon arrival. From May 15 through the end of October, **Trans Canyon Van Service** (☎ 520/638–2820), a South Rim to North Rim shuttle, leaves from Bright Angel Lodge at 1:30 PM and arrives at the North Rim at about 6 PM; the return from Grand Canyon Lodge is at 7 AM, with arrival at the South Rim at about noon. The fare is $60 each way ($100 round-trip), and a 50% deposit is required two weeks in advance.

Contacts and Resources

Banks

An office of **Bank One** (☎ 520/638–2437) is located at the South Rim across from the visitor center in Grand Canyon Village. Services include a 24-hour teller machine operating with Bank One, Plus (Visa), Star, Arizona Interchange Network, and Cirrus (MasterCard) access cards. The bank cashes traveler's checks and exchanges foreign currency, but it does not usually cash personal checks. Banking hours are weekdays 10–3. No banking facilities are located within Grand Canyon National Park at the North Rim.

Bicycling

Bicycles are not permitted on any of the Grand Canyon's designated trails, but there are miles of scenic paved thoroughfares in the national park. Be aware, however, that the park roads have narrow shoulders and are heavily trafficked; use extreme caution. There are no rentals or tours available at either North or South Rim.

Car Rentals

It's imperative to make reservations in advance for the busy summer months; for the rest of the year, you'll avoid disappointment if you book a car well ahead of time. Be sure to ask about weekly rates and unlimited mileage opportunities.

Major companies serving Phoenix and Flagstaff include **Avis** (☎ 800/331–1212), **Budget** (☎ 800/527–0700), **Hertz** (☎ 800/654–3131), and **National Interrent** (☎ 800/227–7368). Budget is also represented at the Grand Canyon Airport.

Emergencies

Police, fire, or **ambulance** (☎ 911).

SOUTH RIM

Grand Canyon Health Center (✉ Grand Canyon Village, ☎ 520/638–2551 or 520/638–2469) offers physician services and receives patients weekdays 8–5:30, Saturday 9–noon. After-hours care and 24-hour emergency services are also available. Dental care (☎ 520/638–2395) is offered by appointment only.

NORTH RIM

The **North Rim Clinic** (✉ Grand Canyon Lodge, Cabin 1, ☎ 520/638–2611, ext. 222) is staffed by a nurse practitioner. The clinic is open for walk-ins and appointments Friday through Monday 9–noon and 3–6, and Tuesday 9–noon. For emergency service dial 911.

PHARMACIES

At the South Rim, the well-stocked **Grand Canyon Clinic Pharmacy** (☎ 520/638–2460) in Grand Canyon Village is open weekdays 8:30–5:30 year-round and also Saturday morning in the summer; it's generally closed for an hour at lunchtime during the week. There is no pharmacy at the North Rim.

Entrance Fees

Fees levied by the National Park Service vary depending on your method of entering Grand Canyon National Park. If you arrive by automobile, the fee is $10, regardless of the number of passengers. Individuals arriving by bicycle or on foot pay $4. The entrance gates are open 24 hours but are generally supervised from about 7 AM until 6:30 or 7 PM. If you arrive when there's no one at the gate, you may enter legally without paying.

Films

An exciting 34-minute historical film, *Grand Canyon—The Hidden Secrets,* is shown on the 70-foot-high screen at the IMAX theater. The script is informative, and some of the shots—especially those of boats running the rapids—are positively dizzying. ✉ *Tusayan,* ☎ *520/638–2203.* *$7.* *Mar. 1–Oct. 31, daily 8:30–8:30; rest of yr, daily 10:30–6:30; shows every hr on the ½ hr.*

Fishing

Contact the **Arizona Game and Fish Department** (✉ 2221 W. Greenway Rd., Phoenix, AZ 85023, ☎ 602/942–3000) to apply for a fishing license.

Food and Camping Supplies

SOUTH RIM

Babbitt's General Store has three locations in the South Rim area: at Grand Canyon Village (☎ 520/638–2262), in the nearby village of Tusayan (☎ 520/638–2854), and at Desert View (☎ 520/638–2393) near the east park entrance. The main store, in Grand Canyon Village, is a department store that has a deli and sells a full line of camping, hiking, and backpacking supplies in addition to groceries.

NORTH RIM

The **North Rim General Store** (☎ 520/638–2611), inside the park across from the North Rim Campground, carries groceries, some clothing, and travelers' supplies.

Guided Tours

BY BOAT

Wilderness River Adventures (☎ 800/992–8022) offers a seven-day excursion that includes hiking and white-water rafting along the Colorado River. Thirty-seven-foot motor rigs head downriver for 102 mi, and you camp for four nights along the way (food and camping equipment, as well as beer, are provided). You arrive at Whitmore Wash, where you are met by helicopters that fly you out to the beautiful Bar Ten Ranch for lunch and a shower. That's not all: A charter plane then picks you up at the ranch and flies you back to either Las Vegas or the Grand Canyon. The price for this excursion is $1,295.

BY BUS

From late May to late September, a free **shuttle bus service** is offered by the National Park Service (☞ Getting Around by Shuttle Bus, *above*) in the South Rim area. This does not provide a guided tour, but you can get a good feel for the region by taking advantage of trips through Grand Canyon Village, to Yavapai Museum, and to Hermits Rest on the West Rim. The **Fred Harvey Transportation Company** (☎ 520/638–2822 or 520/638–2631) in Grand Canyon Village provides a veritable menu of daily motor-coach sightseeing trips along the South Rim and to destinations as far away as Monument Valley on the Navajo reservation. Prices range from $12 for short trips to $80 for all-day tours. Children's half-price fares apply to those under 16 for in-park tours, under 12 on the longer out-of-park tours. For schedules, call the South Rim Reservations number (☎ 520/638–2401) or inquire at any Grand Canyon Lodge transportation desk (☞ Visitor Information, *below*). **TW Recreational Services, Inc.** (☎ 801/586–7686) offers an interpretive van tour of the North Rim ($20 adults, $10 children ages 4–12); schedules and other details are available in the lobby of the Grand Canyon Lodge.

BY MULE

Mule trips down the precipitous trails to the Inner Gorge of the Grand Canyon are nearly as well known as the canyon itself. But, especially for the summer season, it's very hard to get reservations unless you make them months in advance; write to the **Reservations Department** (✉ Box 699, Grand Canyon 86023, ☎ 520/638–2401). These trips have been conducted since the early 1900s, and no one has ever been killed by a mule falling off a cliff. Nevertheless, the treks are not for the faint of heart or people in questionable health. Riders must be at least 4 feet 7 inches tall, weigh less than 200 pounds, understand English, and they cannot be pregnant. Children under 15 must be accompanied by an adult. The all-day ride to Plateau Point costs $102 (lunch included). An overnight with a stay at Phantom Ranch at the bottom of the canyon (☞ East Rim Drive, *above*) is $250.25 ($447.50 for two) for one night, $347.50 ($589 for two) for two nights; meals are included in these prices.

BY PLANE

Flights over the Grand Canyon by airplane or helicopter are offered by a number of companies operating either from Grand Canyon Airport or from heliports in Tusayan. **Air Grand Canyon** (☎ 520/638–2618 or 800/247–4726) and **Grand Canyon Airlines** (☎ 520/638–2407 or 800/528–2413) fly small planes; **AirStar Helicopters** (☎ 520/638–2622 or 800/962–3869), **Papillon Helicopters** (☎ 520/638–2419 or 800/528–2418), and **Kenai Helicopters** (☎ 520/638–2412 or 800/541–4537) operate whirlybirds. Prices and length of flights vary greatly with tours, but they start at about $55 per person for short airplane flights and $90 per person for short helicopter runs. Inquiries and reservations can also be made at any Grand Canyon Lodge transportation desk (☞ Visitor Information, *below*).

BY TRAIN

The **Grand Canyon Railway** began running from Williams to the South Rim in 1989, offering a modern version of a route that was first established in 1901. The railroad had been out of operation since 1968, but an $85 million restoration put the old steam engines and Pullman cars back in business. The ride from the renovated station in Williams, about 2½ hours each way, has refreshments, commentary, and corny but fun on-board entertainment. Club Class, with its fully stocked mahogany bar and complimentary morning pastries and coffee, costs an additional $12. Chief Class, for an additional $50, gets you complimentary snacks, cocktails, and beverages, served in an elegant parlor car with spacious, overstuffed seats and a small, open-air platform. The company also offers a number of good tour and lodging packages. Even if you don't take the train, the impressive 1908 depot, railroad museum, and gift shop are worth visiting. ✉ *518 E. Bill Williams Ave., Williams 86046,* ☎ *800/843–8724.* 🎟 *Round-trip fare $49.* ⏲ *Departures from Williams Mar. 15–Oct. 30, daily 9:30 AM, return arrives in Williams at 5:30 PM.*

ON FOOT

The recently established **Grand Canyon Field Institute** (✉ Box 399, Grand Canyon 86023, ☎ 520/638–2485) leads educational guided hikes around the canyon from April through October. Tour topics include everything from archaeology and backcountry medicine to photography and landscape painting. All levels of hiking expertise are accommodated: Some classes involve easy day hikes, others long backpacking trips over rough terrain. Call or write to GCFI for a current class schedule and price list.

For a very personalized tour (for 5 to 10 people) of the Grand Canyon and surrounding sacred sites, contact **Marvelous Marv** (✉ Box 544, Williams 86046, ☎ 520/635–4948), the Indiana Jones of Williams, whose knowledge of the area is as extensive as his repertoire of local legends.

Hiking

Overnight hikes in the Grand Canyon require a permit that can be obtained only by written request to the **Backcountry Office** (✉Box 129, Grand Canyon 86023, ☎ 520/638–7888). Permits are extremely limited, and the office strongly recommends that reservations be made a full year in advance due to the ever-growing number of visitors to the park. If you arrive without a permit, go to the Backcountry Office at either rim: South Rim near the entrance to Mather Campground, North Rim at the ranger station. There is a slim chance that a cancellation will leave a space available.

SAFETY TIPS

You simply must carry water on hikes to the Inner Gorge—at least 1–1½ gallons per day. To avoid dehydration, it is important to drink frequently, about every 10 minutes, especially during summer months. Dehydration can affect you sooner than you think, and it is a serious danger that can be easily avoided. Likewise, take food—preferably energy snacks such as trail mix, bananas, and fig bars. Do not drink alcohol or caffeine, which accelerate dehydration; for the same reason, avoid processed sugar. Wear hiking boots that have been broken in and proven on previous hikes. Carry a first-aid kit. In case of a medical emergency, stay with the distressed person and ask the next hiker to go for help. Do not attempt to make the round-trip to the Colorado River in one day. The trek down is deceptively easy; the route back up is much longer than most other mountain day-hikes and very fatiguing.

Rafting

Although more than 25 companies currently offer excursions, reservations for raft trips (excluding smooth-water, one-day cruises) often need to be made more than six months in advance. For a complete list of river-raft companies, call ☎ 520/638–7888 from a touch-tone telephone and press 1-3-71, or write to request a *Trip Planner* (☞ Visitor Information, *below*). National Park Service white-water concessionaires include **Canyoneers, Inc.** (☎ 520/526–0924 or 800/525–0924 outside AZ); **Diamond River Adventures, Inc.** (☎ 520/645–8866 or 800/343–3121); **Expeditions, Inc.** (☎ 520/779–3769 or 520/774–8176); and **Outdoors Unlimited** (☎ 520/526–4546 or 800/637–7238).

Smooth-water, one-day-trip companies include **Fred Harvey Transportation Company** (☎ 520/638–2822 or 502/638–2631) and **Wilderness River Adventures** (☎ 520/645–32796 or 800/992-8022). Prices for river-raft trips vary greatly, depending on type and length. Half-day trips on smooth water run as low as $40 per person; trips that negotiate the entire length of the canyon and take as long as 12 days can cost close to $2,000.

Road Service

SOUTH RIM

At Grand Canyon Village, the **Fred Harvey Public Garage** (☎ 520/638–2631) is a fully equipped AAA garage that provides auto and RV repair from 8 to 5 daily (closed 12–1 for lunch) as well as 24-hour emergency service. About ¾ mile down the road, across from the visitor center, **Fred Harvey Chevron** (☎ 520/638–2631) does minor repairs, oil and tire changes, and carries propane and diesel fuel.

NORTH RIM

The **Chevron** service station (☎ 520/638–2611), offering auto repairs, is located inside the park on the access road leading to the North Rim Campground. No diesel fuel is available at the North Rim.

Safety Tips

Be careful when you or your children are near the edge of the canyon or walking any of the trails that descend into it. Guardrails exist only on portions of the rims. Tragically, a few visitors are killed each year in falls from viewing points. Before engaging in any strenuous exercise, be aware that the canyon rims are more than 7,000 feet in altitude. Being at this height can cause some people—even those in good shape—to become dizzy, faint, or nauseated. Before hiking into the canyon, assess the distance of the proposed hike against your physical condition. Although the descent may not be especially difficult, coming back up can be very strenuous. Be sure to take sufficient water and food on hikes into the canyon (☞ Hiking, *above*). During summer months, temperatures in the Inner Gorge can climb above 105°F.

Skiing

Though you can't schuss down into the Grand Canyon, you can cross-country ski in the woods near the rim when there's enough snow. **Babbits General Store** in the South Rim's Grand Canyon Village (☎ 520/638–2234 or 520/638–2262) rents equipment and can guide you to the best trails.

For downhill skiing, you may wish to visit the **Arizona Snowbowl** (☞ Flagstaff and Environs *in* Chapter 4), northwest of Flagstaff. It's larger than the Williams Ski Area (☞ Outdoor Activities and Sports *in* Williams, *above*), though still small by Rocky Mountain standards; it tends to be very crowded in season.

Telephones

You're likely to have a hard time getting through to the Grand Canyon: Trunk lines into the area are limited and often overloaded with people calling this most popular of Arizona's attractions. You'll get a fast busy signal if this is the case. In addition, when you do get through to the National Park Service or South Rim Reservations numbers—which handle many of the services listed in this chapter—you'll have to punch a lot of numbers on a computer-voice system before you reach the service you want. Be patient; it's possible to get through to a human being eventually. Writing ahead for the information-packed *Trip Planner* (☞ Visitor Information, *below*) is likely to save you a phone call. Remember, too, that the park does not accept reservations for backcountry permits by phone; they must be made in writing.

Traveling with Children

The Grand Canyon is family vacation country, and most activities can be enjoyed by all ages. However, many of the daily activities at both the North and South rims, detailed in the free Grand Canyon newspaper, *The Guide,* will appeal especially to children. In addition, the Junior Ranger program, geared toward those ages 4 through 12, introduces kids to the concept of caring for the national parks via an activities checklist found in *Young Adventurer,* a publication available at the South Rim Visitor Center and the Tusayan and Yavapai museums.

Visitor Information

Every arriving visitor at the South or North Rim is given a detailed map of the area. Both rims also publish a free newspaper, *The Guide,* which contains a detailed area map; it is available at the visitor center and many of the lodging facilities and stores. The park also distributes "Accessibility Guide," a free newsletter that details the facilities accessible to travelers with disabilities.

In summer, transportation-services desks are maintained at **Bright Angel Lodge, Maswik Lodge,** and **Yavapai Lodge** in Grand Canyon Village; in winter, the one at Yavapai is closed. The desks provide information and handle bookings, sightseeing tours, taxi and bus services, mule and horseback rides, and accommodations at Phantom Ranch (at the bottom of the Grand Canyon). The concierge at **El Tovar** can also arrange most tours, with the exception of mule rides and lodging at Phantom Ranch.

Grand Canyon Lodge (✉ TW Recreational Services, Inc., Box 400, Cedar City, UT 84720, ☎ 801/586–7686, FAX 801/586–3157) has lodging and general information about the North Rim year-round. For information on local services during the season in which the North Rim is open (generally mid-May through late October, depending on the weather), you can phone the lodge directly (☎ 520/638–2611).

Grand Canyon National Park Lodges (✉ Box 699, Grand Canyon 86023, ☎ 520/638–2401, FAX 520/638–9247) can provide information on lodging, tours, and all other recreation inside the park at the South Rim.

Grand Canyon National Park (✉ Box 129, Grand Canyon 86023, ☎ 520/638–7888) is the contact for general information. Write ahead for a complimentary *Trip Planner,* updated regularly by the National Park Service.

Williams and Forest Service Visitor Center (✉ 200 W. Railroad Ave., at Grand Canyon Blvd., Williams 86046, ☎ 520/635–4061), run jointly by the National Forest Service, the city of Williams, and the Williams Chamber of Commerce, has information on Williams, Kaibab Forest, and the entire Grand Canyon area.

North and South Rim Camping (✉ Mistix, Box 85705, San Diego, CA 92138, ☎ 800/365–2267 or 619/452–0150 outside the U.S.) provides information on camping in the park. When you call this computer-operated system, have the exact dates you'd like to camp on hand.

Weather

Weather information and road conditions for both the North and South rims, updated at 7 AM daily, can be obtained by calling ☎ 520/638–7888.

In general, the South Rim, with an elevation of 7,000 feet, has summer temperatures that range from lows in the 50s to highs in the upper 80s. There are frequent afternoon thunderstorms. The area cools off quickly when the sun goes down, so be sure to bring a sweater or light jacket for the evening. Winter temperatures have average lows around 20°F and highs near 50°F, with the mercury occasionally dropping below zero. In spring and fall, temperatures generally stay above 32°F and often climb into the 70s. The North Rim, accessed through country that ranges in altitude from 8,000 to 9,000 feet, gets heavy winter snow and is thus open to the public only from mid-May through October. Temperatures during this open season range from lows in the 30s to highs in the 70s. As in the South Rim, afternoon rain is common; in May and October, it occasionally snows as well. As you proceed down either rim toward the canyon's Inner Gorge, temperatures rise. In summer along the Colorado River—at an elevation of about 2,400 feet—temperatures range from lows in the 70s to highs above 100°F. Winter sees lows in the 30s, highs around 50°F. It rarely snows at the bottom of the Grand Canyon, even in winter; snow on the rims usually turns to rain as it falls into the Inner Gorge.

3 The Northeast

To the Navajo and Hopi people who inhabit northeastern Arizona, the land is their spiritual guide as well as history book. From the echoing ancestral red canyons to the windswept desert and mountains of towering ponderosa pine, the land is full of sacred symbols, legends, and memories. Visitors to the area are enchanted by the ancient Pueblo ruins at the Navajo National Monument and Canyon de Chelly, the sculpted rock formations of Monument Valley, the brilliant hues of the Painted Desert, and the jade-green waters of rugged Lake Powell.

By William E. Hafford

Updated by Susana C. Sedgwick

A **VAST AND LONELY LAND** of shifting red dunes, soaring buttes, and turquoise skies so clear that horizons are almost always 100 mi or more away, northeastern Arizona covers more than 30,000 square mi. Most of the northeast belongs to the Navajo and Hopi peoples, who have held on to ancient cultural traditions that are based on strong spiritual values and an affinity for nature. Excellent Native American arts and crafts can be found in shops, galleries, and trading posts throughout the region. Visiting here is like crossing into a foreign country—one that is, sadly, less prosperous than much of the rest of the United States. In some respects, life on the Hopi Mesas seems to resemble what it must have been in the last century, and it's not uncommon to hear Navajo spoken in towns such as Tuba City and Window Rock.

The Navajo reservation, known to its people as the Navajo Nation, spreads across some 25,000 square mi of the northeastern corner of Arizona. In its approximate center lie 4,000 square mi of Hopi reservation, a series of stone and adobe villages built on high mesas overlooking cultivated land. And on Arizona's northern and eastern borders, where the Navajo Nation continues into Utah, Colorado, and New Mexico, the stunning topographies of Navajo National Monument and Canyon de Chelly contain some of the haunting cliff dwellings of ancient Pueblo people who lived in the four corners area.

Outside of Navajo country are two of the most popular attractions in the area. Just below the southeastern boundary of the reservation, straddling I–40, the Petrified Forest National Park is an intriguing geological open book of the earth's distant past. The park includes a large portion of the famed Painted Desert, whose name describes the stratified bands of multicolored hills in which ancient life-forms and huge fallen tree trunks have petrified over hundreds of millions of years. Glen Canyon Dam abuts the far northwestern corner of the reservation on U.S. 89. Behind that, more than 120 mi of the emerald waters of Lake Powell are held in precipitous canyons of erosion-carved stone.

Most of the northeast is arid land, with soil and rock formations ranging in astonishing colors from delicate salmon pink to rusty orange and even red—this, too, is painted desert. Immense mesas, rock spires, canyons, cliffs, and some impressive mountain ranges make up the landscape. Inviting stands of ponderosa pine cover the Chuska Mountains to the north and east of Canyon de Chelly. Navajo Mountain to the north and west in Utah soars above 10,000 feet.

Pleasures and Pastimes

Dining

Because northeastern Arizona is a vast area and few communities offer eating establishments, visitors should keep in mind that the following major locations have restaurants: Cameron, Tuba City, Page, Kayenta, Goulding's Trading Post–Monument Valley, Hopi Second Mesa, Keams Canyon, Chinle, Ganado, Window Rock, Fort Defiance, Holbrook, and Winslow. Few restaurants offer fine dining, but there are opportunities to taste very good Native American food. Some eateries serve Mexican dishes; most serve standard American fare. In the smaller reservation communities, only fast food may be available. For the most part, dress is casual, seating is on a first-come, first-served basis, and prices are reasonable. Only in the Page–Lake Powell area at the height of the summer season do we advise making reservations.

CATEGORY	COST*
$$$$	over $25
$$$	$15–$25
$$	$10–$15
$	under $10

**per person, excluding drinks, service, and sales tax (9.5% in Page), except on the Hopi and Navajo reservations, where no tax is charged.*

Fishing

Lake Powell and the area below Glen Canyon Dam are excellent fishing sites. Lake Powell hosts 16 varieties of fish, including largemouth bass, black crappie, striped bass, bluegill, green sunfish, carp, smallmouth bass, threadfin, shad, walleye, rainbow trout, channel catfish, brown trout, and northern pike, while the Colorado River below Glen Canyon Dam is known for its large trout. Keep in mind that Lake Powell stretches through both Arizona and Utah, and an appropriate permit is required depending on where you fish. The eastern region of the Navajo reservation has scattered lakes, most of them remote and small, that contain game fish. Two of the more popular and accessible lakes are in the vicinity of Canyon de Chelly: Wheatfields Lake, on Indian Highway 12 about 11 mi south of the community of Tsaile, and Many Farms Lake, near the community of Many Farms, on U.S. 191. Permits are always required for fishing on the reservation.

Hiking

There are many excellent places to hike at the national monuments, tribal parks, and other points of interest in this vast area. Some of the best hikes are in Canyon de Chelly, up the streambed between the soaring orange-and-white sandstone cliffs, with the remains of the old Pueblo communities frequently in view. Along the sandstone walls lie some of the most pristine of Anasazi ruins anywhere. Among them are Antelope House, White House, Sliding Rock, and Mummy Cave, each a fine example of ancient Anasazi architectural ingenuity. Mummy Cave is especially worth a look: The vast, ancient apartment house lies atop the remains of even earlier structures that are at least 2,000 years old, and its three-story watchtower is nearly perfectly preserved. The more weathered Antelope House and White House stand against the sweeping canyon cliffs—impressive reminders of a bygone era.

Hopi Ceremonies

The Hopi are well known for colorful ceremonial dances, many of which are supplications for rain, fertile crops, and harmony with nature. Most of these ceremonies take place in village plazas and kivas (underground ceremonial chambers) and last two days or longer; outsiders are permitted to watch only certain segments and are never allowed into kivas. Dancers may wear masks and beaded costumes, beat drums, and chant. The best known is the snake dance, in which participants carry live snakes, including poisonous rattlers. However, this ceremony has not been open to the public in recent years. Seasonal kachina dances have also been restricted: Now only those in Moenkopi, Old Oraibi, Hotevilla, and Kykotsmovi may be observed by those who are not Native American. Dances that visitors are allowed to watch usually take place on weekends, extending through the day until dusk. Each tribal clan has its own sacred rituals, starting times, and dates, which are determined by tribal elders. Visitors should be respectful and adhere to the proper etiquette while observing dances.

Lodging

Northeastern Arizona is a large territory with few people and long distances between communities. When you travel here, a top priority is making sure that you have a place to lay your head at the end of the day. Half the battle is knowing which of the scattered communities have motels. During summer months, it is especially wise to make reservations. Fortunately, most motels throughout the northeast are clean, comfortable, and well maintained.

Because of a demand for accommodations in the area, bed-and-breakfasts have begun to proliferate in Page in the last few years. Zoning restrictions currently prevent them from being anything other than informal homestays, but that is likely to change soon.

Although Navajo–Hopi country stretches thousands of square miles across an open and sparsely populated region, visitors are allowed to camp only in posted authorized areas. Most campgrounds are primitive, in many cases nothing more than open, level areas where sleeping bags can be laid out or RVs can be parked; outside the Lake Powell area, only Monument Valley has developed camping facilities.

Unless otherwise indicated, all the establishments listed have air-conditioning, private baths, telephones, and TVs in their rooms.

CATEGORY	COST*
$$$	over $80
$$	$50–$80
$	under $50

**All prices are for a standard double room at summer rates (rates may be lower at other times), excluding hotel tax: 10.5% in the Page area, 8% on the Navajo reservation. No hotel tax is charged on the Hopi reservation.*

Native American Reservations

Visitors to the Navajo Nation and Hopi reservation have the opportunity to gain an understanding of the lives, past and present, of some of our land's true founding mothers and fathers. Both the Hopi and Navajo peoples are friendly to tourists. Their privacy, customs, and laws should be respected:

- Do not wander across residential areas or disturb property.
- Always ask permission before taking photographs of the locals; you may have to pay to take the picture.
- Do not litter.
- No open fires are allowed; fires are permitted only in grills and fireplaces. Bring your own wood or charcoal.
- Observe quiet hours from 11 PM until 6 AM at all camping areas.
- Do not disturb or remove animals, plants, rocks, or artifacts. They are protected by Tribal Antiquity and federal laws, which are strictly enforced.
- The possession and consumption of alcoholic beverages or drugs is illegal.
- No off-trail hiking or rock climbing is allowed.
- A permit is required for fishing in lakes or streams or for hunting game; the use of firearms is otherwise prohibited.
- Off-road travel by four-wheel-drive vehicles, dune buggies, Jeeps, and motorcycles is not allowed.
- Do not wear bikinis or similar scanty clothing in public.
- Pets should be kept on a leash or in a confined area.
- On the Hopi reservation, taking photographs or making videos, tape recordings, and sketches of villages and ceremonies is strictly prohibited. At all sacred events, neat attire and a respectful demeanor are requested. Camping is permitted for a maximum of two nights, but only in designated areas. All Hopi villages have separate rules about visitors; check with the individual village Community Development Offices or call the Hopi Tribe Office of Public Relations (☞ The Northeast A to Z, *below*) in advance for information.

Shopping

Most visitors to the area are tempted by pottery, turquoise and sterling-silver jewelry, handwoven baskets, beautiful and often expensive Navajo wool rugs, and other examples of Native American crafts. In addition to the work of Hopi and Navajo artisans, many of the trading posts also carry the work of New Mexico's tribes, including exquisite inlaid Zuni jewelry and the world-acclaimed pottery of the Pueblo people. Many vendors have roadside stands that resemble Navajo shade arbors. Most products offered on the Hopi and Navajo reservations are authentic, but the possibility of imitations still exists. The trading posts are usually reliable.

Exploring The Northeast

The Navajo Nation, which encompasses the Hopi reservation, occupies most of the northeastern part of Arizona. The Canyon de Chelly is in the eastern part of the reservation, and the Petrified Forest National Park, including much of the Painted Desert, lies to the southeast. In the northwestern corner of the state are Lake Powell and Glen Canyon Dam.

Great Itineraries

Numbers in the text correspond to points of interest on the Northeast Arizona map.

IF YOU HAVE 2 TO 3 DAYS

If you're based in Holbrook or Winslow, you'll have an easy drive to some of the most interesting sights in northeastern Arizona. On your first day you might visit the Petrified Forest National Park ② and, on the second, set out for the Hopi Mesas ⑧–⑩, stopping at the Homolovi Ruins State Park ① along the way. Alternatively, you might consider starting out from Flagstaff or Holbrook and heading to Window Rock ③, visiting the marvels of the Petrified Forest en route. Spend the first night at the Navajo Nation Inn in Window Rock. The next day head west on State Highway 264 for about 70 mi to Keams Canyon Trading Post ⑦, where you can have lunch and do some exploring before pushing on to the Hopi Mesas and a night at the Hopi Cultural Center on Second Mesa ⑨. If you don't want to spend the night in Hopi country, move on to Tuba City ⑪ or to the highly recommended motel at the Cameron Trading Post ⑫.

IF YOU HAVE 5 DAYS

Spend your first night at the comfortable motel at the Cameron Trading Post ⑫. The next morning make your way north on U.S. Highway 89 to Tuba City ⑪, the last stop for gas before heading east at Moenkopi on State Highway 264 for the Hopi Mesas ⑧–⑩. Have lunch at the pleasant restaurant at the Hopi Cultural Center. Returning to Tuba City, head north on U.S. Highway 160 toward Kayenta ⑬, where you can spend your second night. Get up early the next day to visit the Navajo National Monument ⑰ and hike to Betatakin or Keet Seel pueblo (if you have made reservations in advance). Spend your third night at the renowned lodge at Goulding's Trading Post ⑯ in Monument Valley. The next day, visit Monument Valley Navajo Tribal Park ⑭, and then take U.S. Highway 160 north to where it connects with Highway 191 near the town of Mexican Water. Head south for Chinle, a good base for touring magnificent Canyon de Chelly ⑤.

IF YOU HAVE 7 DAYS

We recommend that you extend the itinerary for five days by staying another night in Chinle to explore the Canyon de Chelly ⑤, and spend a night in Holbrook to give yourself time to visit the Petrified Forest National Park ②.

When to Tour the Northeast

Summer is a busy time in the Lake Powell area, and reservations for accommodations are essential. Travelers seeking a quieter vacation should plan a visit during late October through early May, when there are fewer people and lower prices.

September is a good time to be at Window Rock, when the Navajo Nation Annual Tribal Fair takes place. It's the world's largest Native American fair, and includes a rodeo, traditional Navajo music and dances, food booths, and an intertribal powwow.

THE PETRIFIED FOREST NATIONAL PARK AND THE PAINTED DESERT

Numbers in the margin correspond to points of interest on the Northeast Arizona map.

Homolovi Ruins State Park

❶ *65 mi east of Flagstaff, 8 mi northeast of Winslow, 24 mi west of Holbrook.*

Three mi northeast of Winslow off AZ 87 is the site of five major ancestral Hopi pueblos. There are 40 ceremonial kivas thought to date from AD 900, and one pueblo contains more than 700 rooms. The Hopi believe their immediate ancestors inhabited this place, and they still hold the site to be sacred. The Homolovi Visitor's Center is located within the park, about 1½ mi from AZ 87. ✉ *HC 63, Box 5, Winslow 86047,* ☎ *520/289–4106.*

NEED A BREAK? Stop in at one of Winslow's Old Route 66 diners for a blast-from-the-past lunch.

Lodging

☞ Dining and Lodging *in* Petrified Forest National Park, *below.*

CAMPING

⛺ **Homolovi State Park Campgrounds.** The 52 sites and electric hookups are open year-round. Water and showers are available mid-April to mid-October. Prices are $8 per night for non-hookup, $13 for hookup. ✉ *1.3 mi from I–40 off AZ 87,* ☎ *520/289–4106.*

Petrified Forest National Park

★ ❷ *54 mi east of Homolovi Ruins State Park, 30 mi east of Holbrook.*

A visit to the Petrified Forest is a trip back in geological time. In 1984 the fossil remains of one of the oldest dinosaurs ever unearthed—dating from the Triassic period of the Mesozoic era 225 million years ago—were discovered here; other plant and animal fossils in the park date from the same period. Remnants of ancient human beings and their artifacts, dating from some 8,000 years ago, have been recovered at more than 500 sites in this national park.

The park derives its name from the fact that the grounds are also covered with petrified tree trunks whose wood cells were fossilized over centuries by brightly hued mineral deposits—silica, iron oxide, manganese, aluminum, copper, lithium, and carbon. In many places, petrified logs scattered about the landscape resemble a fairy-tale forest turned to stone. Most of the park's 94,000 acres include portions of the vast, pink-hued lunarlike landscape known as the Painted Desert. In the northern area of the park, this colorful but essentially barren and waterless series of windswept plains, hills, and mesas is considered by geologists to be part of the Chinle formation, deposited at an early stage of the Triassic period. Colors are most dramatic at dawn and sunset, when oblique light enhances the earth tones, making smaller chasms glow deep red.

Because so many looters hauled away large quantities of petrified wood in the early years of this century, President Theodore Roosevelt made the area a national monument in 1906. Since then, it has been illegal (not to mention bad karma) to remove even a small sliver of petrified wood from the park (there are plenty of pieces on sale at the visitor-center gift shop if you want a souvenir).

You can easily spend most of a day on the park's 28 mi of paved roads and walking trails. A number of lookouts on the north end of the park provide beautiful Painted Desert vistas. Fascinating Native American petroglyphs survive on boulders at Newspaper Rock. The area around **Jasper Forest** contains stunning hunks of petrified trees scattered on the desert floor. Near the southern end of the park, **Agate House** is a structure assembled from pieces of petrified wood. And the self-guided **Giant Logs Trail** starts at the Rainbow Forest Museum and Visitor Center and loops through a half mile of huge fallen trees. One of the ancient, fallen trunks measures more than 6 feet in diameter.

★ At the north entrance of the park, the Painted Desert Visitor Center shows a movie entitled *The Stone Forest,* tracing the natural history of the area. The **Rainbow Forest Museum and Visitor Center,** located at the south entrance (off U.S. 180), displays three skeletons from the Triassic period, including that of the ferocious phytosaur, a crocodile-like carnivore. The museum has numerous exhibits relating to the world of cycads (tropical plants), ferns, fish, and other early life, as well as artifacts and tools of ancient humans. Within the park's boundaries, visitors also have access to gift shops, a restaurant, a soda fountain, and a service station. Picnicking is allowed inside the park. You may hike into the nearby wilderness areas to camp, but you must obtain a park permit for an overnight stay. Free permits are issued at both visitor centers (☞ *above*). ✉ *North entrance: off I–40, 25 mi east of Holbrook. South entrance: off U.S. 180, 19 mi southeast of Holbrook. Box 2217, Petrified Forest, AZ 86028,* ☎ *520/524–6228.* *$5 per vehicle.* ⏲ *Daily 7:30–5.*

Dining and Lodging

$–$$ ✕ **Butterfield Stage Coach Restaurant.** Easily identifiable by the stagecoach perched on its roof (a landmark from old Route 66 days), the Stage Coach serves predictable but reliable steak-and-roast-beef fare. It also has a salad bar and children's menu. ✉ *609 Hopi Dr., Holbrook 86025,* ☎ *520/524–3447.*

$ **Wigwam Motel.** Classic Route 66 kitsch, the Wigwam consists of 15 bright white cement wigwams where you can sleep inexpensively in a surreal environment. ✉ *811 W. Hopi Dr., Holbrook 86025,* ☎ *520/524–3048.*

NAVAJO NATION EAST

Window Rock

❸ *82 mi northeast of the Petrified Forest National Park, 192 mi northeast of Flagstaff, 26 mi northwest of Gallup, New Mexico (via U.S. 666 and NM 264).*

Named for an immense hole in a massive sandstone ridge nearby, Window Rock is the capital of the Navajo Nation. With a population of fewer than 5,000, this community serves as the business and social center for countless Navajo families from the surrounding areas. It is also the home of the **Navajo Nation Council Chambers,** a handsome structure that resembles a large hogan—the traditional eight-sided, domed Navajo house. Visitors can observe sessions of the council, where 88 delegates representing 100 reservation communities meet on the third Monday of January, April, July, and October. Sessions are conducted mostly in the Navajo language. When the council is not being held, you can walk around the chamber, where colorful murals decorate the walls. Window Rock Navajo Tribal Park is near the Council Chambers. It is a pleasant picnic area with juniper trees and allows for a close view of the huge rock formation. ✉ *Council Chambers: turn east off Indian Hwy. 12, about ½ mi from AZ 264.*

A short drive south of Tribal Park is the **Navajo Tribal Museum,** a small space devoted to the art and culture of the region and the history of the Navajo people; there's an excellent selection of books on the Navajo Nation here. In the same building, the **Navajo Arts and Crafts Enterprise** (☞ Shopping, *below*) displays local artwork, including pottery, jewelry, and blankets. ✉ *On AZ 264, next to Navajo Nation Inn. Museum:* ☎ *520/871–6673.* 🎫 *Free.* ⏲ *Weekdays 8–4:45. Enterprise:* ☎ *520/871–4095.* 🎫 *Free.* ⏲ *Apr.–Oct., Mon.–Sat. 8–6; Nov.–Mar., weekdays 8–5 (often later during busy season, from Thanksgiving to Jan. 1).*

If you're curious about wildlife in northeastern Arizona, stop at the **Navajo Nation Zoological Park,** just east of the Navajo Tribal Museum. Set amid sandstone monoliths are indigenous birds and animals that figure in Navajo legends—golden eagles, hawks, elk, wolves, cougars, and coyotes, among others. ✉ *East of Navajo Nation Inn and north of AZ 264.* 🎫 *Free.* ⏲ *Daily 8–5.*

Window Rock is a good place to stop for food, supplies, and gas. Near the center of downtown, the **Navajo Tribal Fairgrounds** is the site of many all-Indian rodeos (in the Navajo Nation, many Indians are cowboys). The community hosts the annual July 4 Powwow, with a major rodeo, ceremonial dances, and a parade, and the Navajo Nation Tribal Fair, much like a traditional state fair, in early September. *Contact the Navajo Nation Fair Office at* ☎ *520/871–4941 for information about both events.*

Dining and Lodging

$$ ✕🏨 **Navajo Nation Inn.** Native American officials in town on government business frequently stay in this motel in the Navajo Nation's tribal capital. The exterior is typical of contemporary roadside motels, but the rooms have been pleasantly decorated with Spanish colonial furniture and Navajo art. The inexpensive restaurant serves standard American as well as Navajo entrées; the mutton stew is hearty, and the tasty fry-bread taco could easily feed two. ✉ *48 W. Hwy 264, Box 2340, Window Rock 86515,* ☎ *520/871–4108 or 800/662–6189 (reservations only),* FAX *520/871–5466. 56 units. Restaurant, meeting rooms. AE, DC, MC, V.*

CAMPING

⛺ **Summit Campground.** The campground is open year-round and may charge a fee of $1 per person. There are picnic tables but no water. ✉ *Off AZ 264, 9 mi west of Window Rock,* ☎ *520/871–6645.*

⛺ **Tse Bonito Tribal Park.** Set among sandstone monoliths, this campground is a historically significant site: The Navajo camped here before

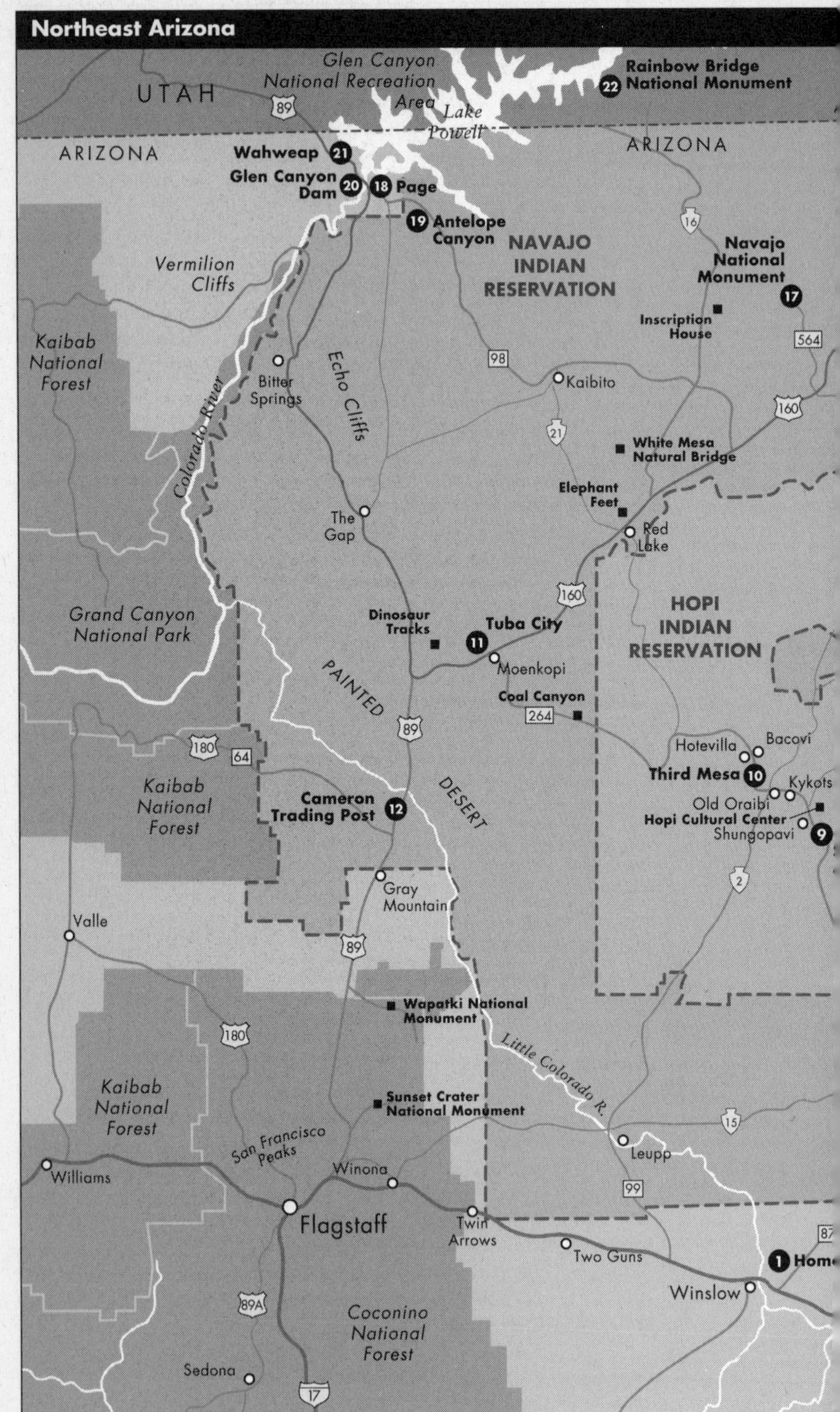
Northeast Arizona
Glen Canyon National Recreation Area
UTAH
89
Lake Powell
Rainbow Bridge National Monument 22
ARIZONA
Wahweap 21
Glen Canyon Dam 20
18 Page
19 Antelope Canyon
ARIZONA
16
NAVAJO INDIAN RESERVATION
Navajo National Monument 17
Inscription House
564
Vermilion Cliffs
Kaibab National Forest
Bitter Springs
Echo Cliffs
98
Kaibito
160
21
White Mesa Natural Bridge
Elephant Feet
Red Lake
Colorado River
The Gap
Grand Canyon National Park
160
Dinosaur Tracks
Tuba City 11
Moenkopi
HOPI INDIAN RESERVATION
PAINTED DESERT
Coal Canyon
264
89
180
64
Hotevilla
Bacovi
Third Mesa 10
Kykots
Old Oraibi
Hopi Cultural Center
Shungopavi
9
Kaibab National Forest
Cameron Trading Post 12
Gray Mountain
2
Valle
89
Wapatki National Monument
180
Little Colorado R.
Kaibab National Forest
Sunset Crater National Monument
15
San Francisco Peaks
Leupp
Williams
Winona
99
Flagstaff
Twin Arrows
87
Two Guns
1 Hom
Winslow
89A
Coconino National Forest
Sedona
17

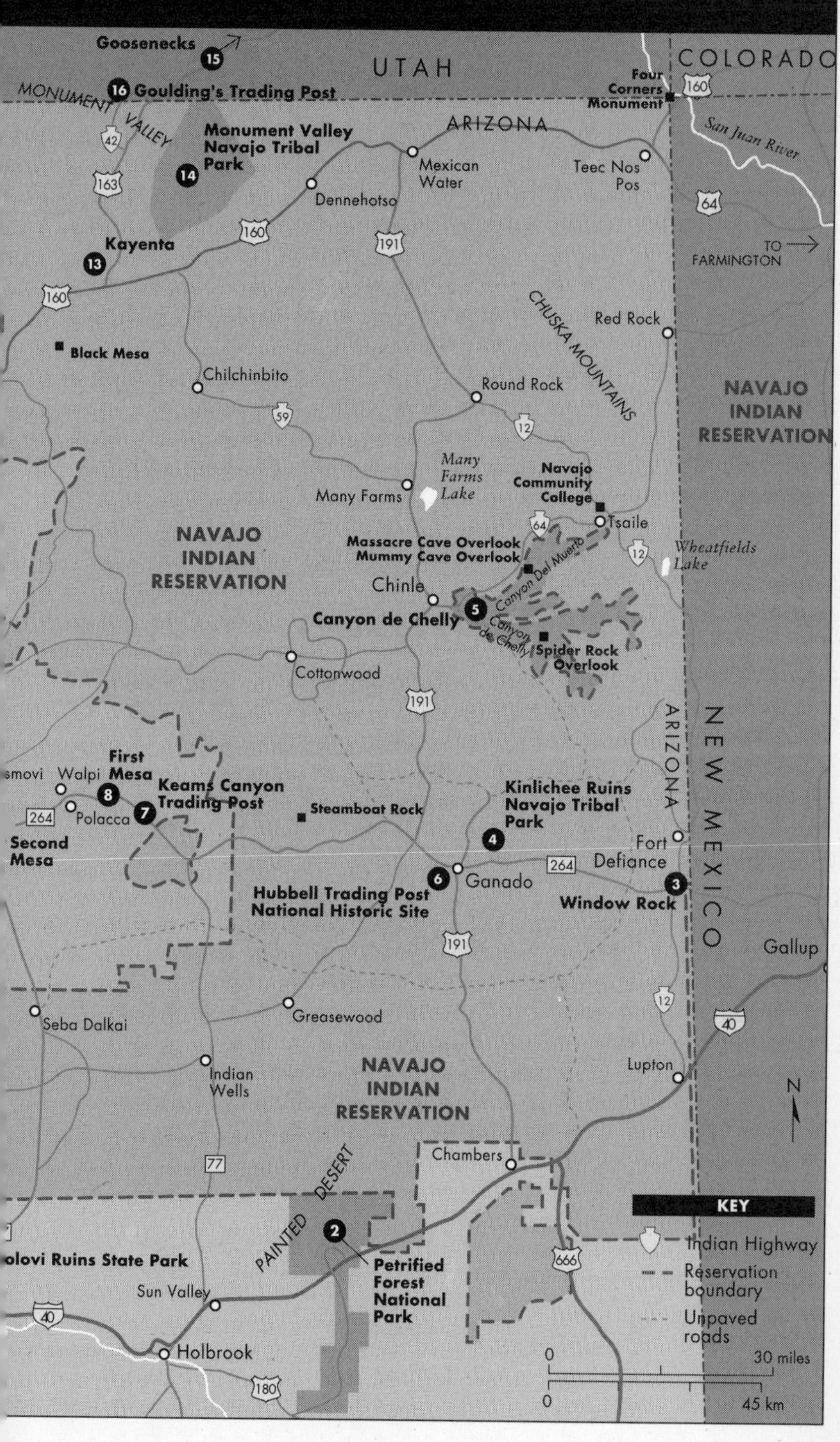
Goosenecks
15
UTAH
16 Goulding's Trading Post
MONUMENT VALLEY
Monument Valley Navajo Tribal Park
14
Kayenta
13
Black Mesa
Dennehotso
Mexican Water
ARIZONA
Four Corners Monument
COLORADO
San Juan River
Teec Nos Pos
TO FARMINGTON
CHUSKA MOUNTAINS
Red Rock
Chilchinbito
Round Rock
Many Farms Lake
Many Farms
Navajo Community College
Tsaile
Wheatfields Lake
NAVAJO INDIAN RESERVATION
Massacre Cave Overlook
Mummy Cave Overlook
Canyon Del Muerto
Chinle
5
Canyon de Chelly
Spider Rock Overlook
Cottonwood
First Mesa
Walpi
8
7
Keams Canyon Trading Post
Polacca
Second Mesa
Steamboat Rock
Kinlichee Ruins Navajo Tribal Park
4
Fort Defiance
6
Ganado
3
Window Rock
Hubbell Trading Post National Historic Site
ARIZONA
NEW MEXICO
Gallup
Seba Dalkai
Greasewood
Indian Wells
Lupton
Chambers
PAINTED DESERT
2
Petrified Forest National Park
olovi Ruins State Park
Sun Valley
Holbrook
KEY
Indian Highway
Reservation boundary
Unpaved roads
0
30 miles
0
45 km
N

being forced on the Long Walk to Fort Summer. There are shaded picnic tables and nearby rest rooms but no water. A fee of $2 per person may be charged. ✉ *Near AZ 264, Window Rock,* ☎ *520/871–6645.*

Shopping

An outlet of the **Navajo Arts and Crafts Enterprises** (✉ Off AZ 264, next to Navajo Nation Inn, ☎ 520/871–4090 or 520/871–4095) stocks authentic Navajo products.

Kinlichee Ruins Navajo Tribal Park

❹ *22 mi west of Window Rock.*

A marked road leads to this 640-acre park, where you'll see dwellings built by ancestral Pueblo people. The park, which is always open, has a self-guided trail that takes you past the ruins and trailside exhibits (you are not permitted to descend into the kiva pit). There are also picnic areas and a primitive campground. A camping fee of $1 per person may be collected.

Canyon de Chelly

★ ❺ *40 mi north of Kinlichee Ruins Navajo Tribal Park.*

The nearly 84,000-acre Canyon de Chelly (pronounced duh-*shay*) is one of the most spectacular national monuments in the Southwest. Its main gorges—the 26-mile-long **Canyon de Chelly** and the adjoining 35-mile **Canyon del Muerto**—have sheer, heavily eroded sandstone walls that reach up to 1,000 feet. Ancient pictographs decorate some of the cliffs. Gigantic stone formations rise hundreds of feet above small streams, hogans, tilled fields, peach orchards, and grazing lands. Although the monument is administered by the National Park Service, the land itself belongs to the Navajo.

The first inhabitants of the canyons, ancestral Pueblo people, arrived more than 2,000 years ago and constructed stone cliff dwellings. Their departure around AD 1300 is widely believed to have resulted from changing climatic conditions, soil erosion, and dwindling local resources. Present-day Hopis see these people as their ancestors, who quite simply moved to find a better place to live. Beginning around AD 780, Hopi farmers settled here, followed by the Navajo around 1000. Centuries-old traditions have been passed down to the Navajo families who now live, farm, and raise sheep in the area.

Both Canyon de Chelly and Canyon del Muerto have a paved rim drive (each takes about two hours) with marvelous views of the great canyon. Prehistoric ruins can be found near the base of cliffs or perched on high, sheltering ledges. The dwellings and cultivated fields of the present-day Navajo lie in the flatlands between the cliffs. The Navajo who inhabit the canyon today farm much the way their ancestors did.

The **South Rim Drive** (36 mi round-trip) of Canyon de Chelly starts at the visitor center and ends at **Spider Rock Overlook,** where cliffs plunge 1,000 feet. Here you'll have a view of two pinnacles, Speaking Rock and Spider Rock; the latter rises about 800 feet from the canyon floor. Other highlights on the South Rim Drive are **Junction Overlook,** where Canyon del Muerto joins Canyon de Chelly; **White House Overlook** (☞ *below*), which allows access to the canyon floor; and **Sliding House Overlook,** where you can see ruins on a narrow, sloped ledge across the canyon.

The **North Rim Drive** (34 mi round-trip) of Canyon del Muerto also begins at the visitor center and continues northeast on Indian Highway 64 toward the town of Tsaile. Major stops on this drive include **Ante-**

lope House Overlook, the site of a large ruin named for the animals painted on an adjacent cliff; the **Mummy Cave Overlook,** where two mummies were found inside a remarkably unspoiled pueblo dwelling, the monument's largest; and **Massacre Cave Overlook,** the last stop on the drive, which marks the spot where 115 Navajo were killed by the Spanish in 1805. In Tsaile, Navajo medicine men worked in conjunction with architects to design the town's six-story **Navajo Community College.** Because all important Navajo activities traditionally take place in a circle (a hogan is essentially circular), the campus was laid out in the round, with all of the buildings within its perimeter. The college's **Hatathli Museum** is devoted to Native American culture. To the north of Tsaile are the impressive **Chuska Mountains,** covered with sprawling stands of ponderosa pine. Although there are no established hiking trails in the mountains, logging roads provide good access. A backcountry-use permit can be obtained at the Parks and Recreation Department (✉ Box 9000, 86515, ☎ 520/871–6647), next to the Navajo Nation Zoo in Window Rock. ✉ *Navajo Community College and Hatathli Museum, Tsaile,* ☎ *520/724–3311.* 🎫 *Donations accepted.* ⏲ *Weekdays 8:30–noon and 1–4; groups by appointment.*

Within Canyon de Chelly National Monument, only one hike—the **White House Ruin Trail,** on the South Rim Drive—can be done without an authorized guide. The easy-to-negotiate trail starts near White House Overlook and runs along sheer walls that drop about 550 feet. The trail leads to the White House Ruin, with dwelling remains of nearly 60 rooms and several kivas. Bring your own water for this 2½-mile hike (round-trip). Other hikes are led by rangers and paid guides (☞ Hiking *in* Outdoor Activities and Sports, *below*), and visitors can also explore the area by truck and Jeep tours (☞ Guided Tours *in* The Northeast A to Z, *below*). The **visitor center** features exhibits on the history of the cliff dwellers and provides information on scheduled hikes, tours, and other programs within the national monument. It also has a good selection of books on the area and on Navajo culture. ✉ *Box 588, Chinle 86503,* ☎ *520/674–5500.* 🎫 *Free.* ⏲ *Memorial Day–Labor Day, daily 8–6; Labor Day–Memorial Day, daily 8–5.*

Chinle is the closest town to Canyon de Chelly. There are three good lodgings with restaurants here (☞ Dining and Lodging, *below*), as well as a large supermarket and a campground. Call ahead for hotel reservations, especially in summer.

Dining and Lodging

$$$ ✕🏨 **Holiday Inn Canyon de Chelly.** This name-brand near Canyon de Chelly is less generic than you might expect: The territorial-style, Navajo-staffed complex stands on the site of a former trading post and incorporates part of the historic structure. Rooms, on the other hand, are predictably pastel and contemporary. The lobby restaurant, low-key by most standards, is the most upscale eatery in town, serving well-prepared specialties like fresh Navajo mountain trout dusted in blue corn meal and sautéed with piñon nuts. Fish and vegetarian entrées, steaks, and burgers are also available. Closed at lunchtime, the hotel restaurant offers to pack a box picnic for its guests. ✉ *BIA Rte. 7, Box 1889, Chinle 86503,* ☎ *520/674–5000 or 800/234–6835,* FAX *520/674–8264. 108 rooms. Restaurant, pool. AE, D, DC, MC, V.*

$$$ ✕🏨 **Thunderbird Lodge.** Set in an ideal spot at the mouth of Canyon de Chelly, this pleasant establishment has stone and adobe units that match the architecture of the site's original 1896 trading post. Some rooms feature roughly hewn beam ceilings, rustic wooden furniture, and Navajo decor. The staff is friendly and knowledgeable about the locale. The manicured lawns and large, sheltering cottonwood trees help create a resortlike atmosphere. A cafeteria offers an inexpensive American menu of soups, salads, sandwiches, and complete meals, including charbroiled steaks, prepared by an all-Navajo staff. ☒ *Box 548 (½ mi south of Canyon de Chelly visitor center), Chinle 86503, ☎ 520/674–5841. 72 rooms. Cafeteria. AE, D, DC, MC, V.*

$$ ✕🏨 **Canyon de Chelly Motel.** This two-story, western-style motel, about 3 mi from Canyon de Chelly, has modern, cheerful rooms with light oak furnishings and Native American–print bedspreads and drapes. All rooms have cable TV and coffeemakers. The Junction Restaurant operates from the motel premises and serves inexpensive American-style food. ☒ *Box 295 (on Rte. 7, ¼ mi east of U.S. 191), Chinle 86503, ☎ 520/674–5875, 520/674–5288, or 800/327–0354. 102 rooms. Restaurant, indoor pool. AE, D, DC, MC, V.*

$$ ✕🏨 **Coyote Pass Hospitality.** You're not likely to encounter a more unusual lodging than this roving B&B run by the Coyote Pass clan of the Navajo Nation. It's not for everyone: You sleep on a mattress on the dirt floor of a hogan (its location depends on the season, but most are near Canyon de Chelly), use an outhouse, and eat a traditional Navajo breakfast prepared on a wood-burning stove. If you don't mind roughing it a bit, this is a rare opportunity to immerse yourself in Native American culture in beautiful surroundings. Guided hikes, nature programs, and other meals are optional extras. ☒ *Contact Will Tsosie Jr., Box 91, Tsaile 86556, ☎ 520/724–3383 or 520/674–9655. Rates per night: $75 per person, $10 each additional person; call for tour and additional meal rates.*

CAMPING

⛺ **Cottonwood Campground.** Free, first-come, first-served camping is offered at 52 RV sites (maximum length 35 feet; no hookups) and 95 tent sites on grounds with cottonwood trees and a picnic area. The campground is open all year, with water and flush toilets available April–September. ☒ *Canyon de Chelly National Monument, near visitor center, Chinle 86503, ☎ 520/674–5500.*

Outdoor Activities and Sports

HIKING

Guides, required for all but the White Horse Ruin Trail, currently charge about $10 per hour with a three-hour minimum for groups of up to four people for day hikes; do not venture into the canyon without a guide, or you'll face a stiff fine. For overnights, there's a $20 surcharge for the guide and usually a $30 charge for permission to stay on private land where the guide will take you; groups of up to 15 people can be accommodated. From Memorial Day through Labor Day, free three-hour ranger-led hikes leave from the visitor center (☞ *above*) at 9 AM. Also during the summer, four-hour hikes costing $10 per person leave from the visitor center in the morning and afternoon; rates for two-hour evening hikes are $5 per person. Some of the hikes are a bit strenuous and precipitous, without clearly defined or gently graded trails. Visitors with health problems or a fear of heights should ask guides about the difficulty of the hike they're considering.

HORSEBACK RIDING

Justin's Horse Rental (☒ Box 881, Chinle 86503, ☎ 520/674–5678), near the South Rim Drive entrance of Canyon de Chelly, offers trips into the canyon for $8 per hour for each horse plus $8 per hour for a guide.

Hubbell Trading Post National Historic Site

❻ *32 mi south of Canyon de Chelly.*

This trading post was established in 1878 by John Lorenzo Hubbell, a native of the Southwest who was born in Pajarito, New Mexico. To the Navajo, Hubbell was not only a merchant but also a good friend and teacher who translated letters, settled family quarrels, explained government policy, and helped the sick. During the 1886 smallpox epidemic in the area, he turned his home into a hospital and personally ministered to the sick and dying. Hubbell died in 1930 and is buried not far from the trading post.

Today the Hubbell Trading Post operates much as it did more than a century ago. At the visitor center, National Park Service exhibits illustrate the post's history, and Navajo men and women frequently demonstrate the crafts of making jewelry and rugs. You may also take a guided tour of Hubbell's house, which contains one of the finest personal collections of Native American artistry anywhere, including rugs and paintings. Tours are given six times daily in summer, four in winter. The affiliated shop, run by the Southwest Parks and Monuments Association, specializes in Navajo rugs (☞ Shopping, *below*). ✉ *On AZ 264, 1 mi west of Ganado,* ☎ *520/755–3475.* *Free.* ⏲ *June–Sept., daily 8–6; Oct.–May, daily 8–5.*

Shopping

Hubbell Trading Post (✉ Off AZ 264, 1 mi west of Ganado, ☎ 520/755–3254) is famous for its "Ganado red" Navajo rugs; the quality is outstanding but prices are accordingly high. Be forewarned, though: It's hard to resist these beautiful designs and colors.

En Route Traveling west on AZ 264, about 20 mi west of the trading post, you'll reach **Steamboat Rock**, an immense, jutting peninsula of stone that resembles an early steamboat, complete with a geologically formed waterline. At Steamboat Rock you are only 5 mi from the eastern boundary line of the Hopi reservation.

THE HOPI MESAS

Most of the Hopi villages are situated on the top of or at the base of a trio of mesas: First Mesa, Second Mesa, and Third Mesa. You'll need permission beforehand to visit Hopi villages. For information, call the **Hopi Tribe Office of Public Relations** (☞ Visitor Information *in* The Northeast A to Z, *below*), which also provides phone numbers for village leaders or village community development offices.

To see the Hopi Mesas at a reasonable pace, it's a good idea to take at least one overnight on this tour, either at the Hopi Cultural Center on Second Mesa in the heart of the reservation or, if you're planning to head north into Navajo country, at a hotel in Tuba City (☞ Dining and Lodging *in* Tuba City, *below*).

Keams Canyon Trading Post

❼ *48 mi west of Hubbell Trading Post.*

The Keams Canyon Trading Post is the main tourist attraction in the Keams Canyon area, established by Thomas Keam in 1875. Originally, it served only Native Americans of the area, but today the trading post also includes a motel, primitive campground, restaurant, and shopping center. An administrative center for the Bureau of Indian Affairs, Keams Canyon also has a number of government buildings.

The first 3 mi of the 8-mile canyon running toward the northeast can be seen by car. At Inscription Rock, about 2 mi down the road, early frontiersman Kit Carson engraved his name in stone. There are several picnic spots in the pretty, wooded canyon.

Dining

$ ✕ **Keams Canyon Restaurant.** At this typical rural roadside dining spot, functionally furnished with Formica tabletops, you can choose from American dishes and a few Native American items, including Navajo tacos, made with Indian fry bread heaped with ground beef, chili, beans, lettuce, and grated cheese. It's open weekdays from 7 AM to 8 PM, weekends until 6 PM. (Note: The inexpensive motel in the same complex cannot be recommended.) ✉ *Keams Canyon Shopping Center (near AZ 264),* ☎ *520/738–2296 and 520/738–2297. MC, V.*

Shopping

Keams Canyon Arts and Crafts (✉ Keams Canyon, ☎ 520/738–2295) sells Hopi wares.

First Mesa

❽ *15 mi west of Keams Canyon.*

On First Mesa you will initially approach Polacca; the older and more impressive villages of Hano, Sichomovi, and Walpi are situated at the top of the mesa. From Polacca, a paved road (off AZ 264) angles up to a parking lot near the village of Sichomovi. For permission to visit Hano, Sichomovi, and Walpi, or for information on the guided walking tours of these villages, call the **First Mesa Visitor's Center at Ponsli Hall.** ✉ *Ponsli Hall,* ☎ *520/737–2262.* 🎫 *Tours free; contribution suggested.* ⏲ *Guided tours can be arranged between 9 AM and 4 PM daily, except when ceremonies are being held.*

All the older Hopi villages have structures built of rock and adobe mortar in a simple architectural style. **Hano** actually belongs to the Tewa, a Pueblo tribe that fled from the Spanish in 1696 and secured permission from the Hopi to build a new home on First Mesa. **Sichomovi** is built so close to Hano that only the residents know the actual boundary line. Constructed in the mid-1600s, this village is believed to have been built to ease overcrowding at Walpi, the highest point on the mesa.

For most outsiders, **Walpi** is usually the most impressive stop on the Hopi reservation, but it can be visited only if you are accompanied by a Hopi guide. Built on solid rock and surrounded by steep cliffs, Walpi stands against an immense expanse of distant earth and sky. At its narrowest point, the mesa measures only 15 feet across. Inhabited for more than 500 years, Walpi's cliff-edge houses seem to grow out of the nearby terrain. Today, only about 30 residents occupy this settlement, which has neither electricity nor running water. Important ceremonial dances frequently take place here.

Second Mesa

❾ *12 mi southwest of First Mesa.*

One of the livelier spots on Second Mesa is the **Hopi Cultural Center.** A cluster of shops carry the work of the Hopi artisans who live in the area; the selection is very good and the prices are reasonable. In addition, the center includes a pueblo-style museum, a good restaurant that serves American and Native American dishes, and a decent motel. It also hails itself to be "at the Center of the Universe," and is one of the best places on the reservation to obtain information and rest for an overnight stop. ✉ *On the north side of AZ 264, west of the junction at AZ 87. Restaurant and motel,* ☎ *520/734–2401; museum,* ☎ *520/734–6650.* 🎫 *Museum $3.* ⏲ *Mid-May–Oct., weekdays 8–5, weekends 9–4; rest of yr, weekdays 8–5.*

Shungopavi, the largest and oldest village on Second Mesa, may be reached by a paved road angling south off AZ 264, between the junction of AZ 87 and the Hopi Cultural Center. The famous Hopi snake dances (now closed to the public) are held here in August during even-numbered years.

The small villages of Sipaulovi and Mishongnovi are situated off a paved road that runs north from AZ 264, about ⅕ mi east of the Hopi Cultural Center. **Mishongnovi,** the easternmost settlement, was built in the late 1600s. If you'd like to visit **Sipaulovi,** the most recently established village, call the Sipaulovi Village Community Center (☎ 520/737–2570).

Dining and Lodging

$ ✕ **Tunosvongya Restaurant.** Also known as the Hopi Cultural Center Restaurant, this clean, comfortable establishment operated by Native Americans provides the opportunity to sample traditional dishes, including Indian tacos, Hopi blue-corn pancakes, fry bread (not unlike a soft pizza crust), and *nok qui vi* (Hopi lamb stew). ✉ *AZ 264, Second Mesa 86043,* ☎ *520/734–2401. DC, MC, V.*

$$ **Hopi Cultural Center Motel.** The only motel in the area, this no-frills pueblo-style lodging set high atop a Hopi mesa offers basic but clean rooms with telephones. One drawback: There's not always a night manager on the premises; guests are given a phone number to reach someone in case there are any problems. ✉ *Box 67, AZ 264, Second Mesa 86043,* ☎ *520/734–2401,* FAX *520/734–2435. 33 units. Restaurant. AE, DC, MC, V.*

CAMPING

Hopi Cultural Center Campground. There's no charge to stay at the modest camping and picnic area on the west side of the Hopi Cultural Center. There are no water hookups, but campers can use rest rooms in the cultural center. ✉ *AZ 264, Second Mesa 86043.*

Shopping

The **Hopi Cultural Center** (✉ AZ 264, Second Mesa 86043, ☎ 520/734–2463) has a collection of shops that feature the work of local artists and artisans. The **Hopi Arts and Crafts/Silvercrafts Cooperative Guild** (✉ Just west of the Hopi Cultural Center, no phone) hosts many craftspeople selling their wares; you might even see some silversmiths at work here. **Tsakurshovi** (✉ 1½ mi east of the Hopi Cultural Center, Second Mesa 86043, ☎ 520/734–2478) is a small, friendly shop brimming with everything you'd expect to find and more. The Hopis sometimes come here to buy kachina dolls and other ceremonial objects, such as bundles of sweetgrass and sage, rustling baskets of deer hooves to make rattles with, and ceremonial belts adorned with seashells.

Third Mesa

10 *8 mi northwest of Second Mesa.*

At the eastern base of Third Mesa is the village of **Kykotsmovi.** Hopi from Old Oraibi descended from the mesa and built this village in a canyon with a perennial spring; the community is known for its greenery and its peach orchards. The town also serves as the home of the **Hopi Tribal Headquarters Chairman's Office** and the **Office of Public Relations** (☞ Visitor Information in The Northeast A to Z, *below*), good sources of information regarding ceremonies and dances.

Old Oraibi, a few miles west and on top of Third Mesa, is widely believed to be the oldest continuously inhabited community in the United States, dating from around AD 1150. It was also the site of a rare, bloodless conflict between two groups of the Hopi people; in 1906, a dispute, settled uniquely by a "push of war," a pushing contest, sent the losers off to establish the town of Hotevilla. Oraibi is a dusty spot, and as an act of courtesy, tourists are asked to park their cars outside and approach the village on foot.

Hotevilla and **Bacavi** are about 4 mi west of Oraibi, and their inhabitants are descended from the former residents of that village. The men of Hotevilla continue to plant crops along the mesa slopes, and in warmer months these gardens on the cliffs are lovely to behold.

Shopping

Along AZ 264 are crafts shops and art galleries. The Third Mesa villages are known for their baskets, kachina dolls, weaving, and jewelry.

En Route Beyond Hotevilla, AZ 264 descends from Third Mesa, exits the Hopi reservation, and crosses into Navajo land, running by **Coal Canyon,** where Indians have long mined coal from the dark seam just below the rim. This canyon of colorful mudstone, dark lines of coal, and bleached white rock has an eerie, ghostlike appearance, especially by the light of the moon. Twenty miles west of Coal Canyon, at the junction of AZ 264 and U.S. 160, is the town of Moenkopi, the last Hopi outpost. Established as a farming community, it was settled by the descendants of former Oraibi residents.

Tuba City

11 *50 mi northwest of Third Mesa.*

Tuba City, with about 12,000 permanent residents, is the administrative center for the western portion of the Navajo Nation. In addition to a motel, hostel, and a few restaurants, this small town has a hospital, bank, and historic trading post. Founded in the early 1880s and recently restored, the octagonal **Tuba City Trading Post** carries authentic Indian rugs, pottery, baskets, and jewelry; it also sells groceries. ✉ *Main St.,* ☎ *520/283–5441.*

About 5½ mi west of Tuba City, between mileposts 316 and 317 on U.S. 160, is a small sign for the **Dinosaur Tracks.** More than 200 million years ago, dilophosaurus, carnivorous bipedal reptiles more than 10 feet tall, left their imprints in soft mud that subsequently turned to sandstone. There's no charge for a look. Four miles west of here on U.S. 160 is the junction with U.S. 89. This is one of the most colorful regions of the **Painted Desert,** with amphitheaters of maroon, orange, and red rocks facing west; it's especially glorious at sunset.

Dining and Lodging

$ ✕ **Pancho's Family Restaurant.** The main fare here is Mexican, but the menu also lists American and Navajo dishes. Mexican entrées are traditionally prepared, with chicken enchiladas and beef tamales as good as any you'll find south of the border. The large dining room looks like a western coffee shop but has beamed wooden ceilings and incorporates such Native American touches as handmade pottery chandeliers and Navajo rugs on the walls. ✉ *Main St., adjacent to Tuba City Motel and Trading Post,* ☎ *520/283–5260. AE, D, DC, MC, V.*

$ ✕ **Tuba City Truck Stop Cafe.** Home cooking is what you'll get at this small, conveniently located fast-service restaurant. Try the delicious Navajo vegetarian tacos. ✉ *Junction of AZ 264 and U.S. 160,* ☎ *520/283–4975.*

$$ **Tuba City Motel.** In the largest community in the western part of Navajo–Hopi country, this property is conveniently situated near

Pancho's Family Restaurant (☞ *above*), a trading post, and shops for essentials, gifts, and souvenirs. The spacious, well-maintained rooms are fine for an overnight stop before or after a visit to the Hopi Mesas. ✉ *Box 247 (at AZ 264–U.S. 160 junction), Tuba City 86045,* ☎ *520/283–4545 or 800/644–8383,* FAX *520/283–4144. 80 rooms. AE, D, DC, MC, V.*

$–$$ **Grey Hills Inn.** Students at Grey Hills High School run this unusual lodging, a former dorm that offers large, clean accommodations. The beds are comfortable, and eclectic decor and kitschy paintings add character to the otherwise plain rooms. Bathrooms and showers are down the hall, and it's hard to find your way to the inn's entrance in the large high school complex at night, but the rates are reasonable, especially for Youth Hostel members. ✉ *Box 160 (off U.S. 160, ½ mi north of junction with AZ 264), Tuba City 86045,* ☎ *520/283–6271, ext. 141, or 520/283–6273 (weekends or after school hrs). 32 rooms. No credit cards.*

Nightlife

There's an inexpensive first-run movie theater in Tuba City.

Shopping

The **swap meet** (✉ On Main St., behind the community center and next to the baseball field), held every Friday from 8 AM on, has good prices on jewelry, rugs, pottery, and other arts and crafts; there are also food concessions and booths selling herbs.

Cameron Trading Post

⓬ *25 mi southwest of Tuba City.*

Established in 1916, the Cameron Trading Post is one of the few remaining authentic trading posts in the Southwest (☞ The Drive to the North Rim *in* Chapter 2).

Dining and Lodging

Cameron Trading Post. This is a good place to stop if you're driving from the Hopi Mesas to the Grand Canyon (☞ Dining and Lodging *in* The Drive to the North Rim, Chapter 2).

CAMPING

Cameron RV Park. This park is adjacent to the Cameron Trading Post (☞ Dining and Lodging *in* The Drive to the North Rim, Chapter 2).

Shopping

The **Cameron Trading Post** has a large selection of goods from a variety of tribes (☞ Shopping *in* Chapter 2).

Fine authentic Navajo products are sold at an outlet of the **Navajo Arts and Crafts Enterprises** (✉ On U.S. 89 at the junction with AZ 64, ☎ 520/679–2244).

En Route Twenty-two miles northeast of Tuba City on U.S. 160 is the tiny community of Red Lake. Off to the left of the highway is a geologic phenomenon known as **Elephant Feet.** These massive eroded sandstone buttes make a good photo stop. Northwest of here, in real Navajo backcountry, is **White Mesa Natural Bridge,** reached via a graded dirt road. The payoff is a view of a massive arch of white sandstone that extends from the edge of White Mesa. The long **Black Mesa** plateau runs for about 15 mi along U.S. 160. Above the prominent escarpments of this land formation, mining operations—a major source of revenue for the Navajo Nation—delve into the more than 20 billion tons of coal deposited there.

NAVAJO NATION NORTH

The magnificent Monument Valley stretches to the northeast of Kayenta into Utah. At a base altitude of approximately 5,500 feet, this sprawling expanse was populated by the ancestral Pueblo people and has been home to generations of Navajo who have farmed and herded livestock in this arid country. The soaring red buttes, eroded mesas, deep canyons, and naturally sculpted rock formations of Monument Valley are easy to enjoy by driving through and pausing from time to time at roadside stops. Many westerns were filmed here, including *She Wore a Yellow Ribbon, How the West Was Won,* and John Ford's *Stagecoach.*

Kayenta

13 *80 mi northeast of Tuba City.*

Kayenta, a small town with a few grocery stores, two motels, and a hospital, is a good base for exploring nearby Monument Valley (☞ *below*).

Dining and Lodging

$$ ✕🏨 **Anasazi Inn at Tsegi.** This unpretentious roadside motel, convenient to both Navajo National Monument and Monument Valley, offers clean, comfortable accommodations and striking views of Tsegi Canyon from its rear-facing rooms. Its restaurant, which features tasty Navajo fry-bread sandwiches and tacos, is one of the best in the area. ✉ *Box 1543 (On U.S. 160, 10 mi west of Kayenta), Kayenta 86033,* ☎ FAX *520/697–3793. 59 units. Restaurant. AE, D, DC, MC, V.*

$$ 🏨 **Holiday Inn.** Except for the contemporary southwestern-style decor, this accommodation about a half mile from Monument Valley provides what you would expect from the Holiday Inn chain. It has one of the few swimming pools in the western section of the region. Children under 19 stay in their parents' room free. ✉ *Box 307 (south of junction of U.S. 160 and U.S. 163), Kayenta 86033,* ☎ *520/697–3221 or 800/465–4329,* FAX *520/697–3349. 164 rooms. Restaurant, pool, travel services. AE, D, DC, MC, V.*

$$ 🏨 **Wetherill Inn Motel.** Named for John Wetherill, a frontier rancher, trader, and explorer who discovered many of the major prehistoric Native American ruins in Arizona, this clean, cheerful, two-story motel with no frills has southwestern decor and a well-stocked gift shop. ✉ *Box 175 (on U.S. 163), Kayenta 86033,* ☎ *520/697–3231. 54 rooms. AE, D, DC, MC, V.*

OFF THE BEATEN PATH

FOUR CORNERS MONUMENT – A simple concrete slab inlaid into the ground marks the only point in the United States where four states meet: Arizona, New Mexico, Colorado, and Utah. Most visitors—in summer, nearly 2,000 a day—stay only a few minutes to record the spot on film; you'll see many people posed awkwardly, with an arm or a leg in each state. ✉ *Off U.S. 160, 7 mi northwest of the U.S. 160–NM 502 junction (near Teec Nos Pos). The monument is a 75-mile drive from Kayenta, near Monument Valley.*

Monument Valley Navajo Tribal Park

14 *24 mi northeast of Kayenta.*

Within Monument Valley lies the 30,000-acre Monument Valley Navajo Tribal Park. The park offers a scenic 17-mile self-guided tour on a rough but passable dirt road. You'll pass the memorable Mittens and Totem Pole formations, among others. Drive slowly, and be sure to walk from North Window around the end of Cly Butte for wonderful views (15 minutes round-trip).

You may also consider taking one of the many guided tours offered by operators in and around the visitor center; most take visitors in enclosed vans and charge about $15 for 2½ hours. A Native American crafts shop and exhibits devoted to both ancient and modern Native American history within the area are also at the visitor center. The park has a 100-site campground, which closes from early October through April. If you are visiting the area in winter (when there are fewer visitors), the rocks may have a beautiful covering of snow. Be sure to call ahead for road conditions. ✉ *Visitor center: 3½ mi off U.S. 163,* ☎ *801/727–3287.* *Park $2.50.* ⏲ *Visitor center May–Sept., daily 7–7; Oct.–Apr., daily 8–5.*

Outdoor Activities and Sports

HORSEBACK RIDING

If you've always wanted to ride off into the sunset at Monument Valley, get in touch with **Ed Black's Horseback Riding Tours** (✉ Box 155, Mexican Hat, UT 84531, ☎ 800/551–4039). Prices for trail rides, which can be as short as 1½ hours or as long as five days, range from $20 to $65 (per overnight). Rides leave from the corral, a half mile north of the Monument Valley Visitor Center.

Goosenecks

⓯ *33 mi north of Monument Valley Navajo Tribal Park.*

Monument Valley's scenic route, U.S. 163, continues from Arizona into Utah, where the land is crossed, east to west, by a stretch of the San Juan River known as the Goosenecks—so named for the type of twists and curves it takes at the bottom of a wildly carved canyon. Set in a lonely, untrafficked domain, this barren, erosion-blasted gorge has a stark beauty that is nearly as awesome as that of the Grand Canyon. The scenic overlook for the Goosenecks is reached by turning west from U.S. 163 onto UT 261, 4 mi north of the small community of **Mexican Hat** (named for the sombrerolike rock formation you'll see on the hills to your right as you drive north), then proceeding on UT 261 for 1 mi to a directional sign at the road's junction with UT 316. Turn left onto UT 316 and proceed 4 mi to the vista-point parking lot. If you visit during the week, you're likely to find yourself alone there, or perhaps joined by one or two Navajo women selling crafts.

Goulding's Trading Post

⓰ *8 mi northwest of Monument Valley Navajo Tribal Park.*

Established in 1924 by Harry Goulding and his wife, this remote outlet was used as a headquarters by director John Ford when he filmed the western classic *Stagecoach*. Because of the numerous Westerns that have been shot in the area, the trading post, motel, and restaurant have gained a measure of international fame. In the old trading-post building, a museum displays prehistoric and modern Indian artifacts as well as memorabilia of the Goulding family. The lodge here is an ideal place for an overnight stay, but call in advance for reservations. You can also rest overnight in or near Kayenta, where there are three motels (☞ Kayenta, *above*).

Dining and Lodging

$$$ ★ ✕ **Goulding's Lodge.** Built near the base of an immense red sandstone butte with spectacular views of Monument Valley from all the rooms, this comfortable motel often serves as headquarters for the location crews

of filmmakers. The lodge has handsome pueblo-style buildings stuccoed in a deep reddish brown that makes them appear to be a part of the surrounding red-rock formations. The cozy rooms are furnished in contemporary style, with southwestern colors and Navajo-design bedspreads. The on-premises Stagecoach restaurant, serving good, standard American fare, is decorated with memorabilia from movies shot in the area; service is excellent, and large windows provide a splendid view across the valley. ✉ *Box 1 (2 mi west of U.S. 163, just north of Utah border), Monument Valley, UT 84536,* ☎ *801/727–3231 or 800/874–0902. 62 rooms. Restaurant, pool, travel services. AE, D, DC, MC, V.*

CAMPING

Goulding's Good Sam Campground. This campground, with tents and RV sites, is open from mid-March to mid-October. The fee is $14 with no hookups, $22 with hookups (plus tax). ✉ *Off U.S. 163, near Goulding's Trading Post, 27 mi north of Kayenta,* ☎ *801/727–3231, ext. 425.*

Mitten View Campground. Here you'll find sites with a table, a grill, and a deck. Water is available, but there are no hookups; the fee is $5 per site, with hot showers extra. More sites are open in summer, but 10 or 15 are open year-round. ✉ *Monument Valley Navajo Tribal Park, near visitor center, off U.S. 163, 25 mi north of Kayenta,* ☎ *801/727–3287.*

Navajo National Monument

17 *53 mi southwest of Goulding's Trading Post.*

At the Navajo National Monument, two unoccupied 13th-century cliff pueblos, Keet Seel and Betatakin, stand under the overhang of soaring orange and ocher cliffs. The largest ancient dwellings in Arizona, these pueblos were also built by ancestral Pueblo peoples. The two large stone-and-mortar complexes were obviously built for permanent occupancy, yet the people lived in them for less than half a century before they departed.

Betatakin (Navajo for "ledge house") consists of a well-preserved, 135-room dwelling situated in a large alcove. It seems almost to hang in midair before a sheer, high sandstone wall. When the complex was discovered in 1907 by a passing American rancher, the apartments were full of baskets, pottery, and preserved grains and ears of corn—as if the occupants had been chased away in the middle of a meal. For an impressive view of Betatakin, walk to the rim overlook about a half mile from the visitor center. You can also hike to Betatakin on tours with ranger guides, offered between early May and mid-October (5 mi round-trip from the visitor center). The trips leave once a day in early May, most of September, and early October, and twice a day from Memorial Day to Labor Day (weather permitting) at 9 AM and noon. They are limited to groups of 25. No reservations are accepted; groups form on a first-come, first-served basis.

Keet Seel (Navajo for "broken pottery") is also in good condition in a serene setting, with 160 rooms and five kivas. Explorations of Keet Seel, which lies at an elevation of 7,000 feet and is 17 mi (round-trip) from the visitor center, are restricted: Only 20 people are allowed to visit per day, and only between Memorial Day and Labor Day, when a ranger is present at the site. A permit—which also allows campers to stay overnight near the ruins—is required. Those interested in horseback trips can make arrangements at the visitor center to rent horses and guides from a Navajo family. Trips to Keet Seel are very popular, and places can be reserved up to (but not beyond) two months in advance. Anyone who suffers from vertigo might want to avoid this trip: The trail leads down a 1100-foot-tall, near-vertical rock face.

The visitor center houses a small museum, exhibits of prehistoric pottery, and a crafts shop. Free campground and picnic areas are nearby, and rangers sometimes present campfire programs in summer. No food, gasoline, or lodging is available at the monument. ✉ *Navajo National Monument, HC 71, Box 3, Tonalea 86044,* ☎ *520/672–2366.* *Free.* *Memorial Day–Labor Day, daily 8–6; Dec.–Feb., daily 8–4:30; rest of yr, daily 8–5.*

Lodging

CAMPING

Navajo National Monument. The campground here has RV and tent sites, water, and rest rooms, but no hookups. Camping is free and is available May–October. ✉ *Reached by turnoff on U.S. 160, 21 mi south of Kayenta,* ☎ *520/672–2366.*

Outdoor Activities and Sports

HORSEBACK RIDING

Native American guides conduct **horseback tours** (contact Virginia Austin, c/o ✉ Navajo National Monument, HC 71, Box 3, Tonalea, AZ 86044, ☎ 520/672–2366 or 520/672–2367) to Keet Seel at Navajo National Monument daily from Memorial Day weekend through Labor Day weekend; rates are approximately $55 per day. Reservations should be made two months in advance; there's often a waiting list.

Shopping

The gift shop at **Navajo National Monument** (☎ 520/672–2366) has an excellent selection of Native American jewelry.

GLEN CANYON DAM AND LAKE POWELL

Lake Powell, with more than 1,900 mi of shoreline, is the heart of the huge (1,255,400-acre) Glen Canyon National Recreation Area. Created by the barrier of Glen Canyon Dam and fed by the mighty Colorado and five other rivers, the jade-green lake extends through eroded canyon country that is nearly devoid of vegetation and so rugged that it was the last major area of the United States to be mapped. The waters of Lake Powell are confined by immense red cliffs that twist off from the main body of the lake into 96 major canyons and countless inlets and coves—so many, in fact, that no single person claims to have explored all of them. In a number of places, huge sandstone buttes jut from the water. Seeing the stark, stunning geography of Lake Powell often makes tourists feel as if they are visiting another planet.

Skies in the Lake Powell area are blue nearly all year, and only about 8 inches of rain falls annually. Summer temperatures range from the 60s to the 90s (sometimes they rise to more than 100°F). Many fall and spring days are balmy, with daytime temperatures often in the 70s and 80s, but it is possible for chilly weather to set in. In winter, the risk of a cold spell increases, but all-weather houseboats and tour boats make year-round cruising possible.

South of Lake Powell the landscape gives way to the immense Echo Cliffs, orange sandstone formations rising 1,000 feet and more above the highway in places. At Bitter Springs, the road ascends the cliffs and provides a spectacular view of the 9,000-square-mile expanse of the Arizona Strip to the west and the sheer, 3,000-foot Vermilion Cliffs to the northwest.

Page

18 *96 mi west of the Navajo National Monument, 136 mi north of Flagstaff.*

Page was born out of the construction of Glen Canyon Dam in 1957. Prior to that, the broad mesa on which it lies was essentially barren land. Initially a construction camp, Page became a tourist stop after Lake Powell formed behind the dam. The town has gradually grown to its present population of about 7,000—the largest community in far-northern Arizona.

Most of the motels, restaurants, and strip shopping centers in Page can be found along Lake Powell Boulevard, the name given to U.S. 89 as it loops through the town's business district in a roughly northwest direction. At the corner of Navajo Drive is the **John Wesley Powell Memorial Museum,** a small building honoring the work of explorer John Wesley Powell, who, between 1869 and 1872, led the first expeditions down the Green River and the rapids-choked Colorado through the Grand Canyon. The one-armed Civil War hero mapped, explored, and kept detailed records of his trips, naming the Grand Canyon and many other geographic points of interest in northern Arizona. The displays—drawings and photographs of the expedition, area fossils, minerals, and Native American crafts—are rather unimpressive, but the museum serves as an information center for the area and a place to book river and lake trips and scenic flights. It also has a good selection of regional books and maps. ✉ *6 N. Lake Powell Blvd.,* ☎ *520/645–9496.* *Requested donation: $1.* ⏲ *May–Oct., Mon.–Sat. 8–6:30, Sun. 10–6:30; Nov. and Mar., weekdays 9–5; Apr., weekdays 8–6.*

Dining and Lodging

$$ ✕ **Salsa Brava.** This cheerful Mexican restaurant, with upholstered booths, lots of windows, and beamed ceilings, emphasizes charbroiled rather than fried preparations and uses vegetable oil instead of lard. Good versions of the standard burritos, tamales, and enchiladas are available along with more unusual fare, such as *carnitas* (slow-cooked pork), chicken with mole, and fish tacos. There's an outdoor patio and a dark and clubby bar. ✉ *635 Elm St., Page,* ☎ *520/645–9058. MC, V.*

$$–$$$ **Arizona Inn.** This modern, well-run motel on a high bluff at the northern end of Page has large rooms with queen-size beds and southwestern-print bedspreads. And, at a slightly higher room rate, you can get views of Lake Powell and Glen Canyon Dam. ✉ *Box C (716 Rim View Dr.), Page 86040,* ☎ *520/645–2466 or 800/826–2718. 103 rooms. Restaurant, bar, pool, hot tub, meeting rooms. AE, D, DC, MC, V.*

$$ **Weston's Empire House.** Built in 1962, this classic 1950s-style motel on Page's main street has comfortable rooms with individual air-conditioning and heating units. The smoky, western bar has a huge jukebox and a big-screen TV. ✉ *Box 1747, 107 S. Lake Powell Blvd., Page 86040,* ☎ *520/645–2406 or 800/551–9005,* FAX *520/645–2647. 69 rooms. Restaurant, bar, lounge, pool. MC, V.*

CAMPING

Page–Lake Powell Campground. More than 70 full-hookup RV sites ($18 per night, $2 extra for cable-TV hookup), and 15 tent sites ($15) are open year-round; reservations are accepted. A coin-op laundry, an indoor swimming pool, and two sets of men's and women's bathrooms and showers are available for no extra charge to both tenters and RVers. ✉ *849 Hwy. 98,* ☎ *520/645–3374.*

Outdoor Activities and Sports

CRUISES

Guided, piloted, 4½-hour rafting excursions cover a portion of the Colorado River that is relatively calm, with no white-water rapids. The scenery through Glen Canyon Dam is spectacular as the rafts glide beneath multicolored sandstone cliffs that are frequently adorned with Indian petroglyphs. The point of departure is the **Wilderness River Adventures office** (✉ 50 S. Lake Powell Blvd., ☎ 520/645–3279 or 800/528–6154) in Page; transportation is furnished to the launch site and back from Lees Ferry, where the raft trip ends. The cost is $42.75.

GOLF

Two-year-old **Lake Powell National Golf Course** (✉ 400 Clubhouse Dr., Page, ☎ 520/645–2023) is a 27-hole, par-72 municipal course that overlooks Glen Canyon Dam and Lake Powell. It boasts wide fairways, tiered greens, and a generous lack of hazards, along with landscaping and an overall course design that take advantage of native plants and elevation changes along the high plateau above the lake.

HORSEBACK RIDING

Trail rides in the Lake Powell area are available from **Rope & Saddle Promotions** (✉ Vermilion Downs on Haul Road, Page, ☎ 520/645–2752 or 520/645–2077); the fee is $20 for the first hour for adults and $10 for each additional hour, $10 for the first hour for children and $5 for each additional hour.

Nightlife

Aside from sitting by a campfire, nightlife in northeastern Arizona is minimal. The Page–Lake Powell area offers the most options. **Mesa Theater** (✉ 42 S. Lake Powell Blvd., ☎ 520/645–9565) is Page's movie house. A combination bowling alley–off-track betting parlor–comedy club–bistro is called **Canyon Bowl** (✉ 24 N. Lake Powell Blvd., ☎ 520/645–2682). **Ken's Old West** (✉ 718 Vista Rd., ☎ 520/645–5160) has country-western music and dancing; you can also get a pretty good steak or barbecued-chicken dinner.

Shopping

Page Factory Stores (✉ 644 N. Navajo Dr. at Lake Powell Blvd., ☎ 520/645–5975) has discount outlets for London Fog, Benetton, and Polo Ralph Lauren. On South Lake Powell Boulevard, just east of Highway 89, **Corral West Ranchwear** (✉ Gateway Park mall, ☎ 520/645–9391) carries a good selection of cowboy and cowgirl duds.

Antelope Canyon

⓳ *4 mi east of Page.*

You'll probably recognize Antelope Canyon from one of many photographs: Red sandstone rising majestically in a corkscrew formation, dramatically illuminated by a chink of light streaming in from above. And, in fact, you're likely to see assorted shutterbugs standing patiently next to tripods, waiting hours for just the right shot. A highlight of any trip to the Lake Powell area, Antelope Canyon is on the Navajo reservation, about 3 mi from Page. If you don't have a four-wheel-drive vehicle (or the time to wait for the rather erratic—and limited—hours that the gate to the site is open), book a tour from Page (☞ Guided Tours *in* The Northeast A to Z, *below*).

Glen Canyon Dam

20 *2 mi west of Page.*

Once you leave the Page business district, the Glen Canyon Dam and Lake Powell behind it immediately become visible. Completed in September 1963, the construction of this concrete-arch dam and its power plant was an engineering feat that rivaled the building of Hoover Dam. Nearly 5 million cubic feet of concrete were required. The dam's crest is 1,560 feet across and rises 710 feet from bedrock and 583 feet above the waters of the Colorado River. Lake Powell is 560 feet deep at the dam at full pool elevation.

Just off the highway at the north end of the bridge is the **Carl Hayden Visitor Center,** a museumlike facility dedicated to telling the story of the creation of Glen Canyon Dam and Lake Powell. Among the several exhibits is a giant, three-dimensional topographic map of Lake Powell country. The center's huge reception and observation room, with floor-to-ceiling glass, provides panoramic views of the dam, the wildly sculpted cliffs that border Lake Powell, and the immense sandstone buttes that protrude, islandlike, from the lake's emerald waters. Between May and October, free guided tours of the dam are offered daily between 8 AM and 4 PM, every hour on the half hour. The rest of the year, visitors can take a 40-minute self-guided tour through the dam complex. ✉ *Glen Canyon Dam,* ☎ *520/645–2511.* 🎟 *Free.* ⏲ *Memorial Day–Labor Day, daily 7–7; Labor Day–Memorial Day, daily 8–5.*

Wahweap

21 *5 mi north of Glen Canyon Dam.*

The most popular destination on Lake Powell, which stretches 180 mi through northern Arizona and southern Utah, is the vacation village of Wahweap. Most recreational activity in the region takes place around here, where everything needed for a lakeside holiday is available: fishing, boat rentals, dinner cruises, and much more. Visitors can easily rent boats and a wide variety of water-sports equipment (☞ Outdoor Activities and Sports, *below*). Stop at **Wahweap Lodge** (☞ Dining and Lodging, *below*) for an excellent view of the lake area.

★ 22 The best way to appreciate the beauty of Lake Powell is by boat. If you don't have access to one, the five-hour excursion cruise to **Rainbow Bridge National Monument** is the way to go. Along the 52-mile route (one-way from Wahweap Marina), you're treated to ever-changing, beautiful, and bizarre scenery, including huge monoliths that look like people turned into stone and a butte that resembles a dinosaur. You might also see eagles perched on ragged outcrops of rock. Finally, after gliding through a deep and twisting canyon waterway, the boat docks near Rainbow Bridge, the massive 290-foot red sandstone arch that straddles a cove of the lake. The world's largest natural stone bridge, it can be reached only by water or by an arduous hike from a remote point on the Navajo reservation (☞ Cruises *and* Hiking *in* Outdoor Activities and Sports, *below*).

The excursion boats, which leave Wahweap daily, are two-tier craft with sundecks upstairs and interior seating with windows downstairs. Experienced pilots provide commentary throughout the trip. Pack a lunch or take snacks; no food is sold on the boats, though coffee and water are provided. And be sure to bring your camera.

Other cruises are offered at the Wahweap Marina, including an all-day trip that stops at Rainbow Bridge and then proceeds farther into the Utah portion of the lake (☞ Boating *and* Cruises *in* Outdoor Activities and Sports, *below*).

Dining and Lodging

$$–$$$ ✗ **Rainbow Room in Wahweap Lodge.** You can't beat the beautiful setting of this attractive semicircular restaurant with panoramic views of Lake Powell and a colony of houseboats bobbing offshore. An extensive menu features southwestern, standard American, and some Continental fare, accompanied by a good wine selection. Specialties include Southwest chicken breast marinated in a honey-and-jalapeño-pepper sauce, and coho salmon with a Dijon-mustard cream sauce. ✉ *Wahweap Lodge (on U.S. 89, 5 mi north of Page),* ☎ *520/645–2433 or 800/528–6154. Reservations accepted in summer. AE, D, DC, MC, V.*

$$$ ★ **Wahweap Lodge.** On a promontory above Lake Powell, Wahweap Lodge serves as the center for recreational activities in the area. This attractively landscaped property offers accommodations with oak furnishings and balconies or patios; many of the rooms have a lake view (rates are a bit higher for these). The brightly colored, southwestern-style suites in the newest building are particularly attractive. Guests can enjoy two pools, a cocktail lounge, a marina, and the Rainbow Room (☞ *above*) for dining. Off-season rates are very reasonable. ✉ *Box 1597 (on U.S. 89, 5 mi north of Page), Page 86040,* ☎ *520/645–2433 or 800/528–6154. 350 rooms. Boating, waterskiing, fishing, travel services. AE, D, DC, MC, V.*

CAMPING

Wahweap Campground. This campground has 180 sites, some near the marina. The fee for campsites with drinking water is $8.50; campers can use the coin-op laundry and showers ($2 extra) at the adjacent RV park (☞ *below*). Open from April 1 to October 31, the campground operates on a first-come, first-served basis. ✉ *5 mi north of Page on U.S. 89 near shore of Lake Powell,* ☎ *520/645–1059.*

Wahweap RV Park. This RV park offers 120 full-service sites with full hookups, showers, and a laundromat; the fee is $21.50. It's open year-round and reservations are accepted. ✉ *5 mi north of Page on U.S. 89 near shore of Lake Powell,* ☎ *520/645–1004 or 800/528–6154.*

Outdoor Activities and Sports

BOATING

The boating opportunities on Lake Powell are almost limitless. If you have your own boat, docks and launching ramps are available at **State Line Marina,** 1½ mi north of Wahweap Lodge. **Wahweap Marina** (☎ 520/278–8888) is the largest of the four full-service marinas on Lake Powell (☞ Boating *in* The Northeast A to Z, *below*), with 850 slips and the most facilities, including a reasonably good diner.

CRUISES

A variety of excursions on double-decker scenic cruisers piloted by experienced guides leave from the dock of Lake Powell's Wahweap Lodge (☞ Dining and Lodging, *above*). The most popular is the one to **Rainbow Bridge National Monument;** half-day cruises cost $59, full days $77. A 2½-hour **sunset dinner cruise** also departs from Wahweap Lodge: A buffet-style dinner is served on the fully glassed lower deck of the 95-foot *Canyon King* paddlewheeler, an 1800s riverboat. The meal includes prime rib with fresh garden vegetables and a baked potato, a salad, and dessert; cocktails are available at an extra charge. The cost of the dinner cruise is $46; those who wish to take the cruise without eating pay $21.

HIKING

Seasoned hikers in good physical condition might want to try either of the two trails leading to **Rainbow Bridge,** the 290-foot sandstone arch in a remote cove on Lake Powell; both trails are about 26–28 mi round-trip. Take Indian Highway 16 north toward the Utah state border. When you come to a fork in the road, take either direction for about 5 mi and you'll come to a trailhead leading to Rainbow Bridge. Excursion boats pull in at the dock at the arch, but no supplies are sold there.

Nightlife

Nightlife in Wahweap revolves around **Wahweap Lodge** (☞ Dining and Lodging, *above*), which has a cocktail lounge and offers a sunset dinner cruise.

THE NORTHEAST A TO Z

Arriving and Departing

By Bus

Greyhound Lines (☎ 800/231–2222) has numerous Arizona destinations, but there is no service into the reservations. If you're coming from out of state and wish to tour northeastern Arizona, take a bus to Phoenix or Flagstaff and then rent a car.

By Car

If you are arriving from southern California or southern Arizona, Flagstaff is the best jumping-off point into northeastern Arizona (☞ Flagstaff and Environs *in* Chapter 4). If you are traveling from Utah or Nevada, you might choose to come in from Utah on U.S. 89, starting your tour at Page, Arizona. For those driving south from Colorado, logical entry points are Farmington and Shiprock, New Mexico, via U.S. 64 (what looks like a more direct route to Canyon de Chelly through Red Rock ends up crossing an unimproved road). Gallup, New Mexico, to the east, is also a convenient starting point for exploring the area.

By Plane

No major airlines fly directly into the reservations. To get closer to the northeastern part of the state, travelers will need to fly to **Sky Harbor International Airport** (☎ 520/273–3300) in Phoenix, the primary hub for air travel coming into Arizona from points out of state, and make connections for either the **Flagstaff Pullium Airport** (☎ 520/556–1234) or the **Page Municipal Airport** (☎ 520/645–2494). **Skywest** (☎ 800/453–9417) has daily flights from Phoenix to Page. (☞ Phoenix and Central Arizona A to Z *in* Chapter 5 *and* North-Central Arizona A to Z *in* Chapter 4.)

By Train

Amtrak (☎ 800/872–7245) provides daily service into Arizona from both the east and the west. It makes scheduled stops in Flagstaff, which is a good jumping-off point for a car trip into the area. No passenger train enters the interior of the Navajo or Hopi reservation.

Getting Around

By Bus

The **Navajo Transit System** (✉ Drawer 1330, Window Rock 86515, ☎ 520/729–5449, 520/729–5457, or, at Navajo Nation Inn, ☎ 520/871–4108) offers regular service on fixed routes throughout the Navajo reservation as well as charter service; write ahead for schedules. The buses are modern, in good condition, and generally on time. However, this method of travel, across vast areas where towns and bus stops are many miles apart, may be too slow for some visitors.

By Car

Because a tour of Navajo–Hopi country involves driving long distances among widely scattered communities, a detailed, recently published road map is absolutely essential. A wrong turn in this lonely country could send you many miles out of your way. Gas stations carry adequate state maps, but two other maps are particularly recommended: the Automobile Association of America's guide to Navajo–Hopi country and the excellent map of the northeastern region prepared by the **Navajoland Tourism Department** (☞ Visitor Information *in* Contacts and Resources, *below*).

Most of the 25,000 square mi of the Navajo reservation and other areas of northeastern Arizona are off the beaten track. Many visitors to the northeast generally stay on paved roads, but this vast, sparsely populated region is crisscrossed with dirt roads. If you don't have the equipment for wilderness travel—including a four-wheel-drive vehicle, water, food, tools, and bedrolls—and do not have backcountry experience, we recommend that you stay off dirt roads unless they are signed and graded, and the skies are clear. Seek weather information if you see ominous rain clouds in summer or signs of snow in winter. Never drive into dips or low-lying road areas during a heavy rainstorm; they could be flooded or could flood suddenly. (For road service locations and emergency and weather information, ☞ Road Service *and* Weather, *below.*) If you heed these simple precautions, car travel through the region will be as safe as travel anywhere else. Paved highways in the interior are well maintained and are patrolled by police officers. Note that it isn't easy to find a place to service your car here; we recommend that you make sure your car is inspected and serviced before your trip.

Contacts and Resources

B&B Reservation Agencies

Among the recommended B&Bs are **A Place Above the Cliff** (✉ Box 2456, Page 86040, ☎ 520/645–3162) and the **American Bed & Breakfast** (✉ Box 213, Page 86040, ☎ 520/645–9752). A brochure listing other members of the new Page/Lake Powell Bed & Breakfast Association is available from the Page/Lake Powell Chamber of Commerce (☞ Visitor Information, *below*).

Banks

Norwest has branch offices with automated teller machines (ATMs) in Window Rock and Tuba City on the Navajo reservation. Adjacent to the reservation, Flagstaff, Page, Winslow, and Holbrook have banks and ATMs.

Boating

There are four full-service marinas at Lake Powell where you can rent small or excursion boats, including houseboats, and water-sports equipment, water sleds and motorized wave cutters: **Wahweap** (☎ 520/278–8888), **Bullfrog** (☎ 801/684–2233), **Halls Crossing** (☎ 801/684–2261), and **Hite Marina** (☎ 801/684–2278). Houseboats—which should be reserved well in advance—range widely in size and price; one that sleeps six (in three double beds) may cost $675 for three nights. Some now have air-conditioning, TVs, VCRs, microwaves, and other amenities. Small boats, too, vary in size and price. An 18-foot powerboat for eight passengers runs about $185 per day. Most of these prices drop after the summer months. A variety of boat-tour and lodging packages are also available. For detailed information on all the Lake

Powell options and prices, contact **ARA Leisure Services** (✉ Box 56909, Phoenix 85079, ☎ 800/528–6154, FAX 520/331–5258).

Bicycling

Biking enthusiasts will find endless miles of paved roads and light traffic. But the mostly two-lane highways do not have paved shoulders, and motorists are unaccustomed to encountering cyclists. As a result, you should practice extreme caution when riding. The roads at Canyon de Chelly National Monument, Navajo National Monument, Monument Valley Navajo Tribal Park, and Kinlichee Navajo Tribal Park are your best bets. There are no bicycle rental companies in Navajo–Hopi country.

Camping and RV Parks

If you plan to stay in national monument and park areas, camping permission can be obtained on-site; for other camping situations, contact the **Navajo Parks and Recreation Department** (☞ Hiking, *below*) to find out whether you need a permit.

CAUTION – Be careful not to camp in low-lying areas, which are subject to extremely dangerous flash floods in sudden summer rains (☞ Lodging *in* Smart Travel Tips A to Z).

Car Rentals

Rental cars in heavily touristed Arizona are plentiful and usually available, but it's still smart to reserve a car in advance of your arrival. Major companies serving Phoenix and Flagstaff include **Avis** (☎ 800/331–1212), **Budget** (☎ 800/527–0700), **Hertz** (☎ 800/654–3131), and **National** (☎ 800/227–7368). Avis and Budget also offer rentals at the Page Municipal Airport. Weekly rates for a compact with unlimited mileage are most reasonable in Flagstaff (about $140 without any discounts), slightly higher in Phoenix (about $150), and much higher in Page (about $225).

Emergencies

POLICE

Canyon de Chelly police: (☎ 520/674–5500). **Navajo tribal police: Chinle** (☎ 520/674–5291), **Tuba City** (☎ 520/283–5242), **Window Rock** (☎ 520/871–6113 or 520/871–6116). **Hopi tribal police: Hopi Mesas** (☎ 520/738–2233).

HOSPITALS/MEDICAL CLINICS

Medical care in Navajo–Hopi country is not as easily accessible as in heavily populated urban areas. People with chronic medical conditions or those in frail health may wish to avoid a trip into Arizona's sparsely populated northeast. Hospital emergency care is generally not more than 60 minutes' driving time from any location on a paved highway.

Page Hospital (✉ N. Navajo and Vista Aves., ☎ 520/645–2424) has emergency-room service. **Sage Memorial Hospital** (✉ Ganado, on the Navajo reservation, ☎ 520/755–3411), a public hospital, offers medical and dental services. **Monument Valley Hospital** (✉ near Goulding's Trading Post off U.S. 163 at the Arizona-Utah border, ☎ 801/727–3241) in Utah has medical and dental services. Emergency care through the **U.S. Public Health Service Indian Hospitals** is available in the reservation communities of Fort Defiance (☎ 520/729–5741), Chinle (☎ 520/674–5281), Tuba City (☎ 520/283–6211), and Keams Canyon (☎ 520/738–2211).

PHARMACIES

There are no pharmacies on the Navajo or Hopi reservation. For emergency medical supplies, *see* the private or public hospitals noted in the Hospital/Medical Clinics section, *above*. In Page, **Safeway** (✉ Page Plaza,

☎ 520/645–5714 or 520/645–5068) is open weekdays 9–9, Saturday 9–6, and Sunday 10–4.

Fishing

Contact the **Navajo Fish and Wildlife Office** (✉ Box 1480, Window Rock 86515, ☎ 520/871–6451 or 520/871–6452) for permits to fish anywhere on the reservation. For the Lake Powell region, fishing licenses are available at the **Wahweap Marina** (✉ on U.S. 89, 5 mi north of Page, ☎ 520/278–8888) and at **Stix Market** (✉ 5 S. Lake Powell Blvd., Page, ☎ 520/645–2891). If you want a fishing guide for Lake Powell or the Colorado River at Lees Ferry, about 15 mi below the Glen Canyon Dam en route to the North Rim of the Grand Canyon, contact **Ed Strasburg** (✉ Box 2699, Page 86040, ☎ 520/645–9489). (☞ Sports *in* Important Contacts A to Z.)

Guided Tours

Except during winter months, the **Navajo Transit System** (☞ Getting Around By Bus, *above*) offers tours departing from Window Rock, the tribal capital. Destinations include Canyon de Chelly, the Painted Desert, and the Petrified Forest. **Nava-Hopi Tours, Inc.** (☎ 520/774–5003 or 800/892–8687), an affiliate of Gray Line Tour, schedules tours into the Navajo and Hopi reservations from Flagstaff. **Crawley's Monument Valley Tours** (☎ 520/697–3463) leaves from the small town of Kayenta. **Goulding's Monument Valley Tours** (☎ 801/727–3231) departs from Goulding's Lodge (☞ Dining and Lodging, *above*). Half- and full-day truck and Jeep tours into Canyon de Chelly on the Navajo reservation depart from nearby **Thunderbird Lodge** (☎ 520/674–5841); the half-day tours leave twice daily (when there is a minimum of six passengers) throughout the year, whereas full-day tours are available only from April to October. The newspaper published by the Navajoland Tourism Department (☞ Visitor Information, *below*) has a listing of operators offering Jeep and horseback tours on the Navajo reservation. Unless you have a four-wheel-drive vehicle or don't mind hiking 8 mi (round-trip) through sand, you'll want to take a guided tour to Antelope Canyon (☞ Antelope Canyon, *above*), one of the most arresting sights in the Page–Lake Powell area. If **Duck Tours'** (☎ 520/645–8581; tickets also available at the Page Chamber of Commerce, ☎ 520/645–2741, and the John Wesley Powell Museum, ☎ 520/645–9496) owner, Lee Woods, is your guide, you're in for a fascinating introduction to the area.

Hiking

For a backcountry hiking permit, contact the **Navajo Parks and Recreation Department** (✉ Box 308, Window Rock 86515, ☎ 520/871–6647). Note that the trails are often poorly marked and ill maintained in this wilderness area. The **Glen Canyon Natural History Association** (✉ Box 581, Page 86040, ☎ 520/645–3532) sells good topographical maps of the region as well as useful publications on hiking here.

CAUTION – Be sure to bring plenty of water with you when hiking and drink often. Dehydration can become a life-threatening condition (☞ Hiking *in* Smart Travel Tips A to Z).

Horseback Riding

Rainbow Trails & Tours (✉ Box 7218, Shonto, AZ 86054, ☎ 520/672–2397) runs pack trips in Lake Powell country from May through September. Tailored to individual interests and skills, Navajo-guided rides include a day trip to Rainbow Bridge and an overnight with teepee accommodations at Desha Canyon near Navajo Mountain. Rates are $75 per person per day, including meals.

Road Service

Contact **Fed Mart Automotive** (☒ AZ 264 near Window Rock, ☎ 520/871–4764), **Tuba City Motors** (☒ Corner of Birch and Oak Sts., Tuba City, ☎ 520/283–5315 during the day, 520/283–5300 at night), **Kayenta Discount Auto Parts** (☒ Kayenta on Hwy. 160, ☎ 520/697–3200), or **Onsae Auto Repair** (☒ Second Mesa, across from the Hopi Cultural Center, Hopi Mesas, ☎ 520/734–2211).

Shopping

Although you may feel more comfortable shopping at an established store, you may find exactly what you want, at a good price, at a reservation roadside vendor. If you would like some tips on quality, the **Navajoland Tourism Department** (☞ Visitor Information, *below*) has printed material on the subject.

Groceries, over-the-counter medicine, gasoline, and other supplies can be purchased in all of the major communities and trading posts on the Navajo and Hopi reservations, including Page, Window Rock, Fort Defiance, Ganado, Chinle, Hopi Second Mesa, Keams Canyon, Tuba City, Kayenta, Goulding's Trading Post, and Cameron Trading Post. Some of the smaller communities offer limited supplies; in general, don't count on a wide selection. Plan your gas stops for the locations cited.

Telephone lines—and thus connections with credit-card verification sources—are often iffy at the Hopi Mesas. It's a good idea to carry cash or traveler's checks to make purchases here or anywhere else outside of the trading posts.

Time

Unlike the rest of Arizona (including the Hopi reservation), the Navajo reservation observes daylight saving time. Thus for half the year—April to October—it's an hour later on the Navajo reservation than everywhere else in the state.

Weather

With elevations in the area generally between 4,000 and 7,000 feet, summer temperatures average about 87°F but can climb beyond 100°F. Winter daytime temperatures range from the 30s to the 60s but can drop to zero or below at night. Although the area gets less than 10 inches of rainfall in an average year, fierce summer thunderstorms can instantly flood low-lying areas. (☞ Driving Precautions *in* Smart Travel Tips A to Z.) Sometimes in winter, heavy snows virtually stop all traffic on dirt back roads.

KTNN radio (AM 660) provides periodic weather information. This station serves Hopi and Navajo reservations from studios in Window Rock. Some programming is in Navajo, but there are news and weather reports in English. You might also telephone Canyon de Chelly police or the Navajo or Hopi tribal police (☞ Emergencies, *above*) for weather updates.

Visitor Information

For more information regarding Navajo–Hopi country, contact the **Navajoland Tourism Department** (☒ Box 663, Window Rock 86515, ☎ 520/871–6659, 520/871–7371, or 520/871–6436) and the **Hopi Tribe Office of Public Relations** (☒ Box 123, Kykotsmovi 86039, ☎ 520/734–2441); both publish tourist-oriented newspapers. The **Native American Tourism Center** (☒ 4130 N. Goldwater Blvd., Scottsdale 85251, ☎ 520/945–0771) sells a map of Arizona reservations including a list of annual festivals and offers tourism brochures and a calendar of Native American events on and off the reservations. In addition, the center can help you contact any of the 14 tribal councils in the state. The **Page/Lake Powell Chamber of Commerce** (✉ 106 S. Lake Powell Blvd., Box 727, Page 86040, ☎ 520/645–2741) and the **National Park Service/Glen Canyon Recreation Area** (✉ Box 1507, Page 86040, ☎ 520/608–6200) are both excellent sources for Lake Powell vacation information and prices.

4 North-Central Arizona

Jerome and Prescott are two of the state's most popular towns, for their Wild West history and scenic settings. Sedona's red rocks, recognizable backdrops in numerous Hollywood westerns, are as captivating as they are easy to hike. Flagstaff offers historic buildings, the most active nightlife in the area, and an array of winter sports to be enjoyed in the dramatic San Francisco Peaks. Outside the city, Wupatki and Walnut Canyon national monuments are windows onto the world of a thousand years past.

By Edie Jarolim

RICH IN NATURAL attractions, north-central Arizona draws visitors to the striking red-rock formations of Sedona, to the limestone hills and desert scrub of the Verde Valley, and, just north of Flagstaff, to the San Francisco Volcanic Field, which has the highest peaks in the state as well as ancient lava flows and cinder cones. Sedona sits at the southern end of Oak Creek Canyon, where the Colorado Plateau meets the Sonoran Desert to the south. Highway 89A, which traverses this wooded canyon en route to Flagstaff, is one of the most scenic drives in the state.

The area is also rich in artifacts from its earliest inhabitants: Several national and state parks—among them Walnut Canyon, Wupatki, Montezuma Castle, and Tuzigoot national monuments—hold well-preserved evidence of the architectural accomplishments of Native American Sinagua and other ancestral Puebloans who made their homes in the Verde Valley and in the region near the San Francisco Peaks. Nor will anyone interested in exploring the West's wild and woolly days be disappointed: Prescott's many Victorian houses attest to the attempt to bring "civilization" to Arizona's territorial capital; the preserved fort at Camp Verde gives an excellent feel for rugged frontier life; and funky old Jerome is living testament to Arizona's former mining madness.

The towns of Verde Valley—Cornville, Clarkdale, Cottonwood—are as sleepy as their names suggest. A visit to the historic sites in the region will take you through a part of America that seems to have changed little since the 1950s. Sedona couldn't provide a greater contrast, with its numerous shops, sophisticated restaurants, upscale accommodations, and New Age entrepreneurs. Prescott's temperate climate, along with its historic hotels, bed-and-breakfasts, and antiques shops, has long attracted weekending Phoenicians and is beginning to lure out-of-staters as well.

Flagstaff, the largest city in north-central Arizona and long considered a jumping-off point for tours of the region, is becoming recognized as an appealing destination in its own right, offering some of the best skiing in the state at reasonable prices, lots of opportunities to explore Arizona history and Native American culture, and pursuits for those with astronomical interests.

Pleasures and Pastimes

Camping

If you look at a map, you'll see that a large part of north-central Arizona is covered by Prescott and Coconino national forests—which means there are a large number of campgrounds in the Flagstaff, Sedona, Prescott, and Jerome area. Campgrounds close to Sedona often fill up in summer, especially those along Oak Creek in Oak Creek Canyon. Two good places to try are Manzanita and Banjo Bill. In Coconino National Forest near Flagstaff, the campgrounds near Mormon Lake and Lake Mary—including Pinegrove, Lakeview, Forked Pine, Double Springs, and Dairy Springs—are popular to the point of overcrowding in summer. Campgrounds near Prescott and Jerome in the Prescott National Forest are generally less visited; Potato Patch and Granite Basin are both scenic, and sleeping out on top of Mingus Mountain is unforgettable.

Dining

Upscale restaurants—and prices—are making rapid inroads into what was once fast-food and meat-and-potatoes territory, giving visitors to north-central Arizona a wide range of noshing options. Sedona remains at the front guard of the haute cuisine incursion, but Flagstaff and Prescott are beginning to see a number of interesting new dining rooms as well. Even Jerome, too small to attract any chain restaurants, has acquired a few good places to chow down. Although many Sedona eateries tend toward the expensive (for Arizona), a number of low-key places can still be found there.

CATEGORY	COST*
$$$$	over $35
$$$	$25–$35
$$	$15–$25
$	under $15

**per person, excluding drinks, service, and sales tax*

Hiking

Hiking options abound in north-central Arizona: You can trek in thickly wooded areas in the Verde Valley and the Prescott National Forest, in the state's highest alpine region near Flagstaff (you can even ascend a volcano), and among the awe-inspiring red-rock formations around Sedona. National Forest Service offices in the Verde Valley, Prescott, Sedona, and Flagstaff can direct trekkers to the best trails.

Lodging

You'll find many comfortable motels in Flagstaff (all the familiar U.S. chains are represented) and some very pleasant bed-and-breakfasts but no real luxury. Sedona offers stunning settings and outstanding amenities but few bargains; prices tend to remain pretty much the same year-round. Prescott, in contrast, has a nice range of interesting accommodations: If you have a penchant for staying in a historic place—or having slot machines close to your room—it's the place to overnight. Little Jerome has finally acquired a hotel and a few reliable bed-and-breakfasts, but it's still smart to call ahead if you think you might want to spend the night there.

CATEGORY	COST*
$$$$	over $150
$$$	$110–$150
$$	$60–$110
$	under $60

**All prices are for a standard double room in high (summer) season, excluding room tax.*

Native American Culture

The achievements of the Sinagua people, who lived in north-central Arizona from the 8th through the 15th centuries, reached their height in the 12th and 13th centuries, when various related groups occupied most of the San Francisco Volcanic Field and a large portion of the upper and middle Verde Valley. Visiting the Sinagua sites around modern-day Camp Verde, Clarkdale, and Flagstaff affords a window onto this venerable culture.

Winter Sports

When nature cooperates, the area around Flagstaff is a delight for those who like to play in the white stuff: Opportunities for snowmobiling, downhill and Nordic skiing, and snowboarding abound, as do places to rent equipment.

Exploring North-Central Arizona

The Verde Valley, in the southern part of the area covered in this chapter, is pleasantly undervisited, but nearby Prescott, which has always been a Phoenician beat-the-heat getaway, is becoming popular among out-of-towners. Jerome, formerly just a day trip from both Prescott and

Sedona, is beginning to acquire enough hotel rooms to allow for an overnight stay. It's hard to believe that Sedona, which is adding movie screens, chic restaurants, and B&Bs at an alarming rate, was sleepy just ten years ago. Flagstaff has long been the population hub for north-central Arizona, and visitors are beginning to linger as the town highlights its attractions.

Great Itineraries

A short stay can give you a little taste of this rich part of the state, but at least five days are necessary for the full flavor. Linger longer if you want to savor the history and spectacular landscape of this region and enjoy some outdoor activities. The following itineraries assume you'll start out in Phoenix, as most visitors do, and head north.

Numbers in the text correspond to points of interest on the North-Central Arizona map.

IF YOU HAVE 3 DAYS

Spend the first two nights in Sedona ⑬. Divide your first day between the town's shops, especially those in the chic Tlaquepaque complex, and its scenery, taking a Jeep tour or a hike in Red Rock State Park ⑭. Visit the ghost town of Jerome ⑥ (with its boutiques and excellent historical museum) on the next day, and on the final day drive through scenic Oak Creek Canyon ⑮ to Flagstaff ⑯, where you might visit the Riordon Mansion Historic State Park or the Museum of Northern Arizona in the afternoon and the Lowell Observatory at night.

IF YOU HAVE 5 DAYS

Expand your time in Sedona ⑬ by shopping and perhaps vortex touring on the first day and exploring the red rocks and Oak Creek Canyon ⑮ on the second. Enjoy a good part of the third day in Jerome ⑥ and then continue on to Prescott ⑦, where you can spend the night in one of the many Victorian-era lodgings. Next day, poke around the town's antiques shops and Sharlot Hall Museum, and in the late afternoon, drive up to Flagstaff ⑯. Both history lovers and hikers will enjoy an excursion to the adjacent Sunset Crater ㉗ and Wupatki ㉘ national monuments, where Native American artifacts may be explored in an inactive volcanic field.

IF YOU HAVE 7 OR MORE DAYS

Take your time driving up from Phoenix to Sedona, spending the morning of the first day exploring Fort Verde State Historic Park ① and Montezuma Castle National Monument ②. In the afternoon, ride the Verde River Canyon Excursion Train and spend the night in Jerome ⑥. Continue on to Prescott ⑦ for a day or two and then head over to Flagstaff ⑯, where you can ski in the winter or view the entire San Francisco Peaks region from the Agassi ski lift in summer. If you finish up your trip in Sedona ⑬, you'll have made a very satisfying circle of the area.

When to Tour North-Central Arizona

If you're not committed to warm weather, winter is an excellent time to visit: It's often easier to find a hotel (except in Sedona around Christmas), and, in Flagstaff and Prescott, rooms are less expensive. Moreover, the stark white of the snow against the red rocks of Sedona or the deep black slopes of the Sunset Crater National Monument volcanic field makes an indelible impression. Prescott and Flagstaff hold most of their festivals and cultural events in summer. Sedona's biggest event, the Jazz on the Rocks Festival, takes place in September.

THE VERDE VALLEY, JEROME, AND PRESCOTT

About 90 mi north of Phoenix, as you round a curve approaching exit 285 of I–17, the valley of the Verde River suddenly unfolds in a stunning panorama of grayish white cliffs, tinted red in the distance and dotted with desert scrub, cottonwood, and pine. With the exception of bustling Sedona at its northern edge, the valley is rather sleepy, but for hundreds of years it was home to many active Native American communities, especially those of the southern Sinagua people. In the second half of the 19th century the discovery of silver and gold in the Black Hills, which border the valley on the southwest, gave rise to such boomtowns as Jerome—and to military installations such as Fort Verde, set up to protect the white settlers and wealth-seekers from the Native American tribes they displaced. Mineral wealth was also the impetus behind the establishment of Prescott, across the Mingus Mountains from Verde Valley, as a territorial capital by President Lincoln and other Unionists who wanted to keep the riches out of Confederate hands.

Numbers in the margin correspond to points of interest on the North-Central Arizona map.

Fort Verde State Historic Park

1 *94 mi north of Phoenix.*

Fort Verde State Historic Park is set on 10 acres overlooking the Verde Valley. Established in 1871–73 as the third of three military posts designed to maintain order in this part of the Arizona Territory and to protect the inhabitants of the valley (mostly farmers and miners) from Tonto Apache and Yavapai raids, this fort oversaw the movement of nearly 1,500 Indians to the San Carlos and Fort Apache reservations. A museum details the history of the area's military installations, and three furnished officers' quarters show the day-to-day living conditions of the top brass; even on the frontier, the married men lived far more comfortably than their bachelor counterparts. If you get off I–17 at any of the three Camp Verde exits, signs will direct you here. ✉ *125 Hollamon St., Camp Verde,* ☎ *520/567–3275.* *$2.* ⊙ *Daily 8–4:30.*

Montezuma Castle National Monument

2 *4½ mi north of Camp Verde (take Main St. to Montezuma Castle Rd.), 2 mi east of I–17, Exit 289.*

Mistakenly named by early explorers who believed it had been built by the Aztecs, this five-story, 20-room cliff dwelling of the southern Sinagua Indians is one of the best-preserved prehistoric ruins in North America—and one of the most accessible. An easy, paved trail (⅓ mi round-trip) leads to the structure and to the adjacent Castle A, a badly deteriorated six-story apartment with about 45 rooms. Visitors are not permitted to enter the ruins, but the viewing area is very close by.

Somewhat less accessible but equally striking is the **Montezuma Well** (☎ 520/567–4521) unit of the national monument. Although there are some Sinagua and Hohokam ruins here, the limestone sinkhole with a limpid blue-green pool lying in the middle of the desert is the site's main attraction. This cavity—55 feet deep and 365 feet across—is all that's left of an ancient subterranean cavern; the water remains at a constant 76°F year-round. It's a short hike up here, but the serene setting and the views of the Verde Valley amply reward the effort. To reach Montezuma Well from Montezuma Castle, return to I-17 and go north

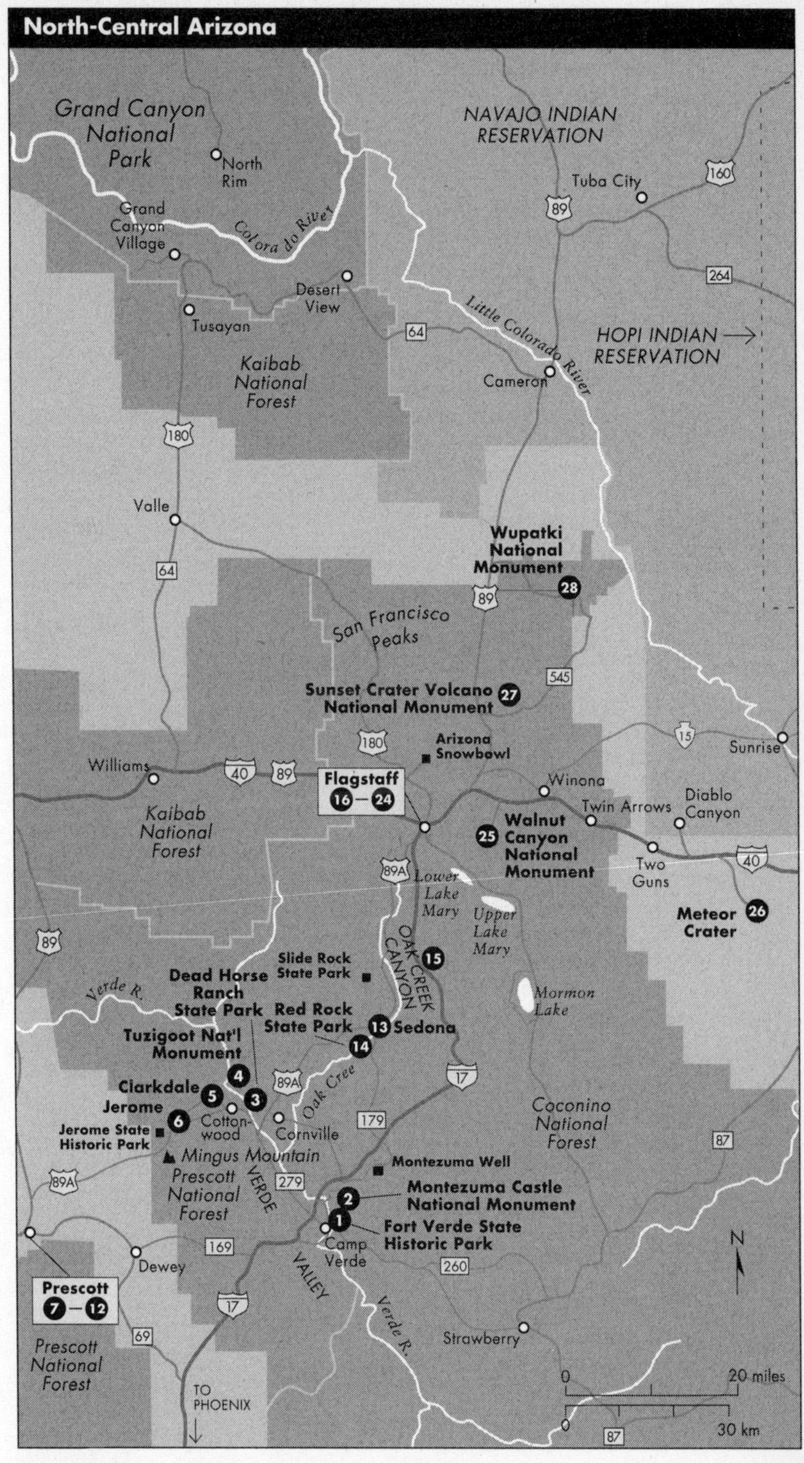
North-Central Arizona
Grand Canyon National Park
North Rim
Grand Canyon Village
Colorado River
Desert View
Tusayan
Kaibab National Forest
NAVAJO INDIAN RESERVATION
Tuba City
HOPI INDIAN RESERVATION
Little Colorado River
Cameron
Valle
Wupatki National Monument
San Francisco Peaks
Sunset Crater Volcano National Monument
Arizona Snowbowl
Williams
Flagstaff
Winona
Twin Arrows
Diablo Canyon
Sunrise
Walnut Canyon National Monument
Two Guns
Meteor Crater
Kaibab National Forest
Lower Lake Mary
Upper Lake Mary
Mormon Lake
Oak Creek Canyon
Slide Rock State Park
Dead Horse Ranch State Park
Red Rock State Park
Sedona
Tuzigoot Nat'l Monument
Clarkdale
Jerome
Jerome State Historic Park
Cottonwood
Cornville
Oak Creek
Verde R.
Mingus Mountain
Prescott National Forest
Verde Valley
Montezuma Well
Montezuma Castle National Monument
Fort Verde State Historic Park
Camp Verde
Coconino National Forest
Dewey
Prescott
Strawberry
Prescott National Forest
TO PHOENIX
N
0
20 miles
30 km

one exit; you'll see the signs for the well, which is 4 mi east of the freeway. The drive includes a short section of dirt road. ✉ *Box 219, Camp Verde 86322,* ☎ *520/567–3322.* 🎟 *$2.* ⏲ *8–5 (hours sometimes longer in spring and summer).*

NEED A BREAK? Two restaurants near Cornville, roughly between Camp Verde and Clarkdale, are worth a detour. The **Manzanita Restaurant & Lounge** (✉ 11425 E. Cornville Rd., ☎ 520/634–8851) serves reasonably priced Continental fare in a lace-curtained dining room; you can dine on sauerbraten with spaetzle for $10.95. **Page Springs Bar & Restaurant** (✉ Page Springs Rd., ☎ 520/634–9954), in two rustic, wood-panel rooms, both overlooking Oak Creek, has more of what you might expect to find out West: great chili, burgers, and steaks.

Outdoor Activities and Sports

The **Verde Ranger District** office of the **Prescott National Forest** (✉ 300 E. Hwy. 260, Camp Verde, ☎ 520/567–4121) is a good resource for places to hike—as well as to fish and boat—along the Verde River.

Dead Horse Ranch State Park

❸ *20 mi northwest of Montezuma Castle National Monument, 1 mi north of Cottonwood.*

In the late 1940s, when Calvin "Cap" Ireys asked his family to help him choose among the ranches he was thinking about buying in the Verde Valley, his son immediately picked "the one with the dead horse on it." Ireys sold the land to the state in 1973 at one-third of its value, with the stipulation that the park into which it was to be converted retain the ranch's colorful name.

The 325-acre spread, which combines high desert and wetlands habitats, is a pleasant place to while away the day. You might fish in the Verde River or the Park Lagoon (it's stocked with panfish, catfish, bass, and, in winter, trout) or hike on some 6 mi of trails that begin in a shaded picnic area and wind along the banks of the river; adjoining forest-service and multiuse agency pathways are available for those who enjoy longer treks. Birders can check off more than 100 species from the Arizona Audubon Society lists provided by the rangers. Many visitors are especially eager to see the bald eagles that perch along the Verde River in winter and the common black hawks—a misnomer for these threatened avians—that nest here in summer. ✉ *675 Dead Horse Ranch Rd., Cottonwood 86326,* ☎ *520/634–5283.* 🎟 *$5 per car for day use, $10 for camping without electricity, $15 with electricity.* ⏲ *Daily 8–7.*

Tuzigoot National Monument

❹ *3 mi north of Cottonwood.*

Not as well preserved as Montezuma Castle (☞ *above)* but more impressive in scope, Tuzigoot is another complex of ruins of the Sinagua people, who lived on this land overlooking the Verde Valley from about AD 1000 to AD 1400. Items used for food preparation, as well as jewelry, weapons, and farming tools excavated from the site, are displayed in the visitor center, where there is also a reconstructed room from the pueblo. ✉ *Box 68, Clarkdale 86324,* ☎ *520/634–5564.* 🎟 *$2.* ⏲ *Daily 8–5.*

Clarkdale

❺ *19 mi northwest of Camp Verde, 23 mi southwest of Sedona, 2 mi southwest of Tuzigoot National Monument.*

There's little to see in Clarkdale itself, but the sleepy town was once home to the smelter for the copper mines in nearby Jerome. The original settlement is said to have arisen from an encampment of prostitutes and hard-core gamblers who were tossed out of a rowdy mining camp in one of its periodic purges of sinners. These days, Clarkdale draws a somewhat more sedate group of train buffs, who come to catch ★ the **Verde River Canyon Excursion Train** (☞ Guided Tours *in* Northeast Arizona A to Z, *below*).

Jerome

★ 6 *3 ½ mi southwest of Clarkdale, 20 mi northwest of Camp Verde, 33 mi northeast of Prescott, 25 mi southwest of Sedona.*

It was once known as the Billion Dollar Copper Camp, but after the last mines closed in 1953, the booming population of 15,000 dwindled to a low of 50 determined souls, earning Jerome the "ghost town" designation it still holds, though the population has risen to almost 450 folks. It's hard to imagine that this town, which doesn't have a single convenience store, used to be home to the largest J.C. Penny in Arizona and to one of the state's first Safeway supermarkets. Jerome saw its first revival during the mid-1960s, when hippies moved in and turned it into a funky art colony of sorts, and it's now becoming an increasingly market-oriented tourist attraction. In addition to its shops and historic sites, Jerome is worth visiting for its scenery: It's built into the side of Cleopatra Hill, and from here you can see Sedona's red rocks, Flagstaff's San Francisco Peaks, and even eastern Arizona's Mogollon Rim country.

Jerome is about a mile above sea level, but structures within town sit at elevations that vary by as much as 1,500 feet, depending on whether they're perched on Cleopatra Hill or at its foot. Blasting at the United Verde (later Phelps Dodge) mine regularly shook buildings off their foundations, and the town's jail slid across a road and down a hillside, where it can still be seen today. That's not all that was unsteady about Jerome. In 1903 a reporter from a New York newspaper called Jerome "the wickedest town in America" because of its abundance of drinking and gaming establishments; town records from 1880 list 24 saloons. Whether due to divine retribution or simply to drunken accidents, the town was burned down several times—some historians say five, others two or three. The mine's financial backers were a bit more respectable: Eugene Jerome, for whom the town was named, was first cousin to Jenny Jerome, Winston Churchill's mother.

Of the three mining museums in town, the most inclusive is part of **Jerome State Historic Park.** Just outside town, signs on Highway 89A will direct you to the turnoff for the park, reached by a short, precipitous road. The museum occupies the mansion of Jerome's mining king, Dr. James "Rawhide Jimmy" Douglas Jr., who purchased Little Daisy Mine in 1912; the house was built in 1917 at the height of Little Daisy's success. (Rawhide Jimmy's first mining fortune was made in southern Arizona; ☞ Douglas *in* Southeast Arizona *in* Side Trips *in* Chapter 6.) Take a look at some of the tools and heavy equipment once used to grind ore. A video details the history of Jerome. The bawdy parts—relating, for example, to the onetime brothel, the House of Joy—have been left out, but you can read between the lines for some sense of the town's wild mining days. Views from the mansion and its surrounding grounds are spectacular. ✉ *State Park Rd.,* ☎ *520/634–5381.* 🎫 *$2.* ⏲ *Daily 8–5.*

The **Mine Museum,** in downtown Jerome, is staffed by the Jerome Historical Society. The museum's collection of mining stock certificates alone is worth the (small) price of admission—the amount of money that changed hands in this town 100 years ago boggles the mind. Among the books available here is the either cap and italicize "the" or delete if not part of title *Ballad of a Laughing Mountain,* featuring fascinating photos of Jerome when it was really a ghost town. ✉ *200 Main St.,* ☎ *520/634–5477.* *50¢.* *Daily 9–4:30.*

NEED A BREAK?

Ask where to have lunch and nearly every shop owner in town will direct you to the **Flatiron Cafe** (✉ 416 Main St., ☎ 520/634–3023), a tiny eatery at the fork in the road (if you don't want to crowd in inside, you can take your goodies to a patio across the street). The menu includes a choice of sophisticated sandwiches, such as black bean hummus with feta cheese, and an array of coffee drinks. Just next door, **Wedge on the Edge** (✉ 421 Main St., ☎ 520/634–5554) features a variety of tasty designer pizzas; the local favorite is the Greek, a sunny Mediterranean concoction.

Jerome, like Sedona on a smaller, slightly less expensive scale, is a shopper's haven, offering 50 retail establishments (that's more than one for every 10 residents). Artsy boutiques and galleries carrying local and imported goods line the streets in the tiny downtown area (☞ Shopping, *below*).

Dining and Lodging

$$$ ✕ **House of Joy.** Situated in a former bordello, this now respectable restaurant attracts patrons from all over the region—perhaps as much for its legendary setting as its food. Two small dining rooms are dimly lit and strung with red lights, but the stuffed animals and dolls on display (and for sale) offset any air of luridness. Book a table several weeks in advance, as this popular restaurant is open only on weekends—and only for dinner, at that. Classic Continental dishes such as chicken Kiev and veal cordon bleu are well prepared. Sample the tasty hot muffins, home-baked breads, and desserts, all of which vary from day to day. ✉ *Hull Ave., just off Main St.,* ☎ *520/634–5339. No credit cards; personal checks accepted. Closed weekdays. No lunch weekends.*

$ ✕ **The Haunted Hamburger/Jerome Palace.** After the climb up the stairs from Main Street to this former boarding house, you'll be ready for the hearty burgers, chili, cheese steaks, and ribs that dominate the menu. Lighter fare, including meatless selections like the guacamole quesadilla and a salad bar, is also available. The hunter-green-and-wood–dominated interior is cozy, but on a fine day you'll want to sit out on the deck overlooking Verde Valley. ✉ *410 Clark St.,* ☎ *520/634–0554. MC, V.*

$$ **Jerome Grand Hotel.** A welcome event in room-short Jerome was the completion in the summer of 1996 of a full-service hotel in the town's former hospital (considered the most progressive facility in Arizona when it was built by the United Verde Mine Company in 1927). The conversion was not yet completed when we visited, but if the finished portions—including a solid oak bar and antique nickelodeon in the lounge—were any indication, it promises to be a winner. The hotel is perched high on Cleopatra Hill, so views from the restaurant and many of the rooms are splendid. All units offer TVs, telephones, and period furnishings. For a treat, book the suite that used to house the delivery room. ✉ *200 Hill St., Box 757, 86331,* ☎ *520/634–8200,* FAX *520/639–0299. 32 rooms, including 5 suites. Restaurant, lounge, video games. MC, V.*

$–$$ **Inn at Jerome.** The funky old Jerome Inn, dating back to the town's heyday in 1899, has been totally redone in recent years, its name changed a bit to reflect the new ownership. Most rooms still share baths and the walls remain thin (a historic hotel liability), but the decor is now a delightful Victorian potpourri, with lots of dried flower arrangements, pretty lace flounces, and period antiques. All rooms have TVs, sinks, armoires, and robes. The rooms with a view of Main Street and beyond are considered the most desirable by many, but there are also those who prefer to share digs with the resident ghost. ✉ *309 Main St., Box 901, Jerome 86331,* ☎ *520/634–5094 or 800/634–5094. 6 rooms with 3 shared baths, 2 rooms with private bath. Restaurant, lounge. AE, DC, MC, V.*

BED-AND-BREAKFASTS

$$ ★ **Ghost City Inn.** This inn, opened in 1994, would be appealing wherever it was located. It's especially welcome in Jerome, considering the dearth of good lodging. Set in a converted 1898 home, it affords sweeping views of the Verde Valley and Sedona from an outdoor veranda. All rooms are beautifully decorated, most in Victorian style, but "Champagne and Propane" and "Satin and Spurs" offer contemporary western touches. Such luxuries as afternoon tea and turn-down with chocolates are especially surprising in a formerly rough-and-ready town. Full breakfast is served outside when weather permits. ✉ *541 N. Main St., Box 382, Jerome 86331,* ☎ FAX *520/634–4678. 4 rooms with 2 shared baths, 1 room with private bath. AE, D, MC, V.*

Nightlife and the Arts

THE ARTS

Some of Jerome's more colorful past events weren't held in 1996, but 1997 may return them to the calendar. You can expect the annual **Jerome Home Tour,** the oldest in the state, in May, and **Spook Night,** on the third weekend in October, but nothing else is certain. Contact the Jerome Chamber of Commerce (☞ Visitor Information *in* North-Central Arizona A to Z, *below*) to find out if anything's happening when you plan to visit.

NIGHTLIFE

On weekends and some Thursday nights, there's live music and a lively scene at the **Spirit Room** (✉ Main St. and U.S. 89, ☎ 520/634–8809); the mural over the bar harks back to the days when it was a popular dining spot for the "ladies" of the red-light district. **Paul & Jerry's Saloon** (✉ Main St., ☎ 520/634–2603) attracts a rowdy crowd to its two pool tables and old wooden bar.

Shopping

Shoppers in Jerome will find a variety of boutiques in houses perched precariously on the side of Cleopatra Hill. The town has its share of art galleries, but they're likely to be a bit more on the funky side than the ones you'll find in Sedona. An exception is the **Anderson-Mandette Art Studios** (✉ Old Mingus High School, Bldg. C, ☎ 520/634–3438). Robin Anderson and Margo Mandette made the building their workplace in 1978; at almost 20,000 square feet, it is considered by many to be the largest private art studio and gallery in the United States. The gallery, which displays paintings in all media as well as sculpture and pottery, is open daily 11–6; guided tours are available on request.

Shopping is simple here; all you need to do is stroll up and down Main Street. But your eyes may begin to glaze over after browsing through one boutique after another, most offering tasteful southwestern paraphernalia. A standout just below Main Street is the **Shaman** (✉ 2 Schoolhouse Road, ☎ 520/639–3577), which carries the ceremonial art of the Huichols, the oldest indigenous tribe in Mexico; the friendly Huichol owners are happy to explain the purpose of each of the exquisite, highly colorful pieces. **Aurum** (✉ 369 Main St., ☎ 520/634–3330) focuses on contemporary art jewelry in silver and gold; about 30 artists are represented, including the owner. You'll be drawn in by the bright patterns and attractively styled women's clothing of **Designs on You** (✉ 233 Main St., ☎ 520/634–7879). **Sky Fire** (✉ 140 Main St., ☎ 520/634–8081) has two floors of items to adorn your person and your house, ranging from Native American pattern dishes to handcrafted Mission-style hutches. **Nellie Bly** (✉ 136 Main St., ☎ 520/634–0255) offers a wide range of walking sticks, perfume bottles, and jewelry, but it's the outstanding collection of kaleidoscopes for which the store is justly renowned.

En Route The drive down a mountainous section of Highway 89A from Jerome to Prescott is gorgeous (if somewhat harrowing in bad weather), filled with twists and turns through Prescott National Forest. If you're coming from Phoenix, the route crosses the Mogollon Rim, overlooking the Verde Valley, and is scenic but less precipitous.

Prescott

33 mi southwest of Jerome, 100 mi northwest of Phoenix.

In a forested bowl at some 5,300 feet about sea level, Prescott is a prime summer refuge for Phoenix-area dwellers. It was proclaimed the first capital of the Arizona Territory in 1864 by President Lincoln and settled by Yankees to ensure that gold-rich northern Arizona would be a Union resource. (Tucson and southern Arizona were strongly pro-Confederacy.) It is believed that ancestors of the Yavapai Indians, whose reservation is today on the outskirts of town, were the area's original inhabitants, but early territorial settlers thought that ruins in the area were of Aztec origin. You can see the results of this notion—inspired by *The History and Conquest of Mexico,* a popular book by historian William Hickling Prescott, for whom the town was named—in such street names as Montezuma, Cortez, and Alarcon.

Despite a devastating downtown fire in 1900, Prescott remains the Southwest's richest store of late-19th-century New England–style architecture (some have called it the "West's most Eastern town"). With two institutions of higher education, Yavapai College and the innovative Prescott College, Prescott could be called a college town, but it doesn't really feel like one, perhaps because its transient youthful population is balanced by the many retirees drawn here by a temperate climate and low cost of living.

Numbers in the margin correspond to points of interest on the Prescott map.

The city's main drag is Gurley Street, named after John Addison Gurley, who was slated to be the first governor; he died days before
7 he was to move to the Arizona Territory. **Courthouse Plaza,** bounded by Gurley and Goodwin streets to the north and south and by Cortez and Montezuma streets to the west and east, is the heart of the city: Here the 1916 Yavapai County Courthouse stands, guarded by an equestrian bronze of turn-of-the-century journalist and lawmaker Bucky O'Neill, who died while charging San Juan Hill with Teddy Roosevelt. At the south end of the plaza, across from the courthouse's main entrance, the **Chamber of Commerce** (☞ Visitor Information *in* North Central Arizona A to Z, *below*) is a good place to get your bearings; those interested in architecture should be sure to get a map of the town's Victorian neighborhoods, most within walking distance of the chamber office—which was formerly the city jail, built out of native stone in 1895. Many of the Queen Anne–style houses have been beautifully

Bead Museum, **9**
Courthouse Plaza, **7**
Phippen Museum of Western Art, **12**
Sharlot Hall Museum, **10**
Smoki Museum, **11**
Whiskey Row, **8**

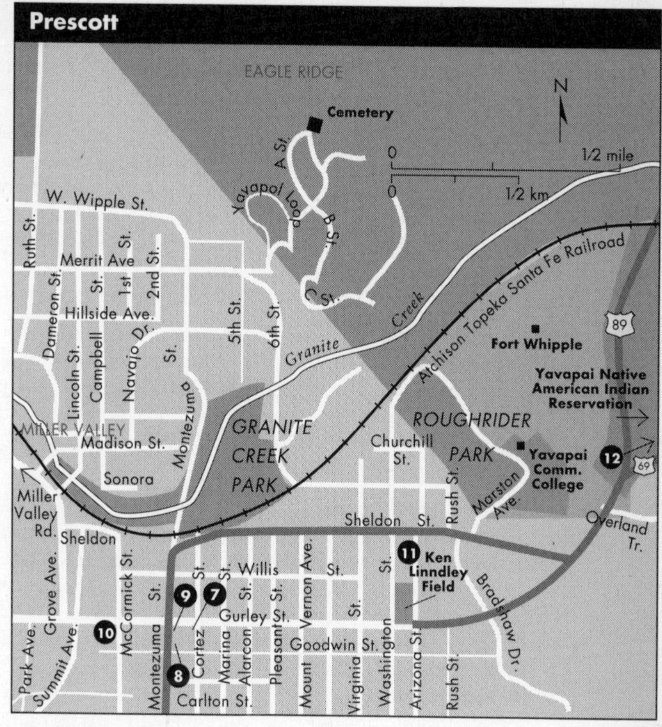

restored, and a number of them are now bed-and-breakfasts. Antiques and collectibles shops line both sides of **Cortez Street** just to the north of the courthouse.

NEED A BREAK?

On the busiest corner of Courthouse Plaza, **Caffé St. Michael** (✉ 205 W. Gurley St., ☏ 520/778–2500) provides equal doses of turn-of-the-century atmosphere and caffeine. You can also get a java jolt at the **Granite Mountain Cafe** (✉ 108 W. Gurley St., ☏ 520/445–2325), a pretty soda fountain–type place with marble-top tables.

8 **Whiskey Row,** named for a string of brawling pioneer taverns, runs along Montezuma Street, flanking Courthouse Plaza's west side; it was once host to 20 saloons and houses of pleasure. Social activity is more subdued these days. The historic bars provide a good escape from the many boutiques that now line the street.

9 The little **Bead Museum,** which sits demurely on Whiskey Row, tells an intriguing story of international trade and intricate bead craft from 3000 BC through today. Jewelry, books, and videos about bead making are sold at the adjoining museum store. ✉ *140 S. Montezuma St.,* ☏ *520/445–2431.* *Free.* *Mon.–Sat. 9:30–4:30, Sun. by appointment.*

10 Lovers of the past won't want to miss the **Sharlot Hall Museum,** a remarkable complex devoted to the history of the area, two blocks west of Courthouse Plaza. Along with the original ponderosa-pine log cabin that housed the territorial governor and the museum named for pioneering historian and poet Sharlot Hall, the parklike setting is home to three fully restored period homes, a working blacksmith shop, and a transportation museum. Territorial times are the focus, but natural history and artifacts of the area's prehistoric peoples are among the

many fascinating displays. It's easy to spend half or all of a day in this place. ⊠ *415 W. Gurley St.,* ☎ *520/445–3122.* 🎫 *$2 donation requested.* ⏲ *Apr.–Oct., Mon.–Sat. 10–5, Sun. 1–5; Nov.–Mar., Mon.–Sat. 10–4, Sun. 1–5.*

11 The stone-and-log structure built in 1935 to house the **Smoki Museum** is almost as interesting as the Native American artifacts inside. A priceless array of baskets as well as pottery, rugs, and beadwork highlight this fine collection, dating from the pre-Columbian period to the present. ⊠ *147 N. Arizona St.,* ☎ *520/445–1230.* 🎫 *$2.* ⏲ *May–Sept., Mon., Tues., Thurs.–Sat. 10–4, Sun. 1–4; Oct., Fri.–Sun. 10–4; Nov.–Apr., no regular hrs;* ☎ *520/778–7754 for appointment.*

12 Included in the permanent collection of the much-respected **Phippen Museum of Western Art,** about 5 mi north of downtown, is work by many prominent artists of the West along with the paintings and bronze sculptures of George Phippen; the rotating shows are often excellent. ⊠ *4701 Hwy. 89 N,* ☎ *520/778–1385.* 🎫 *$3.* ⏲ *Mon. and Wed.–Sat. 10–4, Sun. 1–4.*

Dining and Lodging

$$–$$$ ✕ **Murphy's.** Locals love this large, dark, bustling restaurant and tend to recommend it to out-of-towners. But as interesting as the late-19th-century building may be, the food doesn't always justify the fuss. Still, you'll find decently prepared seafood and steaks here—prime rib is particularly popular—and a nice selection of potent potables. ⊠ *201 N. Cortez,* ☎ *520/445–4044. AE, D, MC, V.*

$$ ✕ **Nolaz.** Come here for tasty New Orleans–style fare—jambalaya, Creole shrimp, or blackened salmon might turn up on the daily chalkboard menu—and a friendly down-home atmosphere to match. The recipes are as spicy as you might expect from a chef whose name is Curry, and the creatures contained therein are often exotic (alligator, say, or frogs' legs), but you can also walk on the mild side if you like. The small, dark dining room, sandwiched between the owner's seafood market and popular bar, really packs them in; call ahead for reservations on the weekends if you don't want to wait. ⊠ *216 West Gurley St.,* ☎ *520/445–3765. AE, MC, V. Closed Sun. No lunch Sat.*

$ ★ ✕ **Prescott Brewing Company.** Good beer, good food, good service, and good prices—for a casual meal, it's hard to beat this cheerful, multilevel restaurant on Prescott's main square. In addition to the pub fare you'd expect, including hearty chili, fish-and-chips, and British-style bangers (sausage) and mash, you'll also find a surprising range of vegetarian selections, including enchiladas made with tofu and pasta salad with sun-dried tomatoes, avocado, broccoli, and two types of cheese. Fresh-baked beer bread comes with many of the entrées. Four fine draughts are brewed on the premises, and you can also choose from the largest selection of single-malt scotch in northern Arizona. ⊠ *130 W. Gurley St.,* ☎ *520/771–2795. AE, D, DC, MC, V.*

BED-AND-BREAKFASTS

$$ **The Marks House.** Victoria still reigns at this bed-and-breakfast, once owned by the mayor of territorial Prescott. It now belongs to Beth Maitland, star of the daytime soap *The Young and the Restless,* and is ably managed by her parents. Rooms are impeccably furnished with period antiques: the suite in the circular turret, overlooking Thumb Butte, is particularly impressive. A full breakfast is served in the formal dining room, at an hour that guests agree upon in advance. ⊠ *203 E. Union St., Prescott 86303,* ☎ *520/778–4632. 2 rooms with private bath (1 adjoining), 2 suites. D, MC, V.*

HOTELS

$$$ **Prescott Resort Conference Center and Casino.** Perched on a hill on the outskirts of town, this upscale property affords forever views of the mountain ranges surrounding Prescott. Many guests hardly notice, so riveted are they by the poker machines and slots in Arizona's only hotel casino. There are plenty of recreational facilities to occupy those who don't have a penchant for one-armed bandits. Attractive, if bland, southwestern-style rooms all have wet bars, refrigerators, and coffeemakers. ✉ *1500 AZ 69, Prescott 86201,* ☎ *520/776–1666 or 800/967–4637,* FAX *520/776–8544. 161 rooms and suites. Restaurant, piano bar, indoor-outdoor pool, sauna, 4 tennis courts, exercise room, racquetball, casino. AE, D, DC, MC, V.*

$$ **Hotel Vendome.** This intimate hostelry, built during World War I and completely overhauled in 1994, has seen miners, health seekers, and celebrities such as cowboy star Tom Mix walk through its doors. Old-fashioned touches such as the original clawfoot tubs remain—and, like many other historic properties, the Vendome has its obligatory resident ghost—but the rooms are mostly decorated in pleasant contemporary fashion. Continental breakfast and local phone calls are included in the room rate. Only a block from Courthouse Plaza, this is a good choice for those who want to combine sightseeing, modern comforts, and good value. ✉ *230 Cortez St., Prescott 86303,* ☎ *520/776–0900,* FAX *520/771–0395. 17 rooms, 4 suites. Wine bar. AE, D, DC, MC, V.*

$$–$$$ ★ ✕ **Hassayampa Inn.** Built in 1927 for early automobile travelers, the Hassayampa Inn oozes character (be sure to look up at the hand-painted ceiling in the lobby). Rooms are individually decorated, a number with original furnishings, like oak headboards inset with tiles. A complimentary cocktail at the elegant lounge and free breakfast—anything you want from the restaurant's extensive morning menu—gild the lily of reasonable rates. The Peacock Room, the hotel's pretty Art Nouveau–style dining room, has tapestried booths, dim lighting, and impressive Continental cuisine. One drawback: The inn's location, just off the town's main square, can mean noisy rooms on weekend nights. ✉ *122 Gurley St., Prescott 86301,* ☎ *520/778–9434 or 800/322–1927 in AZ. 58 rooms, 10 suites. Restaurant, bar. AE, D, DC, MC, V.*

Outdoor Activities and Sports

CAMPING

Campgrounds near Prescott and Jerome in the Prescott National Forest are generally less crowded; Potato Patch and Granite Basin are both scenic, and sleeping out on top of Mingus Mountain is a wonderful experience. Contact the **Prescott National Forest** (✉ 344 S. Cortez St., Prescott 86303, ☎ 520/771–4700) for information (☞ Camping *in* Contacts and Resources *in* North-Central Arizona A to Z).

GOLF

Just outside Prescott, the city-owned **Antelope Hills** (✉ 1 Perkins Rd., ☎ 520/445–0583 or 800/972–6818 in AZ) offers 36 holes on two courses, one of them a Gary Panks creation. Set in the foothills of Bradshaw Mountain, the 18-hole **Prescott Country Club Golf Course** (✉ 14 mi east of Prescott on AZ 69, ☎ 520/772–8984) is open to the public.

HIKING

More than a million acres of national forest land surround Prescott. Thumb Butte is a popular spot for hiking in the area, but there are lots of other trekking and overnighting options. Contact the **Prescott National Forest** (✉ 344 S. Cortez St., Prescott 86303, ☎ 520/771–4700) for information on campsites and trails.

HORSEBACK RIDING

Some 5 mi northeast of Prescott, **Granite Mountain Stables** (✉ HC 29, Box 687, Prescott 86301, ☎ 520/771–9551) has daily guided rides as well as group specials, such as hay-wagon outings.

Nightlife and the Arts

THE ARTS

The mainstay of culture in the community, the **Prescott Fine Arts Association** (✉ 208 N. Marina St., ☎ 520/445–3286) sponsors a wide range of musicals and dramas, a series of plays for children, and a variety of concerts. The association's gallery also offers rotating exhibits by local, regional, and national artists. The **Yavapai Symphony Association** (✉ 107 N. Cortez St., Suite 105 B, ☎ 520/776–4255) hosts performances by the Phoenix and Flagstaff symphonies; call ahead for schedules and venues. The **Prescott Jazz Society** (✉ 129½ N. Cortez St., ☎ 520/445–0000) sometimes offers free concerts on weekend afternoons. The **Satisfied Mind Bookstore** (✉ 113 W. Goodwin St., ☎ 520/776–9766), right next door to the chamber of commerce, is a good place to find out about poetry readings and other literary goings-on about town.

Prescott, which had its first organized cowboy competition in 1888, lays claim to having the world's oldest rodeo; the annual **Frontier Days** (☎ 520/445–3103 for tickets and information) roundup, held on the Fourth of July weekend at the Yavapai County Fairgrounds, is duly revered. In August, the **Cowboy Poets Gathering** (☎ 520/445–3122) brings together campfire bards from around the country. The popular **Prescott Bluegrass Festival** (☎ 520/445–2000) takes place in late August. December sees the **Christmas Parade and Courthouse Lighting.** The **Holiday Home Tour,** designed to evoke festivities of olden days, takes place in December; call the chamber of commerce (☎ 800/266–7534) for details.

NIGHTLIFE

In Prescott, Montezuma Street's Whiskey Row, just off the central Courthouse Plaza, is nowhere near as wild as it was in its historic heyday, but most of the bars have live music—and a lively collegiate crowd—on the weekends; just walk up and down and poke your head in when you hear some sounds you like. Even if there's nothing happening, stop in at the **Palace** (✉ 120 Montezuma, ☎ 520/7788–9941) to see the beautiful mahogany bar brought over from Europe in the late 1800s (you might get distracted by the mooseheads, though; we're talking taxidermy city here). The venerable bar at **Lizzard** (✉ 120 N. Cortez St., ☎ 520/778–2244) was shipped from overseas via the Colorado River. **Nolaz** (✉ 216 West Gurley St., ☎ 520/445–3765) often features good Cajun, bluegrass, or country-western bands. For a more refined atmosphere, head over to the Art Nouveau piano bar at the **Hassayampa Inn** (✉ 122 Gurley St., ☎ 520/778–9434); there's always someone tickling the ivories on the weekend. The main source of entertainment at the **Prescott Resort** (✉ 1500 AZ 69, ☎ 520/776–1666) is its casino, but the mellow tunes of a piano are an alternative to the clank of the slots on Friday and Saturday nights.

Shopping

Shops selling antiques and collectibles line Prescott's Cortez Street, just north of the central Courthouse Plaza. Among the chaotic array of old attic contents, you'll find lots of fun stuff—especially western kitsch—as well as some good buys on valuable pieces. Many of the stores gather together groups of retailers; at 14,000 square feet, the **Merchandise Mart Antique Mall** (✉ 205 N. Cortez St., ☎ 520/776–1727) is the largest of these collections of collectors. When your eyes glaze over, stop in at **Déjà Vu Antiques** (✉ 134 N. Cortez St., ☎ 520/445–6732) for a bit of refreshment at an old-time soda fountain. The plaza itself, and especially Montezuma Street, is lined with a variety of specialty and gift shops. Many of the newer ones match those in Sedona for high quality—and prices. Be sure to check out **Arts Prescott** (✉ 134 S. Montezuma St., ☎ 520/776–7717), a cooperative gallery of talented local crafters and artists. **Bashford Courts** (✉ 130 Gurley St., ☎ 520/445–9798), catercorner from Montezuma Street, offers three floors of artsy stores. **Buffalo Montana Trading Co.** (✉ 142 S. Montezuma St., ☎ 520/445–5774) carries everything from cowboy pancake mix to Santa Fe–style furniture. **St. Michael's Alley,** adjoining the Montezuma Street hotel of the same name, is home to an interesting array of retailers, including Robert Shields Design (don't miss his wonderful ceramic snakes) and From the Heart, featuring romantic tchotchkes.

SEDONA AND ENVIRONS

Sedona, at the north rim of the Verde Valley, is one of Arizona's natural wonders—a Monument Valley in miniature. Its canyons and sensuous red-rock buttes—Cathedral Rock, Bear Mountain, Courthouse Rock, and Bell Rock, among others—will remain long in your mind. Numerous galleries, shops, resorts, and restaurants have become lures of their own. Nearby attractions such as Red Rock State Park and Oak Creek Canyon add to the unforgettableness of a visit here.

Sedona

13 *119 mi north of Phoenix, 60 mi northeast of Prescott, 27 mi south of Flagstaff.*

The former artists' colony is now home to some 15,000 residents, many retired, and many (alas) more interested in making money than in creating beauty. Expansion since the early 1980s has been rapid, and the lack of planning has taken its toll in unattractive strip malls, developments, and increased traffic and congestion, especially on weekends and during busy summer months, when Phoenix residents, overcome by heat, flee north to higher elevations.

That said, it's easy to see what draws so many visitors to Sedona. Deep red rocks reach up into an almost always clear blue sky—these colors both enhanced by inviting dark green pine forests. The rugged landscape once attracted surrealist Max Ernst, writer Zane Grey, and filmmakers, who shot more than 80 westerns in the area in the 1940s and '50s. These days, Sedona—which seems destined to become the next Santa Fe—draws enterprising restaurateurs and gallery owners from the East and West coasts. The town has also become a center of interest to New Age followers, who believe that the area contains some of the earth's more important vortices (energy centers). Several entrepreneurs have set up crystal shops and New Age bookshops here, catering both to the curious and to true devotees.

The wilderness—canyons, creeks, Indian ruins, and the ever-present dreamscape of towering red rock—is readily accessible on foot; there are innumerable trails crisscrossing the red rocks, and the area is thrilling and easy to hike (☞ Hiking *in* Outdoor Activities and Sports, *below*). Another option is to take one of the ubiquitous Jeep tours (☞ Special-Interest Tours *in* North-Central Arizona A to Z, *below*). Those with their own wheels might want to take the stunning drive out to the **Enchantment Resort,** in Boynton Canyon. Even if you're not staying there, you can hike the canyon and stop in for a scenic lunch or late-afternoon drink. Weather permitting, the **Schnebly Hill Scenic Drive** is another ooh-and-ah–inspiring option, and the vistas of the town from **Airport Mesa** at sunset can't be beaten. Many of the most pic-

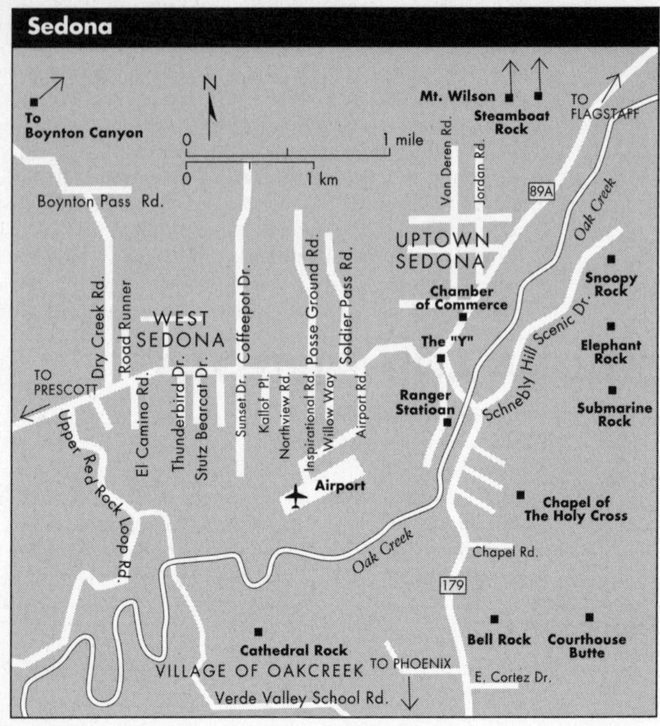

turesque spots in Sedona are considered energy centers; vortex maps of the area are available at most of Sedona's New Age stores.

You needn't be religious to be inspired by the setting and the architecture of the **Chapel of the Holy Cross.** Built by Marguerite Brunwige Staude, a disciple of Frank Lloyd Wright, this striking modern landmark, with a huge cross on the facade, rises between two red-rock peaks. Vistas of the town and the surrounding area are spectacular. There are no regular services, but visitors are welcome for quiet meditation. A small gift shop sells religious articles and books. A trail east of the chapel leads you—after a 20-minute walk over occasional loose-rock surfaces—to a magical seat surrounded by voluptuous red-limestone walls, worlds away from the bustle around the chapel. ✉ *Chapel Rd. (off AZ 179),* ☎ *520/282–4069.* ⏲ *Daily 9–5.*

Although it's set in an area that was inhabited by Native Americans for centuries, the town of Sedona itself is very new—it wasn't incorporated until 1988—so there are few historical sights for visitors to peruse. The main activity in the town proper is shopping, mostly for southwestern-style paintings, clothing, rugs, jewelry, and Native American artifacts (☞ Shopping, *below*). During warmer months it makes sense to visit air-conditioned shops at midday and save hiking and Jeep tours for very early morning or late afternoon, when the light is softer and the heat less oppressive.

NEED A BREAK?

For fresh hot beignets or heavenly focaccia sandwiches (among them an eggplant, goat cheese, and roasted pepper combination), head for the **Muse Literary Cafe** (✉ Country Square, 251 AZ 179, ☎ 520/282–3671). This bookstore, boutique, and restaurant has recently started serving dinner, but great red-rock views and terrific coffee lend themselves best to a daytime visit.

Dining and Lodging

NOTE – A number of Sedona restaurants close for stretches in January and February. Call to make sure that a restaurant will be open before you go. In high season, it's always best to make reservations; the lines can be long at popular restaurants. Lodging prices in Sedona tend to remain pretty much the same year-round (☞ Oak Creek Dining and Lodging, *below*).

$$$ ★ ✕ **Pietro's.** Some savvy entrepreneurs from New York have pulled together the ingredients for a successful Sedona restaurant: good northern Italian cuisine, a friendly and attentive staff, and a lively (it sometimes feels crowded), casual atmosphere. *Gamberi giardinieri* (grilled shrimp with shiitake mushrooms in white wine) makes a fine starter, followed by one of the creative pastas (for example, fettuccine with duck, cabbage, and figs) or a *piatti principali* (main course), such as veal piccata. Desserts like amaretto cheesecake, tiramisù, and zabaglione will take care of whatever's left of your diet. Almost from the start, this has been considered the best Italian restaurant in town, but it's had some stiff competition lately from Dahl & Di Luca (☞ *below*). ✉ *2445 W. Hwy. 89A,* ☎ *520/282–2525. AE, D, MC, V.*

$$$ ✕ **Sedona Swiss.** It's hard to go wrong with a chef who's used to pleasing Swiss embassy diplomats in Washington—and this very *gemütlich* European restaurant doesn't make any mistakes. Breakfast pastry in the adjoining café is light and buttery, and such classic dinner entrées as beef Stroganoff and rack of lamb Provençale are delicately seasoned and well prepared. Lighter alternatives like pasta with fresh salmon are also available. A low-priced buffet lunch draws in the tour-bus crowd (the restaurant sits on a street just off the main Uptown drag), but in the evening the pretty chalet-style dining room is suitably sedate and romantic. French, Italian, and German are spoken here. ✉ *350 Jordan Rd.,* ☎ *520/282–7959. MC, V. Closed Sun.*

$$–$$$ ✕ **Dahl & Di Luca.** The culinary buzz around town is all about this new Italian restaurant, the dream of a Rome-born chef (Andrea Di Luca) and his partner (Lisa Dahl). Updated versions of traditional Italian dishes are served in a cheerful Tuscan yellow dining room, with terra-cotta tile floors, painted ivy on the walls, lots of bright modern art, and soft jazz in the background. If you don't have after-dinner plans, go for the *aglio al forno* (roasted head of garlic with chèvre), followed by linguine and shrimp in a spicy vodka pomodoro sauce or maybe a hearty osso buco. And if you can't handle a rich dessert, linger over a nice grappa. ✉ *2321 W. Hwy. 89A,* ☎ *520/282–5219. AE, D, MC, V.*

$$–$$$ ★ ✕ **Heartline Café.** Attention to detail—fresh flowers on the tables, house salads without a leaf of iceberg—and outstanding, innovative cuisine make this attractive café stand out in a town that's beginning to form a yuppie-restaurant profile. The dinner menu has a southwestern emphasis, as in oak-grilled salmon marinated in tequila and lime or chicken breast with prickly-pear sauce. There are also at least seven appealing vegetarian selections. A temptingly priced sampler for two presents all of the luscious desserts on the menu. On nice days you may want to sit on the rosebush-lined terrace. ✉ *1610 W. Hwy. 89A,* ☎ *520/282–0785. AE, D, MC, V. No lunch Sun.*

$$ ✕ **The Atrium.** After a bit of a rocky start-up, this pretty-in-pink Tlaquepaque eatery has hit its stride. The very reasonably priced menu has moved away from meat and fish entrées (though they're still available as nightly specials) to focus on pastas and meal-size salads. You won't walk away hungry if you go for the barbecued steak salad with grilled onion and *chipotle* (a hot red pepper) dressing, or seafood orecchiette, with squid, mussels, and shrimp in a tomato cream sauce—especially if you begin with the green corn tamale appetizer. This is one

of the few sophisticated places where you can bring your kids and not feel like a pariah. ✉ *Tlaquepaque, AZ 179 (just south of the "Y"),* ☎ *520/282–6060. MC, V.*

$$ ✕ **Takashi.** Those seeking some serenity and a respite from heavy meals will enjoy this lovely Japanese restaurant, which provides aesthetic pleasure in everything from tea (with little bits of floating popcorn and brown rice) to dessert (sweet ginger or red-bean ice cream). A nice array of salads includes a spicy sushi tuna with Japanese mayonnaise on a bed of cabbage and other fresh vegetables. Combination dinners such as sashimi and tempura or two types of teriyaki let you try a little bit of everything, and most entrées come in vegetarian versions. ✉ *465 Jordan Rd.,* ☎ *520/282–2334. AE, D, MC, V. Closed Mon.*

$–$$ ✕ **The Hideaway.** There's nothing pretentious about this southern Italian restaurant and pizzeria, with its wood beam ceiling and red-and-white-checked tablecloths. But, *mama mia,* what a setting: Every one of the many decks (upstairs, downstairs, indoors, outdoors, smoking, nonsmoking) offers eye-popping vistas of Oak Creek and the towering buttes. Go for one of the large antipasto salads at lunch and the hearty lasagna or manicotti at dinner. This is a place that visitors stumble upon and locals tend to keep to themselves. ✉ *Country Square, AZ 179 (just south of the "Y"),* ☎ *520/282–4202. AE, D, DC, MC, V.*

$–$$ ✕ **Shugrue's Restaurant Bakery & Bar.** Combining a coffeeshop—with lots of comfy booths—and a more upscale dining room in the back (used on weekends), Shugrue's in West Sedona attracts a loyal following of locals who come for solid cooking and large portions rather than culinary adventure. Omelets, salads, and burgers are on the menu, along with Mexican fare and, at dinnertime, steaks and seafood. Breakfast is served on weekends. Shugrue's Hillside branch has a more ambitious, more expensive, and somewhat more inconsistent menu—the fish is usually very good, however—as well as a lovely setting overlooking Sedona's red rocks. ✉ *2250 W. Hwy. 89A,* ☎ *520/282–2943; 671 AZ 179 (Hillside Courtyard),* ☎ *520/282–5300. AE, MC, V.*

$ ✕ **Mandarin House.** Its name notwithstanding, the Mandarin House serves everything from standard Cantonese to Szechuan and Hunan fare, with dishes ranging from the exotic (shark-fin salad) to the old standbys (egg foo yong). The lemon chicken is particularly recommended. Everything is fresh—even the noodles and egg rolls are made on the premises—and well prepared. Dark green tablecloths, carved chairs, and dark-wood furnishings lend this restaurant, just down the road from the Oak Creek Factory Stores, a certain elegance. ✉ *6486 AZ 179, Suite 114,* ☎ *520/284–9088. AE, D, MC, V.*

BED-AND-BREAKFASTS

$$$–$$$$ **Casa Sedona.** You can have all the modern amenities—hot tub for two, air-conditioning and heating units—and still be able to commune with nature at this appealing bed-and-breakfast. A large redwood deck, where a full breakfast is served when the weather is fine, has stunning red-rock views, also enjoyed by all of the rooms. The rooms, which all have refrigerators and gas-run fireplaces, are decorated in an eclectic style with differing southwestern themes; one is done in deep blues, burgundies, and tans with a Native American–print bedspread, another in shades of peach and sea green with a light oak closet. ✉ *55 Hozoni Dr., Sedona 86336,* ☎ *520/282–2938 or 800/525–3756,* FAX *520/282–2259. 15 rooms with bath. Air-conditioning, refrigerators, hot tubs. D, MC, V.*

$$–$$$$ ★ **The Lodge at Sedona.** A first-class operation—including a chef who graduated from New York's Culinary Institute—the Lodge still manages to feel intimate and friendly. Rooms in this rambling wood-and-stone house are individually decorated in every style from romantic

Renaissance to cowboy kitsch; some have fireplaces, redwood decks, and/or hot tubs. Of the five public areas where guests can mingle, perhaps the best is the lace-curtained breakfast nook, shaded by trees and looking out onto the red rocks in the distance. ✉ *125 Kallof Pl., Sedona 86336,* ☎ *520/204–1942 or 800/619–4467. 10 rooms with bath, 3 suites. Library, meeting room. MC, V.*

RESORTS, HOTELS, AND INNS

$$$$ ★ ✕🏨 **Enchantment Resort.** Designed as a tennis resort, Enchantment has excellent sports facilities, but it's the stunning setting of Boynton Canyon that makes it unique. Southwest-pattern rooms are set in 56 pueblo-style casitas. Many have fireplaces and kitchenettes, and all have superb views. Fresh-squeezed orange juice and a newspaper are delivered to rooms each morning, and the Yavapai Room has more vistas and excellent Continental cuisine. One drawback: Although flashlights are provided, it's difficult to find one's way around the largely unlighted premises at night; of course, guests can call the front desk for golf-cart transport. ✉ *525 Boynton Canyon Rd., Sedona 86336,* ☎ *520/282–2900 or 800/826–4180,* FAX *520/282–9249. 162 rooms with bath. Restaurant, bar, kitchenettes, 4 outdoor pools, pitch-and-putt golf course, 12 tennis courts, aerobics, croquet, health club, hiking, bicycles, pro shop, children's programs. AE, D, MC, V.*

$$$$ ✕🏨 **L'Auberge de Sedona Resort.** This resort consists of a central building and—the major attraction—a number of sweet, secluded cabins in a wooded setting along a stream. You may wake to the honking of friendly geese, used to gifts of food from generous guests. Phoenix couples flock to these romantic, country-French hideaways and dine in the hotel's French restaurant, one of the most romantic eateries in Arizona. The six-course prix-fixe dinner runs $55—a bit steep even for Sedona—but it comes with a view of Oak Creek; jacket and reservations are required. There's a small heated pool for summertime swimming. ✉ *L'Auberge La. (Box B), Sedona 86336,* ☎ *520/282–1661 or 800/272–6777,* FAX *520/282–2885. 69 rooms, 30 cottages, all with bath. 2 restaurants, pool, spa. AE, D, DC, MC, V.*

$$$$ ★ 🏨 **Los Abrigados.** This place really sparkles at Christmas, when half a million tiny lights illuminate the grounds, but it's a dazzler year-round. All the spacious suites, attractively decorated in earth tones, offer microwaves, minibars, and coffeemakers, as well as two TVs; in addition, some have private spas and fireplaces. A state-of-the-art health club, offering such extras as massages and facials, will help burn off the calories picked up at Joey Bistro, the resort's bustling southern Italian restaurant. Another eatery, Steak & Sticks, has an adjoining billiards lounge and humidor for sophisticated cigar smokers. Guests can picnic at Oak Creek, which runs through the grounds of this 20-acre, tree-lined property. The shops of Tlaquepaque are right next door. ✉ *160 Portal La., Sedona 86336,* ☎ *520/282–1777 or 800/521–3131,* FAX *520/282–2614. 175 suites. 3 restaurants, bar, grill, minibars, pool, 3 tennis courts, health club, volleyball, baby-sitting, children's programs. AE, D, DC, MC, V.*

$$$ 🏨 **Southwest Inn at Sedona.** This recently built, upscale motel in West Sedona is a reasonable alternative to the town's more pricey properties. Rooms have a fresh Santa Fe look, with viga-style ceiling beams, art prints, light wood furnishings, and vibrant colors; all have gas fireplaces and decks or patios (some with red-rock vistas, others with uninspiring views of the parking lot), as well as in-room coffeemakers and refrigerators. Continental breakfast is included in the room rate. The inn does not allow smoking on the property. One of Sedona's newer movie theaters, Cinedona, is right next door. ✉ *3250 W. Hwy. 89A,*

West Sedona 86336, ☎ 520/282–3344 or 800/483–7422, FAX 520/282–0267. 28 rooms and suites with bath. Refrigerators, outdoor pool, hot tub. AE, D, MC, V.

$–$$ ★ **Sky Ranch Lodge.** There may be no better vantage point in town from which to view Sedona's red-rock canyons than the private patios or balconies at Sky Ranch Lodge, perched near the top of Airport Mesa. Some rooms have stone fireplaces, and some have kitchenettes; all are well decorated in dark blues and beiges with ceramic tile trim. Paths on the grounds wind around fountains and, in summer, through colorful flower gardens. This is an excellent value choice. ✉ *Airport Rd., Box 2579, Sedona 86339, ☎ 520/282–6400, FAX 520/282–7682. 92 rooms with bath, 2 cottages. Pool. MC, V.*

Outdoor Activities and Sports

CAMPING

For information on the six **forest-service campgrounds** in the Sedona–Oak Creek Canyon area, call ☎ 520/282–4119 (☞ Campgrounds in Contacts and Resources, North-Central Arizona A to Z, *below*).

GOLF

The **Oak Creek Country Club** (✉ 690 Bell Rock Blvd., ☎ 520/284–1660) is a good semiprivate option. The public is welcome at the **Sedona Golf Resort** (✉ 7260 AZ 179, Oak Creek, ☎ 520/284–9355), where the 18-hole course was designed (by Gary Panks) to take advantage of the many changes in elevation and scenery. The 10th hole, said to be the most photographed hole in all of Arizona, takes in a sweeping view of the Sedona Valley's red-rock splendor—well worth the price of admission. Lake Montezuma, 20 mi from Sedona off I-17, boasts the **Beaver Creek Golf Resort** (✉ Montezuma Ave. and Lakeshore Dr., ☎ 520/567–4487), a championship par-71 course with a 588-yard, par-5 hole, one of the longest in the whole state.

HIKING

For free detailed maps and hiking advice, speak to the rangers at the **Sedona Ranger District Office** (✉ 250 Brewer Rd., ☎ 520/282–4119), which is open Monday through Saturday from 7:30 to 4:30. Ask here or at your hotel for directions to trailheads for Doe's Mountain, beautiful Loy Canyon, Margs Draw, Devil's Kitchen, and Long Canyon. Nearby Red Rock State Park and Slide Rock State Park (☞ *below*) also offer many trekking opportunities.

HORSEBACK RIDING

Kachina Stables of Sedona (✉ 5 J La., Lower Red Rock Loop Rd., West Sedona, ☎ 520/282–7252) includes riding with an Oak Creek swim and a picnic lunch. Among other things, **El Royo Grande Ranch & Stables** (✉ 7 mi west of Uptown Sedona on Hwy. 89A, ☎ 520/282–1898 or 800/362–6926), a 143-acre equestrian center, offers stagecoach excursions, trail rides, and lessons.

Nightlife and the Arts

THE ARTS

Find out about cultural events in Sedona at the **Book Loft** (✉ 175 AZ 179, just south of the "Y," ☎ 520/282–5173), which often hosts poetry readings, theatrical readings, book signings, and lectures. The Sedona **Jazz on the Rocks Festival** (☎ 520/282–1985), held every September, always attracts a sellout crowd that fills the town to capacity; at jazz-festival time it's even more important than usual to book ahead for rooms. The **Sedona Arts Center** (✉ Hwy. 89A and Art Barn Rd., ☎ 520/282–3809) sponsors events ranging from classical concerts to plays; phone for information about upcoming programs. The **Sedona Heritage Day Festival,** sponsored by the Sedona Historical Society (☎ 520/282–7434), is celebrated in early October; this family-oriented event includes pioneer storytellers, square-dance exhibitions, music, and a barbecue.

NIGHTLIFE

Nightlife in Sedona, geared toward a resort crowd, tends to be fairly sedate. On Friday and Saturday nights, you'll find quiet sounds in an intimate setting at **Dahl & Di Luca, Enchantment Resort, Shugrue's** (☞ Dining and Lodging, *above*), and, in nearby Oak Creek, at **Irene's** (✉ 6466 AZ 179, ☎ 520/284–2240) and the **Bell Rock Inn** (✉ 6246 AZ 179, ☎ 520/282–4161); call ahead to see who's playing. The closest you'll come to a rollicking cowboy bar in town is **Rainbow's End** (✉ 3235 W. Hwy. 89A, ☎ 520/282–1593), a steak house with a large dance floor and live country-western bands on weekends.

Shopping

In the so-called Uptown shopping area, running along Hwy. 89A to the east of its intersection with AZ 179, the stores tend to cater primarily to the tour-bus trade. Among them, **Native & Nature** (✉ 248 N. Hwy. 89A, ☎ 520/282–7870) is outstanding for its regional books and Southwest artifacts. At the end of the strip, **North Wind** (✉ 450 N. Hwy. 89A, ☎ 520/282–6505) is a fine arts gallery that hosts some unusual Native American pieces.

For upscale shopping, **Tlaquepaque** (✉ AZ 179, just south of the "Y," ☎ 520/282–4838) gathers together more than 100 artisans, many of them painters and sculptors. Comprising a group of red-tile-roof buildings arranged around a series of courtyards, the complex shares its name and architectural style with a crafts village just outside Guadalajara. It's a lovely place to browse, but prices tend to be high; when asked how to pronounce the name of this shopping complex, locals joke that it's "to-lock-your-pocket." **Isadora** (✉ No. 120, Bldg. A, ☎ 520/282–6232) has beautiful handwoven jackets and shawls. **Carusetta** (✉ No. 109, Bldg. A, ☎ 520/282–7793) showcases gold, silver, lapis, and turquoise jewelry. **Kuivato** (✉ No. 122, Bldg. B, ☎ 520/282–1212) features gorgeous glassware. **Estebans** (✉ No. 103, Bldg. B, ☎ 520/282–4686) focuses on ceramics as well as Native American crafts. A good bet for southwestern art is **El Prado Gallery by the Creek** (✉ No. 101, Bldg. E, ☎ 520/282–7390).

At the junction of AZ 179 and Schnebly Hill Road, a small strip of shops includes **Garland's Navajo Rugs** (✉ 411 AZ 179, ☎ 520/282–4070), with its huge collection of new and antique carpets, as well as Native American kachina dolls, pottery, and baskets. In the same building as Garland's Navajo Rugs, **Sedona Pottery** (✉ 411 AZ 179, ☎ 520/282–1192) features unusual pieces, including life-size ceramic statues by shop owner Mary Margaret Sather.

In the **Hozho Center** (✉ 431 AZ 179, ☎ 520/282–1038), a small, upscale complex set in a beige Santa Fe–style building, the **Lanning Gallery** (☎ 520/282–6865) sells attractive southwestern art and jewelry, and **James Ratliff Gallery** (☎ 520/282–1404) has many pieces by not-yet-established artists; well-heeled buyers can find lots of fun, functional pieces. Drive a minute or two south of the Hozho Center on AZ 179 and you'll come to the **Hillside Courtyard & Marketplace** (✉ 671 AZ 179, ☎ 520/282–4500). Among the 23 shops and galleries, **John M. Soderberg Gallery** (☎ 520/282–3818) specializes in western sculpture.

Inveterate bargain hunters will want to head south on AZ 179 2 mi past Chapel of the Holy Cross to the village of Oak Creek. At the **Oak Creek Factory Outlets** (✉ 6601 S. AZ 179, ☎ 520/284–2150), you'll find such stores as Corning/Revere, Mikasa, Anne Klein, Bass, Jones New York, and Van Heusen.

Red Rock State Park

14 *5 mi southwest of Sedona.*

Two mi west of Sedona on Highway 89A is the turnoff for the 286-acre Red Rock State Park, one of the newest state parks in Arizona (opened in 1991) and one of the most beautiful. An ideal place to enjoy both the red-rock formations of the Sedona area and lovely Oak Creek, it's also a less crowded alternative to the popular Slide Rock State Park (☞ *below*). The 5 mi of interconnected park trails are well marked and provide beautiful vistas. There are bird-watching excursions on Wednesday and Saturday and a guided hike to Eagle's Nest scenic overlook—the highest point in the park—every Saturday. Nature walks are given daily, weather permitting. Call ahead for times, which change with the season. ✉ *HC O2, Box 886, Sedona 86336,* ☎ *520/282–6907.* *$5 per car.* ⏲ *Daily 8–5 winter, 8–6 rest of year.*

Oak Creek Canyon

★ 15 *Begins about 1 mi north of Sedona along Hwy. 89A.*

Whether you want to swim, hike, picnic, or enjoy beautiful scenery framed through a car window, head north on Highway 89A through the wooded Oak Creek Canyon; it's the most attractive route to Flagstaff and the Grand Canyon and worth a drive-through even if you don't have a destination. Although the forest is primarily evergreen, the fall brings enough changing colors to make the view especially glorious then. The road winds through a steep-walled canyon, and visitors crane their necks for views of the dramatic rock formations above. Oak Creek, which runs along the bottom of the canyon, is lined with tent campgrounds, fishing camps, cabins, motels, and restaurants.

Slide Rock State Park is a good place for a picnic. On a hot day, you can plunge down a natural rock slide into a swimming hole—a delightful experience. (Bring an extra pair of jeans to wear on the slide.) The only downside to this trip is the traffic, particularly on summer weekends. ✉ *7 mi north of Sedona,* ☎ *520/282–3034.* *$5 per car.* ⏲ *Daily 8–5 winter, 8–6 spring, 8–7 summer.*

Among the forest-service paths you can hike in the canyon is the popular **West Fork Trail,** which follows Oak Creek. A walk through the woods and a dip in the stream make a great summer combination. You'll find the trailhead about 3 mi north of Slide Rock State Park.

Anglers young and old will enjoy the sure catch at the **Rainbow Trout Farm.** For $1 you'll get a cane pole with a hook and bait. There's no charge if your catch is under 8 inches: it's $2.85 for anything from 8 to 9 inches, $3.85 for 10 to 11 inches, $4.85 from 12 to 13 inches, and $5.85 for 14 inches and larger. The real bargain is that the staff will clean your fish for 50¢ each and pack them in ice for you. ✉ *3 mi north of Sedona on Hwy. 89A,* ☎ *520/282–3379.* ⏲ *Weekdays 9–5, weekends 8–6; summer, daily 8–6, weather permitting.*

Dining and Lodging

BED-AND-BREAKFASTS

$$$–$$$$ ★ **Briar Patch Inn.** Set in a wonderfully verdant canyon with a rushing creek, this bed-and-breakfast has accommodations to match. All the hewn-wood cabins (in Native American and Mexican styles) have kitchenettes; some offer decks overlooking Oak Creek, and many feature fireplaces. On summer mornings you can sit outside and enjoy home-baked breads and fresh egg dishes while listening to classical music performed live. New Age and crafts workshops are held on the premises at various times. ✉ *Off Hwy. 89A, 3 mi north of Sedona, HC 30, Box 1002, Sedona 86336,*

☏ *520/282–2342,* FAX *520/282–2399. 12 2-person cabins, 4 4-person cabins. Kitchenettes, massage, fishing, library. MC, V.*

$$$ ★ **Wishing Well.** Although it's less than a mile from Uptown Sedona, this bed-and-breakfast perched on a plateau at the mouth of Oak Creek Canyon will make you forget there's a town nearby. All the rooms are ultraromantic, with stunning views of Cathedral Rock. A hiking trail behind the house once served as a cattle route for the area's Native American inhabitants. Hosts Valda and Esper Esau, who met in Las Vegas when she was a dancer and he was the stage manager at the Desert Inn, make you feel welcome while respecting your privacy; a lovely Continental breakfast is served on fine china in your room, and chilled champagne or candlelit dinners are easily arranged. ✉ *995 N. Hwy. 89A, Sedona 86336,* ☏ *520/282–4914 or 800/728–9474,* FAX *520/204–9766. 4 rooms with bath. MC, V.*

$$$$ **Garland's Oak Creek Lodge.** In the heart of Oak Creek Canyon, this lodge was built in the 1930s and bought by its current owners, Gary and Mary Garland, in the 1960s. Sixteen comfortably furnished cabins, some including fireplaces and pullout beds for extra guests, share 17 acres of beautiful land (at an elevation of 5,000 feet) with an organic apple orchard. Accommodations look out over the canyon itself or the rugged cliffs surrounding it. The lodge is operated on a Modified American Plan, with excellent breakfasts and dinners included in the room price, along with afternoon tea. Garland's is often booked solid a year in advance—it's open only from April 1 to November 15—but it's worth a phone call to check. ✉ *Hwy. 89A, 8 mi north of Sedona, Box 152, Sedona 86339,* ☏ *520/282–3343. 16 cabins with bath. Restaurant, lake, tennis court, croquet, volleyball. MC, V.*

FLAGSTAFF AND ENVIRONS

Few visitors slow down long enough to explore Flagstaff, a town of 42,000, known locally as Flag. Most stop only to spend the night at one of the town's many motels before making the last leg of the trip to the Grand Canyon, 80 mi north. But the city, set against a lovely backdrop of pine forests and the snowcapped San Francisco Peaks, retains a frontier flavor downtown and is home to many interesting historical attractions as well as to numerous Native American arts exhibits and crafts sales in summer. Flag also makes a good base for day-trips to various Native American ruins and current-day Navajo and Hopi reservations, as well as to the Petrified Forest National Park and the Painted Desert (☞ Chapter 3).

Flagstaff has more fast-food outlets per permanent resident than most cities do, no doubt because of the incredible demand for it: Two major interstate highways crisscross the town; thousands of tourists drive through on the way to the Grand Canyon; thousands of students attending Northern Arizona University reside here; and many Native Americans come in from nearby reservations. Of course, there are other, much better restaurants to enjoy. Traffic to the Grand Canyon is heavy all year, but in summer it skyrockets, increasing the number of overnight visitors. During that time of year, the streets are also filled with Phoenix residents seeking relief from the desert heat.

Phoenicians also come to Flagstaff in winter to ski at the Arizona Snowbowl, a small ski area about 15 mi northeast of town among the San Francisco Peaks. Accommodation rates are low at this time of year, making winter visits an excellent option for downhill and cross-country enthusiasts. At any time of the year, temperatures in Flagstaff are approximately 20°F cooler than in Phoenix. There are plenty of places to stay (though no major hotels or resorts), but it's wise to reserve a room ahead of time in Flagstaff, and during the summer months it's essential.

Flagstaff

146 mi northwest of Phoenix, 27 mi north of Sedona via Oak Creek Canyon.

Numbers in the margin correspond to points of interest on the Flagstaff map.

16 The **downtown historic district** offers a glimpse of Flagstaff in its prime, with some excellent examples of late Victorian and early Art Deco architecture. Allowed to become somewhat seedy over the years, downtown is currently undergoing a major restoration under the auspices of the national Main Street organization. A walking-tour map of the area, prepared by the Arizona Historical Society, is available at the visitor center (☞ Visitor Information *in* North Central Arizona A to Z, *below*), now in the Tudor Revival–style Santa Fe Depot, an excellent place to begin sightseeing. Highlights include the Hotel Monte Vista (☞ Lodging, *below*) and the gabled-roof Orpheum Theatre. You may notice a lot of structures that bear the name Babbitt, after one of Flagstaff's wealthiest founding families. Former Arizona governor and current Secretary of the Interior Bruce Babbitt is just the latest member of the family to wield power and influence. This is also the part of town in which the most interesting shops are concentrated, selling everything from sporting goods to Native American crafts.

NEED A BREAK? Students, skiers, new and aging hippies, and just about everyone else who likes good coffee jams into **Macy's** (✉ 14 S. Beaver St., ☎ 520/774–2243) for the best cup in town. The **Morning Glory Cafe** (✉ 5 San Francisco St., ☎ 520/774–3705) is another popular '60s throwback for a caffeine fix and accompanying light fare.

17 The **Lowell Observatory** was founded in 1894 by Boston businessman, author, and scientist Percival Lowell, who studied the planet Mars from here. His predictions of the existence of a ninth planet led to the discovery of Pluto at Lowell in 1930 by Clyde Tombaugh. V. M. Slipher's observations here between 1912 and 1920 led to the theory of the expanding universe.

The 6,500-square-foot Steele Visitor Center, opened in 1994, hosts exhibits, a lecture hall, and a gift shop; a "Tools of the Astronomer" display explains what professional stargazers do. During the day, the staff welcomes guests and offers slide lectures and tours. There are several interactive exhibits (simple but interesting) for children, who will especially enjoy the Pluto Walk, a scaled-down version of our solar system that is designed for exploring.

On different evenings every month except January and February, weather permitting, the public is invited to peer through the 24-inch Clark telescope, which celebrated its 100th anniversary in 1996; viewings through the smaller Pluto telescope have also been initiated recently. The greatest number of viewings (four a week) are offered from June through August; call ahead for a schedule. The observatory dome is open and unheated—any change in temperature would affect the telescope lens—so dress for an outdoor rather than an indoor activity. To reach the observatory, which is less than 2 mi from downtown, drive west on Route 66 (which resumes its former name, Santa Fe Avenue, before it merges into Mars Hill Road). ✉ *1400 W. Mars Hill Rd.,* ☎

Arizona Snowbowl, **24**
Coconino Center for the Arts, **22**
Downtown Historic District, **16**
Lowell Observatory, **17**
Museum Club, **20**
Museum of Northern Arizona, **23**
Observatory at Northern Arizona University, **19**
Pioneer Historical Museum, **21**
Riordan State Historic Park, **18**

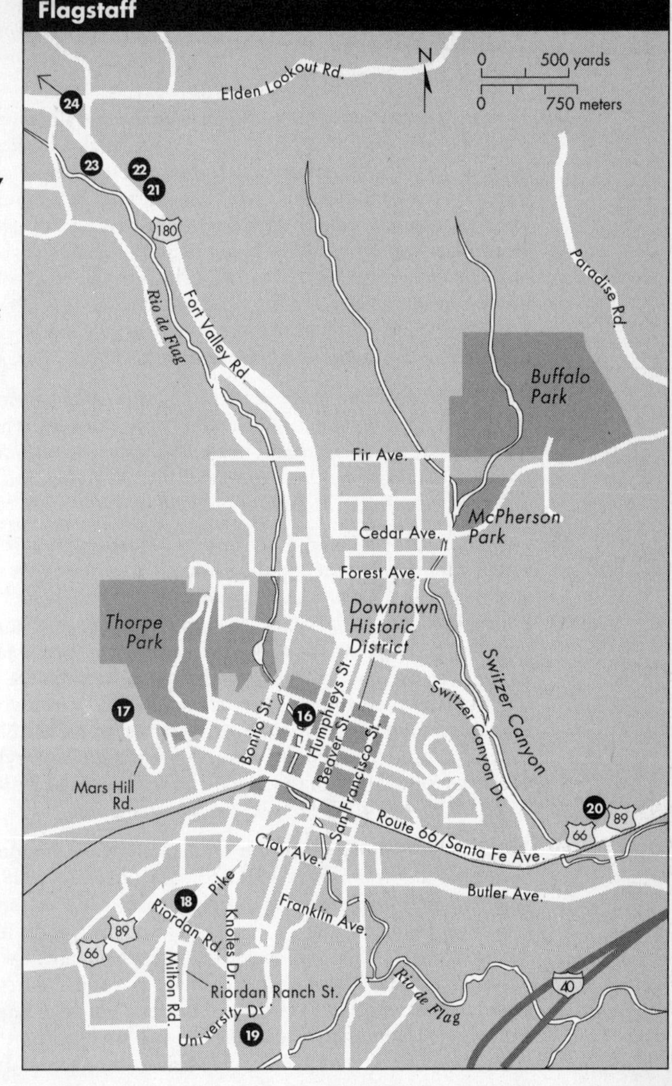

520/774–2096. $3. *Visitor center and night viewing hrs change seasonally; call ahead.*

★ 18 A unique artifact of Flagstaff's logging heyday, **Riordan State Historic Park,** near Northern Arizona University, is a must-see. Its centerpiece is a mansion built in 1904 for Michael and Timothy Riordan, lumber-baron brothers who married two sisters. The 13,300-square-foot, 40-room log-and-stone structure—designed by Charles Whittlesley, who was also responsible for the El Tovar Hotel at the Grand Canyon—contains a good deal of furniture by Gustav Stickley, father of the American Arts and Crafts design movement. Fascinating details abound; one room holds "Paul Bunyan's shoes," a 2-foot-long pair of boots made by Timothy in his workshop. Everything on display—from books to family photos and clothes—is original to the house, half of which was occupied by members of the family until 1986. The mansion may be explored on a guided tour only. Special evening tours given during Halloween week are very popular; they're limited to groups of 15, so book at least a month in advance if you want to be spooked. ✉ *1300 Riordan Ranch St.,* ☎ *520/779–4395.* 🎟 *$3.* ⏲ *May–Sept. daily 8–5, with tours at 9, 10, 11, 1, 2, 3, and 4; Oct.–Apr. daily 11–5, with tours at noon, 1, 2, 3, and 4.*

19 The **observatory at Northern Arizona University,** along with a 24-inch telescope, was built in 1952 by Dr. Arthur Adel, who had been a scientist at Lowell Observatory until he joined the college faculty as a professor of mathematics. His work on infrared astronomy pioneered research into molecules that absorb light passing through the earth's atmosphere. Today's studies of our planet's shrinking ozone layer rely on some of Dr. Adel's early work. Visitors to the observatory—which houses one of the largest telescopes that the public is allowed to move and manipulate—are usually hosted by friendly students and faculty members of the university's Department of Physics and Astronomy.

Public viewings take place every clear Friday night from 7 PM to 10 PM. Tours for individuals and small groups can be arranged any day except Friday by calling at least one week in advance. ✉ *Bldg. 47, Northern Arizona Campus Observatory, Dept. of Physics and Astronomy, S. San Francisco St.,* ☎ *520/523–7170.* 🎟 *Free.*

20 For real Route 66 color, don't miss the **Museum Club,** fondly known as the Zoo because the building housed an extensive taxidermy collection in the 1930s. Most of the stuffed animals—including such bizarre specimens as a one-eyed sheep—are mercifully gone, but some owls still perch above the dance floor of what is now a popular country-western club (Willy Nelson and Waylon Jennings are just a few of the acts who used to play here in the 1960s). Even if you don't like crowds or country music, it's worth coming to see the building, a gigantic log cabin constructed around five trees; the entryway consists of a huge forked pine in the shape of a wishbone. ✉ *3404 E. Rte. 66,* ☎ *520/526–9434.* 🎟 *Free.* ⏲ *Daily noon–1 AM.*

21 The **Pioneer Historical Museum** is operated by the Arizona Historical Society in a volcanic rock building constructed in 1908—Coconino County's first hospital for the poor. You can still see one of the depressingly small patients' rooms, an old iron lung, and a reconstructed doctor's office, but most of the displays touch on more cheerful aspects of Flagstaff history—for example, road signs and children's toys. The museum hosts a folk-crafts festival on the Fourth of July, where you can watch traditional tradespeople, such as blacksmiths, weavers, spinners, quilters, and candle makers, at work. Their crafts, and those of other local artisans, are sold in the museum's gift shop, a tiny space filled with teddy bears, dolls, hand-dipped candles, and hand-stitched quilts. The museum is part of the Fort Valley Park complex, in a wooded residential section at the northwest end of town. ✉ *2340 N. Fort Valley Rd.,* ☎ *520/774–6272.* 🎟 *$1 suggested donation per individual, $3 per family.* ⏲ *Mon.–Sat. 9–5.*

22 The **Coconino Center for the Arts** is a nonprofit community center that puts on two major annual arts-and-crafts festivals (☞ Nightlife and the Arts, *below*) and hosts exhibits, performing arts events, and educational programs throughout the year. A gallery features the work of regionally and nationally known artists, from photographers to sculptors and lithographers, on a rotating basis; write or phone for a calendar of events. Warning: The gift shop, filled with handcrafted jewelry, pottery, and posters by featured artists, can be detrimental to your pocketbook. All proceeds go to the center, though, so you're shopping for a worthy cause—and there's no tax on your purchases. The center is a few hundred feet up a gentle hill from the Pioneer Historical Mu-

seum (☞ *above*). ✉ *2300 N. Fort Valley Rd., Box 296, Flagstaff 86002,* ☎ *520/779–6921.* 🎫 *Free.* ⏲ *Apr.–Sept., Tues.–Sun. 10–5; Oct.–Mar., Tues.–Sat. 10–5. Closed Dec. 24–early Jan.*

★ 23 The **Museum of Northern Arizona** resides in a striking native-stone building shaded with trees. Founded in 1928, the museum is now respected worldwide for its research and for its collections centering on the natural and cultural history of the Colorado Plateau; only 1% of its vast holdings on the archaeology, ethnology, geology, biology, and fine arts of the region is on display at any given time. Among the permanent exhibitions are an extensive collection of Navajo rugs as well as an authentic Hopi kiva (men's ceremonial chamber). Outdoors, a life-zone exhibit shows the changing vegetation in the area from the bottom of the Grand Canyon to the highest peak in Flagstaff, and a nature trail (open only in summer) heads down across a small stream into a canyon and up into an aspen grove.

The museum has been undergoing a good deal of expansion in recent years. Of the two galleries opened in 1992, the one devoted to the geology of the area is particularly popular with children: It includes a life-size model Dilophosaurus, a carnivorous dinosaur that roamed northern Arizona when much of the area was swampland, as well as a number of hands-on displays. And 1995 saw the opening of a new wing with lots of cozy sitting areas and wonderful western details. The Harvey W. Braniger Hall hosts a fascinating 27-minute film, "Sacred Lands of the Southwest," and the Babbitt Gallery will eventually display the museum's extensive ceramics collection.

Every summer, the museum hosts exhibits and sales by Native American artists (☞ Nightlife and the Arts, *below*), whose wares are also sold in the museum gift shop. In addition, the museum's education department sponsors excellent tours of the area and some as far away as New Mexico and California (☞ Guided Tours *in* North-Central Arizona A to Z, *below*). Docent-led tours of the museum are available for individuals or groups, but appointments must be made at least two weeks in advance. ✉ *3001 N. Fort Valley Rd.,* ☎ *520/774–5213.* 🎫 *$5.* ⏲ *Daily 9–5.*

24 The **Arizona Snowbowl** is one of Flagstaff's most popular attractions. It's especially well frequented when the white stuff is on the ground (☞ Skiing *and* Snowboarding *in* Outdoor Activities and Sports, *below*), but in summer the Agassi ski lift doubles as a skyride, which takes you through the Coconino National Forest to a height of 11,500 feet in 25 minutes. From this vantage point, you can see up to 70 mi; views include the North Rim of the Grand Canyon. There's a lodge nearby with a restaurant and bar. ✉ *U.S. 180 to Snowbowl Rd., then 7 mi to skyride entrance,* ☎ *520/779–1951.* 🎫 *$9.* ⏲ *Skyride operates daily mid-June–Labor Day, weekends only (weather permitting) Labor Day–mid-Oct. Operating hrs and prices may change; call ahead.*

Dining and Lodging

By city ordinance, all restaurants in Flagstaff forbid smoking. A number of eateries stay open longer in summer, the time of year when lodging prices are also at their highest.

$$–$$$ ✕ **Chez Marc Bistro.** This classic French restaurant, run by the Cannes-born former head chef of L'Auberge de Sedona Resort, is set in a 1911 mansion built by the influential Babbitt family. In a series of pretty country French–style dining rooms upstairs and downstairs, you can enjoy such entrées as sautéed scallops with white cabbage topped with caviar. The setting is romantic, the wine list impressive, and the food generally good, but service is often unsophisticated. ✉ *503 Humphreys St.,* ☎ *520/774–1343. AE, D, DC, MC, V.*

$$–$$$ ✕ **Cottage Place.** An unexpectedly elegant spot in a town known for hearty food and drive-through service, this cozy restaurant in a 50-year-old cottage has intimate dining rooms decorated in traditional style, with fresh flowers and candles. The menu strays only slightly from Continental to include some classic American dishes, such as charbroiled lamb chops. Try the artichoke chicken breast or chateaubriand for two carved tableside. Dinner includes relish tray, soup, and salad, but save room for signature desserts, like Chocolate Decadence. ✉ *126 W. Cottage Ave.,* ☎ *520/774–8431. AE, MC, V. Closed Mon. No lunch.*

$$–$$$ ✕ **Down Under New Zealand Restaurant.** Dinner is a recent addition to the repertoire of this former tearoom, so the vote's not in yet on such hearty dishes as grilled lamb cutlets with minted lemon sauce or beef Wellington, priced at the high end of the Flagstaff scale; if they meet the standards of the lunch menu, however, they'll be worth it. At midday, local businesspeople flock into the pretty green-and-white dining room (formerly a carriage house) or onto the cheerful outdoor terrace for delicious potato leek soup with sherry and copious Greek salads. Such dishes as New Zealand meat pies and good Australian wines by the glass attest to the owners' far-flung origins. ✉ *413 N. San Francisco St.,* ☎ *520/774–6677. AE, MC, V. Closed Sun. No lunch weekends.*

$$ ✕ **Black Bart's Steakhouse Saloon & Old West Theater.** Fans of the Wild West—or a sanitized version thereof—will enjoy the atmosphere in this rustic, barnlike structure, complete with beamed ceilings and hanging lantern light fixtures. Aged prime beef is grilled over an open oak fire, and the barbecued chicken is tender and flavorful. On weekends, your server is likely to get onstage and belt out a couple of show tunes. When there's no live entertainment, a player piano fills the restaurant with its tinny renditions of old favorites. ✉ *2760 E. Butler Ave.,* ☎ *520/779–3142. MC, V. No lunch.*

$$ ★ ✕ **Sakura Restaurant.** What are the odds of finding a good sushi bar in Flagstaff? Sakura's fish, flown in every other day from the West Coast, is excellent; spicy sushi-style tuna salad will knock your socks off. If sushi doesn't entice you, dine at a large table accompanied by a grill chef's pyrotechnics, and choose from entrées prepared *teppan* (Japanese grill) style; even if you haven't set foot in a Benihana in years, you'll probably enjoy well-seasoned, large portions of steak or seafood with vegetables being flipped in front of you. ✉ *1175 Rte. 66,* ☎ *520/773–9118. AE, D, DC, MC, V. No lunch Sun.*

$–$$ ✕ **Beaver Street Brewery.** Most everyone enjoys the wood-fired pizzas that the open-kitchen of this huge, bustling restaurant turns out—for example, the Enchanted Forest, with Brie, artichoke pesto, portabello mushrooms, roasted red pepper, and spinach. (Whichever you order, expect serious amounts of garlic to be involved.) Sandwiches, such as the southwestern chicken with three types of cheese, come with a hefty portion of tasty fries on the side. You won't regret ordering one of the down-home desserts, like the supergooey chocolate bread pudding. Beer lovers will likely want to imbibe extra calories; among the excellent microbrews, the raspberry ale is a particular local favorite. An outdoor beer garden opens up in summer. ✉ *11 S. Beaver St.,* ☎ *520/779–0079. AE, D, DC, MC, V.*

$–$$ ✕ **Buster's Restaurant.** At lunchtime, families and students from nearby Northern Arizona University frequent the comfortable booths and tables of this popular restaurant. The menu includes fresh seafood, homemade soups, salads, giant burgers, and mesquite-grilled steaks. Try the *lahvosh* appetizer—a giant cracker heaped with a choice of toppings ranging from smoked salmon to mushrooms—or Caesar salad with grilled Cajun chicken. At night, upscale single professionals and skiers crowd the bar and work through its impressive selection of beer. ✉ *1800 S. Milton Rd.,* ☎ *520/774–5155. AE, D, DC, MC, V.*

$–$$ ✕ **Pasto.** This downtown Italian restaurant, comprising two intimate dining rooms in adjacent historic buildings, is extremely popular with a young crowd for its good and plentiful food at reasonable prices. Such southern Italian standards as lasagna and spaghetti with meatballs appear on the menu along with more innovative fare, like artichoke orzo and salmon Caesar salad, and there's a nice selection of beer, soft drinks, wine, and coffee. A courtyard in the back, tucked away among higher buildings, has a romantic urban feel. ✉ *19 E. Aspen St.,* ☎ *520/779–1937. DC, MC, V. Lunch in high season only.*

$ ★ ✕ **Café Espress.** A wholesome, natural-food, all-day restaurant (it's open 7 AM–10 PM Monday–Thursday and 7 AM–11 PM Friday–Saturday), Café Espress serves a largely vegetarian menu (red meat is excluded). Hearty stir-fried vegetables, pasta dishes, Mediterranean salads, tempeh burgers, pita pizzas, fish or chicken specials, and wonderful baked goods made on the premises all come at prices that will make you feel good, too. The atmosphere is gallery hip (the work of local artists hangs on the walls) but friendly. ✉ *16 N. San Francisco St.,* ☎ *520/774–0541. MC, V.*

$ ✕ **Café Olé.** Chili-pepper strings, a neon cactus, and a pastel mural all add to the upbeat atmosphere at this little family-run restaurant, popular with local politicos and university professors. Vegetarian green-chili-and-cheese tamales and the best guacamole in town are among the specialties here, and you can sample a variety of freshly prepared Mexican dishes in well-priced combination plates. ✉ *119 San Francisco St.,* ☎ *520/774–8272. Reservations not accepted. No credit cards. Closed weekends in winter, Sun. in summer.*

$ ✕ **Hunan West Restaurant.** The hands-down local favorite for Chinese food, this west-side restaurant has far more atmosphere than its strip-mall setting would suggest: An imposing dragon decorates the back wall, and white cloths dress the tables. The friendly staff will guide you through a menu that includes many Hunan specialties along with familiar Cantonese fare. The beef in orange-peel sauce is excellent, and you can order the bean curd with mixed vegetables in "spicy" or "not spicy" versions. ✉ *University Plaza Shopping Center, 1302 S. Plaza Way,* ☎ *520/779–2229. AE, D, DC, MC, V. Closed Mon.*

$ ✕ **Salsa Brava.** This cheerful Mexican restaurant, with light-wood booths and bold, colorful designs, eschews heavy Sonoran-style fare in favor of the grilled dishes found in Guadalajara (determined artery-cloggers will still find enough cheese-smothered items on the menu). The fish tacos are particularly popular, and this place has the only salsa bar in town. One annoyance: After the first bowl, additional tortilla chips cost extra. ✉ *1800 S. Milton Rd.,* ☎ *520/774–1083. AE, MC, V.*

$ ✕ **Strombolli's.** Nicer-than-average decor raises Strombolli's above pizza-joint status, but the pizza oven is still the biggest draw. Many come for the huge calzones, which, as with pizza, you can have with any of 25 fresh, tempting ingredients. Of course, you may prefer pasta, like linguine with basil pesto cream sauce. If you're very hungry, consider the delicious spinach dip appetizer, which comes with tortilla chips, odd as that may seem in an Italian place. Reservations aren't accepted, but there is a call-ahead waiting list. ✉ *1435 S. Milton,* ☎ *520/773–1960. Reservations not accepted. AE, D, MC, V.*

BED-AND-BREAKFASTS

$$–$$$ ★ **Inn at Four Ten.** A good alternative to the chain motels in Flagstaff, this bed-and-breakfast offers a quiet but convenient downtown setting. All of the accommodations in this beautifully restored 1907 residence are spacious suites with private baths. Some offer private entrances, fireplaces, and/or hot tubs; all have refrigerators and coffeemakers. The full breakfasts are delicious as well as health-conscious; in the afternoon, the hosts bring out fresh-baked cookies. There's no smoking allowed inside the inn. ✉ *410 N. Leroux St., Flagstaff 86001,* ☎ *520/774–0088 or 800/774–2008,* FAX *520/774–6354. 9 suites (1 accessible to travelers with disabilities). Refrigerators. MC, V.*

$$ **Comfi Cottages of Flagstaff.** Ideal for people who dislike the coldness of motels but don't enjoy breakfasting with strangers in a traditional bed-and-breakfast environment, these individual cottages come stocked with breakfast fixings. They offer most of the conveniences of home (only one doesn't have a washer-dryer), plus such extras as picnic tables, bicycles, and barbecue grills. You can choose from a variety of styles (English country or southwestern, for example) and sizes; the three-bedroom cottage is nice for a family or group of friends. All are in a residential neighborhood less than half a mile from downtown. ✉ *1612 N. Aztec, Flagstaff 86001,* ☎ *520/774–0731. 1 1-bedroom cottage, 3 2-bedroom cottages, 1 3-bedroom cottage. Bicycles. MC, V.*

$$ ★ **Birch Tree Inn.** This historic home, in a lovely tree-filled neighborhood near downtown, is nicely appointed with antiques and has a relaxed atmosphere, in part because the hosts (two friendly couples who trade off innkeeping stints) enjoy chatting with their guests; they even sit down with them during breakfast. The billiard table adjoining the living room gets visitors talking to each other, too. You'll start your day well fueled for sightseeing: The morning meal might consist of a cheese, sausage, and potato casserole accompanied by fresh fruit and banana bread made on the premises. Rates are very reasonable. ✉ *824 W. Birch Ave., Flagstaff 86001,* ☎ *520/774–1042 or 800/645–5805. 3 rooms with private bath, 2 rooms with shared bath. AE, MC, V.*

HOTELS AND MOTELS

$$$ **Best Western Woodlands Plaza Hotel.** This upscale link in the Best Western chain is the glitziest accommodation in town—which isn't saying much in Flagstaff. A brass-and-marble lobby, although tasteful, is somehow oddly eclectic. But the hotel is conveniently located near downtown and major outbound roads; rooms are large, comfortable, and nicely furnished in southwestern pastels; and there are two good restaurants on the premises, including Sakura (☞ *above*). ✉ *1175 W. Rte. 66, Flagstaff 86001,* ☎ *520/773–8888 or 800/528–1234,* FAX *520/773–0597. 183 rooms with bath. Bar, pool, sauna, indoor-outdoor spa, steam room, fitness center. AE, D, DC, MC, V.*

$$ **AmeriSuites.** Look elsewhere if you want character, but if you're seeking mod-cons in a pleasant, convenient setting, you can't go wrong here. This recently built property was designed for business travelers—rooms offer two phones, a well-lighted desk, and free local phone calls—but leisure goers won't mind a 26-inch stereo TV/VCR, minifridge, and microwave. A morning newspaper and nice Continental buffet are included in the room rate. ✉ *2455 S. Beulah Blvd., Flagstaff 86001,* ☎ *520/774–8042 or 800/833–1516,* FAX *520/774–5524. 118 suites. Hot tub, laundry. AE, D, DC, MC, V.*

$$ ★ **Little America of Flagstaff.** This is the biggest motel in town d'd comma and a deservedly popular place. It's far enough from the tracks to allow visitors to sleep undisturbed as trains roar through town, the grounds are surrounded by evergreen forests, and it's one of the few places in Flagstaff that offer room service. Rooms are surprisingly plush: All have brass chandeliers, comfortable sitting areas with French provincial–style furniture, phones in bathrooms, large stereo TVs, and small refrigerators. Other pluses are courtesy van service to the airport and Amtrak station and a 24-hour gift shop with lots of great southwestern stuff.

☒ *Box 3900, 2515 E. Butler Ave., Flagstaff 86004,* ☎ *520/779–2741 or 800/352–4386,* FAX *520/779–7983. 248 rooms with bath. Restaurant, bar, 24-hour coffee shop, kitchenettes, refrigerators, room service, outdoor heated pool, fitness center, hiking, laundry service, playground, airport shuttle. AE, D, DC, MC, V.*

$–$$ **Hotel Monte Vista.** Over the years many Hollywood stars have stayed at this historic downtown hotel built in 1926—so the guest rooms come by the glamorous names attached to them honestly. The restored southwestern-deco lobby, with its shoe-shine stand and curved archways, is appealing, and rates are low, but rooms and hallways are somewhat dark, and the men buying racing forms who hang out at the front desk make this an iffy choice for female travelers. Bunk-bed rooms at less than $15 per person are available. ☒ *100 N. San Francisco St., Flagstaff 86001,* ☎ *520/779–6971 or 800/545–3068,* FAX *520/779–2904. 48 rooms with bath. Restaurant, bar. AE, D, DC, MC, V.*

Outdoor Activities and Sports

BIKING

A map of the Urban Trails System, available at the Flagstaff Visitors Center (☞ North-Central Arizona A to Z, *below*), details biking options in the area. From mid-June through mid-October, the **Flagstaff Nordic Center** (☎ 520/779–1951) opens its cross-country trails to mountain bikers, gratis if you bring your own two wheels; rentals are also available. In town you can rent mountain bikes at **Absolute Bikes** (☒ 18 N. San Francisco St., 520/779–5969) or **Mountain Sports** (☒ 1800 S. Milton Rd., ☎ 520/779–5156 or 800/286–5156). **Arizona Mountain Bike Tours** (☒ Box 816, Flagstaff 86002, ☎ 520/779–4161 or 800/277–7985 in AZ) can guide you along the Colorado Plateau or the volcanic craters near Flagstaff.

CAMPING

Contact the **Coconino National Forest** (☒ 2323 Greenlaw La., ☎ 520/527–3600) for information on camping in the area. (☞ Camping *in* Contacts and Resources *in* North-Central Arizona A to Z, *below.*)

GOLF

In addition to many private clubs in the area, golfers will find semiprivate courses, which accept a limited number of nonmembers, as well as public courses. The best club open to the public in the Flagstaff vicinity is the **Elden Hill Golf Course** (☒ 2380 N. Oakmont Dr., ☎ 520/526–5125).

HIKING

You can explore Arizona's alpine tundra in the San Francisco Peaks, where more than 80 species of plants grow on the upper elevations. The habitat is fragile, so hikers are asked to stay on established trails (and there are lots of them). The **Humphreys Peak Trail** is 9 mi round-trip, with a vertical climb of 3,843 feet to the summit of Arizona's highest mountain (12,643 feet). Those who don't want a long hike will be well rewarded if they do just the first mile of the 5-mile-long **Kachina Trail;** completely flat, this route is surrounded by huge stands of aspen and offers fantastic vistas. It's particularly worthwhile in fall, when changing leaves paint the landscape shades of yellow, russet, and amber. You'll find these two trailheads at the Arizona Snowbowl (☞ Skiing, *below*); others, such as the short but rewarding **Fatmans Loop** on Mt. Eldin, can be accessed in town. Contact the **Coconino National Forest** (☒ 2323 Greenlaw La., ☎ 520/527–3600), which maintains these and other trails, for details on hiking in the area; it's open Monday–Saturday 8–6, Sunday 8–5. Just north of Flagstaff, but still in town, the **Peaks Ranger Station** (☒ 5075 N. U.S. 89, ☎ 520/527–3630) also has excellent hiking and recreational guides.

NOTE – The altitude here will make even the hardiest hikers breathe a little harder, so individuals with cardiac or respiratory problems should be cautious of overexertion.

HORSEBACK RIDING

The wranglers at **Hitchin' Post Stables** (✉ 448 Lake Mary Rd., ☎ 520/774–1719) lead rides into Walnut Canyon and offer horseback or horse-drawn wagon rides with sunset barbecues. In winter, they'll take you through Coconino National Forest on a sleigh—bells and all.

ROCK CLIMBING

Flagstaff Mountain Guides (✉ Box 2383, Flagstaff 86003, ☎ 520/635–0145) offers peak experiences around town or as far away as Sedona. If you'd prefer to hone your skills first, the new **Vertical Relief Rock Gym** (✉ 205 S. San Francisco St., ☎ 520/556–9909) provides the tallest indoor walls in the Southwest.

SKIING

Downhill. To the dismay of schussers, the 1995–96 winter didn't see snow until late February, but the ski season usually starts in mid-November and ends in mid-April. **Arizona Snowbowl** (✉ 7 mi north of Flagstaff on U.S. 180, ☎ 520/779–1951) offers 30 runs (about 30% beginner, 40% intermediate, and 30% advanced), four chairlifts, and a vertical drop of 2,300 feet. Those who've skied Colorado's Rockies might find Snowbowl a bit disappointing—there are a couple of good bump runs, but it's better for skiers of beginning or moderate ability. Still, Arizonans enjoy their local slopes, and it's a fun place to spend the day. The Hart Prairie Lodge and its equipment rental shop recently underwent a huge expansion and added a new SKIwee center for ages 4–8.

For lift tickets, senior citizens ages 65 and over pay only $11, and children ages 7 and under ski free; all-day lift tickets for adults are $31. Half-day discounts are available, and group-lesson packages (including two hours of instruction, an all-day lift ticket, and equipment rental) are a good buy at $47. The kids' program (which includes lunch, progress card, and full supervision 9–3:30) runs $50. Many Flagstaff motels offer ski packages, including transportation to Snowbowl; call ☎ 800/828–7285 for details. For the current snow report, call ☎ 520/779–4577.

Nordic. Cross-country skiers can find 25 mi of well-groomed trails at the **Flagstaff Nordic Center,** owned and operated by Arizona Snowbowl (☞ *above*) and located 9 mi north of Snowbowl Road on Highway 180. A variety of instruction packages and rental combinations are available. The **Mormon Lake Ski Center** (✉ 28 mi southeast of Flagstaff by way of Lake Mary Rd., Mormon Lake, ☎ 520/354–2240) is another cross-country option.

SNOWBOARDING

Don't even suggest to snowboarders that their chosen sport bears some resemblance to skiing—those who ride the snow on a single fat ski the way surfers ride the waves or skateboarders rule the sidewalks have their own distinct dress code and attitude. Nevertheless, aficionados of this latest winter rage share trails with downhill skiers at the **Arizona Snowbowl** (☞ Skiing, *above*) and can rent equipment there; an all-day Snowboard Package (board, boots, all-day lift ticket, and two-hour lesson) runs $60.

SNOWMOBILING

A number of companies around Flagstaff have started capitalizing on the winter-fun market by specializing in snowmobiles. **Adult Toyz Center** (☎ 520/522–0018) offers rentals as well as a variety of guided tours (including ones by moonlight). You can buy or rent your vehicle at **Shed Sled** (✉ 1620 N. 1st St., ☎ 520/779–9497), where rates run from $25 per hour in midweek to $175 per day on weekends and holidays (including gas, helmets, insurance, and permits).

Nightlife and the Arts

For current information on what's going on in town, pick up the free *Flagstaff Live*.

THE ARTS

Between the **Flagstaff Symphony Orchestra** (✉ Box 122, Flagstaff 86002, ☎ 520/774–5107), **Theatrikos** (✉ 11 W. Cherry St., ☎ 520/774–1662), and Northern Arizona University's **College of Creative and Performing Arts** (✉ Ardrey Auditorium, Knoles and Riordon Rds., ☎ 520/523–5661 for the central ticket office), there's bound to be something cultural going on in Flagstaff when you visit. This is especially true in summer: During the month of July, the **Flagstaff Festival of the Arts** (✉ Box 22402, Flagstaff 86002, ☎ 520/774–7750 or 800/266–7740) fills the air with the sounds of music. Events include sunset jazz dinners and chamber music brunches; many of the symphony and pops performers are world renowned.

Other annual events that reflect the area's culture include the **Festival in the Pines,** sponsored annually during the first weekend of August by the Mill Avenue Merchants' Association (✉ Box 3084, Tempe, ☎ 602/967–4877) and featuring an arts-and-crafts fair. The **Coconino Center for the Arts** (✉ 2300 N. Fort Valley Rd., ☎ 520/779–6921) hosts a **Festival of Native American Arts** each July and August and also sponsors the **Trappings of the American West** from mid-May to early June; the latter focuses on cowboy art—everything from paintings and sculpture to cowboy poetry readings. **A Celebration of Native American Art,** featuring exhibits of work by Zuni, Hopi, and Navajo artists, is held at the Museum of Northern Arizona (✉ 3001 N. Fort Valley Rd., ☎ 520/774–5211) from late May through September. Flagstaff's observatories help make September's **Festival of Science** (☎ 800/842–7239 for information) a stellar attraction.

NIGHTLIFE

Flagstaff's large college crowd has lots of places to gather after dark, most of them in the historic downtown district and most of them charging little or no cover. It's easy to walk from one rowdy spot to the next and choose your favorite form of eardrum abuse.

Club Depot (✉ 26 S. San Francisco St., ☎ 520/773–9550) inspires dancing fools to move to either live or DJ sounds. For live entertainment nightly—everything from bluegrass to jazz and rock—in a low-key atmosphere, try the **Main Street Bar and Grill** (✉ 14 S. San Francisco St., ☎ 520/774–1519); the food's good, too, so come early for dinner. **The Monsoons** (✉ 22 E. Rte. 66, ☎ 520/774–7929) books an eclectic array of live music, from alternative to world beat. The **Monte Vista Lounge** (✉ 100 N. San Francisco St., ☎ 520/774–2403) packs them in with nightly live sounds, including blues, jazz, classic rock, punk, and an open mike on Wednesday. The ground floor of the historic **Weatherford Hotel** (✉ 23 N. Leroux St., ☎ 520/779–1919) is home to both **Charly's,** featuring late-night jazz and blues bands, and the **Exchange Pub,** which tends to attract more acoustic, folksy ensembles.

On the east side, the **Museum Club** (✉ 3404 E. Route 66, ☎ 520/526–9434) is the town's cowboy honky-tonk, offering free dance lessons on Thursday night and good country-and-western bands like Mogollon on the weekends (☞ Flagstaff, *above*).

Shopping

Flagstaff's prime shopping area is downtown. Even if you're not looking for anything in particular, it's fun to stroll along San Francisco Street and Route 66 where most of the interesting shops—many in historic buildings—are concentrated.

For fine arts and crafts—everything from ceramics and stained glass to weaving and painting—visit the **Artists Gallery** (⊠ 17 N. San Francisco St., ☎ 520/773–0985), a cooperative that carries the work of more than 30 local artists. A bit north of the town center, the **Carriage House** (⊠ 413 N. San Francisco St., ☎ 520/774–1337) is a collection of 19 antiques shops that offer old clothes, furniture, fine china, and assorted collectibles. You can pick up any sporting-goods items you might be missing at the **Edge** (⊠ 12 E. Aspen Ave., ☎ 520/774–4775). Locals go to **Four Winds Traders** (⊠ 118 W. Rte. 66, ☎ 520/774–1067) for good buys on both pawned and new Native American jewelry. **McGaugh's Newsstand** (⊠ 24 N. San Francisco St., ☎ 520/774–2131) is the place to come for international newspapers and books on any topic you can think of; even nonsmokers will enjoy the aroma of the pipe tobacco sold in the back. **Winter Sun Trading Company** (⊠ 107 N. San Francisco St., ☎ 520/774–2884) carries a full range of medicinal herbs, along with jewelry and crafts, in a soothing New Age atmosphere. **Zani** (⊠ 111-C S. San Francisco St., ☎ 520/774–9409) features hip home furnishings and greeting cards in addition to its futons.

The gift shops at the **Coconino Center for the Arts** and the **Museum of Northern Arizona** (☞ Flagstaff, *above*) both carry high-quality jewelry and crafts.

The **Flagstaff Mall** (⊠ 4650 N. U.S. 89, ☎ 520/526–4827) is just east of town off Exit 201 of I–40. Small (around 65 retailers) by most standards, this mall has the greatest number of department and specialty stores in the area, including Dillards, Sears, and JCPenney. There's also a food court and a two-screen cinema.

East of Flagstaff

The area east of Flagstaff is often neglected by visitors to the region because, regardless of its beauty or historical significance, it gets overshadowed by the Grand Canyon. But traveling east has its unique rewards. If you don't have enough time to do everything, take a quick drive to Walnut Canyon—only about 15 minutes out of town—and stay in this lovely spot for as long as you can.

Numbers in the margin correspond to points of interest on the North-Central Arizona map.

Walnut Canyon National Monument

★ 25 *7½ mi east of Flagstaff at Exit 204 off I–40, then 3 mi south.*

Walnut Canyon National Monument consists of a group of spectacular cliff-dwelling homes constructed by the Sinagua people, who lived and farmed in and around the canyon starting around AD 700. The more than 300 dwellings here were built between 1125 and 1250 and left, like those at so many other settlements in Arizona and New Mexico, around 1300. The Sinagua traded far and wide with other Native Americans, including people at Wupatki (☞ San Francisco Volcanic Field, *below*). Even macaw feathers, which would have come from tribes in what is now Mexico, have been excavated in the canyon. The area wasn't explored by Europeans until 1883, when early Flagstaff settlers shamelessly looted the site for pots and "treasure." Woodrow Wilson declared the site a national monument in 1915, which began a 30-year process of stabilizing the ruins.

Walnut Canyon is a fascinating place to visit, in part because of the opportunity to enter the dwellings and feel ancient life at close range. A number of the Sinagua homes are in near-perfect condition, in spite of all the looting, because of the dry, hot climate and the protection of overhanging cliffs. You can reach them by descending 185 feet on the mile-long, stepped Island Trail, which starts at the visitor center. As you follow the trail, stop occasionally to look across the canyon for other dwellings not accessible on the path.

Island Trail takes about an hour to complete at a normal pace. The entrance to the trail closes one hour before the park does. Those with health concerns should opt for the easier Rim Trail (a half-mile route that most people complete in about a half hour), which has overlooks from which dwellings can be viewed as well as an excavated, reconstructed pit house. Attractive picnic areas dot the grounds and line the roads leading to the park. Park service guides conduct tours on Wednesday, Saturday, and Sunday from Memorial Day through Labor Day. Visitors are permitted to enter about two dozen ruins. ✉ *Walnut Canyon Rd.,* ☎ *520/526–3367.* 🎟 *$2 per person entering on foot or bicycle, $4 per vehicle.* ⏲ *Daily 9–5; hrs extended during summer.*

Meteor Crater

26 *39 mi east of Walnut Canyon National Monument, 43 mi east of Flagstaff.*

This natural phenomenon, set in a privately owned and run park, is impressive if for no other reason than its sheer size. A hole in the ground 600 feet deep, nearly a mile across, and more than 3 mi in circumference, Meteor Crater is large enough to accommodate the Washington Monument or 20 football fields. It was created when a meteorite came hurtling through space at a speed of 43,000 mi per hour and crashed here some 49,000 years ago. The area looks so much like the surface of the moon that NASA made it one of the official training sites for the Project Apollo astronauts.

Visitors can't descend into the crater because of the efforts of its owners to maintain its condition—scientists consider this to be the best-preserved crater on earth—but guided rim tours, given every hour on the hour, weather permitting, afford visitors a bird's-eye view of the hole. Two short, rather corny films, which play every half hour, detail the history of the crater and of astronaut training here. A small snack bar sells soft drinks, coffee, and sandwiches. Rock hounds will enjoy the Lapidary Shop, filled with raw specimens from the area as well as with jewelry made from native stones. ✉ *I–40 east of Flagstaff, Exit 233, then 6 mi south on Meteor Crater Rd.,* ☎ *520/289–2362.* 🎟 *$8.* ⏲ *May 16–Sept. 14, daily 6–6; Sept. 15–May 15, daily 8–5.*

San Francisco Volcanic Field

North of Flagstaff, the San Francisco Volcanic Field encompasses 2,000 square mi of fascinating geological phenomena—ancient volcanoes, cinder cones, and valleys carved by water and ice, and the San Francisco Peaks themselves, some of which soar to almost 13,000 feet—as well as some of the most extensive Native American ruins in the Southwest. If you have any time at all, don't miss Sunset Crater and Wupatki. These national monuments are not only extremely interesting but can be explored in relative solitude during a large part of the year. The area is short on services, so fill up on gas and consider taking along a picnic. There are plenty of lovely spots for lunch along the way. A good source for hiking and camping information in this area is the Peaks Ranger Station (✉ 5075 N. U.S. 89, ☎ 520/526–0866). If you do camp, do not pitch your tent in a low-lying area, where dangerous flash floods can literally wipe you out (☞ Lodging *in* Smart Travel Tips A to Z).

Sunset Crater Volcano National Monument

★ 27 *19 mi northeast of Flagstaff.*

Sunset Crater, a cinder cone that rises some 1,000 feet into the air, was an active volcano 900 years ago. The final eruption contained iron and sulfur, which gives the rim of the crater its glow and thus its name, Sunset. You can walk around the base, but you can't descend into the huge, fragile cone. If you take the Lava Flow Trail, a half-hour, mile-long, self-guided walk, you'll have a good view of the evidence of the volcano's fiery power: lava formations and holes in the rock where volcanic gases vented to the surface. Three smaller cones to the southeast were formed at the same time and along the same fissure.

If you're interested in hiking a volcano, head to **Lenox Crater,** about a mile east of the visitor center, and climb the 280 feet to the top of the cinder cone. Wear closed, sturdy shoes; the cinder is soft and crumbly, without vegetation. From **O'Leary Peak,** 5 mi from the visitor center on Forest Route 545A, there are great views of the San Francisco Peaks, the Painted Desert, and beyond; the road is unpaved and rutted, however, so it's advisable to take only high-clearance vehicles. In addition, there's a gate, about halfway along the route, that's usually closed—in which case, it's a steep 2½-mile hike to the top. ✉ *Santa Fe Ave. east of Flagstaff to U.S. 89, then north for 17 mi; turn right onto the road marked Sunset Crater and go another 2 mi to the visitor center,* ☎ *520/556–7042.* 💳 *$4 per car, $2 to enter on foot or by nonmotorized vehicle; admission includes Wupatki National Monument (☞ below).* ⏲ *Daily 8–5; hours may be extended in summer.*

En Route As you drive from Sunset Crater to Wupatki, you'll see parts of the Painted Desert in the distance. The immediately surrounding landscape is starkly beautiful, with little vegetation.

Wupatki National Monument

★ 28 *20 mi north of the Sunset Crater visitor center along the unmarked Sunset Loop Rd.*

Some 2,700 identified sites contain archaeological evidence of Native American settlement in this area. Families from the Sinagua and other ancestral Puebloans are believed to have lived together in harmony here, farming and trading with one another and with those who passed through their "city." The eruption of Sunset Crater, 20 mi away, may have caused migration to this area—and may have disrupted the settlement more than once around 1064. The earliest inhabitants are believed to have settled here around AD 600, leaving the pueblo by about 1300.

The site for which the national monument was named, the **Wupatki** (meaning "tall house" in Hopi), was originally three stories high, built above a large, unexplored system of underground fissures. The structure had almost 100 rooms and a large, open ball court—evidence in itself of southwestern trade with Mesoamerican tribes for whom ball games were a central ritual. Next to the ball court is a blowhole, a geologic phenomenon in which air is forced upward by underground pressure; scientists speculate that early inhabitants may have attached some spiritual significance to the many blowholes in the region.

Other ruins to visit at the national monument are **Wukoki, Lomaki,** and the **Citadel,** a pueblo that sits on a knoll above a limestone sink. Although the largest remnants of Native American settlements at Wupatki National Monument are open to the public, other sites are off-limits to casual visitors. Permits are available from the park service for limited access beyond the open areas, but rules regarding entering closed sites are strictly enforced. If you are interested in an in-depth tour of the area, consider taking a ranger-led overnight hike to the **Crack-in-Rock Ruin.** The 14-mile trek (round-trip) covers areas marked by ancient petroglyphs and dotted with well-preserved ruins. Anyone who is interested should contact the rangers for details. There are a limited number of trips, conducted in April and October; it's best to call in February and August if you'd like to take part in the lottery for one of the 100 available places on these hikes. The cost is $25. *Between the Wupatki and Citadel ruins, the **Doney Mountain** affords 360° views of the Painted Desert and the San Francisco Volcanic Field. It's a perfect spot for a sunset picnic. In summer, rangers give interpretive lectures on the history of the region. ✉ *HC 33, Box 444A, Flagstaff 86004,* ☎ *520/556–7040.* 🎫 *(collected at Sunset Crater) $4 per vehicle; $2 to enter on foot, bicycle, motorcycle, or nonmotorized vehicle.* ⏲ *Daily 8–5; hrs may be extended in summer.*

NORTH-CENTRAL ARIZONA A TO Z

Arriving and Departing

By Bus

FLAGSTAFF

Greyhound (✉ 399 S. Malpais La., ☎ 520/774–4573 or 800/231–2222) offers daily connections to Phoenix but none to Sedona. Buses also serve San Francisco, Los Angeles, Las Vegas, and other cities. **Nava-Hopi** buses depart daily to the Grand Canyon and offer sightseeing trips to Sedona (☞ Special-Interest Tours, *below*).

PRESCOTT

Greyhound (✉ 820 E. Sheldon St., ☎ 520/445–5470 or 800/231–2222) offers daily service to Phoenix Sky Harbor airport.

SEDONA

The **Sedona/Phoenix Shuttle Service** (✉ Box 3342, West Sedona 86340, ☎ 520/282–2066 or 800/448–7988 in AZ) makes six trips daily between those cities; the fare is $30 one-way, $55 round-trip. The bus leaves from three terminals of Sky Harbor International Airport in Phoenix. Reservations are required.

BY CAR

It makes sense to rent a car at the airport if you fly into Flagstaff, and there are some rental agencies near the Amtrak station (☞ Car and Jeep Rentals, *below*).

Prescott

In Prescott, Highway 89 turns into Gurley Street, the town's main drag, lined with motels and businesses. Gurley leads into Courthouse Square, the heart of the town. The most interesting shops, restaurants, and historic hotels are located within a 10-block radius, and you'll be able to do most of your sightseeing on foot. The local bus service is not very regular; call **Ace City Cab** (☎ 520/445–1616) or **Reliable Taxi** (☎ 520/772–6618) if you don't have a car.

Sedona

Sedona stretches along Highway 89A, its main thoroughfare, which runs roughly east–west through town. Highway 89A is bisected by AZ 179. The more commercial section of Highway 89A east of AZ 179 is known as Uptown; locals tend to frequent the shops on the other side, called West Sedona. To the south of Highway 89A, AZ 179 is lined with upscale retailers for a couple of miles. There is no public transportation in Sedona; if you don't have your own wheels, you'll need to rent some (☞ Car and Jeep Rentals, *below*) or rely on the services of **Bob's Sedona Taxi** (☎ 520/282–1234) or **Bell Rock Taxi** (☎ 520/282–4222).

Contacts and Resources

Car and Jeep Rentals

FLAGSTAFF

Agencies represented at the Flagstaff Pullium Airport include **Avis** (☎ 520/774–8421), **Budget** (☎ 520/779–0306), and **Hertz** (☎ 520/774–4452). Budget also has a downtown office, as does **Sears** (✉ 100 N. Humphreys St., ☎ 774–1879 or 800/527–0770).

PRESCOTT

Budget (✉ 1031 Commerce Dr., ☎ 520/778–3806), **Enterprise** (✉ 202 South Montezuma, ☎ 520/778–6506), and **Hertz** (✉ airport, ☎ 520/776–1399) all have offices in Prescott.

SEDONA

Budget (☎ 520/282–4602) has an office at the Sedona Airport. If you want to explore the back roads of Sedona's red rocks on your own, you can rent a four-wheel-drive vehicle from **Sedona Jeep Rentals** (✉ Sedona Airport, ☎ 520/282–2227) or **Canyon Jeep Rentals** (✉ Oak Creek Terrace Resort, 4548 Hwy. 89A, ☎ 520/282–6061 or 800/224–2229).

Camping and Hiking

There is a large number of campgrounds in the Sedona, Prescott, and Jerome area. For a full listing of campgrounds, consult the *Arizona Camping and Campgrounds Guide,* available from the **Arizona Office of Tourism** (☞ Visitor Information *in* Important Contacts A to Z). Reservations for many of the campgrounds in the area are handled by **Mistix** (☎ 800/365–2267), but you'll need to choose a campground before you call in order to make the most of the automated phone system—it's impossible to get hold of a human being.

If you're staying outside in winter, remember that this area gets quite cold, with frequent snowstorms. In summer, night temperatures can dip to 40°F, whereas daytime temperatures can reach 90°F.

CAUTION – Be sure to bring plenty of water with you when hiking and drink often. Dehydration can become a life-threatening condition (☞ Hiking *in* Important Contacts A to Z). Be careful not to camp in low-lying areas, which are subject to extremely dangerous flash flooding in sudden summer rains (☞ Lodging *in* Smart Travel Tips A to Z).

Emergencies

Call 911 to reach the **fire department, police,** and **emergency medical services.**

FLAGSTAFF

At an altitude of nearly 7,000 feet, Flagstaff has "thin" air; heart and respiratory patients may experience difficulty here, particularly upon exertion.

Hospitals and Doctors. Flagstaff Medical Center (✉ 1200 N. Beaver St., ☎ 520/779–3366), a full-service hospital, has a 24-hour emergency room downtown, about nine blocks north of Route 66. The facility also provides referrals to local doctors and dentists.

Late-Night Pharmacies. The pharmacy at the **Flagstaff Medical Center** (☞ *above*) is open 24 hours. **Walgreen's** (✉ 1500 W. Cedar Ave., ☎

520/773–1011), a few blocks north of downtown, is open Monday through Saturday 9 AM–10 PM, Sunday 9–8. The pharmacy at **Smith's Food and Drug** (✉ 201 N. Switzer Canyon Dr., corner Rte. 66, ☎ 520/774–3389) is open Monday through Saturday 9–9, Sunday 10–4.

PRESCOTT

Hospital. Yavapai Regional Medical Center (✉ 1003 Willow Creek Rd., ☎ 520/445–2700).

Late-Night Pharmacies. The **Apothecary Shop** (✉ 1022 Willow Creek Rd., ☎ 520/445–1161) and **Goodwin Street Pharmacy** (✉ 406 W. Goodwin St., ☎ 520/445–3550) both have 24-hour prescription service.

SEDONA

Hospitals and Doctors. The **Sedona Medical Center** (✉ 3700 W. Hwy. 89A, ☎ 520/204–4900) has a doctor on call 24 hours. Walk-in hours are weekdays 8–5, Saturdays 9–2.

Late-Night Pharmacies. Walgreen's (✉ 180 Coffee Pot Dr., ☎ 520/282–2528) stays open until 9 PM Monday–Saturday, until 8 on Sunday. **Payless** (✉ 2350 W. Hwy. 89A, ☎ 520/282–9577) closes at 9 PM every day except Sunday, when it closes at 8.

Guided Tours

FLAGSTAFF

Orientation. For self-guided tour maps of Flagstaff itself, stop at the **Flagstaff Visitors Center** (☞ Visitor Information, *below*); if you're going to spend any time in town, it's well worth taking the route outlined in the "Historic Downtown Walking Tour" pamphlet.

Special-Interest. The Gray Line of Flagstaff, operated by **Nava-Hopi Tours** (✉ Box 339, 114 W. Rte. 66, Flagstaff 86002, ☎ 520/774–5003 or 800/892–8687), runs bus trips from its downtown bus station to the Grand Canyon ($38 round-trip, not including park entry fee). A tour of Sedona costs $36 per person (plus a $2 entry fee for Montezuma Castle); there are no drop-offs—that is, all passengers must return to Flagstaff on the same bus that evening. The company also offers a variety of package tours, such as the one to the Hopi Indian Reservation ($62 round-trip). All require reservations, which are taken until two hours before departure. Free hotel and motel pickups are included in the price.

The Ventures program, run by the education department of the **Museum of Northern Arizona** (✉ 3001 N. Fort Valley Rd., Flagstaff 86001, ☎ 520/774–5213), offers tours of the area led by local scientists, artists, and historians. Trips might include rafting excursions down the San Juan River, treks into the Grand Canyon or Colorado Plateau backcountry, or bus tours into the Navajo reservation to visit with Native American artists. Prices start at about $400 and go up to $1,200, with most tours in the $500–$600 range.

Plane tours of the area's attractions run by the friendly **Flagstaff Safe Fliers, Inc.** (✉ Flagstaff Pullium Airport, 6200 S. Pullium Dr., Suite 104, Flagstaff 86001, ☎ 520/774–7858 or 800/438–6359) range from 20-minute Red Rock Quick Tours ($28) to Nelson's Ultimate Two-Day Adventure ($679), which includes a bird's-eye view of the Grand Canyon and London Bridge at Lake Havasu, with an overnight at Las Vegas, lunch in Jerome, and dinner in Sedona.

PRESCOTT

Orientation. On Monday and Friday at 10 AM from June through August, knowledgeable volunteer guides offer free orientation tours of the town, which leave from the **Chamber of Commerce** (☞ Visitor Information, *below*). The rest of the year, tours can be booked with **Melissa**

Roughner (☎ 520/445–4567), who'll be wearing territorial garb when she guides you around town.

SEDONA

Orientation. Sedona Trolley (☎ 520/282–6826) offers two types of daily orientation tours, both departing from the main bus stop in Uptown and lasting less than an hour. One goes along AZ 179 to the Chapel of the Holy Cross, with stops at Tlaquepaque and some of the resorts; the other passes through West Sedona to Boynton Canyon (Enchantment Resort). Rates are $6 each or $9 for both.

Special-Interest. One of the most popular things to do in the Sedona area is to take a Jeep tour; several operators headquartered along Sedona's main Uptown drag offer a variety of excursions, some focusing on geology, some on astronomy, some on vortices, some on all three. You can even find a combination Jeep tour and horseback ride. The ubiquitous **Pink Jeep Tours** (✉ 204 N. Hwy. 89A, Box 1447, Sedona 86339, ☎ 520/282–5000 or 800/873–3662), as well as **Sedona Adventures** (✉ 273 N. Hwy. 89A, Box 1476, Sedona 86339, ☎ 520/282–3500 or 800/888–9494) and **Sedona Red Rock Jeep Tours** (✉ 270 N. Hwy. 89A, Box 10305, Sedona 86339, ☎ 520/282–6826 or 800/848–7728), are all reliable operators. Prices start at about $22 per person for one hour and go up to $65 per person for two hours. Car seats are available for youngsters; check with your operator before you book. Although all the excursions are safe, those who dislike heights or bumps should choose one that's easy on the nerves and spine.

Rahelio (✉ 10 Traumeri La., Sedona 86336, ☎ 520/282–6735) offers vortex tours, vision quests, a variety of mystical hikes, and other adventures. Those with New Age inclinations might also contact **Earth Wisdom Tours** (✉ 293 N. Hwy. 89A, Sedona 86336, ☎ 520/282–4714), which features a variety of inner and outer journeys.

A hot-air-balloon tour of Sedona provides a unique perspective of the red-rock landscape. Prices generally start at $135 per person for a one- to two-hour tour. Plan to spend about three or four hours on this venture, including driving time to the launch site and a champagne picnic. The only two companies with permits to fly over Sedona are **Northern Light Balloon Expeditions** (✉ Box 1695, Sedona 86339, ☎ 520/282–2274 or 800/230–6222) and **Red Rock Balloon Adventures** (✉ Box 2759, Sedona 86339, ☎ 520/284–0040 or 800/258–3754).

It's a rare visitor who won't snap a roll or two of film in beautiful Sedona; **Sedona Photo Tours** (✉ 252 N. Hwy. 89A, Box 1650, Sedona 86339, ☎ 520/282–4320 or 800/973–3662) will take you to all the prime spots and help you take your best shot. Rates are $35 per person for a basic two-hour tour; it's an additional $15 per hour for private tours.

Those interested in the photographs of others—and in art in general—might consider a tour of some of the galleries in town; contact **Sedona Art Tours** (✉ 30 Kashmir Rd., Box 10578, Sedona 86339, ☎ 520/282–7686) for information.

VERDE VALLEY

Special-Interest. Along the scenic 22-mile route of the **Verde River Canyon Excursion Train** (✉ Arizona Central Railroad, 300 N. Broadway, Clarkdale 86324, ☎ 800/293–7245), knowledgeable announcers regale riders with the colorful history of the area, pointing out natural attractions along the way—a bald eagle's nest in the side of a cliff, for example. A cowboy balladeer entertains passengers on the return trip. This trip, which takes about four hours, is especially popular in fall-foliage season and in the spring, when the desert wildflowers bloom; make reservations well in advance. Round-trip rides cost $34.95. The train sells snacks, drinks, and sandwiches. For *$52.95* you can ride the comfy, living-room-like first-class cars, where hot hors d'oeuvres, coffee, and champagne are included in the price.

Visitor Information

FLAGSTAFF

Flagstaff Visitors Center (✉ 1 E. Rte. 66, Flagstaff 64001, ☎ 520/774–9541 or 800/842–7293) is open Monday–Saturday 9–6 and Sunday 8–5.

PRESCOTT

Prescott Chamber of Commerce (✉ 117 W. Goodwin St., Prescott 86303, ☎ 520/445–2000 or 800/266–7534) is open weekdays 9–5, weekends 10–4.

SEDONA

The **Sedona–Oak Creek Canyon Chamber of Commerce** (✉ 331 Forest Rd., at the corner of N. Hwy. 89A, Box 478, Sedona 86339, ☎ 520/282–7722 or 800/288–7336) is open Monday–Saturday 9–5, Sunday 9–3.

VERDE VALLEY

Camp Verde Chamber of Commerce (✉ 435 S. Main St., Box 1665, Camp Verde 86322, ☎ 520/567–9294).

Clarkdale Chamber of Commerce (✉ Box 161, Clarkdale 86324, ☎ 520/634–3382).

Cottonwood/Verde Valley Chamber of Commerce (✉ 1010 S. Main St., Cottonwood 86326, ☎ 520/634–7593).

Jerome Chamber of Commerce (✉ Box K, Jerome 86331, ☎ 520/634–2900).

5 Phoenix and Central Arizona

The ever-widening Phoenix metropolitan area provides a tremendous variety of activities—from golfing on championship courses and hiking on some of the country's most-traveled (and appreciated) trails to dining at the restaurants where southwestern cuisine was born and experiencing the last word in pampering at world-class resorts. Scottsdale and the college town of Tempe are packed with great boutiques and art galleries, and the White Mountains are a nearby escape, with Old West towns, the stunning Salt River Canyon, and more great hiking.

Updated by Jenner Bishop

IN CENTRAL ARIZONA, one of the world's great deserts meets one of its great mountain ranges, providing a stunning variety of natural environments for visitors to enjoy in a relatively small area. Central Arizona also combines some of the oldest human dwellings in the Western Hemisphere with the homes of contemporary Native American tribes and America's fastest-growing major urban center: metropolitan Phoenix.

At the heart of central Arizona lies the Valley of the Sun—which gives its name to the common nickname of metro Phoenix, the Valley—named for its 330-plus days of sunshine each year. This 1,000-square-mile valley is the northern tip of the Sonoran Desert, a surprisingly fertile, rolling expanse of prehistoric seabed that stretches from central Arizona deep into northwestern Mexico. The valley is studded with cacti and creosote bushes, crusted with hard-baked clay and rock, and scorched by summer temperatures that can stay above 100°F for weeks at a time. But its dry skin responds magically to the touch of rainwater. Spring is a miracle of poppies strewn among the flower-crowned saguaro cacti, of ruby, ivory, and golden blossoms bursting from the dry spikes of the ocotillo and the thorny beaver-tail pads of the nopal.

As the Hohokam discovered 2,300 years ago, this springtime miracle can be augmented by human hands. Having migrated north from northwestern Mexico, they cultivated cotton, corn, and beans in tilled, rowed, and irrigated fields for about 1,700 years. The Hohokam, like northern Puebloans in the 14th and 15th centuries, moved out of the area as a result of the combination of droughts, longer winters, and other causes. They are believed to be ancestors of the present-day Pimans: the Pima and Tohonó O'odham.

From the time the Hohokam left until the American Civil War, the once fertile Salt River valley lay forgotten, used only by occasional small bands of Pima and Maricopa peoples. Then, in 1865, the U.S. Army established Fort McDowell in the mountains to the east, where the Verde River flows into the Salt. To feed the men and the horses stationed there, Jack Swilling, a former Confederate army officer, had the idea of reopening the Hohokam canals in 1867. Within a year, fields bright with barley and pumpkins earned the area the name of Punkinsville. But by 1870, when the town site was plotted, the 300 inhabitants had decided that their new city would rise "like a phoenix" from the ashes of a vanished civilization.

Phoenix indeed grew steadily. Within 20 years, it had become large enough—at about 3,000 people—to wrest the title of territorial capital from Prescott. By 1912, when Arizona was admitted as a state, the area, irrigated by the brand-new Roosevelt Dam and Salt River Project, had a burgeoning cotton industry. Copper and cattle were mined and raised elsewhere but were banked and traded in Phoenix, and the cattle were slaughtered and packed here in the largest stockyards outside Chicago.

Meanwhile, the climate, so long a crippling liability, became an asset. Desert air was the prescribed therapy for the respiratory ills rampant in the sooty, factory-filled East; Scottsdale began in 1901 as "30-odd tents and a half dozen adobe houses" put up by health seekers. By 1930, visitors looking for warm winter recreation rather than a cure filled the elegant San Marcos Hotel in Chandler and the new Arizona Biltmore, first of the many luxury resorts for which the area is now known worldwide.

Phoenix and central Arizona are places in which to take it easy, go slowly, and dress informally. As old desert hands say, you don't begin to see the desert until you've looked at it long enough to see its colors; and you aren't ready to get up and move until you've seen the sun go down.

NOTE – If you are interested in visiting southwestern Arizona, towns like Ajo, Yuma, and Why, or sights at Organ Pipe Cactus National Monument, *see* the end of Chapter 6.

Pleasures and Pastimes

Dining

Phoenix's culinary traditions arise from a unique blend of Old West and New West cultures. In the mid-19th century, the north-Mexican rancho cooking that had been in Arizona for 150 years was joined by the Anglo-European food of American settlers. Arizona Territory was also an outpost of the West's cattle-ranching boom, and the railroads brought a significant early influx of Chinese settlers.

By the mid-20th century, the Valley was rich in Mexican food, mostly in the style of the adjoining Mexican state of Sonora; steak houses, from cowboy to fancy (Phoenix was a major stockyard center until the 1970s); and Chinese restaurants, mostly Cantonese. There was plenty of family eating, heartburn, and *agita.* When Phoenicians wanted to get fussy, men put on bola ties and women donned silver-and-turquoise jewelry, and they paid someone to pour "Continental" sauces on their steaks.

Then, during the 1970s, things took off. Southeast Asian refugees introduced spicy Asian dishes that were instantly welcome in a city used to salsa and sweet-and-sour. Immigrants from Central America and the Middle East brought more variations on familiar themes, as well as new approaches. Soon, "southwestern international" was born, and by the late '80s, it had taken hold of America's culinary imagination. Still, Arizona being what it is, Phoenix also has plenty of good old meat-and-potatoes and diner fare.

Golf

Phoenix has become a golf mecca, due to the warm weather, azure skies, and serene vistas of the desert. The explosive growth of the area has brought many new courses to the Valley over the past 15 years. Phoenix and the surrounding environs boast world-class courses designed by Jack Nicklaus, Tom Weiskopf and Jay Morrish, Pete Dye, Arnold Palmer and Ed Seay, and Ted Robinson, to name a few. The city provides an impressive array of courses—golfers may choose lush, manicured fairways with tranquil lakes and fountains or get right out in the wild dunes and scrub brush of the natural desert.

Mountains

The Valley of the Sun is ringed by mountains. Squaw Peak is situated within Phoenix, just north of downtown, and Camelback Mountain and the Papago Peaks are landmarks between Phoenix and Scottsdale. South of the city, not 5 mi from downtown, rise the much less lofty peaks of South Mountain Park. This 12-mi-wide chain of dry mountains divides the Valley from the rest of the Sonoran Desert. All of these mountain areas provide the city with wonderful and locally popular outdoor activities.

Past Tempe and Mesa to the east, the barren peaks of the Superstition Mountains—named for their eerie way of seeming just a few miles away and luring unwary prospectors to a dusty death—are the first of a series of mountains that stretch all the way into New Mexico. To the west, past Glendale and Tolleson, the formidable, barren-seeming White Tank Mountains separate the Valley from the empty lands that slope steadily downward toward the Colorado River and the Mojave Desert of California.

But north of Phoenix, behind the dusty Hieroglyphic Mountains (misnamed for Hohokam petroglyphs found there), rises the gigantic Mogollon Rim. This shelf of land, almost as wide as Arizona, was thrust 2,000 to 5,000 feet into the air back in the Mesozoic age; it got its name for posing an overwhelming *mogollon* (obstruction) to Spanish-speaking explorers probing northward. These slopes are green with pine trees, and the alpine meadows are lush with grasses and aspen. Here, after gold was found in the early 1860s, President Lincoln sent the Arizona Territory's first governor to found the capital at Prescott (☞ The Verde Valley, Jerome, and Prescott *in* Chapter 4) and secure mineral riches for the Union.

Today, the northern mountains serve as a cool, green refuge for Valley dwellers. The bumpy wagon roads up the Black Canyon toward Prescott and Flagstaff were key summer escape routes 100 years ago, and their dramatically engineered successor, the four-lane, split-level I–17, leads tens of thousands on exodus every weekend from May to September.

EXPLORING PHOENIX

When low-cost air-conditioning made its summer heat manageable, the Sun Belt boom began. From 1950 to 1990, the Phoenix urban area more than quadrupled in population, catapulting real estate and home-building into two of the state's biggest industries. Cities planted around Phoenix have become its suburbs, and fields that for decades grew cotton and citrus now grow microchips and homes. Glendale and Peoria on the west side, and Tempe, Mesa, Chandler, and Gilbert on the east, make up the nation's third-largest silicon valley.

NOTE – You'll notice a number of options in the exploring sections that follow to take a short break: In the warm months, it's best to allow a half hour sitting out of the sun, sipping a tall, cool drink (not alcohol—it speeds dehydration) for every hour of walking or shopping.

Great Itineraries

IF YOU HAVE 3 DAYS

See the Heard Museum for its internationally acclaimed collection of Native American artifacts, and swing by the Central Library on your way downtown to the Arizona Science Center and Phoenix Museum of History. On day two, rise early and begin your day at Frank Lloyd Wright's Taliesen West; then head south into Scottsdale for a day of gallery browsing and a walk through Old Town. On your final day, take in Phoenix's stunning natural environs: Visit the Desert Botanical Gardens or spend some time exploring the stark beauty of the surrounding desert on horseback, by Jeep, or even by hot-air balloon.

IF YOU HAVE 5 DAYS

Consider some hiking: Even inexperienced hikers will enjoy the walk up to Papago Park's Hole in the Rock or the 1.2-mi trip to the top of Squaw Peak, whereas the more experienced may choose to ascend Camelback Mountain. South Mountain Park has many trails for hikers of all abilities. Proceed to Tempe, where the rest of the day can be spent strolling on Mill Avenue and checking out the unique architecture of the Arizona State University campus. On your fifth day, drive the loop of the Apache Trail (☞ Side Trip to the White Mountains, *below*)—stopping in at the Boyce Thompson Arboretum along the way and enjoying the breathtaking views along AZ 88 on your way back—or drive north to explore the Old West town of Wickenburg or take a tour of Arcosanti (☞ Side Trips near Phoenix, *below,* for both).

IF YOU HAVE 7 DAYS

Expand your drive along the Apache Trail to include an overnight trip up into the pine forests of the White Mountains, or check out the ancient Hohokam ruins at Casa Grande to the south of Phoenix.

Downtown Phoenix

The renovated east end of downtown gives you a look at Phoenix's past and present, as well as a peek at its future. Restored homes from the original townsite give visitors an idea of how far the city has come since its inception around the turn of the last century, while several fine museums point to the Valley of the Sun's increasing sophistication in the coming one.

A Good Walk

Numbers in the text correspond to numbers in the margin and on the Exploring Downtown and the Cultural Center map.

After parking your car in the structure on the southeast corner of 5th and Monroe streets, begin your tour in the blocks known as the Heritage and Science Park; 5th to 7th streets between Monroe and Adams contain **Heritage Square** ①, the **Arizona Science Center** ②, and the **Phoenix Museum of History** ③. From the corner of 5th and Monroe, walk a block north to Van Buren Street. On the northwest corner of the intersection, you'll see two glass-clad office towers with a lane of royal palms between them. Follow the palm trees: They lead to the **Arizona Center** ④. Leaving the Arizona Center, from the corner of 3rd and Van Buren, walk a block west to 2nd Street and two blocks south on 2nd Street, passing the 24-story Hyatt Regency hotel on your right, then another block and a half west on Adams Street to the **Museo Chicano** ⑤. You can catch a DASH shuttle back to Heritage and Science Park from here, or walk two more blocks west toward the striking facade of the **Orpheum Theatre** ⑥.

If you're really an indefatigable walker, continue south through the plaza on the Orpheum's east side to Washington Street; head east on Washington Street, passing Historic City Hall and the county courthouse on your right. At the intersection of Washington and 1st Avenue, you'll see Patriots Square Park on the southeast corner; cross diagonally (southeast) through the park to the corner of Jefferson Street and Central Avenue. Another block east on Jefferson and then a block south on 1st Street will take you to the site of the **America West Arena** ⑦. From the arena, walk back to Jefferson Street and Central Avenue to catch the DASH shuttle back to your car.

Timing

In moderate weather, this walk is a pleasant daylong tour; from late May to mid-October, it's best to break it up over two days. Be sure to take advantage of the 35¢ DASH (Downtown Area Shuttle; ☞ By Bus *under* Getting Around *in* Phoenix and Central Arizona A to Z, *below*).

Sights to See

7 **America West Arena.** This 20,000-seat, multifacility sports palace is the home of the Phoenix Suns, the Arizona Rattlers arena football team, and the Arizona Sandsharks professional soccer team. Almost a mall in itself—with cafés, an athletic club, and shops, in addition to the team offices—it's interesting to tour even when there's no game on. The lobby entrance has displays of postmodern video art, including "Electro-Sym-

America West Arena, **7**
Arizona Center, **4**
Arizona Science Center, **2**
Breck Girl Hall of Fame, **11**
Ellis-Shackelford House, **12**
Heard Museum, **10**
Heritage Square, **1**
Museo Chicano, **5**
Orpheum Theatre, **6**
Phoenix Art Museum, **9**
Phoenix Central Library, **8**
Phoenix Museum of History, **3**

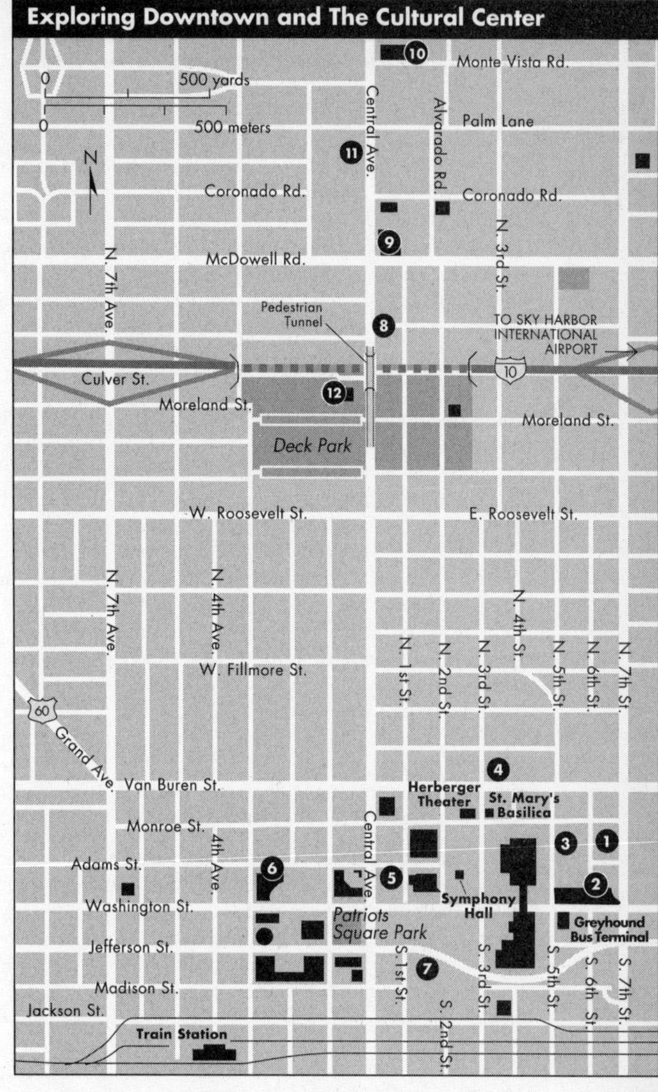

bio Phonics", a neon/video sculpture of three robot figures fashioned out of small televisions. ✉ *201 E. Jefferson St., at 2nd St.,* ☎ *602/379–2000.*

❹ **Arizona Center.** Beyond an oasis of dramatic fountains and manicured, sunken gardens stands the curved, two-tiered structure that is downtown's most impressive shopping venue. There are a variety of chain and specialty stores, from men's and women's clothing to southwestern art and '50s collectibles, and a host of clever cart merchants. In addition to hosting several good eateries, the complex is home to the state's biggest sports bar—would you believe eight restaurant-size spaces spread over two stories, indoors and out? Evenings usually find street performers and live music (including top Valley jazz artists) out in the courtyard, making Arizona Center the downtown spot of choice for cool, shaded outdoor sitting and wandering, even in the heat of summer. ✉ *Van Buren St., between 3rd and 5th Sts.,* ☎ *602/271–4000 or 602/949–4353.*

NEED A BREAK? The most restful refreshment spot in the center is **Amalfi** (✉ 455 N. 3rd St., ☎ 602/257-0605), an Italian sidewalk café that does Caesar salads and great sandwiches and desserts, as well as Italian sodas and steamed coffees.

★ ❷ **Arizona Science Center.** This 120,000-square-foot concrete monolith, designed by architect Antoine Predock, is scheduled to open in the spring of 1997. Lively "please touch" exhibits will provide an entertaining educational experience for kids and grown-ups alike—learn about the physics of making gigantic soap bubbles or the technology of satellite weather systems and components of a computer. Under the 60-foot dome of the planetarium, dazzling computer graphics simulate orbits and eclipses, as well as three-dimensional space flight. State-of-the-art facilities also include the IWERKS theater, with its massive 50-foot-high projection screen. ✉ *600 E. Washington St.,* ☎ *602/258-7250.*

❶ **Heritage Square.** In a parklike setting from 5th to 7th Street between Monroe and Adams, this city-owned block contains the only remaining homes from the original Phoenix townsite. On the south side of the square, along Adams Street, stand four houses built between 1899 and 1901. The midwestern-style **Stevens House** holds the **Arizona Doll and Toy Museum** (✉ 602 E. Adams St., ☎ 602/253-9337). Next to it, in the California-style **Stevens-Haustgen House,** is the **Native Ring Project** (✉ 614 E. Adams St., ☎ 602/534-2243), which rotates exhibits from the Pueblo Grande museum collection and sells hand-crafted Native American jewelry and gifts. The **Teeter House,** the third house in the row, is now a Victorian-style tearoom. The fourth dwelling is the **Silva House,** a bungalow from 1900 restored by the Salt River Project (one of the Valley's two major power companies and its largest irrigator), which features presentations about turn-of-the-century life for settlers in the Phoenix township. Two houses on the south side of Adams Street are in the process of being restored.

The queen of Heritage Square is the **Rosson House,** an 1895 gingerbread Victorian in the Queen Anne style (made famous in San Francisco). Built by a physician who served a brief term as mayor, it is the sole survivor of the fewer than two dozen Victorians erected in Phoenix. It was bought and restored by the city in 1974. A 30-minute tour of this classic is worth the modest admission price. ✉ *6th and Monroe Sts.,* ☎ *602/262-5071.* *$3.* *Wed.–Sat. 10–3:30, Sun. noon–3:30.*

NEED A BREAK? The Victorian-style tearoom in the **Teeter House** (✉ 622 Adams St., ☎ 602/252-4682) serves such authentic tea fare as Devonshire cream, scones with berries, and cucumber sandwiches. Heartier gourmet sandwiches, soups and salads, and a tantalizing array of pastries are also available. The staff will happily box any of your choices, should you prefer to enjoy them on the lawn outside.

★ ❸ **Phoenix Museum of History.** This striking glass-and-steel museum, which opened in 1996, offers a healthy dose of regional history from the 1860s (when Anglo settlement began) through the 1930s. A counterclockwise tour through interactive exhibits allows guests to appreciate the city's multicultural heritage as well as witness its growth. Visitors are invited to play Sniff That Barrel (to guess its contents) at a replica of Hancock Store (a 1860s Circle-K equivalent) or take a turn at packing a toy wagon with color-coded blocks as if for a cross-country trip. Also on display is Phoenix's first jail, a knee-high rock to which criminals were once chained. ✉ *105 N. 5th St.,* ☎ *602/253-2734.* *$5.* *Mon.–Sat. 10–5, Sun. noon–5.*

5 **Museo Chicano.** Artistic works of Hispano-American artists from both the United States and Mexico are showcased here. Exhibits display the broad range of classic and modern Hispanic culture, making this site one of the premier centers for contemporary Latin American art. The gift shop is brimming with interesting, and usually inexpensive, keepsakes. ✉ *25 E. Adams St.,* ☎ *602/257–5536.* *$2.* ⏲ *Tues.–Sat. 10–4.*

6 **Orpheum Theatre.** The Spanish-colonial-revival architecture and exterior reliefs of this 1929 movie palace have long been admired, and now, after an extensive renovation by artisans and craftsmen that was completed in 1996, the eclectic ornamental details of the interior have been meticulously restored. Call for more details. ✉ *203 W. Adams St.,* ☎ *602/252–9678.*

The Cultural Center

The heart of Phoenix's new downtown cultural center is the rolling greensward of the Margaret T. Hance park, also known as Deck Park. Built atop the I–10 tunnel under Central Avenue, it spreads over 1 mi from 3rd Avenue on the west to 3rd Street on the east, and a ¼ mi from Portland Street north to Culver Street. Completed in 1993, it is the city's second-largest downtown park (the largest is half-century-old Encanto Park, 2 mi northwest). Growing at the same rapid rate as the city itself, this neighborhood has received a giant face-lift as of late—efforts to revitalize downtown have included the construction of a new library and the expansion or renovation of nearly all the area's museums.

A Good Walk

Numbers in the text correspond to numbers in the margin and on the Exploring Downtown and the Cultural Center map.

Park free in the lot of the **Phoenix Central Library** ⑧ at the corner of Central Avenue and East Wiletta. Two blocks north on Central, on the other side of McDowell Road, is the modern, green-stone structure of the **Phoenix Art Museum** ⑨. North of the museum, enjoy a brief respite from the noise and traffic of Central Avenue by heading one block east on Coronado Road to Alvarado Road. Follow residential Alvarado north for two longish blocks (zigzagging a few feet to the east at Palm Lane) to Monte Vista Road; turn left onto Monte Vista and proceed 50 yards west to the entrance of the **Heard Museum** ⑩. From the Heard, head south on Central Avenue toward the red-granite Dial Tower, the lobby of which contains the **Breck Girl Hall of Fame** ⑪. Follow Central Avenue south, and just past the library, on the southwest corner of Central Avenue and Culver Street, lies the **Ellis-Shackelford House** ⑫.

Timing

Seeing all of the neighborhood's attractions makes a comfortable day tour in moderate weather; in the warm months, it is too much for one day. Bus 0 runs up and down Central Avenue every 10 minutes on weekdays and every 20 minutes on weekends.

Sights to See

11 **Breck Girl Hall of Fame.** On the ground floor of Dial Tower, one of the two red-granite skyscrapers in the **Dial Corporate Center,** is a campy stop sure to be appreciated by pop-culture enthusiasts. This one-room museum contains more than 150 of the signature pastel portraits from the "Breck Girl" shampoo ads—which date from the 1930s—including pictures of Brooke Shields, Kim Basinger, Cybill Shepherd, and other now-famous former Breck Girls. A guide can detail the life and times of Mr. Edward J. Breck, whose lasting contributions to society include being the first person to differentiate between dry and oily. ✉ *1850 N. Central Ave.,* ☎ *602/207–4000.* *Free.* ⏲ *Weekdays 11–3.*

NEED A BREAK? The grassy park of the Dial Corporate Center, at the north end of the twin towers, is a great place to stop for a rest. A string of tiered fountains snakes through the 2-acre park and sculpture garden, which contains a collection of life-like works in bronze—some so realistic, you might unwittingly pass right by them. Stop to appreciate their whimsical touches, such as the blue-capped window washer's paperback copy of *Rear Window* tucked in his overalls. Inside Dial Tower, the **Palm Grove Food Court** (☎ 602/207–7107) will sell you a snack to enjoy out in the sculpture garden.

12 **Ellis–Shackelford House.** Built in 1917, this two-story, prairie-style building is the lone survivor of the large homes of early civic and business leaders that once lined Central Avenue. It now houses the Phoenix Historic Preservation Office. A restored railcar of the Phoenix Street Railway is kept in back. ✉ *1242 N. Central Ave.,* ☎ *602/261–8699.*

★ 10 **Heard Museum.** In 1928 Dwight and Maie Heard donated their classic Arizona adobe home and impressive southwestern art collection to found what has become the nation's leading museum of Native American art and culture. With a 1996 expansion, the space has increased to better showcase its exceptional collection of fine art, basketry, pottery, weavings, and bead work. Modern Native American arts, interactive art-making exhibits for children, and live demonstrations by artisans are always on hand. Don't miss the kachina-doll room (anchored by the Barry Goldwater collection) or the multimedia presentations. In the spring, you should catch the annual Native American Arts and Crafts Show; call ahead because its dates vary. ✉ *22 E. Monte Vista Rd.,* ☎ *602/252–8840. $5; Native Americans, free; free to all Wed. after 5. Mon.–Sat. 9:30–5, Wed. 9:30–9, Sun. noon–5.*

9 **Phoenix Art Museum.** After an extensive three-year expansion and renovation, completed in 1996, the green quartz exterior of this modern museum adds yet another piece of eye-catching architecture to Central Avenue. More than 13,000 objets d'art are on display inside, including 18th- and 19th-century European paintings and drawings and the American West collection, which features painters from Frederic Remington to Georgia O'Keeffe. A clothing-and-costume collection has items that date from 1750, and the Asian art gallery is filled with fine Chinese porcelain and pieces of intricate cloisonné. In back, niches in the exterior walls house individual sculptures; other pieces are found in the dramatic outdoor pavilion. ✉ *1625 N. Central Ave.,* ☎ *602/257–1222. $4; tours free. Tues. and Thurs.–Sat. 10–5, Wed. 10–9, Sun. noon–5.*

★ 8 **Phoenix Central Library.** Not often is a library on the must-see list for a city, but architect Will Bruder's magnificent 1995 contribution to Central Avenue is absolutely worth a stop. The curved building's copper-penny exterior evokes images of the region's sunburnt mesas; inside, skylights, glass walls, and computer-controlled mirrors keep the structure bathed in natural light. A breathtaking five-story glass atrium, known as the Crystal Canyon, is best appreciated from a speedy ride in one of three glass elevators. At the top, from the largest reading room in North America, check out a cable-suspended steel ceiling that appears to float overhead; catch views to the north and south from 32-foot, floor-to-ceiling windows. Free tours are offered the third Saturday of each month; arrange in advance by calling ☎ 602/262–6582. ✉ *1221 N. Central Ave.,* ☎ *602/262–4636. Mon.–Wed. 9–9, Thurs.–Sat. 9–6, Sun. 1–5.*

Papago Salado

The word "Papago," meaning "bean eater," was a term given by 16th-century Spanish explorers to a vanished native people of the Phoenix area. Farmers of the desert, the Hohokam (as they are more properly called) grew corn, beans, squash, and cotton. They lived in central Arizona from about AD 1 to 1450, at which point their civilization collapsed and disappeared for reasons unknown—some conjecture drought, floods, or internal strife—abandoning the Salt River (Rio Salado) valley but leaving behind remains of villages and a complex system of irrigation canals. The Papago Salado region is located between Phoenix and Tempe and contains the Pueblo Grande ruins, the Desert Botanical Garden, the Phoenix Zoo, and a variety of potential recreational activities in Papago Park.

A Good Drive

Stop at the **Pueblo Grande Museum and Cultural Park,** on Washington Street between 44th Street and the Hohokam Expressway (AZ 143). Follow Washington Street east 3½ mi to Priest Drive and turn north. Priest Drive becomes Galvin Parkway north of East Van Buren Street; off Galvin Parkway, you can follow signs to entrances for the **Phoenix Zoo** and **Papago Park,** or to the **Desert Botanical Garden.** Park wherever you can find a space. To visit the **Hall of Flame** afterward, drive south on Galvin Parkway to East Van Buren Street; turn east on East Van Buren and drive ⅛ mi to Project Drive and turn south.

Timing

Seeing all of the sights requires the better part of a day. You may want to save the Desert Botanical Garden for the end of your tour, as it stays open until 8 PM October–April and 10 PM May–September and is particularly lovely when lit by the setting sun or by moonlight.

Sights to See

★ **Desert Botanical Garden.** Founded in 1937 to study and conserve the ecology of the desert, these 150 acres contain more than 4,000 different species of cacti, succulents, trees, and flowers. A stroll along the ½-mi-long "Plants and People of the Sonoran Desert" trail is a fascinating lesson in the many adaptations that plants, animals, and people have made to desert living; children will enjoy playing the self-guiding game "Desert Detective." The garden boasts a full calendar of special events, including live music on the Ullman Terrace, educational puppet shows, and tours of the Desert House—a prototype for water and energy-conserving homes. Call ahead for a schedule. ✉ *1201 N. Galvin Pkwy.,* ☎ *602/941–1225.* *$6.* *Oct.–Apr., daily 8–8; May–Sept., daily 8 AM–10 PM.*

Hall of Flame. Retired firefighters lead tours through more than 100 restored fire engines and tell harrowing tales of the "world's most dangerous profession." Kids can climb on a 1916 engine, operate alarm systems, and learn lessons of fire safety from the pros. More than 3,000 helmets, badges, and other fire-fighting-related articles are on display, dating from as far back as 1725. ✉ *6101 E. Van Buren St.,* ☎ *602/275–3473.* *$4.* *Mon.–Sat. 9–5, Sun. 12–4; tours at 2 PM.*

Papago Park. A blend of hilly desert terrain, streams, and lagoons, this park has picnic ramadas, a frisbee-golf course, a playground, hiking and biking trails, and even fishing (urban fishing license required for anglers age 15 and over—pick one up at sporting-goods or Circle-K stores). The hike up to landmark Hole-in-the-Rock is popular—but remember that it's much easier to climb up to the hole than to get down. Governor Hunt's Tomb, the pyramid at the top of ramada 16, commemorates the former Arizona leader and provides a quite lovely view. Bring a compass and take part in Papago Park's orienteering courses—instructions and topographic maps are available from the ranger station. ✉ *625 N. Galvin Pkwy.,* ☎ *602/256–3220.* *Daily 6 AM–midnight.*

Phoenix Zoo. Five designated trails wind through this 125-acre zoo, which has replicas of such habitats as an African savanna and a tropical rain forest. Meerkats, warthogs, desert bighorn sheep, and endangered Arabian oryx are among the unusual sights, as is Ruby the Asian elephant, who puts brush to canvas to rival the best of abstract impressionists. In 1997 the zoo opens yet another habitat—the Forest of Uco, home to the endangered spectacled bear from South America's high-mountain rain forests. The Children's Trail introduces young visitors to small mammals from throughout the world, and a stop at the big red barn provides a chance to help groom goats and sheep. The 30-minute narrated tour on the safari train costs $1.50 and provides a good overview of the park. In December, the popular "Zoo Lights" exhibit transforms the area into an enchanted forest of more than 600,000 twinkling lights, many in the shape of the zoo's residents. ⊠ 455 N. Galvin Pkwy., ☎ 602/273–7771. $7. Daily 9–4; call for special summer hours May 1–Labor Day.

Pueblo Grande Museum and Cultural Park. Phoenix's only national landmark, this park was once the site of a 500-acre Hohokam village. In 1929, the city hired archaeologists to begin excavations of the dusty mounds here; the museum, an old adobe building on the north bank of the Salt River, is the repository for the uncovered relics, including such antiquities as shell jewelry and the signature red-on-buff Hohokam pottery. Although you can tour the site on your own, call in advance to arrange a tour of the platform mound. Sections of the park still lie untouched for future excavations with more advanced archaeological technologies. ⊠ *4619 E. Washington St.,* ☎ *602/495–0901.* *$2; free Sun.* *Mon.–Sat. 9–4:45, Sun. 1–4:45.*

Scottsdale

Historic sites, nationally known art galleries, and lots of clever boutiques fill downtown Scottsdale; a quick walking tour can easily turn into an all-day excursion if you browse. Historic Old Town Scottsdale features the look of the Old West, while fashionable 5th Avenue is known for shopping. Cross onto Main Street and enter a world frequented by the international art set (Scottsdale has the third-largest artist community in the U.S.); discover more galleries and interior-design shops along Marshall Way and Craftsman Court. The walk that follows is an overview of the area; the Shopping section, *below,* has specific recommendations.

A Good Walk

Numbers in the text correspond to numbers in the margin and on the Exploring Scottsdale map.

Park in the free public lot on the corner of 2nd Street and Wells Fargo Avenue, east of Scottsdale Road. A portion of the garage is signed for a three-hour limit; go to upper levels that don't carry time restrictions, as enforcement is strict.

From the parking structure, brick-paved sidewalks lead northward to the sculpture- and fountain-filled plaza of Scottsdale Mall. Find the **Scottsdale Center for the Arts** ⑬, to your immediate right, and the Scottsdale Public Library, beyond it to the east. Head over to this plaza's west side to visit the **Scottsdale Chamber of Commerce** ⑭ and **Scottsdale Historical Museum** ⑮. Continue west to the intersection of Brown Avenue and Main Street to reach the heart of **Old Town Scottsdale** ⑯, occupying four square blocks from Brown Avenue to Scottsdale Road, between Indian School Road and 2nd Street. From Main Street in Old Town, cross Scottsdale Road to the central drag of the **Main Street Arts District** ⑰. Turn north onto Goldwater Boulevard and gallery-stroll for another two blocks.

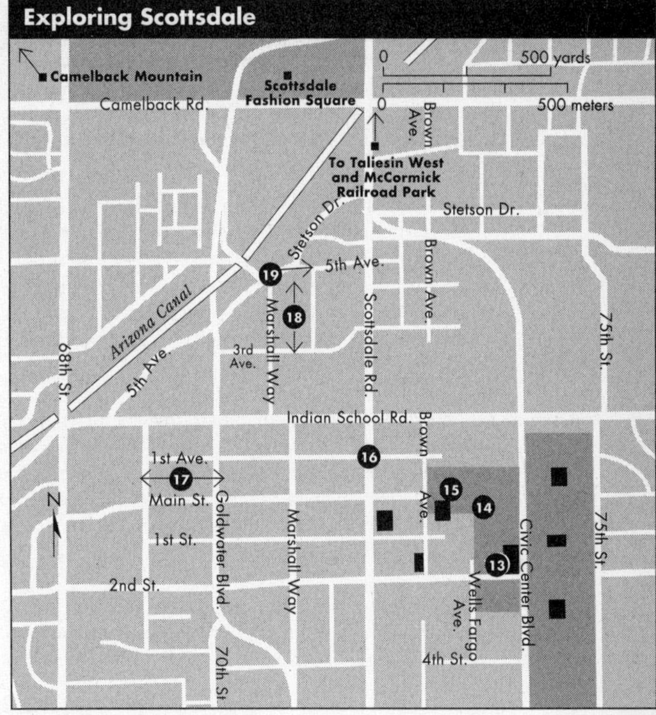

At Indian School Road, head one block east to the **Marshall Way Arts District** ⑱. Continue two blocks north on Marshall Way to the fountain of prancing Arabian horses that marks **Fifth Avenue** ⑲. You can catch the trolley back to Scottsdale Mall here, on the south side of the intersection of 5th Avenue and Stetson Drive, or walk the five blocks south on Scottsdale Road and one block east on Main Street.

Short drives north from downtown Scottsdale are two other worthy attractions: **McCormick Railroad Park** and Frank Lloyd Wright's winter home, **Taliesen West.** You may want to check them out prior to your visit to Old Town or tack them on to the end of a day trip.

Timing

Plan to spend a full day in Scottsdale, as there's a lot to take in between the countless galleries and shops. Although your tour can easily be completed on foot, a trolley ($2 in summer, free rest of year) runs through the downtown area: Ollie the Trolley tours all of Scottsdale and charges $3 for an all-day pass; for information, call ☎ 602/970–9130. Also look for horse-drawn Wagonmasters (☎ 602/423–1449), providing romantic transportation throughout Old Town Scottsdale, as well as props for souvenir snapshots.

The best option, if you're interested in touring the galleries, is to visit on a Thursday and do the Scottsdale **Art Walk** (☎ 602/990–3939), held from 7 to 9 PM each Thursday year-round (except Thanksgiving). Main Street takes on a party atmosphere during the evening hours when everyone is browsing, as do nearby Marshall Way and Fifth Avenue.

Sights to See

19 **Fifth Avenue.** For more than 40 years, this shopping stretch has been home to a fashionable collection of boutiques and specialty shops. Whether you're seeking fine art or handmade Native American arts

and crafts, casual clothing or cacti, you'll find it here—plus colorful storefronts, friendly merchants, even an old "cigar store" Indian. After a full day of paintings, turquoise jewelry, and knickknacks, children especially may enjoy casting their eyes upon the six-story monster screen of the **IMAX Theater** (✉ 4343 N. Scottsdale Rd., ☎ 602/945–4629), located at the east end of the avenue. ✉ *5th Ave., between Goldwater Blvd. and Scottsdale Rd.*

★ 17 **Main Street Arts District.** Gallery after gallery on Main Street and First Avenue, particularly on the blocks between Scottsdale Road and 69th Street, displays artwork of myriad styles—contemporary, western realism, Native American, and traditional. Several antiques shops are also here; specialties include elegant porcelains and china, fine antique jewelry, and Oriental rugs. With very few exceptions, casual visitors are welcome to browse and ogle.

NEED A BREAK? For a cool drink or light meal during daytime gallery-hopping, try **Arcadia Farms**(✉ 7014 E. 1st Ave., ☎ 602/941–5665), where such eclectic sandwiches as rosemary-seasoned focaccia with chicken, roasted eggplant, and feta cheese are brought out to diners on a tree-shaded patio. Leave room for one of the exceptional desserts. This spot can get crowded at lunchtime, so call ahead for a reservation.

18 **Marshall Way Arts District.** Another niche of galleries, concerned predominantly with contemporary art, lines the blocks of Marshall Way north of Indian School Road. Upscale gift and jewelry stores can be found here too. Farther north on Marshall Way across 3rd Avenue, the street is filled with more art galleries and creative stores with a southwestern flair.

OFF THE BEATEN PATH **McCORMICK RAILROAD PARK** – The highlight of this park, a stop for train and history buffs, is the 1928 Roald Amundsen Pullman car, with its stunningly restored rich woods and brass, used in pre-*Air Force One* days by presidents Hoover, Truman, and Eisenhower. Also on display is a 1907 Magma Arizona Railroad Engine (No. 6), a hard-working locomotive that hauled copper ore through the state for 38 years. Model-train displays, stores with railway memorabilia, and items for the train hobbyist are also on site. For $1, children can ride the miniature train or the 1929 antique carousel. ✉ *7301 E. Indian Bend Rd.,* ☎ *602/994–2312.* *Free.* *Daily 10–7.*

16 **Old Town Scottsdale.** Billed as "the West's Most Western Town," this area features rustic storefronts and wooden sidewalks; it's touristy, but it also gives visitors a genuine taste of life here 80 years ago. Many stores carry kitschy souvenirs, but you'll also find high-quality jewelry, pots, and Mexican imports.

NEED A BREAK? The southeast corner of 1st Avenue and Scottsdale Road marks a landmark of sorts: the pink-and-white **Sugar Bowl Ice Cream Parlor** (✉ 4005 N. Scottsdale Rd., ☎ 602/946–0051), run by the Huntress family since 1958 and frequented by Paradise Valley cartoonist Bill Keane (some of his "Family Circus" work is displayed near the entrance). Although sandwiches, soups, and salads are available, you'll miss the point if you don't indulge in the gooey sundaes, floats, and parfaits.

13 **Scottsdale Center for the Arts.** Galleries within this cultural and entertainment complex rotate exhibits frequently, with an emphasis on contemporary art and artists. The airy and bright **Arts Museum gift shop** (☎ 602/874–4644) has a great collection of unusual jewelry, as

well as stationery, posters, and art books. ✉ *7380 E. 2nd St.,* ☎ *602/994–2787.* 🎫 *Free.* 🕒 *Mon.–Sat. 10–5, Sun. 12–5.*

14 **Scottsdale Chamber of Commerce.** Pop inside to pick from local maps, guidebooks, and brochures in abundance. Ask for a walking-tour map of Old Town Scottsdale's historic sites, which the helpful staff will be pleased to provide. ✉ *7343 Scottsdale Mall,* ☎ *602/945–8481 or 800/877–1117.* 🕒 *Weekdays 8:30–5, Sat. 10–5, Sun. 11–5.*

15 **Scottsdale Historical Museum.** Scottsdale's first schoolhouse, this red-brick building houses a version of the 1910 school room, as well as photographs, original furniture from the city's founding fathers, and displays of other treasures from Scottsdale's early days. ✉ *7333 Scottsdale Mall,* ☎ *602/945–4499.* 🎫 *Free.* 🕒 *Wed.–Sat. 10–5, Sun. noon–4. Closed July–Aug. and holidays.*

OFF THE BEATEN PATH

TALIESEN WEST – Ten years after visiting Arizona in 1927 to consult on designs for the Arizona Biltmore hotel, architect Frank Lloyd Wright chose 600 acres of raw, rugged Sonoran Desert at the foothills of the McDowell Mountains, just outside Scottsdale, as the site for his permanent winter residence. Wright and his coterie of apprentices proceeded to construct their "desert camp" here, using "organic architecture"—designed to integrate the buildings with their surroundings and respect the natural setting of the land. The result is an ingenious integration of indoor and outdoor space. In addition to the living quarters, drafting studio, and small apartments of the Apprentice Court, Taliesen West also has two theaters, a music pavilion, and a charming structure of sleeping spaces that surround an open patio and fireplace, known as the Sun Trap. Two guided tours cover different parts of interiors, and a guided "Desert Walk" winds through the petroglyphs and landscape from which Wright drew his vision, as well as the experimental desert residences designed by his apprentices. Tour times vary, so call ahead; all visitors must be accompanied by a guide. ✉ *12621 Frank Lloyd Wright Blvd.,* ☎ *602/860–8810 or 602/860–2700.* 🎫 *Guided tour (1 hr) $10 winter, $8 summer; Behind the Scenes tour (3 hrs) $25 winter, $20 summer; Desert Walk tour (90 min) $12.* 🕒 *Daily 8:30–5:30, winter; 7:30–4:30, summer.*

Tempe

Charles Trumbell Hayden arrived on the east end of the Salt River in the 1860s. There he built a flour mill and began a ferry service to cross the then-flowing Rio Salado, founding the town then known as Hayden's Ferry in 1871. Other settlers soon arrived, including an Englishman who felt—upon approaching the town from Phoenix and seeing the butte, river, and fields of green mesquite—that the name should be changed to Tempe (pronounced tem-*pee*), after the Vale of Tempe in Greek mythology. Hayden took umbrage at the suggested name change but finally relented in 1879.

Today Tempe is Arizona's sixth-largest city and the home of Arizona State University's main campus and a thriving student population. A 20- to 30-minute drive from Phoenix, the tree- and brick-lined Mill Avenue (on which Hayden's mill still stands) is the main drag, rife with student-oriented hangouts, bookstores, boutiques, eateries, and a repertory movie house.

A Good Walk

Parking is available in the public structure just north of University Drive between Ash and Mill avenues. From **La Casa Vieja,** on the southwest corner of Mill Avenue and 1st Street, cross 1st Street and stop in the **Tempe**

City Arts Center. Stroll north 50 feet toward the Rio Salado and two (old and new) Mill Avenue bridges; these banks of the Rio Salado are the future site of a sprawling riverfront commercial and entertainment district. Turn around and head south on Mill Avenue, passing the old Hayden flour mill, as well as "A" Mountain (on which spirited ASU students have painted the state's initial) to your left. Continue south along shop-lined Mill Avenue until you reach 5th Street; walk a block east on 5th toward the inverted pyramid of **Tempe City Hall.** Head the block back west to continue browsing on Mill Avenue. Another two blocks south on Mill, crossing through University Drive and then proceeding the longer block south toward Apache Boulevard, will take you to the Grady Gammage Auditorium and ASU art museums and galleries on the southwest corner of the **Arizona State University** campus. At this point you can walk back up Mill Avenue, catch the northbound 66 or westbound R (Red Line) bus back up Mill Avenue, or wind your way northward through the university campus. Definitely also tour the **Mystery Castle,** a curious sight well worth the short drive from downtown Tempe.

Timing

If you're planning to shop as well as tour the campus and museums, allow four or five hours for exploring (and taking periodic breaks) in downtown Tempe. Allow 1½–2 hours on either end of your agenda for a tour through the Mystery Castle.

Sights to See

Arizona State University. What was formerly the Tempe Normal School for Teachers—in 1886, a four-room redbrick building and 20-acre cow pasture—is now the sprawling 750-acre campus of ASU, home to the largest student population in the Southwest. Stop by the **ASU Visitor Center** (✉ 826 E. Apache Blvd., at Rural Rd., ☎ 602/965–0100) for a copy of a self-guided walking tour. You'll wind past public art and innovative architecture—including a music building that bears a strong resemblance to a wedding cake (designed by Taliesin students to complement Wright's Gammage Auditorium) and a law library shaped like an open book—and end up to the 74,000-seat **ASU Sun Devil Stadium,** home to the school's Sun Devils, headquarters for the NFL's Arizona Cardinals, and the site of 1996's Super Bowl XXX.

Heralded for its superior acoustics, the circular **Grady Gammage Auditorium** was the last public structure completed by architect Frank Lloyd Wright, who detached the rear wall from grand tier and balcony sections in an effort to surround every patron with sound. The stage is large enough to accommodate a full symphony orchestra, as well as the Gammage's 2,909-pipe organ. The Gammage displays art exhibits throughout the lobby and in two on-site galleries. During the school year, free half-hour tours are offered weekdays 1–3:30 PM. ✉ *Mill Ave. at Apache Blvd.,* ☎ *602/965–4050.*

While touring the west end of the campus, stop into the gray-purple stucco **Nelson Fine Arts Center,** just north of the Gammage Auditorium. The center's museum houses some fine examples of 19th- and 20th-century painting and sculpture, contemporary art, and American crafts, as well as an American and European print collection. ☎ *602/965–2787.* ⏲ *Tues. 10–9, Wed.–Sat. 10–5, Sun. 1–5.*

A short walk east, just north of the Hayden Library, ASU's experimental gallery and collection of crockery and ceramics are located in the **Matthews Center.** ☎ *602/965–2875.* ⏲ *Wed.–Sat. 10–5, Sun. 1–5. Call for summer hrs.*

In Matthews Hall, the **Northlight Gallery** exhibits works by both renowned and emerging photographers. Admission to all ASU museums is free. ☎ *602/965-6517.* ⏲ *Mon.–Thurs. 10:30–4:30, Sun. noon–4:30.*

OFF THE BEATEN PATH

MYSTERY CASTLE – At the foot of South Mountain lies a curious dwelling hand-built from desert rocks, railroad refuse, and anything else its builder, Boyce Gulley, could get his hands on. The castle is still a private home; Boyce's daughter Mary Lou, for whom the castle was built, lives here and leads every tour. Chock-full of oddities that will fascinate everyone in the family, the castle has 18 rooms with 13 fireplaces, 90 bottle-glass portholes, a downstairs grotto, and a roll-away bed with a mining railcar as its frame. Be sure to ask how Bing Crosby's golf club became embedded in the ceiling. ✉ *800 E. Mineral Rd., at the end of S. 7th St.,* ☎ *602/268-1581.* 🎫 *$3.* ⏲ *Tues.–Sun. 11–4.*

La Casa Vieja. In 1871, when Tempe was still known as Hayden's Ferry, this "old house" was built as the port for founding father Charles Hayden's ferry across the Salt River. Built of native adobe, the hacienda is modeled after Spanish mansions and was the town's first building. The late Carl Hayden, former U.S. senator from Arizona, was born here. Now a steak house, the structure retains its original dimensions; the lobby and dining rooms contain historical documents and photographic mementos pertaining to the frontier history of the hamlet of Tempe. ✉ *3 W. 1st St.,* ☎ *602/967-7594.* ⏲ *Sun.–Thurs. 11–11, Fri.–Sat. 11 AM–midnight.*

Tempe City Hall. Local architects Rolf Osland and Michael Goodwin constructed this inverted pyramid not just to win awards for its innovative design (which they have) but also to shield city workers from the desert sun. The pyramid is constructed mainly of bronzed glass and stainless steel; the point is buried in a sunken courtyard lushly landscaped with jacaranda, ivy, and flowers, out of which the pyramid widens to the sky. Peek inside through the dramatic terrace-floor entrance. ✉ *31 E. 5th St. (1 block east of Mill Ave.),* ☎ *602/967-2001.* 🎫 *Free.*

NEED A BREAK?

The outdoor patio of the **Coffee Plantation** (✉ 680 S. Mill Ave., ☎ 602/829-7878) is the site of a lively social scene—students cramming, local residents chatting over a cup of joe, and poets and musicians presenting their latest masterpieces.

Tempe City Arts Center. From the old Mill Avenue bridge, an anamorphic image of the Mona Lisa on the roof of this building comes into focus. An indoor gallery and outdoor sculpture garden feature works by local, state, and national artists. ✉ *Northwest corner of Mill Ave. and 1st St.,* ☎ *602/968-0888.* 🎫 *Free.* ⏲ *Tues.–Sun. noon–5.*

DINING

Few restaurants require men to wear jackets and ties (in any situation, a bola tie will always suffice). The *guayabera* (Mexican wedding shirt) is also an appropriate warm-weather option in all but the fanciest places. Similarly, pants or a simple skirt is welcome almost everywhere for women. Only the fanciest places expect an evening dress or pantsuit.

Large parties (six or more) should always make a reservation. Restaurants are open daily (unless otherwise noted), although diners should be aware that Phoenix keeps relatively early hours—dinner is commonly served between 6 and 8.

CATEGORY	COST*
$$$$	over $50
$$$	$30–$50
$$	$15–$20
$	under $15

**per person for a three-course dinner, excluding drinks, service, and sales tax (6%–7%)*

American

$$$ ✕ **Ruth's Chris Steakhouse.** Most meat fanciers agree that steak seldom gets better handling than at this New Orleans–based chain. Amid brass, wood, and glass interiors (plus majestic views at the Scottsdale location), you can get thick, juicy lamb or pork chops, but planks of beef are this restaurant's business. Calorie- and cardiac-watchers, beware: Portions are massive, and everything—even the broiled shrimp—comes swimming in the house butter bath. ✉ *2201 E. Camelback Rd.,* ☎ *602/957–9600; 7001 N. Scottsdale Rd., Scottsdale,* ☎ *602/991–5988. Reservations essential. AE, MC, V.*

$$$ ✕ **Steamers.** New England–style standards like chowder, halibut, and lobster are mainstays of this bright, spacious seafood house. The open kitchen is surrounded by the oyster bar, where patrons watch chefs at work and choose their favorites from the variety of oysters served on the half-shell. Try the "dirty bag shrimp"—a half pound of medium prawns steamed in special spices and served in a brown paper bag. ✉ *2576 E. Camelback Rd.,* ☎ *602/956–3631. AE, D, DC, MC, V.*

$$$ ★ ✕ **Top of the Market.** This smaller, slightly more expensive annex above the noisy, popular Fish Market has the atmosphere of a San Francisco wharf restaurant. And everything on its menu—from charbroiled orange roughy to whole Dungeness crab to handmade pastas—is skillfully handled and imaginatively seasoned. Try crème brûlée or strawberries for dessert. ✉ *1720 E. Camelback Rd.,* ☎ *602/277–3474. Reservations essential. AE, D, DC, MC, V.*

$$ ✕ **American Grill.** Leather, brass, ferns, and etched glass—a large bar at the entry and a lounge with cozy tables and soft, live jazz—all recreate a casual pub feel. But the action is in the glassed-in exhibition kitchen and the booths, where varieties of American Cajun and southwestern cuisine are prepared and consumed. N'awlins barbecued shrimp is a fine appetizer, and chowder in a bowl of toscano bread can't be beat—powerful desserts, too. ✉ *1233 S. Alma School Rd., Mesa,* ☎ *602/844–1918. AE, D, DC, MC, V. No lunch Sun.*

$$ ✕ **Goldie's 1895 House.** This charming downtown Victorian (and former bordello) would fit right in on California's Mendocino coast. Standard dishes get subtle extra touches—baked cod is wrapped in phyllo dough and orange roughy is seasoned with Parmesan-scallion butter—and there are surprises like roast duck in walnut and pomegranate sauce. Upstairs in Goldie's attic, you'll find a small art gallery and the site of mystery dinner theater (performances are at 8 Friday–Sunday). Call ahead if you intend to come here: The hours are as compact as the rooms. ✉ *362 N. 2nd Ave.,* ☎ *602/254–0338. Reservations essential. AE, D, DC, MC, V. No lunch weekends.*

$$ ★ ✕ **Landmark.** After 50 years as a Mormon church and a brief turn as a college, this massive brick Victorian became a restaurant. Expect to wait a half hour downstairs in the small lounge, surrounded by historical photos of a kinder, gentler Mesa. Upstairs, visit the immense "salad room," stocked with well-made Americana, from meatballs to seafood salad and thick, rich soups. A family-style menu of straightforward comfort food features Swiss steak and pot roast like Grandma used to make. After all of that, the Landmark pie is a must for fudge lovers. ✉ *809 W. Main St., Mesa,* ☎ *602/962–4652. Reservations not accepted. AE, D, DC, MC, V. No lunch weekends.*

$$ ✕ **Oscar Taylor.** A staple with the meat-and-potatoes crowd, this 1920s Chicago-style steak house combines beautiful cuts of meat with brisk service and cozy ambience. Prime rib is a house favorite, as are half and full slabs of sweet "Georgia Peach" baby-back ribs. ✉ *2420 E. Camelback Rd.,* ☎ *602/956–5705. AE, D, DC, MC, V.*

$$ ★ ✕ **Rustler's Rooste.** A live steer greets you at the door, floors are strewn with sawdust, and after literally sliding down to the dining rooms, you'll discover this playful western steak house also has a breathtaking view of the Valley. Specialties include mesquite-grilled steaks, as well as juicy barbecued pork ribs and chicken. The Cowboy Stuff Platter ($17) puts a sample of almost everything the restaurant serves (except rattlesnake) on your plate. The Rooste, marked by a star of white lights visible from I–10, is at the east end of South Mountain Park; take the Baseline exit west off the highway. ✉ *7777 S. Pointe Pkwy.,* ☎ *602/431–6474. Reservations essential. AE, D, DC, MC, V. No lunch.*

$$ ✕ **The Stockyards.** When Arizona had cattle barons, they cut their deals and steaks here. The feedlots and barons are gone, but the restaurant remains, a landmark just a ½-mi east of Sky Harbor Airport. Its ornate Victorian interior retains the original brass-trim bar and three salons—the black-leather Cattle Room, the gold-papered Gold Coast Room, and the mural-wall Rose Room. Beef on the menu has been handled with respect, from massive prime rib and steaks to succulent calves' liver and calf fries (Rocky Mountain oysters). ✉ *5001 E. Washington St.,* ☎ *602/273–7378. AE, D, DC, MC, V. No lunch weekends.*

$$ ✕ **T-Bone Steakhouse.** Drive south on 19th Avenue past the end of the pavement and there, on the slopes of South Mountain, is a big outdoor barbecue in a parking lot. Inside the rustic building are wood benches at oilcloth-covered tables. Steak and chicken come to you, and you're swept into vistas of the desert sunset or the Valley lit up at night. Salad and cowboy beans, giant slices of toast, and fresh hot baked potatoes are always on hand. ✉ *10037 S. 19th Ave.,* ☎ *602/276–0945. AE, DC, MC, V. No lunch.*

$ ★ ✕ **Bev's Kitchen.** Some folks call it country, some call it soul food, and some just call it home. Whatever you call it, you may have to wait in line to enjoy it. This handsome downtown diner has gracious staff and great food—the hand-pounded chicken-fried steak, crumbling moist catfish, lively hot links are recommended—plus yams, okra gumbo, and southern-style cabbage with corned-beef hash prepared with care by people who love their vegetables (boiled down some, of course). Your reward for finishing all that is a slice of one of Bev's pies or peach cobbler. The kitchen closes at 9 PM, but on Friday and Saturday nights the live jazz continues into the night. ✉ *4621 S. Central Ave.,* ☎ *243–2788. AE, D, DC, MC, V. No dinner weekdays.*

$ ✕ **Ed Debevic's.** This nostalgic chain diner is a half-accurate, but wholly entertaining, revision of the 1950s, with shiny gold- and red-leatherette dinettes, gum-snapping waitresses, and a working jukebox playing Elvis, Tessy Brewer, and dozens more. The menu has the requisite burgers, malts, and fries, plus blue-plate specials like chili and meat loaf and gravy. With prodding, "Edna" and the girls will provide tableside diversions with their troop of backup singers and dancers. Friday and Saturday nights, the joint comes alive with a sock-hop–style DJ. Forty-plus diners blush to remember, but children love it. ✉ *2102 E. Highland Ave.,* ☎ *602/956–2760. AE, D, DC, MC, V.*

$ ✕ **5 & Diner.** The two branches of this local '50s-style diner offer less elaborate entertainment than their competitor, Ed Debevic's, but tastier food. More than 150 items are on the menu—including juicy burgers and creamy, thick malts and shakes—and they're available 24 hours a day. ✉ *5220 N. 16th St.,* ☎ *602/264–5220; 12802 N. Tatum Blvd., Paradise Valley,* ☎ *602/996–0033. AE, MC, V.*

Adrian's, **58**
American Grill, **77**
Arizona Café & Grill, **30**
Bahía San Carlos, **55**
Bev's Kitchen, **65**
Blue Fin, **49**
Byblos, **72**
Char's, **71**
Chianti, **36**
China Doll, **47**
China Gate, **4, 62, 75**
Chompie's, **6, 13**
Christopher's, **31**
Christo's, **17**
Ed Debevic's, **34**
Eddie's Grill, **23**
The Eggery (Good Egg), **2, 9, 12, 21, 24, 39, 41**
Eliana's, **57**
Felsen Haus, **25**
5 & Diner, **26, 44**
Golden Gate, **73**
Goldie's 1895 House, **48**
Gourmet House of Hong Kong, **52**
Greekfest, **28**
Greektown, **16**
Guiseppe's, **33**
Havana Café, **7, 38**
Indian Delhi Palace, **61**
Korean Garden, **70**
Landmark, **78**
La Hacienda, **8**
Los Dos Molinos, **66**
Macayo, **3, 14, 22, 45, 69, 74**
Marquesa, **8**
Matador, **51**
Mediterranean House, **19**
Mint Thai, **80**
Mrs. White's Golden Rule Café, **54**
Munch a Bagel, **20**
The Olive Garden, **1, 5, 11, 46, 76, 81**
Oregano's Pizza Bistro, **63**
Oscar Taylor, **35**
Pepin, **64**
Richardson's, **18**
RoxSand, **35**
Rustler's Rooste, **68**
Ruth's Chris Steakhouse, **32, 42**
Sam's Cafe, **35, 50**
Samyra's Lebanese Cuisine, **53**
Shogun, **10**
Steamers, **35**

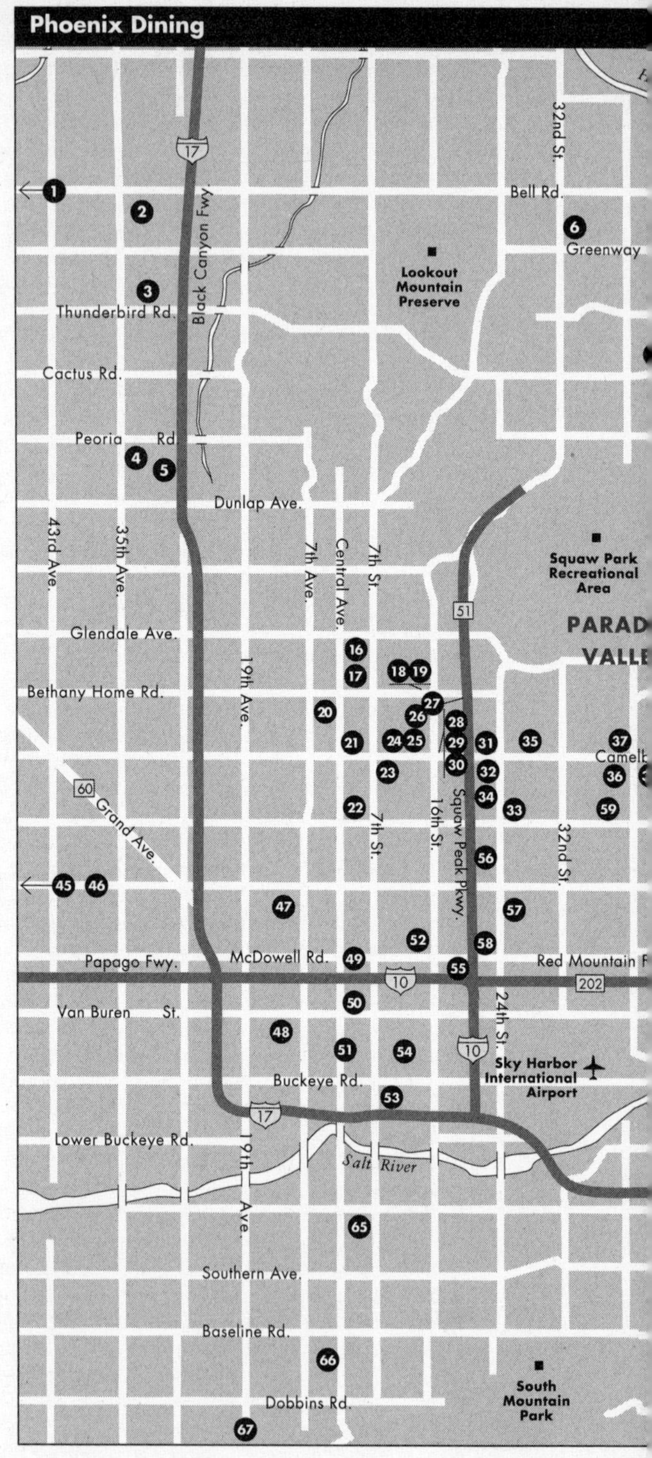

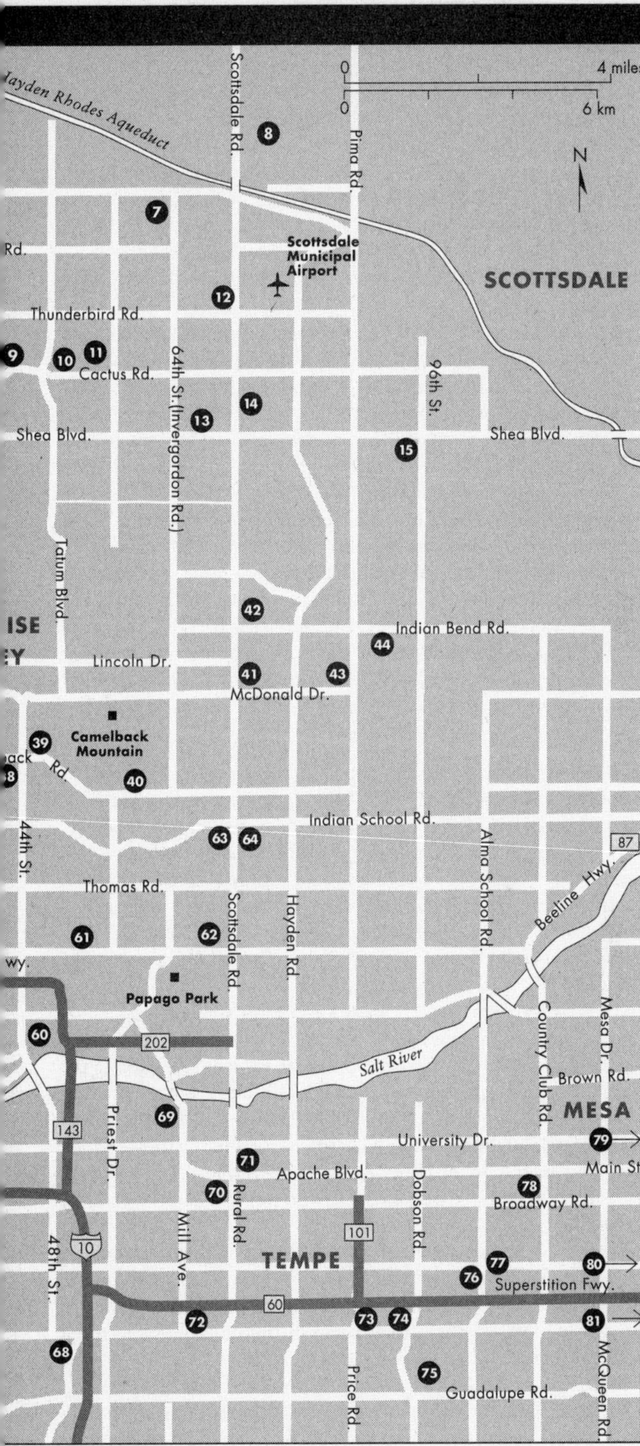

The Stockyards, **60**
Such Is Life, **3, 56**
Tarbell's, **36**
T-Bone Steakhouse, **67**
Texaz Grill, **27**
Thai Lahna, **59**
Timothy's, **29**
Top of the Market, **30**
Vincent Guerithault on Camelback, **37**
Voltaire, **43**
Windows on the Green, **40**
Yamakasa, **15**
Zur Kate, **79**

$ ✕ **The Eggery/The Good Egg.** Country decor and a lengthy menu mark this cheerful, comfy breakfast-and-brunch chain. Besides pancakes, waffles, and an array of cleverly named egg creations, from scrambler skillets to frittatas, there are welcome light options like yogurt, granola, and fruit dishes. Service is brisk and friendly, children are welcome, and there's no rush despite the crowds. ✉ *5109 N. 44th St.,* ☎ *602/840–5734; 4326 E. Cactus Rd. (across from Paradise Valley Mall),* ☎ *602/953–2342; 2957 W. Bell Rd. (northwest),* ☎ *602/993–2797; 50 E. Camelback Rd.,* ☎ *602/263–8554; 906 E. Camelback Rd,* ☎ *602/274–5393; 6149 N. Scottsdale Rd., Scottsdale,* ☎ *602/991–5416; 14046 N. Scottsdale Rd., Scottsdale,* ☎ *602/483–1090. AE, MC, V. No dinner.*

$ ✕ **Texaz Grill.** Tucked in an uptown corner mall, this noisy and crowded spot is decorated with Texas and country-western memorabilia. The kitchen does simple, effective things with steak (including a classic chicken-fried) and serves up some of the best mashed potatoes you've had since you were a youngster. After picking out your steak, ask them to hold the lemon butter—the meat's better by itself. ✉ *6003 N. 16th St.,* ☎ *602/248–7827. AE, MC, V. No lunch Sun.*

$ ✕ **Mrs. White's Golden Rule Cafe.** This little downtown, down-home lunch spot brings smiles to those who love liver and boiled cabbage, as well as fanciers of standard American fare such as fried chicken, red beans, and yams. Food is cooked with a light, loving touch, and every order gets a serving of delicious cornbread; service is friendly, prices are low, and the payin' is by the honor system. Mrs. White serves dinner only until 7PM, so plan accordingly. ✉ *808 E. Jefferson St.,* ☎ *602/262–9256. Reservations not accepted. No credit cards. Closed weekends.*

Chinese

$$ ★ ✕ **China Gate.** Seldom do chain restaurants rise so high or remain so consistent in quality—not to mention offer such a breadth of cuisines, which here ranges from Mongolian to Cantonese, Beijing-style to spicy Szechuan. Mandarin ribs and *shu mai* (shrimp and pork dumplings) are a special experience, as is a combination of shrimp and sea cucumber. Decor is striking, and the layout emphasizes privacy amid open space. ✉ *3033 W. Peoria Ave., Phoenix,* ☎ *602/944–1982;* ✉ *7820 E. McDowell Rd., Scottsdale,* ☎ *602/946–0720;* ✉ *2050 W. Guadalupe Rd., Mesa,* ☎ *602/897–0607. AE, D, DC, MC, V.*

$–$$ ✕ **China Doll.** The venerable Cantonese restaurant still is *the* place for family and association banquets and Chinese New Year feasts. Dinners—including the seasonal ginger fish, which you select from the tank in the lobby—are reliably executed classics, and the dim sum is among the best in town. ✉ *3336 N. 7th Ave.,* ☎ *602/264–0538. AE, DC, MC, V.*

$–$$ ✕ **Gourmet House of Hong Kong.** Get ready for the bustling sounds and incomparable flavors of Hong Kong, squeezed into a tiny downtown restaurant. Staff and owners rush in and out of a narrow, steamy, open kitchen to take your order and serve you, and take-out diners stand between tables, eagerly waiting. The house plate is a succulent, satisfying sampler, and hot-sour chicken wings, king duck, garlic pork, and any seafood special off the board are guaranteed hits. If you're suddenly craving Peking duck, this is one of the only places in town that doesn't require 24 hours' advance notice. ✉ *1438 E. McDowell Rd.,* ☎ *602/253–4859. DC, MC, V.*

$ ✕ **Golden Gate.** Owner and hostess Sue Kao maintains a friendly touch with diners at this charming restaurant serving delicious Mandarin and Szechuan cuisine. Highly recommended are garlic chicken, three kings chicken, Golden Gate shrimp, and moo shu pork. ✉ *2640 W. Baseline Rd., Mesa,* ☎ *602/897–1335. MC, V.*

Delis

$–$$ ★ ✕ **Chompie's.** This cheerful New York deli offers big breakfasts—from blintzes to home fries to hefty omelets—and high-piled sandwiches on fresh-baked bread and rolls at lunchtime (all with pickles, the way it's meant to be). Not only do they make their own bagels, but the huge bakery case is a trip to the old country, with a stunning array of traditional European treats and American inventions. Take a number! ✉ *3202 E. Greenway Rd., Phoenix,* ☎ *602/971–8010; 9301 E. Shea Blvd., Scottsdale,* ☎ *602/860-0475. AE, MC, V.*

$ ★ ✕ **Munch a Bagel.** Just north of Camelback, on one of the main morning routes into downtown, sits one of Phoenix's most popular reasons to leave home early or get to work a little late. A quick breakfast special of eggs, onion-tossed potatoes, and a fresh bagel is worth stopping for, or have a leisurely linger over huge seven-egg omelets—try the Greek, with calamari and feta inside—and a frothy cappuccino or *cafè latte.* Any deli sandwich is guaranteed to send you home with a smile and a doggie bag. ✉ *5114 N. 7th St.,* ☎ *602/264–1975. AE, MC, V. Closed Mon. No dinner.*

French

$$$–$$$$ ★ ✕ **Christopher's.** Christopher Gross, one of the Valley's leading chef-entrepreneurs, offers two choices here: fine dining of the monogrammed-linen-and-silver kind or more upbeat (and less expensive) fare at the marble-tiled bistro next door. Both spots have creative menus and wine lists worthy of the Champs-Elysées. Fish, chicken, and more exotic game are all flawlessly prepared and sauced and given majestic presentations. ✉ *2398 E. Camelback Rd.,* ☎ *602/957–3214. Reservations essential. Jacket required. AE, D, DC, MC, V.*

$$$ ✕ **Voltaire.** The Valley's most consistent classical French cuisine makes its home in a residential Scottsdale neighborhood. Nothing nouvelle here—there may not be a recipe that's less than 100 years old. But when you have the urge to cap off a drive through the desert with escargots, onion soup gratiné, sautéed sand dabs, and perfectly handled rack of lamb, this is the place. And how could one miss crêpes suzette, cherries jubilee, or exquisite crème caramel? ✉ *8340 E. McDonald Dr., Scottsdale,* ☎ *602/948–1005. Reservations essential. AE, DC, MC, V. No lunch. Closed Sun.*

German

$$ ✕ **Felsen Haus.** Owner Klaus Lehmann bids patrons a fond *willkomen* in this half-timbered eatery, bedecked with posters of the Old Country. The full bar offers an extensive collection of wheat beers, available in 1- or 2-liter boots, as well as German cocktails. Authentic German dishes—*Jaeger schnitzel* (pork cutlets smothered in mushrooms), delightfully tangy red cabbage and sauerkraut, and bacony potato salad—are homemade; be sure to try a liberal dollop of the horseradish-infused mustard. If you still have room, indulge in a steaming plate of mellow apple strudel. Spritely polka bands play on weekends on a small stage backed with a trompe l'oeil Matterhorn. ✉ *1008 E. Camelback Rd.,* ☎ *602/277–1119. AE, D, MC, V.*

$$ ✕ **Zur Kate.** Outside you may be in a corner mall on a busy Mesa thoroughfare, but inside Zur Kate you enter a friendly family inn in Bavaria. Steins and Tyrolean caps belonging to regulars line the walls. Soups are good and hearty, and the sauerbraten, *kassler ripchen* (smoked pork loin), dumplings, and tiny spaetzle are wonderful—and that's not to mention the wurst and fresh apple strudel. *Gemütlich* service and weekend live polka complete the pleasures. ✉ *4815 E. Main St., Mesa,* ☎ *602/830–4244. MC, V. Closed Sun.*

Greek

$$ ★ ✕ **Greekfest.** In this tasteful Athens-style taverna, classic dishes are handled exquisitely. Greekfest offers a quietly festive evening with featherlight spanakopita appetizers, succulent lamb, and fresh, tart dolmas. Baklava, anyone? ✉ *1940 E. Camelback Rd.,* ☎ *602/265–2990. Reservations essential. AE, D, DC, MC, V. No lunch Sun.*

$$ ✕ **Greektown.** At this warm family operation cheered by posters and murals, Papa greets, Mama cooks, and Son seats. A combo appetizer samples the Greek islands, and lamb stew and seafood are good bets. When it's time for dessert, there are honey, nuts, and phyllo dough aplenty—and Mama's rice pudding. Wash it down with sweet, cocoay coffee. ✉ *539 E. Glendale Ave.,* ☎ *602/279–9677. AE, MC, V.*

Indian

$ ✕ **Indian Delhi Palace.** Midway between downtown and Tempe, right across from Motorola's semiconductor plant, you'll step through the door of a double storefront right into India. Attentive service and delightful flavors enhance the illusion. Sip tea and nibble home-baked *naan* and *kalcha* breads while perusing the lengthy menu. Tandoori chicken and yogurt lamb are two of many wonderful dishes, but the best bet is the inclusive dinner. A lunch buffet is another fun way to tour India's kitchens. ✉ *5050 E. McDowell Rd.,* ☎ *602/244–8181. AE, D, DC, MC, V.*

Italian

$–$$$ ★ ✕ **Giuseppe's.** In a tiny, noisy storefront in a corner mall, the Carotenuto family serves no pizza but plenty of other Italian favorites: savory pasta and homemade sauces, exquisitely creamy stuffed eggplant and zucchini, manicotti, and rich, moist meatballs. Desserts, from *tiramisù* to hard-shelled ice cream *tartuffo*, are mouthwatering. There's all this and checkered tablecloths, too. ✉ *2824 E. Indian School Rd.,* ☎ *602/381–1237. AE, MC, V. BYOB. Closed Sun.*

$–$$ ✕ **Chianti.** This charming little poster-hung restaurant stays crowded, but the unusually alert service neither forgets nor flusters you. Antipasto salad is a crisp overture of clear, tangy flavors, and pasta is well handled and sauced. Espresso or cappuccino, with gelato, perhaps, or spumoni, closes a delightful meal. ✉ *3943 E. Camelback Rd.,* ☎ *602/957–9840. AE, D, MC, V. No lunch weekends.*

$ ★ ✕ **Oregano's Pizza Bistro.** This small, energetic pizza joint serves not only scrumptious Chicago-style stuffed and thin-crust pizzas but also lasagnas that are out of this world. The majority of seating is out on the patio, where giant murals of the windy city transform parking-lot views into pleasant surroundings and patrons watch the wait staff cross the alley (into the next-door Kaboom Room) with steaming pies. Try a yummy pizzookie for desert—just-baked chocolate-chip dough in a 6-inch pizza pan, served à la mode. ✉ *3622 N. Scottsdale Rd.,* ☎ *602/970–1860. Reservations not accepted. AE, D, MC, V.*

$ ✕ **The Olive Garden.** Plant-filled rooms cleverly cut into private nooks on various levels create a pleasing atmosphere—a good place to go beyond spaghetti and pizza, and a nonthreatening "grown-up" setting for the young. The food does more justice to the range of Italian cuisine than you would expect from a chain—from garlicky bread sticks to fine pesto and very creditable sauces (Alfredo and marinara are both consistently successful). ✉ *10223 N. Metro Pkwy. E (at Metrocenter Mall),* ☎ *602/943–4573; 7889 W. Bell Rd., Sun City,* ☎ *602/977–8378; 1261 W. Southern Ave. (at Fiesta Mall), Mesa,* ☎ *602/890–0440; 4868 E. Cactus Rd., Scottsdale,* ☎ *602/494–4327; 2601 E. Southern Ave., Mesa,* ☎ *602/807–0207; 2626 N. 75th Ave., Phoenix,* ☎ *602/849–6533. AE, D, DC, MC, V.*

Japanese

$$ ✕ **Yamakasa.** Simple and serene in decor and service, this family-run restaurant offers excellent sushi and a tempura- and teriyaki-style menu. Calm consistency makes this a refreshing place in which to enjoy a flavorful Zen evening. ✉ *9301 E. Shea Blvd., Scottsdale,* ☎ *602/860–5605. AE, DC, MC, V.*

$–$$ ★ ✕ **Shogun.** This modified tavern in the corner of a strip mall offers the most enjoyable Japanese-restaurant experience in the Valley, from its cheerful staff to the outstanding sushi bar. At the tables, you can try both finely turned standards (such as teriyaki and tempura) and sumptuous adventures into less familiar areas. Try the *yaki sakana* (catch of the day—usually salmon or squid) served *shioyaki* (salted and broiled). Expect a wait on Friday and Saturday nights. ✉ *12615 N. Tatum Blvd.,* ☎ *602/953–3264. AE, D, DC, MC, V. No lunch Sun.*

$ ✕ **Blue Fin.** Locals pour into this informal, no-frills spot across the street from the Central Library for a quick lunch of generously proportioned *donburi* rice bowls, teriyaki chicken, or select sushi. Photographs of all the menu items hang above the cash register to assist you. If you're going for dinner, make it in before the 7 PM closing time. ✉ *1401 N. Central Ave.,* ☎ *602/254–3171. Reservations not accepted. No credit cards. Closed Sun.*

Korean

$–$$ ★ ✕ **Korean Garden.** Although the decor is unnoteworthy, this friendly, well-staffed restaurant receives high marks for familiar Korean fare, like *bool goki* (grill-your-own marinated beef strips), and more exotic treats, such as *jap chae* (pan-fried clear noodles with vegetables and beef) and *bibim bob* (a bowl of assorted vegetables and beef, with hot sauce, topped with a fried egg). The *kimchi* (marinated chopped cabbage) and *gadduki* (marinated chopped radish) are fiery treats. The menu provides pictures of all entrées for those unfamiliar with Korean cuisine. ✉ *1324 S. Rural Rd., Tempe,* ☎ *602/967–1133. D, MC, V. Closed Sun.*

Mexican and Latin American

$$$–$$$$ ★ ✕ **La Hacienda.** About 20 mi northeast of downtown in the Scottsdale Princess Resort, this tiled-roof hacienda is lavishly appointed with Spanish ceramics and masks, chile *ristas,* and fireplaces. The kitchen elevates Sonoran food to haute cuisine: Dishes range from an enchilada stuffed with crab to the tableside drama of *cochinillo asado* (roast stuffed suckling pig) to the baked sea bass stuffed with crab meat. A strolling mariachi band provides zesty tunes to match the flavors. ✉ *7575 E. Princess Dr. (1 mi north of Bell Rd.), Scottsdale,* ☎ *602/585–2721. Reservations essential. AE, DC, MC, V. No lunch.*

$$ ★ ✕ **Havana Café.** The Cuban cuisine served at this clean, cozy café shows more European than Latin American influence. Pork becomes a marinated, garlic-laden roast, and tamales are moist and sweet, with meat mixed throughout the *masa* (cornmeal), not wrapped in it. Although the *paella a la Havana,* with Valencia rice, Maine lobster, Manilla clams, Spanish chorizo, and threads of imported saffron, takes 45 minutes to prepare, you'll find scads of locals patiently waiting. Don't miss the desserts, and have a cup of espresso at hand. (If you're at the Camelback location and there's a wait for a table, try Arriba, the tapas bar upstairs, for Spanish-style snacks and sherry.) ✉ *4225 E. Camelback Rd.,* ☎ *602/952–1991; 6245 E. Bell Rd.,* ☎ *602/991–1496. AE, MC, V. No lunch Sun.*

$$ ✕ **Richardson's.** This neighborhood haunt can be noisy and crowded, but the chiles rellenos, enchiladas, and other first-rate standbys pack 'em in until midnight. Loose-cushioned, Santa Fe adobe booths surround a small, lively bar, and the open kitchen turns out that fiery fugue of flavors known as New Mexican–style cooking. Green chile stew is to die for—or from, if you're not used to the spicy heat. *Chimayo* chicken is flavorfully stuffed with spinach, dried tomatoes, poblano chilies, and asiago cheese; Santa Fe chicken comes with a sinful jalapeño mayo. ✉ *1582 E. Bethany Home Rd., ☎ 602/265–5886. AE, MC, V. Reservations not accepted.*

$$ ★ ✕ **Such Is Life.** Chef-owner Moises Treves creates a cuisine worthy of Mexico City. Squeeze in and start with *nopal polanco* (broiled prickly-pear cactus), move on to black-bean soup, and then choose a signature salad or an entrée: fillets done in peppers or chipotle sauce; stunning garlic shrimp; chicken Maya or *poblano*-style, or pork shredded in an anise-hinted *achiote* sauce. ✉ *3602 N. 24th St., ☎ 602/955–7822; 7000 E. Shea Blvd., Scottsdale, ☎ 602/948–1753. Reservations essential. AE, D, DC, MC, V. No lunch Sat. Closed Sun.*

$ ✕ **Adrian's.** This modest, creek-rock building with white wrought-iron grilles and a tiny outdoor patio transports you in food and decor south of Sonora to the coastal towns of Sinaloa on the Sea of Cortés (Anglos call it the Gulf of California). Many dishes are similar to Sonoran rancho fare, and Adrian prepares them well, especially pork with *nopalitos* (sliced cactus pads); but local Hispanic families keep coming for such treats as *Vuelve a la Vida* (Return to Life)—a cocktail of shrimp, abalone, oyster, and crab—or garlic-broiled whole pike over which you squeeze tiny, sweet Mexican limes. ✉ *2334 E. McDowell Rd., ☎ 602/273–7957. Reservations not accepted. No credit cards.*

$ ✕ **Bahía San Carlos.** In the shadow of the Squaw Peak Parkway, just down the street from Adrian's, is that restaurant's best competitor in the *mariscos* (seafood) category. This popular, noisy little place is hung with huge posters of Mexico's palm-shaded beaches. Tostadas piled with sweet-tangy *salpicón* (lime-soaked, seasoned, shredded crab) make a splendid appetizer, and *Caldo Siete Mares* (Seven Seas Soup) is a wonderful sampler of fish, squid, shrimp, crab, and more. ✉ *19th St. and McDowell Rd., ☎ 602/340–0892. Reservations not accepted. No credit cards.*

$ ✕ **Eliana's.** Salvadoran food is an interesting variation on the staple themes of Latin American fare, and this family-run storefront has plenty of heart and hearty food. You know tacos and burritos, but now meet *papusas,* crisp crosses between tortillas and puffy pita pockets, stuffed with meat, cheese, and sauces. From tamales, it's a short but tasty leap to these veggie-filled varieties with soft, creamy masa wrappings. Sautéed ripe plantains with sour cream and dessert quesadillas are a treat. ✉ *1627 N. 24th St., ☎ 602/225–2925. Reservations not accepted. MC, V. BYOB. Closed Mon.*

$ ★ ✕ **Los Dos Molinos.** Hot New Mexico–style cooking graces colorful tile tables in this bustling, white-adobe cantina. Chimichangas and shrimp Veracruz are among the collection of spicy delights. Friendly servers will help you gauge the heat on particular choices. Caution: The fresh, homemade green- and red-chile salsas can rip your lips off. The handful of tables and booths are kept full in this popular spot, so anticipate a wait (and a dacquiri or two) out on the patio. ✉ *8646 S. Central Ave., Phoenix, ☎ 602/243–9113. D, MC, V. Closed Sun.*

$ ✕ **Macayo.** This family-run chain has been a Valley standby for half a century, and its six outlets provide well-prepared Sonoran dishes amid colorful folk-art decor. With tacos, tostadas, tamales (especially the sweet green corn), chiles rellenos, chimichangas, refried beans, and creamy flan or honey-filled *sopapillas* (puffy tortillas) for dessert, it's a great place for introducing children to Mexican food. ✉ *4001 N. Central Ave., ☎ 602/264–6141; 7829 W. Thomas Rd., ☎ 602/873–0313; 1909 W. Thunderbird Rd., ☎ 602/866–7034; 11107 N. Scottsdale Rd., Scottsdale, ☎ 602/596–1181; 1920 S. Dobson Rd., Mesa,*

☎ 602/820–0237; (Depot Cantina) 300 S. Ash Ave., ☎ 602/966–6677. AE, D, DC, MC, V.

$ ✕ **Matador.** This downtown tradition, across from the civic center and Hyatt Regency, has a tasteful Maya-modern setting. Dishes are reliable, authentic, and well spiced, and they range from the familiar (tacos, enchiladas, quesadillas) to the adventurous (*menudo,* or tripe soup; *burros de lengua,* or beef-tongue burritos). The steak or chicken picado is highly recommended. It's also a perennially popular breakfast spot for civic leaders and many others. ✉ *125 E. Adams St.,* ☎ *602/254–7563. AE, D, DC, MC, V.*

Middle Eastern

$$ ★ ✕ **Mediterranean House.** On a dozen white-draped tables in a corner-mall storefront, a Korean family serves an array of fine Mediterranean standards. An appetizer platter has hummus and *baba ghanoush* (eggplant dip) with pita triangles for dipping and falafel balls (herbed, deep-fried hummus). Don't miss lemon-garlic Egyptian chicken rolled in sesame flour, creamy herbed Moroccan chicken in yogurt sauce, ambrosial Olympic chicken in a secret marinade with black-olive sauce, or one of the half-dozen vegetarian main dishes (like fettuccine in creamed spinach). ✉ *1588 E. Bethany Home Rd.,* ☎ *602/248–8460. Closed Sun.*

$–$$ ✕ **Christo's.** The sign says RISTORANTE, and the northern Italian food here is nicely done, but Christo and Connie Panagiotakapoulos have in fact scoured the Mediterranean for their cuisine of pasta, lamb dishes, calamari, and other tasty regional specialties. Decor and ambience are contemporary, and service is adroit. ✉ *6327 N. 7th St.,* ☎ *602/264–1784. AE, D, DC, MC, V. Closed Sun.*

$ ✕ **Byblos.** This Lebanese standby in Tempe is not heavy on ambience, but care is taken with the food; the staff usually dines at one of the tables, inquiring regularly as to how you're doing. Hummus and falafel are reliable, but save room for main courses, easily sampled with a mixed grill, which includes three kinds of shish kebab. Try a dessert of *balouza,* a fragrant orange-blossom-scented pudding topped with pistachios. ✉ *3332 S. Mill Ave., Tempe,* ☎ *602/894–1945. Reservations not accepted. AE, DC, MC, V. Closed Mon.*

$ ✕ **Samyra's Lebanese Cuisine.** In this modest, out-of-the-way spot 2 mi south of downtown, Samyra Sopp has been cooking and serving friendly Lebanese lunches for 16 years. Scoop hummus *bitahini* (hummus-and-sesame paste) and baba ghanoush onto chunks of fresh-baked bread; then dig into tangy *yabrak* (lamb and rice rolled in grape leaves) or some *koosa* (lamb-stuffed squash) or *fasoulia* (a lamb–lima bean stew). Delicate strains of Arabic music lull you along to honeyed baklava for dessert. ✉ *713 E. Mohave St.,* ☎ *602/252–9644. No credit cards. No dinner. Closed weekends.*

Southwestern International

$$$–$$$$ ✕ **Vincent Guerithault on Camelback.** Vincent Guerithault is acknowledged to be among the West's master chefs extraordinaire—this is where people come to experience his art. One of the handful of southwestern cuisine's originators, he married his classical country-French training to Mexican traditions to create such specialties as duck tamales, crab cakes in avocado salsa, and grilled lobster with smoky chipotle-chili pasta. Racks of lamb with spicy jalapeño jelly and symphonic pâté are here, too, as are a heart-smart menu and an intelligent wine list. Desserts are simply luscious. ✉ *3930 E. Camelback Rd.,* ☎ *602/224–0225. Reservations essential. Jacket required. AE, DC, MC, V. No lunch weekends. No dinner Mon.*

$$$–$$$$ ★ ✕ **Windows on the Green.** Innovative haute southwestern cuisine rivals views of a lush fairway at the Phoenician resort, where chef Robert McGrath has created such delectable starters as smoked shrimp with red-chile-and-yogurt sauce and an ultrarich cracked-corn custard with lobster and wild mushrooms. A well-educated wait staff will gladly detail the preparation of the entrées, which range from a sugar- and chile-cured venison chop to fajitas of marinated and grilled portabello mushrooms. High ceilings and a creamy, off-white interior add to the elegance of the windowed dining area, which remains informal enough to display a rusty pitchfork on the wall as art. Save room for dessert: A whimsical chocolate taco is "stuffed" with smooth-as-silk white-chocolate mousse and fresh fruit, and soothing cinnamon-flavored *cajeta* ice cream is made on the premises. ✉ *6000 E. Camelback Rd.,* ☎ *602/941–9928. Reservations essential. Jacket required. AE, D, DC, MC, V. No dinner Mon.*

$$$ ★ ✕ **RoxSand.** RoxSand Suarez and Spyros Scocos have woven together Greek, Asian, Continental, and Caribbean influences (among others), creating a unique transcontinental cuisine that adds zest to its Biltmore Fashion Park mall location. Be on the lookout for sizzling sea-scallop salad, air-dried duck tamales, Chilean sea bass with eggplant and artichoke, and an ever-changing array of handmade desserts. It is a nice compliment to customers that solo snackers are as welcome as a hungry foursome. ✉ *2594 E. Camelback Rd.,* ☎ *602/381–0444. Reservations essential. AE, DC, MC, V.*

$$$ ★ ✕ **Tarbell's.** Owner and chef Mark Tarbell likes to call his establishment "a neighborhood restaurant for the nation," a place both comforting and out of the ordinary. Indeed, the wait staff is warm and welcoming, and the space has a spare and relaxed '40s elegance, enhanced by the dramatic curved bar that splits the room. A product of French, Italian, southwestern, and new American influences, the menu has the same friendly intelligence, with a balanced selection of pastas, pizzas, and items from the grill or wood oven. The menu descriptions may be whimsical—see "Mr. Fish of the Moment" or "addictive little biscuits"—but the food is taken seriously. Try meltingly tender house-smoked beef tenderloin or the grilled salmon with a molasses-lime glaze on a crispy potato cake. ✉ *3213 E. Camelback Rd., at 32nd St.,* ☎ *602/955–8100. AE, D, MC, V. No lunch.*

$$–$$$ ✕ **Eddie's Grill.** Under a purple neon sign in a modern office complex 4 mi north of downtown, chef-owner Eddie Matney's inventive new American cuisine with a southwestern flair makes this one of Phoenix's hottest half dozen. Try toasted seafood wanton served with raspberry jalapeño sauce or steak wrapped in country-mashed potatoes and served on a bed of julienned vegetables under cabernet demi-glaze. Mo' Rockin' Shrimp in *chermoula* sauce (lime juice, olive oil, four kinds of pepper, cilantro, and mustard) is to die for. Tasteful blond wood furniture, handmade Italian ceramics, and changing displays by local artists assure the ambience to be as striking and sophisticated as the menu. ✉ *4747 N. 7th St.,* ☎ *602/241–1188. Reservations essential. AE, D, DC, MC, V.*

$$–$$$ ✕ **Timothy's.** In this cozy cottage north of Camelback Road, chef-owner Tim Johnson offers a double treat—southwestern cuisine and live jazz. He does steak au poivre and veal chop with Yucatan potatoes; like the music, the food gets hottest when the voices blend, as in phyllo-dough-wrapped salmon tamales served with red-pepper salsa and green-chili hollandaise. All dinners are served with both soup and salad. It may not be quiet, but service is brisk; dinner and the nightly jazz are served up until midnight. ✉ *6335 N. 16th St.,* ☎ *602/277–7634. AE, D, DC, MC, V. No lunch weekends.*

$–$$ ✕ **Arizona Café & Grill.** Valley restaurateur Christopher Gross, of Christopher's and Christopher's Bistro fame—the Wolfgang Puck of

Phoenix, if you will—combines affordable southwestern dishes with a casual cowboy setting and expansive patio views. Brochettes of duck and yellow bell-pepper soup make for memorable starters, and sauces of red-pepper béarnaise and whiskey peppercorn-grain mustard accompany entrées of oven-roasted prime rib, grilled New York–cut steak, and barbecued ribs. Individual dinner pizzas are also available, topped with chorizo, roasted peppers, or mesquite-smoked chicken. Take advantage of the menu's suggestions for paired wines and microbrewed beers. ✉ *3113 E. Lincoln Dr.,* ☎ *602/957–0777. AE, D, DC, MC, V.*

$–$$ ✕ **Sam's Cafe.** A meal at this casual grill begins with warm, chewy breadsticks with mild red-chile cream cheese; it ends with complimentary white-chocolate tamales, replete with corn-husk wrappings. In between, the menu offers an eclectic variety of Southwest interpretations—from delicious Sedona spring rolls to lasagna and barbecued salmon. If it's a cool enough day for soup, the poblano-chicken chowder is excellent. ✉ *455 N. 3rd St. (in the Arizona Center),* ☎ *602/252–3545; 2566 E. Camelback Rd. (in the Biltmore Fashion Park),* ☎ *602/954–7100. AE, D, DC, MC, V.*

Spanish

$$$ ✕ **Marquesa.** Two soft-hued, intimate rooms at the Scottsdale Princess are accented with huge glass jars of jewel-like vegetables and fruits and graceful giant clay olive-oil urns. Here, traditional Catalan dishes follow authentic tapas appetizers. Paella with lobster, chicken, pork, shellfish, and *chistora* (Spanish sausage) is given a stunning presentation to match the flavors. Service is gracious, wines well chosen, desserts inspired. ✉ *7575 E. Princess Dr., Scottsdale,* ☎ *602/585–2723. Reservations essential. Jacket required. AE, D, DC, MC, V.*

$$ ✕ **Pepin.** At this colorful, festive spot overlooking the fountains, sculptures, and gardens of the Scottsdale Center for the Arts, fragrant garlic and saffron smells seduce a good number of passersby through the painted tile entrance, while locals stop in for mouthwatering tapas. Favorite entrées include the paellas (one is vegetarian), roast pork leg marinated in sour orange, and salmon in cilantro sauce. Nightly live entertainment ranges from classical guitar to the treat of an authentic flamenco floor show. ✉ *7363 Scottsdale Mall, Scottsdale,* ☎ *602/990–9026. AE, D, DC, MC, V.*

Thai

$$ ★ ✕ **Mint Thai.** A tiny, graceful place that has managed to remain remarkable, Mint Thai offers the broadest menu of the Valley's Thai restaurants—if you find a dish not prepared with delicacy and power, you'll be the first. Soups range from the subtly simple *tom ka gai* (hot-sour in coconut milk) to the spectacular *Thai suki* (a beef-pork-chicken-squid-shrimp extravaganza). Curries are gentle, with deep flavors; *rama* beef in peanut sauce is amazing, and you've never had sweet-and-sour like this before. Even their Thai iced tea stands out. ✉ *1111 N. Gilbert Rd., Gilbert,* ☎ *602/497–5366. AE, MC, V. No lunch Sun.*

$ ✕ **Char's.** This austerely simple restaurant gave birth to Phoenix's brood of Thai houses. Meals are carefully prepared and courteously served, from the snappy skewered-chicken *satay* appetizer to *tom yum gai* (hot-sour soup) and *yum yai* salad (chicken and shrimp with peanut dressing) to a noodle-rich *pad Thai* or a belly-warming curry. Tell your server if you'd like the pepper meter set low. ✉ *927 E. University Dr., Tempe,* ☎ *602/967–6013. AE, MC, V.*

$ ✕ **Thai Lahna.** Red booths and Thai knickknacks line the walls of this cozy eatery, where owner Tom Thanom presents exotic Thai dishes created from old family recipes. The menu's wontons and egg rolls are lackluster, but specialties of the house include *khung nahm-prik-pow* (sautéed shrimp in curry paste), *phaht phet pra-duk* (catfish fillet stir-fried with fresh chilies, onion, and mint), and a delicious stir-fried eggplant available with beef, chicken, or pork. All dishes can be ordered *jay* (vegetarian). *✉ 3738 E. Indian School Rd., ☎ 602/955–4658. AE, MC, V. Closed Sun.*

LODGING

Metropolitan Phoenix has a considerable array of lodging options, from world-class resorts and dude ranches to roadside motels, from luxury and executive hotels to no-frills business suites and family-style operations where you can do your own cooking.

Resorts are usually far from the heart of town—too far to be convenient if your interests are in Phoenix proper. The exceptions: the historic Arizona Biltmore, unthinkably far out when it was built and now handily close in; the gigantic Pointe Hilton on South Mountain, less than 3 mi from the airport; and its two sister Pointe resorts, each within 7 mi of downtown. Most of the other resorts are in Scottsdale, a self-contained, very tourist-friendly suburb; a few are scattered 20 to 30 mi out of town. And the dude ranches cluster around Wickenburg, 60 mi northwest.

Business and family hotels are closer to town—and to the average vacation budget. Until 20 years ago, families pulled into any of dozens of downtown courtyard motels with mission-style adobe facades. That is no longer a safe option, as the neighborhood has become seedy; aside from the airport, however, no new downtown hotel district has emerged, so lodging offerings are scattered throughout Phoenix and its suburbs.

Travelers flee snow and ice to bask in the Valley of the Sun. As a result, winter is the high season, peaking in January through March, and summer is giveaway time, when weekend packages at the fanciest resorts cost less than a winter night at a mid-range hotel.

The rise of suite hotels in recent years—with kitchenettes for in-room meal preparation—is rapidly making room service obsolete in all but luxury or resort-class hotels. In its place, such complimentary services as a made-to-order breakfast, poolside or lounge happy hour, and a morning newspaper are becoming standard. Where room service is not noted below, expect some combination of these.

CATEGORY	COST*
$$$$	over $200
$$$	$125–$200
$$	$75–$125
$	under $75

**All prices are for a standard double room, excluding 6.5% state tax, 1% city tax, and 15% service charge.*

Central Phoenix

$$$$ 🏨 **Hyatt Regency Phoenix.** This downtown landmark faces Civic Plaza like a giant kachina figure, its disk-shape rotating restaurant atop 24 floors of dark sandstone. Desert- and Indian-style decor dominate, blended together with Hyatt's trademark atrium design and sky-view elevators. Shops, meeting rooms, and an on-site branch of the visitors bureau attest to the focus on conventions, which crowd the hotel in spring. Rooms are comfortable, utilitarian, and modestly sized; there are balcony rooms on floors 3–7, poolside rooms on 3 (the atrium roof blocks east views on 8–10). The Theater Terrace Café's southwestern food and themed seasonal menus are a cut above standard hotel fare. *✉ 122 N. 2nd St., 85004, ☎ 602/252–1234, FAX 602/254–9472. 712* *rooms. 2 restaurants, bar, pool, health club, meeting rooms, concierge, parking. AE, D, DC, MC, V.*

$$$ **Embassy Suites.** Just 5 mi from downtown, this four-story open-courtyard hotel has lush palms and olive trees hiding bubbling fountains and a huge sunken pool. Free breakfast and an evening social hour are held in the spacious clubhouse at café tables, by a large sunken fireplace–conversation pit, and in front of a wide-screen TV off in a corner. Suites are compact but dramatic, with emerald carpets and drapes, Santa Fe geometric wallpaper and bedspreads. The tiny kitchenette has a microwave, sink, and minifridge. The Squaw Peak Cafe offers wonderful views. ✉ *2333 E. Thomas Rd., 85016,* ☎ *602/957–1910,* FAX *602/955–2861. 183 suites. Restaurant, kitchenettes, pool, airport shuttle, parking. AE, D, DC, MC, V.*

$$$ ★ **Hilton Suites.** A model of excellent design within tight limits, this practical and popular 11-story atrium is likely to become a classic. A more luxurious version of the frequent-traveler suites concept, it sits off Central Avenue, 2 mi north of downtown amid the Phoenix plaza cluster of office towers. The marble-floor, pillared lobby opens into the atrium, with fountains, palms, and the lantern-lighted sidewalk café. Modern fauvist art hangs on the walls, and Navajo-inspired motifs mark carpets and borders. Suites continue the bold design, with bleached wood furniture and rough-cut metal chandeliers. Each large bathroom opens to both living room and bedroom, and every couch is a sofa bed. Each room also has a microwave (the gift shop sells snacks and rents VCR movies). ✉ *10 E. Thomas Rd., 85012,* ☎ *602/222–1111,* FAX *602/265–4841. 226 suites. Restaurant, bar, pool, sauna, exercise room, parking. AE, D, DC, MC, V.*

$$$ **Holiday Inn Crowne Plaza.** This 19-story modern shell is cleverly crafted for the desert, with sand-colored walls, a 14th-century Spanish mosaic in the lobby, and scooped arches shading the window of each room. Soft rose-carpeted halls lead to compact rooms in desert shades. The young staff is gracious, and the scale and services are those of a major hotel, including the revitalized shops and restaurants. ✉ *111 N. Central Ave., 85004,* ☎ *602/257–1525,* FAX *602/254–7926. 533 rooms. Restaurant, bar, pool, health club, jogging, concierge, parking. AE, D, DC, MC, V.*

$$ ★ **Best Western Executive Park.** One of downtown's hidden jewels, this hotel has charm, a great location—and great prices. The small eight-story facility sits on Central Avenue at the new Deck Park (beneath which I–10 passes under the heart of the city). The Heard Museum, Phoenix Art Museum, and central library are within walking distance. Simple and elegant, the rooms are brightened by peach-and-sand-color walls and prints by southwestern masters. Moderate-size rooms have comfortable beds and large, well-lighted desks, compact brass-trim bathrooms with coffee makers, and (above the second floor) commanding city views. The eighth-floor suites are dramatic, with ample balconies and sitting rooms; off the drape-swathed bedroom is a vast dressing room with Roman tub. ✉ *1100 N. Central Ave., 85004,* ☎ *602/252–2100,* FAX *602/340–1989. 107 rooms. Restaurant, bar, pool, sauna, health club, meeting rooms, parking. AE, D, DC, MC, V.*

$$ **Lexington Hotel.** Only 3 mi from downtown, in a nest of midtown corporate-headquarters buildings known as the Central Corridor, this is Phoenix's best bet for sports lovers. The Lexington houses a sports bar (noisy and crowded), 11 racquetball courts (a national tournament site), an aerobics room, a 40-station machine workout center, a full indoor basketball court, and a large outdoor waterfall pool. The ambience is bright, modern, and informal. Rooms range in size from moderate (in the cabana wing, first-floor rooms have poolside patios) to very small (tower wing). In the locker rooms, no amenity is spared.

Arizona Biltmore, **2**
Best Western Executive Park, **13**
The Boulders, **7**
The Buttes, **19**
Camelback Courtyard by Marriott, **3**
Doubletree Suites, **17**
Embassy Suites, **6**
Hampton Inn Airport, **18**
Hilton Pavilion, **23**
Hilton Suites, **5**
Holiday Inn Crowne Plaza, **16**
Hyatt Regency Phoenix, **15**
Hyatt Regency Scottsdale at Gainey Ranch, **9**
Lexington Hotel, **1**
Marriott's Camelback Inn, **10**
Mesa Travelodge, **22**
Motel 6 Scottsdale, **12**
The Phoenician, **11**
The Pointe Hilton on South Mountain, **20**
Ritz-Carlton, **4**
San Carlos Hotel, **14**
Scottsdale Princess, **8**
Tempe Mission Palms Hotel, **21**

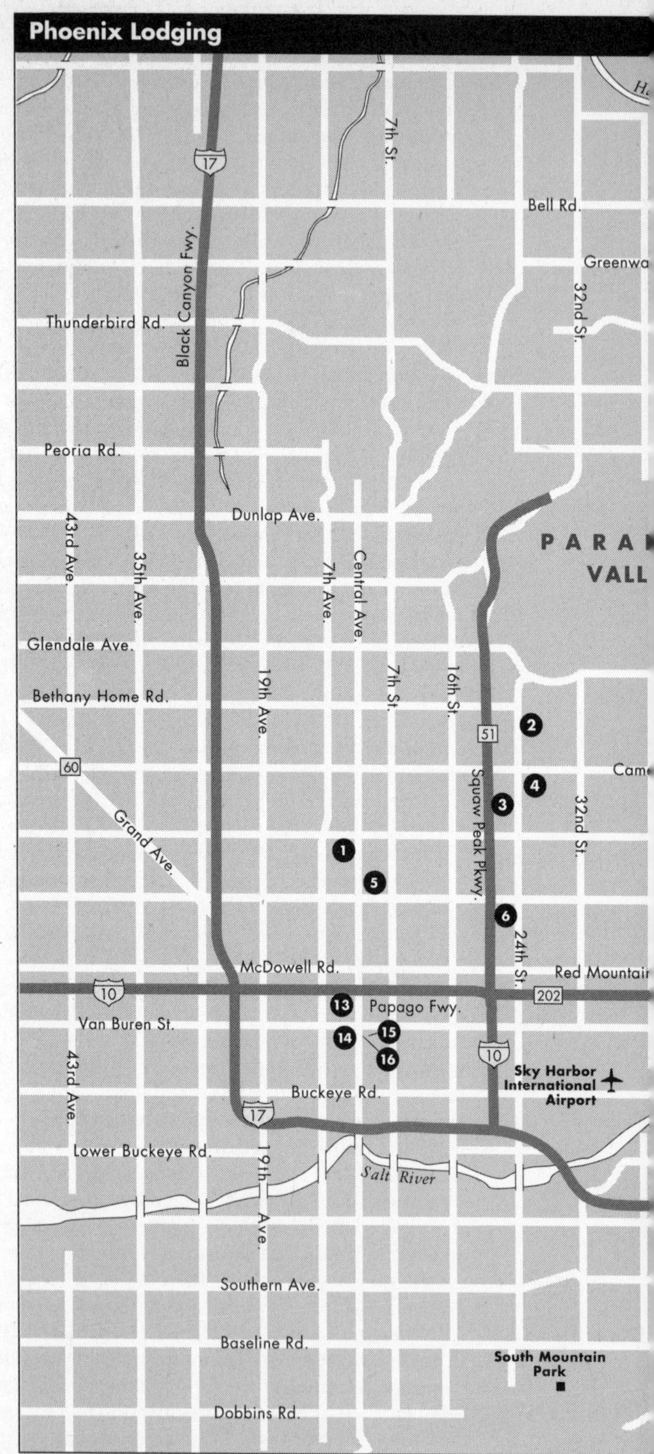

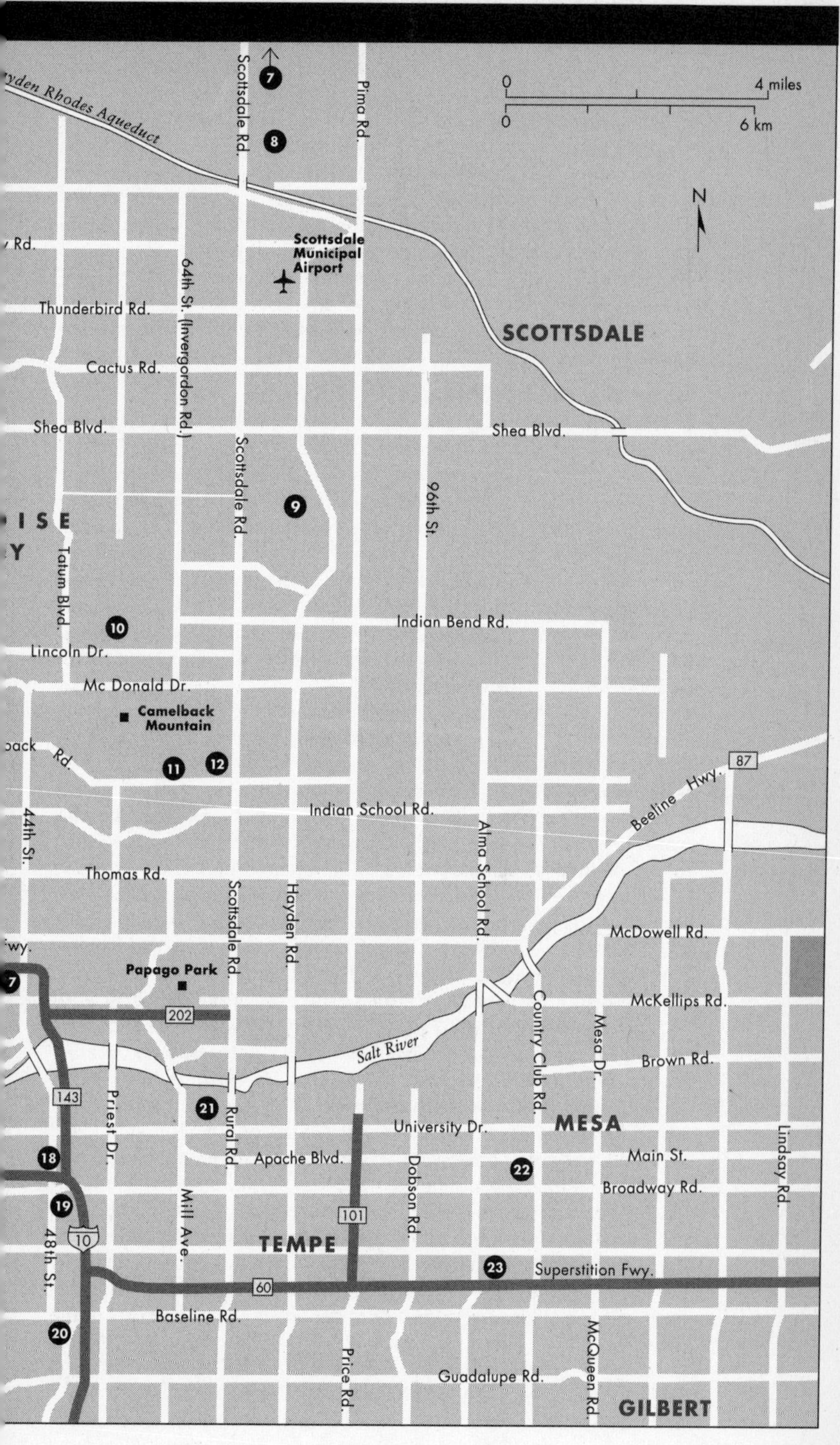

Hayden Rhodes Aqueduct
Scottsdale Rd.
Pima Rd.
0
4 miles
0
6 km
N
Scottsdale Municipal Airport
64th St. (Invergordon Rd.)
Thunderbird Rd.
SCOTTSDALE
Cactus Rd.
Shea Blvd.
Shea Blvd.
Scottsdale Rd.
96th St.
Tatum Blvd.
Indian Bend Rd.
Lincoln Dr.
Mc Donald Dr.
Camelback Mountain
Rd.
87
Beeline Hwy.
Indian School Rd.
44th St.
Alma School Rd.
Thomas Rd.
Scottsdale Rd.
Hayden Rd.
McDowell Rd.
Papago Park
202
McKellips Rd.
Country Club Rd.
Mesa Dr.
Salt River
Brown Rd.
143
Priest Dr.
Rural Rd.
University Dr.
MESA
Apache Blvd.
Dobson Rd.
Main St.
Broadway Rd.
Lindsay Rd.
Mill Ave.
101
48th St.
10
TEMPE
Superstition Fwy.
60
Baseline Rd.
McQueen Rd.
Price Rd.
Guadalupe Rd.
GILBERT
7
8
9
10
11
12
17
18
19
20
21
22
23

This is where visiting teams—and fans—like to stay. ✉ *100 W. Clarendon Ave., 85013,* ☎ *602/279–9811,* FAX *602/285–2932. 180 rooms. Bar, pool, beauty salon, sauna, massage, health club, racquetball, parking. AE, D, DC, MC, V.*

$$ **San Carlos Hotel.** Phoenix's second-oldest hotel, built on the site of the city's first school, has been reborn. Built in 1927, it was a popular downtown hub and landmark for decades; now, its seven stories are nestled in between the Bank Center and other skyscrapers. Fixtures—from the pedestal sinks and old-fashioned toilets to the Austrian crystal chandeliers in the lobby—echo '30s and '40s high style. Rooms are smallish in size, but 3-inch concrete walls ensure quiet. ✉ *202 N. Central Ave., 85004,* ☎ *602/253–4121 or 800/528–5446,* FAX *602/253–6668. 111 rooms. Restaurant, deli, pub, pool, exercise room, meeting rooms, parking. AE, D, DC, MC, V.*

Near Sky Harbor Airport

$$–$$$$ **The Buttes.** Two miles east of Sky Harbor, nestled in desert buttes at I–10 and AZ 60, this hotel joins dramatic architecture (the lobby's back wall is the volcanic rock itself) and classic Southwest design (pine and saguaro-rib furniture, works by major regional artists) with stunning Valley views. Rooms are moderate in size and comfortable, though bathrooms and closets are on the smallish side; decor includes desert colors and live cacti. "Radial" rooms are largest, with the widest views; inside rooms face the huge free-form pools, with waterfall, hot tubs, and poolside cantina. The elegant Top of the Rock restaurant and the quiet luxury of the dawn-to-midnight Market Café are definite pluses. ✉ *2000 Westcourt Way, Tempe 85282,* ☎ *602/225–9000 or 800/843–1986,* FAX *602/438–8622. 353 rooms. 2 restaurants, 3 bars, sauna, pool, 4 tennis courts, health club, hiking, jogging, bicycles, concierge floor, business services, meeting rooms, parking. AE, D, DC, MC, V.*

$$–$$$$ **Doubletree Suites.** In the Gateway Center, just 1½ mi north of the airport, this striking hotel is the best of a dozen choices for the traveler who wants to get off the plane and into a comfortable room. Past the lobby full of modernist regional art lies a honeycomb of six-story towers, linked by mazes of walkways and richly landscaped gardens. The oversize rooms are done in teal, peach, and gray, with comfy furniture. The kitchenettes have microwaves. Topper's, a pleasantly intimate restaurant, offers a relaxed wine bar. Business and sports facilities are extensive; the casual elegance and easy access attract visiting celebrities. ✉ *320 N. 44th St., Phoenix 85008,* ☎ *602/225–0500 or 800/800–3098,* FAX *602/225–0957. 242 suites. Restaurant, bar, pool, sauna, exercise room, meeting rooms, airport shuttle, parking. AE, D, DC, MC, V.*

$$–$$$$ **The Pointe Hilton on South Mountain.** The Southwest's largest resort, 15 minutes from downtown, sits next to South Mountain Park, a 16,000-acre desert preserve that offers hiking, mountain biking, and horseback riding. Rooms and public areas are unremarkable; the facilities are the draw: On site are a premier four-story sports center and three separate restaurants. Golf, tennis, horseback riding, and several pools are among the other amenities. Landscaped walkways and roads link everything on the 750-acre property; carts and drivers are on 24-hour call. The Hilton also runs two identically themed resorts in the area: the Pointe Hilton at Squaw Peak (☎ 602/997–2626, North Phoenix) and the Pointe Hilton Tapatio Cliffs (☎ 602/866–7500). ✉ *7777 S. Pointe Pkwy., Phoenix 85044,* ☎ *602/438–9000,* FAX *602/431–6535. 636 suites. 3 restaurants, 3 lobby lounges, 6 pools, lake, saunas, 10 tennis courts, 18-hole golf course, health club, hiking, horseback riding, jogging, racquetball, volleyball, meeting rooms, parking. AE, D, DC, MC, V.*

$$ 🏨 **Hampton Inn Airport.** This four-story, interior-corridor hotel 9 mi from downtown is both affordable and accommodating. Comfortable rooms, decorated in desert pastels and southwestern art, all have VCRs. Although there's no restaurant on the premises, a free Continental breakfast is available each morning, and a friendly, helpful staff will suggest favorite menu items from the coffee shop directly next door. Take advantage of the 24-hour hotel shuttle. ✉ *4234 S. 48th St., Phoenix 85040,* ☎ *602/438–8688,* FAX *602/431–8339. 134 rooms. Refrigerators (some rooms), pool, meeting rooms, airport shuttle, parking. AE, D, DC, MC, V.*

Scottsdale and Biltmore

$$$$ 🏨 **Arizona Biltmore.** Designed by Frank Lloyd Wright's colleague Albert Chase McArthur, the so-called Jewel of the Desert has been a masterpiece among world-class resorts since it opened in 1929. A vast, dramatic lobby has stained-glass skylights, wrought-iron pilasters, and cozy sitting alcoves that invite guests to linger, especially to enjoy the live piano in the evenings. Impeccably manicured grounds contain open walkways, fountains, and scores of raised flower beds in colorful bloom. The Paradise Pool and its twin towers (which enclose a 92-foot water slide) is truly a sight to behold. Although less impressive than the rest of the extravagant property, rooms are comfortable, featuring natural muted colors, mission-style furnishings, and large tan and off-white marble baths. ✉ *24th St. and Missouri Ave., Phoenix 85016,* ☎ *602/955–6600 or 800/950–0086,* FAX *602/381–7600. 500 rooms, 50 villas. 2 restaurants, lounge, 5 pools, 8 tennis courts, 2 18-hole golf courses, health club, jogging, concierge, parking. AE, D, DC, MC, V.*

$$$$ ★ 🏨 **The Boulders.** The Valley's most serene and secluded luxury resort hides among the hill-size granite boulders in the foothills town of Carefree, 12 mi north of Scottsdale. Golf courses stretch like emerald carpets between the giant 12-million-year-old granite stones, and adobe casitas cluster along open paths that wind through the raw beauty of the natural desert. (Staffers will pick you up and drive you around the sprawling resort in golf carts.) Casitas are compact but comfortable, with exposed log-beam ceilings, ceiling fans, and curving, pueblo-style half-walls and shelves; each has a patio with a view, a miniature kiva fireplace, and a spacious bath and dressing area with a deep tub and adobe vanity. Designed by architect Robert Bacon, the main lodge—with its glass skylights and large fireplaces—is a stunning yet subtle compliment to the surroundings. Creative American and Sonoran cuisine is served from the exhibition kitchen of the Palo Verde restaurant, the Boulders Club features lighter American fare, and the Cantina del Pedregal concocts southwestern creations. The nearby El Pedregal center, a dramatic twin to the resort, has shopping, a satellite extension of the Heard Museum, and more eating options (try delicious pastries from the Bakery Café). ✉ *34631 N. Tom Darlington Dr., Carefree 85377,* ☎ *602/488–9009 or 800/553–1717,* FAX *602/488–4118. 160 casitas, 34 patio homes. 4 restaurants, 2 pools, spa, 6 tennis courts, 2 18-hole golf courses, exercise room, hiking, horseback riding, jogging, business services, meeting rooms, parking. AE, D, DC, MC, V.*

$$$$ 🏨 **Marriott's Camelback Inn.** Founded in the mid-'30s, this historic resort is a swank oasis of comfort and relaxation in the gorgeous valley between Camelback and Mummy Mountains. The 125-acre property, much of which maintains a natural desert feel, contains two landscaped pool areas and two 18-hole golf courses. Don't miss the acclaimed full-service spa, which offers extensive body and beauty treatments for men and women, fitness and wellness classes, a state-of-the-art gym, and stunning views from its pool. Rooms are notably spacious and come in a wide variety of configurations. Ask for accommodations that underwent extensive remodeling in 1995 and '96, where wrought-iron furniture, terra-cotta lamps, and individual balconies or patios are standard. The luxurious bathrooms are accented with custom tile and glass blocks. The Chaparral serves classic French cuisine, with a particular emphasis on dramatic tableside preparations; sample the rich lobster bisque, tender steak Diane, and extensive wine selection. Sprouts, at the spa, offer tasty, healthy items, and the Kokopelli Café has gourmet coffees. ✉ *5402 E. Lincoln Dr., Scottsdale 85253,* ☏ *602/948–1700 or 800/242–2635,* FAX *602/951–8469. 424 rooms, 24 suites. 3 restaurants, 2 lounges, coffee shop, 2 pools, spa, Turkish bath, 2 18-hole golf courses, 8 tennis courts, hiking, horseback riding, business services, meeting rooms, parking. AE, D, DC, MC, V.*

$$$$ ★ **The Phoenician.** Guests enter a bright, airy lobby to find towering fountains, gleaming marble, and smiling faces of a service staff who will do handsprings to satisfy. You may question the suitability of some of the French-provincial decor and authentic Dutch-master paintings for a desert locale, but there's no question that a great deal of attention was paid to details. A 2-acre cactus garden showcases hundreds of varieties of cacti and succulents, the Centre for Well Being spa boasts an inspiring meditation atrium, and the resort's centerpiece oval pool is lined with mother-of-pearl tiles. Rooms at the Phoenician, the highest-priced resort in town, are a spacious 600 square feet, with cream walls, tasteful rattan furnishings in muted tones, Italian marble bathrooms, and private patios. Ask for a room facing south, with views of the resort's pools and the city. Windows on the Green (☞ Dining) offers some of the best southwestern cuisine in the city. ✉ *6000 E. Camelback Rd., Scottsdale 85251,* ☏ *602/941–8200 or 800/888–8234. 440 rooms, 107 casitas, 33 suites. 4 restaurants, 7 pools, barbershop, beauty salon, sauna, steam room, golf course, 11 tennis courts, archery, badminton, basketball, croquet, health club, jogging, volleyball, pro shop, billiards, children's programs, business services. AE, D, DC, MC, V.*

$$$$ **Scottsdale Princess.** On the 450 beautifully landscaped acres of this resort, Mexican-colonial architecture is set against the splendor of the McDowell Mountains. Rooms in the red-tile-roof main building and the casitas are furnished in muted desert hues, with sand-color rugs and bedspreads contributing to the overall airy effect. All rooms have private terraces and large bathrooms that boast vanity areas, double sinks, and silk-padded hangers in walk-in closets. The Marquesa Restaurant (☞ Dining, *above*) has been consistently rated one of the best in the state. ✉ *7575 E. Princess Dr., Scottsdale 85255,* ☏ *602/585–4848 or 800/344–4758,* FAX *602/585–0091. 400 rooms in main building, 125 casitas, 75 villas. 5 restaurants, bar, 3 pools, spa, steam room, 9 tennis courts, 2 18-hole golf courses, health club, racquetball, squash, pro shops, business services. AE, D, DC, MC, V.*

$$$$ **Hyatt Regency Scottsdale at Gainey Ranch.** A fun place for families, this resort has a showy theme-park ambience. A huge neoclassical water park includes fountains and waterfalls, 10 pools, a small sand beach, water volleyball, a water slide, and lagoons plied by gondolas. Three golf courses offer a choice of terrains—dunes, arroyo, or lakes—to suit a fancy for sand or water traps. Public areas are grand and lushly appointed; a large attractive piazza, lined with seating and gurgling steams and fountains, spills out from the lobby. Rooms are comfortable, although of average size and rather bland. ✉ *7500 E. Doubletree Ranch Rd., Scottsdale 85258,* ☏ *602/991–3388 or 800/233–1234,* FAX *602/483–5550. 493 rooms, 7 casitas. 4 restaurants, 2 lounges, 10 pools, 8 tennis courts, 3 9-hole golf courses, croquet, health club, concierge floor, parking. AE, D, DC, MC, V.*

$$$ **Ritz-Carlton.** Like an 11-story false front, this sand-color neo-Federal mid-rise facing Biltmore Fashion Square mall hides a graceful, well-appointed luxury hotel. Built in 1988, it has large public rooms decorated with 18th- and 19th-century European paintings and a handsomely displayed worldwide china collection. Rooms are done in shades of mint and celery, with an armoire holding a TV and refrigerator (stocked), a small closet with a safe, and a marble bath well supplied with amenities. Because the hotel is business-oriented, rates go down on the weekend. The compact, elegant health club and the daily high tea are highlights. ✉ *2401 E. Camelback Rd., Phoenix 85016,* ☎ *602/468–0700 or 800/241–3333,* FAX *602/468–0793. 267 rooms, 14 suites. 2 restaurants, 2 bars, pool, 2 saunas, tennis court, bicycles, exercise room, concierge floor, business services, parking. AE, D, DC, MC, V.*

$$–$$$ **Camelback Courtyard by Marriott.** This four-story hostelry delivers compact elegance in its public areas and no-frills comfort in its rooms and suites. A medium-size lap pool and whirlpool fill the courtyard, landscaped with granite boulders and palms. Standard doubles are handsomely carpeted and draped, while suites are done in blue with rose accents. Considerable savings are achieved by dropping such "hotel" features as 24-hour room service (it's available from 5 to 10 PM) and relying on the attached mall for gift and grooming shops, travel services, and the like. ✉ *2101 E. Camelback Rd., Phoenix 85016,* ☎ *602/955–5200,* FAX *602/955–1101. 144 rooms, 11 suites. Restaurant, bar, pool, spa, health club, meeting rooms, parking. AE, D, DC, MC, V.*

$ **Motel 6 Scottsdale.** The best bargain in Scottsdale lodging is easy to miss, but it's worth hunting for the sign, set back on the north side of Camelback Road. Just steps away from the Scottsdale Fashion Square, this motel is also close to the specialty shops of 5th Avenue and Scottsdale's Civic Plaza. Amenities aren't a priority here, but the price is remarkable considering the stylish and much more expensive resorts found close by. Rooms are small and spare with blue carpets and print bedspreads, but the well-landscaped pool offers a pleasant outdoor respite under the palms. ✉ *6848 E. Camelback Rd., Scottsdale 85251,* ☎ *602/946–2280,* FAX *602/949–7583. 122 rooms. Pool, hot tub, parking. AE, D, DC, MC, V.*

East Valley

$$–$$$ **Hilton Pavilion.** The ambience of this eight-floor property is defined by its atrium's etched glass and brass, tropical greenery, and art deco–style furniture. Rooms are medium-size, with plum and teal carpeting, average-size baths, small closets, and a large lighted table; corner suites and the top two floors have the best views. All rooms have refrigerators. The hotel is in the heart of the East Valley, just off AZ 60, and the area's largest shopping mall, Fiesta Mall, is across the street; downtown Phoenix is 18 mi away. ✉ *1011 W. Holmes Ave., Mesa 85210,* ☎ *602/833–5555 or 800/544-5866,* FAX *602/649–1886. 263 rooms, 62 suites. Restaurant, 2 bars, pool, business services, parking. AE, D, DC, MC, V.*

$$–$$$ **Tempe Mission Palms Hotel.** Set snugly between the Arizona State University campus and Old Town Tempe, this informal courtyard hotel is handy to the East Valley and downtown Phoenix. The tone is set by the spacious lobby and the young, polo-shirted staff. Many visitors come for ASU sports and the pro-football Cardinals (the stadium is virtually next door). Rooms are bright, simple southwestern, and comfortable. The hotel has a pleasant, quiet sports bar (except when a game is on) and a creditable restaurant (the Arches); guests also have Old Town Tempe's wide array of restaurants, shops, and clubs at their feet. ✉ *60 E. 5th St., Tempe 85281,* ☎ *602/894–1400 or 800/547–8705,* FAX *602/968–7677. 303 rooms. Restaurant, bar, pool, sauna, 3 tennis* *courts, exercise room, meeting rooms, business services, parking, airport shuttle. AE, D, DC, MC, V.*

$ **Mesa Travelodge.** This small, plain motel three blocks west of Mesa's downtown center has burgundy carpet, warm muted-tone wallpaper, and bedspreads and art prints in southwestern motifs. The rooms overlook a small pool. The motel's busy corner spot can mean continual street noise, but low prices help compensate. ✉ *22 S. Country Club Dr., Mesa 85210,* ☎ *602/964–5694,* FAX *602/964–5697. 39 rooms. Pool, parking. AE, D, DC, MC, V.*

NIGHTLIFE AND THE ARTS

The Arts

Phoenix performing-arts groups have grown rapidly in number and sophistication, especially over the past two decades. The $19 million **Herberger Theater Center** (✉ 222 E. Monroe St., ☎ 602/252–8497) was specifically designed to meet the complex needs of professional theater and dance companies. The permanent home to the Arizona Theatre Company, Actors Theatre, and Ballet Arizona, it also presents a variety of visiting dance troupes, orchestras, and plays.

Facing the Herberger Theater, **Symphony Hall** (✉ 225 E. Adams St., ☎ 602/262–6225) is home to both the Phoenix Symphony and the Arizona Opera, as well as a venue for touring Broadway shows and top-name performers. After completing an $11 million restoration in 1996, the **Orpheum Theatre** (✉ 203 W. Adams St., ☎ 602/252–9678) showcases various performing arts, including children's theater, and film festivals. Arizona State University splits an impressive performance schedule between the **Gammage Auditorium** (✉ Mill Ave. at Apache Blvd., ☎ 602/965–3434), **Sundome Center** (✉ 19403 R. H. Johnson Blvd., Sun City West, ☎ 602/975–1900) and **Kerr Cultural Center** (✉ 6110 N. Scottsdale Rd., Scottsdale, ☎ 602/965–5377).

The most comprehensive ticket agencies are **Dillard's** (20 locations, as well as outlets in all Dillard's department stores and a Phoenix Civic Plaza location (☎ 602/678–2222) and the **Arizona State University Ticket Office** (Gammage Center, Tempe, ☎ 602/965–3434).

Theater and Shows

Actors Theatre of Phoenix (✉ Box 1924, Phoenix 85001-1924, ☎ 602/253–6701) is the resident theater troupe at the Herberger. The theater presents a full season of drama, comedy, and musical productions.

Arizona Theatre Company (✉ 808 N. 1st St., ☎ 602/256–6995) is the only resident company in the country with a two-city (Tucson and Phoenix) operation. Productions range from classical dramas to musicals and new works by emerging playwrights. The Phoenix season runs October–June at the Herberger.

Black Theater Troupe (✉ 333 E. Portland St., ☎ 602/258–8128) performs at its own house, the Helen K. Mason Center, a half block from the city's Performing Arts Building on Deck Park. It presents original and contemporary dramas and musical revues, as well as adventurous adaptations, such as its recent version of *Mama, I Want to Sing.*

Great Arizona Puppet Theatre (✉ 3302 N. 7th St., ☎ 602/277–1275) mounts a yearlong cycle of inventive puppet productions, mostly original, in a converted church; it also offers puppetry classes.

DINNER THEATERS

Copper State Dinner Theatre (✉ 6727 N. 47th Ave., Glendale, ☎ 602/937–1671), the Valley's oldest troupe, stages light comedy at Max's, a West Valley sports bar, Friday and Saturday nights.

Murder Ink Productions (✉ 1801 S. Jentilly Lane, Suite C-12 Tempe, ☎ 602/967–6800) presents audience-interactive whodunits at Slim & Curly's Steakhouse (Mesa), Avanti (Scottsdale), Beef Eater's (Phoenix), and Le Rhone's Tropicana Cafe (Phoenix).

WILD WEST SHOWS

Pinnacle Peak Patio (✉ 10426 E. Jomax Rd., Scottsdale, ☎ 602/967–8082) has cookouts, mesquite-grilled steaks, old-time photo studios, entertainment, and good ole cowboy fun like steer roping and quick draw contests; wear a tie you don't mind leaving behind.

At **Rawhide Western Town and Steakhouse** (✉ 23023 N. Scottsdale Rd., Scottsdale, ☎ 602/502–1880), the false fronts on the dusty Main Street contain a train depot, saloons, gift shops, and craftspeople. City slickers can take a ride on a stagecoach or burro. Hayrides travel a short distance into the desert for weekend "Sundown Cookouts" under the stars; dinner in the steak house is served nightly.

Rockin' R Ranch (✉ 6136 E. Baseline Rd., Mesa, ☎ 602/832–1539) includes a petting zoo, a reenactment of a wild shoot-out, and—the main attraction—a nightly cookout with a western stage show. Pan for gold or take a wagon ride until the "vittles" are served, followed by music and entertainment. Similar to its competitor, Rawhide, Rockin' R is a better deal because the price of entry is all-inclusive.

Classical Music

Arizona Opera (✉ 4600 N. 12th St., Phoenix, ☎ 602/266–7464), one of the nation's most-respected regional companies, stages a four-opera season, primarily classical, in Tucson and Phoenix.

Phoenix Symphony Orchestra (✉ 3707 N. 7th St., ☎ 602/264–6363), the resident company at Symphony Hall, has reached the first rank of American regional symphonies. Its rich season includes orchestral works from classical and contemporary literature, a chamber series, composer festivals, and outdoor pops concerts.

Dance

A. Ludwig Co. (☎ 602/965–3914), the Valley's foremost modern dance troupe, includes choreography by founder-director Ann Ludwig, an ASU faculty member, in its repertoire of contemporary works.

Ballet Arizona (✉ 3645 E. Indian School Rd., ☎ 602/381–0184), the state's professional ballet company, presents full seasons of classical and contemporary works (including commissioned pieces for the company) in Tucson and in Phoenix, where it performs at the Herberger Theater Center, Symphony Hall, and Gammage Auditorium.

Film

If you're looking for something besides the latest blockbuster, the **Camelview 5** (✉ Goldwater Blvd. and Camelback Rd., Scottsdale, ☎ 602/423–9900) and **Valley Arts Cinema** (✉ 509 S. Mill Ave., Tempe, ☎ 602/829–6668) show major foreign releases and domestic art films.

Cine Capri (✉ 2323 E. Camelback Rd., ☎ 602/956–4200), a classic wide-screen theater from the '60s, occasionally offers such giant-screen revivals as *Dr. Zhivago* and *Spartacus*.

Galleries

The gallery scene in Phoenix and Scottsdale is so extensive that your best bet is to consult the "art exhibits" listings in the weekly *New Times* or the Friday "Weekend" section of the *Arizona Republic Gazette*. Southwestern art—from traditional to avant-garde Native American, from the Cowboy Artists of America to performance art—is varied and abundant. Photography also enjoys a strong tradition in Arizona.

Nightlife

Downtown Phoenix used to close up at sunset—until the advent of the Arizona Center. The heart of town at last has nightclubs, restaurants, and upscale bars that compete with livelier resorts and clubs in Scottsdale, along Camelback Road in north-central Phoenix, and elsewhere around the Valley.

Among music and dancing styles, country-western has the longest tradition here; jazz, surprisingly, runs a close second. Rock clubs and hotel lounges are also numerous and varied. The Valley attracts a steady stream of pop and rock acts; for concert tickets, try **Dillard's** (more than 20 Valley locations, ☎ 602/678–2222).

The best listings and reviews are in the *New Times* free weekly newspaper, distributed Wednesday, and the Friday "Weekend" section of the *Arizona Republic Gazette*.

Country and Western

Handlebar-J (✉ 7116 E. Becker La., Scottsdale, ☎ 602/948–0110) has a lively, 10-gallon-hat–wearing crowd.

At **Mr. Lucky's** (✉ 3660 W. Grand Ave., ☎ 602/246–0686), the granddaddy of Phoenix western clubs, you can dance the two-step all night (or learn it, if you haven't before).

The Red River Opry (✉ 730 N. Mill Ave., Tempe, ☎ 602/829–0607) performs foot-stompin' matinee and evening country and bluegrass shows. Reserve your seat in advance.

The Rockin' Horse (✉ 7000 E. Indian School Rd., Scottsdale, ☎ 602/949–0992) features a country DJ Mondays and live country bands Tuesday–Sunday.

Toolies Country Saloon and Dance Hall (✉ 4231 W. Thomas Rd., ☎ 602/272–3100) books well-known national acts.

Jazz

For a current schedule of jazz happenings, call the **AZ Jazz Hotline** (☎ 602/254–4545).

Azz Jazz Cafe (✉ 1906 E. Camelback Rd., ☎ 602/263–8482) is an intimate spot for combos.

Timothy's (✉ 6335 N. 16th St., ☎ 602/277–7634) joins top jazz performances nightly with fine French-influenced southwestern cuisine.

J. Chew & Co. (✉ 7320 Scottsdale Mall, Scottsdale, ☎ 602/946–2733) is a cozy, popular spot with indoor and outdoor seating. Nadine Jansen sings, plays piano, and lifts her trumpet here Wednesday–Saturday from 8:30 to 12:30, drawing scores of devotees and many visiting celebrities.

Rock and Blues

Blue Note (✉ 8708 E. McDowell, Scottsdale, ☎ 602/946–6227), unlike its famous namesake in New York City, focuses on blues instead of bebop.

Char's Has the Blues (✉ 4631 N. 7th Ave., ☎ 602/230–0205) is the top Valley blues club.

Mason Jar (✉ 2303 E. Indian School Rd., ☎ 602/956–6271) has a nightly schedule of rock bands.

The Rhythm Room (✉ 1019 E. Indian School Road, ☎ 602/265–4842) hosts a variety of local and touring blues artists.

Bars and Lounges

America's Original Sports Bar (✉ 455 N. 3rd St., Arizona Center, ☎ 602/252–2112) is big and boisterous, with 57 TVs (seven giant screens), indoor basketball, and an outdoor volleyball court.

AZ88 (✉ 7353 Scottsdale Mall, Scottsdale, ☎ 602/994–5576) is the closest thing to a sophisticated big-city bar you'll find in the Valley of the Sun.

Chez Nous (✉ 675 W. Indian School Rd., ☎ 602/266–7372), a dark martini lounge, attracts older patrons, as well as retro-chic twentysomething hipsters.

The Plaza Bar (✉ 122 N. 2nd St., ☎ 602/252–1234), on the mezzanine of the Hyatt Regency Phoenix, provides a sparkling downtown view. Tables just outside the bar proper offer a quieter getaway.

Macayo's Depot Cantina (✉ 300 S. Ash Ave., Tempe, ☎ 602/966–6677), in a former train station, is a bustling "meet market" popular with students from the nearby ASU campus.

Top of the Rock Bar (✉ 2000 W. Westcourt Way, Tempe, ☎ 602/431–2370), the lounge in Top of the Rock restaurant at the Buttes, attracts a lively upscale crowd to drink in cocktails and the city's most spectacular view.

Cabaret Entertainment

Paris After Dark (✉ 8525 N. Central Ave., ☎ 602/861–2437) features classy cabaret shows by glamorous and bewitching (and convincing!) she-males Tuesday through Sunday nights.

Comedy

The Improv (✉ 930 E. University Dr., Tempe, ☎ 602/921–9877), part of a national chain, showcases better-known headliners.

Star Theater (✉ 7146 E. 6th Ave., Scottsdale, ☎ 602/423–0120) features the "family sensitive" Oxymoron'z Improvisational Troupe on Friday and Saturday nights.

Clubs

Jetz (✉ 7077 E. Camelback Rd., ☎ 602/970–6001) has three glitzy dance floors, an extensive bar, and a good-looking crowd. The annex, Stixx, is filled with billiard tables.

Martini Ranch (✉ 7295 E. Stetson Dr., Scottsdale, ☎ 602/970–0500) attracts a high number of singles and hosts such bands as Planet Funk and the Boogie Knights on the outdoor stage.

Studebaker's (✉ 10345 N. Scottsdale Rd., Scottsdale, ☎ 602/443–0303) joins bar, buffet, and dancing with live DJs for a noisy place to meet friends Wednesday through Saturday nights.

Microbreweries

Bandersnatch Brew Pub (✉ 125 E. 5th St., Tempe, ☎ 602/966–4438) is a popular, unhurried student hangout that features a large collection of brewed-daily *cervezas*.

Coyote Springs (✉ Camelback Rd. at N. 20th St., ☎ 602/468–0403; 122 E. Washington, ☎ 602/256–6645), the oldest brewpub in Phoenix, has delicious handcrafted ales and lagers, and a thriving patio scene at the Camelback location. Try a raspberry brew.

Hops! (✉ 2584 E. Camelback Rd., Biltmore Fashion Park, ☎ 602/468–0500; 7000 E. Camelback Rd., Scottsdale Fashion Square, ☎ 602/945–4677; 8668 E. Shea Blvd., Scottsdale, ☎ 602/998–7777) serves up bistro cuisine and fills frothy-headed mugs with amber and wheat drafts from the display brewery.

OUTDOOR ACTIVITIES AND SPORTS

Participant Sports

When participating in outdoor activities in Phoenix, be aware that the desert heat imposes its particular restraints—even in winter, hikers and cyclists should wear lightweight opaque clothing, a hat or visor, and high UV-rated sunglasses and should carry a water supply of one quart per person for each hour of activity. The intensity of the sun makes strong sunscreen (SPF 15 or higher) a must, and don't forget to apply it to hands and feet. From May 1 to October 1, don't jog or hike from one hour after sunrise until a half hour before sunset. During those times, the air is so hot and dry that your body will lose moisture—and burn calories—at a dangerous, potentially lethal rate. Don't head out to desert areas at night, however, to jog or hike in the summer; that's when rattlesnakes and scorpions are out hunting.

Bicycling

Although the terrain is relatively level, the desert climate makes special demands on cyclists; note the advice on hours and clothing, *above*. Be sure to have a helmet and a mirror when riding in the streets: There are few adequate bike lanes in the Valley.

Scottsdale's Indian Bend Wash (along Hayden Rd., from Shea Blvd. south to Indian School Rd.) has bikeable paths winding among its golf courses and ponds. **Pinnacle Peak,** about 25 mi northeast of downtown Phoenix, is a popular place to take bikes for the ride north to Carefree and Cave Creek, or east and south over the mountain pass and down to the Verde River, toward Fountain Hills. Mountain bikers will want to check out the **Trail 100,** which runs throughout the Phoenix Mountain preserve (enter at Dreamy Draw park, just east of the intersection of Northern Avenue and 16th Street). **Cave Creek** and **Carefree,** in the foothills about 30 mi northeast of Phoenix, offer pleasant riding with a wide range of stopover options. **South Mountain Park** (☞ Hiking, *below*) is the prime site for mountain bikers, with its 40-plus mi of trails—some of them with challenging ascents and all of them quiet and scenic.

For rentals, contact **Wheels N' Gear** (✉ 7607 E. McDowell Rd., Scottsdale, ☏ 602/945–2881). For detailed maps of bike paths, contact **Phoenix Parks and Recreation** (☏ 602/262–6861.)

To get in touch with fellow bike enthusiasts and find out about regular and special-event rides, contact the **Arizona Bicycle Club** (Gene or Sylvia Berlatsky, ☏ 602/264–5478), the state's largest group. Sunday-morning rides are popular, ending up at a local breakfast spot.

Four-Wheeling

Taking a Jeep through the back country has become a popular way to experience the desert terrain's saguaro-covered mountains and curious rock formations. A number of companies offer four-wheeling packages for $50–$75 for short excursions.

Arizona Awareness (✉ 835 E. Brown St., ☏ 602/947–7852) ventures down to the Verde River on its own exclusive trail.
Arrowhead Jeep Tours (☏ 602/942–3361) has cowboy and gold-prospector guides who take passengers out for open-air Jeep drives, with stops to pan for gold.
Carefree Jeep Adventures (☏ 602/488–0023 or 800/294–5337) travels into the Tonto National Forest on old stage and mining roads, where you can see petroglyphs and rock carvings, taste the fruit of cholla cactus, and hold target practice with tin cans and .22 handguns; riders also have a chance to try their hand at a six-gun target shoot along the way.
Scottsdale Jeep Rentals (☏ 602/951–2191) rents Jeeps and provides free trail maps to those who want to drive themselves.

Golf

Arizona boasts more golf courses per capita than any other state west of the Mississippi River, an embarrassment of riches that, coupled with its surfeit of sunny days, makes the Grand Canyon State a golfer's paradise. Playing fees tend to be low and waiting times short, even though golf draws visitors from all over the world. In the Valley of the Sun, more than 100 courses, from par-3 to PGA championship links, are available (some lighted at night), and the PGA's Southwest section has its headquarters here. For a detailed listing, contact the **Arizona Golf Association** (✉ 7226 N. 16th St., Phoenix 85020, ☎ 602/944-3035 or 800/458-8484).

Ahwatukee Country Club (✉ 12432 S. 48th St., ☎ 602/893-9772), a newer, upscale course just south of of South Mountain Park, is semiprivate but also has a public driving range.

Arizona Biltmore (✉ 24th St. and Missouri Ave., ☎ 602/955-9655), the granddaddy of Phoenix golf courses, offers two 18-hole PGA championship courses, lessons, and clinics.

Encanto Park (✉ 2705 N. 15th Ave., ☎ 602/253-3963) is an attractive, affordable public course.

Gold Canyon Golf Club (✉ 6100 S. Kings Ranch Rd., Apache Junction, ☎ 602/982-9449) is a desert course in the Superstition Mountains area.

Grayhawk Golf Club (19600 N. Pima Rd., Scottsdale, ☎ 602/502-1800), a high-end daily-user course, has championship design by Tom Fazio and immaculate conditioning, making it a favorite of Valley visitors.

Hillcrest Golf Club (✉ 20002 N. Star Ridge, Sun City West, ☎ 602/584-1500) is the best course in the Sun Cities.

Papago Golf Course (✉ 5595 E. Moreland St., ☎ 602/275-8428) is a low-price public course in a scenic city setting.

Raven Golf Club at South Mountain (✉ 3636 E. Baseline Rd., Phoenix, ☎ 602/437-3800) follows a traditional design with thousands of drought-resistant Aleppo pines and Lombardy poplars, making it a cool, shady haven for summertime golfers.

Scottsdale Family Golf Center (✉ 8111 E. McDonald Dr., Scottsdale, ☎ 602/991-0018) combines goofy golf, a driving range, and lessons at all levels; take the kids.

Thunderbird Country Club (✉ 701 E. Thunderbird Trail, Phoenix, ☎ 602/243-1262) has 18 holes of championship-rated play on the north slopes of South Mountain—sweeping views of the city are a bonus.

Tournament Players Club of Scottsdale (✉ 17020 N. Hayden Rd., Scottsdale, ☎ 602/585-3600), a 36-hole course created by Tom Weiskopf and Jay Morrish, is the site of the PGA Phoenix Open.

Troon North (✉ 10320 E. Dynamite Blvd., Scottsdale, ☎ 602/585-5300) offers a challenging 36-hole course, designed by Weiskopf and Morrish, that makes excellent use of the existing desert.

Health Clubs

The Arizona Athletic Club (✉ 1425 W. 14th St., Tempe, ☎ 602/894-2281), near the airport at the border between Tempe and Scottsdale, is the Valley's largest facility. Nonmembers pay a day rate of $10.

Jazzercise (☎ 602/893-1557) has 27 franchised sites in the Valley.

Naturally Women (✉ 2827 W. Peoria Ave., ☎ 602/678-4000; 3320 S. Price Rd., Tempe, ☎ 602/838-8800; 7750 E. McDowell Rd., ☎ 602/947-8300; closed Sun.) focuses on women's needs, from its health profiles to its diet and exercise programs; it offers one free visitor's day, then a day rate of $10 thereafter.

The **YMCA** (☎ 602/257-5165) offers full facilities to nonmembers at six Valley locations. Rates are $3-$6 per day.

Hiking

The Valley boasts some of the best desert mountain hiking in the world—the **Phoenix Mountain Preserve System** (☎ 602/495-0022), in the mountains that surround the city, even has its own park rangers who can help you select and plan your hikes. Phoenix's hiking trails are some of the most heavily used in the world—and for good reason. Call for information and group hiking reservations.

Camelback Mountain (⊠ north of Camelback Rd. on 48th St., ☎ 602/256–3220), another landmark hike, has no park, and the trails are more difficult. This is for intermediate to experienced hikers.

The **Papago Peaks** (⊠ Van Buren St. and Galvin Pkwy., ☎ 602/256–3110) were sacred sites for the Tohonó O'odham tribe and probably the Hohokam before them. The soft sandstone peaks contain accessible caves, some petroglyphs, and splendid views of much of the Valley. This is another good spot for family hikes. The Phoenix Zoo and Desert Botanical Garden are close by.

Squaw Peak Summit Trail (⊠ 2701 E. Squaw Peak Dr., just north of Lincoln Dr., ☎ 602/262–7901) ascends the landmark mountain at a steep 19% grade, but this 1.2-mi trail is a local favorite. Children can handle the hike if adults take it slowly—allow about 1½ hours each direction. Call ahead to schedule an easy hike with a ranger who introduces desert geology, flora, and fauna.

South Mountain Park (⊠ 10919 S. Central Ave., ☎ 602/495–0222) is the jewel of the city's Mountain Park Preserves. At 16,000 acres, it is the nation's largest city park, and its mountains and arroyos contain more than 40 mi of marked and maintained trails—all open to hikers, horseback riders, and mountain bikers. It also has three auto-accessible lookout points, with 65-mi sightlines. The rangers can help you plan hikes some of the 200 petroglyph sites located so far.

CAUTION – Be sure to bring plenty of water with you when hiking and drink often. Dehydration can become a life-threatening condition (☞ Hiking *in* Smart Travel Tips A to Z).

Horseback Riding

More than two dozen stables and equestrian tour outfitters in the Valley attest to the saddle's enduring importance in Arizona—even in this auto-dominated metropolis.

All Western Stables (⊠ 10220 S. Central Ave., ☎ 602/276–5862), one of several stables at the entrance to South Mountain Park, offers rentals, guided rides, hayrides, and at the end of the trail, steak fries.

Old MacDonald's Ranch (⊠ 26540 N. Scottsdale Rd., Scottsdale, ☎ 602/585–0239) provides trail rides, hayrides, and catered cookouts.

Superstition Stables (⊠ Windsong and Meridian Rds., Apache Junction, ☎ 602/982–6353) is licensed to lead tours throughout the entire Superstition Mountains area for more experienced riders; easier rides are also available.

Hot-Air Ballooning

Want to tour Phoenix from above? Check out the many sunrise and sunset hot-air-balloon ascents, which offer a remarkable desert sightseeing experience. More than three dozen companies offer this uplifting experience, the average fee is $135 per person.

Get Carried Away (☎ 602/502–9402 or 800/742–2556) has the Valley's newest and largest balloons—ensuring a comfortable flight and smooth landing—and a high-energy, uniformed staff.

Hot Air Expeditions (☎ 602/788–5555 or 800/831–7610) offers the best ballooning in Phoenix. Flights are long, the staff is gracious and charming, and the gourmet champagne brunch or sunset hors d'oeuvres are prepared by one of the Valley's most venerable chefs, Vincent Guerithault.

Out West Adventures (☎ 602/860–6000 or 800/755–0935) will send you home with a free video of your flight taped from the balloon. **Unicorn Balloon Company** (☎ 602/991–3666 or 800/468–2478) can accommodate large groups of passengers in their gondolas.

Jogging

Phoenix's unique 200-mi network of canals provides a naturally cooled (and often landscaped) scenic track throughout the metro area. Two other popular jogging areas are Phoenix's **Encanto Park,** 3 mi northwest of Civic Plaza, and Scottsdale's **Indian Bend Wash,** which runs for more than 5 mi along Hayden Road—both have lagoons and tree-shaded greens.

Sailplaning

At the Estrella Sailport, **Arizona Soaring Inc.** (✉ Box 858, Maricopa 85239, ☎ 602/568–2318 or 602/821–2903 for 24-hr info) offers sailplane rides in a basic trainer or high-performance plane for prices ranging from $48 to $90. The adventuresome can opt for a wild 15-minute acrobatic flight for $80.

Tennis

Hole-in-the-Wall Racquet Club (✉ 7677 N. 16th St., Pointe Hilton at Squaw Peak Resort, ☎ 602/997–2626) has eight paved courts available for same-day reservation at $15 per hour.
Kiwanis Park Recreation Center (✉ 6111 S. All America Way, Tempe, ☎ 602/350–5201, ext. 0) has 15 lighted premier-surface courts (all can be reserved for $6), as well as drop-in programs for single players weekdays, 10:30–noon.
Mountain View Tennis Center (✉ 1104 E. Grovers Ave., ☎ 602/788–6088), just north of Bell Road, is a Phoenix city facility with 20 lighted courts that can be reserved for $5 for 90 minutes of singles.
Phoenix Tennis Center (✉ 6330 N. 21st Ave., ☎ 602/249–3712), a city facility with 22 lighted hard courts, charges $4.
Phoenix Civic Plaza Sports Complex (✉ 121 E. Adams St., ☎ 602/256–4120) has 4 lighted rooftop courts for $3–$6; reserve seven days in advance.
Pointe Hilton at South Mountain Tennis Club (✉ 7777 S. Pointe Pkwy., ☎ 602/431–6482) has 10 lighted hard courts for $15 per hour.
Watering Hole Racquet Club (✉ 11111 N. 7th St., Pointe Hilton Tapatio Cliffs Resort, ☎ 602/997–7237) has nine hard, lighted courts that rent for $15 per hour.

Tubing

In a region not known for water, one indigenous aquatic sport has developed: Tubing—riding an inner tube down calm water and mild rapids—has become a very popular tradition on the Salt and Verde rivers. Outfitters that rent tubes include **Salt River Recreation Tube Rental & Shuttle** (✉ corner of Usery Pass Rd. and Bush Hwy., Mesa, ☎ 602/984–3305), conveniently located and offering shuttle-bus service to and from your starting point. Tubes are $8 per day, all day (9–4).

Spectator Sports

Auto Racing

Phoenix International Raceway (✉ 7602 S. 115th Ave., Avondale, ☎ 602/252–3833), the Valley's NASCAR track, holds a Winston Cup 500 each October and the IndyCar Slick 50 race each April.

Balloon Racing

The **Thunderbird Hot-Air-Balloon Classic** (☎ 602/978–7208) has grown into a schedule of festivities surrounding the national invitational balloon race, held the first weekend in November.

Baseball

See Pleasures & Pastimes *in* Chapter 1 for information on **Cactus League** spring training.

Basketball

The **Phoenix Suns** (✉ 2nd and Jefferson Sts., ☎ 602/379–7867) have been NBA playoff regulars for several years. Their America West Arena is almost as exciting as their game.

Golf

The **Phoenix Open** (☎ 602/585–4334), played each January at the Tournament Players Club of Scottsdale, is a $1 million PGA Tour event. In March, women compete in the **Standard Register PING Tournament** (☎ 602/942–0000), at the Moon Valley Country Club.

Rodeos

The **Parada del Sol,** held each year by the Scottsdale Jaycees (✉ Box 292, Scottsdale, 85251, ☎ 602/990–3179), includes a rodeo, a lavish parade famed for its silver-studded saddle, and a 200-mi daredevil ride from Holbrook down the Mogollon Rim to Scottsdale by the Hashknife Pony Express. The **Rodeo of Rodeos,** sponsored by the Phoenix Jaycees (✉ 4133 N. 7th St., ☎ 602/263–8671), has one of the Southwest's oldest and best parades. The **World's Oldest Rodeo** (✉ Box 2037, Prescott 86302, ☎ 800/358–1888), held each July as part of Frontier Days, gives the Phoenix rodeos a run for their money.

SHOPPING

Since its resorts began multiplying in the 1930s and 1940s, Phoenix has acquired a healthy share of high-style clothiers and leisure-wear boutiques. But well before that, western clothes were dominant here—jeans and boots, cotton shirts and dresses, 10-gallon hats and bola ties (the state's official neckwear). They still are.

In the past decade, Sun Belt awareness has brought a tide of interest in southwestern furnishing styles as well, from the pastels of the desert mountains and skies to handmade lodgepole furniture of the pueblo and rancho. These—as well as Mexican tiles and tinware, wrought iron and copper work, courtyard fountains and paper flowers—have never died out here. Always an essential part of the way southwesterners shape their homes, work spaces, and public places, these crafts have flourished in the current revival.

On the scene long before, of course, were the arts of the Southwest's true natives—Navajo weavers, sand painters, and silversmiths; Hopi weavers and kachina-doll carvers, Pima and Tohonó O'odham (Papago) basket makers and potters, and many more. Inspired by the region's rich cultural traditions, contemporary artists have flourished here as well, making Phoenix—and in particular Scottsdale, a city with more art galleries than gas stations—one of the Southwest's largest art centers (alongside Santa Fe, New Mexico).

Most of the Valley's power shopping is concentrated in central Phoenix and downtown Scottsdale. But auctions and antiques shops cluster in odd places—and as treasure hunters know, you've always got to have an eye open.

Arts and Crafts

Folklorico (✉ 7216 E. Main St., Scottsdale, ☎ 602/947–0758) is a purveyor of whimsical Oaxacan woodcarvings and southwestern folk arts and crafts.

Gilbert Ortega (✉ 7229 E. Main St., Scottsdale, ☎ 602/947–2805) began as a reliable trader, then mushroomed into an industry with nine Scottsdale locations alone (including two on Main Street). Stores are also found in Phoenix (check in the Hyatt Regency), Tempe, Sun City, and Carefree. Only a fairly experienced Native American–jewelry buyer should shop here.

Godber's Jewelry (✉ 7542 E. Main St., Scottsdale, ☎ 602/949–1133) is one of the oldest, most reliable Native American–jewelry outlets in central Arizona. Begun 60 years ago by a reservation trading-post family, it's a fine place for learning the many styles of southwestern jewelry and discovering your own preferences.

The **Heard Museum** (✉ 22 E. Monte Vista Rd., ☎ 602/252–8344) sells the finest selection of southwestern Native American arts and crafts in the Valley—both traditional and modern—at its gift shop. The museum is also the ideal place for learning about whatever medium or art form interests you and to seeing Native American artists and artisans at work almost every day.

Herman Atkinson's Indian Trading Post (✉ 3957 N. Brown Ave., Scottsdale, ☎ 602/949–9750) is a fine—but eclectic—source for Native American sand paintings, tiles, and pottery. Mixed in is a good deal of inexpensive (but often pretty good) tourist ware.

The **Museo Chicano** (✉ 25 E. Adams St., ☎ 602/257–5536) gift shop has an attractive selection of wares.

Auctions

Barrett-Jackson Classic Car Auction (✉ 5530 E. Washington St., ☎ 602/273–0791) is an internationally recognized dealer in rare and antique autos, and the annual January mega-auction draws collectors from around the world.

John Brunk & Sons Auctions (✉ 4001 N. 7th St., ☎ 602/264–3204) moves a barnful of cast-off furnishings, appliances, tools—and often several decent antiques or collectibles—twice each Wednesday, at 9 AM and from 7 PM until the last lot is gone.

Ron Brunk Inc. Auction (✉ 10109 Grand Ave., ☎ 602/933–7748) has a warehouse auction Sunday at noon in Sun City.

Ware's Auction (✉ 38th Ave. at Indian School Rd., ☎ 602/278–0489) gavels off a diverse gathering of goods starting at 6 PM each Monday.

Markets

Guadalupe Farmer's Market (✉ 9210 S. Av. del Yaqui, Guadalupe, ☎ 602/730–1945) has all the fresh ingredients of Mexican cuisine that you'd find in a rural Mexican market—tomatillos, many varieties of chili peppers (fresh and dried), fresh-ground *masa* (cornmeal) for tortillas, cumin and cilantro, and on and on.

Mercado Mexico (✉ 8212 S. Av. del Yaqui, Guadalupe, ☎ 602/831–5925) carries shelf after shelf of ceramic, paper, tin, and lacquerware, all at unbeatable prices.

Shopping Centers

Biltmore Fashion Park (✉ 24th St. and Camelback Rd., Phoenix, ☎ 602/955–8400) has posh shops lining its open-air walkways, as well as some of the city's most popular restaurants and cafés. **Macy's** (☎ 602/468–2100) and **Saks Fifth Avenue** (☎ 602/955–8000) are its anchors, and designer boutiques are its stock-in-trade—**Banana Republic** (☎ 602/955–9108), **Via Veneto** (☎ 602/956–6661), **Gucci** (☎ 602/957–8710), and **Polo by Ralph Lauren** (☎ 602/952–0155) are among them. Grown-up toy shops include **the Sharper Image** (☎ 602/956–8077) and **Williams-Sonoma** (☎ 602/957–0430). **Cornelia Park** (☎ 602/955–3195) offers an awe-inspiring collection of MacKenzie-Childs, Ltd., glassware as well as furnishings, tiles, and linens.

Borders Books and Music (☎ 602/957–6660) is a great family place, complete with coffee shop. The outpost of **Planet Hollywood** (☎ 602/954–7827) seasons its menu with the hope of spotting one or more of its movie-star owners. Biltmore Fashion Park—home to RoxSand, Steamers, Oscar Taylor's, and Christopher's—also has more fine eating in a small radius than anywhere else in Arizona (☞ Dining, *above*).

The Borgata (✉ 6166 N. Scottsdale Rd., ☎ 602/998–1822), a re-creation of a medieval Italian walled village, may slip into pretentiousness, but it offers a pleasant enough selection of boutiques and galleries. **Dos Cabezas** (☎ 602/991–7004) has won a well-deserved following as a creative source of southwestern interior and apparel design.

Two-tiered **El Pedregal** (✉ Scottsdale Rd. and Carefree Hwy., ☎ 602/488–1072), 30 minutes north of Scottsdale in the town of Carefree, is a serene, attractive shopping plaza. At the foot of a 250-foot boulder formation, it contains posh boutiques, galleries, specialty shops, restaurants, and a satellite of the Heard Museum. In the spring and summer, there are free Thursday-night concerts in the courtyard amphitheater.

Metrocenter (✉ I–17 and Peoria Ave., ☎ 602/997–2641), on the west side of Phoenix, is an enclosed double-deck mall; although this is the largest mall in the Southwest, its Muzak-filled, disinfected environment might just as easily be in St. Louis or Seattle or Secaucus. Anchor department stores include **Robinsons-May** (☎ 602/943–2351). The **Cyber Station** (☎ 602/997–6900) prides itself on having all the latest video games. Adjacent to the mall, **Castles 'N' Coasters** (✉ 9445 N. Metro Pkwy. E, ☎ 602/997–7575) is a miniature-golf park and video-game palace.

Mill Avenue in Tempe is the main drag for ASU's student population; small, interesting shops and eateries make for great browsing or just hanging out. **Urban Outfitters** (✉ 545 S. Mill Ave., ☎ 602/966–7250) sells rough-edged, trendy gear and affordable housewares. The way-cool **Changing Hands Bookstore** (✉ 414 Mill Ave., ☎ 602/966–0203) has three stories of new and used books and an inviting atmosphere that will tempt you to linger—as many students do.

Paradise Valley Mall (✉ Cactus Rd. and Tatum Blvd., ☎ 602/996–8840), in northeastern Phoenix, is an older mall, anchored by the new Macy's department store.

At swank **Scottsdale Fashion Square** (✉ Scottsdale and Camelback Rds., Scottsdale, ☎ 602/990–7800), retractable skylights open to reveal sunny skies above. Besides having Robinsons-May and Dillard's, it is anchored by **Neiman Marcus** (☎ 602/990–2100). The collection of stores runs toward the upscale: J. Crew (☎ 602/945–2739) and **Abercrombie & Fitch Co.** (☎ 602/941–4391) sell sporty men's and women's apparel. **Rodier of Paris** (☎ 602/945–4626) has the latest dressy designs for women. **Artafax** (☎ 602/951–8484) offers a lovely array of home accents and objets d'art in an innovatively designed store. The **Disney Store** (☎ 602/423–5008) and **Warner Bros. Studio Store** (☎ 602/423–1663) are attractions for kids. The Fashion Square's cineplex shows first-run movies.

Superstition Springs Center (✉ AZ 60 and Superstition Springs Rd., Mesa, ☎ 602/832–0212), 30 mi east of Phoenix, has the usual complement of shops and eateries, plus a pleasant outdoor cactus garden to stroll in. The handsome indoor carousel and 15-foot Gila-monster slide keep the kids occupied.

SIDE TRIPS NEAR PHOENIX

North of Phoenix, Arcosanti and Wickenburg make interesting half-day or day trips from Phoenix. Consider stopping along the way to visit the reenactments of life during Arizona's territorial days at the Pioneer Arizona Living History Museum or the petroglyphs of Deer Valley Rock Art Center. You also might consider Arcosanti and Wickenburg as stopovers on the way to or from Flagstaff, Prescott, or Sedona (☞ Chapter 4).

South of Phoenix, an hour's drive takes visitors back to prehistoric times and the site of Arizona's first known civilization, as well as one of its major pioneer western towns. Florence, one of central Arizona's first cities, is rich in examples of territorial architecture. The Casa Grande Ruins National Monument captures vivid reminders of the Hohokam Indians, who began farming this area more than 1,500 years ago.

Numbers in the margin correspond to points of interest on the Side Trips near Phoenix map.

Deer Valley Rock Art Center

20 *15 mi north of downtown Phoenix on I–17. Exit at W. Deer Valley Rd. and drive 2 mi west.*

On the lower slopes of the Hedgepeth Hills, Deer Valley Rock Art Center has the largest concentration of ancient petroglyphs in the metropolitan Phoenix area. Some 1,500 of the cryptic symbols are found here, left behind by various Native American cultures that have lived in the Valley (or passed through) over the past thousand years. Pick up an interpretive trail guide to the ¼-mi path and a viewing tube (a contraption that cuts glare) and head out for an ancient history lesson. Guided tours can be arranged by telephoning in advance. ✉ *3711 W. Deer Valley Rd., Phoenix,* ☎ *602/582–8007.* 🎟 *$3.* ⏲ *Tues.–Fri. 9–2, Sat. 9–5, Sun. noon–5; call for summer hours.*

Pioneer Arizona Living History Museum

21 *25 mi north of downtown Phoenix on I–17, just north of the Carefree Highway (AZ 74).*

The Pioneer Arizona Living History Museum contains 28 original and reconstructed buildings from all over Arizona that set the stage for costumed guides in the blacksmith shop, print shop, schoolhouse, and elsewhere, all demonstrating 19th-century crafts. ✉ *Pioneer Rd. Exit (Exit 225) off I–17,* ☎ *602/993–0212.* 🎟 *$5.75* ⏲ *Oct.–May, Wed.–Sun. 9–4.*

Wickenburg

22 *65 mi from Phoenix. Follow I–17 north for about 15 min to the Carefree Hwy. (AZ 74) junction. About 30 mi west on AZ 74, take the AZ 89/93 north and go another 10 mi to Wickenburg.*

This city, home of dude ranches and tall tales, is named for Henry Wickenburg, whose nearby Vulture Mine was the richest gold strike in the Arizona Territory. On the main drag are the Hassayampa Bridge and the nearby **Jail Tree,** where prisoners were chained, the desert heat sometimes finishing them off before their sentences were served. If you are interested in lore of the American West, the 20,000-square-foot **Desert Caballeros Western Museum** (✉ 21 N. Frontier St., ☎ 520/684–7075) makes a fine stop. If you opt for a longer stay in Wickenburg, there are plenty of dude ranches to accommodate you.

Side Trips near Phoenix

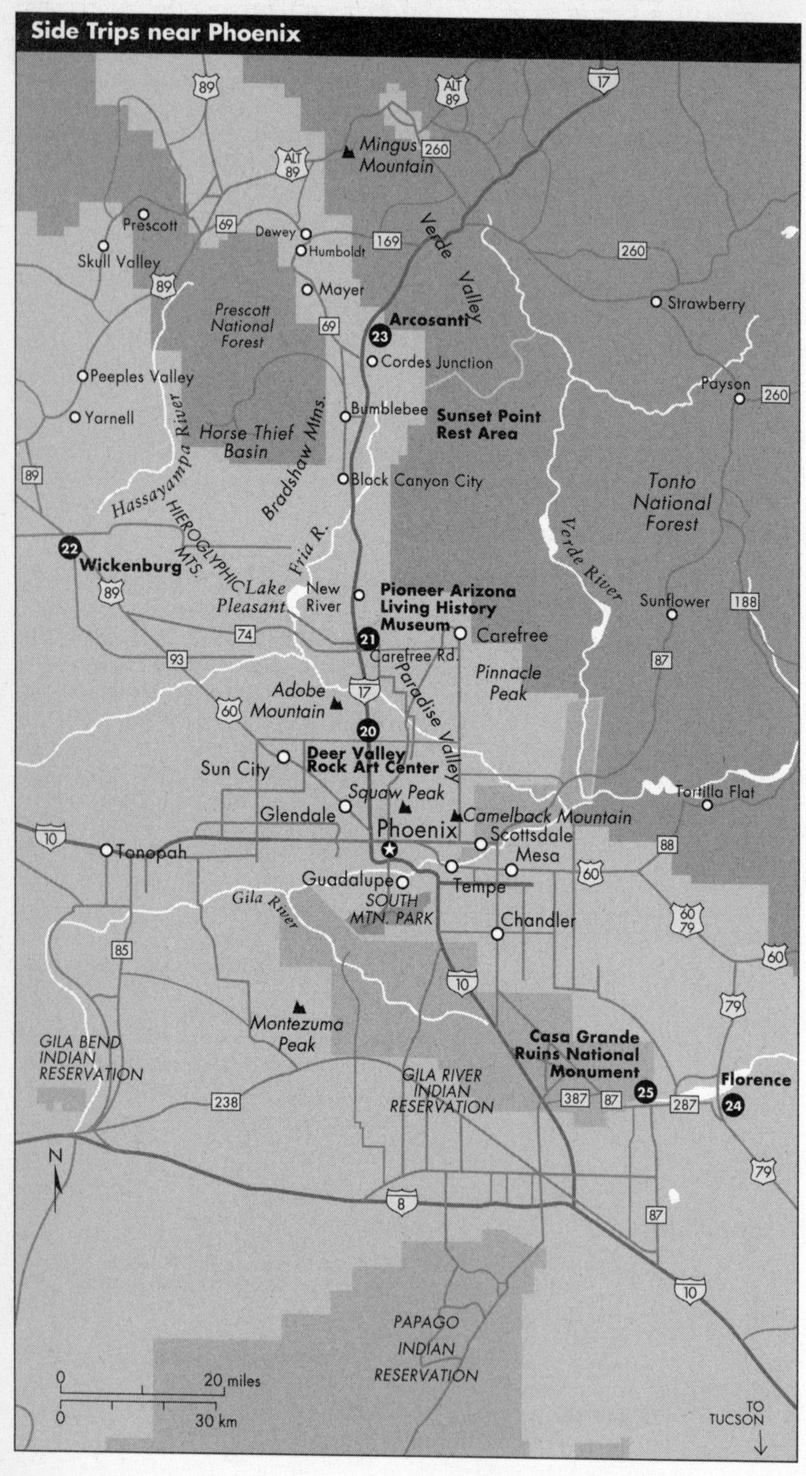

Dining and Lodging

$ ✕ **Anita's Cocina.** Delicious authentic Mexican fare is featured here—fresh, steaming tamales are especially tasty. Try a fruit burrito for dessert. ✉ *57 N. Valentine St.,* ☎ *520/684–5777. No credit cards.*

$ ✕ **Gold Nugget.** At this western-style eating place, perfect for easy refueling, try the homemade soups, prime rib, or fried chicken with corn on the cob. Friday nights there's a fish fry. ✉ *222 E. Wickenburg Way,* ☎ *520/684–2858. AE, D, DC, MC ,V.*

$$$$ ✕🏨 **Rancho de los Caballeros.** Now more of a luxury resort than a dusty dude ranch, this 20,000-acre spread began with 320 acres in 1947 and gradually evolved to include an exclusive housing development, a championship golf course, and a 5,000-square-foot conference center. Trail rides are still a popular feature here, and the annual weeklong Desert Caballeros Trail Ride, starting downtown, is a major event among southwestern horse folk. In the huge main lodge, the original *sala* (living room) has been remodeled; surrounding the copper fireplace now is bright, neo-Mexican decor, and adjacent are game rooms. The American-plan (15% tips included) meals are provided in the bright dining room (breakfast and dinner, restaurant style) and poolside from a half dozen buffet carts. Rooms—from the original brick Sun Terrace duplexes to the Maricopa Suites—are spacious and done in low-key southwestern decor; the baths do not have luxury amenities. The Rancho also has skeet and trap shooting for those who are interested. ✉ *1551 S. Vulture Mine Rd., 85390,* ☎ *520/684–5484,* FAX *520/684–2267. 79 rooms. Pool, 18-hole golf course, 4 tennis courts, horseback riding, parking. Closed mid-May–mid-Oct. No credit cards.*

$$$ ✕🏨 **Kay El Bar Ranch.** Tucked into a hollow beside the Hassayampa River just 3 mi north of town, this is what dude ranches used to be—homey, comfy, and away from it all, with more horses than people, but not too many of either. This National Historic Site, opened as a dude ranch in 1925, was revived in 1980 by two sisters from the East, Jane Nash and Jan Martin. Immense, old salt cedars tower over fat saguaros and some of the biggest mesquite trees in Arizona, all shading the eight-room lodge; the two-bedroom, two-bath cottage (built in 1914); and the brightly decorated cookhouse, where family-style meals are served three times a day. Rooms are compact and clean, with small, modern bathrooms, and decor is down-home western. ✉ *Box 2480, Wickenburg 85358,* ☎ *520/684–7593. 8 rooms, 1 cottage. Bar, pool, golf privileges, horseback riding, Ping-Pong, volleyball, library, parking. MC, V. Closed May–mid-Oct.*

Arcosanti

㉓ *65 mi north of Phoenix on I–17, near the exit for Cordes Junction (AZ 69).*

A mile down a partly paved road northeast from the gas stations and cafés, this evolving complex and community of Arcosanti was masterminded by Italian architect Paolo Soleri to be an urban habitat in which architecture and ecology function in symbiosis. Arcosanti is being built by its residents as a totally energy-independent town. It looks almost like a huge playground or contemporary-art theme park, with desert-rock retaining walls and huge solar greenhouses; it's full of inspiring ideas for dramatic design and ecologically sensitive living. It's worth taking the time out for a tour, a bite at the café, and bringing home one of the hand-cast bronze wind-bells made at the site. ✉ *I–17 at Cordes Junction,* ☎ *520/632–7135.* 🎫 *$5 donation.* ⏲ *Daily 9–5; tours hourly 10–4.*

En Route If you're continuing from Arcosanti to Prescott, consider stopping in at **Young's Farm** (✉ junction of AZ 69 and AZ 169, ☎ 520/632–7272). This farm, family-run since 1947, has hayrides, a nursery, a petting zoo, and a pot-bellied pig named Clementswine. The store has become a beloved purveyor of fresh vegetables, potpies and pumpkins, sweet corn and cider, honey and fresh bread. The Farm Kitchen coffee shop and bakery is open daily, 7–4.

Florence

24 *Take U.S. 60 east (Superstition Freeway) to Florence Junction (U.S. 60 and AZ 79) and head south 16 mi on AZ 79 to Florence.*

This old western town southeast of Phoenix is distinguished by an American Victorian courthouse and more than 150 other sites listed on the National Register of Historic Places. Some visitors may recognize Florence as the location where *Murphy's Romance* was filmed. An annual walking tour of historic Florence is held on the first Saturday in February.

Two attractions are the **Pinal County Historical Museum** (✉ 715 S. Main St., ☎ 520/868–4382), which displays furnishings from early 1900s homes and Native American crafts and tools, and the **McFarland Historical State Park** (✉ Main and Ruggles Sts., ☎ 520/868–5216), where the 1878-era Pinal County Courthouse houses memorabilia of former Governor and U.S. Senator Ernest W. McFarland. The **Pinal County Visitor Center** (✉ 912 N. Pinal St., ☎ 520/868–4331) answers questions and provides brochures weekdays 9–4 September through May, 10–2 June through August.

Casa Grande Ruins National Monument

★ 25 *9 mi west of Florence on AZ 287. When leaving the ruins, take AZ 87 north 35 mi back to U.S. 60.*

Established in 1918, the Casa Grande Ruins National Monument provides a close look at a structure first seen by European explorers in the 17th century. Allow an hour to inspect the site, longer if park rangers are giving a talk at the interpretive ramada or leading a tour.

Start at the visitor center, where a small museum features artifacts and information on the Hohokam, who lived here and farmed irrigated cotton fields until they vanished mysteriously in about AD 1450. Step outside and begin your self-guided tour with an inspection of the 35-foot-tall Casa Grande (Big House), built around 1350 and still close to its original size. It's covered by a modern roof for protection from the sun and wind. Neighboring structures are much smaller, and only a bit of the 7-foot wall around the compound is still in evidence. The original purpose of Casa Grande still puzzles archaeologists; some think it was an ancient astronomical observatory.

Cross the parking lot by the covered picnic grounds and climb the platform for a view of an unexcavated ball court, said to date from the 1100s. Although only a few prehistoric sites can be viewed, more than 60 are included in the monument area.

A small gift shop in the lobby of the visitor center sells books about early Native American civilizations and other aspects of Arizona history. ✉ *1 mi north of Coolidge on AZ 87,* ☎ *520/723–3172.* 🎫 *$2.* ⏲ *Daily 7–6.*

Dining

$ ✕ **Old Pueblo Restaurant.** Of the down-home Mexican and American fare served here, the steak fajita burros, chimichangas, and fish tacos are favorites. The Friday-night all-you-can-eat shrimp and catfish dinner really packs in the locals. ✉ *505 S. Main St., Florence,* ☎ *520/868–4784. AE, D, DC, MC. V. Closed Sat.*

SIDE TRIP TO THE WHITE MOUNTAINS

At elevations ranging from 7,000 to more than 9,000 feet, the White Mountains of east-central Arizona are a winter wonderland and a summer haven. Writing in the 1870s, John Gregory Bourke called the region "a strange upheaval, a freak of nature, a mountain canted up on one side; one rides along the edge and looks down two or three thousand feet into . . . a weird scene of grandeur and rugged beauty." It is still exquisitely grand and rugged, carved by deep river canyons and tall cliffs covered with Ponderosa pine. It is also much less remote than it was in Bourke's time, with a full-scale real-estate boom now under way.

A drive into the White Mountains from Phoenix can be completed as outlined below in two days, or you can chose a shorter daylong excursion on breathtaking Apache Trail loop (head out of Phoenix on U.S. 60, take AZ 88 north just after the town of Claypool, and follow AZ 88 back to the town of Apache Junction). The beauty of the mountains and meadows, not to mention the amount of driving involved, makes at least one overnight stay necessary. If you're going in the winter or early spring, you may need chains—and take ski clothes and equipment and stay for a couple of days.

In fact, it's wise to bring sporting equipment in any season: The White Mountains' stunning scenery and wide range of activities draw sports and outdoor enthusiasts from far and near. Although many specific trails and facilities are listed under the towns below, some region-wide recreational information is worth noting here.

BIKING

Many White Mountains towns actively promote mountain biking, and there are plenty of rental and service facilities in Pinetop–Lakeside and Show Low. Most routes follow forest-service roads, which carry heavy traffic during the logging season from April to November; be alert for logging trucks traveling at high rates of speed along these bumpy, narrow paths. One locally popular route of medium difficulty follows Forest Service Road 224 north of the now nearly abandoned logging town of McNary to its junction with FS 9, skirting the base of the mountains to FS 96, and returning then back to 224. The total ride is about 10 mi, passing through prime elk habitat. Inquire about local conditions for other routes.

CAMPING

Private campgrounds abound in the White Mountains, and public facilities are found throughout the Apache–Sitgreaves National Forest. Call or write the **U.S. Forest Service** (✉ 2022 White Mountain Blvd., Pinetop–Lakeside 85935, ☎ 520/368–5111) for a brochure—at last count, it maintained 31 separate campgrounds, most of them open April–November only—or contact the **White Mountain Apache Tribe** (✉ Box 220, Whiteriver 85941, ☎ 520/338–4385), which maintains an additional 32 camping areas throughout its 1.6-million-acre reservation.

FISHING

Some 39 lakes and reservoirs dot the White Mountains, almost all of them stocked with German brown and rainbow trout, bluegill, smallmouth bass, catfish, and crappie. Among the most popular spots are 450-acre **Big Lake,** 19 mi southwest of Eagar on AZ 260; the slightly smaller **Hawley Lake,** 9 mi south of AZ 260 on Forest Service Road 473, which commonly posts Arizona's coldest wintertime temperatures; and tiny but well-stocked **Nelson Reservoir,** just outside the hamlet of Nutrioso on U.S. 191. An Arizona fishing license is required at these sites; on tribal land, a separate White Mountain Apache fishing license is required (☞ Camping, *above*).

SKIING

Famous regionally as a winter skiing destination, the White Mountains offer hilly, wooded landscapes that invite cross-country exploration. Most trails are not marked, but the towns of Pinetop–Lakeside, Show Low, and Greer each have equipment-rental facilities at which you can inquire about local conditions; the area around Greer is also laced with forest-service roads that double as cross-country trails in wintertime.

Numbers in the margin correspond to points of interest on the White Mountains map.

Superstition Mountains

From Phoenix, take I–10 and then U.S. 60 (the Superstition Freeway) east through the suburbs of Tempe, Mesa, and Apache Junction.

As the Phoenix metro area gives way to cactus- and creosote-dotted desert, the massive escarpment of the Superstition Mountains heaves into view and slides by to the north. The Superstitions are supposedly home to the legendary **Lost Dutchman Mine,** the location—not to mention the existence—of which has been hotly debated since pioneer days.

Weaver's Needle

26 *About 11½ mi southeast of Apache Junction, off U.S. 60, take the Peralta Trail Rd. (about 3 mi past King's Ranch Rd.). An 8-mi, rough gravel road leads to the start of the Peralta Trail.*

The 4-mi round-trip Peralta Trail winds 1,400 feet up a small valley for a spectacular view of Weaver's Needle, a monolithic rock formation that is one of Arizona's more famous sights. Allow a few hours for this rugged and challenging hike, bring plenty of water and a snack or lunch, and don't hike it in the middle of the day in summer.

Boyce Thompson Southwestern Arboretum

★ 27 *12 mi east of Florence Junction (U.S. 60 and AZ 79).*

A "living museum" at the foot of Picketpost Mountain, the Boyce Thompson Southwestern Arboretum is one of the treasures of the Sonoran Desert. From the visitor center, well-marked, self-guided trails traverse 35 acres, winding through all of the desert's varied habitats—from gravelly open desert to lush creekside glades—rich with native flora that coexists alongside imported exotic specimens that have acclimated to the southwestern desert. The **Smith Interpretive Center,** a National Historic Site, houses displays on such topics as geology and mining plus two greenhouses with cacti and other succulents. Bring a picnic lunch and enjoy the arboretum's lovely picnic grounds. ✉ *37615 Hwy. 60, Superior 85273,* ☎ *520/689–2811.* 🎫 *$4.* ⏲ *Daily 8–5.*

En Route A few miles farther, **Superior** is the first of several modest mining towns and the launching point for a dramatic winding ascent through the Mescals to a 4,195-foot pass that affords panoramic views of this copper-rich range and its huge, dormant, open-pit mines. Collectors

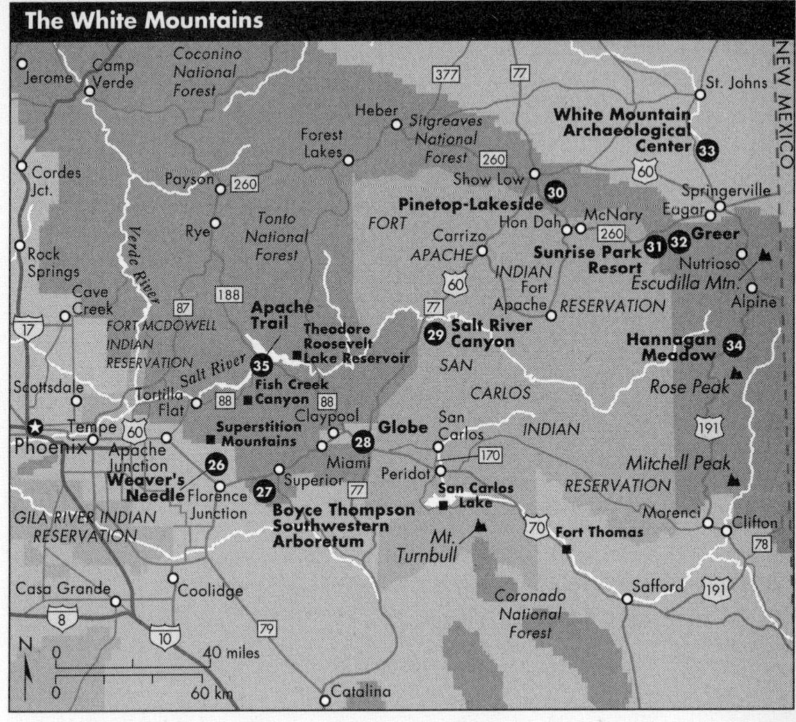

will want to watch for antiques shops through these hills, but be forewarned that quality varies considerably. A gradual descent will take you into **Miami** and **Claypool,** once-thriving boom towns that have carried on quietly since major-corporation mining ground to a halt in the 1970s. Working-class buildings are dwarfed by the mountainous piles of copper tailings to the north.

Globe

28 *25 mi east of Superior.*

In the southern reaches of Tonto National Forest, Globe is the last and most cosmopolitan of area mining towns. The **Besh-Ba-Gowah Ruins** (✉ 150 N. Pine St., ☎ 520/425–0320) consist of more than 200 rooms that were occupied by Salado Indians during the 13th and 14th centuries. In the basement of the old courthouse, the **Globe Downtown Association** (✉ 101 N. Broad St., ☎ 520/425–9340) will provide a walking-tour map of more than 25 sites in historic downtown Globe. Have a bite and fill the gas tank if necessary, because this is the last appreciable town for about 90 mi of mostly mountainous country.

Dining

$ ✕ **Chalo's.** This casual roadside spot offers some of the best Mexican food you'll find north of the border. Locals know to order stuffed *sopapillas* (puffed Indian bread filled with pork and beef, beans, and red or green chilies.) ✉ *902 E. Ash St.,* ☎ *520/425–0515. No credit cards.*

$ ✕ **Jerry's Restaurant.** This humble, busy café serves up steaks, meatloaf, liver and onions, and other standard American fare 24–7. ✉ *933 E. Ash St.,* ☎ *520/425–5282. AE, D, DC, MC, V.*

Salt River Canyon

29 *40 mi past Globe on U.S. 60 north.*

As you approach the Salt River Canyon and the highway climbs through rolling hills, the terrain changes to the Tonto's Ponderosa pine forests. After entering the San Carlos Indian Reservation, U.S. 60 drops from the Natanes Plateau into a vast gorge, makes a series of hairpin turns, and crosses the Salt River. Stop before crossing the bridge to stretch your legs and wander along the banks of the Salt, enjoying its rock-strewn rapids (on hot Arizona days you can slip your shoes off and dip your feet into the chilly water for a cool respite).

En Route The road out of the Salt River Canyon climbs along the canyon's northern cliffs, providing views of this truly spectacular chasm, unfairly overlooked in a state full of world-famous gorges. The highway continues some 50 mi northward to the **Mogollon Rim**—a huge geologic upthrust that bisects Arizona from northwest to southeast—and its cool upland pinewoods. **Show low,** 60 mi north of the Salt River on U.S. 60 in the Apache Sitgreaves National Forest, is a crossing point for east–west traffic along the rim and traffic headed for Holbrook and points north.

Pinetop–Lakeside

30 *At Show Low, turn right and head southeast on AZ 260 about 15 mi.*

The tourist-retirement community of **Pinetop–Lakeside** was formed when the two towns joined in 1984, although they retain separate post offices. The slowly curving highway through these twin towns is usually dotted on the weekends with fruit and vegetable stands purveying modestly priced, wonderfully fresh Arizona produce. Nearby are the White Mountains' three premier golf courses and an excellent hiking trail.

Dining and Lodging

$$–$$$ ✕🏨 **Coldstream B&B.** Decorated with lovely antiques, this historic 1920s residence has elegant country charm. Guests are encouraged to deposit their troubles in the "Worry Box" at the entrance, so as to have nothing interfere with relaxing by a roaring fireplace or out on the patio and manicured lawns. Social tea is a favorite ritual here, served daily at 4 PM. ✉ *3042 Mark Twain Dr., Pinetop 85935,* ☎ *520/369–0115. 5 rooms with bath. Hot tub, golf privileges, horseback riding, billiards. AE, D, MC, V.*

Outdoor Activities and Sports

GOLF

White Mountain Country Club (☎ 520/367–4357), the most challenging of Pinetop–Lakeside's courses, is a par-72 forest course with steep fairways and several dog-legs. Holes three through six are especially tough; five is a 618-yard, uphill par 5 that has broken not a few golfers' hearts—to say nothing of their clubs. **Pinetop Country Club** (☎ 520/369–4375) boasts several uphill holes, including a wicked number nine played through a dense grove of Ponderosa pines. **Pinetop Lakes Country Club** (☎ 520/369–4184) has fewer trees, but it offers several water hazards by way of compensation. All three clubs are open to the public, but you must reserve tee times, and play is restricted to availability.

HIKING

One popular and very easy path follows the 19th-century **Crook Trail** along the Mogollon Rim; the path, with a trail head just west of the Pinetop–Lakeside city limits, is well marked with interpretative signs describing local wildlife and geography.

En Route From Pinetop–Lakeside, AZ 260 east dips into the Fort Apache Indian Reservation. At the tiny crossroads town of **Hon Dah** (you'll see the casino on your left), AZ 260 swings east again. **McNary** is next, a Native American community built among the pines. Slow down if you see a tent and a sign advertising Indian fry bread. Try this doughy fried dish with honey or other fillings for a taste of Native American cuisine. Already more than a mile above sea level, the highway continues its gradual but steady climb after McNary into the White Mountains, leaving the reservation for the Apache National Forest. The thin, pine-scented air tends to be cool even in the middle of a summer day.

Sunrise Park Resort

31 *12 mi past McNary, take AZ 273 south.*

In winter and early spring, skiers may want to visit **Sunrise Park Resort** (✉ Box 217, McNary, 85930, ☎ 800/772–7669 or 602/735–7676 for skiing reports), the state's largest ski area. The resort has five day lodges, 11 lifts, and 65 trails on three mountains rising to 11,000 feet; "guaranteed to ski in one day" classes are available, and for skiers who do not require classes, one-day slope tickets are about $15, cross-country passes $4. Operated by the White Mountain Apaches, the resort is one of the most successful Native American business enterprises in the United States. The tribe also operates a modest outdoor-sports center, which rents a variety of equipment, from cross-country skis to mountain bikes.

Greer

32 *5 mi past the AZ 273 turnoff, take AZ 373 south.*

Built around a meadow and trout ponds, Greer is a tiny, charming community. This area of gently sloping National Forest land is dotted with meadows, lakes, and small reservoirs and is dominated by 11,590-foot Baldy Peak. It's a wonderland for outdoor activities—hunting, fishing, horseback riding, hiking, boating, and camping. Much of the area remains under the control of the Apache nation, so visitors must take care to respect the land and Apache law.

Lodging

$$–$$$ **Greer Lodge.** Cozy overnight accommodations are available year-round in one of two lodges or in rustic log cabins; the friendly help keeps a fire stoked and roaring through the cool alpine evenings. ✉ *Box 244, Greer 85927,* ☎ *520/735–7216,* FAX *520/735–7720. 14 rooms, 7 cabins. Restaurant, bar, pond, croquet, horseback riding, cross-country skiing, fishing. AE, MC, V.*

$$–$$$ **White Mountain Lodge.** This charming property serves tasty (and huge) full breakfasts with the price of a room or cabin. ✉ *Box 143, Greer, 85927,* ☎ *520/735–7568,* FAX *520/735–7498. 7 rooms, 3 cabins. Fishing, cross-country skiing. No credit cards.*

Hiking

A difficult but still accessible trail begins at Sheeps Crossing, 9 mi southwest of Greer; in just over 10 mi, it climbs the northern flank of 11,403-foot Mount Baldy, the second-highest peak in Arizona, from the heights of which you can see spectacular views of the Salt River Canyon and Mogollon Rim. The very summit of Baldy is on the White Mountain Apache Reservation and is off-limits to non-Apaches. The boundary is marked by a turnstile. Please respect it, regardless of how much you might wish to continue on to the peak.

White Mountain Archaeological Center

33 *10 min east of the Greer turnoff on AZ 260 are Eagar and Springerville. At Springerville, AZ 260 joins U.S. 60, which continues east into New Mexico. The Archaeological Center is 12 mi north of Springerville on AZ 191.*

For a pleasant stop and a step back 1,000 years, check out the White Mountain Archaeological Center. At Raven Site Ruin, on a former cattle ranch, James and Carol Cunkle lead amateurs, students, and professionals in unearthing evidence of a pottery-making Native American culture that flourished from about AD 1000 to 1450. Half-day hikes and horseback rides visit nearby petroglyphs; daylong programs add hands-on training in ruin-sifting. The tiny museum is a marvel. ✉ *HC 30, St. Johns 85936,* ☎ *520/333–5857.* *$3.50, including 1-hr guided tour.* *May 1–Oct. 15, daily 10–5.*

Hannagan Meadow

34 *52 mi south of Springerville on U.S. 191.*

Formerly AZ 666, U.S. 191 coming down from the Painted Desert is still known as the Devil's Highway. Surely one of the world's curviest roads, this steep, winding highway passes through Nutrioso under 10,912-foot Escudilla Mountain and eventually rises to Hannagan Meadow, one of Arizona's most splendid camping areas and the site of a former famous face-off between the region's sheep and cattle ranchers. Lush and isolated, it provides a home to elk, deer, and range cattle. Don't miss the splendid overlooks on the way.

Dining and Lodging

$–$$ **Hannagan Meadow Lodge.** Standing by the roadside in the middle of a meadow is this log lodge. You can enjoy a meal or stay for a month in a setting of unparalleled peace and beauty, with people who have true appreciation for life outside the city, but not life without amenities. Cabins have wood-burning stoves, and some have kitchens. ✉ *HC 61, Box 335, Alpine 85920,* ☎ *520/339–4370. 9 rooms, 8 cabins. Restaurant, hiking, horseback riding, cross-country skiing. AE, MC, V.*

En Route From Hannagan Meadow, the road south twists and turns as it descends into a huge wilderness devoid, for the most part, of humans, and crosses under Rose and Mitchell peaks. After passing through the mining towns of Clifton and Morenci, AZ 191 then swings back west, links up with U.S. 70, and provides a fairly straight shot through Safford and across rather uninteresting desert toward Globe. As you near **Fort Thomas,** keep your eyes peeled—$28,000 in gold pieces, meant to pay the soldiers there, was stolen back in May 1889 and still hasn't been found. About 12 mi farther along on your left, you'll see towering 8,282-foot Mt. Turnbull, then the spreading expanse of **San Carlos Lake,** a reservoir behind Coolidge Dam; dedicating it in 1927, Will Rogers observed, "If that was my lake, I'd mow it."

Apache Trail

35 *From Globe (approximately 75 mi after AZ 191 links back up with U.S. 70), retrace your original route back along U.S. 60 to Phoenix or wind back to town via AZ 88, a shortcut through the Superstition Mountains (AZ 88 rejoins U.S. 60 at the town of Apache Junction).*

Scenic AZ 88, also known as the Apache Trail, departs from Claypool to the north, passing several ranches en route to the massive **Theodore Roosevelt Lake Reservoir,** a favorite aquatic recreational area flanked by the desolate Mazatzal and Sierra Anchas mountain ranges. Past the dam, the trail becomes a dirt road, eventually winding its way back to Apache Junction via the magnificent, bronze-hued **Fish Creek Canyon,** with views of the sparkling lakes, towering saguaros, and a vast array of wildflowers.

NEED A BREAK? Close to the end of the Apache Trail are the old-time restaurant, bar, and country store of **Tortilla Flat** (✉ 1 Main St., Tortilla Flat 85290, ☎ 602/984–1776). This is a fun place to stop for a well-earned rest and refreshment—miner- and cowboy-style grub, of course—before heading back the last 20 mi to civilization. Save room for prickly-pear-cactus ice cream.

PHOENIX AND CENTRAL ARIZONA A TO Z

Arriving and Departing

By Bus

Greyhound Lines (✉ 5th and Washington Sts., ☎ 602/271–7423 or 800/231–2222) has statewide and nationwide routes from its main terminal downtown.

By Car

If you're coming to Phoenix from the west, you'll probably come in on I–10. This transcontinental superhighway's last link was joined in 1990 in a tunnel under downtown Phoenix. The trip from the Los Angeles basin, via Palm Springs, takes six to eight hours, depending on where you start. From San Diego, I–8 slices across low desert to Yuma and on toward the Valley on what the Spanish called El Camino del Diablo (the Devil's Highway); at Gila Bend, take AZ 85 up to I–10. The trip takes a total of six to seven hours. From the east, I–10 takes you from El Paso, across southern New Mexico, and through Chiricahua Apache country into Tucson, then north to Phoenix (a total of about 9–11 hours).

From the northwest, I–40 crosses over from California and runs along old Route 66 to Flagstaff. East of Kingman, however, U.S. 93 branches off diagonally to the southeast, becoming U.S. 60 at Wickenburg and continuing into Phoenix.

The northeastern route, I–40 from Albuquerque, crosses Hopi and Navajo historic lands to Flagstaff, where I–17 takes you south to Phoenix—an eight-hour journey. For a scenic shortcut, take AZ 377 south at Holbrook to Heber and the pines of the Mogollon Rim; then take AZ 260 down the 2,000-foot drop to Payson and AZ 87 through the forests of saguaro cactus into Phoenix.

By Plane

Most air travelers visiting Arizona fly into **Sky Harbor International Airport** (☎ 602/273–3300). Just 3 mi east of downtown Phoenix, it is surrounded by freeways linking it to almost every part of the metro area. Although it is the nation's ninth-busiest airport, it is also one of the most compact.

Sky Harbor has three commercial terminals, each with rental luggage carts, taxi stands, car-rental booths, ATM banking, and courtesy telephones. Terminals 3 and 4 (there is no longer a Terminal 1) also have several shops and restaurants, and 24-hour car-rental booths. **Answers & Apples** (☎ 602/267–7994) passenger-service desks at all three terminals offer fax, notary, and insurance services. The airport **chaplain's office** (☎ 602/244–1346) aids travelers in distress.

AIRLINES

Sky Harbor is the home airport of **America West** (☏ 800/235–9292) and a hub for **Southwest** (☏ 800/435–9792). Other airlines with frequent flights to Sky Harbor are **Alaska** (☏ 800/426–0333), **American** (☏ 800/433–7300), **Continental** (☏ 800/525–0280), **Delta** (☏ 800/221–1212), **TWA** (☏ 800/221–2000), **United** (☏ 800/241–6522), and **USAir** (☏ 800/428–4322).

For flights to the Grand Canyon, Page, Lake Havasu, and other Arizona points, try **America West** (☏ 800/235–9292), **Scenic Airlines** (☏ 520/282–7935 or 800/634–6801), and commuter **Skywest** (☏ 800/453–9417).

BETWEEN THE AIRPORT AND DOWNTOWN

It's easy to get from Sky Harbor to downtown Phoenix (3 mi west) and Tempe (3 mi east). The airport is also only 20 minutes by freeway from Glendale (to the west) and Mesa (to the east). Scottsdale (to the northeast) is harder to reach, requiring a jaunt on the Squaw Peak Parkway (AZ 51) or a route of all surface streets; both options take 30–45 minutes by car, depending on traffic.

Sky Harbor has limited bus service, ample taxi service, and very good shuttle service to points throughout the metro area. Very few hotels offer a complimentary limo or shuttle, but most resorts do. You should definitely rent a car, either at the airport or wherever you are staying (most rental firms deliver).

By Bus. In about 20 minutes, **Valley Metro** buses (☏ 602/253–5000) will get you directly from Terminal 2, 3, or 4 to the bus terminal downtown (1st and Washington Sts.) or to Tempe (Mill and University Aves.). With free transfers, the bus can take you from the airport to most other Valley cities (Glendale, Sun City, Scottsdale, etc.), but the trip is likely to be slow unless you take an express line. Adults pay $1.25, senior citizens and children ages 6–12 pay half-fare; children 5 and under (accompanied by an adult) ride free.

The **Red Line** runs westbound to Phoenix every half hour from about 6 AM until after 9 PM weekdays (Saturday, you take Bus 13 and transfer at Central Avenue to Bus 0 north; there is no Sunday service). The Red Line runs eastbound to Tempe every half hour from 3:30 AM to 7 PM weekdays (no weekend service); in another 25 minutes, it takes you to downtown Mesa (Center and Main Sts.).

By Car. Tempe is 10 minutes from the airport by car; Glendale and Mesa are 25 minutes away; and Scottsdale and Sun City, 30–45 minutes. The following companies have airport booths or free pickup from nearby lots: **Alamo** (☏ 800/327–9633), **Avis** (☏ 800/831–2847), **Budget** (☏ 800/527–0700), **Dollar** (☏ 800/800–4000), **Hertz** (☏ 800/654–3131), **National** (☏ 800/227–7368), **Thrifty** (☏ 800/367–2277), and, if you care more about your wallet than about appearances, **Rent-a-Wreck** (☏ 602/252–4897 or 800/828–5975).

By Limousine. A few limousine firms are allowed to cruise Sky Harbor, and many more provide airport pickups by reservation. All of these are on 24-hour call. **AAA Transportation** (☏ 602/242–3094) charges $15–$50, depending on distance. **Classic Limousine** (☏ 602/252-LIMO) will take up to six passengers (by reservation only) for $65, depending on how far you're going. **Scottsdale Limousine** (☏ 602/946–8446) also requires reservations but offers a toll-free number (☏ 800/747–8234); it costs from $40 to $70, plus tip.

By Shuttle. The blue vans of **Supershuttle** (☏ 602/244–9000) cruise Sky Harbor, each taking up to seven passengers to their individual destinations, with no luggage fee or airport surcharge. Fares range from competitive with the cheapest taxi for a short run, such as downtown Phoenix or Tempe, to 25% or more below the best taxi fares on longer trips. You can reserve a Supershuttle back to the airport (call ahead to schedule pickup, and allow one hour at the airport before your flight). Wheelchair vans are also available. Drivers expect tips.

By Taxi. Only three firms are licensed to pick up at Sky Harbor's commercial terminals. All add a $1 surcharge for airport pickups, do not charge for luggage, and are available 24 hours a day. A trip to downtown Phoenix can range from $6.50 to $12. The fare to downtown Scottsdale averages about $15–$16. **AAA Cab** (☎ 602/253–8294), **Checker/Yellow Cab** (☎ 602/252–5252), and **Courier Cab** (☎ 602/232–2222) all charge about $2 for the first mile and $1.30 per mile thereafter. All expect tips.

By Train

Amtrak (☎ 800/872–7245) has only one connection, the former Southern Pacific line between New Orleans and Los Angeles, that passes through Phoenix (eastbound, 7:48 AM Tuesday, Friday, and Sunday; westbound, 10:05 PM Tuesday, Thursday, and Sunday). It stops at the downtown terminal (✉ 4th Ave. and Harrison St., ☎ 602/253–0121) in what is now the industrial part of town, and you may have to phone for a taxi. The much more heavily used former Santa Fe line between Los Angeles and Chicago runs through Flagstaff, 150 mi north of the Valley; Amtrak buses leave from the downtown terminal daily at various times.

Getting Around

To get around Phoenix, *you will need a car.* The metro area developed in the automobile era, and only a few downtowns (Phoenix, Scottsdale, Tempe) are pedestrian-friendly. There is no mass transit beyond a bus system that does not even run seven days a week.

By Bus

Valley Metro (☎ 602/253–5000) is a good rudimentary bus system, with 19 express lines and 51 regular routes that reach most of the Valley suburbs. But there are no 24-hour routes; only a skeletal few lines run between sundown and 10:30 PM or on Saturday, and there is no Sunday service. Fares are $1.25, with free transfers; senior citizens and children 6–19 pay half-fare, and children 5 and under ride free, although they must be accompanied by an adult. The City of Phoenix also runs a 35¢ **Downtown Area Shuttle (DASH),** with purple minibuses circling the area between the Arizona Center and the state capitol at 10-minute intervals. The system also serves major thoroughfares in several suburbs—Glendale, Scottsdale, Tempe, Mesa, and Chandler. The City of Tempe operates the **Free Local Area Shuttle (FLASH),** which serves the downtown Tempe and Arizona State University area from 7 AM until 8 PM. In addition, **Dial-a-Ride** services (☎ 602/253–4000) are available throughout the Valley on Sundays.

By Car

Driving is easy in the Valley of the Sun: Rain and fog are rare, and snow gets major headlines. Most metro-area streets are well marked and well lighted, and the freeway system is making gradual progress in linking Valley areas. Arizona requires seat belts on front-seat passengers and children 16 and under. (For car-rental firms, *see* Between the Airport and Downtown, *above.*)

Around downtown Phoenix, AZ 202 (Papago Freeway), AZ 143 (Hohokam Freeway), and I–10 (Maricopa Freeway) make an elongated east–west loop, embracing the state capitol area to the west and Tempe to the east. At mid-loop, AZ 51 (Squaw Peak Freeway) runs north into Paradise Valley. And from the loop's east end, I–10 runs south to Tucson, 100 mi away; U.S. 60 (Superstition Freeway) branches east to Tempe and Mesa.

Driving in the Valley presents one major challenge: Phoenix and all its suburbs are laid out on a single, 800-square-mile grid of horizontal and vertical streets. Even the freeways all run north–south and east–west. (Grand Avenue, running about 20 mi from northwest downtown to Sun City, is the *only* diagonal.) This makes places easy to find, but it also means you must allow a lot of driving time to get from point A to point B, since you have to trace two legs of a right triangle to do it.

Central Avenue is the main north–south grid axis: All roads parallel to and east of Central are numbered *avenues*; all roads parallel to and west of Central are numbered *streets*. The numbering begins at Central and increases in each direction.

Weekdays, 6–9 AM and 4–6 PM, the center or left-turn lanes on the major surface arteries of 7th Street and 7th Avenue become one-way traffic-flow lanes between McDowell Road and Dunlap Avenue. These specially marked lanes are dedicated mornings to north–south traffic (into downtown) and afternoons to south–north traffic (out of downtown).

By Taxi

Taxi fares are unregulated in Phoenix, except at the airport. (For a listing of leading firms and their fares, *see* Between the Airport and Downtown, *above*.) The 800-square-mile metro area is so large that one-way fares in excess of $50 are not uncommon; you might want to ask what the damages will be before you get in. Except within a compact area, such as central Phoenix, travel by taxi is not recommended.

Contacts and Resources

Emergencies

Police, fire, ambulance or **highway** emergencies (☎ 911).

DOCTORS AND DENTISTS

The **Maricopa County Medical Society** (☎ 602/252–2844) and the **Arizona Osteopathic Medical Association** (☎ 602/840–0460) offer referrals during business hours on weekdays. The **American Dental Association Valley** chapter (☎ 602/957–4864) has a 24-hour referral hot line.

HOSPITALS

Samaritan Health Service (☎ 602/230–2273) has four Valley hospitals—Good Samaritan (downtown), Desert Samaritan (east), Maryvale Samaritan (southwest), and Thunderbird Samaritan (northwest)—and a west Valley urgent-care clinic; all share a 24-hour hot line. **Scottsdale Memorial Hospital** (☎ 602/481–4000 or 602/860–3000) has two campuses in the northeastern valley. **Maricopa County Medical Center** (☎ 602/267–5011) has been rated one of the nation's best public hospitals.

LATE-NIGHT PHARMACIES

Walgreens has fourteen 24-hour locations throughout the Valley. The easiest way to locate the one nearest you is to call ☎ 800/925–4733. **Osco Drug** (☎ 800/881–6726) has 24-hour outlets, including central Phoenix (✉ 3320 N. 7th Ave., ☎ 602/266–5501), west Phoenix (✉ 35th and Glendale Aves., ☎ 602/841–7861), Scottsdale (✉ Scottsdale and Shea Rds., ☎ 602/998-3500), and Mesa (✉ 1836 W. Baseline Rd., ☎ 602/831–0212).

Guided Tours

Reservations for tours are a must all year, with seats often filling up quickly in the busy season, October–April. All tours provide pickup services at area resorts, but some offer lower prices if you drive to the tour's point of origin. For various outdoor excursions, *see* Outdoor Activities and Sports, *above*.

ORIENTATION TOURS

Gray Line Tours (✉ Box 21126, Phoenix 85036, ☎ 602/495–9100 or 800/732–0327) offers a seasonal, three-hour narrated drive through Phoenix and Scottsdale for $27, touring downtown Phoenix, the Arizona Biltmore hotel, Camelback Mountain, mansions in Paradise Valley, Arizona State University, Papago Park, and Scottsdale's Old Town.

Open Road Tours (✉ 748 E. Dunlap, No. 2, Phoenix 85020, ☎ 602/997–6474 or 800/766–7117) offers excursions to Sedona and the Grand Canyon, Phoenix city tours, and a Native American–cultures trip to the Salt River Pima Indian reservation.

For $35, **Vaughan's Southwest Custom Tours** (✉ Box 31312, Phoenix 85046, ☎ 602/971–1381 or 800/513-1381) offers a five-hour city tour for 11 or fewer passengers in custom vans, stopping at the Heard Museum, the Arizona Biltmore, and the state capitol building. Vaughan's will also take visitors east of Phoenix on the Apache Trail, a scenic route that passes through old mining towns and includes a narrated boat ride on Dolly's Steamboat Cruises at Canyon Lake. The cost is $60, with the tour available September through May, weather permitting.

SPECIAL-INTEREST TOURS

Arizona Scenic Tours (✉ 2801 E. Victor Hugo Ave., Phoenix 85032, ☎ 602/971–3601) heads past Pinnacle Peak toward the Verde River on dirt desert roads. Two people can expect to pay $50 each (beverages included) for four hours, but the price drops to $45 per person if more than two make the trip.

Cimarron Adventures and River Co. (✉ 7714 E. Catalina Dr., Scottsdale 85251, ☎ 602/994–1199) arranges half-day float trips down the Salt, Verde, and Gila rivers. Trips cost about $55 per person. Multiday wilderness tours are available on the Upper Gila River and the scenic Upper Verde River.

Wagonmasters (✉ 7319 E. Second St., Scottsdale 85251, ☎ 602/423–1449 or mobile phone 602/501–3239) leads 15-minute to one-hour horse-drawn-carriage tours around Old Scottsdale for $20–$70. They are also available for weddings, birthdays, and other special events.

WALKING TOUR

A 45-minute self-guided walking tour of **Old Scottsdale** takes visitors to 14 historic sites in the area. Maps showing the route can be picked up in the **Scottsdale Chamber of Commerce** (✉ 7343 Scottsdale Mall, ☎ 602/945–8481 or 800/877–1117) weekdays 8:30–5, Saturday 10–5, and Sunday 11–5.

Opening and Closing Times

Generally, banks are open Monday–Thursday 9–4, Friday 9–6. Selected banks have Saturday-morning hours, and a few large grocery stores have bank windows that stay open until 9 PM. Most enclosed shopping malls are open weekdays 10–9, Saturday 10–6, and Sunday noon–5; some of the major centers (☞ Shopping, *above*) are open later on weekends. Many grocery stores are open 7 AM–9 PM, but several stores within major chains throughout the Valley are open 24 hours.

Radio Stations

AM

KTAR 620: news, talk, sports. **KIDR 740:** children. **KFYI 910:** news, talk. **KOOL 960:** oldies. **KISO 1230:** adult contemporary. **KOPA 1440:** classic rock. **KPHX 1480:** Spanish-language.

FM

KBAQ 89.5: classical. **KJZZ 91.5:** jazz, National Public Radio. **KKFR 92.3:** Top 40. **KOOL 94.5:** oldies. **KHTC 96.9:** '70s favorites. **KSLX 100.7:** classic rock. **KZON 101.5:** alternative rock. **KNIX 102.5:** country. **KEDJ 106.3:** modern rock. **KVVA 107.1:** Spanish-language.

Visitor Information

Arizona Office of Tourism. ✉ *2702 N. 3rd. St., Suite 4015, Phoenix 85004,* ☏ *602/230–7733 or 800/842–8257.*

Phoenix Chamber of Commerce. ✉ *Bank One Plaza, 201 N. Central Ave., Suite 2700, Phoenix 85073,* ☏ *602/254–5521.*

Phoenix and Valley of the Sun Convention and Visitors Bureau. ✉ *Arizona Center, 400 E. Van Buren St., Suite 600, Phoenix 85004; Hyatt Regency Phoenix, 2nd and Adams Sts.;* ☏ *602/254–6500 for both.*

Weather

Pressline (☏ 602/271–5656, then press 1010) gives tomorrow's forecast and up-to-date Valley conditions. **Weatherline** (☏ 602/265–5550) provides three-day forecasts.

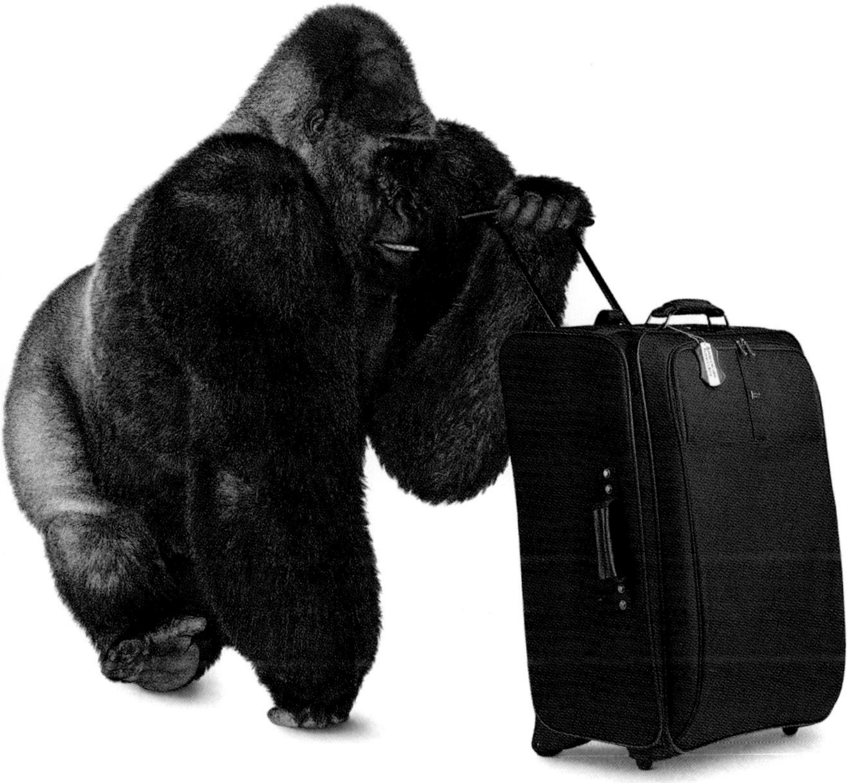

It helps to be pushy in airports.

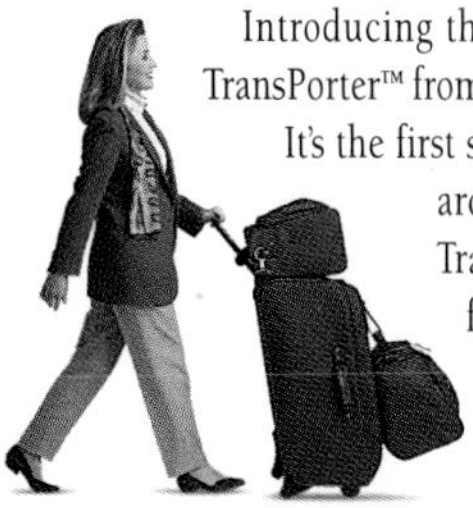

Introducing the revolutionary new TransPorter™ from American Tourister®. It's the first suitcase you can push around without a fight. TransPorter's™ exclusive four-wheel design lets you push it in front of you with almost no effort–the wheels take the weight. Or pull it on two wheels if you choose. You can even stack on other bags and use it like a luggage cart.

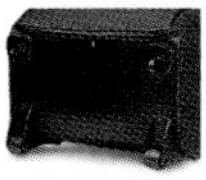

Stable 4-wheel design.

TransPorter™ is designed like a dresser, with built-in shelves to organize your belongings. Or collapse the shelves and pack it like a traditional suitcase. Inside, there's a suiter feature to help keep suits and dresses from wrinkling. When push comes to shove, you can't beat a TransPorter™. For more information on how you can be this pushy, call 1-800-542-1300.

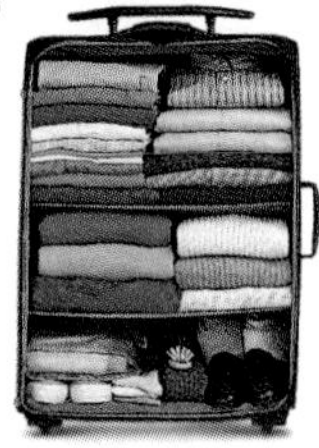

Shelves collapse on command.

American Tourister
Making travel less primitive®

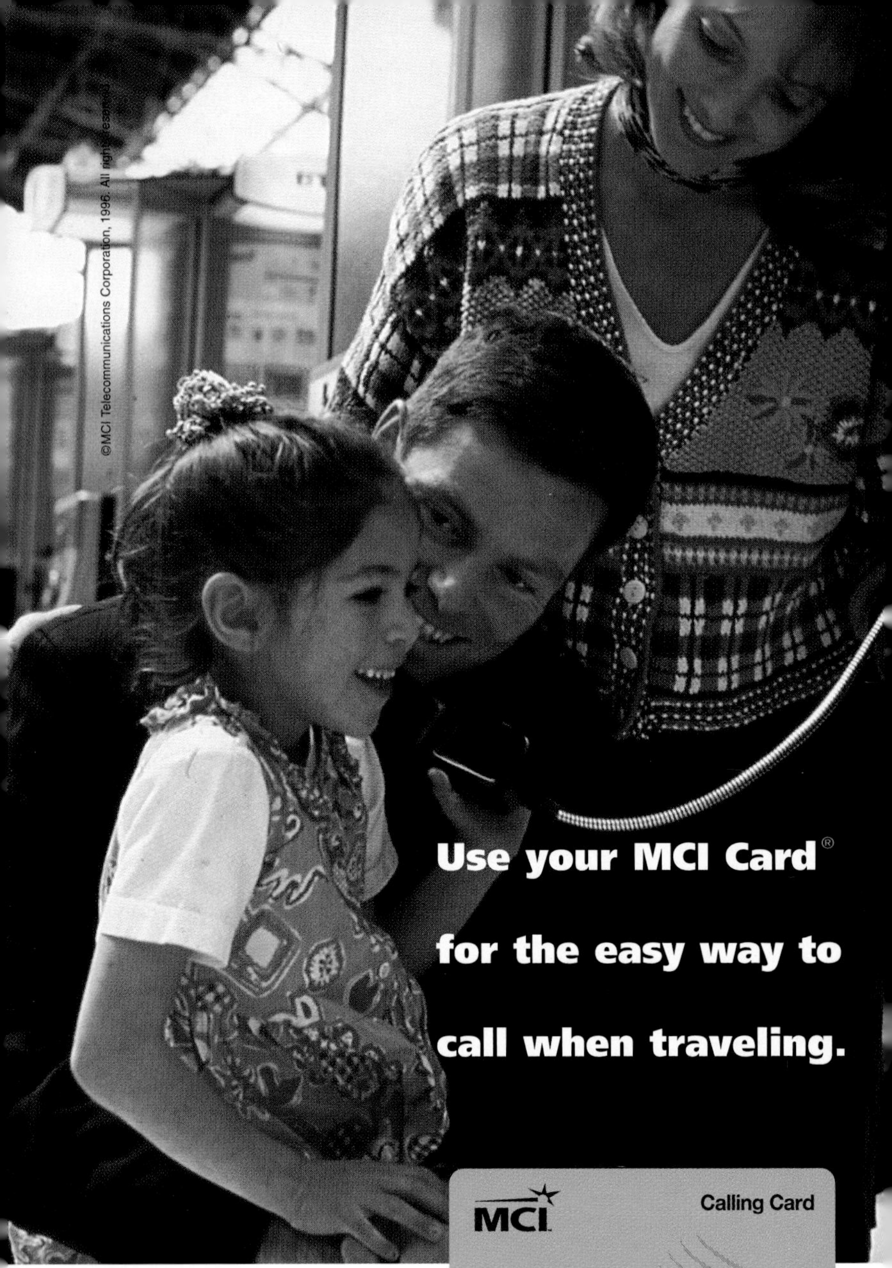

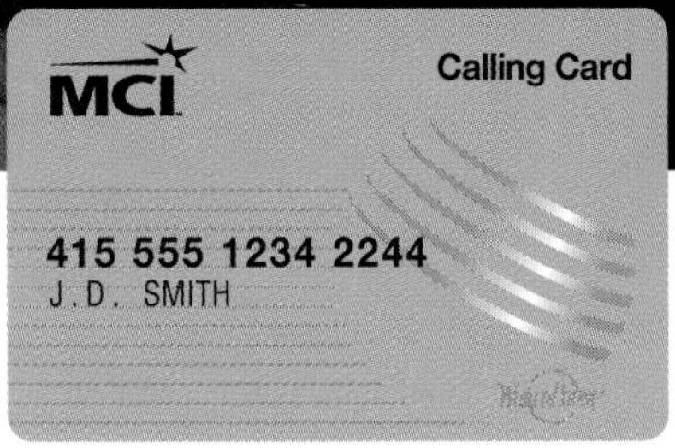

Convenience on the road

- Your MCI Card® number is your home number, guaranteed.
- Pre-programmed to speed dial to your home.
- Call from any phone in the U.S.

MCI

1-800-754-8941

http://www.mci.com

6 Tucson and Southern Arizona

Tucson may have buried most of its Spanish roots, but you'll find remnants of its early days in its El Presidio neighborhood and, just outside of town, in the Mission San Xavier del Bac, an architectural masterpiece set in the midst of the Tohonó O'odham Reservation. Farther from the city, visit the legendary Tombstone and other mining towns or pop over the border to Nogales, Mexico. Lovers of nature should explore Saguaro National Park locally and then head for Ramsey Canyon, Organ Pipe National Monument, and Chiracahua National Monument.

By Edie Jarolim

A GATEWAY TO southern Arizona, Tucson offers travelers history, culture, shopping, and the great outdoors: fascinating Spanish colonial adobe architecture; ballet, symphony, theater, and the University of Arizona's museums; astronomical observatories; western gear and Native American crafts; five surrounding mountain ranges and a national park with the world's highest concentration of saguaro cactus; superb golf courses—and more.

Although it is Arizona's second-largest city, Tucson feels like a small town—one enriched by its deep Native American, Spanish, Mexican, and Old West roots. It is at once a bustling center of business and a kicked-back university and resort town. Metropolitan Tucson has more than 700,000 year-round residents, increased by "snowbirds," who come to the area in winter to enjoy the warm sun that shines on the city more than 320 days a year. Winter temperatures hover around 65°F during the day and 38°F at night. Summers are unquestionably hot—with July averaging 104°F during the day and 75°F at night—but, as Tucsonans are fond of saying, "it's a dry heat" (Tucson averages only 11 inches of rain a year). There are plenty of places to escape from the sun, including Sabino Canyon and Mount Lemmon.

In a part of the world where everything seems new and buildings more than 50 years old are viewed as historic places, Tucson is an exception. Historians have dated Tucson's earliest citizens to AD 100, when the Hohokam Indians made their home in the fertile farming valley. During the 1500s, Spanish explorers arrived to find Pima Indians enjoying the mild weather and growing crops.

The name Tucson came from the Indian word *stjukshon* (pronounced "*stook*-shahn"), meaning "spring at the foot of a black mountain." (The springs at the foot of Sentinel Peak, made of black volcanic rock, are now dry.) The name became Tucson (originally pronounced "*tuk*-son") in the mouths of the Spanish explorers who built the *presidio* (walled city) of San Augustin del Tuguison in 1776 to keep Native Americans from reclaiming the city. Replacing the presidio that had previously been established to the south in Tubac, this new walled city was affectionately called the Old Pueblo by early settlers, and the nickname has stuck till this day.

Father Eusebio Francisco Kino, a Jesuit missionary, first visited the village in 1687 and returned a few years later to build missions in the area. His influence is still strongly felt throughout the region, especially at the noteworthy Mission San Xavier del Bac south of Tucson on the Tohonó O'odham reservation.

Four flags have flown over Tucson—those of Spain, Mexico, the U.S. Confederacy, and the Union. Arizona didn't become a state until 1912, and its colorful days as a territory are still very much a part of the area's lore. In the 1850s the Butterfield stage line was extended to Tucson, bringing adventurers, a few settlers, and more than a handful of outlaws. The arrival of the railroad in 1880 marked another spurt of growth, as did the opening of the University of Arizona in 1891.

Tucson's growth really took off during World War II, thanks to Davis-Monthan Air Force Base. It was also around this time that air-conditioning made the desert hospitable to visitors and residents alike. Today the city's economy relies heavily on tourism, the university, and high-tech industries. The resident population is now almost one-quarter Hispanic, and some of the best Mexican food north of the border is served in restaurants here. The influence of Spanish and Mexican settlers is also strongly felt in the city's architecture and culture.

Tucson is a good jumping-off point for excursions around southern Arizona, a wonderful assemblage of mountains, deserts, canyons, and dusty cowboy towns that remains largely undiscovered by travelers. Among the area's myriad attractions are the old mining towns of Tombstone, Bisbee, Douglas, and Ajo; Cochise's Stronghold; the ominous, towering rock formations of Chiricahua National Monument; many pristine Nature Conservancy preserves; and the lively shops and restaurants in Nogales, across the Mexican border. Several day trips can be coordinated from the city, but plan on an overnight stay to experience the mining towns fully. As you might expect, the desert areas are popular in winter, and the cooler mountain areas are more heavily visited in summer months.

Pleasures and Pastimes

Astronomy

Stargazers can visit the internationally known observatory at Kitt Peak or peer through the telescope at the Flandrau Space and Science Center. City ordinances against "light pollution" allow viewing of the usually clear desert skies at night, even in the center city.

Bird-Watching

The area surrounding Tucson has been ranked as one of the five best for bird-watching in the United States; almost 500 species have been spotted in southern Arizona. Birds can be seen in the city in such places as Sabino Canyon and Mt. Lemmon; Madera Canyon, the Patagonia-Sonoita Creek Preserve, the Buenos Aires National Wildlife Refuge, and the Ramsey Canyon Preserve are among the many nearby places famed for their abundance of avian visitors.

Dining

Tucson's culinary reputation is growing, and there are restaurants in town to satisfy every appetite. Southwestern cuisine, in its element here, ranges from barbecue and cowboy steaks to light nouvelle recipes that use such innovative ingredients as cactus and blue corn.

Tucson's residents have long boasted about their city's Mexican food, some rather grandly proclaiming their town "Mexican Food Capital of the U.S." (a title regularly challenged by San Antonians and Phoenicians). Most of the Mexican food in Tucson is Sonoran style—that is, derived from the cooking native to the adjoining Mexican state of Sonora. It's the type that's familiar to most Americans, featuring cheese, mild peppers, corn tortillas, and beef or chicken. Although Sonoran Mexican food has a well-earned reputation for being high in calories and saturated fats, many restaurants in Tucson now feature otherwise authentically prepared dishes cooked without lard. (Note that the salsa served with baskets of tortilla chips may be spicier than what you are used to. Proceed with caution. Similarly, when you ask the staff whether a dish is "hot," remember that their definition may be quite different from yours.) If you can take the heat, you've come to the right place.

Golf

You can easily dedicate a vacation to golf in Tucson, which has some of the best desert courses in the country and plenty of sunshine in which to play them. Options range from spreads in posh resorts to very reasonably priced but excellent municipal courses.

Hiking

Tucson abounds with desert trails to explore in the winter and, in summer, offers lots of cooler trekking options in nearby mountain ranges. Among the places to hike are Saguaro National Park, Mt. Lemmon, Sabino Canyon, "A" Mountain, and Catalina State Park. Farther afield, you can trek around Nature Conservancy preserves such as Ramsey Canyon, Arivaipa Canyon, the Patagonia-Sonoita Creek Sanctuary, and Muleshoe Ranch; Organ Pipe and Chiricahua national monuments; and dramatic mountain ranges such as the Huachucas, the Patagonias, the Rincons, the Whetstones, and the Dragoons.

Horseback Riding

It wouldn't be a trip to the Southwest without at least one day on the back of a horse. Tucson has plenty of stables and lots of scenic places to trot around.

Lodging

In Tucson you can enjoy the luxury of a desert resort or the more basic accommodations offered by small motels. A number of guest ranches—some of them from the 1800s when they were real working cattle ranches—can be found on the outskirts of town. There is also a variety of bed-and-breakfasts in the area, ranging from bedrooms in modest homes to private cottages nestled on wildlife preserves.

Mexican Culture

You can see Tucson's south-of-the-border soul in everything from the city's tile-roof architecture to its mariachi festivals and abundance of Mexican restaurants.

Native American Culture

The reservations of the Pascau Yaqui and the Tohonó O'odham peoples border Tucson; many events in town celebrate the culture of these tribes as well as that of other Native Americans in Arizona. Native American crafts range from exquisite jewelry and basketry to the more pedestrian (but still authentic) tourist items.

Shopping

There are plenty of places to find unique gift items in Tucson—everything from cactus to salsa. Shoppers can also head south for the artisans colony of Tubac and the bustling booths of Mexican crafts in Nogales.

Western Lore

The west was never lost in Tucson, where city slickers mingle with cowboys at guest ranches, country-and-western dance clubs, steakhouses, and western-wear stores.

EXPLORING TUCSON

Tucson covers more than 500 square mi in a valley ringed by mountains (the main surrounding ranges are the Santa Catalinas to the north, the Santa Ritas to the south, the Rincons to the east, and the Tucson Mountains to the west). For the most part, touring the area requires having a car. The central portion of town, where most shops, restaurants, and businesses are located, is roughly bounded by Wilmot Road on the east, Oracle Road on the west, River Road to the north, and 22nd Street to the south. The older downtown section, accessible just east of I–10 off the Broadway–Congress exit, is much smaller and easy to navigate on foot. (Streets there don't run true to any sort of grid, however, and many of them are one-way, so it's best to get a good, detailed map.) Those accustomed to living in humid areas may find themselves unprepared for Tucson's dry climate: If you're out walking in the hot weather, stop for frequent fluid breaks.

Great Itineraries

Numbers in the text correspond to numbers in the margin and on the Downtown Tucson, University of Arizona, Tucson, Southeast Arizona, and Southwest Arizona maps.

IF YOU HAVE 3 DAYS

Spend the first day at Saguaro National Park West ㉕ and the Arizona-Sonora Desert Museum ㉖, with a stop at Old Tucson Studios ㉗ if you're traveling with kids. The next morning, drive out to the Mission San Xavier del Bac ㉙ and enjoy Indian fry bread for lunch in the plaza. Military buffs might want to continue south to the Titan Missile Museum ㉚ and Fort Huachuca ㊸; shoppers will enjoy trips in the same direction to Tubac ㉟ and Nogales ㊲, Mexico. On the third day, head downtown to the El Presidio district to explore Tucson's early history and, in the afternoon, visit one of the University of Arizona's excellent museums ⑩–⑭ (art lovers, photographers, and astrononomy and history buffs will all find something to enjoy here).

IF YOU HAVE 5 DAYS

What you do on the fourth day depends on the weather: If it's hot, visit Sabino Canyon ⑲ or Mt. Lemmon ㉑ to cool off; if it's not, you might enjoy breakfast at Tohonó Chul Park ㉓, followed by a visit to Biosphere II ㉒. On the fifth day take a day trip, either west to the Kitt Peak National Observatory ㉛ and Organ Pike Cactus National Monument ㉞, or east to Tombstone ㊷ and Bisbee ㊺.

IF YOU HAVE A WEEK OR MORE

Follow the four-day itinerary and then plan on overnighting elsewhere in southern Arizona. You might want to spend a night each in Tombstone ㊷ or Bisbee ㊺, making sure to include a visit to the Amerind Foundation en route. Nature lovers will want to hike the Chiracahuas ㊽ and perhaps spend a couple of nights at the Nature Conservancy cabins near Willcox ㊿. If you head west, visit Kitt Peak National Observatory (51) and Organ Pipe Cactus National Monument (54) and then sleep in one of the bed-and-breakfasts in the former mining town of Ajo (53). Those wishing to explore the lower Colorado River and a fascinating historical state park should visit Yuma (55).

Downtown

The area flanked by Franklin and Pennington streets on the north and south and by Church and Main avenues on the east and west encompasses more than 130 years of the city's architectural history, dating from the original walled El Presidio del Tucson, a Spanish fortress built in 1776, when Arizona was still part of New Spain. A good deal of Tucson's history was destroyed in the 1960s, when large sections of downtown were bulldozed to make way for high-rises and parking lots, but it's still possible to explore parts of the original Spanish settlement and to see a number of the posh residences that accompanied the arrival of the railroad.

Numbers in the margin correspond to points of interest on the Downtown Tucson map.

Timing

If you're in town from November through March, don't miss the Naciemento, a traditional Mexican Christmas display in La Casa Cordoba. The entire room is filled with folk-art miniatures arranged in elaborate scenes from the Old and New Testaments and from Mexican rural life. And for the eight nights from December 15 through Christmas Eve, you can witness Las Posadas, a traditional procession started

"A" Mountain, **1**
El Tiradito, **9**
La Casa Cordova, **4**
Pima County Courthouse, **5**
Sosa-Carillo-Fremont House, **6**
St. Augustine Cathedral, **7**
Stevens Home, **3**
Tucson Children's Museum, **8**
Tucson Museum of Art and Historic Block, **2**

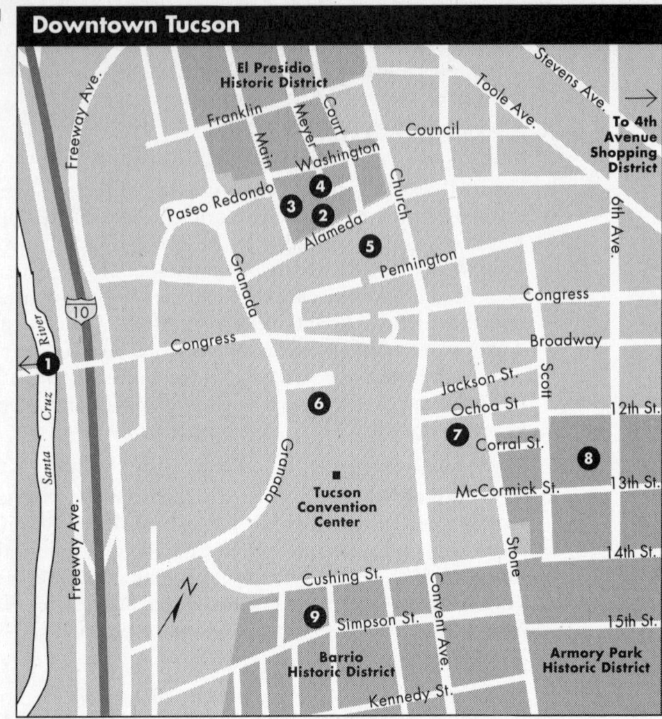

in Mexico in 1587 to introduce Christmas to the Aztecs. The faithful sing traditional songs and prayers while carrying statues of the Holy Family through the streets of downtown, where they symbolically seek shelter at various houses. On the final night, the procession ends up at St. Augustine's cathedral.

Sights to See

❶ **"A" Mountain (Sentinel Peak).** The original name of this mountain, just west of downtown, was derived from its function as a lookout point for the Spanish. In 1915, fans of the University of Arizona football team whitewashed a large "A" on its side to celebrate a victory, and the tradition has been kept up ever since. The Pima Indian village and the cultivated fields that once flanked the peak are long gone, but you can still see the ruins of an early (1870–80) adobe residence and flour mill at its base. During the day, it's a great place for visitors to get an overview of the town's layout; at night, it's generally crowded with amorous teenagers. ✉ *Off Congress St., on Sentinel Peak Rd.*

❾ **El Tiradito (The Castaway).** No one seems to know the details of the story behind this little shrine, but everyone agrees a tragic love triangle was involved. A bronze plaque indicates only that it is dedicated to a sinner who is buried here on unconsecrated ground. The many candles that line the cactus-shrouded spot attest to its continuing importance in local Catholic lore. A modern-day miracle: The shrine's inclusion on the National Register of Historic Places helped prevent a freeway from ploughing through the Barrio Historico District. ✉ *Main Ave., just south of Cushing St.*

❹ **La Casa Cordova.** One of the best examples of the simple but elegant Sonoran row house, a Spanish style adapted to adobe construction, La Casa Cordova is also one of the oldest buildings in Tucson: The original part was constructed in about 1848. It's now home to the Mexican Heritage Museum; when you enter through the double doors on Meyer Avenue, the room on your right has an exhibit of the history of the presidio, while three rooms off the patio display furnishings of the Indian and pioneer settlers of the period. After visiting the museum, you'll understand why adobe—brick made of mud and straw, cured in the hot sun—was so widely used in early Tucson. It offers a natural insulation from the heat and cold, and it is durable in Tucson's dry climate. In some cases the woody cactus ribs built into the walls and ceilings for extra support poke through the hard-packed adobe. ✉ *175 N. Meyer Ave.,* ☎ *520/624–2333.* 🎫 *Free.* 🕓 *Sept.–Apr., Mon.–Sat. 10–4, Sun. noon–4. Closed Mon. June–Aug.*

NEED A BREAK? On the patio of Old Town Artisans, a 13-room marketplace set in a 19th-century adobe building, the pretty **Old Town Grill** (✉ 186 N. Meyer Ave., ☎ 520/622–0351) is a nice spot for a quiche, salad, or sandwich; you'll even enjoy sitting outside in summer, when it's mist-cooled.

★ ❺ **Pima County Courthouse.** This Spanish colonial–style building with its landmark mosaic-tile dome is among Tucson's most beautiful historic structures. It was built in 1927 on the site of the original single-story adobe court of 1869; a portion of the old Presidio wall can be seen in the south wing of the courthouse's second floor, and another section of the fortress was recently excavated in front of the building. To the side of the building, the County Assessor's office hosts a diorama depicting the area's early days (if the location seems odd, remember that the Spanish were big on taxation, too). The courthouse is on the eastern side of **El Presidio Park,** a modern square once occupied by the Plaza de las Armas, the largest plaza in the El Presidio area. ✉ *115 N. Church St. (between Alameda and Pennington Sts.).*

❻ **Sosa-Carillo-Fremont House.** The only building spared when the surrounding barrio was torn down to build the Tucson Convention Center, this is one of Tucson's oldest adobe residences. Originally purchased by José Maria Sosa in 1860, it was owned by the Carillo family for 80 years. Arizona's territorial governor, John C. Fremont, may have spent a night or two here when the place was briefly rented out to his daughter in 1880. The restored house, now a branch of the Arizona Historical Society, is furnished in 1880s fashion and has rotating displays of territorial life. ✉ *Convention Center Complex, between the Music Hall and the Arena (parking at 151 S. Granada Ave.),* ☎ *520/622–0956.* 🎫 *Free; walking tours of the Presidio and Tucson Historic District $4.* 🕓 *Wed.–Sat. 10–4; tours Oct.–Apr., Sat. at 10.*

❼ **St. Augustine Cathedral.** Construction began in 1896 on one of downtown's most striking structures, set in what had earlier been the Plaza de Mesilla. Although the imposing pink building was modeled after the Cathedral of Queretaro in Mexico, a number of its details reflect the desert setting: Above the entryway, next to a bronze statue of St. Augustine, are carvings of a saguaro cactus, yucca, and horned toad. Compared with the magnificent facade, the modernized interior is a bit disappointing. ✉ *192 South Stone Ave.*

❸ **Stevens Home.** It was here that wealthy politician and cattle rancher Hiram Stevens and his Mexican wife, Petra Santa Cruz, entertained many of Tucson's leaders—including Edward and Maria Fish—during the 1800s. A drought brought the Stevenses' cattle ranching to a halt in 1893, and Stevens killed himself in despair, after unsuccessfully attempting to kill his wife (the bullet was deflected by the comb she wore in her hair). The 1865 house, just north of the Fish House (☞

below) and architecturally similar, was restored in 1980 and is now home to one of Tucson's most elegant restaurants, Janos (☞ Dining, *below*). ✉ *150 N. Main Ave.*

8 **Tucson Children's Museum.** Kids are encouraged to touch and explore the exhibits, which are oriented toward science, language, and history: They can crawl inside a giant model of the heart and lungs or turn on the electricity in the streets of a model town. Art supplies, dress-up clothes, and musical instruments add to the fun. Ages 1 through 12 will enjoy this 8,000-square-foot playground. ✉ *200 S. 6th Ave.,* ☎ *520/792–9985.* *$5.* *Sat. 10–5, Sun. noon–5; call for weekday hrs.*

2 **Tucson Museum of Art and Historic Block.** Tucson's past is interpreted for visitors in downtown's main cultural center. The museum itself is fine, especially its new western wing, but a major draw is also the chance to explore the town's earliest settlement. The five historic buildings on this block are listed in the National Register of Historic Places; you can enter **La Casa Cordova** (☞ *above*), the **Stevens Home** (☞ *above*), and the **Edward Nye Fish House.** The other two residences, the **Romero House,** believed to incorporate a section of the presidio wall, and the **Corbett House,** occupied for 56 years by the influential Tucson family for whom Hi-Corbett Field is named, are not open to the public. In the center of the museum complex is the **Plaza of the Pioneers,** honoring Tucson's early citizens.

The modern Tucson Museum of Art building houses a permanent collection of pre-Columbian art and hosts some interesting traveling shows, most of them contemporary. The highlight here may well be the gift shop, featuring a colorful array of work by local artisans. The opening in December 1995 of the John K. Goodman Pavilion of Western Art in the Edward Nye Fish House was big art news in town. The museum's fine permanent and changing exhibitions of western art fill the 1868 adobe that belonged to an early merchant, entrepreneur, and politician, and his wife, Maria Wakefield Fish, a prominent educator; it's notable for its 15-foot beamed ceilings and saguaro-cactus-rib supports. ✉ *140 N. Main Ave.,* ☎ *520/624–2333.* *$2; Tues. free. Free docent tours Wed. and Thurs. at 1:30.* *Mon.–Sat. 10–4, Sun. noon–4. Closed Mon. Memorial Day–Labor Day.*

NEED A BREAK? **Wild Johnny's Wagon** (✉ 150 N. Main Ave., 520/884-9426), an outdoor outpost of Janos (☞ Dining, *below*), is parked at the Plaza of the Pioneers. Chic southwestern salads and sandwiches such as grilled chicken with cilantro pesto are available here at reasonable prices.

The University of Arizona

A university might not seem to be the most likely spot for a vacation visit, but this one is unusual. Not only is the institution itself of historical importance, but it also hosts museums for special interests ranging from astronomy to photography. For all of the university's institutions, it's best to call ahead and verify opening and closing hours; budget cuts have caused schedule changes in a number of cases. If you drive, you're best off leaving your car in a university lot. A central one, on 2nd Street between Highland and Mountain avenues, charges $5 from 7 to 1, $3 from 1 to 5, and $2 from 5 to 8. There's also a large parking garage at the junction of Speedway Boulevard and Park Avenue.

The U of A, as the University of Arizona is known locally (versus ASU, its rival state university in Phoenix), covers 325 acres and is a major economic influence on the city. Approximately 38,000 students attend graduate and undergraduate classes here. The original land for the university was "donated" by a couple of gamblers and a saloon owner in 1891 (their benevolence was reputed to have been inspired by a bad hand of cards), and $25,000 of territorial money was used to build Old Main (the original building) and hire six faculty members. Money ran out before the Old Main's roof was placed, but a few enlightened local citizens pitched in with the funds to finish it. Most of the city's populace was less enthusiastic about the institution: They were disgruntled when the 13th Territorial Legislature granted the University of Arizona to Tucson and awarded rival Phoenix with what they considered to be the real prize—an insane asylum and a prison.

Numbers in the margin correspond to points of interest on the University of Arizona map.

Timing

It's hard to see everything there is to see on the huge university campus in a single day—allot your time accordingly. During the school semesters, you're better off visiting on the weekend, when there's no fee for parking and it's less of a hassle to find a legal spot; there's no problem in summer, when most of the students leave campus.

Sights to See

11 **Arizona Historical Society's Museum.** Well-displayed exhibits transport visitors through Arizona history, starting with the Hohokam Indians and Spanish explorers and highlighting important influences such as mining and cattle ranching. Children will especially enjoy the dark (and slightly spooky) replica of a mine shaft and the old cars and wagons in the transportation section. A gift shop includes items from the late 1800s (many reproductions but also antiques) as well as Native American crafts and Mexican folk art. The library houses an extensive collection of historical Arizona photographs and sells reprints of most of them for a small fee. (If you're driving and this is your first stop, park your car in the lot at the corner of 2nd and Euclid streets and then inquire at the museum about the token system.) ⊠ *949 E. 2nd St.,* ☎ *520/628–5774.* *Suggested donation $3.* *Mon.–Sat. 10–4, Sun. noon–4.*

12 **Arizona State Museum.** Just inside the main gate of the university is the oldest museum in the state, dating from territorial days (1893). Exhibits in the original (south) building focus on the state's ancient history, including fossils and a fascinating sample of tree-ring dating. In the north building is the extensive, new "Paths of Life: American Indians of the Southwest" exhibit, occupying some 10,000 square feet; it was completed in 1995. The cultural traditions, origins, and contemporary lives of native tribes of Arizona and of Sonora, Mexico, are explored through a variety of displays and video programs. The museum's new gift shop is also in this building. ⊠ *Park Ave.,* ☎ *520/621–6302.* *Free.* *Mon.–Sat. 10–5, Sun. noon–5.*

NEED A BREAK? Just outside the campus gate, University Boulevard is lined with student-oriented eateries. **Geronimoz** (⊠ 800 E. University Blvd. at Euclid, ☎ 520/623-1711) stands out with its good burgers and salads. Beer aficionados should head over to the newly expanded and upscaled **Gentle Ben's** (⊠ 865 E. University Blvd., ☎ 520/624-4177), the only brewpub in Tucson. You can enjoy deli sandwiches and rotisserie chicken downstairs; upstairs is a 6,000-square-foot bar and open deck.

★ 13 **Center for Creative Photography.** Ansel Adams conceived the idea of this museum, which houses a superb collection of his work and that of many other major 20th-century photographers, including Paul

Arizona Historical Society's Museum, **11**
Arizona State Museum, **12**
Center for Creative Photography, **13**
Grace H. Flandrau Science Center and Planetarium, **14**
University of Arizona Museum of Art, **10**

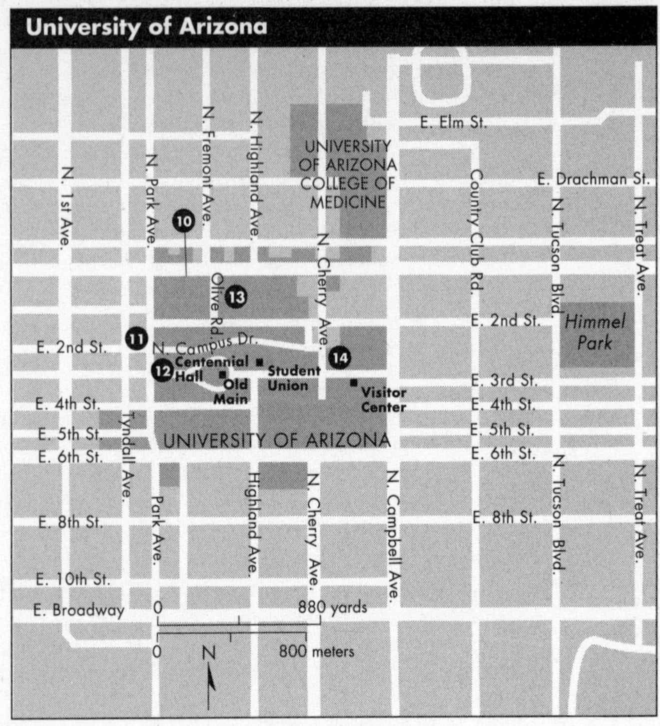

Strand, W. Eugene Smith, Edward Weston, and Louise Dahl-Wolfe. Changing exhibits in the main gallery highlight various holdings of the collection, but if you'd like to spend an hour looking at the pictures of a particular photographer in the center's archives, call to arrange an appointment. ✉ *1030 N. Olive Rd. (north of 2nd St.),* ☏ *520/621–7968.* 🎟 *Free.* ⏲ *Weekdays 11–5, Sun. noon–5.*

14 **Grace H. Flandrau Science Center and Planetarium.** Attractions here include a 16-inch public telescope; the impressive Star Theatre, where a multimedia show brings astronomy to life; an interactive meteor exhibit; and, in the basement, a small Mineral Museum, which exhibits more than 2,000 rock and gem samples, some rather rare. Laser light shows are held at night. Bring a camera—special adapters allow you to take pictures through the telescopes. ✉ *Cherry Ave. and University Blvd.,* ☏ *520/621–4515.* 🎟 *Exhibits $2, laser light show $5, exhibits plus theater $4.50; no children under 3.* ⏲ *Mon.–Tues. 10–5, Wed.–Thurs. 10–5 and 7–9, Fri. 10–5 and 7–midnight, Sat. 1–5 and 7–midnight, Sun. 1–5. Show times vary;* ☏ *520/621–7827 for recorded message. Telescope hrs: in summer, Tues.–Sat. 8–10 PM; in winter, Tues.–Sat. 7–10 PM.*

10 **University of Arizona Museum of Art.** This small museum features a wide-ranging collection of European paintings from the Renaissance through the 17th century. Two of the museum's highlights are the 26 astounding panels of Fernando Gallego's 1488 Ciudad Rodrigo altarpiece and the second largest collection in the world of bronze, plaster, and ceramic sculpture by Jacques Lipschitz. ✉ *Fine Arts Complex, Bldg. 2 (southeast corner of Speedway Blvd. and Park Ave.),* ☏ *520/621–7567.* 🎟 *Free.* ⏲ *Sept.–mid-May, weekdays 9–5, Sun. noon–4; mid-May–Aug., weekdays 10–3:30, Sun. noon–4.*

Central Tucson

The University of Arizona, built in 1891, determined the direction that the city would grow. Sights worth seeing near the university include a city park, a zoo, and botanical gardens.

Numbers in the margin correspond to points of interest on the Tucson map.

Sights to See

18 **Fort Lowell Park and Museum.** This restful city park was once the site of a Hohokam Indian village and, many centuries later, a fort. At a small museum run by the Arizona Historical Society, the reconstructed commanding officers' quarters gives visitors a glimpse of military life in territorial days. There are also rotating exhibits of photographs and frontier artifacts. ☒ *2900 N. Craycroft Rd.,* ☎ *520/885–3832.* 🎫 *Free.* ⊙ *Wed.–Sat. 10–4.*

16 **Playmaxx/The Yozeum.** A member of the Duncan (of yo-yo fame) family has put together a delightful historical exhibit of the wood-and-string toys, dating from 1929 through the 1980s. Attractions on the guided tours include films of old yo-yo contests and demonstrations of yo-yo assembly. Anyone who buys a yo-yo here can come in the first Saturday of the month for complimentary instruction classes. ☒ *2900 N. Country Club Rd.,* ☎ *520/322–0100.* 🎫 *Free.* ⊙ *Weekdays 9–5, Sat. 9-1.*

15 **Reid Park Zoo.** This small but well-designed zoo won't tax the children's—or your—patience. Ask who's new when you arrive; the many baby animals born here each year are adorable. The zoo was recently expanded by 2½ acres to include a South American enclosure, replete with rain forest and exotic birds. If you're visiting in the summertime, go early in the day when the animals are active. ☒ *Reid Park, Lake Shore La., off 22nd St. between Alvernon Way and Country Club Rd.,* ☎ *520/791–4022 (recorded hours) or 520/791–3204 (administration).* 🎫 *$3.50.* ⊙ *Daily 9–4.*

17 **Tucson Botanical Gardens.** This 5-acre oasis in the center of town includes a tropical greenhouse; a sensory garden, where visitors are encouraged to touch, smell, or listen to various plants; historical gardens, which display the Mediterranean landscaping that the property's original owners planted in the 1930s; a garden designed to attract birds; and a cactus garden. The grounds are also home to Native Seeds/SEARCH, an organization that helps farmers throughout the Southwest and northern Mexico by collecting, growing, and selling seeds of crops that thrive in arid areas. The Prima Donna Café, open in high season, uses native foods to create sandwiches and salads. ☒ *2150 N. Alvernon Way,* ☎ *520/326–9686.* 🎫 *$3.* ⊙ *Garden daily 8:30-4:30; gift shop Mon.–Sat. 9–4, Sun. noon–4.*

Northern Tucson

Even those who have no sense of direction are guided around town by the imposing presence of the Santa Catalina Mountains on the northern rim of the Tucson valley. Whether as destinations in themselves or as a backdrop to other sights, the peaks are most impressive.

Numbers in the margin correspond to points of interest on the Tucson map.

Arizona-Sonora Desert Museum, **26**
Biosphere 2, **22**
Botanical Gardens, **17**
Colossal Cave, **32**
De Grazia's Gallery in the Sun, **20**
Fort Lowell, **18**
G-P Toy Train Museum, Ltd., **24**
Int'l Wildlife Museum, **28**
Mission San Xavier del Bac, **29**
Mt. Lemmon, **21**
Old Tucson Studios, **27**
Pima Air Museum, **31**
Playmaxx/The Yozeum, **16**
Reid Park Zoo, **15**
Sabino Canyon, **19**
Saguaro N. P. East, **33**
Saguro N. P. West, **25**
Titan Missile Museum, **30**
Tohonó Chul Park, **23**

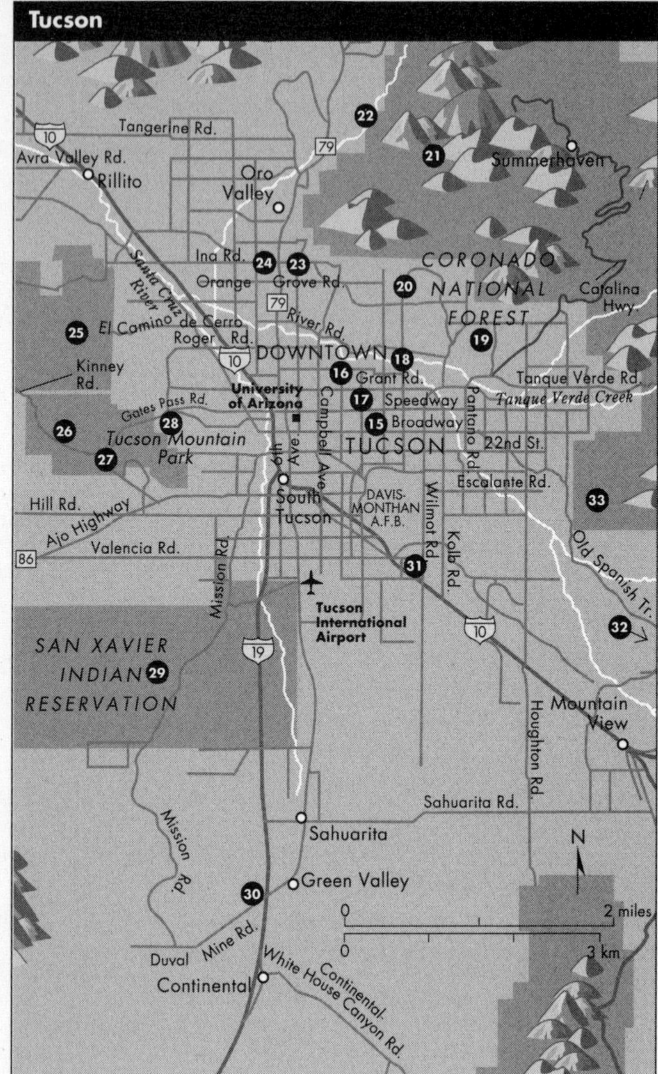

Sights to See

22 **Biosphere 2.** You may have heard some of the publicity surrounding the once controversial project taking place in the little town of Oracle, some 45 minutes north of central Tucson. The least flattering accounts described it as eight cultists locked up together in a terrarium for two years in preparation for colonizing Mars. But not long after the original "crew" left the enclosure in 1994, Biosphere 2 went legit: The bankroller of the project, Texas oil billionaire Edward P. Bass, ejected the original directors and hired a group of distinguished scientists to do research on the sealed

ecosystem. In November 1995, Columbia University and Biosphere 2 signed a five-year agreement under which Columbia's Lamont-Doherty Earth Observatory will manage and direct all the Biosphere's scientific, educational, and visitor-center operations. (The university hasn't been wild about the release of the 1996 Pauly Shore comedy, *Bio-Dome,* which pokes fun at the project's early flakiness.)

The miniature world created within Biosphere includes tropical rain forest, savanna, desert, thorn scrub, marsh, ocean, and agricultural areas, including almost 4,000 plant and animal species. Guided walking tours, which last about two hours, don't enter the sealed sphere, but a film and cut-away model explain the project, and visitors are able to look inside through observation areas. The Canyon Café, overlooking the Santa Catalina Mountains, offers health-oriented meals and snacks, and there are plenty of gift shops to browse through. Reasonably priced hotel suites with excellent views are available on Biosphere's premises. Pets and picnicking are not permitted on the site. ⊠ *AZ 77, mile marker 96.5,* ☎ *520/896–6200 or 800/828–2462.* 🎫 *$12.95.* ⏲ *Daily 9–5; guided tours 9–4 (every hr on the hr).*

20 **De Grazia's Gallery in the Sun.** First-time visitors to the area will especially enjoy the museum, gallery, workshop, former home, and grave site of the Arizonan artist Ted De Grazia, who depicted Southwest Indian and Mexican life. Built by the artist himself with the help of Native American friends, the sprawling, spacious single-story museum utilizes only natural material from the surrounding desert. None of De Grazia's original oil paintings, sculptures, or watercolors are for sale, but the museum's gift shop offers a wide selection of cards, prints, lithographs, ceramics, and books by and about the colorful artist. ⊠ *6300 N. Swan Rd.,* ☎ *520/299–9191.* 🎫 *Free.* ⏲ *Daily 10–4.*

24 **Gadsden-Pacific Toy Train Museum, Ltd.** Children of all ages will enjoy this museum in the northern sector of the Foothills Mall, across from the administrative offices. Visitors can make the 11 little locomotives run around the room by pushing various buttons; miniature cranes, milk cars, and forkloaders add to the action. Collectors'-edition trains, produced by members of the club that operates the nonprofit museum, are sold here. ⊠ *7401 N. La Cholla Blvd. at Ina Rd.,* ☎ *520/742–7191 (mall number; no* ☎ *in museum).* 🎫 *Free.* ⏲ *Fri. 10–7, Sat. 10–6, Sun. noon–5.*

21 **Mt. Lemmon.** One of the Santa Catalina Mountains, Mt. Lemmon is the southernmost ski slope of the continental United States, but you don't have to be a skier to visit. In spring and fall you can enjoy picnicking and hiking in this lovely area, which has some 150 mi of well-marked and well-maintained trails; in summer the mountain's 9,157-foot elevation brings welcome relief from the heat. If you're making the trip in winter, check road conditions by calling ☎ 520/741–4991. And be sure to fill up the tank before you leave town any time of year, because there are no gas stations on Mt. Lemmon Highway, the road that winds and twists its way for 28 mi up the mountainside.

The journey up the mountain is interesting in itself: Every 1,000 feet of elevation is equivalent to traveling 300 mi north, so you'll move from typical Sonoran Desert plants in the foothills to vegetation similar to that found in southern Canada at the top. Along the way, you'll see rock formations that look as though they were carefully balanced against each other by architects from another planet.

At milepost 18, on the left hand side of the road when you're ascending, the **Palisades Ranger Station** can give you current information on the mountain's campgrounds, hiking trails, and picnic spots; it's also a good place to buy maps and books. It's open daily 9–4:30 in summer, 9–5 in winter. The station does not have a published telephone number, but you can call the Coronado National Forest at 520/749–8700 if you have any questions.

Just before you reach the ski resort, the tiny alpine-style village of **Summerhaven** features a couple of casual restaurants, lots of gift shops, and a few pleasant lodges.

Mt. Lemmon Highway ends at **Mt. Lemmon Ski Valley** (☎ 520/576–1321, or 520/576–1400 for a recorded snow report). Skiing here depends on natural conditions—there's no artificial snow—so call ahead. There are 16 runs, open daily, ranging from beginner to advanced. Lift tickets cost $25 for an all-day pass and $20 for a half day (starting at 1 PM); children 12 and under ski for $10 ($8 after 1 PM). Ski equipment can be rented, and private instruction starts at $30 an hour for private lessons; it's $10 for a two-hour group lesson. A $36 first-time skier's package includes equipment rental, a lesson, and a lift pass upon completion of the lesson. Even in off-season, visitors will enjoy a ride on the double chairlift that whisks them to the top of the slope—some 9,100 feet. The cost is $5 for adults and $2 for children 12 and under; for $10, a family pass will admit two adults and up to four children. Many ride the lift and then head out on one of several trails that crisscross the summit. ✉ *Take Tanque Verde Rd. to the Catalina Hwy., which becomes Mt. Lemmon Hwy. as you head north.*

NEED A BREAK? The **Iron Door** (☎ 520/576–1321) in Mt. Lemmon Ski Valley is open weekends 10–5:30, weekdays 10:30–5:30 (give or take half an hour, depending on the weather). In winter, the focus is on burgers, chili, corn bread, and soups; in warmer weather, lots of salads turn up on the menu. This place is popular on the weekends—parking can be tough.

★ ⑲ **Sabino Canyon.** All year round, but especially during summer, locals flock to this oasis in the northeast corner of town. Part of the Coronado National Forest but filled with saguaros and other desert flora and fauna, this is a good spot for hiking, picnicking, or enjoying the waterfalls, streams, natural swimming holes, and shade trees that provide a respite from the heat. No cars are allowed, but a narrated tram ride (about 45 minutes round-trip) takes you to the top of the canyon. You can hop off and on at any of the nine stops. There's also a tram ride to adjacent Bear Canyon. Magical nighttime tram tours are available by prepaid reservation only (☎ 520/749–2327) when there's a full moon and the weather is warm enough. ✉ *Sabino Canyon Rd. in the Santa Catalina foothills,* ☎ *520/749–2861 (recorded tram information) or 520/749–8700 (visitor center).* *Tram $5; Bear Canyon tram $3. Call for schedules.* ⏲ *Visitor center weekdays 8–4:30, weekends 8:30–4:30.*

★ ㉓ **Tohonó Chul Park.** A peaceful 48-acre retreat designed to promote the conservation of arid regions, Tohonó Chul—the name means "desert corner" in the language of the Tohonó O'odham Indians—features a demonstration garden, greenhouse, geology wall, and other exhibits that educate visitors about the unique area. Shady nooks and nature trails allow for leisurely sitting or strolling. Two gift shops, a small art gallery, a tearoom (☞ Dining, *below*), and, next door, the Haunted Bookshop (☞ Shopping, *below*) are additional reasons to visit this lovely landscaped setting. ✉ *7366 N. Paseo del Norte,* ☎ *520/742–6455.* *$2 suggested donation.* ⏲ *Park daily 7 AM–sunset; building Mon.–Sat. 9:30–5, Sun. 11–5.*

Western Tucson

If you're interested in the flora and fauna of the Sonoran Desert—as well as some of its appearances in the cinema—west is an ideal direction for you to take.

Numbers in the margin correspond to points of interest on the Tucson map.

Timing

Although the distances between the attractions in this area are not small, it's easy to tour all the sights in a single day since they're on a fairly direct route. The best plan is to set out in the cooler early morning to Saguaro National Park, which has no shaded areas (it's also the best time to see the wildlife at its liveliest). Just south of Saguaro National Park, the 17,000-acre Tucson Mountain Park contains the Arizona–Sonora Desert Museum and Old Tucson Studios theme park. Spend the rest of the morning at the Desert Museum, where you can have lunch at the Ironwood Terrace (in any case, allow at least two hours for your visit). The hottest time of the afternoon can be spent ducking in and out of attractions at Old Tucson or visiting the air-conditioned International Wildlife Museum, which is on the way back to town.

Sights to See

★ 26 **Arizona–Sonora Desert Museum.** The name "museum" is misleading; this delightful site is more like a beautifully planned zoo. In this microcosm of a desert environment, hummingbirds, cactus wrens, rattlesnakes, scorpions, bighorn sheep, and prairie dogs all busy themselves in natural habitats ingeniously planned to allow the visitor to look on without disturbing them. An Earth Sciences Center features a damp limestone cave and meteor and mineral displays that encourage visitors to feel the texture of the stones and inspect them under magnifying glasses. Exhibits and interactive programs change with the season. For example, during the spring visitors are invited to help identify local wildflowers.

The Ironwood Terrace restaurant, near the hummingbird exhibit, offers a variety of hot and cold sandwiches, along with burgers, soups, salads, and Mexican entrées. There's also a small coffee bar near the gift shop (which carries a tempting array of Native American jewelry as well as many terrific items made from minerals). Wheelchairs and strollers are available at the museum, but pets aren't allowed, so don't take them along. Confining them to the car in Arizona heat can kill them. ✉ *2021 N. Kinney Rd.,* ☎ *520/883–2702.* *$8.95.* ⏲ *Mar.–Sept., daily 7:30–6; Oct.–Feb., daily 8:30–5. Last ticket sales 1 hr before closing.*

28 **International Wildlife Museum.** A Petting Menagerie at this facility allows kids to touch a variety of animal skins; they can also learn about more than 200 species of birds and mammals from all over the world via interactive computers. There's a theater that shows wildlife films, an art gallery, a gift shop, and a vending machine area (the restaurant is currently closed but may be open by the time you read this). ✉ *4800 W. Gates Pass Rd.,* ☎ *520/617–1439.* *$5.* ⏲ *Daily 9–5.*

27 **Old Tucson Studios.** This film set–cum–theme park was seriously damaged by fire in 1995 and is currently under reconstruction. To find out

which of the former activities and exhibits will be reopened by early 1997—among them gunfights, magic shows, stunt shows, a petting farm, stagecoach rides, trail rides, and souvenir shops—and for current hours and prices, call when you get to town. ✉ *201 S. Kinney Rd. (inside Tucson Mountain Park),* ☎ *520/883-0100.*

★ 25 **Saguaro National Park West.** This is the smaller (24,000 acres) and most visited section of the national park that flanks Tucson, its eastern and western portions divided by the city. Together the sections are home to the world's largest concentration of the huge saguaro (pronounced "suh-*war*-oh") cactus, which is native to the Sonoran Desert and known for its towering height (often 50 feet) and arms that reach out in weird configurations. The cactus is ribbed vertically with accordion-like pleats that expand to store water gathered through its shallow roots during the infrequent desert rain showers. In the springtime (usually April or May), the giant succulent sports a tiny party hat of white blooms. At any time of year, the sight of these kings of the desert ruling over their quiet domain is awe-inspiring.

The slow-growing cacti (they can take up to 15 years to grow 1 foot) are protected by state and federal laws, so enjoy but don't disturb them. In recent years, they have suffered a decline because a decrease in the coyote population has led to an abundant rabbit population. Rabbits and other small animals nibble at the base of the young saguaro, gathering nutrients and water for survival and thereby hindering or halting the cactus's slow growth.

Before you venture into the desert, it's worth stopping in at the impressive visitor center. A sophisticated slide show (given every half hour from 8:30 to 4:30) offers a Native American perspective of the Saguaro cactus. An extremely lifelike display simulates the flora and fauna of the region. Walkways from the side of the center lead out onto short nature trails; you can obtain information about longer hiking trails that wind through the park. Ask how to get to Signal Hill, where you can inspect petroglyphs (rock drawings) left by the Hohokam Indians centuries ago. Keep in mind that desert critters such as snakes and scorpions aren't necessarily hostile unless you crowd them, so just watch your step and respect their habitat. ✉ *Kinney Rd.,* ☎ *520/733-5158.* *Free.* *Visitor center daily 8:30-5; park roads 6 AM-sunset.*

Southern Tucson

Those with an interest in the military and Spanish missions should head east on I-10; all these southern Tucson sights are easily accessible from the freeway.

Numbers in the margin correspond to points of interest on the Tucson map.

Sights to See

★ 29 **Mission San Xavier del Bac.** The oldest Catholic church in the United States still serving the community for which it was built, San Xavier was founded in 1692 by Father Eusebio Francisco Kino, who established 22 missions in northern Mexico and southern Arizona. It was constructed out of native materials by Franciscan missionaries between 1777 and 1797. Today it is owned by the Tohonó O'odham Indian tribe (the name means "desert people who have come from the earth").

The beauty of the mission, with elements of Spanish, Baroque, and *mudejar* (Spanish Islamic) architectural styles, is highlighted by the stark landscape against which it is set—thus the early nickname White Dove of the Desert. Inside, there's a wealth of painted statues, carvings, and frescoes. The mission has been called the Sistine Chapel of the United States by Paul Schwartzbaum, who worked on restoring Michelangelo's masterwork in Rome and is helping to supervise the restoration of the mission's artwork. Begun in 1992, the project is not expected to be completed until 1997. A visitor center in the front part of San Xavier del Bac offers displays of the history and architecture of the church. It's adjoined by a gift shop, open 9–5 in winter, 8–6 in summer.

Mass is celebrated daily at San Xavier. On Sunday and religious holidays, there's often a mariachi band—one of the many Mexican influences in evidence here. Call ahead for information about special celebrations.

Across the parking lot from the mission, **San Xavier Plaza** has a number of shops that sell fine Native American crafts. Look especially for jewelry, pottery, and baskets featuring man-in-the-maze designs and for friendship bowls, both particular to the Tohonó O'odham tribe. Works of the northern Arizona Hopi and Navajo are also represented. ✉ *San Xavier Rd., 9 mi southwest of Tucson on I–19,* ☎ *520/294–2624.*

NEED A BREAK? For wonderful Indian fry bread—large, round pieces of dough taken fresh from the hot oil and topped with all sorts of delicious possibilities—stop in the **Wa:k Snack Shop** (☎ 520/573-9191) at the back of San Xavier Plaza. You can also have breakfast or a Mexican lunch here.

31 **Pima Air Museum.** This huge facility ranks among the largest private collections of historic aircraft in the world. More than 200 flight machines are displayed on 65 acres both indoors and outdoors. You'll see a full-scale replica of the Wright brothers' 1903 Wright Flyer and a mock-up of the X-15, the world's fastest aircraft. Visitors can tour the surprisingly low-key presidential plane used on official business by both John F. Kennedy and Lyndon B. Johnson. World War II veterans find the museum particularly moving, but all ages should enjoy this walk through U.S. aviation history. ✉ *6000 E. Valencia Rd.,* ☎ *520/574–9658.* *$6; tram ticket $2.* *Daily 9–5 (last admission at 4).*

30 **Titan Missile Museum.** During the Cold War, Tucson was ringed by 18 Titan II missiles. Of the total 54 such missiles that existed in the U.S., the only one that was left intact when the Salt II treaty with the Soviet Union was signed has been turned into this rather sobering museum. Guided tours take visitors down into the command post where a ground crew of four lived. Among the fascinating sights is a 114-foot, 165-ton, two-stage liquid-fuel rocket. Now empty, it originally held a nuclear payload with 214 times the explosive power of the bomb that destroyed Hiroshima. ✉ *1580 W. Duval Mine Rd.,* ☎ *520/791–2929.* *$6.* *Nov.–Apr., daily 9–5; May–Oct., Wed.–Sun. 9–5 (last tour at 4).*

Eastern Tucson

Tucson's last frontier, eastern Tucson is gradually succumbing to development, but it still remains a relatively unspoiled area.

Numbers in the margin correspond to points of interest on the Tucson map.

Sights to See

32 **Colossal Cave.** The limestone grotto that lies 20 mi east of Tucson and 6 mi north of I–10 is the largest dry cavern in the world. Indeed, parts of it have yet to be explored. Informed guides discuss the fascinating crystal formations and relate the many romantic tales surrounding the cave, including the legend that an enormous sum of money stolen in a stagecoach robbery is hidden here and has never been recovered. ✉ *In-*

tersection of Colossal Cave Rd. and Old Spanish Trail Rd., ☎ *520/647–7275.* 🎫 *$6.50.* ⏲ *Oct.–mid-Mar., Mon.–Sat. 9–5, Sun. and holidays 9–6; mid-Mar.–Sept., Mon.–Sat. 8–6, Sun. and holidays 8–7.*

33 **Saguaro National Park East.** The eastern portion of the national park that sandwiches Tucson covers more than 67,000 acres and climbs through five climate zones; it offers the opportunity for dramatic hikes through the foothills of the Rincon Mountains. An 8-mile paved Cactus Forest Drive leads to a variety of trailheads and picnic areas. Ask for a detailed map at the visitor center. See the Saguaro National Park West listing in the Western Tucson section, *above*, for more information about the unique cactus that are concentrated here. ✉ *Old Spanish Trail; signs will direct you to the visitor center, about 16 mi east of the center of town,* ☎ *520/733–5153.* 🎫 *$4 per vehicle, $2 individuals entering by bicycle or on foot.* ⏲ *Visitor center daily 8:30–5; park roads 7 AM–sunset.*

DINING

Dress is more casual in Tucson than in many cities its size. Very few restaurants request that men wear jackets to dinner. The issue of whether to wear a tie takes on a new slant here—there's at least one cowboy steak house where anyone caught wearing such formal neckwear will have it snipped off and added to the restaurant's collection of city-slicker garb.

Late fall, winter, and early spring make up the high season for travel here. It's a good idea to call ahead for reservations during these busy months. Some restaurants close for a portion of the summer, taking advantage of the slow time to make repairs or give staff vacations. Again, it's wise to call ahead, this time to ensure that your intended destination is open and hasn't altered its hours. Don't assume, incidentally, that you'll have to dine indoors in summer—many Tucson restaurants cool their outdoor patios with a misting system.

While Tucson's variety of restaurants is akin to that of its big-city cousins, the city doesn't offer much in the way of late-night dining. Most restaurants in town are shuttered by 10 PM. Some spots that keep later hours are noted below. In addition, two locations of **Coffee, Etc.** (✉ 2830 N. Campbell Ave., ☎ 520/881–8070; 6091 N. Oracle Rd., ☎ 520/544–8588), which has good coffee and a varied menu, are open 24 hours.

CATEGORY	COST*
$$$$	over $35
$$$	$25–$35
$$	$15–$25
$	under $15

**per person, excluding drinks, service, and 7% sales tax (5% state plus 2% city)*

American

$$$ ✕ **Rancher's Club.** The four wood grills on which most of the foods are prepared are the key to the success of this upscale western-style restaurant, with its dark wood, mounted animal heads, and sidesaddles. As the friendly staff explains, different woods impart different flavors to foods, so diners must be ready to make a choice from two grills: Mesquite wood is offered every day, and hickory, sassafras, and wild cherry alternate during the week. The lobster is especially good, and the steaks are excellent, too (a note on the menu advises "Our steaks are copious and we encourage you to share"). An array of sauces, butters, and condiments provides diners with interesting ways to flavor their food. ✉ *5151 E. Grant Rd.,* ☎ *520/321–7621. AE, DC, MC, V. Closed Sun. No lunch Sat.*

$$–$$$ ★ ✕ **The Kingfisher Grill.** A relatively new kid in town, the Kingfisher has drawn critical kudos and a loyal following for its fine regional American cuisine. The chic setting—low lighting, bright turquoise and neon contrasting with warm brick walls and comfy black banquettes—is matched by the innovative menu (which changes seasonally). You might find mesquite-grilled pork loin chops or crayfish étouffée n the menu. From 10 to midnight, a late-night menu features soups, salads, burgers, and selections from the oyster bar. ✉ *2564 E. Grant Rd.,* ☎ *520/323–7739. AE, D, DC, MC, V. No lunch weekends.*

Continental

$$$$ ✕ **Anthony's.** *The* special-occasion restaurant for many Tucsonans, Anthony's offers elegance and a superb view of the city. Pink linen, stemmed crystal, pink-rim china, and—on the glassed-in terrace—lighting that precludes your seeing your dining companion very well, add to the romantic atmosphere. Such dishes as the seafood relleno (an Anaheim chili stuffed with Jack cheese, shrimp, and scallops) or the veal Sonoita (sliced veal tenderloin with roasted garlic, sun-dried tomatoes, and goat cheese) put a contemporary spin on the Continental menu. Chateaubriand and lamb Wellington are classic examples. The wine list is among the largest in Arizona, and service is uncharacteristically formal for Tucson. A classical pianist who plays from 7 PM nightly draws locals to the cocktail lounge. ✉ *6440 N. Campbell Ave.,* ☎ *520/299–1771. AE, DC, MC, V. No lunch weekends.*

$$$$ ★ ✕ **Ventana Room.** This lovely dining room in the Loews Ventana Canyon Resort is a triumph of understated elegance. Muted colors and low ceilings don't compete with the spectacular views, either of the lights of Tucson or the towering waterfall on the resort property. The contemporary Continental menu, which changes seasonally, has a California-inspired emphasis on lower-fat, lower-cholesterol preparation and beautiful presentation. Daily specials might include grilled loin of venison with pecans or seared ahi tuna crusted with coriander. The award-winning wine list meets the high standards of the menu, and service is impeccable without being overbearing. ✉ *7000 N. Resort Dr.,* ☎ *520/299–2020. Jacket required in high season. AE, D, DC, MC, V. No lunch.*

$$$ ✕ **Arizona Inn Restaurant.** This Tucson classic welcomes old friends and new visitors alike. Sit out on the patio for a lovely view of the grounds of this historic lodging, or enjoy the view through huge windows in the dining room, a light, airy place with many 1930s southwestern details. A fire warms the room on chilly evenings. Steamed fish of the day served with ginger and leeks is a specialty, and the mesquite-smoked quail is also popular. Locals love to come in for Sunday brunch or a civilized afternoon high tea in the library (Thanksgiving through Easter only). There is no longer a dress code, but you'll fit in best if you put on a bit of the ritz for dinner. ✉ *2200 E. Elm St.,* ☎ *520/325–1541. AE, MC, V.*

French

$$$–$$$$ ✕ **Le Rendez-vous.** The clientele is a bit blue-haired and the service a tad hovering, but you'll hardly notice as you concentrate on the excellent cuisine. The most expensive French restaurant in town prepares duck à l'orange that is as crispy as it should be and veal medallions with Calvados as tender. If you start with the garlicky escargots, you won't be disappointed, but be prepared if you decide to finish with the excellent tart Tatin: All eyes will be drawn to your table when your dessert is immolated in brandy. Recently, a spa menu and bistro menu have been introduced at dinnertime for those who are watching their

weight and their wallets. The lunch menu is wide-ranging and rather moderately priced. The intimate dining rooms are light, with colorful art deco prints, and the sommelier is as entertaining as he is helpful. ✉ *3844 E. Fort Lowell Rd.,* ☎ *520/323–7373. AE, D, DC, MC, V. Closed Mon. No lunch weekends.*

$$$ ✕ **Le Bistro.** Set in a nondescript building on a busy road near the university, Le Bistro is one of the prettiest restaurants in town: Potted palms tower over tables covered with chic burgundy-and-black cloths splashed with pink flowers, and Art Nouveau–style etched mirrors grace the walls. The setting is matched by the creations of young chef-owner Laurent Reux. Born in Brittany, he offers many fish and shellfish dishes inspired by the seascape of his native region, such as supreme of salmon in a ginger crust with lime butter. Another popular specialty is Long Island duck in a raspberry vinaigrette. A revolving glass dessert display at the entrance will leave you pondering throughout the meal whether to opt for the triple-chocolate mousse cake, say, or the Key-lime tart. Lunch prices are very reasonable. ✉ *2574 N. Campbell Ave.,* ☎ *502/327–3086. D, MC, V. No lunch weekends.*

$$–$$$ ✕ **Café Beaujolais.** Opened in 1995 on the northwest side of town, this appealing eatery has already etched its niche in Tucson's dining scene. Tapestry chairs with wrought-iron ivy designs, pink walls, and the sounds of Mozart or Bach provide a nice backdrop for the short, classic bistro menu. Mushrooms baked in a puff pastry shell with a touch of Stilton are a delicious but rich starter; you won't be settling if you opt for the house salad, crunchy with walnuts and fresh greens. The lamb chops with garlic mashed potatoes are the ultimate in comfort food; the lighter mussels in a white wine and shallot sauce won't disappoint, either. Interesting and reasonable wines are available by the glass. Crème brûlée aficionados will be very happy with the almond-redolent version made in house, as all the desserts are. ✉ *5931 N. Oracle Rd.,* ☎ *520/887–7359. AE, D, MC, V. Closed Mon. No lunch weekends.*

Guatemalan

$ ✕ **Maya Quetzal.** This friendly, family-owned restaurant on trendy 4th Avenue is inexpensive enough to allow those unfamiliar with Guatemalan food—and who isn't?—to sample lots of different dishes. Try the vegetarian *paches* (potato-meal tamales topped with a mild red pepper sauce) or the *pollo en jocón* (chicken with cilantro-flavor green sauce). Friday's chicken special comes in a rich, yogurt-based sauce. A large, brightly colored mural, Guatemalan crafts, and a pleasant patio all add to the congenial atmosphere. The food may be a bit bland for palates expecting Mexican fire, but you'll be eating for a good cause. A portion of all profits go to help Guatemalan refugees. ✉ *429 N. 4th Ave.,* ☎ *520/622–8207. Reservations not accepted. MC, V. Closed Sun.*

Indian

$–$$ ✕ **New Delhi Palace.** Vegetarians, carnivores, and seafood lovers will all find something to enjoy at this elegant Indian restaurant. The congenial staff is helpful in explaining the menu, which features a wide variety of tandoori dishes, curries, rice, and breads. The "heat" of each dish can be adjusted to individual preference by the chef. If you're undecided, a lunch buffet and complete dinners offer nice samplings of several dishes. The atmosphere is quiet, with Indian music played softly, and tasteful displays of Indian objets d'art. ✉ *6751 E. Broadway,* ☎ *520/296–8585. AE, DC, MC, V.*

Italian

$$$–$$$$ ✉ **Daniel's.** A fine northern Italian menu, an excellent wine and beer list, the largest selection of single-malt Scotches in town, and service that is attentive but not overbearing draw a sophisticated crowd to this chic art deco–style restaurant. The polenta and Gorgonzola appetizer, the veal scaloppini with wild mushrooms, and *spaghetti alla putanesca* with olives, capers, and tomatoes are among the many recommended standards. Dining on the terrace during one of St. Phillips Plaza's outdoor concerts is a real treat. ✉ *St. Phillips Plaza, 4340 N. Campbell Ave.,* ☎ *520/742–3200. AE, DC, MC, V. No lunch.*

$$–$$$ ★ ✕ **Boccata.** In a tasteful mall in the foothills of the Santa Catalina Mountains, this pretty restaurant serves excellent northern Italian cuisine, with some southern French dishes for good measure. The flowered tablecloths match the delicate aubergine and Tuscan-yellow walls, and the artwork ranges from contemporary to Victorian whimsy. A good wine list complements such entrées as penne *ciao bella* (with grilled chicken and a delicate white wine and Gorgonzola sauce) and filet mignon with a Madera truffle and foie gras sauce; the steamed mussel appetizer is plentiful. Go Gallic for dessert: The profiteroles, with fresh-made vanilla ice cream and dripping warm chocolate sauce, are superb. Boccata serves Sunday brunch. ✉ *5605 E. River Rd.,* ☎ *520/577–9309. AE, DC, MC, V. No lunch.*

$$–$$$ ✕ **Vivace.** Daniel Scordato has had his hand in some of the best Italian restaurants in town, and his latest venture continues to be a big hit. During high season, Vivace fills up even on weekday nights, mostly with a well-heeled, well-turned-out crowd. It's all very industrial chic—gray columns, black iron chairs, open kitchen—but this is still Arizona, which means the black-and-white–clad servers are not SoHo frosty to match. Appetizers are a little pricey compared with the rest of the menu, though the grilled shrimp in a phyllo cup with a tomato, basil, and garlic sauce is hard to resist. Go for one of the good salads or a wonderful side dish of sautéed spinach with garlic if you're looking to economize. For a lighter alternative to such dishes as rich osso buco, try the linguine with grilled salmon; that way, you'll have room for spumoni, made on the premises to perfection. One caveat: The room can get very noisy. ✉ *4811 E. Grant Rd., Suite 155,* ☎ *520/795–7221. MC, V. No lunch Sun.*

$$ ✕ **Gavi.** Tucson has its share of good Italian restaurants, but this is one of the few that really feel . . . well, ethnic, even though it's in a strip mall on a major road on the far east side of town. There's almost always a line to get into the small dining room, decorated with pictures of the Milan championship soccer team. An open kitchen lets you watch while specials such as clams Terrantini (fresh clams with marinara sauce over spaghettini) or staples like rich fettuccine carbonara are being prepared. The huge wine list includes a Chianti by the glass for a retro $1.25. ✉ *7865 E. Broadway Blvd.,* ☎ *520/290–8380. AE, D, DC, MC, V. No lunch.*

$ ✕ **Pappy's.** Come here for huge portions of Italian standards served in a pleasant atmosphere—plush booths, white tablecloths, and a small, tree-shaded patio. You can order a variety of pastas with assorted chicken, seafood, meat, or vegetable toppings, or opt for the hearty lasagna or fettuccine Alfredo. Prices are generally very reasonable, and the cold pasta primavera with chicken is a serious bargain at $4.95. Just down the block from the Temple of Music and Art, Pappy's is ideal for a pretheater dinner (just leave the garlic-redolent doggy bag in the car when you go to the show). Call ahead for hours, which vary throughout the week and seasons. ✉ *375 S. Stone Ave.,* ☎ *520/882–8908. DC, MC, V.*

Japanese

$$ ✕ **Yamato.** Colorful paper lanterns line the walls of this modest eatery, tucked away in a strip mall near the university. A sushi bar serves fish flown in daily from California, and a number of combination dinners

such as shrimp tempura and teriyaki chicken are available. *Yaki soba* (beef and vegetables heaped on wheat noodles) makes a tasty, hearty meal. Many of Yamato's Japanese patrons gather on Saturday night from 10 PM to 1 AM for laser karaoke sing-alongs. ✉ *857 E. Grant Rd.,* ☎ *520/624–3377. AE, MC, V. Closed Sun. No lunch Sat.*

Malaysian

$ ✕ **Seri Melaka.** Malaysian food, like Thai, uses plenty of curry, coconut, and other tasty condiments in its sauces. This popular restaurant on the east side of town is an excellent place to try the cuisine and to indulge in good versions of such dishes as *satay* (grilled meat on a skewer with peanut sauce) and *lemak* (shrimp or chicken with vegetables in a sweet curry sauce). An extensive selection of well-prepared Chinese dishes is also on the menu. There's a buffet at lunchtime seven days a week. ✉ *6133 E. Broadway,* ☎ *520/747–7811. AE, D, DC, MC, V.*

Mediterranean

$$ ✕ **Athens.** A Greek oasis of tranquillity off bustling 4th Avenue, Athens creates a serene Mediterranean atmosphere with its lace curtains, wooden wainscoting, white stucco walls, and potted plants. Order a dish of creamy *taramasalata* (Greek caviar). Follow it with *kotopoulo stin pita* (grilled chicken breast with a yogurt-cucumber sauce on fresh-baked pita), a better deal than the skewered version of the same dish. If it's Greek comfort food you're after, order the moussaka or the *pastitsio* (a pasta-, meat-, and bechamel-filled lasagna). There's a nice selection of retsina wine. ✉ *500 N. 4th Ave., No. 6,* ☎ *520/624–6886. AE, D, DC, MC, V. Closed Sun. No lunch.*

$$ ✕ **Olive Tree.** In an appealing Santa Fe–style building, the Olive Tree serves up fine versions of such Greek standards as moussaka, shish kebab, and stuffed grape leaves but also includes more unusual dishes on its menu. The Lamb Bandit is baked in foil with two types of cheese, potatoes, and vegetables. Daily fresh-fish specials are broiled in garlic, oregano, and olive oil and served with a well-prepared orzo. This is not light cuisine. If you don't have room for supersweet baklava, a cup of strong Greek coffee makes for a satisfying finish. ✉ *7000 E. Tanque Verde Rd.,* ☎ *520/298–1845. DC, MC, V. No lunch Sun.*

$–$$ ✕ **Le Mediterranean.** A generally nondescript dining room, pleasant enough in a pastel contemporary mode, gives little hint of the exotic fare on the menu. In addition to Greek dishes like moussaka and lamb kebab, there are also good versions of Middle Eastern specialties, such as shawarma (beef marinated with tahini sauce) and falafel. When ordering, keep in mind that the portions are hefty. The mashed eggplant appetizer, for example, comes with huge amounts of olives, carrots, and radishes. On weekends, a belly dancer winds her way through the tables. ✉ *4955 North Sabino Canyon Rd.,* ☎ *520/529–1330. AE, D, DC, MC, V.*

Mexican

$–$$ ★ ✕ **Café Poca Cosa.** Arguably Tucson's best restaurant, Café Poca Cosa serves consistently innovative Mexican fare in a colorful, lively setting. Eschewing the cheese-saturated Sonoran standbys, Mexico City–born chef-owner Susana Davila creates exciting recipes inspired by different regions of her native land. The menu, which changes daily, might include *pollo à mole* (chicken in a spicy chocolate-based sauce) or pork *pìbil* (made with a tangy Yucatan barbecue seasoning). Locals were happy for Susana's success after she got a huge write-up in *Gourmet* magazine, but are grumpy because it's so much harder to get a table these days. Call in advance for dinner reservations in high season. The tiny original restaurant across the street (20 S. Scott Ave.), also a lively treat, is open for breakfast and lunch during the week. ✉ *88 E. Broadway,* ☎ *520/622–6400. MC, V. Closed Sun.*

$–$$ ✕ **El Charro Café.** Started by Monica Flin in 1922 and run by her grandniece and her grandniece's husband today, El Charro still serves excellent versions of the American-Mexican staples Flin claims to have originated—chimichangas (flour tortillas rolled around seasoned beef or chicken and deep-fried) and cheese crisps, most notably. Daily "fitness-fare" specials such as seafood enchiladas are delicious as well as healthful. You can dine outside on the front porch or inside in one of the bright, cheerful dining rooms. A lounge serves appetizers and drinks. Next door, a gift shop sells mementos of this Tucson classic. ✉ *311 N. Court Ave.,* ☎ *520/622–1922. AE, D, MC, V.*

$–$$ ✕ **El Minuto Café.** This brightly decorated, bustling restaurant in Tucson's historic barrio is a good bet for those seeking a late meal downtown. It's open until 1:30 AM Friday and Saturday, 10 PM the rest of the week. In business for more than 50 years, El Minuto serves up crispy chimichangas, huge burritos, and green corn tamales (in season) made just right. The spicy menudo is a great hangover remedy (just don't ask what's in it if you don't already know). All the ingredients are fresh, and the Mexican beer selection is large. ✉ *354 S. Main Ave.,* ☎ *520/882–4145. Reservations essential for 6 or more. AE, D, DC, MC, V.*

$–$$ ✕ **South Tucson/4th Avenue.** Every Tucsonan you meet will argue the merits of a favorite "real" Mexican restaurant, but invariably it's on or near 4th Avenue in South Tucson. Technically a separate city, South Tucson has a large Mexican-American population and thus many authentic and inexpensive places to find good south-of-the-border cuisine. Among the most popular are **Crossroads** (✉ 2602 S. 4th Ave., ☎ 520/624–0395), **Gran Guadalajara** (✉ 2527 S. 4th Ave., ☎ 520/620–1321); **Guillermo's Double L** (✉ 1830 S. 4th Ave., ☎ 520/792–1585), **La Hacienda** (✉ 4207 S. 6th Ave., ☎ 520/889–6613), **Micha's** (✉ 2908 S. 4th Ave., ☎ 520/623–5307), and **Mi Nidito** (✉ 1813 S. 4th Ave., ☎ 520/622–5081), all open for both lunch and dinner. You'd be hard-pressed to have a bad meal—or a bad time—at any of these friendly, informal places. Many have mariachi bands on the weekends. MasterCard and Visa are accepted at most.

Southwestern

$$$–$$$$ ★ ✕ **Janos.** Notable both for its setting—the historic Stevens House, an adobe home built in 1855—and its food, this downtown restaurant adjacent to the Tucson Museum of Art offers innovative and superlative Southwest menus created by chef-owner Janos Wilder. A series of small, flower-filled dining rooms create an intimate, elegant atmosphere. Typical offerings include a mushroom-and-Brie-stuffed chili appetizer and pan-seared salmon with a smoky maple syrup glaze; the baklava with apricots and macadamia nuts is amazing. Combinations are usually very successful, but the high prices make the occasional failure all the more disappointing. The summer and fall $12.95 dinner specials allow the less well-heeled to indulge in a meal here. ✉ *150 N. Main Ave.,* ☎ *520/884–9426. AE, DC, MC, V. Closed Sun. Nov.–mid-May; Sun. and Mon. late May–Nov. No lunch.*

$$$–$$$$ ✕ **The Tack Room.** This restaurant has won many awards for its food, and the setting—in a rustic but elegant old adobe on the grounds of a former resort—is romantic, but the service is a tad overfussy and the menu has rested on its laurels for too long. It's also irritating to pay extra for such standard accompaniments to expensive entrées as potatoes and vegetables. That said, it's still worth coming here for a dress-up splurge. Dark-wood beams and furnishings and a blue-and-maroon color scheme are complemented by the lighter dusty-rose linen. Walls are hung with southwestern landscapes by local artists. Arizona four-

pepper steak flavored with different chilies is a favorite, as is the rack of lamb for two, prepared with mesquite honey, cilantro, and southwestern limes. ✉ *2800 N. Sabino Canyon Rd., ☎ 520/722–2800. AE, D, DC, MC, V. Closed Mon. mid-May–mid-Dec. and 1st 2 wks of July. No lunch.*

$$–$$$ ✕ **Café Terra Cotta.** Everything about this restaurant says Southwest—from the decor, with its bright pastels and bleached woods, to the food, which features such contemporary Southwest specialties as prawns stuffed with herbed goat cheese, pork tenderloin with black beans, and pizza with artichokes and herbed mozzarella. The garlic-custard appetizer is superb. Café Terra Cotta offers an impressive by-the-glass California wine list and a tasty Sunday brunch. This is the place for native yupsters and their out-of-town guests. ✉ *St. Philip's Plaza, 4310 N. Campbell Ave., ☎ 520/577–8100. AE, D, DC, MC, V.*

$$–$$$ ✕ **Presidio Grill.** If it weren't for the saguaro cactus flanking the window, you might at first think you were in one of New York's chic downtown haunts, with stylish black booths and art deco room dividers. But the food is southwestern all the way. Dinner entrées include chicken Santa Fe, served with black beans, flour tortillas, grilled scallions, and two types of salsa; and an eggplant, artichoke-heart, onion, and sun-dried tomato pizza. In the University of Arizona area and across the street from the city's main art cinema, this place is open unusually late (for Tucson) on weekends. The bar, which has a nice selection of beer and wines by the glass, sees a lot of singles action. ✉ *3352 E. Speedway Blvd., ☎ 520/327–4667. AE, MC, V.*

$$ ✕ **Tohonó Chul Tea Room.** The food is fine, though it's not the reason to make the drive to the northwest part of town. What's unique here is the setting. The tearoom is nestled in a wildlife sanctuary and surrounded by a fantastic cactus garden. Although the tearoom is typically southwestern, with lots of Mexican tile and light wood and a cobblestone patio, the menu covers southwestern, Mexican, and American dishes. House favorites include chicken enchiladas made with Monterey Jack cheese, corn, and green chilies, and a sliced-tomato-and-basil sandwich served on French sourdough bread. Sunday brunch is especially good—which can mean long waits in high season. It's open from 8 to 5. ✉ *7366 N. Paseo del Norte, ☎ 520/797–1711. AE, D, MC, V.*

Steakhouses

$$ ✕ **Li'l Abner's.** This Old West institution in the Butterfield Express stagecoach rest stop, which dates from the early 1800s, draws locals, who go straight for the mesquite-broiled 2-pound porterhouse steaks. There's nothing here for vegetarians, except for the salad, beans, salsa, and garlic bread that come with all the entrées. On Friday through Sunday, you can chow down to the sounds of a live country band. It's about a 20-minute drive from downtown. ✉ *8501 N. Silverbell Rd., ☎ 520/744–2800. MC, V. No lunch.*

$$ ✕ **Pinnacle Peak Steakhouse.** No nouvelle-cuisine fans welcome here: Anybody caught eating fish tacos or cactus jelly would probably be hanged from the rafters—along with all the ties snipped from loco city slickers. This is a cowboy steak house that the tourists love. It's fun, it's Tucson, and the food ain't half bad, either, partner. Excellent mesquite-broiled steak comes with salad and pinto beans. If you can handle more after all that, try the hot apple cobbler with vanilla ice cream. The restaurant is part of Trail Dust Town, a re-creation of a turn-of-the-century town, complete with an "opera" house featuring cancan girls and a barbershop quartet, souvenir shops, and an old-time photographer's studio, where you can have your picture taken in western garb. ✉ *6541 E. Tanque Verde Rd., ☎ 520/296–0911. Reservations not accepted. AE, D, DC, MC, V. No lunch.*

Vegetarian

$ ✕ **Govinda.** One of two places in town with a strictly nonmeat menu, this Hare Krishna–run restaurant offers reasonably priced all-you-can-eat lunch and dinner buffets that include vegan options. Selections of hot and cold dishes vary daily, but ingredients are consistently fresh and the food is tasty, if not particularly spicy. There are three areas to eat: one with low tables and cushions (diners must remove their shoes to eat in here); an adjoining light-wood dining room; and an outdoor patio with a snack bar from which you can hear the squawks of the resident peacocks. No alcohol is served or permitted. ✉ *711 E. Blacklidge Dr.,* ☎ *520/792–0630. Reservations not accepted. MC, V. Closed Sun.–Tues.*

$ ✕ **Sprouts.** A Japanese-style spareness lends a soothing, zenlike quality to this place, which doubles as a gallery for local art. Items on the small, organic menu are tasty and well prepared. The huge veggie burger, served with a generous side salad, is among the best around, and those who like to pretend they're eating meat will also enjoy the Thursday-night special, a pork-style barbecue made of tempeh. Pass on the boring desserts and go for a fruit smoothie if you crave something sweet. The menu is the same for lunch and dinner, making this popular 4th Avenue locale a little steep for the middle of the day but a bargain at night. Only brunch is served on Sunday. ✉ *621 N. 4th Ave.,* ☎ *520/620–1938. Reservations not accepted. AE, MC, V. No dinner Sun.*

LODGING

The **Arizona Association of Bed and Breakfast Inns** (✉ Box 7186, Phoenix 85011, ☎ 602/277–0775) can provide referrals to member inns in the area. Seven of the larger, more professionally run inns in town have formed **Premier Bed & Breakfast Inns of Tucson** (✉ 316 E. Speedway Blvd., 85705, ☎ 520/628–1800 or 800/628–5654, FAX 520/792–1880). Write or call for a brochure. **Old Pueblo HomeStays** (✉ Box 13603, Tucson 85732, ☎ FAX 520/790–2399 or 800/333–9776) specializes in smaller, more casual bed-and-breakfasts in southern Arizona and northern Mexico but also lists a number of the larger inns.

Prices vary widely between seasons. Room rates in summer—generally defined as April 15 through October 1—are sometimes as much as 60% lower than those in the winter, and visitors who don't mind warmer weather can get real deals at resorts that are quite pricey during the busy time. Note: Unless you book months in advance, you'll be hard-pressed to find a hotel room at any price in Tucson the week before and during the huge gem and mineral show (February 13–16 in 1997).

CATEGORY	COST*
$$$$	over $160
$$$	$110–$160
$$	$70–$110
$	under $70

**All prices are for a standard double room, excluding room tax (9.5% in Tucson and 6.5% in Pima County). Prices given here are winter, or high-season, rates.*

Hotels

$$$–$$$$ ★ 🏨 **Arizona Inn.** This sprawling lodging, which has remained in the same family since it opened in 1930, is an oasis in the center of town: Although close to the university and many sights, the inn's beautifully landscaped 14 acres seem far away from it all. The spacious rooms are

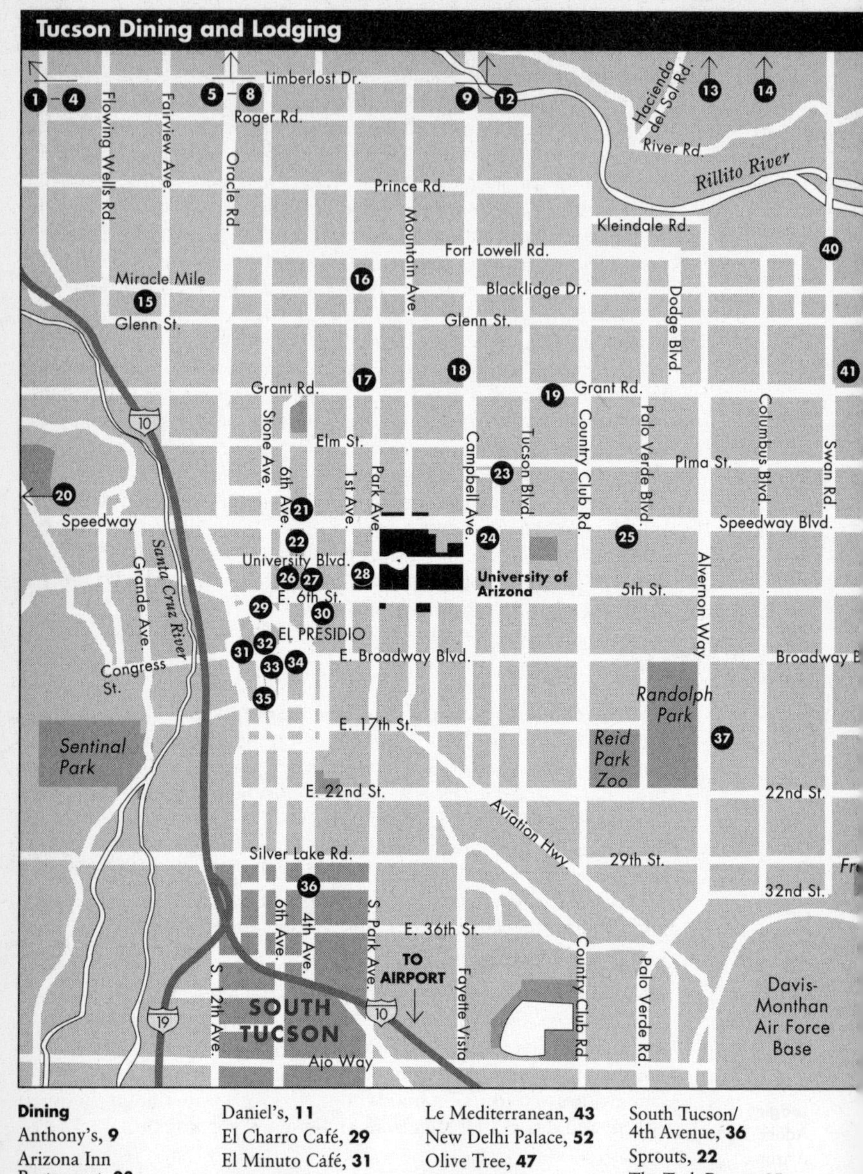

Dining

Anthony's, **9**
Arizona Inn Restaurant, **23**
Athens, **27**
Le Bistro, **18**
Boccata, **42**
Café Beaujolais, **5**
Café Poca Cosa, **33**
Café Terra Cotta, **10**
Daniel's, **11**
El Charro Café, **29**
El Minuto Café, **31**
Gavi, **54**
Govinda, **16**
Janos, **32**
The Kingfisher Grill, **19**
Li'l Abner's, **1**
Maya Quetzal, **30**
Le Mediterranean, **43**
New Delhi Palace, **52**
Olive Tree, **47**
Pappy's, **35**
Pinnacle Peak Steakhouse, **48**
Presidio Grill, **25**
Rancher's Club, **49**
Le Rendez-Vous, **40**
Seri Melaka, **51**
South Tucson/ 4th Avenue, **36**
Sprouts, **22**
The Tack Room, **45**
Tohonó Chul Tea Room, **2**
Ventana Room, **38**
Vivace, **41**
Yamato, **17**

Lodging

Adobe Rose Inn, **24**
Arizona Inn, **23**
Best Western Ghost Ranch Lodge, **15**
Canyon Ranch, **44**
Casa Alegre, **21**
Casa Tierra, **20**
Catalina Park Inn, **26**
Doubletree Hotel, **37**
Embassy Suites Tucson-Broadway, **50**
Hacienda del Sol, **13**
Hotel Congress, **34**
Lazy K Bar Guest Ranch, **39**
Loews Ventana Canyon Resort, **38**
Park Inn/ Santa Rita, **33**
Peppertrees, **28**
Ramada Inn Foothills, **46**
Sheraton Tucson El Conquistador, **7**
Tanque Verde Ranch, **55**
Triangle L Ranch Bed & Breakfast, **8**
Tucson Hilton East, **53**
Tucson National Golf & Conference Resort, **4**
Westin La Paloma, **14**
Westward Look Resort, **6**
White Stallion Ranch, **3**
The Windmill Inn at St. Phillip's Plaza, **12**

spread out in pink stucco houses; all have patios and lovely period furnishings, and many offer fireplaces. Rent a guest house—reasonably priced when shared by three or more—if you really want to luxuriate. The unobtrusively friendly service sets a standard for hotel hospitality. Locals as well as guests frequent the hotel's restaurant (☞ Dining, *above*) and its cocktail lounge, which often has a piano player. ✉ *2200 E. Elm St., 85719,* ☎ *520/325–1541 or 800/933–1093,* FAX *520/881–5830. 83 rooms. 2 restaurants, bar-lounge, tea shop, pool, 2 tennis courts, croquet, Ping-Pong, library. AE, MC, V.*

$$$–$$$$ **Doubletree Hotel.** Convenient to the airport and to the center of town, this comfortable, contemporary-style property is also across the road from the municipal golf course at Randolph Park, which hosts the LPGA tournament every year. Most of the participants stay here. Rooms are large and done in earth tones with southwestern-style furnishings. The pretty Cactus Rose Restaurant serves excellent nouvelle southwestern cuisine, and the Javelina Cantina in the lobby is a fun place to have a beer. ✉ *445 S. Alvernon Way, 85711,* ☎ *520/881–4200 or 800/222–8733,* FAX *520/323–5225. 295 rooms. Restaurant, bar, pool, beauty salon, hot tub, 3 tennis courts, exercise room. AE, D, DC, MC, V.*

$$$ **Embassy Suites Tucson–Broadway.** This centrally located hotel is 10 mi from Tucson International Airport, 5 mi from downtown, and a bit less than 5 mi from the University of Arizona. Accommodations are two-room suites (with a kitchenette) opening onto an atrium full of plants. Furnishings are tasteful if not exciting. Among the extras are a free cooked-to-order breakfast every morning and complimentary happy hour every evening. ✉ *5335 E. Broadway, 85711,* ☎ *520/745–2700 or 800/362–2779,* FAX *520/790–9232. 142 suites. Kitchenettes, pool, coin laundry, free parking. AE, D, DC, MC, V.*

$$$ **Tucson Hilton East.** This east-side property is convenient to Sabino Canyon and Saguaro National Monument East as well as to Davis–Monthan Air Force Base. An airy glass-atrium lobby takes full advantage of the view of the Santa Catalina Mountains. Rooms are nicely furnished, with modern light-wood fittings, pastel carpeting, and vibrant southwestern bedspreads. The VIP level offers extra service and luxuries such as complimentary hors d'oeuvres, and deluxe Continental breakfast. ✉ *7600 E. Broadway, 85710,* ☎ *520/721–5600 or 800/648–7177,* FAX *520/721–5696. 232 rooms. Restaurant, bar, pool. AE, D, DC, MC, V.*

$$ ★ **Best Western Ghost Ranch Lodge.** The bleached-out cow skulls popularized by Georgia O'Keeffe are now a Southwest cliché, but they weren't in 1936 when the New Mexico artist gave the then-unusual logo to conservationist Arthur Pack as a wedding gift. The neon sign he made with this design still lights up the entrance to the former hotel Pack, opened in 1941 on what was then the main road into Tucson. A less central Miracle Mile now connects two larger thoroughfares, I–10 and AZ 77 (Oracle Road)—a convenient location for touring. The Spanish tile-roof units are spread out over 8 acres that encompass an orange grove and garden with 400 varieties of cactus. Rooms have all been freshly redone with modern motel furnishings but still retain such original features as brick walls and sloped wood-beam ceilings. The cottages, with a separate kitchen, sitting area, and carport, are a bargain. Continental breakfast is complimentary. ✉ *801 W. Miracle Mile, 85705,* ☎ *520/791–7565 or 800/456–7565,* FAX *520/791–3898. 83 units. Restaurant, bar, pool, hot tub, shuffleboard. AE, D, DC, MC, V.*

$$ **Ramada Inn Foothills.** Families as well as business travelers stay in this upscale link in the Ramada Inn chain on the northeastern side of town, close to restaurants, Sabino Canyon, and mall shopping. An attractive light stucco building with rounded corners, this property has the expected generic rooms, but they're fairly new and more than serviceable. A Continental breakfast is complimentary, as are beer and wine in the afternoon. Free passes to a local health club are available, and golf and tennis facilities are nearby. ✉ *6944 E. Tanque Verde Rd., 85715,* ☎ *520/886–9595 or 800/228–2828,* FAX *520/721–8466. 113 rooms. Restaurant, lounge, pool, sauna. AE, D, DC, MC, V.*

$$ ★ **The Windmill Inn at St. Phillip's Plaza.** Located in a chic shopping plaza filled with glitzy boutiques and good restaurants (☞ Daniel's *and* Café Terra Cotta *in* Dining, *above*), this all-suites hotel offers attractive, Southwest-contemporary accommodations. Each suite has a separate sitting area, microwave, wet bar, minifridge, two TVs, and three telephones (local calls are free). A few dollars extra will buy you a view of the pool rather than the parking lot. Complimentary coffee, muffins, and a newspaper are delivered to your door. All in all, it's a good deal for the price. *4250 N. Campbell Ave., 85718,* ☎ *520/577–0007 or 800/547–4747,* FAX *520/577–0045. 122 rooms. Pool, bicycles, library, laundry. AE, D, DC, MC, V.*

$ **Hotel Congress.** Loved by many for its idiosyncratic charm, this downtown hotel was built in 1919 and restored to its original western version of Art Deco style. The rooms, which vary in size, are individually furnished: All have black-and-white tiled baths and the original iron beds, and some have desks and tables. Near the Greyhound and Amtrak stations and the main Sun Tran terminal, and close to downtown art galleries and restaurants, this is an excellent choice for those who don't have a car. The downside of this convenient, hip location is noise, compounded on weekend nights, when music from the popular Club Congress filters up to the rooms. ✉ *311 E. Congress St., 85701,* ☎ *520/622–8848 or 800/722–8848,* FAX *520/792–6366. 40 rooms. Restaurant, bar, beauty salon, nightclub, shop. AE, MC, V.*

$ **Park Inn/Santa Rita.** Modern furnishings, hand-painted Mexican tile, and stuccoed walls brighten the lobby, but rooms here are fairly generic and the place sometimes shows its age in the plumbing. Still, the price is right, and the hotel is conveniently located near the downtown arts district and across the street from the visitor center. It's also home to the excellent Café Poca Cosa (☞ Dining, *above*). Continental breakfast, happy hour, and local phone calls are all on the house. ✉ *88 E. Broadway, 85701,* ☎ *520/622–4000 or 800/437–7275,* FAX *520/620–0376. 163 rooms. Restaurant, pool, beauty salon, sauna. AE, D, DC, MC, V.*

Bed-and-Breakfasts

$$ **Adobe Rose Inn.** With its thick adobe walls, lodgepole pine furnishings, and kiva (beehive) fireplaces, this welcoming inn incorporates the best of Southwest style. The clean, unfussy lines of the 1933 house make it a perfect setting for the latest in Santa Fe designs. Each room has its own color TV; a cottage with a separate entrance also offers a refrigerator, coffeemaker, and private phone. A central but quiet location, a bougainvillea-draped ramada overlooking an inviting pool, and no-holds-barred breakfasts—amaretto French toast with macadamia nuts, say—make this a most appealing place to stay. ✉ *940 N. Olsen Ave., 85719,* ☎ *520/318-4644 or 800/328–4122,* FAX *520/325–0055. 3 rooms with bath, 1 cottage. Pool, hot tub. AE, D, MC, V.*

$$ ★ **Casa Alegre.** You'll enjoy poking around the knickknacks and antiques—everything from a hand-hewn Mexican mine shovel to an ornate 19th-century French clock—in friendly Phyllis Florek's "Happy House," as comfortable as it is fascinating. The 1916 Craftsman-style bungalow is near the university, 4th Avenue, and downtown, and it's a straight shot west from here to the desert museum and other west-side attractions. A plunge into the pool and hot tub in the ramada-shaded

backyard are an ideal end to a day of sightseeing. Breakfasts are copious and delicious. ✉ *316 E. Speedway Blvd., 85705,* ☎ *520/628–1800 or 800/628–5654,* FAX *520/792–1880. 5 rooms with bath. Pool, hot tub, free parking. D, MC, V.*

$$ ★ **Casa Tierra.** For a real desert experience, head out to this bed-and-breakfast on 5 acres of land near the Arizona–Sonora Desert Museum and Saguaro National Monument West. For the last 1½ mi you'll be driving along a dirt road. This adobe house, built by Lyle Hymer-Thompson in 1989 expressly to serve as a bed-and-breakfast, has three guest rooms, each with private bath, kitchenette, and a private entrance from individual back patios; all look out onto a lovely central courtyard with a paloverde tree and other desert foliage. The southwestern-style furnishings include Mexican *equipales* (chairs with pigskin seats), tiled floors, and viga-beam ceilings. The delicious breakfasts prepared by Karen Hymer-Thompson might include blue-corn pancakes, breakfast burritos, or oatmeal apple waffles. There is always a lot of fresh fruit and baked goods to accompany them. ✉ *11155 W. Calle Pima, 85743,* ☎ FAX *520/578–3058. 3 rooms with bath. Kitchenettes, hot tub. No credit cards. 2-night minimum stay. Closed June–Aug.*

$$ **Catalina Park Inn.** Classical music plays softly in the living room of this beautifully restored 1927 neoclassical house, still a bastion of civilization, though Tucson is no longer the rough-and-tumble desert town it was when this home was built. The original Art Nouveau tilework and butler's pantry are among the many architectural details you're likely to ogle. Lots of niches and porches afford views of tranquil Catalina Park or the pretty back garden. A newspaper and Continental breakfast delivered to your door allow you to be as antisocial as you like in the morning. Phones, TVs, robes, irons, and hairdryers in all the rooms are among other luxurious touches at this conveniently located lodging. ✉ *309 E. 1st St., 85705,* ☎ *520/792–4541 or 800/792–4885,* FAX *520/792–0838. 4 rooms with bath. AE, MC, V.*

$$ **Peppertrees.** This restored Victorian just off the University of Arizona campus allows guests their privacy along with the usual bed-and-breakfast camaraderie. Two appealing classic contemporary–style guest houses at the rear of the tree-shaded main house have full kitchens, washers and dryers, and individual patios; 1½ baths are shared by two bedrooms in each unit. Rooms are also available in the antiques-filled main house (furnished with pieces from innkeeper Marjorie Martin's family in England) and in a separate studio apartment. Martin, a gourmet cook who has published a book of her recipes, prepares elaborate morning repasts for her visitors. ✉ *724 E. University Blvd., 85719,* ☎ *520/622–7167 or 800/348–5763,* FAX *520/622–5959. 5 rooms with bath, 2 2-bedroom guest houses. MC, V.*

$–$$ **The Triangle L Ranch Bed & Breakfast.** Out near Biosphere 2 and Catalina State Park, a 45-minute drive northeast of Tucson at an elevation of 4,500 feet, Triangle L offers four private cottages scattered about the property's 80 acres. Buffalo Bill was among the regular visitors to the ranch, which was built in the 1880s. The cottages are furnished with comfortable antiques. All offer porches and one has a fireplace. Co-owner Tom Beeston repairs stringed instruments (there's an amazing collection of historic ones on the premises) and will take you out to see his studio. This place is a bird-watcher's paradise; songbirds, hawks, ravens, and quail abound in the area. A hearty ranch breakfast of eggs, homemade breads, and fresh fruit is accompanied by plenty of terrific coffee. ✉ *2805 N. Triangle L Ranch Rd., Box 900, Oracle 85623,* ☎ *520/896–2804 or 800/266–2804. 4 private cottages with bath. D, MC, V.*

Guest Ranches

NOTE – Unless otherwise indicated, price categories for guest ranches include all meals and most activities.

$$$$ **Lazy K Bar Guest Ranch.** In the Tucson Mountains, 16 mi northwest of town at an altitude of 2,300 feet, this family-oriented guest ranch will please children as well as adults. Steak cookouts are held every Saturday night, and the daily fare in the community dining room is hearty and good. As you might expect, horseback riding is a focus, with mounts available for greenhorns as well as those with experience. Riders are entertained with tales of the Old West as they explore the Saguaro National Park West on horseback. Guest rooms are situated in eight *casitas,* or cottages. Those in the older structures, made of Mexican Indian stucco, feature fireplaces and wood-beam ceilings, whereas rooms in the newer, adobe-brick buildings are larger and more modern. Rates for children 17 and under are very reasonable. ✉ *8401 N. Scenic Dr., 85743,* ☏ *520/744–3050 or 800/321–7018,* FAX *520/744–7628. 23 rooms. Pool, library. AE, D, MC, V. 3-day minimum stay.*

$$$$ **Tanque Verde Ranch.** The most upscale of Tucson's guest ranches and one of the oldest in the country, Tanque Verde sits on more than 600 beautiful acres in the Rincon Mountains between Coronado National Forest and Saguaro National Monument. There's plenty to do, from guided nature walks and trail rides to tennis and swimming. Rooms in the main ranch house or in private casitas are all furnished in tasteful southwestern style; most have patios and some have fireplaces. Service is relaxed but very attentive. Cookouts and indoor meals are delicious. Many of the guests have been coming here for years. Everything runs smoothly in high season, but we've had reports of spotty room maintenance in summer. ✉ *14301 E. Speedway Blvd., 85748,* ☏ *520/296–6275 or 800/234–3833,* FAX *520/721–9426. 64 rooms and 3 houses. Indoor and outdoor pools, spa, 5 tennis courts, exercise room, basketball, horseback riding, horseshoes, volleyball, fishing. AE, D, MC, V.*

$$$$ ★ **White Stallion Ranch.** If you feel as if this place is right out of the film *High Chaparral,* you won't be imagining things. Many scenes from the movie were shot on the ranch, which sits on 3,000 acres of desert mountain land. The True family—Cynthia, Russell, and Michael—has run the White Stallion for almost 30 years, and it feels very homey. Children are welcome and large groups are easily accommodated. Horseback rides, a weekend rodeo, cookouts, and hikes along mountain trails are just a few of the activities offered. A herd of longhorn cattle and a wide variety of birds, desert cottontail rabbits, and peacocks make their home on the grounds. Children will enjoy the petting zoo, where llamas, potbellied pigs, and miniature horses are among the residents. There are no telephones or TVs in the spare but comfortable rooms. ✉ *9251 W. Twin Peaks Rd., 85743,* ☏ *520/297–0252 or 800/782–5546,* FAX *520/744–2786. 29 rooms. Bar, pool, hot tub, 2 tennis courts, basketball, horseback riding, Ping-Pong, shuffleboard, volleyball, billiards. No credit cards. Closed May–Sept.*

Resorts

$$$$ **Loews Ventana Canyon Resort.** One of the newer desert resorts, Ventana Canyon is unquestionably luxurious, but also snootier than most other Tucson properties. The setting is spectacular: Expect to see desert cottontails around the 93-acre grounds, along with hummingbirds, quail, and other birds. Rooms are modern and chic, furnished in soft pastels and light woods; each bath has a miniature TV and an oversize tub with a nice supply of bubble bath. The center of this open, airy property is an 80-foot waterfall that cascades down the Catalina Mountains

into a little lake. Four restaurants offer guests a choice of casual poolside snacks and elegant dining; there's also a daily afternoon tea in the lobby lounge. The upscale Ventana Room (☞ Dining, *above*) serves first-rate Continental cuisine. ✉ *7000 N. Resort Dr., 85715,* ☎ *520/299–2020 or 800/234–5117,* FAX *520/299–6832. 398 rooms. 4 restaurants, bar, lobby lounge, 2 pools, beauty salon, spa, 2 18-hole golf courses, 8 tennis courts, exercise room, hiking. AE, D, DC, MC, V.*

$$$$ ★ **Sheraton Tucson El Conquistador.** You'll know you're in the Southwest when you step into the cathedral-ceiling lobby of this golf and tennis resort: It has a huge copper mural filled with cowboys and cacti, as well as a wide-window view of one of the pools set against a backdrop of the rugged Santa Catalina Mountains. This friendly, relaxing place draws families and out-of-town conventioneers as well as locals, who take advantage of summer rates for the Sheraton's excellent sports facilities. Rooms, either in private casitas or the main hotel building, have stylish light-wood furniture with tinwork and pastel-tone spreads and curtains, as well as balconies or patios (some suites have kiva-shape fireplaces). The White Dove, the resort's dining room, has an innovative Italian menu. Biosphere 2 is a 10-minute drive up the road from here. ✉ *10000 N. Oracle Rd., 85737,* ☎ *520/544–5000 or 800/325–7832,* FAX *520/544–1224. 428 rooms. 4 restaurants, piano bar, 4 pools, sauna, 3 18-hole golf courses, 31 tennis courts, 2 exercise rooms, basketball, horseback riding, racquetball, volleyball, bicycles. AE, D, DC, MC, V.*

$$$$ **Tucson National Golf & Conference Resort.** Perfect for couples with separate sybaritic interests, Tucson National features both an excellent golf course (it hosts the PGA's Northern Telecom Open annually) and a full-service spa, where you can be coiffed, waxed, wrapped, worked over, and scrubbed to your heart's content. Smaller than most of Tucson's major resorts, it's also closer to town and thus to sightseeing and shopping. Public areas and guest rooms have just undergone a $10 million overhaul. Oddly, of the six levels of accommodations available, the most expensive (hacienda) are the least attractive. The Catalina Grill, the resort's fine-dining room, has a good American regional menu and a great view of the lush greens; Legends is a classic sports bar, replete with pool table and happily guzzling golfers. ✉ *2727 W. Club Dr., 85741,* ☎ *520/297–2271 or 800/528–4856,* FAX *520/742–2452. 167 rooms. 3 restaurants, 3 bars, 2 heated outdoor pools, beauty salon, spa, 27-hole golf course, 4 lighted tennis courts, exercise room, basketball, croquet, volleyball, bicycles. AE, D, DC, MC, V.*

$$$$ ★ **Westin La Paloma.** Vying with the Sheraton and Loews Ventana for convention business, this sprawling pink resort also offers lots of options for individual and family relaxation. The resort's golf, fitness, and beauty centers are top-notch; a huge pool has the only swim-up bar in Tucson and Arizona's longest resort water slide; and reasonably priced child care at a special play lounge as well as the addition of an adults-only and kids-only pool help both parents and kids enjoy their stay. Service is excellent all around. Newly refurbished rooms, with southwestern colors and copper accents, have private balconies with views of the city lights, golf course, or grounds. The casual Desert Garden restaurant affords wonderful views of the Santa Catalina Mountains. ✉ *3800 E. Sunrise Dr., 85718,* ☎ *520/742–6000 or 800/876–3683,* FAX *520/577–5878. 487 rooms. 5 restaurants, 2 bars, 3 pools, beauty salon, 3 hot tubs, 27-hole golf course, 12 tennis courts, aerobics, croquet, exercise room, jogging, racquetball, volleyball, business services. AE, D, DC, MC, V.*

$$$$ **Westward Look Resort.** When the dust settles on this resort, set on 80 acres in the Santa Catalina foothills north of town, it will have a newly old look. A resort since 1943 (it was built as a residence by William

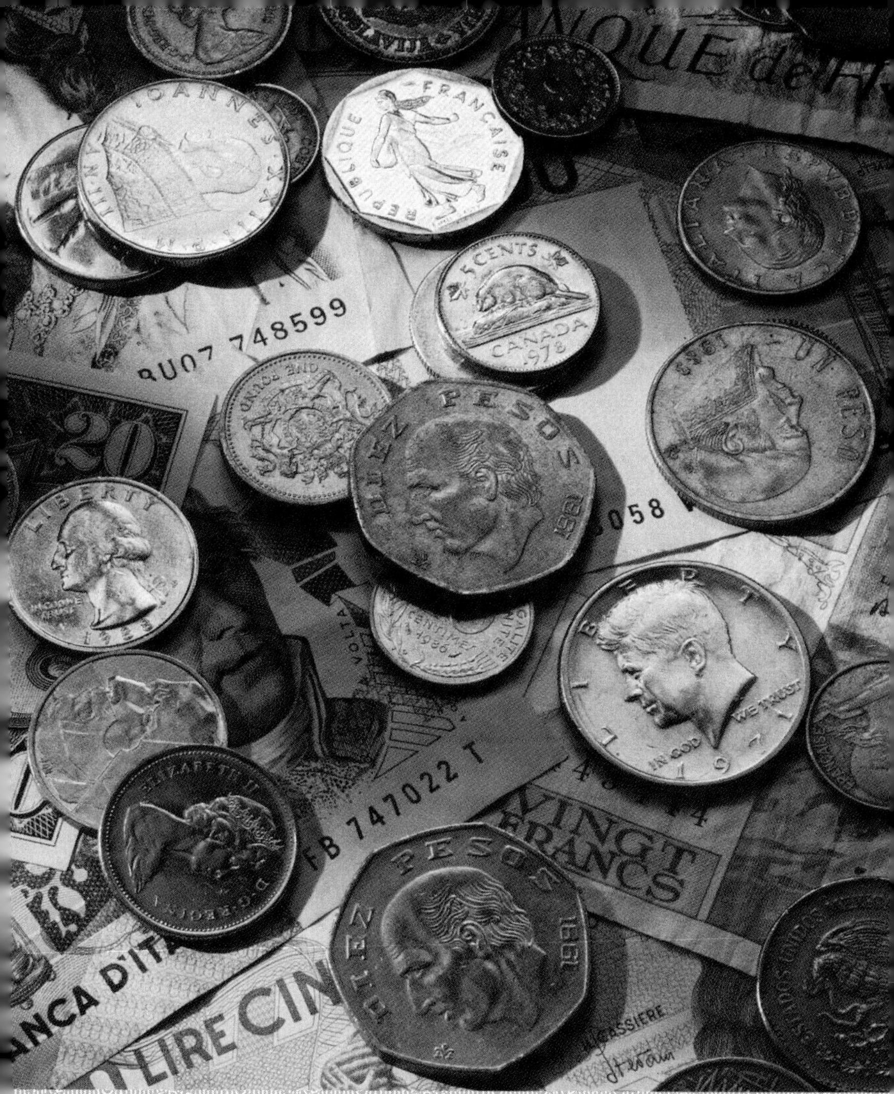
RÉPUBLIQUE FRANÇAISE
5 CENTS
CANADA 1978
PESOS
FB 747022 T
VINGT FRANCS
LIRE
LIBERTY

and Mary Watson in 1912 and converted to a guest ranch in the 1920s), Westward Look acquired new owners in 1995 and underwent a massive renovation in 1996. The lobby is now in what was once the Watsons' traditionally Southwest–style living room; the couple probably couldn't have envisioned the additional patio with a cappuccino machine, nor the property's new wellness center, offering all kinds of New Age treatments. Guest rooms have been redone in earthy olive, terra cotta, and rust tones, with comfy leather chairs, wrought-iron bed frames, and Mission–style furniture; all offer coffeemakers and irons. The hotel's fine dining room serves innovative American fare, including ostrich. ✉ *245 E. Ina Rd., 85704,* ☎ *520/297–1151 or 800/722–2500,* FAX *520/297–9023. 244 rooms, including 8 suites. 2 restaurants, coffee bar, deli, 3 pools, 3 spas, 8 tennis courts, exercise room, horseback riding, mountain biking, shops. AE, D, DC, MC, V.*

$$$ **Hacienda del Sol.** It's hard to categorize this place, which sits on 32 acres in the Santa Catalina foothills: It's part guest ranch, part resort, and entirely gracious. Built in Santa Fe style in 1929, it was originally a posh finishing school for girls and attracted stars—among them Katherine Hepburn and Spencer Tracy—when it was converted to a guest ranch during World War II. After years of neglect, new owners have restored the lovely landscaping and have redecorated rooms in the main house with deep, rich colors. Some of the one- and two-bedroom casitas have fireplaces and private porches looking out on the Tucson Mountains. Hacienda del Sol was already renting some rooms when we visited, but it doesn't officially open until November 1996. With plans for a full roster of activities such as yoga, massage, and hiking, this promises to be a relaxing getaway. ✉ *5601 N. Hacienda del Sol Rd., 85718,* ☎ *520/299–1501,* FAX *520/299–5554. 32 units, including 9 suites. Restaurant, pool, tennis court, horseback riding, library. AE, D, MC, V.*

Spas

$$$$ ★ **Canyon Ranch.** Opened in 1979 on the site of the old Double U Guest Ranch, Canyon Ranch draws an international crowd of glitterati to its superb spa facilities (it's been voted World's Best Spa by the readers of *Condé Nast Traveler* five times since 1990). Set on 70 acres in the desert foothills northeast of Tucson, two activity centers include a 62,000-square-foot spa complex and an 8,000-square-foot Health and Healing Center, where dietitians, exercise physiologists, behavioral-health professionals, and medical staff attend to body and soul (you can have your astrological chart done and your tarot cards read). The unobtrusively healthful food has proved so popular that it's sold outside the spa. This is a wonderful place to be pampered, but beware: Unless you're seriously rich, the benefits of the stress reduction programs may be wiped out when you get the bill. ✉ *8600 E. Rockcliff Rd., 85715,* ☎ *520/749–9000 or 800/742–9000,* FAX *520/749–1646. 153 rooms and suites. Indoor pool, 3 outdoor pools, beauty salon, spa, 8 tennis courts, aerobics, health club, basketball, squash, racquetball. AE, D, MC, V.*

OUTDOOR ACTIVITIES AND SPORTS

Participant Sports

Ballooning

What better way to take advantage of Arizona's mild winter months than to take a quiet hot-air-balloon ride in the early morning hours and get a bird's-eye view of the frisky desert wildlife down below? **Southern Arizona Balloon Excursions** (✉ Box 5265, 530 W. Saguaro, Tucson 85703, ☎ 520/624–3599) welcomes individuals and groups and offers champagne celebrations and daily flights (from September through May) by pilots who are licensed by the Federal Aviation Administration (FAA). Prices range from about $115 to $250 per person, depending on the season and the length of the flight over the Tucson valley. Individual members of the **Saguaro Aerostat Association** offer tours that can range farther afield, with launches in the San Pedro River valley and along the Mexican border. For information, contact association president Fran Reynolds (✉ 984 W. Lyman La., Tucson 85704, ☎ 520/888–2954).

Bicycling

Tucson, ranked among America's top-five bicycling cities by *Bicycling* magazine, has designated bikeways, routes, lanes, and paths for bikers all over the city—through rugged terrain, up and down winding roads, and along frequently used byways in the Tucson area. The Tucson Transportation Department (☎ 520/791–4372) will mail you city bike maps, or you can pick them up at the office of the **Pima Association of Governments** (✉ 177 N. Church St., Suite 405, 520/792–1093). If you want even more isolated and scenic locations, try biking in southern Arizona. Tour maps are available at the **Metropolitan Convention and Visitors Bureau** (☞ Visitor Information *in* Tucson A to Z, *below*).

Most bike stores in Tucson carry the monthly newsletter put out by the Tucson chapter of **GABA** (Greater Arizona Bicycling Association, ✉ Box 34273, Tucson 85733), which lists rated group rides. Visitors are welcome. Reliable, centrally located bike renters include the **Bike Shack** (✉ 940 E. University Ave., ☎ 520/624–3663) and **Full Cycle** (✉ 3232 E. Speedway Blvd., ☎ 520/327–3232); the latter is also headquarters for **SAMBA** (Southern Arizona Mountain Biking Association).

Bird-Watching

In the Huachuca Mountains, the Nature Conservancy's 300-acre **Ramsey Canyon Preserve** (90 mi southeast of Tucson, off AZ 92, ☎ 520/378–2785) is home to more than 200 species of birds, as well as dozens of species of butterflies, deer, snakes, frogs, and mountain lions. Even closer to Tucson, in the nearby Santa Rita Mountains, **Madera Canyon** is another bird lovers' haven. So, too, is the **Patagonia-Sonoita Creek Preserve** (☎ 520/394–2400 for details), 4 mi west of Patagonia off Route 82. Operated by the Nature Conservancy, the preserve harbors more than 270 bird species from hawks to trogons and kingfishers—many experienced birders head here to round off their life lists.

You can find out what's flying by phoning the **Tucson Audubon Society**'s 24-hour line (☎ 520/798–1005); the latest sightings of rare or interesting avians in the area are recorded regularly. The society's **Audubon Nature Shop** (✉ 300 E. University Blvd., Suite 120, ☎ 520/629–0510) carries field guides, bird-feeders, and binoculars, along with a wide range of natural history books. The **Wild Bird Store** (✉ 3522 E. Grant Rd., ☎ 520/322–9466) is another excellent resource for bird-watching books, maps, and trail guides. Tours are offered by **Wings, Inc.** (✉ Box 31930, Tucson 85751, ☎ 520/749–1967), **Victor Emanuel Nature Tours** (✉ Box 33008, Austin, TX 77647, ☎ 800/328–8368), and **Borderlands** (✉ 2550 W. Calle Padilla, Tucson 85745, ☎ 520/882–7650). The Tucson office of the **Nature Conservancy** (✉ 300 E. University Blvd., Suite 230, ☎ 520/622–3861) offers seasonal bird-watching tours ranging in length from a few hours to several days; call or write for information.

Camping

There are at least 100 camping areas scattered throughout the southern region of Arizona. Though it can get very chilly at night in the desert, the weather's usually good enough year-round to make sleeping out under the vast, starry night sky an appealing option. Summertime is the time to camp in the state's cooler higher-altitude campgrounds.

The closest public campground to Tucson is probably at **Catalina State Park** (✉ 11570 N. Oracle Rd., ☎ 520/628–5798), about 9 mi north of town on AZ 77. Located in the desert foothills of the Santa Catalinas, the campground accommodates tents as well as RVs. It fills up quickly in good weather because it's close to town. Unfortunately, there is no reservation system.

Recreational vehicles can park in any number of facilities around town. The **Metropolitan Tucson Convention and Visitors Bureau** (☞ Visitor Information *in* Tucson A to Z, *below*) can provide information about specific locations.

CAUTION – Be careful not to camp in low-lying areas, which are subject to extremely dangerous flash flooding in sudden summer rains (☞ Lodging *in* Important Contacts A to Z).

Golf

The Tucson & Southern Arizona Golf Guide, published by Tucson Guide Quarterly, Inc. (✉ Box 42915, Tucson 85733, ☎ 520/322–0895), describes and rates all the local courses; send $5 for a copy. For a golf package based on your budget, interests, and experience, you might contact **Tee Time Arrangers** (✉ 6286 E. Grant Rd., ☎ 520/296–4800 or 800/742–9939). If you're planning to stay a week or more, **Tucson's Resort Golf Card** (✉ 6286 E. Grant Rd., Tucson 85712, ☎ 520/886–8800), offering year-round discounts at seven of the area's best courses, is a good deal. Write or call for information.

MUNICIPAL COURSES

One of Tucson's best-kept secrets is that the city's five municipal courses are maintained to standards that in most parts of the country can be found only at the best country clubs. The flagship of these low-priced municipal golf courses within the city of Tucson (Randolph North, Randolph South, El Rio, Fred Enke, and Silverbell) is the centrally located **Randolph North,** which hosted the PGA and LPGA Tour for many years. To make reservations at these city-operated courses, contact the Tucson Parks and Recreation Department (☎ 520/791–4336) at least a week in advance.

PUBLIC COURSES

Canoa Hills (✉ 1401 W. Calle Urbano, ☎ 520/648–1880) is a good 18-hole choice for average golfers.

Dorado Golf Course (✉ 6601 E. Speedway Blvd., ☎ 520/885–6751), on the east side of town, has an executive course that's good for those who just want to play a few short rounds.

The Raven Golf Club at Sabino Springs (✉ 9945 E. Snyder Rd., ☎ 520/760–1253), opened in December 1995, is an 18-hole, par-71 course in a gorgeous setting.

Rio Rico Resort & Country Club (✉ 1550 Camino a la Posada, ☎ 520/281–8567), south of Tucson, near Nogales, was designed by Robert Trent Jones, Jr. An excellent 18-hole course, it's one of Arizona's lesser-known gems.

San Ignacio Golf Club (✉ 4201 S. Camino del Sol, ☎ 520/648–3468), in Green Valley, was designed by Arthur Hills and is a challenging 18-hole desert course in a beautiful setting.

RESORTS

Many avid golfers check into one of the tony local resorts (most are described in more detail *in* Lodging, *above*) and do nothing but tee off for a week. Golf vacation specialists include **Tucson National Golf & Conference Resort,** cohost of a PGA winter open in early January, with 27 holes and beautiful, long par 4's, designed by the great Robert Bruce Harris; **Westin La Paloma,** which has a 27-hole layout designed by Jack Nicklaus (rated among the top 75 resort courses by *Golf Digest*); **Sheraton Tucson El Conquistador,** its 45 holes in the Santa Catalina foothills affording 360° views of the city; the 36-hole Tom Fazio–designed course at **Lodge at Ventana Canyon** (✉ 6200 N. Clubhouse La., 85715, ☎ 520/577–1400 or 800/828–5701); and **Starr Pass Golf Resort** (✉ 3645 W. Starr Pass Blvd., 85745, ☎ 520/670–0500 or 800/503–2898), which now has guest casitas for those who want to devote as much time as possible to playing its 18 magnificent holes in the Tucson Mountains. The Arnold Palmer–managed club was developed as a Tournament Player's Course and has become a favorite of visiting pros; playing its Number 15 signature hole has been likened to threading a moving needle. Those who don't mind getting up early to beat the heat will find some excellent golf packages at these places in the summer.

Health Clubs

5th Street Fitness (✉ 5555 E. 5th St., ☎ 520/571–7000) has an indoor swimming pool, sauna, hot tub, and a wide array of aerobics classes. Nonmembers receive a free one-day pass; additional days cost $15 for all facilities.

Naturally Women (✉ 6880 E. Broadway, ☎ 520/722–3700; 4343 N. Oracle Rd., ☎ 520/292–0500) offers a range of diet and exercise programs for women of all ages. Visitors can spend their first day free; on subsequent visits, a rate of about $10 is charged.

Tucson Athletic Club (✉ 4220 E. Bellevue, ☎ 520/881–0140) is the city's largest facility, at 35,000 square feet. The sports bar serves full meals and snacks, and the club offers, among other attractions, lighted tennis courts, an indoor track, a 40-meter outdoor pool, and massage therapy. The club issues nonmembers a free one-day pass, with subsequent day rates of $10 for all facilities, $5 for handball and racquetball only.

Hiking

For hiking inside Tucson city limits, you might test your skills climbing trails up Sentinel Peak ("A" Mountain). State and city parks in the area also offer a variety of hiking experiences. There are literally hundreds of trails in the immediate Tucson area. **Catalina State Park** (☞ Camping, *above*) is crisscrossed by hiking trails. One of them, an easy two-hour walk, leads to the Romero Pools, a series of natural *tinajas,* or stone tanks, that are full of water for much of the year. Keep your eyes open along the trail for the elusive desert bighorn, a few of which still live in the rugged middle altitudes of the Santa Catalina Mountains but are very seldom seen.

If you want to go a bit farther afield, head south past the Huachuca Mountain range, where you can wander in and out of old **ghost towns** such as Fort Duquesne, Pearce, and Washington Camp in the Patagonia Mountains. To the east of Tucson, beyond the Rincons and the Whetstone Mountains, the Dragoon Mountains are both beautiful and of historical interest. **Cochise's Stronghold** was the Apache chief's hideout with his people during 11 years of battle with U. S. troops. Farther east, **Chiricahua National Monument** (☞ Southeast Arizona, *below*) offers a number of well-marked trails in a striking setting.

The local chapter of the **Sierra Club** (✉ 738 N. 5th Ave., Suite 214, Tucson 85705, ☎ 520/620–6401) welcomes out-of-town visitors on their weekend hikes around the area. There's a $2 suggested donation per person for nonmembers. For hiking on your own, a good source of information is **Summit Hut** (✉ 5045 E. Speedway Blvd., ☎ 520/325–1554), which has an excellent collection of hiking reference materials and a friendly staff who will help you plan and outfit your trip. Packs, tents, bags, and climbing shoes can be rented here.

CAUTION – Be sure to bring plenty of water with you when hiking and drink often. Dehydration can become a life-threatening condition in the desert.

Horseback Riding

Desert-High Country Stables (✉ 6501 W. Ina Rd., ☎ 520/744–3789), in the northwest part of town, offers trail rides, hayrides, and cookouts.

Pusch Ridge Stables (✉ 13700 N. Oracle Rd., ☎ 520/825–1664), adjacent to Catalina State Park, serves up a cowboy-style breakfast at the end of your trail ride; gentle children's walks are also available.

Rockhounding

Although the heyday of mining has passed, there are still plenty of gems and minerals to be found in these parts, if you know what you're looking for. Just be sure to check in advance that you're not removing anything from protected areas such as national parks or Indian reservations. Amateur traders and buyers might consider joining the thousands of professionals who come to town in February for the huge **Tucson Gem and Mineral Show** (✉ Box 42543, Tucson 85733, ☎ 520/322–5773), the largest of its kind in the world. Many precious stones as well as affordable samples are displayed and sold here, and even if you don't buy a thing, it's fun to look at all the fascinating rocks and gems. The main show, sponsored by the Tucson Gem and Mineral Society, is held at the Tucson Convention Center, but many satellite shows run at the same time—some as informal as dealers operating out of hotel rooms. If you do plan to attend, make reservations far in advance. In 1997 every hotel and car-rental agency in town is likely to be booked up from February 13 through February 16, when the show runs, as well as the entire week before.

Tennis

A number of the hotels and resorts in town have tennis facilities. Many courts are at Loews Ventana Canyon, Sheraton Tucson El Conquistador, Westin La Paloma, Westward Look, and Canyon Ranch resorts (☞ Lodging, *above*). The **Randolph Tennis Center** (✉ 50 S. Alvernon Way, ☎ 520/791–4896) offers 25 courts, 11 lighted, at very reasonable rates. **Fort Lowell Park** (✉ 2900 N. Craycroft Rd., 520/791–2584) and **Himmel Park** (✉ Tucson Blvd., a block south of Speedway Blvd., ☎ 520/791–3276) each have 8 lighted courts and similarly low prices. **Catalina High School** (✉ 3645 E. Pima), famed singer Linda Ronstadt's alma mater and a favorite among local tennis enthusiasts, has good, well-lighted courts at no charge.

Spectator Sports

Baseball

In 1993 Tucson welcomed the **Colorado Rockies** to their inaugural season of Cactus League practice games (☞ Pleasures and Pastimes *in* Chapter 1); since then the city has taken to the fledgling major-league team. Call ☎ 520/327–9467 for schedule and ticket information (tickets can be hard to come by during the exhibition season, especially when the Rockies face the locally popular Chicago Cubs and San Francisco Giants). The Rockies share Hi-Corbett Field (✉ 3400 E. Camino Campestre), which recently got a facelift and new grandstands, with the **Tucson Toros** (☎ 520/325–2621), a minor-league team. Picnickers and squirrels sit side by side in adjacent Randolph Park to enjoy the games of both teams. Inside the stadium, during training games, beer is sold behind first and third bases. Parking isn't easy to come by in the area, so park in any of the Randolph Park lots west of Hi-Corbett Field and take a short, pleasant walk through the park to get to the stadium.

Rodeo

From February 19 to 23, Tucson hosts the largest annual winter rodeo in the United States, a five-day extravaganza with more than 600 events and a crowd of more than 44,000 spectators per day, at the **Tucson Rodeo Grounds** (✉ 4823 S. 6th Avenue, ☎ 520/294–8896). The rodeo kicks off with a 2-mile-long parade through downtown Tucson, billed as the "world's longest nonmotorized parade," featuring Mexican *charros,* horse-drawn floats, and marching bands from all over Arizona. Bleacher seating for the parade is $4; otherwise the parade is free. Daily seats at the rodeo itself range from $6 to $12.

NIGHTLIFE AND THE ARTS

The Arts

Tucson, known as the most cultured of Arizona's cities, is one of only 14 cities in the United States that are home to a symphony as well as to opera, theater, and ballet companies. Winter is the high season for most of Tucson's cultural activities because that's when most of the visitors come, but there's something going on all the time.

Summer is when **Downtown Saturday Night,** a year-round event, really comes alive. On the first and third Saturday nights of each month (about 7–10 PM), Tucson's downtown arts district opens up its galleries, studios, and cafés. There's dancing in the street—everything from calypso to square dancing—and musical performances ranging from jazz to gospel. Most of the activity takes place along Congress Street and Broadway (from 4th Avenue to Stone Street) and along 5th and 6th avenues. You can also explore this area via a free, docent-led **Thursday Night Artwalk.** For more information about these events and about festivals, free workshops and classes, and performances in the downtown arts district, contact the **Tucson Arts District Partnership, Inc.** (☎ 520/624–9977), which also offers material on self-guided gallery and historic district walking tours.

The cost of attending any cultural event in Tucson will be a pleasant surprise to anyone who's accustomed to paying East or West Coast prices—symphony tickets can be purchased for as little as $5 for some concerts, and tickets to a touring Broadway musical can often be had for $22. Parking is frequently free. Most of the city's cultural activity takes place either downtown in the arts district, where the **Tucson Convention Center** (✉ 260 S. Church St., ☎ 520/791-4101 or 791–4266 [box office]) complex and the El Presidio neighborhood are, or at the University of Arizona, where the UA Artist Series is held at **Centennial Hall** (✉ off Park Ave. and University Blvd., ☎ 520/621–3341). The 1996 season included everything from the New York City Opera's *La Traviata* to *Ain't Misbehavin'* with the Pointer Sisters. Tickets to Tucson arts and entertainment events can often be purchased through **Dillard's Box Office** (☎ 800/638–4253).

The free *Tucson Weekly,* published every Wednesday and found in most supermarkets and convenience stores, and the Friday edition of *The Arizona Daily Star* both have complete listings of what's on in town.

Dance

Tucson shares its professional ballet company, **Ballet Arizona** (☎ 520/882–5022), with Phoenix. Performances, which range from classical to contemporary, are held at the Music Hall in the Tucson Convention Center (☞ *above*). The most established of the modern companies, **Orts Theatre of Dance** (✉ 930 N. Stone Ave., ☎ 520/624–3799), schedules a variety of outdoor and indoor performances.

Music

The **Tucson Symphony Orchestra** (✉ 443 S. Stone Ave., ☎ 520/882–8585 [box office] or 520/792–9155 [main office]), part of Tucson's cultural scene since 1929, holds concerts in the music hall in the Tucson Convention Center complex and at the Pima Community College Center for the Arts (✉ 12202 W. Anklam Rd.). A variety of concerts and recitals, many of them free, are offered by the **University of Arizona's School of Music and Dance** (☎ 520/621–2998 for a recorded listing of events in the upcoming week). A chamber-music series is hosted by the **Arizona Friends of Chamber Music** (☎ 520/298–5806) at the Leo Rich Theater in the Tucson Convention Center from October through April. The **Arizona Opera Company** (☎ 520/293–4336), centered in Tucson, puts on five major productions each year at the Tucson Convention Center's Music Hall. The **Southern Arizona Light Opera Co.** (✉ 908 N. Swan Rd., ☎ 520/323–7888 or 520/326–5155) is becoming increasingly popular. All of the performances are at the Tucson Convention Center's Music Hall.

Tucson's jazz scene encompasses everything from afternoon jam sessions in the park to Sunday jazz brunches at resorts in the foothills. The **Tucson Jazz Society Hot Line** (☎ 520/743–3399) offers information about the many events around town.

From late February through late June, the Tucson Parks and Recreation Department hosts a series of **free concerts** on the weekends. The Tucson Pops Orchestra plays at the De Meester Outdoor Performance Center in Reid Park, while the Arizona Symphonic Winds performs at Morris T. Udall Park (Tanque Verde and Sabino Canyon Rds.). There are also special events, such as concerts by the Old Time Fiddlers and the Civic Orchestra. It's smart to arrive at least an hour before the music starts (usually at 7:30) so that you can position your blanket exactly where you want it. In 1996, a series of lunchtime concerts was initiated at the main library, downtown, on Wednesdays from late February to early May. Call ☎ 520/791–4079 for schedules and directions.

Poetry

The **Tucson Poetry Festival** (☎ 520/321–2163 or 520/623–7277 for details) is held in early spring. A large range of poets, some internationally acclaimed—Allen Ginsberg and Amiri Baraka have been participants—come to town for three days of readings and related events.

The **University of Arizona Poetry Center** (✉ 1216 N. Cherry Ave., ☎ 520/321–7760) runs a free series open to the public. Phone during fall and spring semesters for information on scheduled readers.

Theater

Theater groups in town include Arizona's state theater, the **Arizona Theatre Company** (☎ 520/884–8210), which performs everything from classical to contemporary drama at the Temple of Music and Art (✉ 330 S. Scott Ave., ☎ 520/622–2823) from September through May. It's worth coming just to see the beautifully restored Spanish colonial/Moorish–style theater, and dinners served at the adjoining bed-and-breakfast Cafe (☎ 520/792–2623 for reservations), coordinated to show times, are tasty preludes to a performance. The **a.k.a. theatre** (✉ 125 E. Congress St., ☎ 520/623–7852) specializes in avant-garde productions. **Invisible Theatre** (✉ 1400 N. 1st Ave., ☎ 520/882–9721) presents contemporary plays and musicals.

Children love the old-fashioned melodramas at the **Gaslight Theatre** (✉ 7010 E. Broadway, ☎ 520/886–9428), where hissing the villain and cheering the hero are part of the audience's duty. There is free popcorn, and beer, wine, soft drinks, and pizza are sold.

Nightlife

Bars and Clubs

Although Tucson doesn't have the huge selection of bars and clubs available in some major cities, there's something here to suit nearly every taste. In addition to the places listed below, most of the major resorts have nightspots that offer late-night drinks and sometimes dancing.

COUNTRY AND WESTERN

An excellent house band gets the crowd two-stepping every night except Sunday at the **Maverick** (✉ 4702 E. 22nd St., ☎ 520/748–0456). On Sunday night the **Cactus Moon Cafe** (✉ 5470 E. Broadway Blvd., ☎ 520/748–0049) has a terrific all-you-can-eat buffet for $3 and free dance lessons. It's worth a drive to **A Little Bit of Texas** (✉ 4385 W. Ina Rd., ☎ 520/744–7744), the Southwest's largest country-and-western nightclub, with two dance floors, pool tables, free dance lessons (Tues.–Fri.), and a western clothing boutique. Concerts feature popular C&W performers like Hal Ketchum and Diamond Rio, as well as big-time Tejano artists.

JAZZ

Of the various clubs around town, **Cafe Sweetwater** (✉ 340 E. 6th St., ☎ 520/622–6464) is the most consistent in the quality of its jazz acts—and the food's pretty good, too. There's usually a lively jazz pianist at the **Arizona Inn** (☞ Lodging, *above*).

ROCK/VARIETY

Berky's (✉ 5769 E. Speedway Blvd., ☎ 520/296–1981) has live music—R&B and rock and roll—every night; there's a new location on lively 4th Avenue (✉ 424 N. 4th Ave., ☎ 520/622–0376). The **Chicago Bar** (✉ 5954 E. Speedway Blvd., ☎ 520/748–8169) features reggae on Wednesday, Thursday, and Saturday nights, rocking blues on Friday nights, and a variety of live bands the rest of the week. **Club Congress** (✉ 311 E. Congress St., ☎ 520/622–8848) is the main venue in town for cutting-edge rock bands who play on Friday and sometimes Sunday. At the **Cushing Street Bar and Restaurant** (✉ 343 S. Meyer Ave., ☎ 520/622–7984) the focus is on blues, though live jazz and rock acts are also booked. The **Outback** (✉ 296 N. Stone Ave., ☎ 520/622–4700) hosts performers like Kansas, Electric Light Orchestra, and Mick Fleetwood, who wouldn't fill the convention center but draw a good crowd. Go totally retro at the **Shelter** (✉ 4155 E. Grant Rd., ☎ 520/326–1345), a former bomb shelter where the early '60s still reign.

Casinos

After a long struggle with the state of Arizona, two Native American tribes now operate casinos on their Tucson-area reservations. The Pascua Yaqui tribe runs the **Casino of the Sun** (✉ 7406 S. Camino de Oeste,

☎ 520/883–1700 or 800/344–9435), which has lots of slot and video-gambling machines, as well as keno and high-stakes bingo. The Tohonó O'odham tribe's **Desert Diamond Bingo and Casino** (✉ 7350 S. Old Nogales Hwy., ☎ 520/294–7777) offers 500 one-arm bandits and video poker in addition to live keno and bingo. Both are open daily, 24 hours a day. No alcohol is sold or permitted at either casino.

SHOPPING

San Xavier Plaza, across from San Xavier mission, carries the work of a variety of native peoples, including the Tohonó O'odham, upon whose reservation the church is located (☞ Southern Tucson *in* Exploring, *above*). Those looking for work by other regional artists might drive down to Tubac, a community 45 mi south of Tucson. Hard-core bargain hunters usually continue south to the Mexican border and Nogales (☞ South of Tucson *in* Side Trips, *below*).

In Tucson itself, much of the retail activity is focused around malls, but you'll find shops with more character in two areas. The downtown district hosts a number of art galleries, antiques shops, and crafts stores. Congress Street is a particularly good block to browse, and the **Old Town Artisans complex** (✉ 186 N. Meyer Ave., ☎ 520/623–6024), near the Tucson Museum of Art, has a large selection of southwestern wares. The adjoining 4th Avenue neighborhood, near the University of Arizona, is also fertile ground for unusual items. The **Fourth Avenue Merchants Association** (✉ 329 E. 7th St. at 4th Ave., ☎ 520/624–5004) represents the many artsy boutiques and restaurants that line 4th Avenue between 2nd and 9th streets.

Specialty Shops

ART GALLERIES

Philabaum Contemporary Glass (✉ 711 S. Sixth Ave., ☎ 520/884–7404) offers beautiful designs in a difficult medium, mastered by Tom Philabaum. The more cutting-edge downtown galleries include **Etherton Gallery** (✉ 135 S. 6th Ave., ☎ 520/624–7370) and **Dinnerware** (✉ 135 E. Congress St., ☎ 520/792–4503). ***Art Life in Southern Arizona*** ✉ Box 36777, Tucson 85740, ☎ 520/797–1271), published annually, lists local galleries and artists.

BOOKS

Tohonó Chul Park (☞ Northern Tucson *in* Exploring, *above*) shares its lovely grounds with the **Haunted Bookshop** (✉ 7211 N. Northern Ave., ☎ 520/297–4843), with its outstanding selection for bibliophiles of all ages. There's a coffeepot on the porch in the wintertime, plenty of nooks for a quiet read, and a tunnel for children to crawl through. In central Tucson, the **Book Mark** (✉ 5001 E. Speedway Blvd., ☎ 520/881–6350) also has very well stocked shelves, covering a wide range of topics.

Near the University of Arizona is **Books West Southwest** (✉ 2452 N. Campbell Ave., ☎ 520/326–3533), focusing on regional works. The store often hosts signings by local authors. Pick up your topographical maps and specialty guides to Arizona at **Tucson's Map and Flag Center** (✉ 3239 1st Ave., ☎ 520/887–4234). Seekers of books by and about women should stop in at **Antigone** (✉ 411 N. 4th Ave., ☎ 520/792–3715), which also sells creative feminist cards and T-shirts.

CACTI

You won't need to stick a cactus in your suitcase if you want to take back a spiny souvenir (it's illegal anyway): **B&B Cactus Farm** (✉ 11550

E. Speedway Blvd., ☎ 520/721–4687), on the far eastern side of town, has a huge selection of desert plants and will ship all over the country.

GIFTS

Sangin Trading Co. (✉ 300 N. 6th Ave., ☎ 520/882–9334) is set in a huge historic warehouse filled with baskets, home furnishings, folk art, and jewelry—some imported, some made by local artists. Very reasonably priced ethnic jewelry, clothing, and crafts can be purchased at the **United Nations Center** (✉ 2911 E. Grant Rd., ☎ 881–7060).

JEWELRY

For a splurge, consider buying something by **Beth Friedman** (✉ Old Town Artisans, 186 S. Meyer Ave., ☎ 520/622–5013); her designs in silver and semiprecious stones are unsurpassed.

NATIVE AMERICAN ARTS AND CRAFTS

Bahti Indian Arts (✉ St. Philip's Plaza, 4300 N. Campbell Ave., ☎ 520/577–0290) specializes in Native American art, including high-quality jewelry, pottery, baskets, and more. **Huntington Trading Co.** (✉ 111 E. Congress, ☎ 520/628–8578) carries masks and pottery made by the Yaqui and Tarahumara Indians. The **Kaibab Shops** (✉ 2841 N. Campbell Ave., ☎ 520/795–6905) have been selling a wide variety of Native American crafts in Tucson for 50 years.

WESTERN WEAR

Corral Western Wear (✉ 4525 E. Broadway Blvd., ☎ 520/322–6001), with a large array of shirts, hats, belts, jewelry, and boots, caters to both urban and authentic cowboys and cowgirls. **Stewart Boot Manufacturing** (✉ 30 W. 28th St., South Tucson., ☎ 520/622–2706) has been making handmade leather boots for more than 50 years. Factory imperfects are available.

Malls and Shopping Centers

El Con Mall (✉ 3601 E. Broadway at Alvernon Way, ☎ 520/795–9958) is Tucson's oldest mall and has more than 135 stores, including JCPenney, Foley's, Dillard's, and Montgomery Ward. It also is home to a popular movie theater.

Foothills Mall (✉ 7401 N. La Cholla Blvd. at Ina Rd., ☎ 520/742–7191), the most upscale of the malls, hasn't been very crowded since its two anchor department stores, Dillard's and Foley's, departed, but there is hope that a new Barnes and Nobles superstore will draw other retailers in. Right now the mall features a variety of tony boutiques, a 16-plex cinema, the Gadsden-Pacific Toy Train Museum (☞ Exploring Northern Tucson, *above*), and a good restaurant, Keaton's.

Park Mall (✉ 5870 E. Broadway at Wilmot Rd., ☎ 520/747–7575) is a family shopping mecca, one of those utilitarian places where you can get all that practical stuff checked off your list in one trip. It has more than 120 stores, including Sears, Dillard's, and Macy's.

St. Philip's Plaza (✉ 4280 N. Campbell Ave. at River Rd., ☎ 502/529–2775) arranges its chic shops around a series of Spanish-style outdoor patios. After shopping such boutiques as Nicole Miller, Obsidian, El Presidio, and Turquoise Door galleries, you can enjoy a meal at Café Terra Cotta, Ovens, or Daniel's, all among Tucson's top eateries.

Tucson Mall (✉ 4500 N. Oracle Rd. at Wetmore Rd., ☎ 520/293–7330) is probably the most heavily shopped mall in town, serving both the sophisticated and the family shopper with two floors of stores, including Foley's, Dillard's, Macy's, Mervyn's, Sears, JCPenney, and almost 200 specialty shops. For tasteful southwestern T-shirts, belts, jewelry, and posters, try Señor Coyote, on Arizona Avenue, a section of the first floor devoted to regional items.

SIDE TRIPS

South of Tucson

There's something for everyone—history buffs, bird-watchers, hikers, Mexican-food lovers, and folks whose idea of heaven is to shop until they drop—en route from Tucson to Nogales along I–19. The road roughly follows the Camino Real (King's Road), which the conquistadors and missionaries traveled from Mexico up to what was once the northernmost portion of New Spain. A return to Tucson via Patagonia and the wine country makes this an ambitious but extremely rewarding day trip.

Numbers in the margin correspond to points of interest on the South of Tucson map.

Madera Canyon

34 *61½ mi southeast of Tucson.*

At Madera Canyon, the Coronado National Forest meets the Santa Rita Mountains—among them Mt. Wrightson, the highest peak in southern Arizona at 9,453 feet. With approximately 200 mi of scenic trails, the **Madera Canyon Recreation Area** (☎ 520/670–5464 in Tucson) is a favorite destination for hikers. Higher elevations and thick pine cover make it especially popular in summer with Tucsonans looking to escape the heat. Birders flock here year-round; about 400 avian species have been spotted in the area. As you enter the recreation area, you'll see a small visitor center, open only on weekends and operated by the volunteer Friends of Madera Canyon. Nearby, the Box Springs campground has 13 sites with toilets, potable water, and grills, available on a first-come, first-served basis (🎫 $5 per vehicle per night). ✉ *Exit 63 off I–19, then east on White House Canyon Rd. for 12.5 mi (it turns into Madera Canyon Rd.).*

Tubac

★ 35 *45 mi south of Tucson.*

Tubac is the site of the first European settlement in Arizona in 1726. A year after the Pima Indian uprising in 1851, a military garrison was established here to protect early Spanish settlers, missionaries, and peaceful Indian converts of the nearby Tumacacori Mission (☞ *below*) from further attack. It was from here that Juan Bautista de Anza led the expedition of 240 colonists across the desert that resulted in the founding of San Francisco in 1776. Arizona's first newspaper, the *Weekly Arizonian,* was printed here in 1859, and in 1860 Tubac was the largest town in Arizona. Today, the quiet little town is a popular art colony. Crafts sold in the more than 80 shops—mostly staffed by the artists who make the goods sold in them—range from carved wooden furniture and hand-thrown pottery to delicately painted tiles and silkscreen fabrics. The annual **Tubac Festival of the Arts** has been held in February for more than 30 years. For dates or other information about the town, contact the Tubac Chamber of Commerce (☎ 520/398–2704) or visit the Tubac Presidio State Historic Park (☞ *below*).

There's an archaeological display of portions of the original 1752 fort at the **Tubac Presidio State Historic Park and Museum** in the center of town. In addition to the visitor center, which has an exhibit area detailing the history of the early colony, the park includes Tubac's 1885 schoolhouse and a pleasant picnic area. ✉ *Presidio Dr.,* ☎ *520/398–2252.* 🎫 *$2.* ⏲ *Daily 8–5.*

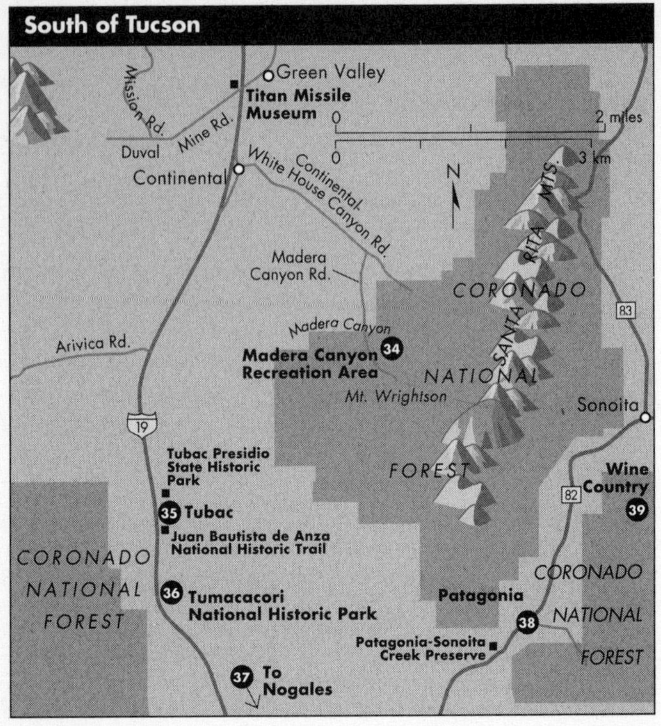

DINING

Tubac Country Market. Just north of Tubac on the road paralleling I–19, this combination gift shop, deli, and grocery also features a patio restaurant—with a stunning vista—that's open every day for breakfast and lunch. Try the jalapeño popper, a deep fried pepper stuffed with sour cream or cheddar cheese. Reasonably priced and well-prepared American dinners are available Thursday through Saturday by reservation only. The entrées on the set menu ($11.95) change every month but might include stuffed shrimp or beef tenderloin. ✉ *401 E. Frontage Rd.,* ☎ *520/398–9532 or 520/884–1914. MC, V.*

En Route You can tread the same road as the conquistadors: The first 4½ mi of the de Anza National Historic Trail from Tumacacori to Tubac were dedicated in 1992. You'll have to cross the Santa Cruz River (which is usually pretty low) three times in order to complete the hike, and the path is rather sandy, but it's a pleasant journey along the tree-shaded banks of the river.

Tumacacori National Historic Park

36 *3 mi south of Tubac.*

The site where Tumacacori National Historic Park now stands was visited by missionary Father Eusebio Francisco Kino in 1691, but the Jesuits didn't build a church here until 1751. Visitors can still see some ruins of this simple structure, but the main attraction is the mission of San José de Tumacacori, built by the Franciscans around 1799–1803. A combination of circumstances—Apache attacks, a bad winter, and Mexico's withdrawal of funds and priests—caused the friars to flee in 1848, and persistent rumors of wealth left behind by both the Franciscans and the Jesuits led treasure-seekers to pillage the site unsuccessfully. It was finally protected in 1908, when it became a national monument.

Information about the mission and the de Anza trail is available at the visitor center. Guided tours are also offered daily (more in winter than in summer). A small museum displays some of the mission's original artifacts, and the patio garden boasts a variety of native plants. In 1990, when Tumacacori became a national historic park, two mission ruins were added, both about 15 mi to the south. They are currently being excavated, however, and are not open to the public. In addition to a Christmas Eve service, costumed historical high masses are held at Tumacacori in spring and fall. An annual fiesta held here in the first week of December features arts and crafts and food booths. ✉ *Exit 29 off I–19,* ☎ *520/398–2341.* 🎫 *$2.* 🕒 *Daily 8–5.*

Nogales

37 *15 mi south of Tumacacori, 63 mi south of Tucson.*

A bustling border town, Nogales can get fairly rowdy on weekends, when underage Tucsonians head south to drink, but it offers some good restaurants and fine-quality crafts and furnishings in addition to the usual border schlock. If you're just coming for the day, it's best to park on the Arizona side of the border (you'll see many guarded lots that cost about $4 or $5 for the day) and walk across. Practically all the good shopping is within easy strolling distance of the border.

DINING

$$ ✕ **El Balcon de la Roca.** Lots of Tucsonans head down to this elegant restaurant on the sprawling second floor of a stately old stone house for special-occasion dinners. A balcony overlooks a charming patio with magnolia trees. Among the excellent variety of meat or seafood dishes is *carne tampiqueña,* an assortment of grilled meats that comes with a chile relleno and an enchilada. ✉ *Calle Elias 91,* ☎ *631/2–07–60 or 631/2–08–91. AE, DC, MC, V.*

$ ✕ **Elvira.** The free shot of tequila that comes with each meal will whet your appetite for Elvira's fine fish dishes, chicken mole, or chile rellenos. This large, friendly restaurant (divided into more intimate dining areas) is at the very end of Avenida Obregón next to the border and popular with frequent visitors to Nogales. ✉ *Av. Obregón 1,* ☎ *631/2–47–73. Reservations not accepted. DC, MC, V.*

SHOPPING

The shopping area centers mainly on Avenida Obregón, which begins a few blocks west of the border entrance and runs north–south; just follow the crowds. You'll find a wide selection of handicrafts, furnishings, and jewelry here. Except at shops that indicate otherwise, bargaining is not only acceptable but expected. The following shops, however, tend to have fixed prices:

El Changarro (✉ Calle Elias 93, ☎ 613/2–05–45), east of the railroad tracks and off the beaten tourist path, carries high-quality furniture, antiques, pottery, and handwoven rugs.

El Sarape (✉ Av. Obregón 161, ☎ 631/2–03–09) specializes in sterling silver jewelry from Taxco and designer clothing for women.

Firenze (✉ Av. Obregón 111, ☎ 613/2–22–52) features gifts, fine perfumes and beauty products, and crafts.

Mickey & CIA (✉ Av. Obregón 128–130, ☎ 631/2–22–99) has two floors of handcrafted Mexican treasures, *equipale* (pigskin) furniture, Talavera ceramic dishes, pottery, glassware, and liquors.

Patagonia

38 *18 mi northeast of Nogales, 82 mi southeast of Tucson.*

Art galleries and boutiques coexist with real western saloons in Patagonia, a tiny, tree-lined town surrounded by rolling hills and choice cattle-grazing land. For the most scenic route here from Tucson, take I–10 to AZ 83 south and then pick up AZ 82 in Sonoita. The cheerful Ovens of Patagonia (✉ corner 3rd Ave. and AZ 82, ☎ 520/394–2483) is a pleasant place to stop for a quiche or a cappuccino, and the Mesquite Grove Gallery (✉ 371 McKoewn Ave., ☎ 520/394–2358) carries an appealing array of local crafts. Both are in the center of town, as is the Santa Cruz Winery (☞ Wine Country, *below*).

At the **Patagonia–Sonoita Creek Preserve,** 750 acres of riparian habitat are protected along the Patagonia–Sonoita Creek. More than 275 bird species have been sighted here, along with deer, javelina, coatimundi, desert tortoise, snakes, and more. A new visitor center offers interpretive exhibits and guided walks, and a self-guided nature trail has just been established. You must call ahead and make reservations before you visit. ✉ *To get here, make a right on 4th Ave., which comes to a dead end, and then make a left. This paved road soon becomes dirt and leads to the preserve in about ¾ mi;* ☎ *520/394–2400.* 🎫 *Donations appreciated.* ⏲ *Wed.–Sun. 7:30–3:30.*

Wine Country

39 *Region southeast of Tucson.*

Wyatt Earp might have been hooted out of town if he had swaggered up to a bar and ordered a glass of cabernet, but wine is in these days in cowboy country. Connoisseurs debate the merits of the various wineries that have sprung up in the region southeast of Tucson since 1974, but if you want to decide for yourself, you might start a tour with **R. W. Webb** (✉ 13605 E. Benson Hwy., ☎ 520/762–5777). Take I–10 east about 12 mi, and get off at Vail, Exit 279. Most of the other growers are in the area where Routes 82 and 83 intersect: Get back on I–10 for two more exits, and then drive south on Route 83 for 24 mi to Sonoita. Growers in the scenic ranching region nearby include **Sonoita Vineyards** (✉ 3 mi southeast of Elgin, ☎ 520/455–5893), the kosher **Santa Cruz Winery** (✉ 154 McKoewn Ave., Patagonia, ☎ 520/394–2888), and **Arizona Vineyards** (✉ 1830 Patagonia Hwy., 4 mi northeast of Nogales on Rte. 82, ☎ 520/287–7972). Santa Cruz is open for tastings Thursday through Sunday; the others are open daily. Call ahead for hours.

DINING

Wine country hosts two surprisingly sophisticated but reasonably priced restaurants.

✕ **Er Pastaro.** This homey, low-key place established by a former manager of Regine's in New York offers a variety of sauces for its pastas, as well as a good choice of Italian wines. ✉ *3084 Hwy. 82, Sonoita,* ☎ *520/455–5821. MC, V. Closed Mon., Tues. No lunch.*

✕ **Karen's Wine Country Cafe.** Karen's could be straight out of Sonoma, California, with its country French–style patio and innovative menu focusing on salads and pasta dishes—and, of course, a good selection of wines by the glass. ✉ *471 Upper Elgin Rd., Elgin,* ☎ *520/455–5282. MC, V. Closed Mon.–Wed. No dinner Thurs., Sun.*

Southeast Arizona

The southeast corner of Arizona is a mix of ghost towns, rugged rock formations;dense, deep forests; and mountain mining towns. It's the site of Chiricahua National Monument, one of Arizona's best-kept secrets, and a paradise for birders, hikers, and antiquers—and anyone else who has an interest in frontier history. Many consider this to be Arizona's most scenic region.

Much of this area is part of Cochise County, named in 1881 in honor of the chief of the Chiricahua Apache. Cochise waged war against troops and settlers for 11 years, but he was respected by Indian and non-Indian alike for his integrity and leadership skills. Today Cochise County is dotted by small towns, many of them much smaller—and all much tamer—than they were in their heyday. It's hard to imagine now, but Tombstone, headquarters for most of the area's gamblers and gunfighters, was once bigger than San Francisco. These days it derives most of its revenue from tourism.

The area's terrain ranges from the rugged forests of its mountains to the desert grasslands of Sierra Vista. Cochise County is home to six and part of the seventh of the 12 mountain ranges—including the Huachucas, Mustangs, Whetstones, and Rincons—that compose the 1.7-million-acre Coronado National Forest.

Numbers in the margin correspond to points of interest on the Southeast Arizona map.

Benson

40 *50 mi east of Tucson.*

Once the hub of the Southern Pacific Railroad and a stop on the Butterfield Stagecoach route, Benson is now a fairly sleepy little town. With the start-up of the **San Pedro & Southwestern Railroad** (☞ Guided Tours *in* Southeast Arizona A to Z, *below*) in early 1995, Benson began to draw a few more visitors. As you pass through Benson on I–10, watch for Ocotillo Avenue, Exit 304. Take a left and drive about 2¼ mi, where a mailbox with a backward SW signals that you've come to the turnoff for **Singing Wind Bookshop** (✉ Ocotillo Ave., ☎ 520/586–2425). Make a right at the mailbox and drive ¼ mile until you see a green gate. Let yourself in, close the gate, and go another ¼ mile to the store. If you don't see the proprietor, who also runs the ranch, ring the large gong out front and she's sure to come out and welcome you. This unique bookshop-on-a-ranch has an excellent selection of books on Arizona wildlife, history, and geology.

NEED A BREAK? For a good green-chili burrito or a patty melt, stop in at the **Horseshoe Cafe** (✉ 154 E. 4th St., ☎ 520/586–3303), which has occupied its current site on Benson's main street for more than 50 years. The neon horseshoe on the ceiling, the macramés of local cattle brands, and the large Wurlitzer jukebox all give this casual restaurant and lounge a unique western character.

Texas Canyon

41 *12 mi of east Benson, 63 mi east of Tucson.*

Signs on I–10 will tell you that you're entering Texas Canyon, but you'll know just from looking around you. The rock formations here are exceptional—huge boulders appear to be delicately balanced against each other.

Texas Canyon is also the home of the **Amerind Foundation** (a contraction of "American" and "Indian"), founded by amateur archaeologist William Fulton in 1937 to foster understanding about Native American cultures. The research facility and museum, built between 1930 and 1959, are housed in a beautiful Spanish colonial revival–style

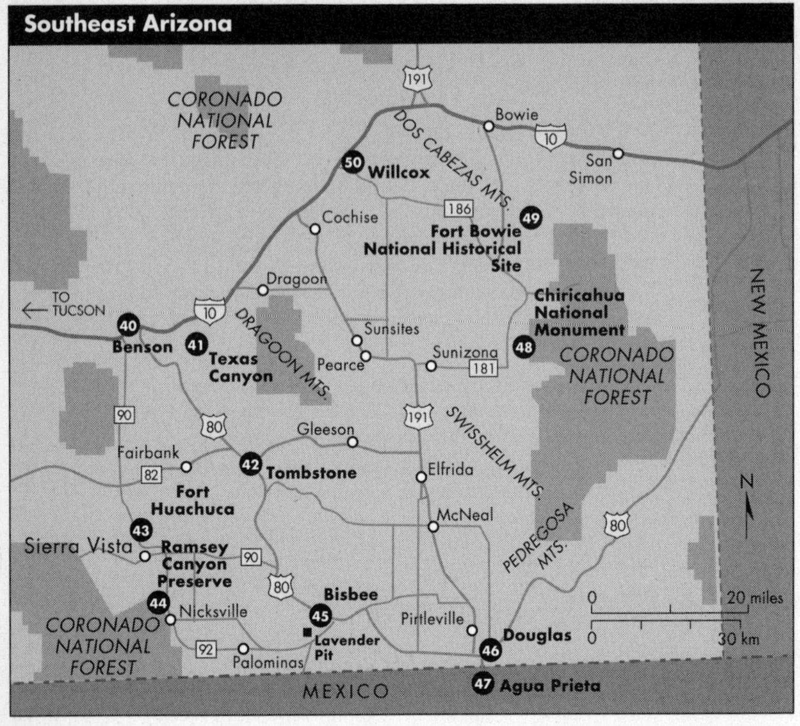

structure designed by noted Tucson architect H. M. Starkweather (the landmark Arizona Inn in Tucson is another example of his work).

Visitors to the museum are given an overview of Native American cultures of the Southwest and Mexico through well-designed rotating displays of archaeological materials, crafts, and photographs. The museum store is well stocked with books on history and Native American cultures, as well as items created by Native American craftspeople. The adjacent Fulton–Hayden Memorial Art Gallery offers an interesting assortment of art collected by William Fulton, mostly from the Southwest. The natural setting and the quality of the exhibits at the foundation make a visit here delightful as well as educational. ✉ *Dragoon Rd., 1 mi southeast of I–10 (Exit 318),* ☎ *520/586–3666.* 🎫 *$3.* ⏲ *Sept.–May, daily 10–4; June–Aug., Wed.–Sun. 10–4.*

Tombstone

42 *24 mi south of Benson.*

The legendary headquarters of Wild West rowdies, Tombstone was part of an area called Goose Flats in the late 1800s and was prone to attack by nearby Apache tribesmen. The intrepid prospector, Ed Schieffelin, wasn't discouraged by those who cautioned that "all you'll find there is your tombstone." In 1877 he struck one of the West's richest veins of silver in the tough old hills and gave the town its name as an "I told you so." He called the silver mine Lucky Cuss, figuring that he fit the description himself.

The promise of riches attracted all types of folks, including outlaws. Soon gambling halls, saloons, and houses of prostitution sprang up all along Allen Street. In 1881 the Earp family and Doc Holliday battled to the death with the Clanton boys at the famous shoot-out at the OK Corral. Over the past 100 years or so, scriptwriters and storytellers have done much to rewrite the exact details of the confrontation, but it's a fact that the town was the scene of several gunfights in the 1880s. On Sunday, visitors are treated to replays of some of these on Allen Street.

Tombstone's rough-and-ready heyday was popularized by Hollywood in the 1930s and capitalized on by the local tourist industry in the decades that followed, but there's more to the town than the OK Corral, the souvenir shops on Allen Street, and the staged shoot-outs. "The town too tough to die" (it survived two major fires, an earthquake, the closing of the mines, and the moving of the county seat to Bisbee) was also a cultural center, and many of its original buildings remain intact. Check with the **Tombstone Office of Tourism** (☞ Southeast Arizona A to Z, *below*) for a walking tour that includes several of the town's currently unmarked sights.

Boot Hill Graveyard, where the victims of the OK Corral shoot-out are buried, is on the northwestern corner of town, facing U.S. 80. The commercialism of the place may turn you off (you enter through a gift shop that sells novelty items in the shape of tombstones), but the site itself is interesting. Chinese names in one section bear testament to the laundry and restaurant workers who came from San Francisco during the height of Tombstone's mining fever. About a third of the more than 350 graves dug here from 1879 to 1974 are unmarked.

The **Tombstone Courthouse State Historic Park** offers an excellent introduction to the town's—and the area's—past. The largest settlement between San Francisco and St. Louis in 1881, Tombstone was chosen as the seat of the newly established Cochise County. The courthouse built the next year was an expensive, stylish affair. Displays include a reconstruction of the original courtroom, numerous photographs of prominent—and notorious—town figures, and such area artifacts as the dozens of types of barbed wire used by local cattle ranchers. ✉ *Toughnut and 3rd Sts.,* ☎ *520/457–3311.* 🎫 *$2.* ⏲ *Daily 8–5.*

Originally a boardinghouse for the Vizina Mining Company and later a popular hotel, the **Rose Tree Inn Museum,** with its 1880s period rooms and huge rose bush on the patio (listed in the *Guinness Book of Records* as the largest in the world), displays the gentler side of life in Tombstone. ✉ *Toughnut and 4th Sts.,* ☎ *520/457–3326.* 🎫 *$2.* ⏲ *Daily 9–5.*

You'll get a dramatic version of the town's history, narrated by Vincent Price, in the **Historama** on Allen Street, a block to the north. At the adjoining **OK Corral,** a recorded voice-over details the town's most famous event, while life-size figures of the gunfight's participants stand poised to shoot. Photographer C. S. Fly, whose studio was next door to the corral, didn't record this bit of history, but Geronimo and his pursuers were among the historical figures he did capture with his camera. Many of his fascinating Old West images may be viewed at the **Fly Exhibition Gallery.** ✉ *Allen St., between 3rd and 4th Sts.,* ☎ *520/457–3456.* 🎫 *Historama $2, OK Corral and Fly Exhibition Gallery $2.* ⏲ *Daily 8:30–5; Historama shows every hr on the hr 9–4.*

Allen Street, the town's main drag, is lined with restaurants and curio shops. Many of the street's buildings still bear bullet holes from their livelier days, and some of the remaining artifacts are interesting—including the original printing presses for the town's newspaper, the *Tombstone Epitaph* (✉ 9 S. 5th St., ☎ 520/457–2211), founded in 1880 and still publishing. (If the town's other newspaper, the *Nugget,* had survived instead, the Clanton boys might be mourned as martyrs today, but it was the Earp-supporting *Epitaph* and its version of history that endured.)

NEED A BREAK?

Sightseeing is thirsty work, and what better place to wet your whistle than one of Tombstone's saloons? The **Crystal Palace** (✉ Allen and 5th Sts., ☎ 520/457–3611) has a beautiful mirrored mahogany bar, wrought-iron chandeliers, and tinwork ceilings. Locals come here on weekends to dance to live country-and-western music.

A Tombstone institution, the **Bird Cage Theater** is a former music hall where Caruso, Sarah Bernhardt, and Lillian Russell—among others—performed. The displays are dusty and chaotic, but if you poke around, you can find such treasures as the 1881 Black Maria hearse that brought all the victims of the OK Corral shoot-out—and everyone else who died in Tombstone—to the Boot Hill cemetery. ✉ *6th and Allen Sts.,* ☎ *520/457–3421).* *$3.50.* *Daily 8–6 or 6:30.*

DINING AND LODGING

$$ ✕ **Bella Union.** A good spot for a leisurely dinner—service is none too swift here—the Bella Union offers well-priced American standards such as steaks and chops in a nice setting. The 1881 building, off the main commercial drag, has a tastefully restored front saloon with a piano and low-key dining-room decor. An old gazette-style menu highlights breakfast combinations, blue-plate lunch specials, and a wide range of dinner entrées. A country-western singer croons on weekend evenings. ✉ *401 E. Fremont St.,* ☎ *520/457–3656. AE, D, MC, V.*

✕ **Nellie Cashman's.** You can order up anything from a burger to a hearty dinner platter of juicy pork chops or chicken-fried steak in this homey spot, named for the original owner, a Tombstone pioneer who opened a hotel and restaurant in 1882. The restaurant's walls are hung with old photographs and postcards, and there is a massive stone fireplace, with an assortment of family photos on the mantel. Nellie's is also a great place for a country breakfast complete with biscuits and gravy. ✉ *5th and Toughnut Sts.,* ☎ *520/457–2212. AE, D, MC, V.*

$–$$ **The Best Western Look-Out Lodge.** Set off U.S. 80 on the way into town, this motel has a lot of character. The rooms feature western-print bedspreads, Victorian-style lamps, and locally made wood-hewn clocks. All have views of the Dragoon Mountains and desert valley. A Continental breakfast is included in the rate. The front desk and switchboard close at 10 PM, so you'll need to check in and receive any phone calls before then. ✉ *U.S. 80 West, Box 787, 85638,* ☎ *520/457–2223 or 800/652–6772,* FAX *520/457–3870. 40 rooms with bath. Pool. AE, D, DC, MC, V.*

$ **Tombstone Boarding House.** Two meticulously restored 1880s adobes sit side by side in a quiet residential neighborhood. Guests of this friendly bed-and-breakfast sleep in one house and go next door to have a hearty country breakfast. It's ideal for those who like the intimacy of a bed-and-breakfast but feel a bit odd about staying in someone's house. Complimentary drinks are offered in the afternoon at a nearby restaurant. ✉ *108 N. 4th St., Box 906, 85638,* ☎ *520/457–3716. 8 rooms with bath. No credit cards.*

Fort Huachuca

43 *24 mi southwest of Tombstone.*

Historic Fort Huachuca, currently the headquarters of the army's Global Information Systems Command, is the last of the great western forts still in operation. It dates back to 1877, when the Buffalo Soldiers, the first all-black regiment in the U.S. forces, came to aid settlers battling invaders from Mexico, Indian tribes reluctant to give up their homelands, and assorted American desperadoes hiding out from crimes committed back east. Three miles from the fort's main gate is the Fort

Huachuca Museum, housed in a late-19th-century frame building that originally served as bachelor officers' quarters. The museum and its annex across the street provide a fascinating record of military life on the frontier. ⊠ *AZ 90, west of Sierra Vista,* ☎ *520/538–7111.* 🎟 *Free.* ⏲ *Weekdays 9–4, weekends 1–4.*

Ramsey Canyon Preserve

44 *30 mi southwest of Tombstone.*

Hikers and bird-watchers alike flock to the Ramsey Canyon Preserve, managed by the Nature Conservancy. Between April and October, 14 species of hummingbird come to the area, and coatimundi and white-tail deer are among other wildlife that make it their home. There are, of course, hiking trails through the preserve as well. Reservations are required on weekends and federal holidays, and the 13 parking spots fill up quickly on weekdays in the busiest months of April, May, and August. Reserve well in advance for one of the Conservancy's fully equipped cabins in the preserve. Register at the visitor center, where maps and books on the area's natural history, flora, and fauna are available. ⊠ *27 Ramsey Canyon Rd., Hereford (off AZ 92 a few miles north of Nicksville),* ☎ *520/378–2785.* 🎟 *$5 suggested donation for nonmembers.* ⏲ *Daily 8–5.*

Bisbee

45 *31 mi east of Ramsey Canyon Preserve, 24 mi south of Tombstone.*

Like Tombstone, Bisbee was a mining boomtown, but its wealth was in copper, not silver, and its success much longer lived. It wasn't until 1975 that the last mine closed and the city went into decline. However, it was rediscovered in the early 1980s by burned-out city dwellers and revived as a kind of Woodstock West. The permanent population is a mix of retired miners and their families, aging hippie jewelry-makers, and enterprising young restaurateurs and antiques dealers. The three rather disparate groups seem to get along fine—Bisbee is that kind of place.

When you drive through Mule Mountain Tunnel on U.S. 80, you'll be getting close. You'll see the pretty, compact town hugging the steep mountainside on your left. If you want to head straight into town, get off at Brewery Gulch interchange. You can park here and cross under the highway, taking Main or Commerce or Brewery Gulch Street, all of which meet here.

Another option is to continue driving on U.S. 80 about ¼ mile to where it intersects with AZ 92. Pull off the highway on the right into a gravel parking lot, where a short, typewritten history of the **Lavender Pit Mine** can be found attached to the hurricane fence surrounding the area (Bisbee isn't big on formal exhibits). The hole left by the copper miners is huge, with piles of lavender-hue "tailings," or waste, creating mountains around it. Arizona's largest pit mine yielded some 94 million tons of copper ore out of more than 280 million tons of raw materials before the town's mining activity came to a halt.

For a real lesson in mining history, take the **Copper Queen mine tour.** The mine is less than a half mile to the east of the Lavender Pit, across U.S. 80 from downtown at the Brewery Gulch interchange. Tours are led by one of Bisbee's several retired copper miners, who are wont to embellish their official spiel with tales from their mining days. They're also very capable, safety-minded people (any miner who survives to lead tours in his older years would have to be), so don't be concerned about the precautionary dog tags (literally—they're donated by a local veterinarian) issued to each person on the tour.

The tours, which depart daily at 9, 10:30, noon, 2, and 3:30 (you can't enter the mine at any other time), last anywhere from 1 to 1½ hours, and visitors go into the shaft via a little open train, like those the miners rode when the mine was active. Before you climb aboard, you're outfitted in miner's garb—a yellow slicker and a hard hat that runs off a battery pack strapped to your waist. You may want to wear a sweater or light coat under your slicker because the temperature in the mine is a brisk 47°F on average. You'll travel by train thousands of feet into the mine, up a grade of 30 feet (not down, as many visitors expect). Those who are a bit claustrophobic might consider taking one of the surface tours that depart from the building at the same times as the mine tours (excluding 9 AM). They cover Old Bisbee and the perimeter of the Lavender Pit mine, as well as the old leaching plant. ✉ *478 N. Dart Rd.,* ☎ *520/432–2071.* 🎫 *Mine tour $8, surface tour $7.* ⏲ *Daily.*

The **Mining and Historical Museum** is housed in the old redbrick Phelps Dodge general office (Phelps Dodge was the operator of the town's copper mines), right across the street from the Copper Queen mine. The museum is filled with old photographs and artifacts from the town's mining days and explores other aspects of the first 40 years of Bisbee's history, from 1887 to 1920. It's fun to walk out of the museum and view the same buildings you've just seen depicted inside. ✉ *No. 5 Copper Queen Plaza,* ☎ *520/432–7071.* 🎫 *$3.* ⏲ *Daily 10–4.*

The venerable old **Copper Queen Hotel** (☞ Dining and Lodging, *below*), built a century ago, is behind the Mining and Historical Museum. It has housed the famous as well as the infamous: "Black Jack" Pershing, John Wayne, Teddy Roosevelt, and mining executives from all over the world made this their home away from home.

Brewery Gulch, a short street running north and south, is adjacent to the Copper Queen Hotel (walk out the front door of the Copper Queen, make a left, and you'll be there in about 20 paces). Largely abandoned, it's lined with boarded-up storefronts. In the old days, the brewery housed there allowed the dregs of the beer that was being brewed to flow down the street and into the gutter.

NEED A BREAK?

Café Maxie (✉ No. 2 Copper Queen Plaza, ☎ 520/432–7063), once the Phelps Dodge General Mercantile Store and now the town's convention center, is a good place for homemade soups and sandwiches. A white silk parachute covers the ceiling. Take a trip upstairs to the rest rooms for a view of the lobby down below, with its rich copper (what else?) light fixtures and handrails.

Bisbee's **Main Street** is very much alive and retailing. This hilly commercial thoroughfare is lined with appealing crafts shops, boutiques, and restaurants, many of them in well-preserved turn-of-the-century brick buildings.

DINING AND LODGING

$$–$$$ ✕ **Stenzel's.** Although this intimate, attractive restaurant, set in a white clapboard cottage off the side of the road, is touted by locals for its seafood specialties, the succulent barbecued ribs and well-seasoned grilled chicken breast are equally fine. Or you might try the fettuccine Alfredo, an outstanding specialty. There's a decent wine list. ✉ *207 Tombstone Canyon,* ☎ *520/432–7611. MC, V. Closed Wed. No lunch weekends.*

$$ ★ ✕ **Café Roka.** Roka is the deserved darling of the hip Bisbee crowd. The constantly changing northern Italian–style evening menu is small, but you can count on whatever you order—chicken with ricotta and basil cannelloni, sea scallops with spinach pasta—to be wonderful. Portions are generous, and the entrée price ($8.50–$15.50) includes soup, salad, and a pasta-based main course preceded by a sorbet. The dining room, with exposed brick walls and the original 1906 tinwork ceiling, looks onto a central bar, which offers a nice selection of wines and cognacs. Smoking is not permitted. ✉ *35 Main St.,* ☎ *520/432–5153. MC, V. Closed Sun.–Tues. No lunch.*

$$ ★ 🏨 **Copper Queen Hotel.** Built by the Copper Queen Mining Company (which later became the Phelps Dodge Corporation) at a time when Bisbee was the biggest copper-mining town in the world, this hotel in the heart of downtown Bisbee has been operating since 1902. The upstairs halls are lined with photos of its early days. Some of the accommodations are small or oddly laid out and the walls between them are thin, but all have a Victorian charm. Ask for a room that's been renovated. Guests over the years have included a host of wild and crazy prospectors as well as more respectable types. Today's visitors are also a varied lot, as likely to include a film producer scouting locations as a retired snowbird from Minnesota. ✉ *11 Howell Ave., Drawer CQ, 85603,* ☎ *520/432–2216 or 800/247–5829,* FAX *520/432–4298. 43 rooms with bath. Dining room, bar, pool. AE, D, DC, MC, V.*

$–$$ 🏨 **The Clawson House.** Terrific views of the town from the sun porch, a light-filled kitchen, and generous but health-conscious breakfasts are among the reasons to seek out this bed-and-breakfast on Old Bisbee's Castle Rock. The owners' art and antiques collections grace a beautifully restored former residence, built in 1895 for the superintendent of the Copper Queen Mine. If the Clawson House is full, you'll be offered alternate accommodations in the same owners' Main Street Inn (✉ 26 Main St., ☎ 520/432–5237), two 1888 buildings with one suite and 8 guest rooms furnished in handsome southwestern style. ✉ *116 Clawson Ave., Box 454, 85603,* ☎ *520/432–5237 or 800/467–5237. 1 room with bath, 2 rooms with shared bath. AE, D, MC, V.*

$–$$ 🏨 **High Desert Inn.** In the heart of downtown Bisbee, the High Desert Inn is housed in the old (1901) Cochise County Jail building. Behind an imposing classical facade highlighted by four monumental Doric columns, this sophisticated but friendly hostelry offers modern rooms that include color TV and private telephones (a rarity in Bisbee accommodations). Decor includes wrought-iron beds from France, wicker and wrought-iron tables, and wicker chairs. The inn has a small bar and a dining room (open for dinner Thursday through Sunday) run by a Cordon Bleu–trained chef. ✉ *8 Naco Rd., Box 145, 85603,* ☎ *520/432–1442 or 800/281–0510. 6 rooms with bath. D, MC, V.*

$–$$ 🏨 **School House Inn.** You'll flash back to your classroom days at this former school house, built in 1918 at the height of Bisbee's mining days and now transformed into a spacious bed-and-breakfast inn. Perched on the side of a hill, the two-story brick building has a pleasant outdoor patio shaded by an oak tree. In keeping with its educational past, the inn's rooms all have a theme—music, history, geography, arithmetic—reflected in the decor (though, surprisingly, there is no writing desk in the writing room). Twelve-foot-high ceilings contribute to an overall airy effect. ✉ *818 Tombstone Canyon Rd., Box 32, 85603,* ☎ *520/432–2996 or 800/537–4333. 9 rooms with bath. AE, D, DC, MC, V.*

Douglas

46 *23 mi southeast of Bisbee.*

This town on the U.S.–Mexico border was founded in 1902 by James Douglas to serve as the copper-smelting center for the mines in Bisbee. Douglas's house, now owned by the Arizona Historical Society, is open to the public as the **Douglas/Williams House Museum** (✉ 1001 D Ave., ☎ 520/364–2687 or 520/364–2636). There's not much to see here and hours are limited, but there are some interesting old photographs and mementos.

The must-see historic landmark in town and still the center of much of Douglas's activity is the **Gadsden Hotel** (☞ Lodging, *below*), built in 1907. The lobby contains a solid white Italian-marble staircase, two authentic Tiffany vaulted skylights, and a 42-foot stained-glass mural. One thousand ounces of 14-karat gold leaf were used to decorate the capitals. When you leave the hotel and walk out onto G Avenue, Douglas's main thoroughfare, you'll be taking a stroll back through time. A film company shooting here had to do very little to make the restaurants and shop fronts fit its 1940s plot line.

Before Douglas became the smelter for Bisbee, the site was the annual roundup ground for local ranchers, Mexican and American—among them John Slaughter, who was the sheriff of Cochise County after Wyatt Earp. The 300-acre **John Slaughter Ranch/San Bernardino Land Grant** offers a glimpse of life near the border in the late 19th and early 20th centuries. This National Historic Landmark includes the Slaughter family ranch house, filled with period furnishings and old photographs, as well as a number of the ranch's original outbuildings. A car shed holds a 1915 Model T Ford identical to the one owned by John Slaughter. You can also visit ruins of a military outpost established here in 1911 during the Mexican civil unrest and maintained by the U.S. Army until 1923. Much of the ride out to the ranch is via a graded dirt road that traverses a strikingly western landscape of rolling hills and desert scrub. ✉ *16 mi east of Douglas (from town, go east on 15th St., which turns into Geronimo Trail and leads to the ranch),* ☎ *520/558–2474.* 🎫 *$3.* ⏲ *Wed.–Sun. 10–3.*

LODGING

$–$$ 🏨 **The Gadsden Hotel.** Although recently refurbished, the rooms at this hotel—declared a National Historic Monument in 1976—are rather strangely decorated: Some fine antique pieces are thrown in among mismatched rugs, bedspreads, and drapes. Shower curtains are discordantly modern. And you'll sometimes hear clinking radiators at night. But the accommodations, which include suites and apartments with kitchenettes, are clean, comfortable, and very reasonably priced, and the art deco public areas are beautifully maintained. The hotel bar, with its array of local brands and local characters, looks as if it's straight out of *The Life and Times of Judge Roy Bean,* which was filmed here. ✉ *1046 G Ave., 85607,* ☎ *520/364–4481,* FAX *520/364–4005. 160 rooms with bath. Restaurant, bar, coffee shop, beauty salon. AE, DC, MC, V.*

Agua Prieta

47 *10 blocks from the center of Douglas, which extends to the Mexican border.*

Agua Prieta doesn't fit the stereotype of a Mexican border town. Like Douglas, it is a clean, pleasant place, but it's easy to imagine you're far from the States when you sit in the leafy plaza in the center of town. Agua Prieta's prime attraction for U.S. visitors is its assorted array of stores, offering inexpensive Mexican glassware, onyx and silver jewelry, pottery, cowboy boots, and ironwood carvings done by the Seri Indians. Since Agua Prieta is a free port, you can buy liquor at very reasonable prices. **Las Novedades Curios** (✉ Calle 3, 304, ☎ 633/8–07–30) is among the shops you'll find near the border crossing on Avenida Panamericana (the continuation of Douglas's Pan American Ave.). Note that most shops close for afternoon siesta and all day Sunday. You can have a decent Mexican lunch at **La Hacienda** (✉ corner of Calle 6 and 1st St., ☎ 633/8–06–74; turn left from Av. Panamericana at the border crossing). Tacos, burritos, enchiladas, and such are served in a pleasant setting sparked by colorful jugs of artificial flowers, pottery, and hanging plants. You can leave your car at the free (though unsupervised) parking lot at the corner of 3rd Street and Pan American Avenue in Douglas and walk across the border.

En Route En route from Douglas to Chiracahua National Monument, just past the town of Elfrida on U.S. 191, you'll see a turnoff for the ghost towns of Gleeson and Courtland. There's little to see here now except a few adobe ruins, but it's an interesting side trip if you've got time—and good shocks. As you approach Gleeson, the paved road becomes rutted dirt.

Chiracahua National Monument

48 *58 mi north of Douglas.*

The vast fields of desert grass that characterize most of the immediate area are suddenly transformed into a landscape of forest, mountains, and striking rock formations as you enter the 12,000-acre Chiricahua National Monument. Dubbed the Land of the Standing-Up Rocks by the Chiricahua Apache—who lived in the mountains for centuries and, led by Cochise and Geronimo, tried for 25 years to prevent white pioneers from settling here—this is an unusual site for a variety of reasons. The vast outcroppings of volcanic rock worn by erosion into strange pinnacles and spires are set in a forest where autumn and spring occur at the same time. Because of the particular balance of sunshine and rain in the area, in April and May visitors will see brown, yellow, and red leaves coexisting with new green foliage. Summer in Chiricahua National Monument is exceptionally wet: From July through September, there are thunderstorms nearly every afternoon. In addition, few other areas in the United States have such a variety of plant, bird, and animal life. Along with the plants and animals of the Southwest, the Chiracahua Mountains also host a number of Mexican species. Deer, coatimundis, peccaries, and lizards live among the aspen, ponderosa pine, Douglas fir, oak, and cypress trees—to name just a few. This is a natural mecca for bird-watchers, and hikers have more than 17 mi of scenic trails, ranging from half a mile to 13 mi long. At the visitor center, you can purchase a brochure describing the trails for 25¢. Lists of the mammals, snakes, and birds in the region are also available, and in spring and summer rangers give interpretive talks at the visitor center or at the campground amphitheater. ✉ *Dos Cabezas Route, Box 6500, Willcox 85643,* ☎ *520/824–3560.* 🎫 *$4 per car.* ⏲ *Visitor center daily 8–5.*

DINING AND LODGING

$$$–$$$$ ★ ✕🏨 **Grapevine Canyon Ranch.** This guest ranch in the Dragoon Mountains, approximately 80 mi southeast of Tucson in the town of Pearce, adjoins a working cattle ranch. Visitors get the chance to watch—and, in some cases, participate in—real day-to-day cowboy activities. Horses for all levels of experience are on hand, and there are lots of trails for hiking this quintessentially western terrain. Grapevine is also a good base from which to explore towns such as Douglas, Tombstone, and Bisbee, and nearby Chiricahua National Monument. Accommodations, either in adjacent cabins or private casitas, vary—some are rather plain, whereas others have striking southwestern-style furnishings—but all have spacious decks and porches. ✉ *Box 302, 85625,* ☎ *520/826–3185 or 800/245–9202,* FAX *520/826–3636. 12 rooms with bath. Pool, hot tub, horseback riding, coin laundry. AE, D, MC, V. 4-night minimum in peak season, 2-night minimum off-season.*

Fort Bowie National Historical Site

49 *5 mi north of Chiracahua National Monument.*

Arizona's last battle between Native Americans and U.S. troops is commemorated at Fort Bowie National Historical Site, in the Dos Cabezas (Two-Headed) Mountains. The nearby **Butterfield stage stop,** in the heart of Chiricahua Apache land, was a crucial link in the journey from east to west in the mid-19th century. Chief Cochise and the stagecoach operators ignored one another until sometime in 1861, when hostilities broke out between U.S. Cavalry troops and the Apache. After an ambush by the chief's warriors at Apache Pass in 1862, U.S. troops decided a fort was desperately needed in the area, and Fort Bowie was built within weeks. There were skirmishes for the next 10 years, followed by a peaceful decade. Renewed fighting broke out in 1881. Geronimo, the new leader of the Indian warriors, finally surrendered in 1886. The fort was abandoned eight years later and fell into disrepair.

To reach the site, take AZ 186 east from Chiracahua National Monument. About 5 mi north of the junction with AZ 181, you'll see signs directing you to the well-maintained gravel road leading to the fort. In order to get to the fort from the parking lot at the trailhead you must take a 1½-mile unpaved footpath. The site is virtually in ruins now, but there's a small ranger-staffed visitor center (☎ 520/847–2500) with a book-sale area, some historical displays, and rest rooms. The center is open daily 8–5, and admission to the site is free.

Willcox

50 *26 mi northwest of Fort Bowie, 78 mi east of Tucson.*

With fewer than 4,000 residents, Willcox is a major cattle-shipping center. Its downtown looks like an Old West movie set. An elevation of 4,167 feet renders the climate here moderate in summer and a bit chilly in winter. Apple-pie fans from all over Arizona know this little town as apple-growing headquarters. Enterprising Willcox cooks bake pies for customers as far away as Phoenix. If you visit in winter, you can see some of the more than 10,000 sandhill cranes that roost at the Willcox Playa, a 37,000-acre area resembling a dry lake bed some 12 mi south of Willcox. They migrate in late fall and head north to various nesting sites in February. Also near Willcox is the headquarters for the **Muleshoe Ranch Cooperative Management Area** (☎ 520/586–7072), nearly 49,000 acres of riparian desert land in the foothills of the Galiuro Mountains that are jointly owned and managed by the Nature Conservancy, the U.S. Forest Service, and the U.S. Bureau of Land Management. It's a 30-mile drive on a dirt road to the ranch—it takes about an hour to get there—but the scenery, wildlife, and hiking are well worth the bumps. Backroad Jeep tours or horseback rides and pack trips can be arranged by the ranch, and a variety of overnight accommodations are also available (☞ Lodging, *below*).

The **Rex Allen Arizona Cowboy Museum,** in Willcox's historic district, was set up as a tribute to Willcox's most famous native son, cowboy singer Rex Allen. He starred in several rather average cowboy movies during the '40s and '50s for Republic Pictures, but he's probably most famous as the friendly voice that narrated Walt Disney nature films. In 1994 the Willcox Cowboy Hall of Fame, saluting local cattlemen and rodeo riders, was moved here. ⊠ *155 N. Railroad Ave.,* ☎ *520/384–4583.* 🎟 *Suggested donation $2 single, $3 couple, $5 family.* ⏲ *Daily 10–4.*

The **Willcox Commercial Store** (⊠ 180 N. Railroad Ave., ☎ 520/384–2448), less than a block down the street from the Rex Allen Cowboy Museum, was established in 1881; it's the oldest retail establishment in Arizona that's still operating in its original location. Locals like to boast that Geronimo used to shop here. Today it's a clothing store, with a large selection of western wear.

The Chamber of Commerce is home to the **Museum of the Southwest,** which focuses on the Native American and military history of the area. You can see a sword belonging to Civil War general Orlando Willcox, for whom the town was named, though his only contact with it was a single ride-through on the train. Across the parking lot, you'll see Stout's Cider Mill (on the frontage road to I–10); it's a good place to pick up an apple pie. ✉ *1500 N. Circle I Rd.,* ☎ *520/384–2272 or 800/200–2272.* 🎫 *Free.* ⏲ *Mon.–Sat. 9–5, Sun. 1–5.*

LODGING

$–$$ **Muleshoe Ranch.** A former late-19th-century health spa is now a uniquely appealing property run by the Arizona chapter of the Nature Conservancy. Accommodations vary—four furnished housekeeping casitas have kitchens or kitchenettes, baths, and linens, whereas one is more rustic—but all are in a beautiful natural setting on a dirt road. There's a camping area ($6 per night per vehicle, with water and cold showers provided) as well as a visitor center, a nature trail, natural hot springs (for use by casita guests only), and a common room. The Conservancy runs natural-history workshops and, occasionally on Saturday, guided hikes. Overnight horseback riding packages are available in fall and spring. A 50% deposit is required when you make your reservation. ✉ *30 mi northwest of Willcox, R.R. 1, Box 1542, 85643,* ☎ *520/586–7072. 5 cabins, camping area. 2-night minimum Sept.–May and holiday weekends. No credit cards.*

Southeast Arizona A to Z

ARRIVING AND DEPARTING

#Do "By Bus" etc. need separate, coded heads?

By Bus. Greyhound Lines (☎ 800/231–2222) has service from Tucson to Douglas and Bisbee. You'll need to book a tour if you want to take the bus to Tombstone.

By Car. From Tucson, take I–10 east. When you reach the town of Benson, take U.S. 80 south (turn off at Benson) to reach Tombstone, Bisbee, and Douglas.

By Train. Amtrak (☎ 800/872–7245) trains run three times a week from Tucson to Benson.

GUIDED TOURS

The 3½-hour round-trip departs from Benson's new depot and follows the San Pedro River to Charleston, a ghost town between Tombstone and Sierra Vista. ✉ *796 E. Country Club Dr.,* ☎ *520/586–2266.* 🎫 *$15 one-way, $25 round-trip. Call ahead for schedules. Trains run Fri.–Sun.*

VISITOR INFORMATION

Benson–San Pedro Valley Chamber of Commerce (✉ 363 W. 4th St., Box 2255, Benson 85520, ☎ 520/586–2842).

Bisbee Chamber of Commerce (✉ 7 Main St., Box BA, Bisbee 85603, ☎ 520/432–5421).

Douglas Chamber of Commerce (✉ 1125 Pan American, Douglas 85607, ☎ 520/364–2477).

Tombstone Office of Tourism (✉ Box 917, Tombstone 85638, ☎ 520/457–3548 or 800/457–3423).

Willcox Chamber of Commerce & Agriculture (✉ 1500 N. Circle I Rd., Willcox 85643, ☎ 520/384–2272 or 800/200–2272).

Southwest Arizona

Many people just speed through southwest Arizona on their way to California, but the area has much to offer travelers willing to slow down for a closer look. The turbulent history of the West is writ large in this now-sleepy part of the state. It's home to the Tohonó O'odham Indian reservation (the largest in the country after the Navajo Nation's) and site of such towns as Ajo, created—and almost undone—by the copper-mining industry. Yuma, abutting the California border, was a major crossing point of the Colorado River as far back as the time of the conquistadors.

Natural history is also a lure in this starkly scenic region: Organ Pipe Cactus National Monument provides a number of trails for desert hikers, while birders and other nature-watchers will revel in the many unusual species to be observed at the little-visited Imperial National Wildlife Refuge on the lower Colorado.

On warm weekends and especially during semester breaks, the 130-mile route from Tucson to Ajo is well traveled by cars headed southwest to Puerto Penasco (Rocky Point), Mexico, the closest outlet to the sea for Arizonans. Much of the time, however, one can go for long stretches west on AZ 86 without seeing another vehicle. A great part of the way the landscape is flat, abundant with low-lying scrub and cactus as well as mesquite, ironwood, paloverde, and other desert trees.

Numbers in the margin correspond to points of interest on the Southwest Arizona map.

Kitt Peak National Observatory

51 *56 mi southwest of Tucson.*

Funded by the National Science Foundation and managed by a group of more than 20 universities, Kitt Peak National Observatory is part of the Tohonó O'odham reservation. After much discussion back in the late 1950s, tribal leaders agreed to share their 4,400 square mi with the observatory's 19 telescopes. Among these is the McMath, the world's largest solar telescope, which is cooled by piped-in coolant. From a visitors' gallery, you can see into the telescope's light-path tunnel, which goes down hundreds of feet into the mountain. In addition to the vital research into aspects of the sun carried out here, Kitt Peak scientists have also observed distant galaxies. The scientists and staff are friendly and knowledgeable and keen to share their enthusiasm for astronomy. Nor will the superb setting, including a close-up of the imposing Baboquivari Peak, sacred to the Tohonó O'odham people, fail to impress.

The museum's visitor center has exhibits on astronomy and information about the telescopes at the facility. Tapes, mostly about the making of telescopes and the work at the observatory, run continuously in a minitheater. Free guided tours, which take about an hour, depart from the center daily at 10:30 and 1:30. Complimentary brochures enable you to take self-guided tours. A gift shop sells excellent examples of Tohonó O'odham handiwork as well as astronomy-related items. To reach Kitt Peak from Tucson, take I–10 to I–19 south, and then AZ 86. After 44 mi on AZ 86, turn left at the AZ 386 junction and follow the winding mountain road 12 mi up to the observatory. (In inclement weather, contact the highway department to confirm that the road is open.) There's a picnic area about 1½ mi below the observatory. Aside

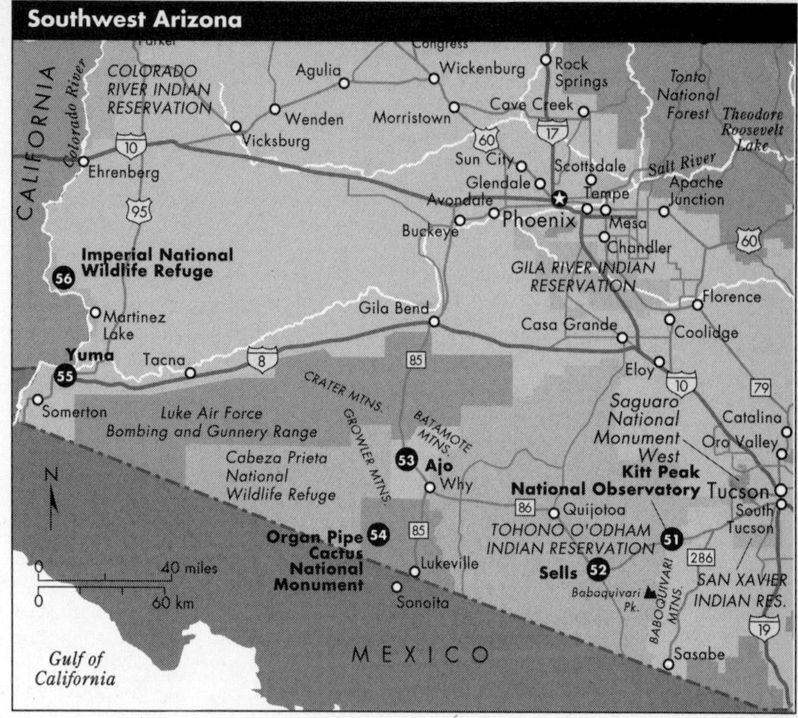

from vending machines in the observatory buildings, there's no place to get food or gas within 20 mi of Kitt Peak. ✉ *Kitt Peak National Observatory,* ☎ *520/318–8726 or 520/318–7200 for recorded message.* 🎫 *Suggested donation $2 per person.* ⏲ *Visitor center daily 9–3:45.*

En Route To the south of Kitt Peak, the 7,730-foot Baboquivari Peak is considered sacred by the Tohonó O'odham as the home of their deity, I'itoi ("elder brother"). Baboquivari sits on the eastern boundary of the Tohonó O'odham reservation, which covers some 4,400 square mi between Tucson and Ajo, stretching south to the Mexican border and north almost to the city of Casa Grande.

Sells

52 *32 mi southwest of Kitt Peak, 64 mi southwest of Tucson.*

A little less than halfway between Tucson and Ajo, the tribal capital of the Tohonó O'odham is a good place to stop for gas or a soft drink. If you want something more substantial, head for the Sells Shopping Center where you'll see **Basha's Deli & Bakery** (✉ Topawa Rd., ☎ 520/383–2546). It's a good-size market and can supply all the makings for a picnic, including a picnic table near the store's entrance. Much of the time there's little to see or do in Sells, but in March an annual rodeo and fair attract thousands of visitors. For details, call ☎ 520/383–2978.

En Route At Why, approximately 60 mi from Sells, AZ 86 forks off into the north and south sections of AZ 85. Originally the name of the community at this Y-shape intersection was spelled, simply and descriptively, "Y," but in 1950 the town was told that it had to have a three-letter name in order to be assigned a postal code. Hence the querulous appellation that has kept travelers wondering ever since.

Ajo

90 mi northwest of Sells.

"Ajo" (pronounced "*ah*-ho") is Spanish for garlic, and some say the town got its name from the wild garlic that grows in the area. Others claim the word is a bastardization of the Indian word "au-auho," referring to red paint derived from a local pigment.

For many years Ajo, like Bisbee to the east, was a thriving Phelps Dodge company town. Copper mining had been attempted in the area in the late 19th century, but it wasn't until the 1911 arrival of John Greenway, general manager of the Calumet & Arizona Mining Company, that the region began to be developed profitably. Calumet and Phelps Dodge merged in 1935, and the huge New Cornelia pit mine produced millions of tons of copper until the mine finally closed in 1985. With the town's main source of revenue gone, Ajo looked for a time as though it might shut down, but many retirees are now being lured here by the warm climate and low-cost housing.

Set in a desert valley flanked by low mountain ranges to the north, south, and west, Ajo is indeed a very pretty place in which to live. At the center of town and of community activities is a sparkling white Spanish-style **plaza,** designed in 1917 by Isabella Greenway, wife of the Calumet mine manager and an important figure in her own right: In the 1930s she opened the Arizona Inn in Tucson, and she was friends with such dignitaries as Eleanor Roosevelt. The shops and restaurants that line the plaza's covered arcade today are rather modest. Unlike Bisbee, Ajo hasn't yet drawn an artistic crowd—or the upscale boutiques and eateries that tend to follow.

The **New Cornelia Open Pit Mine Lookout Point** provides a panoramic view of the town's huge open pit mine, almost 2 mi wide. Some of the abandoned equipment remains in the pit, and various stages of mining operations are diagrammed at the visitors' ramada, where there's also a separate viewing area for a 30-minute film about Phelps Dodge's mining operations. ✉ *Indian Village Rd.,* ☎ *520/387–5396.* 🎫 *$1 suggested donation.* ⏲ *Generally 10–4 in high season. Closed Sun. and May 1–Oct. 1.*

The **Ajo Historical Society Museum** has collected a mélange of articles related to Ajo's past from local townspeople. The displays are rather disorganized, but some of the historical photographs and artifacts are fascinating, and the museum is inside the Territory-style St. Catherine's Indian Mission, built around 1916. ✉ *160 Mission St.,* ☎ *520/387–7105.* 🎫 *Free.* ⏲ *Generally 10–4 in high season; call ahead to confirm. Closed May 1–Oct. 1.*

The 860,000-acre **Cabeza Prieta National Wildlife Refuge,** about 10 minutes from Ajo, was established in 1939 as a preserve for endangered bighorn sheep and other Sonoran Desert wildlife. A permit is required to enter, and only those with four-wheel-drive vehicles, needed to traverse the rugged terrain, can obtain one. For additional information or for an entry permit, contact the refuge office (✉ 1611 N. 2nd Ave., Ajo 85321, ☎ 520/387–6483).

DINING AND LODGING

$ ✕ **Señior Sancho.** Just about everybody in Ajo comes to this unprepossessing roadhouse at the north end of town for generous portions of Mexican food, well prepared and very reasonably priced. This friendly spot has light-wood booths and colorful murals with a Mexican motif. All the standard favorites are on the menu—hearty combination platters, tacos, enchiladas, chile rellenos, flautas, and even a good chicken mole. ✉ *663 N. 2nd Ave.,* ☎ *520/387–6226. Reservations not accepted. No credit cards.*

$$ 🏨 **The Mine Manager's House Inn.** Another remnant of the town's Phelps Dodge heyday, this 5,000-square-foot, 1919 mansion overlooks the entire town from its site atop the highest hill in Ajo. The high-ceiling guest rooms have period furnishings and artwork. Full breakfasts are served on linens and fine china in the former mine superintendent's light-filled formal dining room. The patio barbecue and refrigerator (stocked with complimentary soft drinks) are a bonus. ✉ *1 Greenway Dr., 85321,* ☎ *520/387–6505,* FAX *520/387–6508. 5 rooms with bath. Coin laundry. MC, V.*

$ 🏨 **Guest House Inn.** Built in 1925 to accommodate visiting Phelps Dodge VIPs, this lodging is one of six Southwest "Bird 'n' Breakfast Fly-Inns": Guests can head out early to nearby Organ Pipe National Monument or just sit on the patio and watch the quail, cactus wrens, and other warblers that visit the Sonoran Desert. Rooms are furnished in a range of southwestern styles, from light Santa Fe to rich Spanish colonial. ✉ *3 Guest House Rd., 85321,* ☎ *520/387–6133. 4 rooms with bath. AE, DC, MC, V.*

Organ Pipe Cactus National Monument

54 *32 mi southwest of Ajo.*

Anyone interested in exploring the flora and fauna of the Sonoran Desert should head for Organ Pipe Cactus National Monument, abutting Cabeza Prieta National Wildlife Refuge (☞ Ajo, *above*) but much more accessible to visitors. The monument is the largest gathering spot north of the border for organ pipe cacti. These multiarmed cousins of the saguaro are fairly common in Mexico but rare in the States. Because they tend to grow on south-facing slopes, you won't be able to see many of them unless you take one of the two scenic loop drives, the 21-mile **Ajo Mountain Drive** or the 53-mile **Puerto Blanco Drive,** both on winding, graded dirt roads. The latter trail, which takes half a day to traverse, brings you to Quitobaquito, a desert oasis with a flowing spring. ✉ *Rte. 1 (from Ajo, backtrack to Why and take AZ 85 south for 22 mi to reach the visitor center),* ☎ *520/387–6849.* 🎟 *$4 per vehicle.* ⏲ *Visitor center daily 8–5.*

Yuma

55 *170 mi northwest of Ajo.*

Many people tend to think of Yuma as a convenient en-route stop—these days, between San Diego and Phoenix or Tucson—and this was equally true in the past. It's difficult to imagine the lower Colorado River, now dammed and bridged, as either a barrier or a means of transportation, but up until the early part of the century, this section of the great waterway was a force to contend with. Records show that since at least 1540 the Spanish were using Yuma (then the site of a Quechan Indian village) as a ford across a relatively shallow juncture of the Colorado.

Some three centuries later, the advent of the shallow-draft steamboat made the settlement a point of entry for fortune seekers heading up through the Gulf of California for mining sites in eastern Arizona. Fort Yuma was established in 1850 to guard against Indian attacks, and by 1873 the town was a county seat, a U.S. port of entry, and an army quartermaster depot. The building of the Yuma Territorial Prison in 1876 helped stabilize the economy.

The steamboat shipping business, undermined by the completion of the Southern Pacific Railroad line in 1877, was finished off by the building of Laguna Dam in 1909, which controlled the overflow of the Colorado River and made agricultural development in the area possible. In World War II, Yuma Proving Ground was used to train bomber pilots, and General Patton readied some of his desert war forces for battle at a number of classified areas near the city. Many people who served here during the war returned to Yuma to retire, and the city's economy now relies largely on tourism. According to weather statistics, the sun shines more on Yuma than on any other U.S. city.

Most of the interesting sights in Yuma are at the north end of town. Stop in at the Convention and Visitors Bureau (☞ Visitor Information *in* Southwest Arizona A to Z, *below*) and pick up a walking-tour guide to the **historic downtown area.** Highlights include the Century House, which now hosts the **Arizona Historical Society Museum.** This adobe structure, built around 1870 and once owned by prominent businessman E. F. Sanguinetti, exhibits artifacts from Yuma's territorial days and details the military presence in the area. It's in a pretty complex with rose gardens, an aviary, small shops, and a restaurant. ✉ *240 S. Madison Ave.,* ☏ *520/782–1841.* 🎟 *Free.* 🕓 *Tues.–Sat. 10–4.*

If you cross the railroad tracks at the northernmost part of town, you'll come to **Yuma Crossing National Historic Landmark,** which consists of the Quartermaster Depot, the Territorial Prison, and Fort Yuma to the north. The mess hall of the former fort, later used as a school for Indian children, now serves as the small **Fort Yuma Quechan Indian Museum.** Historical photographs, archaeological items, and Quechan arts and crafts, including beautiful beadwork, are on display here. ✉ *On CA 24, 1 mi north of town,* ☏ *619/572–0661.* 🎟 *$1.* 🕓 *Weekdays 8–5, Sat. 10–4.*

On the other side of the river from Fort Yuma, the **Quartermaster Depot,** created toward the end of the Civil War period, was responsible for resupplying army posts to the north and east. Freight brought upriver by steamboat was unloaded here and distributed by wagon overland to Arizona forts. The depot's earliest building (1853) originally served as the home of riverboat captain G. A. Johnson. Dubbed the Williamsburg of the West by *Arizona Highways* magazine, the site has costumed interpreters who adopt the roles of people who might have made the crossing. Historical events are reenacted on weekends. There's a museum in the quartermaster's office, which is furnished in period pieces, as is his former residence. Five covered wagons dating from the 1850s stand outside. ✉ *Off 4th Ave. between 1st St. and the Colorado River Bridge,* ☏ *520/329–0404.* 🎟 *$3.* 🕓 *Daily 10–5.*

The most notorious—and fascinating—tourist sight in town, **Yuma Territorial Prison** was built largely by the convicts who were incarcerated here from 1876 until 1909, when the prison outgrew its usefulness. The hilly site on the Colorado River, chosen for security purposes, precluded further expansion.

Visitors gazing today at the tiny cells that held six inmates each, often in 115°F heat, are likely to be appalled, but the prison was once considered a model of enlightenment: In an era when beatings were common, the only punishments meted out were solitary confinement and assignment to a dark cell. The complex housed a hospital as well as the only library in Yuma, open to the public. The 25¢ fee charged townspeople for a prison tour financed the acquisition of new books. The inmates' food was sufficiently varied and plentiful to inspire locals to dub the place the Country Club of the Colorado.

The 3,069 people who served time at this penal institution, the only one in the Arizona Territory during its tenure, included men and women from 21 different countries. They came from all social classes and were sent up for everything from armed robbery and murder to violation of the Mexican Neutrality Act and polygamy. R. L. McDonald, incarcerated for forgery, had been the superintendent of the Phoenix public school system. Chosen as the prison bookkeeper, he absconded with $130 of the inmates' money when he left. Pearl Hart, convicted of stagecoach robbery, gained such notoriety for her crime that she attempted a career in vaudeville after her release.

Different groups continued to come, more or less voluntarily, after the prison closed. When the local high school burned down, classes were held for four years (1910–14) in the former hospital. In the 1920s railriders took a break from the freights to sleep in the unsupervised buildings, and during the Great Depression the abandoned cells provided shelter for many homeless people. A number of films, including *Red River Valley*, were shot here in the 1930s and '40s. The site of the former mess hall opened as a museum in 1940, and the entire prison complex was designated a State Historic Park in 1961. ✉ *Near Exit 1 off I–8,* ☎ *520/783–4771.* 🎫 *$3. Free interpretive programs at 11, 2, and 3:30.* ⏲ *Daily 8–5.*

Surrounded by citrus orchards and ranches, the 40-acre **Saihati Camel Farm** is at the far southern end of town. The landscape near Yuma inspired Saudi Arabia native Abdul-Wahed Saihati to raise and breed his favorite animals here along with more exotic desert-loving breeds, such as oryx (antelope) and wildcats. It's fun to help feed the well-groomed, friendly dromedaries—not a biter or spitter among 'em—and to see some rare animal species, many of them purchased from the San Diego Zoo, at close range. ✉ *15672 S. Ave. 1 E (between County 15th and County 16th Sts.),* ☎ *520/627–2553.* ⏲ *Guided tours Mon.–Sat. at 10 and 2, Sun. at 2. Reservations advised.* ⏲ *Guided tours $3.*

DINING AND LODGING

$ ✕ **Chretin's Mexican Food.** A Yuma institution, Chretin's opened as a dance hall in the 1930s before it became one of the first Mexican restaurants in town in 1946. Don't be put off by the nondescript exterior or the entryway, which leads back past the kitchen and cashier's stand into three large dining areas. The food is all made on the premises, right down to the chips and tortillas. Try anything that features *machaca* (shredded spiced beef or chicken). If you're really hungry, go for the enchilada-style burritos, smothered with cheese and sauce. ✉ *485 S. 15th Ave.,* ☎ *520/782–1291. D, MC, V. Closed Sun.*

$ ✕ **Lutes Casino.** Almost always packed with locals at lunchtime, this large, funky restaurant and bar, at the historic North End of town, claims to be the oldest pool hall and domino parlor in Arizona. Decorated with photos of the bad old days, this is the place for a brew and a burger. Try potato tacos or the "Especial" hot dog–cheeseburger combo, which tastes a lot better than it sounds. ✉ *221 S. Main St.,* ☎ *520/782–2192. Reservations not accepted. No credit cards.*

$$ ★ 🏨 **Best Western Coronado Motor Hotel.** This Spanish tile–roof lodging, convenient to both the freeway and downtown historical sights, was built in 1938 and is run by the son of the original owner. Bob Hope used to stay here during World War II, when he entertained the gunnery troops training in Yuma. Photos of Yuma's territorial days line the walls of the hotel's restaurant, where guests enjoy a free Continental breakfast. The rooms have such extras as VCRs (with two free films each night), refrigerators, microwaves, hair dryers, and modem phone jacks. Some have hot tubs. Family suites with full kitchens are available. ✉ *233 4th Ave., 85364,* ☎ *520/783–4453 or 800/528–1234,* FAX *520/782–7487. 49 rooms, including 20 family suites. Restaurant,*

lobby lounge, refrigerators, in-room VCRs, pool, coin laundry. AE, D, DC, MC, V.

$$ **Radisson Suites Inn.** This sprawling, attractive hostelry has an inviting southwestern look, with a pink stucco facade accented with burgundy window awnings. One wing surrounds a well-manicured courtyard, which features a central fountain and several orange trees; another faces the heated outdoor pool and Cabana Club, where the complimentary Continental breakfast and happy-hour drinks are served. This is an all-suites property, and each accommodation has a separate sitting area with a desk, and such amenities as an in-room coffeemaker, refrigerator, and microwave oven. There's a free shuttle to the airport and to a nearby health club. ✉ *2600 S. 4th Ave., 85364,* ☎ *520/726–4830 or 800/333–3333,* FAX *520/341–1152. 164 suites. Lobby lounge, pool, hot tub, coin laundry, airport shuttle. AE, D, DC, MC, V.*

Imperial National Wildlife Refuge

56 *40 mi north of Yuma.*

Guided tours (☞ Southwest Arizona A to Z, *below*) are the best way to visit the 25,765-acre Imperial National Wildlife Refuge, created by backwaters formed when the Imperial Dam was built. Something of an anomaly, the refuge is home both to species indigenous to marshy rivers and to creatures that inhabit the Sonoran Desert, which lines its banks here—desert tortoises, coyotes, bobcats, and bighorn sheep. Most of all, though, this is bird-lovers' heaven. Thousands of waterfowl and shorebirds live here year-round, and migrating flocks of swallows pass through in the spring and fall. During those seasons, expect to see everything from pelicans and cormorants to Canada geese, snowy egrets, and a variety of rarer species. Canoes can be rented at Martinez Lake Marina, 3½ mi southeast of the refuge headquarters. It's best to visit from mid-October through May, when temperatures are lowest and the ever-present mosquitoes are least active. From Yuma, take U.S. 95 north past the Proving Ground and follow the signs to the refuge. ✉ *Red Cloud Mine Rd., Box 72217, 85365,* ☎ *520/783–3371.* *Free.* *Visitor center mid-Apr.–mid-Oct., weekdays 8–4:30; rest of yr, weekdays 8–4:30, weekends 10–4.*

Southwest Arizona A to Z

ARRIVING AND DEPARTING

By Bus. You can get to Yuma from a variety of directions via **Greyhound Lines** (☎ 800/231–2222). The **Ajo Stage Line** (☎ 800/242–9483) has bus service three times a week from Tucson and twice weekly from Phoenix to Ajo.

By Car. Ajo lies on AZ 85 (north–south), Yuma at the junction of I–8 and U.S. 95. For a scenic route to Ajo from Tucson (126 mi), take AZ 86 west to Why and turn north on AZ 85. Yuma is 170 mi from San Diego on I–8, and it is 300 mi from Las Vegas on U.S. 95.

By Plane. Both **Sky West** (☎ 800/453–9417), a Delta subsidiary, and **America West** (☎ 800/235–9292) have frequent direct flights to Yuma from Phoenix. Sky West also flies nonstop from Los Angeles.

By Train. Amtrak (☎ 800/872–7245) runs trains to Yuma from Tucson and Los Angeles three times a week.

GUIDED TOURS

You can take a boat ride up the Colorado with **Yuma River Tours** (✉ 1920 Arizona Ave., Yuma 85364, ☎ 520/783–4400). Twelve-person jet-boat excursions run by Smokey Knowlton, who has been exploring the area for more than 36 years, offer a unique look at the formerly active life of the river. Speed past Indian petroglyphs as well as abandoned steamboat landings and mining camps. The options are a three-hour trip ($25 per person, including lunch or dinner) or a full-day excursion ($49, including lunch), both departing from Fisher's Landing at Martinez Lake, 23 mi north of Yuma.

VISITOR INFORMATION

The **Ajo Chamber of Commerce** (✉ AZ 85, just south of the plaza, 321 Taladro, Ajo 85321, ☎ 520/387–7742) is open Monday–Saturday 9–3, more limited hours during the summer.

The **Yuma Convention and Visitors Bureau** (✉ 377 S. Main St., Box 10831, Yuma 85366, ☎ 520/783–0071, ⏲ weekdays 9–5) is open weekdays 9–5.

TUCSON A TO Z

Arriving and Departing

By Bus

Buses to Los Angeles, El Paso, Phoenix, Flagstaff, Douglas, and Nogales (Arizona) depart and arrive regularly from Tucson's **Greyhound Lines** terminal (✉ 2 S. 4th Ave. at E. Broadway, ☎ 520/792–3475). For travel to Phoenix, **Arizona Shuttle Service, Inc.** (☎ 520/795–6771) runs express service from three locations in Tucson every hour on the hour, 4 AM–9 PM every day; the trip takes approximately 2½ hours. One-way fares are $19 for adults, $10 for children under 12. Call 24 hours in advance for reservations.

By Car

From Phoenix, 111 mi northwest, I–10 east is the road that will take you to Tucson. Also a major north–south traffic artery through town, I–10 has well-marked exits all along the route. At Casa Grande, 70 mi north of Tucson, I–8 connects with I–10, bringing travelers into the area from Yuma and San Diego. From Nogales, 63 mi south on the Mexican border, take I–19 into Tucson.

By Plane

Check plane fares carefully when you're planning your trip. Though you may not want to spend time in Phoenix, sometimes it's cheaper to fly into that city and then take a scenic 2½-hour drive down the Pinal Pioneer Parkway (U.S. 79), or a speedier (½-hour) trip on I–10, to Tucson.

Tucson International Airport (☎ 520/573–8000) is 8½ mi south of downtown, west of I–10 off the Valencia exit. Carriers include **Aeromexico** and its subsidiary, **Aerolitoral** (☎ 520/573–8315); **American** and its subsidiary, **American Eagle** (☎ 800/433–7300); **America West** (☎ 800/235–9292),; **Arizona Airways** (☎ 520/889–8100), **Continental** (☎ 520/623–3700); **Delta** (☎ 800/221–1212); **Northwest** (☎ 800/225–2525); **Reno Air** (☎ 800/736–6247); **Southwest** (☎ 800/444–5660); and **United** (☎ 800/241–6522).

BETWEEN THE AIRPORT AND DOWNTOWN

In addition to the modes of transportation listed below, many hotels provide courtesy airport shuttle service; inquire when making reservations.

By Car. It makes sense to rent at the airport; all the major rental-car agencies—Avis, Budget, Hertz, and National Interrent—are represented, along with Alamo, Dollar, and Value. The driving time from the airport to the center of town varies, but it's usually less than half an hour; add 15 minutes during rush hours (7:30–9 AM and 4:30–6 PM). Parking is not a problem in most parts of town.

By Taxi. Taxi rates vary widely; they are unregulated in Arizona. It's always wise to inquire about the cost of a trip before getting into a cab. You shouldn't pay much more than $18 from the airport to central Tucson. A few of the more reliable cab companies are **ABC** (☎ 520/623–7979), **Airline Taxi** (☎ 520/887–6933), and **Fiesta Taxi** (☎ 520/622–7777), whose drivers speak both English and Spanish.

By Van or Bus. Arizona Stagecoach (☎ 520/889–1000), with an office at the airport, takes groups and individuals to all parts of Tucson for $8.50–$26, depending on the location. If you're traveling light and aren't in a hurry, you can take a city **Sun Tran** (☎ 520/792–9222) bus to central Tucson. Bus 11, which leaves every half hour from a stop at the left of the lower level as you come out of the terminal, goes north on Alvernon Way, and you can transfer to most of the east–west bus lines from this main north–south road; ask the bus driver which one would take you closest to the location you need. You can also transfer to a variety of lines from Bus 25, which leaves less frequently from the same airport location and heads to the Roy Laos center at the south of town (☞ Getting Around, *below*).

By Train

Amtrak serves the city with westbound and eastbound trains three times a week; the station is downtown at 400 East Toole Street (☎ 520/623–4442).

Getting Around

A car is almost a requirement if you're really going to explore Tucson and southern Arizona. You can get around the small downtown area on foot and by bus or taxi, but Tucson is generally very spread out and public transportation is somewhat limited when it comes to sightseeing.

By Bus and Trolley

Within the city limits, public transportation is available through **Sun Tran** (☎ 520/792–9222), Tucson's bus system. On weekdays, buses start running at around 5 AM; some lines operate until 10 PM, but most only go until 7 or 8 PM. Service is more limited on weekends. A one-way ride costs 75¢; transfers are free, but be sure to request them when you pay your fare, for which exact change is required. Those with valid Medicare cards can ride for 30¢. Call for information on Sun Tran bus routes. Note: At press time, prices on Sun Tran were to be raised, but no rate information was available.

The city-run **Van Tran** (☎ 520/620–1234) offers transportation in specially outfitted vans for riders with disabilities. Call for information and reservations.

By Car

Much of the year, traffic in Tucson isn't especially heavy, but during the busiest winter months (December through March), streets in the central area of town can get congested. There's a seat-belt law in the state, as well as one that requires children under the age of four to ride in a secure child-restraint seat. Don't even think of drinking and driving; if you do, you'll spend your vacation in jail. Arizona's strict laws against driving under the influence are strongly enforced.

CAUTION – When driving off major highways in low-lying areas, watch for rain clouds. Flash floods from sudden summer rains can be deadly (☞ Driving Precautions *in* Smart Travel Tips A to Z).

Contacts and Resources

Car Rental Agencies

If you haven't rented a car at the airport (☞ Between the Airport and Downtown, *above*), you might try **U-Save Auto Rental** (☎ 520/790–8847 or 520/745–2119), **Enterprise** (☎ 520/881–0484) or **Rent-a-Ride** (☎ 520/750–1900 or 520/622–0162), all in the city center. In addition, **Carefree Rent-a-Car** (☎ 520/790–2655) offers reliable used cars at good rates. If you think you might be interested in driving to nearby Mexico, check in advance to make sure that the rental company will allow you to bring the car over the border.

Emergencies

For the **police, ambulance, fire department,** dial 911, a free call from public pay phones.

DOCTORS AND DENTISTS

From Monday through Friday, the **Pima County Medical Society** (☎ 520/795–7985) will refer visitors to Tucson physicians, and the **Arizona State Dental Association** (☎ 520/881–7237) can recommend a dentist in the area.

HOSPITALS

El Dorado Hospital and Medical Center (✉ 1400 N. Wilmot Rd., ☎ 520/886–6361), **Northwest Hospital** (✉ 6200 N. La Cholla Blvd., ☎ 520/742–9000), **St. Joseph's Hospital** (✉ 305 N. Wilmot Rd., ☎ 520/296–3211), **Tucson General Hospital** (✉ 3838 N. Campbell Ave., ☎ 520/327–5431), **Tucson Medical Center** (✉ 5301 E. Grant Rd., ☎ 520/327–5461), **University Medical Center** (✉ 1501 N. Campbell Ave., ☎ 520/694–0111).

LATE-NIGHT PHARMACIES

Several **Walgreen's** (☎ 800/925–4733 for the location nearest you) drugstores in the city have 24-hour prescription service. A number of **Osco Drug** stores also offer 24-hour prescription service; if you call ☎ 800/654–6726 and give the zip code of the place where you're staying, you'll be referred to the closest open pharmacy.

Guided Tours

ADVENTURE AND ECO-TOURS

Sunshine Jeep Tours (☎ 520/742–1943) and **Trail Dust Jeep Tours** (☎ 520/747–0323) both offer trips to the Sonoran Desert in open-air four-wheel-drive vehicles. **Baja's Frontier Tours** (☎ 520/887–2340) and **Desert Path Tours** (☎ 520/327–7235) explore the natural history of the area. **Southern Arizona Offroad Adventures** (☎ 520/882–6567 or 800/689–2453) run an array of mountain bike excursions, ranging from gentle half-day sessions in Tucson to "extreme" tours through rough terrain and weeklong trips through southern Arizona.

ORIENTATION TOURS

Great Western Tours (☎ 520/721–0980) and **Tucson Tours & Entertainment** (☎ 520/297–2911) take individuals and groups to such popular sights as Old Tucson, Sabino Canyon, and the Arizona–Sonora Desert Museum and also offer in-depth tours of the city and its neighborhoods. **Old Pueblo Tours** (☎ 520/575–1175), with a slightly different itinerary—including "A" Mountain and San Xavier del Bac Mission—provides a fine historical overview of the area. Many tour operators are on limited schedules (or close altogether) during the summer, but **Off the Beaten Path Tours** (☎ 502/529–6090) has excellent customized excursions year-round.

SPECIAL-INTEREST TOURS

In the spring and fall, those interested in visiting the area's historic missions can contact **Kino Mission Tours** (☎ 520/628–1269), which has professional historians and bilingual guides on staff.

WALKING TOURS

Tucson's historic districts make for great walks. For one easy-to-follow self-guided tour, head for the **Convention & Visitors Bureau** (☞ Visitor Information, *below*). The friendly, knowledgeable docents of the **Arizona Historical Society** (☎ 520/622–0956) conduct walking tours of El Presidio neighborhood (departing from the Sosa-Carillo-Fremont House) every Saturday at 10 AM from October through April; the cost is $4 for adults. **Old Pueblo Walking Tours** (☎ 520/323–9290) gears its weekend strolls around historic neighborhoods to visitors' interests—for example, architecture or photography; the cost ($10 per person if there's a group of at least 10) includes an information packet with reproductions of historic photos.

Radio Stations

The following are a few of the many popular stations in Tucson.

AM

KNST 790: News, talk; **KTKT 990:** Sports Entertainment Network; **KJYK 1490:** Top 40; **KUAT 1550:** National Public Radio, jazz.

FM

KUAT 89.1: National Public Radio, jazz; **KUAZ 90.5:** Classical; **KXCI 91.3:** Alternative rock, folk, blues; **KLPX 96.1:** Rock; **KIIM 99.5:** Country.

Visitor Information

Located downtown, the **Metropolitan Tucson Convention and Visitors Bureau** (✉ 130 S. Scott Ave., 85701, ☎ 520/624–1817 or 800/638–8350) is open weekdays 8–5 and weekends 9–4.

OTHER USEFUL NUMBERS

Chamber of Commerce (☎ 520/792–1212); local and state road conditions (☎ 520/573–7623); Tucson Parks and Recreation Department (☎ 520/791–4873); weather (☎ 520/881–3333).

7 Portraits of Arizona

THE NATIVE SOUTHWEST

CONSIDERING THE ARIDITY of the Southwest, the tremendous cultural productivity of its native civilizations is not simply a fascinating anthropological fact, it is one of the best examples of humankind's working with the challenges of nature to produce a meaningful existence. Over time, tribal interaction became a vital, even necessary, part of that existence. It is easy to think of such interaction in terms of trade—the troves of goods that poured into the Southwest from as far away as southern Mexico, such as macaw feathers. But the most dramatic social change resulted from the influence of Mesoamerican agricultural techniques and ritual practice on native southwesterners. That influence sparked the wondrous achievements visible in pottery and cliff dwellings, informed peoples' spiritual beliefs, and planted its legacy in the Hopi and New Mexican Pueblo cultures of today. As understanding of native cultures deepens, then, the patterns of southwestern life are revealed as a rich interweaving of various groups that shared and built on their experience of desert life. Arizona is the single best place to learn about that experience, both past and present.

Following Ice Age migrations from Asia to North America, over the land bridge that has since been covered by the waters of the Bering Strait, nomadic peoples began populating the Southwest. Three Paleo-Indian groups (*paleo* meaning "old") are the earliest identifiable inhabitants. One group hunted large game, first wooly mammoth until they became extinct, then bison. They carved spear points and knives roughly and used *atlatls,* spear-and-stick throwing weapons, to bring down their prey. Evidence of their presence from Clovis, New Mexico, dates back 11,500 years. One thousand years later, they moved east to follow the bison. Fossil remains from Fulsom, New Mexico, suggest another group with different hunting techniques. Other sites around the Colorado–New Mexico border indicate an even wider variety of activities and tool use.

Traces of more permanent settlements appear from 9,000 years ago in what archaeologists call the Archaic Period. New groups moved south into deserts and canyonlands that earlier hunters couldn't use, taking smaller game and gathering extensively. They were still quite mobile and took full advantage of seasonal plants, fruit, and nuts to supply their nourishment. And they prospered—there is quite an abundance of sites from the Archaic Period. Just how the groups at different sites interacted may not be clear, but similarities among artifacts suggest patterns of intertribal communication that would continue for thousands of years.

The next stage of development in the Southwest, about 4,000 years ago, marks a major transition in cultures around the world as people gradually adopted agriculture and a more sedentary way of life. In the southwest, pioneers brought the cultivation of corn, squash, and beans north from Mesoamerica. One group in particular, the Hohokam, is seen to have done this. In an area straddling the Arizona-Mexico border, the Hohokam developed a highly productive agricultural system. Some archaeologists believe that they migrated from northwestern Mexico with knowledge of planting, growing, and irrigating. Others picture an evolution of Archaic peoples who gradually took on Mesoamerican practices. Either way, they had great success and in turn influenced their northern and eastern neighbors for more than a thousand years. Their artisans produced ritual objects, jewelry, and stone and ceramic wares with great skill. They continually traded with Mesoamerican tribes, and Pacific-coast trade brought in raw materials for their own and other regional artisans.

The flowering of Hohokam culture began around 2,300 years ago. The period of their growth, expansion, and eventual decline, when they began to take new ideas in from the north, lasted about 1,500 years—twice as long as the Roman Empire. During that time, they cultivated corn, beans, squash, agave, and cotton, using remarkable irrigation methods. Some of their networks of canals stretched 3 miles from the Salt and Gila rivers to planted fields. Their contact with Mesoamerican cultures periodically brought new strains of corn to the Southwest along with religious beliefs, ritual practices, and the ball game and ball courts well known from the Maya. The Hohokam culturally fertilized the region, providing a base for the Pueblo culture that has survived into the modern era.

The Mogollon were another group, occupying an area stretching from eastern-central Arizona into New Mexico from 2,000 to 500 years ago. They took on Hohokam and so-called Anasazi cultural patterns, but they never fully embraced an agricultural lifestyle. They became skillful potters, especially those living near the Mimbres River. Their contact with the Anasazi resulted in the production of some of the Southwest's most outstanding pottery. The principle Mimbres Mogollon site is now the Gila Cliff Dwellings National Monument in New Mexico.

ROMANTICIZED, mythicized, and perhaps misunderstood, the so-called Anasazi left wondrous architectural remains, most notably at Mesa Verde in Colorado, Chaco Canyon in New Mexico, and Canyon de Chelly, Betatakin, and Keet Seel in Arizona. Composed of various groups living around the Four Corners area, they have generated the most intense interest. We take up with them 2,000 years ago where we left off with the Archaic peoples. For centuries they lived seminomadically, hunting, gathering, and marginally cultivating corn, squash, and beans. They eventually settled into villages and adopted much of the Hohokam culture, more than their Mogollon neighbors did.

These various Ancestral Pueblos were not pueblo dwellers yet, however. They were slow to establish year-round communities. Perhaps they weren't convinced that the Hohokam model would work in their rugged, dry canyonlands. With fewer and smaller rivers, they couldn't irrigate on the Hohokam scale. About 1,500 years ago the Pueblo cultural pattern called Anasazi began to take shape, owing, perhaps, to the introduction of a new, more productive strain of corn.

Ancestral Pueblo peoples made a significant contribution to southwestern culture with their architecture. Their remarkable stone masonry evolved out of the pithouse style used by Archaic peoples. A precursor of the kiva, the pithouse was constructed around a shallow, circular dugout with mud walls packed around vertical pole supports. The new stone-and-mortar houses, on the other hand, were very often rectangular in plan. In small communities they were built on a scale to house groups of a few families. These groups would have individual clan *kivas* (the Hopi word for underground ceremonial chambers) or single great kivas.

The soaring cliff dwellings of Canyon de Chelly, Betatakin, Keet Seel, and Mesa Verde represented another type of settlement, more protected from the elements and, perhaps, raiders. Villagers cultivated the land around them. All of these communities had kivas, ritual spaces central to the lives of deeply spiritual people.

Ancestral Pueblo culture reached its height about 1,000 years ago. Hitherto Puebloans had continued to refine their use of water, not actually irrigating, but using sporadic rainfall to the greatest advantage. They would line stones across slopes and cut ditches to distribute rainfall and limit erosion. Occasionally they dug canals in order to channel rainwater into planted fields. Unquestionably, they were expert dry farmers, coaxing abundance out of a harsh environment.

At the time of this climax, some people began moving from smaller, widespread communities into larger, denser settlements—perhaps like today's migrations to cities. The volume of trade in nearly all directions was tremendous, and Pueblo artisans were making superb pottery. Decorative techniques varied from region to region: black-on-white, black-on-red, black-on-orange, red-on-orange, and expressive combinations of these. People also etched petroglyphs into, and painted pictograms onto, rock faces. Rock art is found at almost all Anasazi and Sinagua sites. The quantity of artifacts that they left behind—utility and ceremonial items alike—is unparalleled among Native North American groups.

Around 850 years ago, a cultural decline began. Drought and climatic change put pressure on the Pueblos' settled, agricultural lifeways. Longer winters shortened growing seasons in which less rain fell. Villagers continued to move into denser settlements. By the late 1200s, Canyon de Chelly was unoccupied. Chaco Canyon had been vacant for 100 years. Settlements at Wupatki continued a little longer, into the 1300s. The Hopi Mesas, on the other hand, first built in the 1100s, were growing. They absorbed some of their migrating neighbors, and their traditions testify to their assimilation of ancient Pueblo culture.

There are also a great number of transitional settlements, many yet to be excavated, that accommodated groups leaving the immediate Four Corners area. Some of them are quite substantial. Archaeologically speaking, then, the scenario that used to be construed as the disappearance of a vast culture can now take a more human shape. The Anasazi didn't vanish—they chose to move. Over a couple of centuries they gradually migrated to new locations, slightly altering their lifestyles. (Some of them may have been doing that on and off for hundreds of years anyway.) In the process they passed on their knowledge to the people they joined: the Hopi, the New Mexican Zuñi, the Acoma, or other Pueblos. And while archaeologists look for external forces that might have caused this movement—drought, climatic change, deforestation, disease, warfare—the Zuñi see the migration as a process of searching for "the center place," a place of spiritual rightness. That center place is where present-day Pueblos are living.*

MANY OTHER PEOPLES also lived within current Arizona borders in the pre-European Southwest. One of them, the Sinagua (meaning "without water" in Spanish), belonged to a diverse group called the Hakataya, spread out across central Arizona. Wupatki, Walnut Canyon, Tuzigoot, and the inappropriately named Montezuma Castle are all Sinagua sites. These people absorbed Hohokam, Mogollon, and Anasazi cultural patterns: agriculture, village life, and the Mesoamerican ball game; stone masonry and cliff-dwelling architecture; and pottery.** Situated in the middle of these three groups, they became a composite but separate culture.

As the so-called Anasazi waned, Hopi and Navajo cultures grew. The Navajo are an Apachean group linguistically related to the Athabascans of western Canada. They gradually moved into the Southwest 500 years ago. Migrating southward along the Rocky Mountains, they finally settled in unoccupied places around Pueblo villages. Hunting and gathering were just about all that the land would support. Over time they learned farming techniques from the Pueblos and traded with them and as a result took on a character distinct from other Apachean groups, such as the 19th-century Chiracahua and Mescalero Apache. Living in small, dispersed groups, Navajos also raided Pueblo farms and villages—a practice in retrospect notoriously Apachean.

Soon after the Navajo came the Spanish, invading the Southwest early in the 16th century. Unlike Anglo-European conquerors, they did allow elements of native cultures to survive, provided that they accept a transfusion of Catholicism and alien governance. Of course, their intrusion into southwestern life was far from cordial. Their first contact was with New Mexican Pueblos, whose understandable lack of interest in accepting Spanish rule met with the sword. Pueblo retaliation brought further hostility from the invaders, who murdered hundreds of natives and destroyed villages.

The Spanish didn't have the chance to overrun the Apacheans, whose scattered settlements were more difficult to locate than were pueblos. Some of the eastern Apaches entered into slave trade with the conquerors, selling them captives taken during raids. Then after the Pueblo Revolt of 1680, which drove the Spanish away only to have them return 12 years later, the Navajo periodically housed Pueblos seeking refuge from reprisals. In return, the Pueblos taught them rituals, customs, agricultural techniques, and arts—in some of which, like weaving, they eventually surpassed their teachers. In the 1700s, drought led many Hopis to seek refuge among the Navajo in the formerly vacated Canyon de Chelly—a poignant example of the long-standing cooperative relationship of the two groups.

The Navajo also picked up European skills, some of them from the Pueblos. Directly from the Spanish they learned about silversmithing, raising cattle, and riding horses—and they became superior horsemen. Horses extended their gathering range and gave them greater mobility for trading and raiding. The Navajo were not nomadic, however. Many of them had different seasonal residences, log-and-earth hogans, as they continue to do today. But these are maintained as permanent dwellings.

After independent Mexico ceded New Mexico to the United States in 1848, the Southwest's new proprietors decided to put an end to Indian raids. Over the next 16 years U.S. troops and the Navajo clashed repeatedly. The United States set up army posts within Navajo territory. They attempted to impose treaties, but U.S. agents often arranged them with headmen who had no authority that the Navajo as a whole could accept.

This misunderstanding of Navajo organization had tragic results. When raids continued, the U.S. territorial governor believed he had been betrayed and decided that drastic measures were necessary to safeguard the so-called frontier. He called in Colonel Kit Carson to destroy Navajo crops and livestock. Over the next few months, the People, as the Navajo call themselves, began to give themselves up. In 1864, as many as 8,000 Navajo made the grueling Long Walk to captivity in Fort Sumner, 300 miles to the southeast.***

The People were allowed to return to their land after four years of concentration-camp life. Fewer in number and greatly demoralized, they had to reconstruct their lives from scratch, rebuilding customs and lifestyles that had been impossible, if not forbidden, in the camps. Since then, Navajo ingenuity and an impressive ability to seize opportunities have gained them a measure of success in modern America. Their democratically governed community—they call it Navajo Nation—numbers more than 250,000.

THE HOPI didn't suffer that kind of brutality. The Spanish had set up a mission at Hopi by 1629. But the Hopi drove them out in the 1680 revolt. Spanish missionaries returned to attempt another conversion, and again the Hopi got rid of them, this time by destroying their own, Christianized village of Awatovi, thus maintaining the purity of Hopi ritual. Because of their otherwise noncombative stance, the U.S. government has left the Hopi more to themselves than any other Native American group.

In their proper observance of tradition and ritual the Hopi are unique even among traditional Native Americans. In fact it was to Hopi spiritual leaders that many Native American traditionalists turned in the 1950s in what eventually became the Indian Unity Movement. Hopi beliefs focus on the relationship between the people, the land, and the Creator, whose Life Plan locks them all in balance. In this strict moral order, prayer and ritual—including the kachina rain power being dances—are necessary to keep the natural cycle in motion and to ensure the flow of life-sustaining forces. The earth is sacred, and they are its keepers.

The Hopi may well be the best dry farmers on the planet, successfully harvesting crops on a precarious 8 to 15 inches of rain per year—and no irrigation. Doubtless they manage this because they have perfected ancient Ancestral Pueblo techniques. The mesas on which they chose to live contain precious aquifers, particularly essential to life in such an arid territory. These vast water sources no doubt sustained them and their migrant guests when Pueblo peoples left places like Wupatki and Walnut Canyon and Canyon de Chelly 700 years ago. Unfortunately, the Hopi Tribal Council, which represents the progressive Christianized members of the Hopi, has sold sacred land to strip miners who in turn have destroyed parts of Black Mesa and depleted the aquifer. This is one indication of the rift at Hopi between modernizers and those continue to practice traditional ways. The traditionalists reside in the villages of Oraibi, Hotevilla, and Shungapovi. They are, understandably, intolerant of whites. They follow the Hopi Way even as contemporary life and the Tribal Council pose ever greater threats to it.

The present-day Tohonó O'odham (called Papago by the Spanish) and the Pima, in central-southern Arizona, are descendants of the Hohokam. The Spanish first encountered them in the 17th century cultivating former Hohokam territory, using some of the ancient irrigation canals. Both tribes are Pimans, and both continue some Hohokam practices: living in rancherías along canals and performing costume dances and other rituals that link them to Uto-Aztecan language groups nearby in Mexico. The Pima live on the Salt River Reservation south of Phoenix, and the Tohonó O'odham reservation stretches north from the Mexican border.

Like the Southwest's history, perspectives on Native American cultures are complex and fascinating—and have become confused in the clash of Euro-American and Native American ways. Take, for example, the enchanting and mysterious word *Anasazi,* which enters into almost any discussion of native Arizonans. This Navajo word, meaning both "ancient ones" and "enemy ancestors," automatically implies one perspective. Another of equal cultural value is that of the Hopi, whose name for the ancient culture, *Hisatsinom,* means "people of long ago." Yet another perspective is that of the New Mexican Zuñi, who prefer the word *Enote:que,* "our ancient ones, our ancestors."*

To scientifically trained Euramerican archaeologists, the term *Anasazi* conveniently groups together a variety of ancient Pueblo peoples who had similar lifestyles but often divergent adaptations to southwestern conditions. In past decades researchers encouraged the myth of a lost Anasazi civilization and posed virtually unanswerable questions about who the people were and how and why they "vanished" from the scene. Had they taken the beliefs and statements of the Hopi and of New Mexican Pueblos seriously—acting as both archaeologists and anthropologists—certain answers would have been clear. The *Hisatsinom-Enote:que-Anasazi* would have fit seamlessly into the continuity of Native American life.

The perspective we can never know is that of the Ancestral Pueblos themselves—we don't even know the language they spoke. Yet we can try to get a sense of their worldview by listening to contemporary Pueblos. If we project their uniquely American customs into the past, aspects of their ancestral culture come to life. And while western tradition has its own ancient echoes, in a world rushing to keep up with continually accelerating values, traditional Pueblo ways speak of a balanced life, rooted in its relationship with the earth.

Sources

Ancient Ruins of the Southwest: An Archaeological Guide. David Grant Noble. Flagstaff: Northland Publishing Co., 1981.

Indian Country. Peter Mathiessen. New York: The Viking Press, 1984.

****The Navaho.* Clyde Kluckhon and Dorothea Leighton. Cambridge, Mass.: Harvard University Press, 1974.

North American Indians: A Comprehensive Account. Alice Beck Kehoe. Englewood Cliffs, N.J.: Prentice-Hall, Inc., 1981.

***Those Who Came Before: Southwestern Archaeology in the National Park System.* Robert H. Lister and Florence C. Lister. Flagstaff, Ariz.: Southwestern Parks and Monuments, 1983.

**What Happened to the Anasazi? Why Did They Leave? Where Did They Go? A Panel Discussion at the Anasazi Heritage Center.* Jerold G. Widdison, ed. Albuquerque: Southwest Natural and Cultural Heritage Association, 1990.

— Stephen Wolf

Stephen Wolf is a staff editor at Fodor's.

THE WHAT AND THE WHY OF DESERT COUNTRY

ON THE BRIGHTEST and warmest days my desert is most itself because sunshine and warmth are the very essence of its character. The air is lambent. A caressing warmth envelops everything in its ardent embrace. Even when outlanders complain that the sun is too dazzling and too hot, we desert lovers are prone to reply, "At worst that is only too much of a good thing."

Unfortunately, this is the time when the tourist is least likely to see it. Even the winter visitor who comes for a month or more is likely to choose January or February because he is thinking about what he is escaping at home rather than of what he is coming to here. True, the still-warm sun and typically bright skies make a dramatic contrast with what he has left behind. In the gardens of his hotel or guest ranch, flowers still bloom and some of the more obstreperous birds make cheerful sounds, even though they do not exactly sing at this season. The more enthusiastic visitors talk about "perpetual summer" and sometimes ask if we do not find the lack of seasons monotonous. But this is nonsense. Winter is winter, even in the desert.

At Tucson's elevation of 2,300 feet it often gets quite cold at night, even when shade temperatures during the day rise to 75°F or higher. Most vegetation is pausing, though few animals hibernate. This is a sort of neutral time when the desert environment is least characteristic of itself. It is almost like late September or early October, just after the first frost, in southern New England. For those who are thinking of nothing except getting away, rather than learning to know a new world, this is all very well. But you can't become acquainted with the desert itself at that time of year.

By April the desert is just beginning to come into its own. The air and the skies are summery without being hot; roadsides and many of the desert flats are thickly carpeted with a profusion of wildflowers such as only California can rival. The desert is smiling before it begins to laugh, and October and November are much the same. But June is the month for those who want to know the true desert. That is the time to decide once and for all if it is, as for many it turns out to be, "your country."

It so happens that I am writing this not long after the 21st of June, and I took special note of that astronomically significant date. This year, summer began at precisely 10 hours and no minutes, mountain standard time. That means that the sun rose higher and stayed longer in the sky than on any other day of the year. In the north there is often a considerable lag in the seasons as the earth warms up, but here, where it is never very cold, the longest day and the hottest are likely to coincide pretty closely. So it was this year. On June 21 the sun rose almost to the zenith so that at noon it cast almost no shadow. And it was showing what it is capable of.

Even in this dry air, 109°F in the shade is pretty warm. Under the open sky the sun's rays strike with an almost physical force, pouring down from a blue dome unmarked by the faintest suspicion of even a fleck of cloud. The year has been unusually dry (even for the desert). During the four months just past, no rain—not even a light shower—has fallen. The surface of the ground is as dry as powder. And yet, when I look out of the window, the dominant color of the landscape is an incredible green.

On the low foothills surrounding the steep rocky slopes of the mountains, which are in fact 10 to 12 miles away but in the clear air seem much closer, this greenness ends in a curving line following the contour of the mountains' base, inevitably suggesting the waves of a green sea lapping the irregular shoreline of some island rising abruptly from the ocean. Between me and that shoreline the desert is sprinkled with hundreds, probably thousands, of evenly placed shrubs, interrupted now and then by a small tree—usually mesquite or what locals call a cat's-claw acacia.

More than a month ago all the little perennial flowers and weeds, which spring up after winter rains and rush from seed to flower and to seed again in six weeks, gave up the ghost at the end of their short lives. Their hope of posterity lies now invisible, either upon the surface of the bare ground or just below it. Yet even when summer thunderstorms come in late July or August, these seeds will not make the mistake of germinating. They are triggered to explode into life only when they are both moist and cool—which they will be February or March when their season comes again. Neither the shrubs nor the trees seem to know that no rain has fallen during these long months. The leathery, somewhat resinous leaves of the dominant shrub—the attractive plant unattractively dubbed creosote bush—are not at all parched or wilted. Nor are the deciduous leaves of the mesquite.

Earlier in the year the creosote was covered with bright yellow pealike flowers, the mesquite with pale yellow catkins. Now the former is heavy with gray seed and on the mesquite are forming long pods that Indians once ate and that cattle now find an unusually rich food.

It looks almost as though the shrubs and trees could live without water. But of course they cannot. Every desert plant has its secret, though not always the same one. In the case of mesquite and creosote it is that their roots go deep and that, below 6 feet, there is no wet or dry season in the desert. What little moisture is there is pretty constant throughout the year, in dry years as well as wet. Like the temperature in some caves, it never varies. The mesquite and creosote are not compelled to care whether it has rained for four months or not. And unlike many other plants, they flourish whether there has been less or more rain than usual.

Plants with substantial root systems that do not reach very deep are more exuberant some years than others. Thus the Encelia, the brittlebush, which in normal years literally covers many slopes with thousands of yellow, daisylike flowers, demands a normal year. Though I have never seen it fail, I am told that in very dry years it comes into leaf but does not flower, whereas in really catastrophic droughts it does not come up at all, as the roots lie dormant and hope for better times. Even the creosote bush, which never fails, profits from surface water, and when it gets the benefit of a few thunderstorms in late July or August, it will flower and fruit a second time, sprinkling the desert expanse once again with yellow. . . .

On such a day as this, even the lizards, so I have noticed, hug the thin shade of the bushes. If I venture out, the zebratails scurry indignantly away, the boldly banded appendages that give them their name curved high over their backs. But I don't venture out very often during the middle of the day. It is more pleasant to sit inside where a cooler keeps the house at a pleasant 80 degrees. And if you think that an advocate of the simple life should not succumb to a cooler, it is you rather than I who is inconsistent. Even Thoreau had a fire in his cottage at Walden, and it is no more effete to cool oneself in a hot climate than it is to get warm before a stove in a cold one. The gadget involved is newer, but that is all.

In this country "inclemency" means heat. One is "sunbound" instead of snowbound, and I have often noticed that the psychological effect is similar. It is cozy to be shut in, to have a good excuse for looking out of the window or into oneself. A really blazing day slows down the restless activity of a community very much as a blizzard does in regions that have them. Where there is either, a sort of meteorological sabbath is usually observed even by those who keep no other.

OBVIOUSLY the animals and plants that share this country with me take it for granted. To them it is just "the way things are." By now I am beginning to take it for granted myself. But being a man, I must ask what they cannot: What *is* a desert, and why is it what it is? At 32° latitude one expects the climate to be warm. But the desert is much more than merely warm. It is a consistent world with a special landscape, a special geography, and, to go with them, special flora and fauna adapted to that geography and that climate.

Nearly every striking feature of this world, be it the shape of the mountains or the habits of its plant and animal inhabitants, goes back ultimately to the grand fact of dryness—the dryness of the ground, of the air, of the whole sum total. And the most inclusive cause of dryness is the simple lack of rain.

Some comparisons with wetter regions may bring that into sharper focus. Take, for example, southern New England. By world standards it gets a lot—namely some 40 inches—of rain per year. Certain southern states get even more: about 50 inches for east Tennessee, nearly 60 for New Orleans. Some areas on the West Coast get fantastic amounts, like the 75 inches at Crescent City, California, and the unbelievable 153 inches—nearly four times what New York City gets—recorded one year in Del Norde County, California.

Nevertheless, New England's 40 is a lot of water, either comparatively or absolutely. The region around Paris, for instance, gets little more than half that amount. Forty inches is, in absolute terms, more than most people imagine. One inch of rain falling on an acre of ground means more than 27,000 gallons of water. No wonder irrigation in dry regions is a formidable task even for modern technology.

In terms of vegetation, 40 inches is ample for the kind of agriculture and natural growth that we tend to think of as "normal." It means luxuriant grass, rapid development of second-growth woodland, a veritable jungle of weeds and bushes in midsummer. In inland America, rainfall tends to be less than in coastal regions. Moving west from the Mississippi, it declines sharply and begins to drop below 20 inches a year at about the 100th meridian or, very roughly, at a line drawn from Sioux Falls, South Dakota, through Oklahoma City. This means too little water for most broad-leafed trees and explains why the southern Great Plains were as treeless when the white man first saw them as they are today.

OUR TRUE DESERTS lie farther west still: the Great Basin Desert in Utah and Nevada, the Chihuahuan in New Mexico, the Sonoran in Arizona, and the Mohave in California. The four differ among themselves but they are all arid, and they all fulfill what is probably the most satisfactory definition of "desert": namely, a region where the ground cover is not continuous—where the earth remains bare of vegetation between the plants that manage to grow. Over these American deserts rainfall varies considerably, and with it the character and extent of vegetation. In southern Arizona, for instance, there are about 4 inches of rain at Yuma, nearly 11 around Tucson. Four inches means sand dunes that look like pictures of the Sahara that the word "desert" calls to most people's minds. Eleven means that where soil is suitable, well-separated individuals of such desert plants as cacti and paloverde trees will flourish.

But if scant rainfall makes for deserts, what makes for scant rainfall? To that there are two important answers. One is simply that most nonmountainous regions tend to be dry if they lie in that belt of permanently high atmospheric pressure extending some 30 or 35 degrees on each side of the equator where calms are frequent and winds erratic. Old sailors used to call this region "the horse latitudes," though nobody knows exactly why. (You can take your choice of three equally unconvincing explanations. One is that horses tended to die on ships lying long in the hot calms. Another: The boisterous changeableness of winds when they do come suggests unruly horses. A third is that they were originally named after an English explorer, Ross, whose name Germans mistook for their old word for "horse.") In any event, Tucson falls within the "horse latitudes." Most of the important deserts of the world, including the Sahara and the Gobi, lie within this belt.

Mountains lying across the path of moist winds also make for scant rainfall. In our case, the Coast Ranges of California lie between us and the Pacific. From my front porch, which looks directly across the desert to some of the southernmost Rockies, I can see, on a small scale, what happens. So many times a moisture-laden mass of air reaches as far as these mountains. Dark clouds form, and sometimes the whole range is blotted out. Torrential rain is falling—but not a drop on me. Either the sky is blue overhead or the high clouds that have blown my way dissolve before my eyes as they reach warm air rising from the sun-drenched flats. I live in what geographers call a "rain shadow" cast by the mountains. At their summit rainfall is nearly twice as much as it is down here, and as a result they are clothed with pines from 6,000 or 7,000 feet right up to the 9,000-foot peak. When I do get rain in midwinter and midsummer, it is usually because winds have brought moisture up from the Gulf of Mexico by an unobstructed southern route, or because in summer a purely local thundershower has formed out of hot air rising from the sun-beaten desert floor. Most of the time the sun is hot, even in winter, and the air is usually fantastically dry, the relative humidity being often less than 10.

NATURALLY the plants and animals living in such a region must be specially adapted to survive under such conditions, but the casual visitor usually notices the strangeness of the landscape before he is aware of flora or fauna. Peculiar features of the landscape are also the result of dryness, even in ways that are not immediately obvious.

The nude mountains reveal their contours, or veil them as lightly as late Greek sculptors veiled their nudes, because only near the mountaintops can anything grow tall enough to obscure the outlines. A little less obvious is the fact that the beautiful "monuments" of northern Arizona and southern Utah owe their unusual forms to the sculpting of windblown sand—or that sheer cliffs often rise from a sloping cone of rocks and boulders because there is not enough draining water to break them down and distribute them over the surrounding plain as they would be distributed in regions with heavier rainfall. But the most striking example of all is the greatest single scenic wonder of the region, the Grand Canyon itself. This narrow gash, cut a mile deep through so many strata that the river now flows over some of the oldest rock exposed anywhere on earth, could have been formed only in a very dry climate.

As recently as 200 years ago the best-informed observer would have taken it for granted that the river was running between those sheer walls at the bottom of the gorge simply because it had found them out. Today few visitors are not aware that the truth is the other way around, that the river cut its own course through the rock. But most laymen do not ask the next questions: Why is the Grand Canyon unique, or why are such canyons, even on a smaller scale, rare? The answer to those questions is that a set of very special conditions was necessary.

First, there must have been a thick series of rock strata slowly rising during a period when a considerable river flowed over it. Second, that considerable river must have carried an unusual amount of hard sand or stone fragments in suspension so that it could cut downward at least as rapidly as the rock over which it flows rose. Third, that considerable river must have coursed through very arid country. Otherwise rain, washing over the edges of the cut, would widen it at the top as the cut went deeper. That is why broad valleys are characteristic of regions with normal rainfall and canyons require arid country.

And the Grand Canyon is the grandest of all canyons because at that particular place all the necessary conditions were fulfilled more exactly than at any other place. The Colorado River carries water from a relatively wet country through a dry one, it bears with it a fantastic amount of abrasive material, the rock over which it flows has been slowly rising during several millions of years, and too little rain falls to rapidly (in geological time) widen the gash that it cuts. Thus in desert country everything from the color of a mouse or the shape of a leaf to the largest features of mountains is more likely than not to have the same explanation: dryness.

So far as living things go, all this adds up to what even an ecologist may call, forgetting himself for a moment, an "unfavorable environment." But like all such pronouncements, this one doesn't mean much unless we ask "unfavorable for what and for whom?" For many plants, for many animals, and for some people it is very favorable indeed. Many of the first two would languish and die if transferred to some region where conditions were "more favorable." It is here, and here only, that they flourish. Likewise, many people feel healthier and happier in the bright dry air than they do anywhere else. And since I happen to be one of them, I not unnaturally have a special interest in the plants and animals that share my liking for just these conditions. For many years now I have been amusing myself by inquiring of them directly what habits and what adjustments they have found most satisfactory. Many of them are delightfully ingenious and eminently sensible. . . .

I HAVE LIVED in this house and been lord of these few acres for nearly five years, and the creatures who share the desert with me have already summed me up as a softy and have grown contemptuously familiar. It is not only that the cactus wrens sit on the backs of my porch chairs. The round-tailed ground squirrels—plain, sand-colored, chipmunk-like animals—are digging rather too many burrows rather too close about the house. The jack rabbits—normally the most timid as well as the fleetest of creatures—take nibbles at the few plants I have set out and refuse to leave off until I arrive shouting and waving my arms a few feet from where they are. Sooner or later something may have to be done to discourage this impudent familiarity, but for the present I am getting some good looks at creatures who usually don't wait to be looked at. Yesterday, for instance, I saw what at first I thought was a bird eating seeds from the upper branches of a creosote bush. It turned out to be a ground squirrel belying his name by climbing several feet above ground among the slender swaying branches of the creosote to eat the small fuzzy seeds. This is doubtless no addition to Knowledge with a capital K. But it is an addition to my knowledge, and that is the next best thing. I like to investigate such matters for myself when I can. "What on earth do they live on?" is a common question from those newcomers not too egotistical to notice that creatures other than those of their own kind do live here somehow. Obviously "creosote seeds" is one answer so far as the ground squirrel is concerned.

People of many races have been known to speak with scorn of those who live where nature makes things easy. In their inclement weather, the stoniness of their soil, or their rigorous winters, they find secret virtues to make even a thing like London fog praiseworthy. Making a virtue out of necessity is not itself a virtue. But there may be something of value in that process. We grow strong against the pressure of a difficulty and test our ingenuity by solving problems. Individuality and character are developed by challenge. We tend to admire trees, as well as people, who bear the stamp of success from struggles with adversity. People who have not had too easy a time of it develop character. And there is no doubt about the fact that desert life has character. Plants and animals are so clearly what they are because of the problems they have solved. They are part of some whole. They belong. Animals and plants, as well as people, become especially interesting when they fit their environment, when to some extent they reveal what their response to it has been. And nowhere more than in the desert do they reveal it.

— Joseph Wood Krutch

Joseph Wood Krutch (1898-1970), one of America's noted natural-history writers, contributed to *The Nation* for many years as a drama and literary critic and lived his last 18 years outside Tucson. *The Voice of the Desert*, from which this essay was excerpted, *Grand Canyon*, and *Henry David Thoreau* are among Krutch's 21 books.

ARIZONA CRAFTS

WHETHER YOU HAVE $10 or $1,000 to spend, shopping for crafts can make your trip to Arizona memorable, and not only for what you'll take home with you. The pursuit of local wares may take you down desert roads to remote studios, introduce you to snazzy urban galleries and historic trading posts, or involve you in lively festivals. Regional crafts also provide an intimate introduction to an area's history, culture, and peoples, as well as its contemporary interests and trends.

In the Southwest, several cultures have strong craft traditions, some predating European contact by more than 1,000 years. Native American, cowboy, and contemporary crafts—many made from native materials or by capturing local colors, themes, and spirit—are all well developed in this region.

Native American Crafts

Arizona visitors will see Native American crafts everywhere—in specialty shops, airports, motel gift shops, drugstores, and even gas stations. The problem is finding authentic work. Some so-called Native American crafts are made in Taiwan or Mexico. Others labeled "genuine Indian made" are mass-produced with shoddy material and inferior workmanship.

If you haven't read any books on the subject, study Native American collections at the Heard Museum (Phoenix) or the Museum of Northern Arizona (Flagstaff). These museums have their own gift shops, which sell good-quality items at reasonable prices. Long-established trading posts, galleries, and Native American dealers are another option. Most first-rate shops will have a range of prices and knowledgeable salespeople who can answer your questions. If everything in a shop is inexpensive, it's probably attributable to the poor quality of the goods rather than to low overhead. It's a good idea to shop elsewhere.

One way to ensure authenticity and at the same time add an adventurous detour to your trip is to buy directly from craftspeople on the reservations. Look for signs that say "pottery," "rugs," or "baskets" hanging outside homes. Although visiting craftspeople is not a guarantee of quality, it does provide an opportunity to ask questions and learn about the work you are purchasing. And it's fun to watch artisans at work, to see their raw materials being turned into finished pieces.

Reservation gift shops are another option for authentic wares, although quality and prices vary tremendously. Crafts are also sold at Native American festivals, fairs, and powwows (ceremonial gatherings), which also have tribal dances and storytelling groups and serve food. One recommended event is Flagstaff's annual six-week Festival of Native American Arts, held each summer at the Coconino Center for the Arts (2300 N. Fort Valley Rd., Flagstaff, ☎ 520/779–6921). This juried festival offers high-quality, traditional and contemporary tribal arts, including work rarely found elsewhere, such as colorful Pueblo moccasins and miniature pottery. Visitors can also watch jewelry-making, cloth- or basket-weaving demonstrations or participate in various workshops, including one that teaches children how to make Native American masks.

Arizona's 14 tribes each make distinctive art. The works of the Hopi, Navajo, and Tohonó O'odham (Papago) are best known, but the Chemehuevi, Maricopa, Mojave, Paiute, and Pima tribes create equally fine pieces.

Hopi pottery, baskets, and weaving reflect ancient traditions and techniques, whereas the tribe's silver work is of more recent vintage. Each of the reservation's three mesas has a craft specialty. First Mesa is home to potters who fashion hand-coiled vessels with pale cream or deep red glazes decorated with stylized birds and figures. Second Mesa's specialty is baskets of thickly coiled yucca joined with colorfully dyed lengths of yucca leaves; wicker baskets decorated with brightly colored designs can be found on Third Mesa. When buying pottery and baskets, look for symmetrical shapes, smooth rims, and neatly painted or evenly woven designs.

Hopi artisans also create kachina dolls, colorfully costumed, masked figures embellished with feathers, textiles, and leather. Modeled after the ceremonial kachina dancers, the dolls are used to teach children their religious heritage. Hopi men weave colorful sashes and narrow decorative bands used on clothing on belt looms. The vertical threads (warp) on these unusual looms stretch from one rod, tied to a tree, to another rod held taut by a belt wrapped around the weaver's waist. While making a sash, the weaver leans forward to loosen the warp and insert the woof, then backward to tighten it. Although Hopi woven fabrics are created primarily for their own use, some pieces are occasionally available through the reservation's crafts cooperative.

Hopi silver work, begun as a craft in the late 1890s, reflects a union of contemporary silver-working techniques and ancient motifs. Hopi silversmiths create some of the Southwest's finest jewelry. Two-layer designs use a number of motifs, ranging from simple sun shapes to those depicting elaborate tribal legends. Patterns are carefully cut through a top layer, which is then soldered to a bottom layer. Tiny parallel lines are chiseled into the design, and pieces are then oxidized to make motifs stand out from the polished silver surrounding it. Some of the best pieces have smoothly cut patterns with neatly stamped, parallel interior lines.

Navajo jewelry traces its origin to the mid-19th century. Tribal craftsmen learned smithery from Mexican artisans, later adding their own styles and designs. Early pieces were made from hammered silver coins and decorated with stamp work. Although turquoise beads date from prehistoric times, Navajos did not combine the stone with silver until the late 1800s. Today, in addition to using turquoise, artisans incorporate coral, lapis, and other semiprecious stones into their designs.

Contemporary Navajo jewelry ranges from simple rings and cast silver bracelets to massive necklaces and concha belts (named for the stamped silver disks strung together on narrow leather strips). Because there are so many variables in the quality of stones and workmanship, purchase Navajo jewelry only from reputable dealers. Many Indian traders and jewelry shops throughout the Southwest have one case displaying items of Native American–made jewelry that have been pawned and not retrieved by their owners. Although you can occasionally find older pieces of exquisite quality in these cases, be wary about assertions as to an item's age or caliber.

The Navajo are also known for the variety and quality of their woven wool rugs. Sheepherders for centuries, they learned weaving skills from Pueblo peoples during the 18th century. At first they produced blankets and clothing in natural brown-and-white stripes. During the late 19th century, colors, particularly red, and a wide range of complex designs were added. At this time, most weavers also switched from making pieces for personal use to creating rugs for traders. Today Navajo rug patterns range from traditional eye dazzlers with bold zigzag patterns and pictorials featuring animals and other figures to *yei* rugs that duplicate sandpainting designs and two-faced rugs with different patterns on each surface.

If you purchase a Navajo rug, make sure that it is made entirely of wool (no linen or cotton threads), that the wool is of even thickness throughout the piece, that the design is neatly woven, and that colors are uniform throughout. A good source of Navajo rugs and other Native American crafts is the Hubbell Trading Post, a National Historic Site in Ganado, on the Navajo reservation 22 miles west of Window Rock. Established in 1878, the post looks exactly as it did in the 19th century when Navajos brought John Lorenzo Hubbell their rugs and jewelry to trade for groceries and other goods. These artisans still bring their crafts for sale or trade, but now they arrive in pickups instead of on horseback.

Although Hopi and Navajo crafts are the best-known Arizona Native American arts, other tribes also produce good-quality items that provide an introduction to their cultural history. Among these, traditional Tohonó O'odham baskets are coiled, waterproof vessels with intricate designs using techniques and materials that have remained virtually unchanged for more than 11 centuries. Most baskets, made from two southwestern desert plants, are broad and slightly sloping, with geometric patterns. Black designs, the most highly prized, are fashioned from black devil's claw, an increasingly rare plant that yields strong strips of jet-black fiber. Red motifs are woven with the root of banana yucca, a more common plant found in Arizona's higher elevations. One traditional Tohonó O'odham design is the legendary Man in the Maze, a stylized male figure standing at the top of the basket, about to enter a complex white-and-black labyrinth.

Baskets are also made by the Pima and Paiute. The Pima use coils of cattail stems bound with willow and favor complex zigzag designs. Traditional Paiute baskets have plain, functional shapes, reflecting the fact that they were once used to carry water, harvest or store seeds, and cradle babies. Mojave, Maricopa, and Chemehuevi tribal arts are more difficult to find, but they are worth the effort. Mojave beadwork can be exquisite, especially large, collar-shape necklaces created in traditional network designs resembling intricate lace. Maricopa artisans specialize in cream-color pottery, decorated with black designs that incorporate both geometric shapes and curvilinear symbols. Finely woven Chemehuevi baskets, another rare but exquisite craft, are made from coiled fiber, sometimes decorated with colorful feathers.

Cowboy Crafts

Even if you don't own horses or cattle, consider buying cowboy crafts: They can add vicarious fun to your wardrobe or decor. Watch them being created by talented artisans.

Arizona ranchers may use computers to keep track of their businesses, but no one has devised the technology to replace cowboys. Although his (and sometimes her) job may include time in a pickup, the daily routine is still dominated by horses, cattle, and traditional equipment rarely influenced by 20th-century innovations. Everyday cowboy trappings—saddles, spurs, bridles, and hats—form a craft tradition that spans centuries. Some items originated with Native Americans, while others were adopted from Mexican or California-Spanish styles.

Arizona cowboy crafts can be found in many shops, and even in department stores, but it's more fun to buy them directly from craftspeople or in tack shops that sell everything a horse and its rider need. Look in telephone books under "tack shops," "horse furnishings," or specific crafts such as "saddlery" or "hats." For a thorough immersion, attend Flagstaff's annual 5½-week Trappings of the American West Festival, sponsored by the Coconino Center for the Arts; it runs from early May until the second week of June. The festival includes cowboy craft demonstrations and workshops where you can learn rawhide braiding and boot making.

Although cowboy crafts are often decorative, they are first of all functional tools of the trade. Hats protect the wearer from weather, branches, and rocks and double as containers for carrying water and feed. Boots, designed to be pulled off easily and fit comfortably in stirrups, protect feet from mud and brush. Chaps shield the legs from prickly cactus and other hazards. The brush in Arizona is particularly heavy, so cowboys here prefer Arizona bell-bottom chaps made from very heavy leather that is flared at the bottom so they bend with the leg. What is the best of each?—hats made from beaver-fur felt, custom-made boots, and used chaps with that trail-worn look.

Saddles, which are custom-made to fit horse and rider, are often covered with carved or stamped designs of elaborate floral and leaf motifs. Some cowboys claim that deep carving keeps them from slipping in the saddle. For urban cowpokes, many saddlers create stamped or carved leather purses, belts, wallets, and even wastebaskets.

The oldest cowboy craft is leather and horsehair braiding. Conceived by Native Americans, braiding was later adopted by Mexican and American cowboys. Complex patterns decorate braided horse gear, from bridles and reins to other items whose exotic names belie their practicality: bosals and hobbles, romals and quirts. Look also for braided hatbands, belts, and bracelets.

Other cowboy accoutrements include bits and spurs with ornate inlaid designs that are seen only by the cowboy and his horse. Texas cowboys generally favor massive inlaid silver stars and geometric patterns, whereas California and Arizona cowboys prefer gear embellished with flowers and flourishes. Many smiths also fashion decorative silver work for saddles, as well as buckles, money clips, and jewelry. Knives, another cowboy necessity, can be found in great variety. Look for those with handles made from exotic materials and engraved or inlaid with precious metal and stones.

Contemporary Crafts

Arizona's contemporary artisans work in every medium, but particularly in clay, textiles, and wood. Although the focus of their work varies from abstract to functional, many of the crafts reflect Arizona colors: the glowing hues of a desert sunset, the subtle pastels of cactus flowers, the myriad reds of Sedona's cliffs. There's also a healthy dose of humor in many items: prickly ceramic cactus vases, howling wood dogs, flirty roadrunner sculptures, chairs with coyote armrests. The use of native materials is also common—for example, you may come across cactus-spine baskets or mesquite armoires.

Phoenix, Scottsdale, and Tucson offer a bonanza of contemporary crafts galleries. On a smaller scale, Tubac, an artists' community 35 miles south of Tucson, has numerous crafts studios open to the public. Tubac artisans create everything from avant-garde jewelry and textiles to copper fountains shaped like cacti. To find galleries throughout Arizona, consult *Art Life,* two comprehensive guides (one covering northern Arizona, the other southern Arizona) that describe galleries, provide detailed maps, and include indexes arranged by style, subject, and medium. The guides are available free in many Arizona galleries.

— Suzanne Carmichael

Author of *The Traveler's Guide to American Crafts,* Suzanne Carmichael also writes articles on travel and crafts for such publications as *The New York Times, USA Weekend,* and *Northwest* magazine.

BOOKS AND VIDEOS

Books

Essays and Fiction

Going Back to Bisbee, by Richard Shelton, *Frog Mountain Blues,* by Charles Bowden, and *The Mountains Next Day,* by Janice Emily Bowers, are all fine personal accounts of life in southern Arizona. The hipster fiction classic *The Monkey Wrench Gang,* by Edward Abbey, details an ecoanarchist plot to blow up Glen Canyon Dam. *Stolen Gods,* a thriller by Jake Page, is set largely on Arizona's Hopi reservation and in Tucson. Three novels by Tucson-based writers skillfully evoke the interplay between Native American culture and contemporary Southwest life: *Pigs in Heaven,* by Barbara Kingsolver, *Almanac of the Dead,* by Leslie Marmon Silko, and *Yes Is Better Than No,* by Byrd Baylor. Wild West adventure, with all of the mythological glory that Hollywood has tried to capture, abounds in Zane Grey's novels—buy a new copy or look for any of the charming illustrated hardcover editions in used- or out-of-print bookstores. Tony Hillerman's mysteries will put you in an equally southwestern mood.

General History

Arizona Cowboys, by Dane Coolidge, is an illustrated account of the cowboys, Indians, settlers, and explorers of the early 1900s. Buried-treasure hunters will be inspired by *Lost Mines of the Great Southwest,* by John D. Mitchell, which is just enough of a nibble to start you sketching maps and planning strategy. First printed back in 1891, *Some Strange Corners of Our Country,* by Charles F. Lummis, takes readers on a century-old journey to the Grand Canyon, Montezuma Castle, the Petrified Forest, and other Arizonan "strange corners." For a dip into the backroads of the past, try *Arizona Good Roads Association Illustrated Road Maps and Tour Book,* a 1913 volume, replete with hotel ads, reprinted by Arizona Highways magazine. *Roadside History of Arizona,* by Marshall Trimble, will bring you up to date on many of the same thoroughfares. *Ghost Towns of Arizona,* by James E. and Barbara H. Sherman, gives historical details on the abandoned mining towns that dot the state and provides maps to find them. For an anthology that covers the entire state's literature, consult *Named in Stone and Sky: An Arizona Anthology,* edited by Gregory McNamee.

Native American History

Two books provide excellent surveys of the ancient and more recent Native American past and cover in more depth sites mentioned in this guidebook. *Those Who Came Before: Southwestern Archaeology in the National Park System,* by Robert Lister and Florence Lister, provides a well-researched and completely accessible summary of centuries of life in the region informed by both contemporary Indian and archaeological perspectives, and it contains wonderful photographs and descriptions of numerous sites. David G. Noble's *Ancient Ruins of the Southwest* covers similar territory more briefly and portably and includes directions for driving to sites. *Hohokam Indians of the Tucson Basin,* by Linda Gregonis, offers an in-depth look at this prehistoric tribe. In *Hopi,* by Susanne Page and Jake Page, the daily, ceremonial, and spiritual life of the tribe is explored in detail. Study up on the history of Hopi silversmithing techniques in *Hopi Silver,* by Margaret Wright. The beautifully illustrated *Hopi Indian Kachina Dolls,* by Oscar T. Branson, details the different ceremonial roles of the colorful Native American figurines. Navajo homes, ceremonies, crafts, and tribal traditions are kept alive in *The Enduring Navajo,* by Laura Gilpin. Navajo legends and trends from early days to the present are collected in *The Book of the Navajo,* by Raymond F. Locke.

A superb new collection of Native American stories, songs, and poems, *Coming to Light,* edited by Brian Swann, includes material from all over the country, not only the Southwest. Introductions to individual pieces provide invaluable and fascinating cultural information.

Natural History

A Guide to Exploring Oak Creek and the Sedona Area, by Stewart Aitchison, provides natural-history driving tours of this very scenic district. In *100 Desert Wild-*

flowers in Natural Color, by Natt N. Dodge, you'll find a color photo and brief description of each of the flowers included. Also written by Natt N. Dodge, *Poisonous Dwellers of the Desert* gives precise information on both venomous and nonvenomous creatures of the Southwest. *Cacti of the Southwest,* by W. Hubert Earle, depicts some of the best-known species of the region with color photos and descriptive material. For comprehensive information on Grand Canyon geology, history, flora and fauna, plus hiking suggestions, pick up *A Field Guide to the Grand Canyon,* by Steve Whitney. *Common Edible and Useful Plants of the West,* by Muriel Sweet, gives the layperson descriptions of medicinal and other plants and shrubs, most of which were first discovered by Native Americans. *Roadside Geology of Arizona,* by Halka Chronic, is a good resource for finding the causes of the striking natural formations you'll see throughout the state.

Crafts

The Traveler's Guide to American Crafts: West of the Mississippi, by Suzanne Carmichael, gives browsers and buyers alike a useful overview of Arizona's traditional and contemporary handiwork.

General Interest

Arizona Highways, a monthly magazine, features exquisite color photography of this versatile state. Useful general travel information, fine pictures, and well-written historical essays all make *Arizona,* by Larry Cheek, a good pretrip resource.

Videos

For a glimpse of the Arizona landscape, check out the following videos: *Broken Arrow* (1995), directed by John Woo and starring John Travolta and Christian Slater; *Grand Canyon* (1991), starring Kevin Kline, Steve Martin, and Danny Glover; *Red Rock West* (1991), directed by John Dahl and starring Nicholas Cage; *Raising Arizona* (1986), directed by Joel Coen and starring Nicholas Cage and Holly Hunter; *National Lampoon's Vacation* (1982), starring Chevy Chase; *The Outlaw Josey Wales* (1975), directed by and starring Clint Eastwood; *Zabriskie Point* (1968), directed by Michaelangelo Antonioni; and *The Searchers* (1954) and *Stagecoach* (1938), both directed by John Ford and starring John Wayne.

INDEX

NOTES

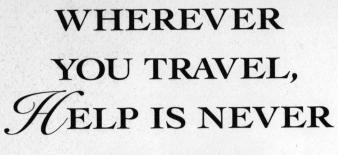